# gilbert
## LAW SUMMARIES

# SECURITIES REGULATION

Fifth Edition

**Niels B. Schaumann**

Professor of Law
William Mitchell College of Law

A COMPLETE PUBLICATIONS CATALOG IS
FEATURED AT THE BACK OF THIS BOOK.

**HARCOURT BRACE LEGAL AND PROFESSIONAL PUBLICATIONS, INC.**

EDITORIAL OFFICES: 176 W. Adams, Suite 2100, Chicago, IL 60603

## gilbert
LAW SUMMARIES

REGIONAL OFFICES: New York, Chicago, Los Angeles, Washington, D.C.
*Distributed by:* **Harcourt Brace & Company** 6277 Sea Harbor Drive, Orlando, FL 32887 (800)787-8717

PROJECT EDITOR
Steven Levin, B.A., J.D.
Attorney At Law

QUALITY CONTROL EDITOR
Blythe C. Smith, B.A.

# gilbert
## LAW SUMMARIES

# Titles Available

Administrative Law
Agency & Partnership
Antitrust
Bankruptcy
Basic Accounting for Lawyers
Business Law
California Bar Performance
  Test Skills
Civil Procedure
Commercial Paper &
  Payment Law
Community Property
Conflict of Laws
Constitutional Law
Contracts
Corporations
Criminal Law
Criminal Procedure
Dictionary of Legal Terms
Estate & Gift Tax
Evidence

Family Law
Federal Courts
First Year Questions & Answers
Future Interests
Income Tax I (Individual)
Income Tax II (Corporate)
Labor Law
Legal Ethics (Prof. Responsibility)
Legal Research, Writing,
  & Analysis
Multistate Bar Exam
Personal Property
Property
Remedies
Sales & Lease of Goods
Securities Regulation
Secured Transactions
Torts
Trusts
Wills

## Also Available:

First Year Program
Pocket Size Law Dictionary
The Eight Secrets Of Top Exam Performance In Law School

# SUMMARY OF CONTENTS

# gilbert

## capsule summary

# securities regulation

not available when the securities being offered are fractional undivided interests in oil and gas rights or securities of investment companies . . . . . . . . . . . . . . . . . . . . . . . . . . . . . [399]

   3) **Limitation on dollar amount of securities offered:** The securities offered under regulation A are limited to $5 million in any one-year period. In addition, all security holders together may not sell more than $1.5 million of securities in any one-year period, and the securities sold by security holders are counted against the issuer's $5 million limit . . . . . . . [400]

      a) **Limitation due to integration of issues:** Regulation A contains a safe harbor, providing that sales made in reliance on regulation A will not be integrated with prior offers or sales of securities sold in compliance with the 1933 Act or subsequent offers and sales that are (i) registered under section 5, (ii) made in reliance on Securities Act ("SA") rule 701 (relating to employee benefit plans), (iii) made in reliance on regulation 5 (concerning unregistered offers and sales made outside the U.S.), or (iv) made more than six months after completion of the regulation A offering . . . . . . . . . . . . . . . . . [405]

(b) **Filing and process procedures**

   1) **Offering statement**

      a) **Part I:** Part I of the offering statement under regulation A (Form 1-A) is a notification which is filed with the S.E.C. and is publicly available, but is not circulated to investors . . . . . . . . . . . . . . . . . . . . . . [407]

      b) **Part II:** There are three possible formats: . . . . . . . . . [408]

        1/ *Model A* is an extensive, fill-in-the-blank form;

        2/ *Model B* provides a "pool" of disclosure materials; and

        3/ *Form SB-2* is available for corporations.

      c) **Part III:** Part III specifies exhibits that must be filed in a regulation A offering . . . . . . . . . . . . . . . . . . . . . . . . [409]

   2) **S.E.C. processing procedures:** There is a 20-day waiting period before the offering statement becomes effective. The S.E.C. can review the statement and recommend changes. The S.E.C. may accelerate the effective date when all S.E.C. comments have been addressed . . . . . . . . . . . . [410]

   3) **Reports of sales and use of proceeds:** An issuer under regulation A must file a report of sales and use of proceeds of the offering every six months after the offering statement is qualified and within 30 days after the offering is completed . . . . . . . . . . . . . . . . . . . . . . . . . . . . . . . . . . . [414]

   4) **S.E.C. enforcement procedures—suspension of offering:** The S.E.C. may order a temporary suspension of the regulation A offering if it has reason to believe the requirements of the exemption have not been met, the statement contains misleading statements or omissions, etc. . . [415]

   5) **Substantial and good faith compliance:** Failure to comply with all of the requirements of regulation A does not result in a loss of the exemption as to a sale to a particular person if (i) the failure did not pertain to a term intended to protect that particular person; (ii) the failure was insignificant; and (iii) there was a good faith attempt to comply with all applicable regulation A requirements . . . . . . . . . . . . . . . . . . . . . . [418]

(c) **Offers and sales pursuant to regulation A**

1) **Solicitation of interest document:** Before committing to an offering under regulation A, an issuer may publish or deliver to perspective purchasers a written document or scripted radio or television broadcast to determine whether there is any interest in a contemplated securities offer, as long as the document or script states, among other things, that no money is being solicited, that no sales will be made until delivery of an offering circular, and that an indication of interest involves no obligation or commitment by the prospective purchaser. Also, the issuer's chief executive officer must be identified and its business or products described . ........ [419]

2) **Preliminary offering circular:** After the offering statement is filed, but before it is qualified by the S.E.C., a solicitation of interest document may no longer be used, but the offering statement may be used in the form in which it was filed as long as it contains a legend alerting potential investors that the document has not yet been qualified under regulation A. Oral offers are also permitted, as are "tombstone" ads . . . . . . . . . . . . . . . . . . . . . . . . . . . . . . . . . . . . . . . . . [423]

3) **Final offering circular required after qualification:** After the offering statement is qualified, written offers may be made by means of the final offering circular, which may be accompanied or followed by other written materials. "Tombstone" ads are also permitted. Generally, a sale may not be made unless the purchaser is furnished with a copy of the offering circular . . . . . . . . . . . . . . . . . . . . . . . . . . . . . [427]

(3) **Registrations on form SB-2:** A small business issuer (*i.e.*, an issuer that is a U.S. or Canadian entity that is *not* an investment company and has annual revenues of less than $25 million) can register using form SB-2 . . . . . . . . . . . . . . . . . . . . . . . . . . . . . . . . . [437]

f. **Intrastate offering exemption:** Securities offered and sold only to persons residing within a single state, by an issuer that is also a resident of and doing business in that state, are exempt from registration under section 5 . . . . . . . . . . . . . . . . . . . . . . . . . . . . . . . . . . . . . . . . . . . . . [440]

(1) **Requirements for statutory intrastate offering exemption—section 3(a)(11):** Under section 3(a)(11), the entire issue must be intrastate, and resales to nonresidents can destroy the exemption unless the offering has "come to rest" (the point at which the securities are purchased with the intention of keeping them for investment). Note that the issuer, offerees, and purchasers must all reside in the same state . . . . . . . . . . . . . . . . . . . . . . . . . . . . . . . . . . . . . . . . . . . [445]

(2) **Rule 147 criteria for intrastate offering exemption:** Rule 147 provides the following, objective criteria for determining what is exempt under section 3(a)(11) . . . . . . . . . . . . . . . . . . . . . . . . . . . . . . . . . [457]

(a) **Integration of offerings:** Transactions covered by section 3 exemptions or by the section 4(2) exemptions, and which occur either six months or more before or at least six months after a section 3(a)(11) transaction will not be integrated with the intrastate offering as long as there are no offers or sales of the same or similar class of securities by or for the issuer during either of these six-month periods . . . . . . . . . . . . . . . . . . . . . . . . . . . . . [458]

(b) **Requirement of coming to rest:** Rule 147 provides an objective standard for the "coming to rest" test. No sales can be made to persons residing outside the state of issue during the time the securities are being offered and sold by the issuer *and* for an additional *nine months* following the last sale by the issuer.

Moreover, the issuer must (i) place a legend on each securities certificate that the securities are not registered and are subject to rule 147's "coming to rest" provisions, (ii) issue instructions to its transfer agent prohibiting the transfer of the securities until they have "come to rest," and (iii) obtain a written representation from each purchaser as to the purchaser's residence . . . . . . . .

(c) **Requirement of residence**

   1) **Issuers:** To be doing business in a state, the issuer must derive 80% of its gross revenues from business within the state, have at least 80% of its assets within the state, use at least 80% of the proceeds from the securities transaction in question in the state, and have its principal office within the state . . . . . . . . . . . . . . . . . . . . . . . . . . . . . .

   2) **Offerees and purchasers:** Corporations and business organizations are deemed to be residents of the state in which their principal business office is located . . . . . . . . . . . . . .

g. **Exemptions for reorganizations and recapitalizations**

  (1) **Exemptions where no "offer or sale for value":** Section 5 of the 1933 Act applies only when a security is offered or sold "for value." Thus, no registration is required when the issuer gives its stockholders rights to purchase additional shares or stock dividends, because there is no transfer "for value" . . . . . . . . . . . . . . . . . . . . . . . . . . . . .

    (a) **Spin-off transactions:** In a conventional spin-off, a parent corporation distributes the stock of its subsidiary to the parent's shareholders, often for purposes of downsizing. Enterprising promoters abused spin-offs, *e.g.*, by issuing stock of a privately held company to a public company with no assets, which then distributes the stock to its shareholders. The S.E.C. has taken the position that spin-offs are "sales" under the 1933 Act, and therefore require registration . . . . . . . . . . . . . . . . . . . . . . . . . . . . . .

  (2) **Exemption for exchanges between an issuer and existing shareholders:** Any security that an issuer exchanges *voluntarily and exclusively* for its outstanding securities—with *no commission or other remuneration* for soliciting the exchange—is exempt from the registration requirements of section 5 . . . . . . . . . . . . . . . . . . . . . .

    (a) **"Clean exchange" required:** Although generally, the transaction is exempt only if it involves a "clean exchange" of the old securities for the new ones, payments from security holders are allowed if necessary to ensure that all holders of a class of securities receive the same treatment. Also, the exchange may call for cash payments from the issuer . . . . . . . . . . . . . . . . . . . . . . . .

  (3) **Exemption for approved reorganizations:** The 1933 Act exempts from registration approved business reorganizations in which new securities are issued in exchange for outstanding securities, claims, or property interests . . . . . . . . . . . . . . . . . . . . . . . . . . . . . . . . . . . .

    (a) **Authorized agencies:** Agencies that can approve such reorganizations include the courts, an agency of the United States, and state banking or insurance commissions . . . . . . . . . . . . . . . . . .

  (4) **Exemption for selling or merging businesses—rule 145:** Rule 145 makes it clear that certain transactions—such as mergers—involve offers and sales and must be registered if no exemption is available. It replaces former S.E.C. rule 133, which formalistically provided that a "sale" occurred only if there was a volitional act on the part of the seller (thus exempting many reorganizations in which a corporation, rather than its shareholders, performed this act) . . . . . . . . . . . . . . .

    (a) **Transactions covered by rule 145:** Rule 145 provides that,

## G. LIABILITIES UNDER THE 1933 ACT

### 1. Introduction

#### a. Conduct resulting in liability

#### b. Remedies for 1933 Act violations

### 2. Express Civil Liabilities

(a) *Every person who signs the registration statement* (issuer, principal executive officers, principal financial officer, controller or principal accounting officer, and a majority of the board of directors must sign the statement);

(b) *Every director of the issuer;*

(c) *Every person about to become a director,* who consents to being named in the registration statement;

(d) *Every "expert"* who consents to being named as having prepared or certified part of the registration statement;

(e) *Every underwriter* involved in the distribution; and

(f) *Control persons* of the issuer, unless they are without knowledge of the facts on which liability is based.

(2) **Elements of plaintiff's cause of action**

    (a) **Material misstatements or omissions:** Material facts are those to which there is a substantial likelihood that a reasonable investor would attach importance in deciding whether to purchase the security . . . . . . . . . . . . . . . . . . . . . . . . . . . . . . . . . . . . . . . . [652]

    (b) **Limited reliance requirement:** There is *no* reliance requirement *unless* the issuer sends out an earnings statement covering the period of one year *after* the effective date of the registration statement (a person thereafter acquiring some of the registered securities must prove reliance on the misrepresentation or omission to recover) . . . . . . . . . . . . . . . . . . . . . . . . . . . . . . . . . . . [656]

    (c) **Tracing required:** The purchaser must establish that the purchased securities were among those sold in the offering that was the subject of the registration statement . . . . . . . . . . . . . . . . . . . . [659]

    (d) **Causation of damages:** Plaintiff need *not* prove that the loss was caused by defendant's misrepresentation. (But *defendant* can prove that all or some portion of the damages is due to some cause other than the misrepresentation) . . . . . . . . . . . . . . . . . . . [660]

(3) **Defenses**

    (a) **General affirmative defenses:** Any defendant may plead the following defenses . . . . . . . . . . . . . . . . . . . . . . . . . . . . . . . . . . . . . . [662]

        1) *The alleged misstatements were true;*

        2) The facts misstated or omitted were *not material*;

        3) *Plaintiff knew* of the misrepresentations and invested anyway; and

        4) *The statute of limitations* has run.

    (b) **Due diligence defenses:** All defendants, *except* the issuer, have a due diligence defense . . . . . . . . . . . . . . . . . . . . . . . . . . . . . . . . [663]

        1) **Statements made by experts:** Experts may avoid liability as to the portions of the registration statement they certified if they can show that they *actually believed that the statements made were true,* and that their belief was *reasonable* (*i.e.*, they made a *reasonable investigation* of the supporting facts) . . . . . . . . . . . . . . . . . . . . . . . . . . . . . [664]

        2) **Statements made by nonexperts:** Nonexperts are held to the same standard as experts. A reasonable investigation for a nonexpert must be the kind of investigation that a *prudent person* in the same position, with the same responsibilities, skill, and background would have made (*e.g.*, a nonexpert director-attorney drafting part of the registration statement must conduct an independent investigation to verify the material facts stated in the registration statement) . . . . . . . . . . . . . . . . . . . . . . . . . . . . . . . . . . . . [665]

        3) **Nonexperts reviewing statements made by other nonexperts:** To avoid liability under the Act for statements made in the registration statement by other nonexperts, a nonexpert not involved in the actual drafting of the registration statement (*e.g.*, an underwriter or a member of the issuer's board of directors) must show that she exercised due diligence appropriate to her position and background. The standard of diligence required is the same as for nonexperts concerning their own representations in the registration statement . . . . . . . . . . . . . . . . . . . . . . . . . . [671]

        4) **Nonexperts reviewing statements made by experts:** Here the standard of care is lower. *No investigation* need be made by the nonexpert, since nonexperts are entitled to

rely to a greater extent on the statements of experts. The reviewing nonexpert need only show that she did not believe and had no reasonable ground to believe the statements made by the expert to be false ................. [676]

    (4) **Measure of damages**

      (a) **If the stock is sold prior to filing suit:** Plaintiff may recover the difference between the price paid for the stock (but not exceeding the price at which the security was offered to the public) and the price at which it was sold prior to suit ............... [680]

      (b) **If the stock has not been sold prior to suit:** Plaintiff may recover *either* the difference between the price paid (not exceeding the offering price) and the value of the security at the time of suit, *or* the price at which the stock was sold after suit was instituted, but before judgment, if such damages are less than those that result from using value at the time of suit ............... [681]

      (c) **Plaintiff not required to mitigate damages:** The plaintiff need not sell if the market price rises .......................... [683]

      (d) **Joint and several liability:** All persons who are liable under section 11 are jointly and severally liable .................. [686]

  b. **Section 12(1)—liability for offers or sales in violation of section 5:** Under section 12(1), any person who offers or sells a security in violation of any of the provisions of section 5 of the Act is liable to the purchaser for (i) the *consideration paid* (with interest) less the amount of any income received on the securities (*i.e.*, a suit for rescission); or (ii) for *damages* if the purchaser no longer owns the security ........................ [687]

    (1) **Any violation of section 5:** Liability attaches for any violation of any provision of section 5 (*i.e.*, a sale of unregistered securities, failure to deliver the required prospectus, etc.) ........................ [688]

      (a) **"Control persons":** Persons who control any other person liable under section 12(1) may be jointly and severally liable with those primarily liable ..................... [689]

      (b) **Participant liability:** "Sellers" liable under section 12(1) include the person who actually passes title to the security and persons who solicit the purchase from the purchaser, but not persons whose sole motivation in acting is to benefit the buyer ........ [692]

    (2) **Defenses to a section 12(1) cause of action:** The most common defense to a section 12(1) action is that the privity requirement has not been met; *i.e.*, direct privity of contract between plaintiff-purchaser and the seller-defendant is necessary. *Lack of any violation* and running of the *statute of limitations* are also defenses ............. [693]

  c. **Section 12(2)—general civil liability under the Act:** Section 12(2) of the 1933 Act prohibits fraud in the interstate offer or sale of securities. It provides that any person (i) who offers for sale a security by the use of any means of interstate commerce, (ii) by means of a prospectus or oral communication that contains an untrue statement or omission of material fact, and (iii) who cannot sustain the burden of proof that he did not know and in the exercise of reasonable care could not have known of such untruth, is liable to the purchaser of such security ......................... [699]

    (1) **Plaintiff's cause of action:** Plaintiff may sue for rescission or damages, but in any case must show the following: ................. [701]

      (a) *Sale* of a *security;*

      (b) Use of some means of *interstate commerce;*

      (c) An *untrue statement or omission* of material fact;

      (d) Sale by means of an *oral communication or prospectus;* and

      (e) Plaintiff must *plead* that *defendant knew* or, in the exercise of reasonable care, *should have known* of the untrue statement or omission of material fact. However, defendant carries the burden of proof on this issue.

## III. REGULATION OF SECURITIES TRADING—THE SECURITIES EXCHANGE ACT OF 1934
The SEA regulates the trading of securities subsequent to their original distribution.

C. **TENDER OFFER AND REPURCHASES OF STOCK**
   A "tender offer" is an offer by a person (the "bidder") to purchase the securities of a

## D. REGULATION OF PROXY SOLICITATIONS

Text
Section

  (2) **Representations as to price:** A broker-dealer may not represent to a customer that a transaction is taking place "at the market price" unless there are reasonable grounds to believe that a trading market for the security in fact exists (other than one created by the broker-dealer). Also, every sale by a broker-dealer carries the implied representation that the price charged is reasonably related to prevailing open market price (*see* "shingle theory," above) ............. [1810]

  (3) **Single market makers:** A firm that is the only market maker in a security is ***closely scrutinized*** to see that its disclosures to customers are proper. At a minimum, the broker-dealer must tell the customer it is the only firm making a market in the security ................ [1811]

 d. **Prohibition against causing sales:** It is unlawful for a broker-dealer to cause a customer to accept a transaction not actually agreed upon ...... [1815]

 e. **Prohibition against "churning":** The SEA also prohibits "churning" (*i.e.,* excessive trading by a broker-dealer in a customer's account, for the primary purpose of generating commission income) ................... [1817]

4. **Broker-Dealer's Duty to Disclose Adequate Information:** Broker-dealers must ascertain and disclose relevant information in making recommendations to clients ......................................................... [1824]

 a. **"Boiler room" operations:** These are high pressure sales operations (*e.g.,* direct mail offers and telephone follow-up) in which the broker-dealer typically provides incomplete or false information about the security being sold) ................................................................ [1825]

  (1) **Proceeding against broker-dealer:** The SEA authorizes the S.E.C. to proceed directly against a broker-dealer to revoke its registration . [1826]

  (2) **Private cause of action:** Customers damaged by misrepresentations or material omissions may proceed under rules 10b-5 or 15c1-2 against the ***individual salespersons*** or the broker-dealer ........ [1827]

  (3) **Direct action against salesperson:** And the S.E.C. may proceed against ***"any person"*** (including the broker-dealer's individual salespeople) to censure or bar them from associating with ***any*** broker-dealer, if such person has willfully violated the securities laws ... [1829]

 b. **"Know thy customer" rules:** NASD and NYSE rules require all broker-dealers to have reasonable grounds for believing that any purchase or sale recommended to a customer is "suitable" to the customer ............. [1830]

  (1) **Duty applies to salespeople:** This rule applies to all individual salespeople employed by broker-dealers ........................... [1831]

  (2) **Duty to investigate:** The NASD rule does not expressly require a broker to investigate the customer's financial situation. The NYSE rule requires investigation of the essential facts relative to the customer .. [1833]

  (3) **Violations of the rules:** Violations include recommending a speculative security as "safe," failing to instruct sales employees of the suitability requirement, and making overly optimistic statements about a company's prospects ...................................... [1836]

 c. **Duty of broker-dealers in submitting security quotations:** The S.E.C. has imposed a duty of care on broker-dealers in submitting quotations on over-the-counter securities to any inter-dealer quotation system or any other "publication" of such quotations. Essentially, the issuer of the security must be filing the reports required of companies registered under the SEA, or the broker-dealer must obtain similar information regrading the issuer from a reliable source, before making public quotations of the issuer's securities . [1842]

5. **Broker-Dealer's Duty to Supervise:** The SEA provides for the censure, denial of, suspension, or revocation of a broker-dealer's registration for failure adequately to supervise its associates (salespeople and employees), where the result is a violation of the securities laws ............................. [1844]

6. **Margin Requirements:** Regulations adopted under SEA section 7 governing

**XL—Securities Regulation**

## V. APPLICATIONS OF THE FEDERAL SECURITIES LAWS TO MULTINATIONAL TRANSACTIONS

### A. IN GENERAL

### B. REGISTRATION UNDER THE 1933 ACT

### C. APPLICATION OF THE 1934 ACT

## VI. REGULATION OF SECURITIES TRANSACTIONS BY THE STATES

### A. IN GENERAL
Both the SA and SEA preserve the power of the states to regulate securities transactions. Every state has adopted some form of securities regulation. Hence, every securities transaction may be subject to the law of one or more states, as well as to federal law ....... [1888]

### B. UNIFORM SECURITIES ACT
1. **Provision of Act:** The Commissioners on Uniform State Laws have adopted a Uniform Securities Act, divided into sections on (i) fraud, (ii) broker-dealer registration, (iii) registration for new securities offerings, and (iv) remedy provisions ....... [1889]
2. **Adoption by the States:** In drafting their own securities laws, most states have adopted some part of the Uniform Securities Act, as well as some provisions of their own choosing and some parts of the federal acts. Nearly all states regulate the original distribution of securities and the subsequent trading thereof (including the registration of broker-dealers) ....... [1890]

### C. ORIGINAL DISTRIBUTION OF SECURITIES
An issuer making an original distribution within a state must comply with both the SA and relevant state law ....... [1892]
1. **Blue Sky Laws:** State statutes regulating the original distribution of securities are called "blue sky" laws. The four basic types of regulatory systems used by the states are: ....... [1893]
   a. **Prohibition of fraud:** Some states simply prohibit fraud or misrepresentation in the purchase and sale of securities and provide civil and criminal sanctions for violations ....... [1894]
   b. **Registration by notification:** Other states require issuers to file with state authorities certain material information about themselves and the securities to be issued. After a stated period of time, the registered securities may be issued. Civil and criminal sanctions are provided for violations ... [1895]

# TEXT CORRELATION CHART

| Gilbert Law Summary Securities Regulation | Jennings, Marsh, Coffee **Securities Regulation** 1992 (7th ed.) 1994 Supp. (with Seligman) | Ratner, Hazen **Securities Regulation** 1991 (4th ed.) 1994 Supp. | Soderquist **Securities Regulation** 1994 (3rd ed.) |
|---|---|---|---|
| **I. INTRODUCTION TO FEDERAL SECURITIES REGULATION** | 1-4 | | 1-2 |
|   A. The Securities Industry Generally | 4-98; Supp. 1-22 | 2-5 | 2, 26-36 |
|   B. The Securities and Exchange Commission | 98-102 | 9-15, 23 | 2-11 |
|   C. Securities Acts Administered by the S.E.C.—An Overview | 98-110, 151-162, 440-448; Supp. 23-33 | 5-9, 15-24 | 2-8, 11-17 |
|   D. Jurisdiction and Interstate Commerce | 103, 392-393, 1252-1254 | 5, 372-373 | 13-14, 40-41 |
| **II. REGULATING THE ORIGINAL DISTRIBUTION OF SECURITIES—THE SECURITIES ACT OF 1993** | | | |
|   A. Introduction | 81-98, 103-110; Supp. 23-29 | 6, 25-32, 842-847 | 2, 18-36 |
|   B. Persons Covered by the 1933 Act | 85-98, 104, 322-328, 459-491 | 63-64, 70-71, 232, 324-350 | 3, 27-28, 78-79, 218-220 |
|   C. Property Interests Covered by the 1933 Act | 2, 6, 264-321 | 232-279; Supp. 7, 50 | 130-165 |
|   D. Transactions Covered by the 1933 Act | 110-150 | 44-77, 218; Supp. 42-47 | 40-79, 165-174 |
|   E. The Registration Statement | 151-263; Supp. 30-33 | 77-164, 217-225; Supp. 1-6, 48 | 24-25, 80-129, 166-171 |
|   F. Exemptions from Registration Requirements | 317-458, 469-530; Supp. 43-52 | 70-71, 276-358, 633-637, 716-720, 1046-1048; Supp. 7-8, 51-53, 60-62 | 78-79, 175-241 |
|   G. Liabilities Under the 1933 Act | 185-194, 784-789, 817-827, 836-839, 899-900, 911-923, 951-972, 1056-1067, 1086-1087, 1094-1096, 1113-1125, 1131, 1145-1162, 1173-1181, 1236-1237, 1252-1265, 1310-1313, 1334-1341, 1467-1472; Supp. 34-42, 101-132 | 151-158, 164-231, 327-329, 358-380, 452, 463-464, 466, 485-486, 495-499, 550-558, 919-932, 947-954; Supp. 8-11, 15, 22, 54 | 242-319, 582 |
| **III. REGULATION OF SECURITIES TRADING—THE SECURITIES EXCHANGE ACT OF 1934** | | | |
|   A. Overview of the 1934 Act | 98-100, 531-537, 786-789, 823-836, 839-848, 1281-1303 | 7-9, 11-14, 401, 452-455, 475-486, 533-538, 628-640, 749-750, 787-788, 837-838, 981-982; Supp. 15, 27 | 4-8, 320-331, 552-554, 571-573 |
|   B. Civil Liability Under Rule 10b-5 of the 1934 Act | 784-787, 812-833, 849-873, 951-1096, 1189-1313, 1320-1338, 1341-1349; Supp. 71-100, 133-171 | 452-532, 550-706, 912-913, 932; Supp. 15-36 | 406-512, 582-588 |
|   C. Tender Offers and Repurchases of Stock | 652-783, 793-801, 833-836, 908-910, 928-933, 954-965, 1097-1098, 1313-1320, 1334-1338, 1341-1349, 1583-1594; Supp. 53-83 | 707-714, 747-836; Supp. 57-59, 64 | 362-405, 683-696 |
|   D. Regulation of Proxy Solicitation | 789-801, 832-833, 900-910, 958-961, 967-972, 1072-1076, 1096-1097, 1189, 1251, 1335, 1473, 1483-1487; Supp. 23-29 | 65-66, 480-484, 628-637, 716-746; Supp. 29-36, 63 | 5, 332-359 |
|   E. Insider Liability for Short-Profits | 1350-1403 | 402-451; Supp. 13-14, 55-56 | 513-540 |
|   F. Liability of Participants in and Advisors to Securities Transactions | 900-910, 1099-1188; Supp. 84-125 | 189-217, 220-225, 358-364, 455-464, 485-486, 513-549, 745-746, 899-919, 947-954; Supp. 22, 54, 65 | 249-263, 470-475, 523-530, 626-669 |

| Gilbert Law Summary<br>**Securities Regulation** | Jennings, Marsh, Coffee<br>**Securities Regulation**<br>1992 (7th ed.)<br>1994 Supp. (with Seligman) | Ratner, Hazen<br>**Securities Regulation**<br>1991 (4th ed.)<br>1994 Supp. | Soderquist<br>**Securities Regulation**<br>1994 (3rd ed.) |
|---|---|---|---|
| G. **S.E.C. Enforcement Actions** | 105, 632-639, 1404-1472; Supp. 172-185, 196-201 | 15-19, 21-23, 463, 475-477, 513-541, 633-637, 926-927, 981-1006; Supp. 38 | 7-8, 10-14, 320-325, 366-367, 577-604, 612-625 |
| H. **Criminal Enforcement and RICO** | 1473-1527; Supp. 186-195 | 338-340, 466, 574-583, 593-594, 618-622 | 223-224, 243-247, 604-612 |
| **IV. REGULATION OF THE SECURITIES MARKETS** | | | |
| A. **Regulation of the National Securities Exchanges** | 16-25, 62-75, 98-102, 104, 531-580, 607-617, 683, 801-811, 842-848, 1465-1466; Supp. 9-23, 172-185 | 2-4, 842-859, 969-1034; Supp. 39 | 7-8, 25, 102-103, 320-331, 552-556 |
| B. **Regulation of the Over-the-Counter Market** | 61-65, 99-102, 563-570, 632-651 | 2-4, 477, 837-847, 982-984; Supp. 15 | 24-27, 541-553 |
| C. **Regulation of Market Manipulation and Stabilization** | 500-503, 581-624, 786 | 797-802, 859-887, 976-981 | 541-552 |
| D. **Regulation of Trading Activities of Broker-Dealers** | 61-67, 98-100, 257-258, 501, 533-562, 573-651, 784-789, 801-811, 842-848, 1046-1047, 1404-1472; Supp. 172-185, 196-201 | 837-941, 947-954, 969-972; Supp. 37, 65 | 553-576 |
| **V. APPLICATION OF FEDERAL SECURITIES LAWS TO MULTINATIONAL TRANSACTIONS** | | | |
| A. **In General** | 1528-1532 | | |
| B. **Registration Under the 1933 Act** | 1540-1558, 1566-1575, 1579-1583 | 1034-1035, 1041-1048, 1049 | |
| C. **Application of the 1934 Act** | 1532-1540, 1550-1573, 1575-1612; Supp. 186-195 | 1034-1041, 1044-1046, 1048-1057 | |
| **VI. REGULATION OF SECURITIES TRANSACTIONS BY THE STATES** | | | |
| A. **In General** | | 5-6 | 17 |
| B. **Uniform Securities Act** | 345, 1616-1617 | 5-6, 380-381 | 681-683 |
| C. **Original Distribution of Securities** | 1613-1659 | 380-399, 810-836 | 670-696 |

# _approach to exams_

Law school courses in Securities Regulation generally focus on two federal statutes—the Securities Act of 1933 and the Securities Exchange Act of 1934. These laws regulate: (i) the original issuance and subsequent trading of securities; (ii) the markets in which securities are traded; and (iii) the parties that do the trading. However, federal law is not exclusive, and state securities laws (commonly called "blue sky" laws) may impose similar or additional restrictions on securities transactions.

You should use the following general approach to identify the relevant issues in exam questions. (Refer also to the more detailed chapter approaches at the beginning of each chapter.)

## A. THE SECURITIES ACT OF 1933

1. **Coverage of the Act:** The 1933 Act applies to the original distribution and, in limited circumstances, the secondary distribution of securities. Thus, the first question when a fact situation involves the distribution of securities is whether there is a _"distribution of securities"_ covered by the 1933 Act.

   a. **Original distributions:** An "original distribution" is an offering by the issuer to the public of securities that have never been sold before.

   b. **Secondary distributions:** A "secondary distribution" has two important aspects:

      (1) **Offering by shareholder(s):** A secondary distribution is an offering to the public of the issuer's securities, but by one or more _shareholders_ of the issuer, rather than by the issuer itself.

      (2) **Shareholders standing in for issuer:** In a secondary distribution, shareholders are standing in for the issuer; they are not merely persons who purchased the securities as a routine investment, but rather are either:

         (i) "Control persons" of the issuer (_i.e.,_ those who can influence the issuer); and/or

         (ii) Persons who purchased the securities in a non-public transaction or series of transactions.

      _Note:_ A single group of selling shareholders in a secondary distribution may include persons within one or the other, or both, of the above categories.

   c. **Definition of "security":** The 1933 Act applies only to the distribution of securities, but the universe of possible investments is much larger. In other words, not every investment offered to the public is a security. In general, therefore, it is a good idea to verify that the exam question involves a security; if it does not, the Act does not apply.

2. **Factors to Consider in Covered Distributions:** Where a fact situation involves an original or secondary distribution, consider the following:

   a. **Jurisdiction:** Are the facilities or means of interstate commerce involved in the offering?

b. **Exemptions from registration:** If at all possible, the offeror (issuer or selling shareholder) will desire to avoid by some exemption the time and expense of registering with the S.E.C.:

    (1) **Exemptions for original distributions**

        (a) Is it a "private offering"? Or, do the "small issue" exemptions apply? If so, then no registration is required.

        (b) Is the offer or sale of the securities for "value"? If not, registration is not required.

        (c) Is the sale pursuant to a "reorganization" or "recapitalization"? If so, there may be an exemption from registration.

        (d) Is the transaction subject to approval by a court or other governmental agency? If so, there may be an exemption from registration.

        (e) Is the offer or sale an "intrastate offering"? If so, the intrastate offering exemption may apply.

        (f) Are brokers or dealers involved in the distribution chain? If so, an exemption from registration for these persons may be available.

    (2) **Exemptions for secondary distributions**

        (a) Is the sale a public offering? If not, the selling shareholder is exempted from the registration requirements.

        (b) Is the sale exempt from registration under rule 144?

        (c) Is the transaction one *not* involving an issuer, underwriter, or dealer? If so, it is exempt under SA section 4(1). *Note:* A sale by an ordinary investor of securities purchased in a routine investment transaction (and not in a private placement) is exempt because the investor can use the section 4(1) exemption, and the broker-dealer through whom the investor sells can use either the dealer's exemption in section 4(3) or the brokers's exemption in section 4(4). Beware, however, of sales by persons who either are *control persons* of the issuer or who purchased the securities *in private transactions*; such sales often involve "statutory underwriters" and are therefore not exempt under section 4(1).

c. **Registration:** If the offering is *not* exempt, it must be registered, and the following issues may arise:

    (1) **Type of registration:** Is the registration covered by the regulation A exemption (a shorter form for registering limited offerings), by the regular S-1 registration (for most commercial or industrial companies), or by some other form of registration statement (*e.g.,* for "corporate act" transactions under rule 145)?

    (2) **Timing requirements:** Have the issuer and the other parties involved in the registered offering complied with the requirements of:

       (a)   The pre-filing period?

       (b)   The waiting period?

       (c)   The post-effective period?

   (3)  **Disclosure:** Has the registration statement disclosed all material facts concerning the issuer and its business?

   (4)  **Processing issues:** Are there issues regarding the processing of the registration statement with the S.E.C.?

       (a)   Has a stop order (or some other S.E.C. order) been issued?

       (b)   Is a post-effective amendment or a supplemental prospectus required?

  d.  **Liability under the 1933 Act:** Finally, there may be issues involving the liability provisions of the 1933 Act that apply to failure to register a non-exempt offering, and to misstatements or omissions of material facts in a covered securities offering.

## B.  THE SECURITIES EXCHANGE ACT OF 1934

1.  **Coverage of the Act:** The 1934 Act generally covers the *trading of securities* in the market after the original or secondary distribution.

2.  **Registered Securities:** The 1934 Act requires issuers to register securities meeting certain criteria.

  a.  **Listed securities:** Are the securities (equity or debt) traded on a national securities exchange? If so, they must be registered under the 1934 Act.

  b.  **OTC securities:** Does the issuer have more than $5 million in assets? If so, the issuer must register under the 1934 Act each class of equity security that is held of record by 500 or more persons.

3.  **Reporting Companies:** All issuers with securities registered under the 1934 Act must file periodic reports with the S.E.C. Such issuers are often referred to as "reporting companies." The filed reports are public, and may be inspected and copied at the S.E.C.'s offices in Washington, D.C. These reports are of several kinds:

  a.  Annual reports on Form 10-K (or Form 10-KSB, for small business issuers);

  b.  Quarterly reports on Form 10-Q (or Form 10-QSB, for small business issuers);

  c.  Current reports on Form 8-K (triggered by the occurrence of significant events);

  d.  Proxy statements (which must be sent directly to shareholders as well as filed with the S.E.C.), prior to each shareholders meeting at which directors are to be elected; and

  e.  Annual reports to shareholders, which must accompany or precede each proxy statement.

4. **Jurisdiction:** Since most provisions of the 1934 Act apply only if *interstate commerce* is involved, has this jurisdictional requirement been met?

5. **Regulation of Broker-Dealers:** Does the transaction involve a broker-dealer? If so, has there been a violation of the NASD or S.E.C. rules relating to the conduct of broker-dealers?

    a. **Market-making:** If the broker-dealer was "making a market" in the security, has she violated a duty of disclosure?

    b. **Margin trading:** Were the securities sold on "margin" and, if so, have the rules relating to margin trading been violated?

    c. **"Churning":** Was there excessive trading, raising a "churning" issue?

6. **Market Manipulation and Stabilization:** Did any party attempt artificially to fix or determine the market price or volume of trading in a security? Or did any party unlawfully attempt to "stabilize" the market price for a security?

7. **Tender Offers and Repurchases of Stock:** Has there been an attempt to purchase shares of a company directly from the shareholders? If so, was this a "tender offer" subject to the 1934 Act? Were all of the rules applicable to tender offers met?

8. **Short-Swing Trading:** Has there been trading in an equity security by corporate "insiders" within a six-month period? If so, section 16 may apply.

9. **Proxy Solicitation:** Have proxies been solicited from shareholders? If so, the rules and regulations applicable to proxy solicitations may apply.

10. **Rule 10b-5:** In every securities transaction, consider whether rule 10b-5 is applicable. This general fraud provision is very broad and may apply wherever there is some nexus of fraud with a securities transaction.

## C. LIABILITY OF "COLLATERAL PARTICIPANTS"

Consider whether any "collateral participants" might be liable for a violation of the securities laws. "Collateral participants" are those who are involved in, but not directly responsible for the transaction (*e.g.*, lawyers, accountants, underwriters, etc.).

1. **Liability Under the 1933 Act:** Although the "collateral participant" is not directly responsible for the securities transaction, has she "participated " to such a degree that she may be held liable? Could she be held liable as a "control person"?

2. **Liability Under the 1934 Act:** Could the person be held liable as a "control person" or co-conspirator under rule 10b-5 or under one of the other general liability provisions of the 1934 Act?

## D. STATE LAW

Finally, consider whether the *statutory or common law* of one or more states might apply to regulate either an original distribution or the subsequent trading of securities.

# I. INTRODUCTION TO FEDERAL SECURITIES REGULATION

## _chapter approach_

The public has a strong interest in the regulation of securities and securities markets. Securities are an important form of private property affecting the financial well-being of a large segment of the population; and the condition of the securities markets has a major impact on the flow of capital to industry and therefore on the economy as a whole.

This chapter provides an introduction to Securities Regulation, giving you a broad overview of the securities industry, the federal securities acts, and the Securities and Exchange Commission. Although most of the information in this chapter is important only for a general understanding of this area of law, you may find a question on your exam asking you to determine whether interstate commerce is involved and thus whether the federal securities laws apply to the particular transaction.

## A. THE SECURITIES INDUSTRY GENERALLY

1. **Securities Markets:** [§1]   Securities markets are the systems through which securities are bought and sold. The two basic types of securities markets are primary markets and secondary markets. Primary markets are the markets for the original distribution of securities; secondary markets are for the continuous trading of outstanding securities.

   a. **Primary markets:** [§2]   Primary markets are the facilities through which the securities are *first* issued or distributed to the public. For example, if XYZ Corp. is formed and issues some of its common stock to the public, this issuance occurs in the primary market.

   b. **Secondary markets:** [§3]   Secondary markets are markets that exist for the ongoing trading of securities *after* their original distribution. Securities already distributed may be bought and sold in one of two ways: through a stock exchange, or with the help of a securities firm in the "over-the-counter" ("OTC") market.

      (1) **Stock exchanges:** [§4]   The securities of most large corporations are traded over stock exchanges. These exchanges (the most important of which is the New York Stock Exchange—"NYSE") have physical locations with organized facilities, including trading "floors" upon which stocks are bought and sold.

         (a) **Note:** To be traded on the floor of an exchange, securities must be "listed" (*i.e.*, registered and qualified) with that exchange. (*See* further discussion *infra*, §1605.)

      (2) **Over-the-counter trading:** [§5]   Securities traded outside the stock exchanges are said to be traded "over the counter"—which means that they are traded back and forth by securities firms called "broker-dealers" (discussed below). There is no physical location or exchange facility for

the over-the-counter market. Instead, securities firms in many locations are linked through various communication systems (such as computer networks) used to match buyers and sellers.

(a) **NASDAQ:** [§6]   The National Association of Securities Dealers has implemented an automated quotation system—"NASDAQ"—which, by ensuring timely price information, makes the OTC market increasingly attractive to investors and issuers.

    1)   **Note:** Securities traded over NASDAQ must meet standards similar to (but generally less demanding than) those required of securities that are listed on a securities exchange.

(3) **Other securities markets:** [§7]   There are also other markets for the trading of securities. One is the so-called "third market"; *i.e.*, securities are listed on stock exchanges and traded by broker-dealers in the over-the-counter market. Another is the "fourth market"; *i.e.*, individual persons or firms owning securities trade them without the assistance of a market intermediary, such as a broker-dealer.

(4) **National market system:** [§8]   Note also that section 11A(a)(2) of the Securities Exchange Act of 1934 directs the Securities Exchange Commission ("S.E.C.") to facilitate the establishment of a "national market system," which is slowly developing through computerized systems that provide information from many sources and locations on the trading of securities.

2.   **Securities Firms—Brokers and Dealers:** [§9]   Besides regulating securities markets, the federal securities laws also regulate the activities of firms engaged in trading securities. These firms function both as "brokers" and as "dealers." The definitions of "broker" and "dealer" given below are general, functional definitions. The securities acts also define the terms in several places where they are relevant to specific regulatory purposes. The definitions in the acts may or may not coincide with the general, functional definitions given here.

a.   **"Brokers":** [§10]   These are generally defined as agents who buy and sell securities for their customers on a commission basis. For example, assume A wishes to buy 100 shares of XYZ Corp. If B buys the shares for A at $10 per share and charges A a 5% commission, B has acted as a broker.

b.   **"Dealers":** [§11]   Dealers, on the other hand, act as principals—buying the securities for their *own account* and subsequently reselling them to their customers at a marked-up price. Thus, in the above example, instead of charging A a 5% commission, B could have purchased the XYZ stock for $10 and resold it to A for $12 per share.

c.   **Dual functions common:** [§12]   Note that the same person or firm can be a "broker" in one transaction and a "dealer" in another transaction. Most firms in the securities business function in both capacities, and hence are referred to as "broker-dealers." Note that broker-dealers employ a variety of personnel, including salespeople, clerks, traders, and supervisory personnel.

d.   **Different functions on exchanges and in the over-the-counter market:** [§13]   When a customer executes a purchase or sale order over an exchange, the firm through which he deals acts as a broker for the customer. The broker typically executes the order through a "specialist" (a person authorized by the exchange to buy and sell specific listed securities for his own account) on the floor of the exchange. (*See* discussion *infra*, §1648 concerning specialists.)

(1) **Compare:** When a customer executes a purchase or sale order in the over-the-counter market, the firm through which the customer deals may act either as a broker (buying or selling for the customer on a commission basis) or as a dealer (buying or selling for its own account and charging the customer a markup). (*See* discussion *infra*, §§1783-1784.) Note that many securities firms operate both in the exchange markets and in the over-the-counter market.

3. **Changing Role of Banks:** [§14]   Since 1933, the Glass-Steagall Act has prohibited banks from underwriting corporate securities. Efforts by the banking industry to repeal or amend Glass-Steagall have not been successful. However, in recent years the Federal Reserve Board has permitted banks to engage in more and more securities-related activities, and these administrative decisions have generally been upheld by the courts.

4. **Other Financial Markets:** [§15]   Increasingly, the operation and regulation of the United States securities markets is affected by other financial markets, both foreign and domestic.

   a. **Foreign markets:** [§16]   Growth in foreign markets, especially the so-called "Euromarket," has led the S.E.C. to seek to coordinate requirements among regulators from the United States and other countries. In particular, United States regulators are concerned that if the United States markets are seen as over-regulated, United States issuers might flee to foreign markets to raise capital, and foreign issuers might avoid the United States markets.

   b. **Domestic markets:** [§17]   The 1980s saw an explosion of new financial products, especially "derivative instruments" such as interest rate swaps, futures on financial indices, and options on other financial instruments. Not all of these instruments are securities. (*See* discussion of the definition of "security," *infra*, §§123-140.) But they nevertheless form an important part of the context in which the securities industry functions.

      (1) **The money market:** [§18]   The money market involves primarily "commercial paper," *i.e.*, short-term debt instruments issued by corporations.

      (2) **The government securities market:** [§19]   Government securities include direct obligations of the United States and obligations of agencies of the United States government.

      (3) **The municipal securities market:** [§20]   The market for municipal securities resembles in many respects that for government securities, except that there is a much greater risk of default by a municipality than by the United States.

(4) **Derivative products markets:** [§21]   This market includes a variety of financial products, the most important of which are discussed below.

    (a) **Traded options:** [§22]   Options are contracts giving the buyer of the option the right to buy or sell an asset at a price determined in advance. The holder of an option is *not obligated* to exercise it. Traded options are options written on standardized terms and issued by the Options Clearing Corporation, a corporation jointly owned by the exchanges on which options are traded.

    (b) **Futures:** [§23]   Futures contracts create an *obligation* to sell or to buy an asset at a future date, at a price determined in advance. Futures on stock market indices, for instance the Standard & Poor's 500 index, give one of the parties the right to receive a sum of cash based on the price of the securities in the index. Which party gets paid depends on whether the index has risen or fallen since the parties entered into the futures contract. Futures are regulated by the Commodities Futures Trading Commission ("C.F.T.C.").

        1) **1987 market crash:** Most commentators attribute the October 19, 1987, stock market crash at least partly to futures trading. On that day, many investors sold stock while simultaneously purchasing index futures. The resulting flood of stock onto the market contributed to the decline of stock prices.

    (c) **Swaps:** [§24]   Swaps are agreements whereby two parties agree to make periodic payments to each other. A typical *interest rate swap* involves one side paying interest at a fixed rate, while the other side pays a floating rate (for example, the prime rate in effect on each payment date). In a typical *currency swap,* one side agrees to pay a dollar amount to the other, and the other makes its payment in a foreign currency (for example, Swiss francs).

    (d) **"Portfolio insurance":** [§25]   Portfolio insurance is not really insurance at all. The term refers to a variety of complex hedging strategies, often employing one or more of the financial instruments described immediately above. The aim of these strategies is to hedge (that is, to reduce the risk of severe loss in) an investor's securities portfolio.

5. **Regulatory Issues:** [§26]   The proliferation of new financial instruments has produced conflict between the S.E.C. and the C.F.T.C., as each agency tries to assert jurisdiction over a new instrument. Which agency succeeds in a given case depends on whether the instrument in question is a security, an option on a security, or a futures contract. Many new instruments, however, fit into more than one of these categories.

    a. **Both a security and a futures contract:** [§27]   If an instrument is both a security and a futures contract, then the C.F.T.C. has sole jurisdiction. [7 U.S.C. §2a(ii); *and see* Chicago Mercantile Exchange v. S.E.C., 883 F.2d 537 (7th Cir. 1989)]

b. **Both an option on a security and a futures contract:** [§28]  If an instrument is both an option on a security and a futures contract, then the S.E.C. has sole jurisdiction. [7 U.S.C. §2a(i); *and see* Chicago Mercantile Exchange v. S.E.C., *supra*]

## B.  THE SECURITIES AND EXCHANGE COMMISSION

1. **S.E.C. Functions:** [§29]  The S.E.C. is the agency responsible for administering and enforcing the federal securities laws. The basic functions of the S.E.C. are:

   a. **Rulemaking:** [§30]  The S.E.C. adopts substantive rules to implement the federal securities laws. The S.E.C. has the authority to adopt such rules pursuant to a congressional delegation of authority in the federal securities acts.

   b. **Interpreting:** [§31]  The S.E.C. interprets the securities laws and S.E.C. rules issued thereunder. The Commission does this in two principal ways:

      (1) **General policy statements:** [§32]  Periodically, the S.E.C. will issue "releases" to the general public which state the views of the S.E.C. on matters of current concern.

      (2) **No action letters:** [§33]  In addition, private parties (such as a lawyer for a corporate client) may inquire of the S.E.C. as to whether a specific transaction may be carried out in a specific manner without violating the securities laws. If the staff agrees that the action as described will not violate the securities laws, its response is called a "no action" letter, since the S.E.C. staff indicates that it will not recommend enforcement action to the Commission if the transaction is carried out in the manner specified.

   c. **Investigating:** [§34]  The S.E.C. also investigates possible violations of the laws and rules.

   d. **Initiating formal proceedings:** [§35]  The S.E.C. initiates formal proceedings against a wrongdoer—*i.e.*, seeks statutory remedies and sanctions for violation of the securities laws. *Examples:*

      (i) *Civil injunctions* may be sought in the federal district courts;

      (ii) *Criminal prosecutions* may be brought by the U.S. Department of Justice; and

      (iii) *Administrative remedies* (*e.g.*, suspension of a securities firm from trading, or issuance of a cease and desist order) may be pursued by the S.E.C. in administrative proceedings.

      *Note: Private actions* may be brought by private (*i.e.*, nongovernmental) plaintiffs when they have been injured by a violation of the securities laws and when the law provides for either an express or implied cause of action.

2. **S.E.C. Administrative Procedures:** [§36]  All administrative proceedings brought by the S.E.C. are conducted in accordance with rules conforming to the Federal

Administrative Procedure Act ("A.P.A."). These rules are designed to meet the requirements of constitutional due process—*i.e.*, proper notice, confrontation and cross-examination of witnesses, etc. (*See* Administrative Law Summary.) Briefly, the procedures are as follows:

a. **Hearing before administrative law judge:** [§37]   The first step in S.E.C. proceedings is a hearing conducted by an administrative law judge appointed by the S.E.C. This judge makes the initial decision in the matter.

b. **Commission review:** [§38]   Following the hearing, either or both of the parties may seek review of the administrative law judge's decision by the full Commission. Alternatively, the S.E.C. may decide to review the decision on its own motion.

c. **Appeal to the courts:** [§39]   Finally, an aggrieved party may seek review of the S.E.C.'s decision by a United States Court of Appeals.

## C.   SECURITIES ACTS ADMINISTERED BY THE S.E.C.—AN OVERVIEW

1. **Securities Act of 1933:** [§40]   The Securities Act of 1933 ("SA" or "1933 Act"; discussed in detail, *infra*) primarily regulates the *original issuance* of securities—*e.g.,* where XYZ Corp. desires to issue 100,000 shares of its common stock to the public for $10 per share.

   a. **Purpose of the Act:** [§41]   The primary purpose of the 1933 Act is to *compel full disclosure of all material facts* in public offerings. [SA §5] A secondary purpose is *to prevent fraud and misrepresentation* in the interstate offer or sale of securities. [SA §12]

2. **Securities Exchange Act of 1934:** [§42]   The Securities Exchange Act of 1934 ("SEA" or "1934 Act"; also discussed at length, *infra*) governs trading in securities that are already issued and outstanding. The 1934 Act has a much broader scope than the Securities Act, and regulates a wide variety of securities transactions. These include:

   a. **Registration and reporting:** [§43]   The 1934 Act requires a company to register its securities with the S.E.C. and thereafter to file periodic financial reports with the S.E.C. if the company's securities are (i) traded on a regulated *national securities exchange or* (ii) traded over the counter, and the company has assets of *more than $5 million and 500 or more shareholders* of a class of equity securities (such as common stock). Corporations subject to the registration and filing requirements are called "registered companies." [SEA §§12, 13]

   b. **Proxy solicitation:** [§44]   The SEA also regulates the solicitation of voting proxies from the shareholders of registered companies. [SEA §14; *and see infra*, §§1128 *et seq.*]

   c. **Insider trading:** [§45]   Provisions of the SEA restrict and penalize trading in a registered company's shares by company "insiders" (*i.e.*, company officers or directors, or owners of 10% of the outstanding shares of a registered class of equity securities). [SEA §16; *and see infra*, §§1282 *et seq.*]

d. **Margin trading:** [§46]   The 1934 Act permits regulation by the S.E.C. of margin trading (*i.e.*, buying securities on credit). [SEA §§7, 8; *and see infra,* §1848]

e. **Market surveillance:** [§47]   The Act likewise authorizes the S.E.C. to regulate certain security market trading practices which are based on fraud or market manipulation. [SEA §9; *and see infra,* §§1720 *et seq.*]

f. **Registration of securities exchanges, broker-dealers, and securities associations:** [§48]   National securities exchanges (such as the NYSE) and broker-dealers who conduct an interstate over-the-counter securities business must register with and make periodic reports to the S.E.C. [SEA §§6—regulation of national exchanges; 15—regulation of broker-dealers; *and see infra,* §1695]

   (1) **S.E.C. regulation:** [§49]   The 1934 Act authorizes the S.E.C. to make rules and regulations governing the activities of broker-dealers and the national exchanges. [SEA §§19(b)-(c), 15]

   (2) **Self-regulation:** [§50]   The Act also permits the exchanges to make their own self-policing rules. In addition, self-policing associations of broker-dealers may organize and register with the S.E.C. [SEA §§15, 15A, 19]

g. **Tender offer solicitations:** [§51]   The 1934 Act also regulates situations in which one company seeks to acquire control of another by a direct offer to purchase stock from shareholders of the target company. [SEA §§13, 14; *and see infra,* §978]

h. **Antifraud provisions:** [§52]   And, finally, the 1934 Act contains a number of provisions that impose liability for fraud in the purchase or sale of securities—the most important of which is contained in section 10(b) and rule 10b-5 of the 1934 Act. (*See infra,* §§795 *et seq.*)

3. **Other Federal Acts Administered by the S.E.C.:** [§53]   The S.E.C. administers certain other federal securities acts not normally covered in a law school course in Securities Regulation. Briefly, these are:

   a. **Public Utility Holding Company Act of 1935:** [§54]   This Act is designed to correct abuses in the financing and operation of public utility holding companies.

   b. **Trust Indenture Act of 1939:** [§55]   This Act regulates large issues of debt securities (*i.e.*, in excess of $10 million in total value). This Act contains provisions designed to protect security holders, such as a requirement that the trust indenture covering the securities (*i.e.*, the documents stating the terms under which the securities are issued) meet certain standards insuring the independence and responsibility of the indenture trustee.

   c. **Investment Company Act of 1940:** [§56]   This Act governs the activities of publicly owned companies that invest and trade in securities (*e.g.*, mutual funds). It regulates the composition of management, the capital structure of the company, its investment policies, etc.

d. **Investment Advisers Act of 1940:** [§57] This Act provides for registration and regulation of those in the business of advising others on securities investments.

4. **Other Federal Statutes:** [§58] Although they are not administered by the S.E.C., the following federal statutes are also helpful to an understanding of the S.E.C.'s function and of the securities industry in general:

   a. **Bankruptcy Act:** [§59] This Act authorizes the S.E.C. to serve as an adviser to United States district courts in federal bankruptcy proceedings—involving reorganization of debtor corporations—where there is a "substantial public interest." In this capacity, the S.E.C. may be asked to advise the court on the selection of the trustee, on the appropriateness of the reorganization plans for the debtor corporation, and other related matters.

   b. **Securities Investor Protection Act of 1970:** [§60] This Act creates a non-profit membership corporation to which most broker-dealers must belong. It is funded by assessments. If a securities firm fails and cannot pay its customer accounts, then (up to certain maximum amounts) this corporation makes up the difference.

5. **Integrated Disclosure:** [§61] As the above material makes clear, there are many disclosure requirements under the securities laws. With respect to the two main acts (Securities Act of 1933 and Securities Exchange Act of 1934), originally there were two separate and distinct disclosure systems established. This dual system spawned separate sets of registration statements, periodic reports, etc., each with its own set of instructions. Eventually, the S.E.C. lightened the burden of compliance by integrating the reporting requirements of the two Acts. Regulation S-K now prescribes a single standard set of instructions for filing forms under the two Acts, so that when the same type of information is required by the various forms under these Acts, a single set of instructions applies. Also, revisions to several rules and forms resulted in a uniform set of financial disclosure requirements for all documents required to be filed under the 1933 or 1934 Acts. Finally, the S.E.C. adopted forms for registration of offerings under the 1933 Act (*see infra*, §§218-224), which in some cases permit incorporation by reference of information in 1934 Act reports.

## D. JURISDICTION AND INTERSTATE COMMERCE

1. **In General:** [§62] The provisions of the federal securities laws are based on Congress's power to regulate interstate commerce. Therefore, these acts generally apply only where the facilities or instrumentalities of interstate commerce are involved.

2. **"Interstate Commerce"**

   a. **Definition under 1933 Act:** [§63] Under the 1933 Act, "interstate commerce" is defined as "trade or commerce in securities or any transportation or communication relating thereto among the several states." [SA §2(7)]

      (1) **Expansive interpretation:** [§64] The S.E.C. and the courts have adopted a broad interpretation of what constitutes "interstate commerce" in order to realize the underlying objectives of the 1933 Act.

(a) **Use of means of interstate commerce:** Under modern interpretations of the Act, interstate commerce is not only involved whenever a transaction touches more than one state, but also when the "means" of interstate commerce (*e.g.*, the telephone, mails, etc.) are used in any part of a securities transaction.

1) **Example:** Thus, even *intrastate* telephone calls or mailings have been held to support federal jurisdiction under the 1933 Act, since the *means* of interstate commerce were used.

b. **Definition under 1934 Act:** [§65]   Under the 1934 Act, the term "interstate commerce" includes trade, commerce, transportation or communication among the several states—plus *intrastate* use of any facility or instrumentality of interstate commerce, such as a national securities exchange or a telephone. [SEA §3(a)(17)]

c. **Effect—nearly all transactions covered:** [§66]   As a result of the expansive interpretation of these definitions, very few securities transactions are exempt from the 1933 or 1934 Acts on the grounds they do not involve "interstate commerce."

# II. REGULATING THE ORIGINAL DISTRIBUTION OF SECURITIES— THE SECURITIES ACT OF 1933

## ___chapter approach___

This chapter covers the Securities Act of 1933. A lot of material is covered here, so to help you study, the most likely topics for exam questions are discussed below.

1. **Persons Covered by the Act:** The registration and prospectus requirements of the Act apply to the *"issuer," "control person," "underwriter,"* and *"dealer,"* unless they are otherwise exempted. Be sure you understand the definition of each category. Especially remember that the person or firm *helping the issuer distribute* securities to the public may be an "underwriter" (and must comply with the registration provisions of the Act). Also, if the person selling securities to the public is *able to influence the affairs* of the company whose securities are being sold (*i.e.*, is a control person), he is treated as an issuer. Finally, be aware that people who *sell for control persons* may be underwriters.

2. **Property Interests Covered by the Act:** Nearly all Securities Regulation exams will have a question on whether some investment interest is a "security" and thus covered by the 1933 Act. Therefore, study this section carefully. The most likely issue would be whether an investment contract is involved. This analysis requires you to look at all of the facts of the situation and determine whether some investment interest should be treated as a security. To do this, consider the five factors listed in §136.

   Another possible problem for an exam question would involve an investment interest that is one of the instruments *specifically named* as a security, but as to which the circumstances and economic realities of the situation make application of the Act questionable. Consider *Landreth Timber Co. v. Landreth* (*infra*, §126) (stock and the "sale of business" doctrine), *United Housing Foundation, Inc. v. Forman* (*infra*, §126) (stock in a housing cooperative) and *Reves v. Ernst & Young* (*infra*, §130) (notes).

3. **Transactions Covered by the Act:** This part of the chapter contains very technical, detailed statutory and S.E.C. rule information. It will probably *not* show up in an essay question, but it is good material for multiple choice or true-false questions. To master this material, you need to read carefully the S.E.C. rules and relevant sections of the 1933 Act. Read the rules and statute and the material in this chapter until you understand what exactly can be done to market securities that are being registered with the S.E.C. in the *prefiling period*, the *waiting period* before the registration statement is effective, and the *posteffective period* (*i.e.,* after the registration is effective).

4. **The Registration Statement:** The main thing to note here is what type of information must be disclosed in a registration statement: financial information, information about the issuer's management, etc.

5. **Exemptions from Registration Requirements:** The importance of this topic cannot be overemphasized. Registration is time-consuming and expensive, so issuers always try to avoid registering if possible. Thus, almost every exam will have at least one question

asking whether one or more of the possible exemptions to registration apply to a given transaction. Some helpful hints:

a.  Exempted security *transactions* are emphasized more than the exempted *securities*.

b.  The *broker's exemption* is important to know since, when a security is sold outside the public offering itself, a broker is usually involved and the broker may need to appeal to this exemption.

c.  The *private offering* exemption is a favorite test subject. Also likely are the *intrastate exemption* and the *Regulation D* exemptions. (Regulation A offerings or the exemptions relating to reorganizations and recapitalizations are less likely subjects, although you should study rule 145 carefully.)

d.  The material on *restrictions on the resale* of securities that are first issued under a transaction exemption is very important for you to know (*e.g.*, if the issuer sells to X in a private offering, what happens if X then sells to Y?). Be sure you know the details of rule 144 (*infra*, §§549 *et seq.*).

6.  **Liabilities Under the Act:** Be sure that you understand the various situations where the remedy provisions of the 1933 Act apply (*e.g.*, section 11 of the Act applies only to misstatements in a registration statement, while section 12(2) applies generally to fraud in the sale of securities). Be sure that you understand the interrelation between the remedy provisions so that you know which might apply to a given situation and which may be preferable to sue for. Finally, integrate these remedies sections with the material on rule 10b-5 (*see infra*, §795), a general liability section.

---

## A.  INTRODUCTION

As noted above, the Securities Act of 1933 regulates the original distribution of securities by the issuer to the general public.

1.  **Distribution Process:** [§67]   The distribution of securities (called an "underwriting") involves the moving of securities from the issuer through the underwriter, dealers, and initial investors into the hands of those purchasers who intend to hold the securities for investment (*i.e.*, for some substantial period of time).

    a.  **Example:** XYZ Corp. contracts to have Merrill Lynch (a securities firm) underwrite 100,000 shares of its capital stock. Merrill Lynch, as the managing underwriter, may organize a group of other underwriters to help it sell the issue of XYZ securities. Merrill Lynch and the other underwriters buy the stock from XYZ at $10 per share, and then arrange for other dealer firms to purchase a portion of the shares at $11 per share. The dealers then sell the securities to retail customers at $12 per share. The managing underwriter, who negotiates the deal with XYZ and assembles the underwriting group, charges each of the other underwriters in the group a commission for its services.

    b.  **Pattern of distribution:** [§68]   Thus, the sequence of events in a typical underwriting is as follows:

(1) **Decision to issue:** [§69] The issuer (XYZ Corp.) decides to sell 100,000 shares of its common stock to the public in order to raise capital.

*Issuer*
(XYZ Corp.)

*Underwriter(s)*

*Dealers*

*Retail Purchasers*

(2) **Agreement with underwriter:** [§70] XYZ goes to a securities firm (the underwriter) and enters into an agreement to have this firm "underwrite" the securities issue: The securities firm will either buy the securities from the issuer, or take responsibility for their sale on some other basis (*see infra*, §§74-78).

(3) **Agreement with dealers:** [§71] The underwriter then enters into agreements with a number of other securities firms ("dealers") to have them buy the securities for resale to their retail customers.

(4) **Sale to retail customers:** [§72] Finally, the dealers sell the XYZ securities to their retail customers.

c. **Initial investors:** [§73] In a normal securities distribution, dealers often sell to retail customers who intend to hold for only a short time, hoping to make a quick profit by selling once the newly issued securities move up in price (which often occurs in the first hours or days of a new offering). A sale to such an investor does not mean the completion of a "distribution"; this occurs only when the securities come to rest in the hands of those investors who intend to hold them for a *substantial* period of time.

(1) **Example:** XYZ Corp. issues 100,000 shares of its common stock to the public through A, an underwriter. B, a dealer who has an allotment from A to sell 10,000 shares, sells 1,000 shares to C, a retail purchaser. C holds the XYZ stock for only one day (while the price goes up) and then resells the stock to D, who intends to hold it for a substantial period of time. The distribution is complete only when the stock is sold to D.

d. **Types of underwriting agreements:** [§74] Several types of underwriting agreements may be used between issuers and underwriters, and the 1933 Act applies in the same manner to each of these arrangements.

(1) **"Stand-by" underwriting:** [§75] In this form of underwriting, the issuer itself advertises the issuance of the securities and sells directly to the public. In the event that the issuer does not sell all of its securities, the underwriter agrees (for a fee) to buy the unsold portion. Thus, the underwriter acts, in effect, as an insurer of the success of the distribution.

(2) **"Firm-commitment" underwriting:** [§76] Here, the issuer actually sells its securities outright to the underwriter, who then resells the securities to dealers and/or the general public.

(3) **"Best-efforts" underwriting:** [§77] In this form of underwriting, the underwriter acts as a sales agent for the issuer on a commission basis. The

underwriter agrees to use its best efforts to market the securities to the public, but makes no guarantee that the issue will be completely sold.

(4) **Complete control by issuer:** [§78]  In some situations, a company might not use an underwriter at all, even as an "insurer." Such situations generally occur where the company is well established (and does not need an underwriter) or is a poor financial risk (and cannot find an underwriter).

    (a) **Note:** A company is a poor financial risk where there is a high degree of uncertainty whether the issuer's securities will maintain or exceed the issuing price in subsequent trading due to poor financial performance by the issuer (and investors become dissatisfied as a result).

e. **Regulation of underwriter's compensation**

(1) **Under state law:** [§79]  The securities laws of many states limit the amount and type of compensation that an underwriter may receive in an original distribution.

(2) **By NASD standard:** [§80]  The National Association of Securities Dealers ("NASD"), an organization to which all registered broker-dealers must belong, has also undertaken to regulate underwriter compensation. In general, the standard used is that compensation must be "fair and reasonable" under all of the circumstances.

    (a) **Advance review:** [§81]  Underwriting agreements for "unseasoned companies" (*i.e.*, new companies or those without an established earnings record) must be reviewed in advance of the underwriting.

    (b) **Securities received as compensation:** [§82]  All types of the issuer's securities received or purchased by the underwriter in connection with the distribution are considered part of the underwriter's compensation for doing the underwriting (*e.g.*, the underwriter may receive options to purchase 10,000 shares of XYZ's common stock, good for five years, as compensation for underwriting an issue of 100,000 shares of XYZ stock).

    (c) **Factors considered:** [§83]  Factors considered in determining underwriter compensation are: the underwriting expenses payable by the issuer, cash commissions received by the underwriter, consulting and advisory fees received, and options and warrants to purchase the issuer's securities granted to the underwriter.

    (d) **Excessive compensation:** [§84]  Compensation that exceeds 18-20% of the gross dollar amount received by the issuer from the offering is probably excessive.

2. **Objectives of 1933 Act:** [§85]  Congressional inquiries into the stock market crash of 1929 determined that securities were often initially distributed to investors without any disclosure of facts relevant to the buyer's investment decision, and that the remedies provided by state law for fraudulent practices in these transactions were inadequate. Enactment of the 1933 Act therefore had as its objectives: (i) *full disclosure* of all material facts in public offerings; and (ii) *prevention of fraud and misrepresentation* in the interstate offer or sale of securities.

a. **Full disclosure to potential investors:** [§86]   The primary objective of the 1933 Act is to provide investors with all material investment information relating to the original issuance of securities.

    (1) **Registration statement:** [§87]   To accomplish this goal, the Act requires the issuer to file a "registration statement" with the S.E.C. prior to issuing its securities. This statement must disclose all material facts about the issuer and the issuer's securities. [SA §5; *see* detailed discussion *infra*, §§209-264]

    (2) **Prospectus:** [§88]   Part I of the registration statement is the "prospectus." It is the most important part of the registration statement, and it must be distributed to investors prior to (or at least simultaneously with) delivery of the issuer's securities. [SA §5(b)(2); *see infra*, §195]

b. **Prevention of fraud and misrepresentation in interstate sale of securities:** [§89]   The second objective of the 1933 Act is to prevent fraud and misrepresentation in the interstate sale of securities. To accomplish this, the Act includes several liability provisions affording defrauded purchasers more liberal remedies than those available at common law. (*See* detailed discussion *infra*, §§619 *et seq.*)

3. **Scope of the 1933 Act:** [§90]   The provisions of the 1933 Act apply only to certain *transactions* (offers and sales in interstate commerce) by certain *parties* (issuers, underwriters, and dealers) involving certain *property interests* (securities). The following three sections of this chapter discuss the coverage of the 1933 Act in terms of these categories.

## B. PERSONS COVERED BY THE 1933 ACT

1. **In General:** [§91]   Although section 5 of the 1933 Act provides that a public distribution of securities by *any person* be registered with the S.E.C., section 4(1) of the Act *exempts* from this requirement securities transactions by persons *other than* "issuers," "underwriters," or "dealers." Thus, the registration and prospectus requirements really apply only to *"issuers," "underwriters,"* and *"dealers."*

2. **Issuers:** [§92]   The first group covered by the Act is "issuers." Section 2(4) of the 1933 Act defines "issuer" as including every person who issues or proposes to issue any security. An issuer is subject to the registration requirements of the Act whenever it makes an "original distribution" of its securities to the public. [SA §5; *compare* "secondary distributions," *infra*, §111]

3. **Underwriters:** [§93]   The second group covered by the Act is "underwriters." Three classes of persons are considered "underwriters" within the meaning of the registration requirements of the 1933 Act: (i) persons who purchase securities from the issuer with a view toward public distribution; (ii) persons who offer or sell securities for an issuer in connection with a distribution; and (iii) persons who "participate" in a distribution. [SA §2(11)]

a. **Purchasers who intend to distribute securities:** [§94]   One who purchases securities from an issuer with an eye toward *"distribution"* is an underwriter. "Distribution" essentially means a *public offering*—*i.e.*, an offering to a substantial number of unsophisticated investors. [SA §2(11); *and see infra*, §341]

b. **Persons who offer or sell for an issuer:** [§95]   The definition of "underwriter" also encompasses persons who actually offer or sell securities *for an issuer* in connection with the issuer's public distribution.

    (1)   **Example:** Members of a Chinese benevolent society in this country who gratuitously undertook to solicit offers for the purchase of Chinese government liberty bonds (without a contract or remuneration from the issuer) were held to be underwriters within the "selling for" definition. [S.E.C. v. Chinese Consolidated Benevolent Association, 120 F.2d 738 (2d Cir. 1941)]

c. **Participants in a distribution:** [§96]   People who participate in a distribution are underwriters of the issuer's securities within the meaning of SA section 2(11).

    (1)   **Test of "participation":** [§97]   The test of participation is simply whether the person in question took part in some *significant* fashion in the underwriting. It does not depend on whether the person receives any monetary compensation for the services.

    (2)   **Presumptive underwriter doctrine:** [§98]   The S.E.C. has formulated an administrative rule of thumb—the *"presumptive underwriter doctrine"*—providing that any person who purchases 10% or more of the securities offered in a registered public offering and then turns around and sells the securities without registering them is an "underwriter." However, the seller will not be charged with being an underwriter if the resales are in limited quantities—*i.e.*, according to the limits set in rules 144 or 145 (*see infra*, §§499, 549). [*See* Nathan, "Presumptive Underwriters," 8 Review of Securities Regulation 881 (1975)]

    (3)   **Exemptions:** [§99]   The 1933 Act exempts from underwriter status certain persons who participate in underwritings and would otherwise be deemed underwriters.

        (a)   **Purchasers of unsold securities:** [§100]   Persons unaffiliated with the issuer or any principal underwriter who enter into an agreement with one of the principal *underwriters* (but *not* with the issuer), to purchase all or a portion of the securities unsold after a specified period of time, are excluded from underwriter status if their purchase of the securities is for *investment purposes*—*i.e.*, they intend to hold the securities for a significant period as an investment. [*See* SA Rule 142]

            1)   **Example:** An institutional investor, such as an insurance company, makes an advance commitment to the underwriter to purchase those securities not otherwise sold in the issuer's public distribution. This investor may purchase the securities at a discount from the public offering price without incurring liability as an underwriter.

        (b)   **Dealers selling for a normal commission:** [§101]   Dealers who are part of the selling group in an underwriting would normally come within the participation test and hence be "underwriters." However, where such dealers merely receive from the underwriter or another dealer a commission which is "not in excess of the usual and customary distributors' or sellers' commission," they are *excluded* from the definition of "underwriters." [SA §2(11); SA Rule 141]

1) **No payment from issuer:** [§102]   To qualify for this exemption, the dealer must receive the commission from an *underwriter or other dealer*; the commission may *not* be received directly from the issuer. [SA §2(11)]

2) **"Usual and customary commission":** [§103]   In addition, the commission must be for the "usual and customary" amount; *i.e.*, it may not exceed the amount typically allowed to other persons for comparable services in similar underwritings.

   a) **"Spreads":** [§104]   Permissible commissions include remuneration commonly known as a "spread"—the difference between the purchase price and the sale price (*i.e.*, the amount received by a dealer who buys and sells as a principal)—as long as this is not more than customary or normal in the circumstances.

3) **Compare—dealers performing additional functions:** [§105]   Note that if a dealer's function is to *manage the distribution* of all or a substantial part of the particular issue of securities, or if she otherwise performs the normal functions of an underwriter or underwriting syndicate, she will be deemed an underwriter regardless of the amount of her commission. [*See* SA §2(11)]

d. **Underwriters for "control persons":** [§106]   As defined above, an "underwriter" is a person who buys from, sells for, or participates in the issuer's public distribution of securities. Section 2(11) of the 1933 Act provides that for the purpose of determining who is an underwriter, the term "issuer" includes "control persons." Thus, the term "underwriter" also includes a person who buys from, sells for, or participates in a distribution for a "control person" who makes a public distribution of her stock.

(1) **"Control person" defined:** [§107]   A "control person" is someone having the power to direct the management and policies of the issuer. [SA Rule 405]

   (a) **Source of control:** [§108]   The control person's power may come through stock ownership, a position in management, influence with management, or a combination of these factors.

      1) **Example:** A owns 25% of the common stock in XYZ Corp. and is on the firm's board of directors. A would probably be a "control person" since she is in a position to influence the management and policies of XYZ.

   (b) **Control groups:** [§109]   Groups of persons who have the power to act in concert to influence the affairs of the issuer may be a "control group." Members of control groups are treated as control persons for the purposes of the Act.

(c) **Control power need not be exercised:** [§110]   Power to control, not exercise of the power, is what makes someone a "control person." Thus, where the principal creditor of a corporation (who was also the principal source of its business) had options to acquire the interests of others in the company, and received 90% of the company's profits, the S.E.C. found that the creditor was a "control person" even though the creditor had not actively participated in the management of the company's business. [*In re* Walston & Co., 7 S.E.C. 937 (1940)]

(2) **Offerings by a control person:** [§111]   The public sale of securities owned by a control person or control group is called a "secondary distribution," since the stock was first issued by the issuer to the control person in the original distribution.

(3) **Examples of underwriters:** Key to understanding the 1933 Act is understanding that there are several ways to be an "underwriter," as defined by the Act, and that one can inadvertently (and unknowingly) achieve underwriter status. The following are examples of statutory underwriters.

(a) **Example:** A owns 22% of XYZ Corp. common stock, has contributed another 67% of the stock to a trust whose trustees are his sons, controls another corporation that owns an additional 2% of the XYZ stock, and is the president of XYZ. A is a control person. Thus, an offering to the public of a substantial amount of A's stock over the New York Stock Exchange is a "secondary distribution" and must be registered. Furthermore, any broker-dealer who participates in the public distribution on behalf of A will be held to be an underwriter. [*In re* Ira Haupt & Co., 23 S.E.C. 589 (1946)]

(b) **Example:** XYZ sells 85,000 shares of common stock to S, the chairman of its board of directors. S already owns half of XYZ's common stock and a substantial percentage of the company's outstanding preferred stock convertible into common stock. S immediately converts the preferred stock into common stock and sells the converted stock and the newly acquired common stock to numerous persons without registration. S is a control person making an unlawful public distribution, and those selling for S in this distribution or buying from S and redistributing the stock to others are underwriters. [*In re* Hazel Bishop, Inc., 40 S.E.C. 718 (1961)]

e. **Pledgees of securities:** [§112]   The problem of defining who is an "underwriter" frequently arises when securities are pledged to a lender (such as a bank) as collateral for a loan. For example, suppose A, a control person owning stock in XYZ Corp., pledges his stock with a bank to secure a loan and then defaults on the loan. If the bank sells the shares publicly to repay the loan, is the bank an "underwriter" because it sold the securities to the public "for" a control person?

(1) **Spurious pledge:** [§113]   Where there is no bona fide pledge involved (*i.e.*, the "loan" is really a device to give the control person cash, and the pledgee bank intended from the beginning to sell the securities for reimbursement), the bank will be considered an underwriter. [S.E.C. v. Guild Films Co., 279 F.2d 485 (2d Cir. 1960)]

(2) **Weak loan:** [§114]   The result is the same where the bank has not reasonably investigated whether it is making a good loan—*i.e.*, where there is no reasonable basis for determining that the pledgor can repay the loan without a sale of the securities. [*See* S.E.C. v. Guild Films Co., *supra*]

(3) **Bona fide pledge and loan:** [§115]   The difficult cases occur where the loan is bona fide.

    (a) **Note:** No court has expressly held that a good faith loan and pledge requires registration of the control person's shares before the pledgee bank can publicly sell them.

    (b) **Compare:** The court in *Guild Films, supra,* indicated in dictum that *all* pledgees take with a view to distribution and must therefore register under the 1933 Act before making any public distribution of the securities. [*But see* Fox v. Glickman Corp., Fed. Sec. L. Rep. (CCH) §91,682 (S.D.N.Y. 1966)—*contra*]

4. **Dealers:** [§116]   The third group covered by the 1933 Act are "dealers." Thus, under section 4(1), dealers are also subject to the registration and prospectus requirements of the Act.

    a. **Those included as dealers:** [§117]   The definition of "dealer" given in section 2(12) of the Act is based on a person's general activities rather than on conduct in a particular offering. A dealer is defined as any person who, either full or part-time, is *engaged in the business* of offering, buying, selling, or otherwise dealing or trading in securities issued by another person as *agent, broker,* or *principal.*

        (1) **Note:** This definition of dealer expressly includes those performing the function of a broker.

    b. **Exemptions for dealers**

        (1) **Limited "dealer's exemption" from prospectus delivery requirements:** [§118]   Section 4(3) of the Act provides dealers with a limited exemption from the prospectus delivery requirements of the Act. In general, dealers need not deliver a prospectus in the "post-distribution" period—*i.e.*, the period starting 40 days after the registration statement becomes effective and selling begins (*see infra*, §323).

            (a) **Note:** In the case of an *initial public offering* (*i.e.*, an offering for an issuer that has never before publicly issued securities), the "post-distribution period" begins 90 days, rather than 40 days, after the registration statement becomes effective. The rationale is that the public is not well-informed about such issuers, and therefore dealers should provide information (by delivering a prospectus to each investor) for a longer period of time than for issuers who have previously "been to the market."

        (2) **Dealer's exemption from underwriter status:** [§119]   Note that since dealers "participate" in the underwriting process, they would usually be defined as "underwriters," and hence would be subject to section 5

regardless of any exemption for "dealers." However, dealers are specifically *exempted* from underwriter status if they perform only normal dealer functions in return for a normal dealer's commission (*see supra*, §101).

c. **Exemption for brokers:** [§120]   In addition to the limited exemption from registration provided for dealers, the Securities Act also provides an exemption for brokers (*see infra*, §326).

d. **Limitation on exemptions—underwriters:** [§121]   If a dealer or broker is acting as an underwriter in a particular distribution, the dealer or broker may *not* rely on the dealer or broker transaction exemption for transactions that are part of the distribution.

e. **Customers:** [§122]   Even if the dealer or broker has an exemption, the selling customer must have his own exemption to avoid the prospectus delivery requirement. Usually the selling customer is not an "issuer, underwriter, or dealer," and so is exempt under section 4(1).

## C. PROPERTY INTERESTS COVERED BY THE 1933 ACT

1. **Act Applies Only to "Securities":** [§123]   To come within the registration requirement of section 5 of the 1933 Act, the property interest that is offered or sold must be a "security."

2. **Securities Subject to Registration:** [§124]   Section 2(1) of the 1933 Act defines three basic categories of "securities" subject to registration:

   a. **Interests or instruments specifically mentioned in the Act:** [§125]   The Act expressly classifies financial instruments or interests as "securities." However, the Act also provides that its definition of securities will not apply if "the context otherwise requires." Thus, even items expressly classified as securities in the Act may not be securities if the context dictates otherwise. The Supreme Court has provided some guidance for two such items: stocks and notes.

      (1) **Stock:** [§126]   If so-called "stock" *possesses the characteristics normally associated with stock—i.e.,* it carries dividend and voting rights, it is negotiable, it can be pledged, and it can appreciate in value—then it is a security under the 1933 Act.

         (a) **Example:** A purchaser of 100% of the stock in a corporation can bring a claim under the 1933 and 1934 Acts, even though the transaction involved the purchase of an entire business, and even though the parties could have structured the transaction so as to avoid transferring stock (*e.g.*, by transferring the assets of the business). [Landreth Timber Co. v. Landreth, 471 U.S. 681 (1985)]

            1) **Note:** It may seem obvious that stock in a corporation is a security. However, before *Landreth, supra*, some courts had applied the "sale of business doctrine" to sales of 100% of the stock in closely held corporations. Under that doctrine, the federal securities laws did not apply.

(b) **Compare:** If so-called "stock" *lacks the normal indicia of stock*, then the courts may look to the economic realities of the situation to determine that no security is involved. Thus, the Supreme Court refused to hold that the sale of stock in a nonprofit housing cooperative involved a security. The stock lacked the usual indicia of stock: it was not transferable, there was no right to receive dividends, etc. The purchasers essentially bought living quarters for their personal use and were not investing in "stock." [United Housing Foundation, Inc. v. Forman, 421 U.S. 837 (1979)]

(2) **Promissory notes:** [§127]   Like stock, notes are specifically listed as "securities" in section 2(1) of the 1933 Act. Notes, however, present a special problem, because many notes clearly are not securities (*e.g.,* mortgage notes, or the note signed by a consumer buying a refrigerator).

   (a) **"Family resemblance" test:** [§128]   To determine whether a note is a security, courts apply the "family resemblance" test. The test includes a presumption and exceptions to the presumption.

   1) **Presumption that a note is a security:** [§129]   Because notes are specifically mentioned as securities in the 1933 Act, there is a presumption that every note is a security.

   2) **Exceptions:** [§130]   Recognizing, however, that not all notes are securities, the Supreme Court in *Reves v. Ernst & Young,* 494 U.S. 56 (1990), adopted a list of notes that are not covered by the presumption. These notes, and notes bearing a "family resemblance" to them, are deemed not to be securities under the 1933 Act. The list includes notes delivered in the following kinds of transactions:

   a)   Consumer financing;

   b)   Home mortgages;

   c)   Short-term loans secured by assets of a small business;

   d)   "Character" loans to bank customers;

   e)   Short-term secured financing of accounts receivable;

   f)   Short-term open-account debts incurred in the ordinary course of business (especially when the debt is collateralized); and

   g)   Commercial bank loans for current operations.

   3) **Four factors for interpretation:** [§131]   In *Reves, supra,* the Supreme Court provided some guidance for deciding when a note bears a family resemblance to a note on the above list. Four factors should be examined:

a) The *motivations* of the seller and buyer of the note (*e.g.*, was the transaction one for investment, or instead to finance the purchase of a consumer item?);

b) The *plan of distribution* of the instrument, if any (*e.g.*, if the instrument is traded, the likelihood that it is a security increases);

c) The *reasonable expectations of the investing public* (*e.g.* does the public reasonably expect to have the protections of the 1933 Act in this kind of transaction?);

   1/ *Note:* In *Reves,* the Court stated that public expectations may result in defining a note as a security *even when an economic analysis of the transaction suggests that the note is not a security;* and

d) Finally, the *existence of a comparable scheme of regulation* diminishes the likelihood that a note is a security in a particular case. (*See* further discussion of the effect of comparable regulations, *infra* §139.)

(3) **Other interests or instruments specifically mentioned in the Act:** [§132] The Act also expressly classifies the following additional items as "securities":

   (a) *Preorganization subscriptions* for securities;

   (b) *Fractional, undivided interests in oil, gas, or other mineral rights;*

   (c) *Collateral trust certificates* (a type of bond secured by collateral, frequently other securities, deposited with a trustee);

   (d) *Certain types of receipts for securities,* including American deposit receipts for foreign securities (*i.e.*, where a foreign company issues deposit receipts in this country for shares deposited in banks in the foreign country) [*see* SA §2(4)]; and

   (e) *Equipment trust certificates* and certificates of interest in unincorporated investment trusts (*e.g.*, Massachusetts Trusts) [*see* SA §2(4)].

b. **Investment contracts:** [§133] The most important classification of securities in section 2(1) is the broad, catchall reference to "investment contracts." The S.E.C. and the courts have broadly construed this phrase so as to apply the registration requirements of the 1933 Act to a wide variety of financial schemes.

(1) **Traditional "*Howey* test":** [§134] The traditional test for whether a property interest constitutes an investment contract is the so-called "*Howey* test," set forth by the Supreme Court in *S.E.C. v. W.J. Howey Co.,* 328 U.S. 293 (1946). This case holds that an "investment contract" is *any* contract or *profit-making scheme* whereby a person *invests his money* in a *common enterprise* and *expects to make a profit* solely from the *efforts of the promoter* or a third party who is responsible for management.

(2) **Modern trend:** [§135]  For many years, court decisions tended to expand the scope of property interests regulated as securities under this provision of the Act. Thus, the cases occasionally went beyond the criteria of the *Howey* test to require registration in situations where the investors *participated* to some extent in management and where the benefits derived by them were something *other than cash profits.*

(a) **Factors determining "investment" or "participation":** [§136]  Under the modern test, the criteria for determining whether a particular property interest is an "investment contract" or "participation in a profit-making venture" are:

1) Does the investor make an investment of *money or something else of value?*

2) Does the investor derive *something of substantial benefit* from the venture?

3) Is there a *common enterprise*? This test suggests that there are a number of investors who stand in a similar relationship to a business in which they invest in common.

4) Is management *principally provided by a third party* other than the investors; or, even if the investors are active in management, does the scheme involve the raising of capital to finance the venture, which is then controlled by a third party (the so-called "risk capital" test)?

5) Do the investors *need the protection* of the 1933 Act?

(b) **Requirement of a common enterprise:** [§137]  Under the so-called "horizontal" test for a common enterprise, there must be a sharing or pooling of funds or other assets by several investors and profits derived from these combined funds.

1) **Example:** There was *no* common enterprise where plaintiff invested funds in a discretionary futures trading account with defendant-management firm (agreeing to share 25% of the trading profits with defendant as compensation for its services) because there was no sharing or pooling of funds by more than one investor. [*See* Hirk v. Agri-Research Council, Inc., 561 F.2d 96 (7th Cir. 1977)]

2) **Horizontal test sometimes discounted:** [§138]  Note, however, that many courts seem to pay little attention to this horizontal (several investors) test. Instead, they rely on a "vertical" common enterprise test—a common enterprise will be found if the investor is relying on the efforts of the promoter to make a profit. Thus, "a common enterprise is one in which the fortunes of the investor are interwoven with and dependent upon the efforts and success of those seeking the investment." [S.E.C. v. Glen W. Turner Enterprises, Inc., 474 F.2d 476 (9th Cir. 1973)]

a) **Narrower test:** A narrower vertical common enterprise test requires that the investment manager's fortunes rise and fall with those of the investor. For example, if a broker managing a discretionary commodities account is paid a fixed commission based on the dollar value of the trades he executes (and does not participate in the profits made in the account), some courts would hold that there is *no* vertical common enterprise but only a broker providing a service; thus, there is no security. [*See* Schofield v. First Commodity Corp., 638 F. Supp. 4 (D. Mass. 1985), *aff'd*, 793 F.2d 28 (1st Cir. 1986)]

(3) **The "comparable regulation" limitation:** [§139] Recently, the Supreme Court has begun to limit the scope of the federal securities laws to the regulation of the public trading markets and interstate investment promotions. This trend has also narrowed somewhat the definition of a security. Thus, the Supreme Court has held that if a detailed scheme of federal regulation applies to a particular instrument or contract, the 1933 Act may not apply. [Marine Bank v. Weaver, 455 U.S. 551 (1982)]

(a) **Example:** Plaintiffs purchased a six-year certificate of deposit from a bank. The bank then encouraged plaintiffs to pledge the certificate in a loan guarantee for one of the bank's customers. The bank never disbursed the loan but used it instead to pay off the customer's other loans and checking accounts that were in default. Four months later, the customer went bankrupt and the bank took the pledged certificate of deposit to pay off the remainder of the customer's loan. Plaintiffs sued the bank under rule 10b-5 of the 1934 Act, but the Supreme Court held that the certificate of deposit was not a security because banks were heavily regulated and the certificate was guaranteed by the Federal Deposit Insurance Corporation, and that the agreement to guarantee a loan to one of the bank's customers was not a security since it was negotiated one on one, was private in nature, and was never intended to be publicly traded. [Marine Bank v. Weaver, *supra*]

(b) **Example:** Plaintiff was a participant in a noncontributory, compulsory union pension plan. Eligibility to receive benefits under the plan was determined by years of service. When plaintiff was found ineligible to receive benefits, he sued the union under rule 10b-5 of the 1934 Act and section 17 of the 1933 Act. The Supreme Court held that the enactment of ERISA (which requires pension plans to disclose specified information to employees and governs the substantive terms of pension plans) made application of the 1933 and 1934 Acts unnecessary. "Whatever benefits employees might derive from the effect of the securities acts are now provided in more definite form through ERISA." [International Brotherhood of Teamsters v. Daniel, 439 U.S. 551 (1979)—*see infra*, §155, for further discussion]

c. **Any interest or instrument commonly known as a security:** [§140] In addition to the items specifically listed in section 2(1) and the ambiguous "investment contract," the 1933 Act also includes a catchall provision that sweeps into the definition of a security "in general, any interest or instrument commonly known as a 'security.'"

3. **Application of Definitions:** [§141]   The above definitions provide the courts with three tests for determining whether a property interest is a "security" within the 1933 Act: (i) is it *specifically mentioned* in the Act?; (ii) is it an *investment contract?*; or (iii) is it an *interest commonly classified as a security?*

    a. **Examples:** The following are examples of property interests to which the foregoing criteria have been applied.

        (1) **Interests in land:** [§142]   A "security" has been found where small tracts of land were sold to investors to be used for growing fruit. *Rationale*: The seller's company managed the land for the investors and was responsible for growing, harvesting, and selling the crops; the investors received a percentage of the net profits. [S.E.C. v. W.J. Howey Co., *supra*, §134]

           (a) **And note:** A security was found where leasehold rights on small plots of land were sold to investors in connection with the lessor's advertisement that he would drill a test well for the property. [S.E.C. v. C.M. Joiner Leasing Corp., 320 U.S. 344 (1943)]

        (2) **Partnership and joint venture interests**

           (a) **General partnerships:** [§143]   The sale of a general partnership interest normally does *not* constitute the sale of a security, since general partners ordinarily take an active part in the management of the business.

              1) **Example:** In *Goodwin v. Elkins & Co.*, 730 F.2d 99 (3d Cir. 1984), the court held that a terminated general partner could not sue the partnership under rule 10b-5 of the 1934 Act because no "security" was involved. Despite the fact that the partnership agreement provided for an executive committee and a managing partner, state law still legally allocated significant management responsibilities to all other general partners, and the partnership agreement itself provided (i) that a majority of partners could vote both the executive committee and the managing partner out of power and (ii) that all partners should devote their full time to the business of the partnership. Hence, partners could take an active part in the business and were not mere "passive" investors.

              2) **But note:** Interests that technically are partnerships, but which are marketed to individuals who do not function as partners (*e.g.*, the partner is really a passive investor or the investor-partner is so inexperienced or unknowledgeable in the business that he is incapable of exercising his partnership powers, etc.) may be securities under the Act.

           (b) **Compare—limited partnership interests:** [§144]   Limited partnership interests are often held to be securities, since limited partners obtain an interest in the partnership in return for a contribution of cash or other property, but have little or no role in managing the business.

        (3) **Franchises:** [§145]   The basic issue regarding franchises is the same as that for partnerships: Is the investor active in management of the franchise

or merely a passive investor? Where the franchisee is active, there is normally no security.

(a) **Example:** P paid $12,500 for a franchise to operate a tax center in a specified geographic area. The franchisor's participation was limited to providing initial training and assistance in establishing the center (in return for 10% of the gross sales). The court found that no security had been sold since the franchisee had to play a very active role in management. [Wieboldt v. Metz, 355 F. Supp. 255 (S.D.N.Y. 1973)]

(4) **Pyramid sales plans:** [§146]   A "pyramid sales plan" exists where the promoter of a product creates a franchise system whereby she sells to franchisees both the right to distribute the product *and* the right to sell further distribution rights to others. The franchisees receive a flat fee for recruitment, or an override on sales by these "subdistributors." In essence, the scheme is one in which the participants (*i.e.*, each successive group of purchasers) try to sell distributorships and subdistributorships rather than the product itself.

(a) **Investor's role:** [§147]   To avoid being classified as a "security" under the *Howey* test (*see supra*, §134), these plans initially required the purchasers to perform some minor management duties (*e.g.*, filing reports). However, the investors generally did not assume the major duties normally required of a person buying a business.

(b) **Investor's benefit:** [§148]   The S.E.C. has also indicated that the benefit expected by the investor from such schemes need not necessarily be a share of cash profits in the enterprise. Any "economic benefit" may make the requisite property interest a "security." [SA Release No. 5211 (1971)]

(c) **Example:** In one case, the court held that a pyramid scheme involved the sale of a security where:

(i) There was an initial *investment of money* to buy distributorships;

(ii) There was a *common enterprise* (the return to the investor-distributor depended in part on the efforts of the promoter to assist those who had already bought distributorships to sell others); and

(iii) The success of the scheme depended on the *promoter's essential management efforts,* even though the investor-distributors also contributed their own efforts.

[S.E.C. v. Koscot Interplanetary, Inc., 497 F.2d 473 (5th Cir. 1974)]

(5) **Condominiums:** [§149]   There are situations in which condominiums can be securities—generally when the purchaser, in addition to buying the condominium, receives some type of investment interest. For example, condominium units have been held to be securities where there is a rental arrangement whereby the condominium project manager rents the units to

others when the owners are not using them and all units share expenses and revenues from rentals on a project basis. [SA Release No. 5347 (1973)]

(6) **Club memberships:** [§150] Memberships in social organizations or clubs (*e.g.*, memberships in country clubs) are normally not considered "securities"; however, memberships in clubs that have *some business aspect* are generally held to involve the sale of securities (*e.g.*, certificates issued to members for loans constitute "investment contracts" and hence are securities). [United States v. Monjar, 47 F. Supp. 421 (D. Del 1942)]

    (a) **Construction of facilities:** [§151] Where memberships are sold to raise the *"risk capital"* to build a club, the promoters of the club operate it for their personal profit, and club members have an irrevocable right to use the club, a security is involved. [Silver Hill Country Club v. Sobieski, 55 Cal. 2d 811 (1961)]

        1) **Rationale:** In *Sobieski, supra,* the California Supreme Court reiterated that profitmaking is not the only criterion of a security, but that the purpose of the securities laws was to protect against all schemes used to raise "risk capital."

        2) **Scope of *Sobieski*:** Note that although *Sobieski* is a state securities law case, it has been frequently cited in *federal* decisions interpreting the 1933 Act.

    (b) **Compare—no "risk capital":** [§152] Whereas the court in *Sobieski* stressed the "risk capital" aspect of the venture, the court in *Wieboldt v. Metz, supra,* §145, held that the "risk capital" test did *not* apply there since the franchisor had been in business for several years and was not using the money derived from franchises to start the business.

(7) **Employee pension and profit-sharing plans:** [§153] Qualified employee pension and profit-sharing plans are tax-motivated arrangements. They allow employers to make a deductible contribution to a fund that defers any tax to the benefited employees, with respect to both the employer's contribution and the amounts of income generated by the plan, until the employee actually receives a deferred distribution (typically on retirement at age 65) from the plan. All such plans are conceivably investment contracts involving the pooling of individual investments in a medium through which profits are expected as a result of the efforts of another. The S.E.C.'s historical approach to such arrangements, however, has been dictated in large part by the extent to which it perceives the need to protect an investor interest.

    (a) **Voluntary contribution plans:** [§154] Where the offer or sale of an interest in these types of plans contemplates that the employee will make voluntary contributions to the plan, this has historically been held to be the offer and sale of a security. [*See* S.E.C. Release No. 33-6188 (1980)]

        1) **Compare:** Where the contributions are used merely for the purchase of annuity or insurance contracts (themselves exempt

under section 3(a)(8) of the Act), it may be that the plan does not involve the offer of a "security."

(b) **No contributions or compulsory contribution:** [§155] Where the plan has no contributions by employees or where employee contribution is compulsory (*i.e.*, involuntary), historically the S.E.C. regarded such plans as involving no "sale" of a security and hence not covered by the Act. This position was affirmed in *International Brotherhood of Teamsters v. Daniel*, *supra*, §139. There, the court held:

1) *The plaintiff-employee's interest* in an involuntary and non-contributory union pension fund is *not* a "security."

2) *Plaintiff's interest is acquired "involuntarily"* (by becoming an employee), so there is no "sale" of the security to the plaintiff for value.

3) *The employee does not make an investment;* he does not give up specific consideration in return for a separable interest with the characteristics of a security. He becomes an employee and as a result receives (commingled with many other rights) a compensation package. He is selling his labor to make a living—not primarily to make an investment. Also, the employer did not make a contribution specifically on behalf of the individual employees; the employer made contributions on the basis of actual weeks worked, and all qualifying employees (whether in service 20 or 40 years) got the same benefit.

4) *The return from the pension fund* comes to the employees mostly from employer contributions and only a minor amount from investment earnings on the contributed funds. Also, qualification to receive funds is not primarily a result of the management efforts of others, but rather of whether the individual can meet the requirements of the pension fund (such as length of service).

5) *The enactment of ERISA* in 1974 (which requires pension plans to disclose specified information to employees and governs the substantive terms of pension plans) severely undercuts all arguments for extending the federal securities acts to non-contributory, compulsory pension plans. The possible benefits employees might have derived from the securities acts are now provided in definite form by ERISA.

(8) **Commodity silver purchases:** [§156] With the increased popularity of commodity "investment plans," the S.E.C. and the courts have begun to scrutinize closely such programs. Nevertheless, where the defendant firm offered and sold silver bars, touted silver as being a superior investment, and promised to buy the silver back at the spot price quoted in the *Wall Street Journal* on the date of sale, it was held that no security existed. [Noa v. Key Futures, Inc., Fed. Sec. L. Rep. (CCH) ¶97,568 (9th Cir. 1980)] In reaching its decision, the court noted that any profits to be derived

depended on the fluctuations of the silver market and not on the investment firm's management efforts. Also, the buy-back agreement saved the investor a brokerage fee but did not amount to an engagement in a common enterprise.

## D.  TRANSACTIONS COVERED BY THE 1933 ACT

1. **In General:** [§157]   Section 5 of the 1933 Act provides rules concerning the making of *offers to sell* and the actual *sale* of securities through the facilities of interstate commerce. Section 5 divides the underwriting process into three time periods related to the sequence of events in the registration process: pre-filing period, waiting period, and post-effective period (each discussed *infra*, §§158, 176, 193). Then it sets forth rules regulating offers and sales of securities during each of these periods. (Remember that the section 5 rules for making offers and sales in the three periods apply only to issuers, underwriters, and dealers.)

2. **Sales Activity Prohibited During the Pre-Filing Period:** [§158]   During the period when an issuer is contemplating a public offering of its securities—but before a registration statement has been filed with the S.E.C. (*i.e.*, the "pre-filing" period)—it is unlawful for issuers, underwriters, and/or dealers *to buy or offer to buy* or to *sell or offer to sell* the issuer's securities (when means of interstate commerce are used). [SA §5(a), (c)]

   a. **Rationale—no pre-selling:** This prohibition is to ensure that investors are not "pre-sold" on the issuer's securities by information other than that contained in a registered prospectus.

   b. **Exception for agreements between issuer and underwriter:** [§159] However, negotiations and agreements between the issuer and an underwriter are exempted from the prohibition against offers and sales during the pre-filing period. [SA §2(3)]

      (1) **Rationale:** This exception allows the issuer to make a firm contract to sell its securities to an underwriter prior to incurring the expense of preparing the registration statement.

      (2) **But note:** Negotiations among underwriters are permitted also, but negotiations or agreements further downstream (*e.g.,* among underwriters and *dealers*) are *not* permitted during this period. [*See* SA §2(3); SA Rule 141]

   c. **Meaning of "offers" and "sales":** [§160]   The ban against "offers or sales" in the pre-filing period encompasses more than "offers" as defined in state contract law. Since the objective is to see that potential purchasers are not influenced by information other than that ultimately contained in the prospectus, the terms "offer" and "sale" in section 5(a) and (c) have been given broader meaning than the contract concept of "offer," or "offer and acceptance." [SA Release No. 3844 (1957); SA §2(3)]

      (1) **No conditioning of market:** [§161]   The term "offer" has been held to include the dissemination of any material that might "condition the market" prior to the actual offer of securities for public sale pursuant to a registration statement. "Condition the market" means to raise expectations to whet the public's appetite for the securities in order to stimulate sales when

securities are issued. For example, speeches by company officials, press releases, company advertising, etc., could all be "offers" in violation of section 5(c) if they had the proscribed effect.

## (2) Dissemination of information by issuers

(a) **Normal business conduct permitted:** [§162]   The S.E.C. does not want unreasonably to interfere with an issuer conducting its business in a normal manner (*e.g.*, by advertising its products, communicating with shareholders, etc.), and such normal business activities are therefore permitted.

(b) **Press releases soliciting advance orders prohibited:** [§163] However, an issuer and underwriter cannot disseminate a news release naming those who will underwrite a new company's securities, giving promotional information about the assets and liabilities of the new company, where the purpose and effect of such a news release is to *procure or solicit advance* interest in participating in the underwriting and advance purchase orders for the securities to be underwritten. [*In re* Loeb, Rhoades & Co. and Dominick & Dominick, 38 S.E.C. 843 (1959)] Whether a press release or other communication is "promotional" or in the ordinary course of business is a fact question to be determined from all of the circumstances.

1) **"Checklist approach" for press releases—rule 135:** [§164] To provide objective guidelines as to what information can be disseminated by issuers in news releases, the S.E.C. has adopted a "checklist" for such releases [SA Rule 135]:

a) **Mandatory items:** [§165]   Certain items *must* be mentioned in the press release, such as the fact that the offering will be made only by means of a prospectus.

b) **Permissible items:** [§166]   In addition, an issuer *may* communicate certain other facts, including the title of the security, the basic terms, the time of the offering, and the name of the issuer.

c) **Prohibited items:** [§167]   Other facts, such as the identity of the underwriter, may *not* be mentioned in the news release.

2) **Checklist exclusive:** [§168]   One court has held that rule 135 is an *exclusive* list of what an issuer may communicate in a press release. Thus, an issuer was not permitted to mention the "offering price" or the "value of the securities" being issued, since these items are not included in rule 135. [Chris-Craft Industries, Inc. v. Bangor Punta Corp., 426 F.2d 569 (2d Cir. 1970)]

(c) **Proscription against sales activity vs. policy of disclosure:** [§169] The section 5(c) restrictions on disclosures during the pre-filing period may conflict with other policies of the securities laws requiring that a company with already publicly traded securities disclose material information to the investing public.

1) **Example:** In the *Chris-Craft Industries* case (above), Bangor Punta planned a registered offering of its securities to buy Piper Aircraft. One issue was whether the "value" of the securities offered had to be disclosed to Piper shareholders, Bangor Punta shareholders, and the investing public generally.

   a) The policy of the Securities Exchange Act of 1934 (discussed *infra*, §740) is to require disclosure of material information—*i.e.*, information that might affect the decision of investors in the trading markets. However, rule 135 specifically prohibits a disclosure of the "value" in the pre-filing period.

   b) In the *Chris-Craft* case, the court held that rule 135 considerations dominated, and therefore the price could not be disclosed.

2) **Response of S.E.C.:** [§170] Recognizing this conflict in policies, the S.E.C. has stated that a company *does* have a duty to publicly disclose material developments, even when it is "in registration" (*i.e.*, contemplating a registered offering of its securities). However, so as not to violate section 5(c), the disclosures should be *limited to factual reports;* forecasts, projections, predictions, and/or opinions as to value must be avoided. Furthermore, the issuer should avoid initiating situations with securities and financial firms where disclosures are made, but the issuer can respond to legitimate, unsolicited inquiries with appropriate factual information. [SA Release No. 5180 (1971)]

   a) **Regular meetings with analysts:** [§171] The S.E.C. has also indicated that a company that has a history of regular and periodic meetings with securities and financial analysts may continue this practice during the pre-registration period (as long as the information distributed is not promotional), but that a company with no such history might violate section 5(c) if it begins such a program immediately before registering its securities.

   b) **Forecasts and projections:** [§172] In SA Release No. 5180 (noted above), the S.E.C. stated that disclosures by issuers "in registration" should be limited to factual statements only, and should not include opinions, forecasts, projections, predictions and the like. This was consistent with the S.E.C.'s views on disclosure of such information in general. Beginning in the late 1970s, however, the S.E.C. modified substantially its position on disclosure of such "soft information." (*See infra*, §§245-256.) To date, however, the S.E.C. has not revised its public statements concerning disclosure of soft information during the pre-filing period.

(3) **Dissemination of information by underwriters and dealers:** [§173] In addition to the rule 135 checklist for issuers, the S.E.C. has established guidelines for underwriters and dealers (including those who will participate in the offering and those who will not) as to the information they may disseminate about the issuer and its securities prior to the effective date of the registration statement. In general, the S.E.C. guidelines allow underwriters and dealers to conduct their normal business operations—such as the publication of regular market reports and security analyses—as long as these do not unduly interfere with the objectives of the 1933 Act. [SA Rules 137-39; SA Release Nos. 5009 (1969), 5101 (1970)]

    (a) **Example:** Where the issuer is filing reports under the 1934 Act (*see supra*, §43) and proposes to register securities for an offering under the 1933 Act, a dealer or underwriter acting in the regular course of business may (under certain conditions, below) publish information, an opinion, or a recommendation with respect to the securities that will be registered. Such a publication will not constitute an offer in violation of section 5(c) of the 1933 Act. [SA Rule 139(a), (b); SA Release Nos. 5009 (1969), 33-6550 (1984)]

        1) **Note:** The underwriters and dealers who are allowed to publish such information if done in the regular course of business include dealers who might later be part of the dealer selling group, and underwriters who might later be part of the underwriter selling group.

        2) **Limitation:** [§174]   If the issuer does *not* qualify to use registration form S-3 (*see infra*, §§219-221), then the information or opinion may be published only if the publication is distributed with reasonable regularity in the normal course of business, and either contains similar information, opinions, or recommendations regarding a substantial number of companies in the industry of the intended registrant, or contains a comprehensive list of securities currently recommended by the dealer. Also, the information about the issuer's securities may be given no greater prominence than is given to the other securities listed in the publication, and the dealer or underwriter must have published an equally favorable recommendation in the last previous edition of the publication. [*See* SA Rule 139(b)]

        3) **Compare—registrants qualifying to use form S-3:** [§175] Where an intended registrant qualifies to use form S-3, then rule 139(a) allows broker-dealers to publish information if the publication is distributed with reasonable regularity in the normal course of business by the broker-dealer.

3. **Regulation During the Waiting Period:** [§176]   Once the registration statement has been filed with the S.E.C., but before the S.E.C. declares it to be effective (so that the sale of securities pursuant to the statement may begin), the objective of regulation changes. Although actual sales of the securities are still not permitted [*see* SA

§5(a)] (except between the issuer and the underwriters or among the underwriters), underwriters may now arrange with brokers and dealers for their assistance in selling the issue to retail customers. In addition, both underwriters and dealers *may solicit offers to purchase,* so that when the registration statement becomes effective, thc securities may be sold very rapidly. However, only certain types of information may be used in making selling arrangements and in conducting this pre-selling. [SA Release No. 3844 (1957)]

a. **Permissible communications:** [§177] During the waiting period, securities can be marketed either through oral offers or through certain written communications, but sales must not be concluded. Oral offers during the waiting period are not regulated by the Act. Written offers are regulated: Section 5(b)(1) prohibits the use of "prospectuses" during the this period and section 2(10) defines "prospectus" to include almost any written communication (plus television and radio advertisements) regarding the securities *except* the communications described below.

(1) **Note—terminology:** [§178] Although section 2(10) of the 1933 Act defines "prospectus" to include almost any written communication regarding an offering, business persons normally use the term to refer only to a prospectus that meets the requirements of either section 10(a) (in which case its is called a "final" or "statutory" prospectus) or section 10(b) (in which case it is called a "preliminary" or "red herring" prospectus). The final prospectus is used after the registration statement is declared effective. (*See infra*, §§193-208.) The preliminary prospectus is discussed below.

(2) **Tombstone ads:** [§179] "Tombstone ads" and the slightly longer "identifying statement" are short announcements about a proposed offering of registered securities that typically appear in publications such as the *Wall Street Journal.* They, and other similar communications, may be published during the waiting period as long as they include:

(i) The *issuer's name;*

(ii) The *kind of security* that will be offered;

(iii) The *price* at which the security will be offered;

(iv) The *identity of the person who will be executing purchase orders;*

(v) The person *from whom a prospectus may be obtained;* and

(vi) A *statement that no offer to purchase can actually be accepted* during the waiting period and that the ad itself does *not constitute a solicitation* of an indication of interest from a prospective purchaser.

[*See* SA §2(10)(b); SA Rule 134] The communication may also include a brief description of the issuer's business, the date on which the offering is expected to commence, and the like.

(a)  **Example:**

This announcement is neither an offer to sell nor a solicitation of an offer to buy these securities. The offer is made only by the Prospectus.

New Issue / December 22, 1994

## 2,070,000 Shares

## General DataComm Industries, Inc.

## Common Stock
($.10 par value)

## Price $29.875 Per Share

Copies of the Prospectus may be obtained in any State in which this announcement is circulated only from such of the undersigned as may legally offer these securities in such State.

| | |
|---|---|
| Salomon Brothers Inc. | SoundView Financial Group, Inc. |
| Alex. Brown & Sons <br> Incorporated   CS First Boston | NatWest Securities Limited |
| Yamaichi International (America), Inc. | Brean Murray, Foster Securities Inc. |
| Cowen & Company | Ladenburg, Thalmann & Co. Inc. |

Reprinted with permission of Salomon Brothers Inc.

(b)  **Expanded use:** [§180]  Note that a rule 134 communication (including a tombstone ad) may be used to actually solicit offers if it is preceded or accompanied by a regular section 10 prospectus—including a "preliminary" or "summary" prospectus (below). [SA Rule 134(d)]

(3)  **Preliminary (or "red herring") prospectus:** [§181]  During the waiting period, written offers may also be made through use of a preliminary prospectus. A preliminary prospectus is similar to the final prospectus (which contains the most important information in the registration statement), but it is missing certain information that would be included in the final prospectus because the information is not yet available. For example, because the price of securities can change rapidly and approval of a registration statement can take many days (*see infra,* §190), the preliminary prospectus will not include the offering price or any other information based on the price.

(a)  **Terminology:** [§182]  A preliminary prospectus is often called a "red herring" prospectus because it must include a red ink warning that it is only a preliminary prospectus.

(b)  **Limited period of use:** [§183]  Once the registration statement becomes effective and a complete prospectus is available, use of the preliminary prospectus must be discontinued.

1)  **Note:** Securities Act rule 430A provides that a registration statement for securities offered for cash may be ***declared effective before the price of the securities is set.*** Until the price is determined, the preliminary prospectus may be used for informational purposes after effectiveness of the registration statement. However, it may not be used to satisfy 1933 Act section 5(b)(2) (requirement that a final prospectus be delivered with or before delivery of a security in interstate commerce). [SA Rule 430A(c)]

(4) **Summary prospectus prepared by issuer:** [§184]   The third and final written communication permitted during the waiting period is a summary prospectus. [SA §10(b); SA Rule 431]

(a) **Requirements for use:** [§185]   A summary prospectus can be used only if the form used to register the securities (*see infra*, §§217-224) specifies that a summary prospectus is available. In addition, only issuers that: (i) meet certain financial requirements, (ii) file reports under the 1934 Act, and (iii) are "seasoned" (*i.e.*, have been 1934 Act reporting companies for at least three years and have timely filed all 1934 Act reports required in the last year), are permitted to use the summary prospectus. [SA Rule 431]

1)  **Note:** The financial and other requirements for use of the summary prospectus are essentially the same as the registrant requirements for use of form S-3 (*see infra*, §220), but the summary prospectus is available for forms S-1 and S-2 (and ***not*** for form S-3).

(b) **Period of use:** [§186]   The summary prospectus may be used after effectiveness. It may not, however, be used to satisfy section 5(b)(2), which requires delivery of a final prospectus before or simultaneously with delivery of any securities sold.

b.  **Impermissible communications during waiting period:** [§187]   As in the pre-filing period, the issuer, underwriters, and dealers must be careful not to make unlawful offers—*i.e.*, by using means or materials other than those specifically permitted above. Furthermore, no sales are permitted during the waiting period, and consequently ***no offers may be accepted until the registration statement has become effective.*** One technique often used to avoid inadvertently making a sale is to solicit offers to purchase (which must then be accepted by the offeror) rather than making offers to sell (which the customer might accept, creating a sale).

(1) **Example:** It is an unlawful offer for the underwriter to indicate by letter to a prospective purchaser that he will sell to the purchaser "when, as, and if issued" shares in a company whose registration statement for a new offering has been filed but is not yet effective. [Diskin v. Lomasney, 452 F.2d 871 (2d Cir. 1971)]

(2) **And note:** The result in *Diskin* was not changed by the fact that the purchaser received and read an approved prospectus prior to actually paying for the stock after the registration statement did become effective.

c. **Required distribution of preliminary prospectus:** [§188] Technically, the 1933 Act merely permits and does not require the distribution of a preliminary prospectus during the waiting period. This is because the primary aim of the statute during the waiting period is to prevent illegal offers and sales. However, most investors make their investment decisions during the waiting period, and so the S.E.C. also wants to ensure that information about the offering is distributed to all persons who should have it. To accomplish this goal, the S.E.C. uses its ability to control *acceleration* of the registration statement to influence *issuers* to cooperate in the distribution. The S.E.C. also uses its power to regulate and license brokers and dealers to obtain their cooperation in distributing the preliminary prospectus. Both of these techniques are discussed below.

(1) **S.E.C. acceleration policy:** [§189] As a practical matter, an issuer needs to have the effective date of its registration statement *accelerated* (*see* below). The S.E.C. will not issue an order accelerating effectiveness unless the preliminary prospectus has been distributed to certain persons.

(a) **Need for acceleration order:** [§190] Under the 1933 Act, a registration statement becomes effective 20 days after it is filed, unless it is amended (which starts the 20-day period anew) or unless the S.E.C. declares it effective before the end of the 20-day period. [SA §8] Usually, a registration statement is amended a number of times before it is declared effective. The last amendment before effectiveness (sometimes called the *pricing amendment*) sets the price of the securities, which is based in part on prevailing market conditions. Once the price has been set, the underwriters will want to begin selling immediately, before market conditions change. If they have to wait 20 days until they can sell, the price will be "stale" and the registration statement will need another amendment—which of course starts the 20-day period over again. Thus, as a practical matter, acceleration of the effective date of a registration statement is a necessity.

(b) **Required distribution of preliminary prospectus:** [§191] The S.E.C. has adopted a rule that it will not grant acceleration unless the preliminary prospectus has been distributed to all underwriters and dealers who can reasonably be expected to participate in the distribution. [SA Rule 460]

1) **Note:** Furthermore, if the securities are being issued by a company that has never before offered its securities to the public—and hence is not a reporting company under the 1934 Act—the S.E.C. will not accelerate the offering date unless the underwriters and dealers have sent copies of the preliminary prospectus to *all persons* who are reasonably expected to become purchasers of the securities. [SA Release No. 4968 (1969)]

(2) **Disclosure policy of 1933 Act:** [§192] Distribution of the preliminary prospectus during the waiting period is also required by the S.E.C. in some other instances.

(i) *The managing underwriter* must take reasonable steps to see that *broker-dealers* participating in the distribution receive copies of the preliminary prospectus;

    (ii) *A broker-dealer* participating in the offering must take reasonable steps to see that *each salesperson* who will offer the securities gets a copy of the preliminary and final prospectus; and

    (iii) *A broker-dealer* participating in the offering must take reasonable steps to see that *persons desiring a copy of* the preliminary or final prospectus get one.

[SA Release No. 5101 (1970)]

4. **Regulation During the Post-Effective Period:** [§193] Once the registration statement is declared effective by the S.E.C., the "post-effective period" commences and actual sale of the registered securities may begin. Offers solicited during the waiting period are usually accepted at this time. [SA §5(a)(1)]

  a. **Objective of regulation:** [§194] The objective of the 1933 Act during the post-effective period is to see that all purchasers receive a copy of the final prospectus, called the "statutory prospectus," which summarizes the investment information contained in the registration statement. [*See* SA §§10(a), 5(b)(2)]

  b. **Distribution of statutory prospectus**

    (1) **With written offers—"free writing":** [§195] Section 5(b)(1) of the 1933 Act prohibits the use of jurisdictional means to transport a prospectus (*i.e.*, almost any written offer) relating to a security that is the subject of a registration statement, *unless* that prospectus meets the requirements of section 10 of the Act. After the registration statement is declared effective, however, the Act *permits* written offers in any form, as long as they are either accompanied or preceded by a copy of the final, statutory prospectus. This permission to distribute written offers is often referred to as the "free writing privilege."

      (a) **Basis of "free writing":** [§196] The 1933 Act implements the free writing privilege in a rather unusual manner—by manipulating the definition of "prospectus." As we have seen, the Act defines "prospectus" generally as any written communication regarding a security. However, *after the effective date* of the registration statement, the Act provides that a written communication is *not a prospectus if it is accompanied or preceded by a statutory prospectus.* [SA §2(10)(a)]

    (2) **With supplementary sales literature:** [§197] After the effective date, sales literature may be used to supplement the statutory prospectus, as long as the statutory prospectus accompanies or precedes the mailing of the sales literature to the prospective purchaser. [SA §2(10)(a)]

    (3) **With written confirmations:** [§198] After the effective date, written confirmations of sale sent by interstate means may be distributed if accompanied or preceded by a statutory prospectus. [SA §§2(10)(a), 5(b)(2)]

    (4) **With delivery of securities:** [§199] After the effective date, a statutory prospectus must also generally *precede or accompany* the delivery of securities where the mails or other interstate facilities are used in the delivery process. [SA §5(a)(2), (b)(2)]

(a) **Exemptions:** [§200]  There are, however, certain exemptions from this rule:

1) **Exemption for dealers:** [§201]  Generally, once the registration statement has been effective for 40 days (90 days in the case of an initial public offering), *dealers* need not deliver a prospectus with the security, *if* they have finished selling their allotments of securities in the offering. [SA §4(3)]  The S.E.C. also excuses delivery of a prospectus *during* the 40- (or 90-) day period (and even excuses delivery of a prospectus by a dealer selling its allotment) in the following cases:

   a) **Issuer is a 1934 Act reporting company:** Dealers who are *not* part of the dealer selling group or those who are part of the group but who have already sold all of their original allotment are *excused* from the prospectus delivery requirement if the issuer is filing periodic reports with the S.E.C. under the provisions of the 1934 Act (*see supra*, §43). [SA Rule 174]

      1/ **Rationale:** In such a case, a prospectus is not needed because equivalent information about the issuer is already available to the purchaser.

   b) **Offered security listed on an exchange or quoted in NASDAQ:** [§202]  Even if the issuer is not a 1934 Act reporting company, if the security has been listed on a securities exchange (*see supra*, §4) or is quoted in the NASDAQ quotation system (*see supra*, §6), the period during which the dealer must deliver prospectuses is *shortened to 25 days*. [SA Rule 174]

2) **Exemption for sales made to brokers over a stock exchange:** [§203]  There is also an exemption from the prospectus delivery requirement for sales made by an underwriter to a broker over a stock exchange of which the broker is a member if the stock exchange has been supplied with enough prospectuses to meet the requests of its members *and* the exchange delivers a copy to any member upon written request. [SA Rule 153]

3) **Exemption for unsolicited broker's transactions:** [§204]  Finally, the Act provides that a broker executing a transaction upon a customer's order, either on an exchange or in the over-the-counter market, need not deliver a prospectus. [SA §4(4)]

   a) **Note:** The Second Circuit has held, however, that this broker's exemption does not apply to transactions in which the "customer" of the selling broker is an underwriter of the securities. [Bairns v. Faulkner, Dawkins & Sullivan, 550 F.2d 1303 (2d Cir. 1977)]

c. **Loophole in the 1933 Act:** [§205]  Note that under the above rules, sales may be consummated in person or by telephone in the post-effective period without furnishing the buyer with a statutory prospectus in advance—as long as the prospectus accompanies or precedes any later written confirmation of the sale or delivery of the security using interstate means. Thus, despite the objective of full disclosure, some sales of registered securities may legitimately take place even though the investor is committed to the purchase prior to seeing the prospectus.

d. **Length of time prospectus must be used:** [§206] The statutory prospectus must be used as long as the original distribution is taking place (*i.e.*, during the period in which any securities in the original issue have yet to be sold for the first time) and, in any event, for at least 40 days after selling begins (90 days, if it is the issuer's first public offering)—whether or not the original distribution has ended. (There are exceptions in limited circumstances—*see* rule 174, discussed *supra*, §201.)

(1) **Mandatory updating:** [§207] If the period of use of the statutory prospectus extends beyond nine months, the information may not be more than 16 months old. In most cases, this means that the prospectus *must* be updated. [SA §10(a)(3)]

(2) **Updating to avoid liability:** [§208] Furthermore, the issuer *should* update the prospectus *any time* new material facts develop, since use of a prospectus which is misleading as to a material fact can result in liability under the 1933 Act. [SA §§11, 12, 17(a)]

(a) **Rationale:** Implicit in the statutory requirement that a prospectus contain all material information is the requirement that the information given be true and correct. According to one court, a misleading prospectus violates section 5 of the Act, and liability may result from its use. [S.E.C. v. Manor Nursing Centers, Inc., 458 F.2d 1082 (2d Cir. 1972); *and see infra*, §§619 *et seq.*]

## E.  THE REGISTRATION STATEMENT

1. **In General:** [§209] As previously indicated, prior to the original public issuance of securities, the issuer must file a registration statement with the S.E.C., the purpose of which is to disclose all of the material facts relating to the securities being offered. The prospectus, discussed above, constitutes Part I of the registration statement, and contains the most important information in the registration statement. (Part II contains supplementary information.) It is the prospectus that is actually given to a purchaser prior to purchase or when the securities are delivered.

2. **Preparing the Registration Statement**

a. **Investigation:** [§210] After the issuer decides to issue the securities, the issuer and its attorney normally conduct an investigation of the proposed underwriting firm. Similarly, the underwriting firm usually does a research study of the issuer before deciding whether to underwrite the securities issue (and if so, at what price).

b. **Negotiation:** [§211] The underwriter and issuer generally do not sign a formal underwriting agreement until shortly before the registration statement is to be declared effective by the S.E.C. and the actual offering price of the security to be offered is determined. However, following their investigations, the issuer and underwriter do negotiate the terms of the underwriting—including the tentative offering price and the underwriter's commission—and they may sign a *letter of intent* (*i.e.*, an "agreement to agree"). At this point, the parties are ready to prepare the registration statement.

c. **Drafting process:** [§212] Typically, the first step in drafting the underwriting agreement is to draw up a schedule of events assigning responsibility for each event to the various parties.

(1) **Legal responsibilities:** [§213] The legal duties in preparing the offering are generally split between counsel for the issuer and counsel for the underwriter, according to the background and experience of each. Normally, counsel for the underwriter prepares the underwriting agreement while counsel for the issuer drafts the registration statement.

(a) **Dual role of counsel for issuer:** [§214] The biggest concern during preparation of the registration statement is what the issuer must disclose in the statement. The law requires that all material facts be disclosed, but the issuer may balk at disclosing anything negative, wanting to make the statement as positive as possible for selling purposes. Counsel for the issuer may therefore find herself in a difficult position: She must represent the client's interests, but at the same time see that the client complies with the law.

(2) **Sources of guidance for drafter:** [§215] Drafting a registration statement is difficult, and much of the ability required to do an effective job can be acquired only by actual practice. However, the starting point for learning what is required is the statutory guidelines and the rules and forms prescribed by the S.E.C.

(a) **Applicable sections and rules:** [§216] The drafter of a registration statement should look first to sections 6 and 7 of the 1933 Act (governing the registration process) and regulation C (setting forth the rules that apply to the registration statement itself).

(b) **Registration forms:** [§217] In addition, the S.E.C. has prescribed a number of forms for use in complying with the registration requirements. These forms incorporate requirements stated in schedule A of the Act.

1) **Basic registration forms:** [§218] The S.E.C. has adopted a set of registration forms, including three basic forms:

a) **Form S-3:** [§219] Form S-3 requires the least amount of disclosure and incorporates by reference 1934 Act reports filed by the issuer. To use form S-3 in a particular transaction, the *issuer* must meet the *registrant requirements* and the *transaction* must meet the *transaction requirements.*

1/ **Registrant requirements:** [§220] Form S-3 may be used by firms that (i) have been filing reports under the 1934 Act for at least three years; (ii) have *timely* filed all reports under the 1934 Act for the preceding 12 months; and (iii) can meet certain standards of financial stability.

2/ **Transaction requirements:** [§221] Form S-3 is available for the following kinds of transactions:

a/ *Offerings of securities for cash,* if the issuer's "public float" (*i.e.*, the amount of voting stock held by nonaffiliates of the issuer) is at least $150 million, *or* the public float is at least $100 million and has an annual trading volume of three million shares or more;

b/ *Offerings by the issuer of debt and nonconvertible preferred stock, for cash,* if the securities offered are rated "investment grade" by at least one nationally recognized rating agency;

c/ *Secondary offerings* (*i.e.*, offerings of the issuer's securities by persons other than the issuer), if securities of the same class are listed on a stock exchange or quoted in the NASDAQ system; and

d/ *Rights offerings, dividend (or interest) reinvestment plans, and conversions or warrants.*

b) **Form S-2:** [§222] Form S-2 allows those companies that qualify (the tests are the same as the "registrant requirements," above, for Form S-3) to incorporate certain 1934 Act filing information by reference and either to deliver their annual reports to potential purchasers or to include substantially the same information in the prospectus to investors.

c) **Form S-1:** [§223] Form S-1 permits the least amount of incorporation by reference. This form is the general form used for the registration of the securities of most companies unless another form is prescribed or authorized.

2) **Other registration forms:** [§224] Other, particularized forms also exist, such as form S-8 (for stock option plans) and form S-18 (a generalized but simplified form for offerings of less than $5 million).

d. **Contents of the registration statement:** [§225] As noted above, the objective of the registration statement is disclosure of material information—*i.e.*, providing potential investors with *all* of the information that a reasonable investor would consider important in deciding whether to buy the securities registered.

(1) **S.E.C. discretion:** [§226] The S.E.C. exercises broad discretion in deciding what information is material and must therefore be included in the

registration statement. For example, the registration statement must ordinarily contain the information specified in schedule A of the 1933 Act (*e.g.*, name of issuer, state of organization, location of principal office, etc.). [SA §7] Securities Act section 7, however, authorizes the S.E.C. to require more or less disclosure in a registration statement than is specified by Schedule A. The primary way in which the S.E.C. exercises this discretion is in promulgating the various forms for registration statements. (*See, e.g.*, form S-3, discussed above, which abbreviates required disclosures for certain issuers on the theory that most such information has already been disclosed in reports the issuer filed under the 1934 Act.)

(a) **Additional information:** [§227] The form for a registration statement is only the starting point for disclosure. A registration statement must contain ***all additional information needed to make the registration statement, as a whole, not misleading.*** [SA Rule 408] For example, it would be misleading to include required information about a particular product manufactured by the issuer, but omit the fact that the issuer's management has plans to discontinue that product in the near future. Experienced practitioners include such information from the outset, without waiting for the S.E.C. to request it.

(b) **Effect of exercise of discretion:** [§228] Although the S.E.C. does not approve or disapprove the investment merits of the securities being registered—*i.e.*, it does not protect the investor from risk, but merely sees that all material information is disclosed—the S.E.C.'s exercise of discretion over what must be put into the registration statement may affect whether people ultimately buy the registered securities.

(2) **Financial information:** [§229] To make a wise investment decision, a potential investor will want to project the issuer's future sales and net earnings. Thus, financial data about the issuer are obviously an important part of the information that must be disclosed in the registration statement.

(a) **Balance sheet:** [§230] The issuer must release a balance sheet (*i.e.*, a statement showing its present or current financial condition) normally dated not more than ***90 days*** before filing; and if there is a delay in the effective date of the registration statement, the balance sheet must be updated. [SA Schedule A]

(b) **Profit and loss statements:** [§231] The S.E.C. also generally requires that the issuer include statements of its net income for at least the past three years (plus a statement for the year-to-date).

(c) **S.E.C. accounting regulations:** [§232] The S.E.C. has its own accounting regulations setting forth what it considers "generally accepted accounting principles." [*See* Regulation S-X] These regulations must be adhered to in preparing all financial information submitted to the S.E.C. in connection with the registration statement.

1) **Example:** S.E.C. accounting regulations require that balance sheets and profit and loss statements be prepared so as to permit

meaningful financial analysis by investors. Thus, a profit and loss statement might have to be broken down so that investors can determine the source of the issuer's revenues by division, major product lines, etc.

(d) **Certification by independent accounts:** [§233] The accountants who certify that the issuer's financial statements comply with generally accepted accounting principles must be independent of the issuer.

1) **Conflicts of interest:** [§234] The standard for independence is an objective conflict of interest test: Are there circumstances that a reasonable person might find would prevent the accountants from rendering an independent opinion on the financial affairs of the issuer?

a) **Example:** Accountants who certify the issuer's financial statements cannot hold a direct financial interest in the issuer, nor have a business or partnership relationship with the issuer, nor serve as an officer, director, or employee thereof.

(3) **Other material facts that require disclosure:** [§235] Various Securities Act Releases and court cases, taken together, indicate that the following information is material and should be included in the registration statement:

(a) **Facts affecting price or value of the securities:** [§236] Facts affecting the price or value of the securities should be disclosed. These include:

1) *The difference between the book value* (*i.e.*, the excess of assets over all liabilities, or net assets) of the issuer's presently issued shares and the *offering price* of the new shares [*In re* Universal Camera Corp., 19 S.E.C. 648 (1945)];

2) *Any substantial disparity* between the public offering price and the cost of shares owned by officers, directors, promoters, etc. [Regulation S-K, Item 506];

3) *Those factors used to determine the offering price* of the securities where the issuer is a new company [Regulation S-K, Item 505];

4) *The use to be made by the issuer of proceeds* from the offering [Regulation S-K, Item 504]; and

5) *Any restrictions on use* of the issuer's earned surplus (*e.g.*, because of loan agreements) which might limit the possibility of future dividends [SA Release No. 5278 (1972)].

(b) **Facts that may make the securities a high risk:** [§237] Facts that make the securities a high risk should be disclosed. These include:

(i) *Absence of any operating history* for the issuer;

(ii) *No earnings history,* or an erratic pattern of earnings;

(iii) *Competitive conditions in the industry;* and

(iv) *The issuer's reliance on only one product* or a limited product line.

[Regulation S-K, Item 503]

(c) **Facts regarding status of issuer:** [§238] Facts regarding the status of the issuer should be disclosed. These include:

1) *Government regulations* that could affect the business (*e.g.,* cost estimates of compliance with environmental laws) [Regulation S-K, Item 101(c)(xii); *see* SEA Release No. 34-16223 (1979)];

2) *Pending or threatened litigation* of a substantial nature against the issuer [Regulation S-K, Item 103]; and

3) *Proposals to (or the intention of) the issuer to enter new businesses* or lines of business [SA Release No. 5395 (1973); *see* Regulation S-K, Item 101(c)].

(d) **Facts regarding conflicting interest transactions:** [§239] Transactions (and proposed transactions) aggregating $60,000 or more must be disclosed, if they are between the issuer (or any subsidiary) and any of the following:

(i) Any *director or executive officer* of the issuer;

(ii) Any *nominee for election* as a director;

(iii) Any *security holder owning or voting more than 5%* of any class of voting securities of the issuer, *if* the issuer knows of this ownership or voting power; or

(iv) Any member of the *immediate family of any of the above.*

[Regulation S-K, Item 404; *see In re* Franchard Corp., 42 S.E.C. 163 (1964)]

(e) **Facts regarding legal proceedings against directors and executives:** [§240] Certain kinds of legal proceedings against directors, director-nominees, and executive officers of the issuer must be disclosed.

1) **Disclosure required by Regulation S-K:** [§241] The following proceedings must be disclosed, if they took place with respect to a director, director-nominee, or executive officer *within five years before filing* the registration statement:

    a)   Bankruptcy;

    b)   Criminal convictions and pending criminal proceedings;

    c)   Securities or commodities law violations; and

    d)   Any injunction or order barring the executive from engaging in any type of business activity.

2)   **Other required disclosure:** [§242] In addition, all other material facts of this nature, including facts regarding events that took place more than five years ago, and also *including material pending civil litigation*, must be disclosed. [*See* Zell v. InterCapital Income Securities, Inc., 675 F.2d 1041 (9th Cir. 1982); Bertoglio v. Texan International Co., 488 F. Supp. 630 (D. Del. 1980); SA Release No. 5758 (1976)]

    a)   **Scope of "materiality":** [§243] Because these disclosure requirements are so broad, courts have sometimes limited the concept of what is considered material in order to render harmless the failure to disclose particular misconduct. Generally, claims that a director or officer received a personal benefit from a transaction are more likely to be deemed material than claims merely alleging illegality, without the element of personal profit to the individual director or officer. [*See, e.g.,* Gaines v. Haughton, 645 F.2d 761 (9th Cir. 1981)]

(f)   **Facts regarding environmental litigation:** [§244] Environmental litigation to which the *government is a party* must be disclosed unless the issuer reasonably believes that any resulting sanction will not exceed $100,000. [Regulation S-K, Item 103, instr. 5]

(g)   **"Soft" information:** [§245] One of the most important items of information to a prospective investor is whether the price of the security will go up or go down. This requires analysis of the issuer's likely future revenues, earnings, plans for expansion, and so on. Such information, which relies in part on subjective analysis and judgment, is often referred to as "soft" information, as distinguished from "hard" facts concerning past performance.

1)   **Safe harbor provisions adopted:** [§246] The S.E.C. historically discouraged the use of soft information in a registration statement, because of its potentially misleading impact on investors. Over time, however, and in response to increasing criticism of its disclosure rules, the S.E.C. modified its stance and in 1979 adopted safe harbor rules for the disclosure of soft information. [SA Rule 175; SEA Rule 3b-6] Indeed, the S.E.C. actively encourages the disclosure of projections and other forward-looking information by the issuer. [Regulation S-K, Item 10]

2) **Safe harbor requirements:** [§247] Under the S.E.C.'s safe harbor rules, a forward-looking statement should comply with the following requirements:

a) **Good faith and reasonable basis:** [§248] The projection must be made in "good faith" and with a "reasonable basis." Experience or past accuracy in making projections may indicate that projections were made in good faith and with a reasonable basis.

  1/ **Burden of proof:** [§249] To prove a cause of action where actual results do not match earlier made projections, a *plaintiff has the burden of proof* to establish the absence of a reasonable basis and good faith in making the projection. [Wielgos v. Commonwealth Edison Co., 892 F.2d 509 (7th Cir. 1989)]

  2/ **Disclosure of assumptions:** [§250] Disclosure of assumptions behind projections is *not* mandatory, *but* in many cases may be necessary for the projections to meet the good faith and reasonable basis part of the test.

b) **Duty to update:** [§251] Projections must be updated and assumptions must be restated when new information indicates that the earlier statements no longer have a reasonable basis.

c) **Compliance with annual reporting requirements:** [§252] Companies that are required to file 10K (annual) reports with the S.E.C. under the 1934 Act must have filed their most recent report to qualify for the safe harbor protection.

3) **Scope**

a) **Financial projections:** [§253] The safe harbor rule covers projections of revenues, earnings, and earnings per share and *other projections of financial items* such as capital expenditures and financing, dividends, capital structure, statements of management plans and objectives for the future, etc.

b) **Statements of outsiders:** [§254] Statements made by or on behalf of the issuer, or by *an outside* (expert) *reviewer* retained by the issuer, are also covered by the safe harbor rules.

c) **Reporting companies and registered companies:** [§255] Companies that file reports under the 1934 Act *or* that are filing registration statements under the 1933 Act are covered. (Note that projections of these companies made prior to or subsequent to these filings are also covered—not just their filings with the S.E.C.—if similar projections are also filed with the S.E.C., the companies are registered under the 1934 Act, or the projections are made in an annual report under the proxy rules of the 1934 Act.)

    d) **Investment companies:** [§256] The safe harbor rule does *not* apply to investment companies.

  (h) **Management's Discussion and Analysis:** [§257] Issuers must include a section entitled "Management's Discussion and Analysis" ("MD&A") in registration statements and in certain Securities Exchange Act filings. The MD&A affirmatively *requires* a certain amount of forward-looking disclosure.

    1) **Purpose of MD&A:** [§258] The MD&A section is intended to give the investor an opportunity to look at the company through the eyes of management by providing both a short- and long-term analysis of the business of the company. It requires management to address key variables and other factors peculiar to and necessary for an understanding and evaluation of the individual company. [SA Release No. 6835 (1989)]

    2) **Compliance with MD&A requirements:** [§259] Historically, few issuers have complied with the literal requirements of the MD&A. To encourage better compliance, the S.E.C. has made the MD&A an enforcement priority. [*See, e.g.*, Matter of Caterpillar, Inc., SEA Release No. 34-30532 (1992)]

3. **Organization of Material in the Registration Statement:** [§260] In addition to requiring that certain kinds of information be disclosed, the S.E.C. closely regulates the organization of the material, including the contents of the registration statement, the use of graphs, charts, etc., to ensure that the material included is communicated clearly.

4. **Liability Based on Contents of Registration Statement:** [§261] Section 11 of the 1933 Act imposes civil liability on those associated with preparation of a registration statement (including the prospectus) that contains material misstatements or omissions. (This topic is discussed in detail, along with other liability provisions, *infra*, §§644 *et seq.*)

5. **Criticisms of S.E.C. Disclosure Policy:** [§262] Several commentators have criticized the S.E.C.'s policies concerning disclosure, generally on the ground that they do not achieve their goal of ensuring that an investor will receive all material information concerning the offered securities. The following criticisms are among those heard most frequently.

  a. **Emphasis on negative information:** [§263] There has been criticism of the fact that the S.E.C. requires the registration statement to focus on the negative aspects of the issuer (to avoid potential liability under the 1933 Act for misrepresentation), rather than allowing it to present a balanced picture of the company (relating the positive as well as the negative aspects of the company). The critics argue that since registration statements thus lack much information that is relevant to making an intelligent investment decision, and since all registration statements are uniformly negative, they may no longer be taken seriously by investors.

b. **Presentation of complex information:** [§264] Some also argue that the complex information the S.E.C. requires to be disclosed (*e.g.*, information on sophisticated products, financial information, accounting data, etc.) is impossible to present in a way that is understandable to the "average" investor. The solution offered by the commentators would be to draft the registration statement for the sophisticated or expert securities analyst, to whom the average investor looks for advice, and to dispense with the charade of trying to inform the investor himself.

c. **Reliance on the "efficient capital market hypothesis":** [§265] The S.E.C. policies concerning disclosure are based to some extent on the idea that the market for securities is "efficient," that is, that prices of securities in the market are affected, if not dictated, by the information available with respect to those securities. Recently, these ideas have come under scrutiny, and the impact of other factors on securities prices (such as investor "sentiment," various trading strategies that are not based on information about issuers, etc.) has been examined. Ultimately, while no one theory adequately explains pricing in the securities market, it is probably safe to assume that information about the issuer and security will continue to be viewed as an important factor and that disseminating that information will continue to be a dominant goal of securities regulation.

6. **Processing the Registration Statement**

a. **Effective date of statement:** [§266] The registration statement becomes effective on the *twentieth* day after its filing with the S.E.C., unless it is the subject of a refusal or stop order issued by the S.E.C. (*see infra*, §§275 *et seq.*) or becomes effective sooner by an S.E.C. acceleration order (*see supra*, §§189-191).

   (1) **Amendments to the statement:** [§267] Usually, several amendments will be required by the S.E.C. before it declares the registration statement effective. An amendment starts the 20-day waiting period running anew. However, the S.E.C. normally accelerates the effective date as soon as all of the problems with the registration statement have been worked out, so that the issuance is not adversely affected by a delay (*see supra*, §§189-190).

b. **Review of the registration statement:** [§268] Once the registration statement is filed, the S.E.C. begins an examination of the statement to ensure that the issuer has complied with all disclosure requirements. [SA §8(e)] The Act provides that it is unlawful to offer or sell securities that are the subject of any proceeding under section 8(e) which was filed by the S.E.C. prior to the effective date of the registration statement. [SA §5(c)]

   (1) **S.E.C. authority:** [§269] The S.E.C. cannot legally compel the issuer to amend a defective registration statement; but by entering a "stop order" (*see* below), the S.E.C. can prevent the registration statement from becoming effective and thus effectively force the issuer to make the suggested amendments. Also, although there is no time limit on the duration of a

section 8(e) examination, a court *can* compel the S.E.C. to make a determination whether to terminate the examination or institute a section 8(d) proceeding (*see* below), at least where the S.E.C.'s inaction has the effect of prohibiting the sale of securities due to an unreasonably delayed completion of the section 8(e) examination. [*See* Las Vegas Hawaiian Development Co. v. S.E.C., 466 F. Supp. 928 (D. Hawaii 1979)]

(2) **S.E.C. review procedures:** [§270] The S.E.C. employs four different review procedures for examining registration statements. [SA Release No. 5231 (1972)]

    (a) **Deferred review:** [§271] If an initial review of the registration statement indicates that it is poorly prepared or has other serious problems, the S.E.C. will simply notify the registrant of that fact (without specific comments) and allow the registrant to consider whether to go forward, withdraw, or amend the statement.

    (b) **Cursory review:** [§272] If, after an initial review, the registration statement appears to be proper, the S.E.C. will indicate to the registrant that only a cursory review has been made and that the statement will be declared effective on the date and at the time requested in letters from the issuer and the managing underwriter. These acceleration requests are treated by the S.E.C. as a declaration that the various parties are aware of their statutory responsibilities under the Act.

        1) **Effect:** This procedure saves the S.E.C. the administrative time normally consumed in a "customary review" (below), but exposes the issuer to the risk of having mistakes in the documents which a more exhaustive review by the S.E.C. might have revealed.

    (c) **Summary review:** [§273] This type of review means that the S.E.C. notifies the issuer that the statement will be declared effective on receipt of: (i) the same type of letters as required in a cursory review; *plus* (ii) adequate responses to limited comments made by the S.E.C. in its review.

    (d) **Customary review:** [§274] Here the S.E.C. gives a *complete* accounting, financial, and legal review—either on its own or when the issuer refuses to agree to the more limited cursory or summary review. The S.E.C. gives the customary review to all first-time issuers.

c. **Formal proceedings by the S.E.C.**

(1) **Refusal and stop orders:** [§275] If, following an examination of the registration statement, the S.E.C. finds that the issuer has failed to comply with the Act's disclosure requirements, the S.E.C. may issue an order delaying or suspending the effectiveness of the registration statement.

    (a) **Refusal order:** [§276] A "refusal order" may be issued within 10 days after the filing of a statement that is clearly inadequate on its face. Such an order *delays* the effective date in order to allow the S.E.C. to take appropriate action; therefore it must always be issued *prior to* the effective date of the registration statement. [SA §8(b)] The impracticability of acting within 10 days after a registration statement is filed has made the refusal order rare, and the stop order (below) is the more common form of S.E.C. action.

    (b) **Stop order:** [§277] A "stop order" either delays the effective date *or* stops the selling of securities (if it has begun), so as to permit an investigation of the issuer and the securities offered. The S.E.C. may issue a stop order at any time—whether before or after the effective date. [SA §8(d)]

  (2) **Effect of formal proceedings on underwriter:** [§278] The institution of S.E.C. administrative proceedings against an underwriter can have a devastating effect on the underwriter's business. For example, in one case where the S.E.C. was investigating an underwriter's involvement in a regulation A offering, it sent letters to all issuers that were using the underwriter, indicating they would have to disclose in their registration statements that the S.E.C. was investigating the underwriter. [Koss v. S.E.C., 364 F. Supp. 1321 (S.D.N.Y. 1973)]

  (3) **S.E.C.'s use of acceleration power:** [§279] As a practical matter, the S.E.C. and issuers do not resort to formal grounds to delay the effective date. Issuers simply state on the registration statement that it will not be effective until S.E.C. approval. As a quid pro quo, the S.E.C. then grants acceleration immediately after the price amendment is filed.

    (a) **Comment:** Depending on the S.E.C. to grant acceleration gives the S.E.C. a lot of informal power over what goes into a registration statement.

d. **Withdrawal of registration statement:** [§280] If, after filing, there are problems with the issuing company or its registration statement, the issuer may simply seek to withdraw the statement—in order to avoid adverse publicity and/or potential liability under the Act.

  (1) **S.E.C. approval required:** [§281] The S.E.C. will grant the issuer's application for withdrawal only if withdrawal is consistent with the public interest and protection of investors. [SA Rule 477]

  (2) **Timing of request:** [§282] A withdrawal request filed *before* the institution of stop order proceedings is *always* honored.

    (a) **Compare:** If a stop order has been instituted in the *post-effective* period, the S.E.C. obviously will *not* permit withdrawal—since the stock (or part of it) has already been sold.

e. **Shelf registrations:** [§283] Many issuers are almost constantly involved in issuing new securities. It would be convenient for such issuers to simply prepare one registration statement, thereby registering all securities that they may offer at any time in the future (a so-called "shelf registration").

  (1) **Problem—inadequate disclosure:** [§284] The difficulty with this approach to registration is that the single registration statement may not

provide adequate disclosure to investors; *i.e.*, material events may occur subsequent to the filing of the registration statement that would make some of the information in the registration statement incorrect.

(2) **General prohibition on shelf registrations:** [§285] As a result, the Act provides that the registration statement is deemed effective only as to the securities *specified* therein. [SA §6(a)]

   (a) **And note:** The S.E.C. has indicated that it is materially misleading for an issuer to include in a registration statement more securities than are going to be offered *presently*; *i.e.*, it is misleading to include securities that are to be offered at some remote future date. [*In re* Shawnee Chiles Syndicate, 10 S.E.C. 109 (1941)]

(3) **Exceptions to prohibition:** [§286] There has always been, however, a number of situations where "shelf registrations" were permitted; for example, where Company A is merged into Company B, and the controlling shareholders of Company A may wish to later offer their shares to the public but cannot without registration. (*See* discussion of rule 145, *infra*, §499.)

(4) **Form S-3 registrants:** [§287] There are advantages to shelf registrations for the issuer (flexibility in responding to changing markets, cost savings, etc.). The main concerns are the ability of underwriters to conduct their due diligence investigations (*i.e.*, their investigation of the facts about the issuer and their verification that the statements made in the registration statement are true) and the adequacy of disclosure by the issuer. Despite these concerns, in 1983 the S.E.C. expanded the situations where shelf registrations are available. [*See* SA Rule 415]

   (a) **Application—form S-3 companies:** In addition to listing formally the traditional offerings for which the S.E.C. permits shelf registration, Rule 415 permits companies that may use registration form S-3 to shelf register their securities. S-3 companies are those that are widely followed in the market place and that file reports pursuant to the 1934 Act. These reports may be incorporated by reference, and the information in them need not be repeated again in the prospectus delivered to investors.

   (b) **Rationale:** The S.E.C. has suggested that continuous due diligence programs are developing that can take care of the problems of not permitting the underwriter of such shelf registrations to conduct a sufficient due diligence investigation before the securities are offered to the public. Such programs include making sure that a single law firm acts as the underwriter's counsel for all parts of the shelf registration offerings and holding periodic due diligence meetings with management; also, due diligence requirements in this situation may be different than in regular underwriting situations. [*See* SA Rule 176]

f. **Refusal of underwriter to proceed—material misstatements:** [§288] The underwriter normally conducts an independent investigation of the issuer during the waiting period to determine whether all material facts have been disclosed in the registration statement. (This relates to the underwriter's defense of "due diligence" in case there are material misstatements or omissions in the registration statement; *see infra* §663.) If there are material misstatements, the underwriter may *refuse* to proceed with the underwriting despite its contractual obligation to purchase and sell the issue (*see supra,* §70).

(1) **Rationale:** An underwriting contract that violates the 1933 Act because of material misstatements in the registration statement is void and therefore unenforceable. [Kaiser-Frazer Corp. v. Otis & Co., 195 F.2d 838 (2d Cir. 1952)]

(2) **Opinion from counsel for issuer:** [§289]  The underwriter also usually requires that the issuer's counsel (if the drafter of the registration statement) render the underwriter a legal opinion that he has no reason to believe that the registration statement contains any material omissions or misstatements.

g. **Blue sky qualification:** [§290]  The securities of a company going public must also be qualified under the "blue sky" or securities laws of each state in which they are intended to be offered, unless there is an exemption from qualification available under applicable state law.

h. **NASD clearance:** [§291]  The issuer must also receive clearance from the National Association of Securities Dealers that the underwriting commissions being paid are "fair" according to NASD rules.

7. **Post-Effective Amendments and Updates to Registration Statement:** [§292]  There are two possible sources of error in the registration statement: (i) an intentional or unintentional material misstatement or omission may exist at the time the registration statement becomes effective; or (ii) everything may be correct at the time the registration statement becomes effective, but subsequent events may outdate the registration statement so that it contains material misstatements or omissions at the date of use. The Securities Act provides for a way to update the registration statement and the prospectus in each of these situations.

a. **Errors existing at time of effectiveness:** [§293]  Where the registration statement contains an error at the time it is declared effective, but the error is discovered only *after* the effective date, the appropriate way to update the prospectus is to file a "post-effective" amendment with the S.E.C. [SA Rule 423]

(1) **Note:** Such filing is necessary in that section 11 of the 1933 Act (discussed *infra*, §621) makes the issuer, underwriters, and others associated with the registration statement liable if the registration statement contains misstatements and omissions when it becomes effective.

(2) **And note:** Since the amended statement is processed by the S.E.C., it has a new effective date and becomes a new registration statement. Section 11 liability is thus imposed on the parties when the registration statement is updated in this manner.

b. **Errors caused by subsequent developments:** [§294]  Where developments *after* the effective date of the registration statement make the information in the registration statement or prospectus misleading or false (although it was accurate at the effective date), a correction may be made simply by placing a sticker on the cover of the prospectus and supplying the correct information in the body of the prospectus. No filing or advance processing by the S.E.C. is required as it is where errors existed at the effective date (above). [SA Rule 424]

(1) **Note:** In this situation, section 11 liability does not apply. However, section 12(2) (prohibiting misrepresentation in the interstate sale of securities generally) *does* cover this situation (*see infra*, §699). Consequently, correct information must be included in the prospectus whenever it is used if those connected with the offering are to avoid liability under the Act.

c. **Updating requirement:** [§295] Whether or not any errors are discovered, the Act requires that a prospectus still in use nine months after the effective date be updated to ensure that it contains information as of a date not more than 16 months prior to its use. The provision puts an outside limit on what can be considered "currently" accurate. [SA §10(a)(3)]

d. **Special provisions for "blank check" offerings:** [§296] During the 1980s, many promoters (*i.e.*, issuers, underwriters, and dealers) of "penny stock" (generally, low-priced stock that is not traded on a national exchange) were abusing the securities market with so-called "blank check" offerings. In a blank check offering, the promoter does not specify what the proceeds of the issuance will be used for. Such offerings usually involved start-up companies with no operating history or assets, and there were frequent allegations that the promoters diverted the offering proceeds into their own pockets. The Securities Enforcement Remedies and Penny Stock Act of 1990 was enacted to combat these abuses.

(1) **Scope:** [§297] The 1990 Act applies only to offerings by "blank check companies." The Act defines a "blank check company" as a development stage company that is issuing penny stock, and that either has no business plan or purpose, or has indicated that its business plan is to merge with an unidentified company or companies. [SA §7(b); SA Rule 419]

(a) **Distinguish:** "Blind pool offerings" are not the same as "blank check offerings." Blind pool offerings are somewhat less prone to abuse, and involve offerings by ventures that propose to invest in unspecified *businesses of a certain type*, for example, commercial real estate, or motels.

(2) **Definition of "penny stock":** [§298] Penny stock is defined in SEA rule 3a51-1, and includes any equity security *other than* a security:

(i) Registered on a national securities exchange (with an exception for certain "emerging companies");

(ii) Issued by a registered investment company;

(iii) That is a put (*i.e.*, option to sell) or call (*i.e.*, option to buy) issued by the Options Clearing Corporation (*see supra*, §22);

(iv) That has a price of $5 or more;

    (v)    Authorized for quotation on NASDAQ;

    (vi)   Whose issuer has at least: (i) $2 million in assets (if in operation at least three years), or (ii) $5 million in assets (if in operation less than three years), or (iii) average annual revenues of at least $6 million.

[SEA §3(a)(51); SEA Rule 3a51-1]

(3) **Additional investor protection:** [§299] The "blank check" rules mandate certain forms of investor protection in addition to the usual disclosure obligations imposed by federal securities law. The regulations include the following:

    (a)   **Escrow provisions:** [§300] Securities sold in a "blank check" offering and the proceeds of the sale must be promptly deposited into an escrow account at a qualified institution. [SA Rule 419] Trading in such securities is not permitted as long as they are in escrow. [SEA Rule 15g-8]

    (b)   **Disclosure and rescission:** [§301] When the issuer acquires assets for its business, it must describe the transaction in a post-effective amendment to the registration statement. A new prospectus describing the transaction must be distributed to the investors, who then have the right, if they wish, to rescind the transaction and to receive back their money. [SA Rule 419]

## F.   EXEMPTIONS FROM REGISTRATION REQUIREMENTS

1. **In General:** [§302] The cost and time required for a registered offering are very great. Expenses include the S.E.C. registration fee, accounting and legal fees, printing costs (including stock certificates), state filing fees (in each state where the securities are sold), and insurance against Securities Act liabilities. The time required for the full registration and selling process is generally between 90 and 120 days. Therefore, if issuers can avoid having to go through the registration process, they will make every effort to do so. Thus, an issue frequently encountered under the 1933 Act is whether a particular distribution of securities qualifies under one or more of the *exemptions* from registration provided in the 1933 Act for certain types of *securities*, and certain types of securities *transactions.*

2. **Exempted Securities:** [§303] Certain types of securities are themselves exempt from registration under section 5 of the 1933 Act; *i.e.,* they may be sold and resold without ever being subject to registration. (*Note:* Such securities may be subject to the general antifraud and civil liability provisions of the Act; *see infra.*) Most of the exemptions for securities are covered in section 3 of the 1933 Act.

    a.   **Bank and government securities:** [§304] Section 3(a)(2) of the 1933 Act exempts from the registration requirements: (i) securities issued or guaranteed by the United States, its territories, or the states themselves; and (ii) securities issued by banks.

    b.   **Short-term notes and other debt instruments:** [§305] Notes or drafts arising out of current transactions are exempt if their maturity date does not exceed *nine months*. [SA §3(a)(3)]

c. **Charitable organizations:** [§306]  Securities issued by religious, educational, or charitable organizations are also exempt from registration. [SA §3(a)(4)]

d. **Savings and loan associations:** [§307]  Securities issued by savings and loan or related institutions are exempt if the issuer is supervised by state and/or federal authorities. [SA §3(a)(5)]

e. **Railroad equipment trusts:** [§308]  Securities issued by common carriers to finance the acquisition of rolling stock are exempt. [SA §3(a)(6)]

f. **Bankruptcy:** [§309]  Likewise, securities issued by a receiver or trustee in bankruptcy with the approval of the court are exempt. [SA §3(a)(7)]

g. **Insurance policies:** [§310]  Finally, insurance, endowment, or annuity policies issued by companies supervised by state agencies are exempt. [SA §3(a)(7)]

3. **Exempted Security Transactions:** [§311]  It is important to distinguish exempted securities from exempted securities *transactions*. If the security *itself* is exempted, as above, it can be sold and resold without ever being subject to the registration requirements of section 5. On the other hand, if only the security *transaction* is exempt, the initial sale is not subject to section 5, but a later resale of the same securities might be. For example, if XYZ Corp. issues stock to A under a transaction exemption, and A later transfers the stock to B, the transfer to B may not be exempt. However, if XYZ issued the stock to A under a security exemption, the transfer from A to B would be exempt. Exempted securities transactions are covered in section 4 of the 1933 Act and some subsections of section 3.

a. **Integration:** [§312]  When an issuer has on separate occasions attempted several offerings under transaction exemptions, a question may arise as to whether the offerings were truly separate or only one offering intended to look like two or more offerings so that the issuer can avoid registering a distribution that would otherwise be required to be registered. While the issuer might attempt to convey the appearance of having made two or more offerings, the S.E.C. might decide that the several offerings are *integrated* (*i.e.*, that all of the offerings are part of the same offering). The effect of having several offerings declared integrated can be disastrous, because when several offerings are integrated into one, it is unlikely that the integrated offering will qualify for a transaction exemption, and because the issuer has not registered the offering, it will violate the Securities Act. There are two basic approaches to integration under the Securities Act: the S.E.C.'s general five-factor test and safe-harbor tests particular to specific exemptions. The general five-factor test is discussed below. Each specific safe-harbor test will be discussed, *infra*, along with the particular exemption to which it applies (*see infra*, §§370, 405, 457-471).

(1) **Five-factor test:** [§313]  In several releases pertaining to different exemptions, the S.E.C. has provided a list of five factors that it considers in determining whether offerings will be integrated:

(i) Whether the offerings are *part of a single plan of financing*;

(ii) Whether the offerings involve *issuance of the same class of security*;

(iii) Whether the offerings are *made at or about the same time*;

(iv) Whether the *same type of consideration* is to be received; and

(v) Whether the offerings are *made for the same general purpose*.

[*See, e.g.*, SA Release No. 4434 (1961)—§3(a)(11); SA Release No. 4552 (1962) —§4(2)]

(a) **Note:** It is important in considering the transaction exemptions, discussed below, to keep in mind the concept of integration and the possibility that a series of offerings might be integrated by the S.E.C.

b. **Mortgage transactions:** [§314] When certain mortgages are initiated by regulated financial institutions and participating interests (*i.e.*, portions of the loan rights and duties) are sold to investors, the transactions may be exempt from registration. [SA §4(5)]

c. **Transactions by particular persons**

(1) **Transactions by persons other than issuers, underwriters, or dealers:** [§315] As noted *supra*, §91, the registration requirements of the 1933 Act apply only to issuers, underwriters, and dealers. Hence, transactions by other persons (for example, ordinary investors) are exempt from those requirements. [SA §4(1)]

(2) **Dealer's transaction exemption:** [§316] Once a registration statement has been filed, every dealer is subject to the prospectus delivery requirements of section 5 during the statutory distribution period (below), on the theory that it is essential during this period for investors to receive a prospectus. However, dealer transactions after the distribution period are exempt from the section 5 prospectus delivery requirements. [SA §4(3); *see supra*, §§188-192]

(a) **Definition of "dealer":** [§317] A "dealer" in this context is any person who spends all or part of his time (directly or indirectly) as an agent, broker, or principal in the offering, buying, selling or other trading of securities issued by another person. [SA §2(12)]

1) **Note:** This definition includes persons who are also considered "brokers" (*see supra*, §10).

2) **And note:** Classification as a "dealer" depends on the party's usual activities—not merely his role with respect to a particular offering or transaction.

(b) **Statutory "distribution period":** [§318] For purposes of the dealer exemption under SA section 4(3), the "distribution" period is defined as a specific time period—*i.e.*, 40 days following the effective date of the registration statement *or* 40 days following commencement of the offering, whichever is later. Thus, dealers must deliver a prospectus as part of any sales transactions they conduct during this period.

1) **Extension of statutory period for new companies:** [§319] When a company is offering its securities to the public for the

first time, the distribution period on that issuance is deemed to last 90 days rather than 40. [SA §4(3)]

2) **No forty-day period for issues by reporting companies:** [§320] The 40-day prospectus delivery requirement of section 4(3) is eliminated for dealers trading in the securities of corporations already required to file regular and periodic reports with the S.E.C. under sections 13(a) or 15(d) of the 1934 Act. (*See* discussion *infra*, §671; *and see* SA Rule 174 *supra*, §201.)

   a) **Rationale:** The information normally required in a prospectus is included in these reports, and interested investors may therefore obtain it from the S.E.C.

   b) **Note:** This exemption does *not* apply when the dealer is participating in the offering and is still selling securities from his original underwriting allotment. [SA §4(3)(B)]

3) **Dealers affected:** [§321] The requirement that a prospectus be delivered to investors during the distribution period applies to *all* dealers—both those participating in the offering and those who are merely trading in the securities.

   a) **Rationale:** In the 40-day period after the offering begins, resales of securities included in the "distribution" will be taking place, and dealers not participating in the underwriting may be involved in these resales.

4) **Securities involved:** [§322] If the issuing corporation has already issued common stock and now makes an offering of additional shares of common, only the *new shares* are subject to the registration and dealer prospectus delivery requirements. However, a dealer may not be able to distinguish between the two and, to avoid possible liability, may thus be forced to deliver prospectuses as to *all* transactions in the corporation's common stock during the "distribution period."

(c) **Dealers exemption during post-distribution period:** [§323] The "post-distribution trading period," during which the dealer's exemption operates, commences after the statutory "distribution period"—generally 40 days. Dealer's transactions occurring after the expiration of this period are not subject to the prospectus delivery requirement of section 5. [SA §4(3)]

1) **Exemption as to unregistered offerings:** [§324] The exemption applies even when a registration statement should have been filed but was not. In such case, if the unregistered securities are offered to the public, dealers are exempt from the prospectus delivery requirements starting 40 days after such offering first begins.

a) **Rationale:** Even though the offering was illegal, unsuspecting dealers trading in the securities should not be held to have violated the Act.

2) **Exemption does not apply to original allotment:** [§325] However, the exemption from prospectus delivery in the post-distribution trading period does *not* apply to dealers participating in the offering who have not yet sold their original full allotment of securities.

a) **Rationale:** As long as securities that are part of the offering are being sold for the first time, the distribution is still going on and investors still need the protection of receiving a prospectus. [SA §4(3)(C)]

(3) **Broker's transaction exemption:** [§326] Brokers (*i.e.*, persons who sell a customer's securities for a commission) are exempt from the prospectus delivery requirement when they execute a customer's order to sell securities on any exchange or in the over-the-counter market. [SA §4(4)]

(a) **Applies to specific transaction:** [§327] The broker's exemption is only for a specific transaction—*i.e.*, the broker need only be acting as a broker (*e.g.*, on a commission basis) *in this transaction* to qualify. Also, unlike a "dealer" seeking to qualify for the dealer's exemption, a *person need not normally or usually act as a broker* for the broker's exemption to be available.

1) **Application to dealers:** [§328] The Securities Act definition of "dealer" *see supra*, §11) is broad enough to include persons performing the function of a broker. If a dealer transaction does not qualify for the dealer exemption, *supra*, the dealer might be able to rely on the broker's exemption—at least for transactions in which the dealer is performing a broker's function—since the broker-dealer's usual functions are immaterial.

(b) **Not limited to "post-distribution" period:** [§329] The 1933 Act contemplates that the ordinary investor should be able to sell her securities (purchased as part of a new offering) at any time—even when an S.E.C. stop order may have halted the original distribution process involving the issuer, the underwriters, and participating dealers. Hence, there is no 40-day "distribution" restriction on the broker's exemption, as there is in the case of the dealer's exemption.

1) **Rationale—"open market" for investors:** [§330] The broker's exemption allows brokers to execute *unsolicited* sell orders *at any time*, without complying with the prospectus delivery requirements. This ensures that there is always an open market in the securities, so that they may be traded at a price reflecting their current trading value.

2) **Example:** XYZ Corp. issued 100,000 shares of its common stock to the public in a registered offering through A, an

underwriter. B, a dealer, had an allotment of 10,000 shares. A stop order would halt these parties from further distribution activity. But if B had already sold 1,000 shares to C, then even during the period when the stop order was in effect, C could sell her 1,000 shares through B (with B using the broker's exemption), and receive whatever an unsolicited buyer was willing to pay.

(c) **Does not apply to customer:** [§331] The exemption applies only to the broker and does *not* extend to the selling customer. The customer must find her own exemption to sell the securities without violating the Act.

  1) **Note:** The ordinary customer usually has no trouble in this regard, since she is usually not an "issuer, underwriter, or dealer" subject to the provisions of the Act (*see supra,* §315).

  2) **But note:** Sales by a *control person* through a broker may result in liability for both the control person and the broker, because in such a case the broker will often be deemed to be an "underwriter" under section 2(11) of the Securities Act (*see supra,* §§93-115; *and see* below). Similarly, sales by anyone of "restricted stock" may result in liability. [*See* SA Rule 144; *see supra,* §§93-115; *see infra,* §§549 *et seq.*]

(d) **"Usual brokerage function":** [§332] The broker exemption applies only where the broker is performing no more than the usual broker's function in this particular transaction.

  1) **More than usual commission:** [§333] Receipt of more than the usual brokerage commission may take the transaction beyond the usual broker's function and eliminate the exemption.

  2) **Delegation of unusual authority:** [§334] The transaction may also be deemed to be beyond the broker's function if the seller of the securities delegates unusual authority to the broker (*e.g.,* as to time and manner of executing the sell order).

    a) **Example:** Authority to sell a "substantial block of securities" exceeds the usual brokerage function, since under such circumstances it is likely that the broker will *solicit* orders to buy so that he can dispose of the seller's block of securities (*see* below).

    b) **But note:** The broker can always prove that the presumption of solicitation is wrong, thereby bringing himself within the exemption.

  3) **Broker's sales for control persons:** [§335] The rules concerning a broker's sales for control persons are complex, mostly because the SA section 2(11) definition of underwriter deems control persons of issuers to be issuers. As a result, the following rules apply:

a) **Where control person has exemption:** [§336] If the control person has an exemption from the sale of unregistered securities (*e.g.*, under rule 144; *see infra*, §549), the broker that assists the control person in the sale may properly rely on the broker exemption in section 4(4).

b) **Where control person has no exemption:** [§337] However, where the control person has no exemption, and the broker knows or has reasonable grounds for believing this fact, the broker may be acting as an "underwriter" in selling the control person's stock (*see supra*, §106), in which case, he *cannot* rely on the broker's exemption. [*In re* Ira Haupt & Co., *supra*, §111]

c) **Duty to investigate seller's status:** [§338] Therefore, to claim the broker's exemption, the broker must make a reasonable investigation prior to any sale to determine whether the sale is for a control person and, if so, whether the control person has the requisite exemption. [SA Release No. 5168 (1971); SEA Release No. 9239 (1971)]

(e) **No broker solicitation of buy orders:** [§339] The broker's exemption is lost if the broker *solicits* orders to buy the seller's stock.

1) **Rationale:** The 1933 Act is designed to protect *buyers* rather than sellers. Hence, buyers should normally receive all of the disclosure information required by the Act.

2) **What constitutes "solicitation":** [§340] General business advertising does not amount to the solicitation of buy orders. Also, a broker *may* call another broker or dealer who has already bid on the security (*e.g.*, through printed or computer security quotation services), or may simply execute the other's sell order over the exchange.

a) **Compare:** But the broker may *not* call another broker or dealer on the telephone, or approach another member of the exchange, to "see if he is interested."

d. **Private offering exemption:** [§341] The registration requirements of section 5 apply only to an offering of securities that is made *to the public*. Therefore, transactions by an issuer that constitute a "private" (rather than public) offering of securities are exempt from registration. [SA §4(2)]

(1) **Bases for exemption:** [§342] The statutory base for the private offering exemption is contained in section 4(2) of the 1933 Act, which excludes from the registration requirements of SA section 5 "transactions by an issuer not involving any public offering." However, as we will see shortly, this statutory exemption is quite vague. In response to protests by issuers, underwriters, and their respective counsel, the S.E.C. adopted a rule clarifying the circumstances under which the requirements of section 4(2) will

be deemed to be met. (Such rules are often called "safe harbors," because compliance with the rule provides shelter from the stormy seas of statutory interpretation and litigation.) The modern section 4(2) safe harbor is SA rule 506, contained in regulation D. (*See infra*, §§363 *et seq.*, discussing regulation D in detail.) An understanding of the private offering exemption, therefore, requires knowledge of both the *statutory exemption* under section 4(2), and the *rule 506 safe harbor* under regulation D. This section discusses the statutory exemption; a discussion of the safe harbor follows in the discussion of regulation D.

(2) **Statutory (section 4(2)) exemption for private offerings:** [§343] Whether an offering will be considered to be "private" under section 4(2), and hence exempt from registration, is a *question of fact* in each case. The party claiming the exemption has the burden of proof to show that the offering is private.

    (a) **Criteria for distinguishing private vs. public offerings:** [§344] The following factors are considered by the courts in determining whether a given offering is public or private.

        1) **Need for protection of 1933 Act:** [§345] In many courts, the primary question is whether, given the circumstances of the offering, potential purchasers need the protection of the registration provisions. [*See* S.E.C. v. Ralston Purina Co., 346 U.S. 119 (1953)]

            a) **Sophistication of investors:** [§346] In answering this question, the basic issue is the sophistication of the persons to whom the securities are offered for sale: are they knowledgeable enough to ask the right questions, demand and get the information they need to make an intelligent investment decision, appreciate and bear the risk of securities investment, etc.?

                1/ If so, the offer of securities may well be considered *private.*

                2/ If not, the offering may be deemed *public* and therefore subject to registration.

        2) **Access to investment information:** [§347] Investor sophistication by itself is not enough to establish applicability of the private offering exemption. The investor must *also* have access to all information material to the investment decision—*i.e.,* the same information as would be included in a registration statement. [SA Release No. 5487 (1974)]

            a) **Application:** This has been held to mean that the offerees in a private offering must have a close relationship to the issuer and its management since this provides the needed access to relevant information. [S.E.C. v. Continental Tobacco Co., 463 F.2d 137 (5th Cir. 1972)]

3) **Receipt of material information:** [§348] Some courts have indicated that mere access to information is not enough; the issuer must also *actually distribute* to its offerees the same type of material information as would be contained in a formal registration statement, as well as provide access to any additional information they request (no matter how sophisticated the offerees are). [S.E.C. v. Continental Tobacco Co., *supra*]

4) **Number of offerees:** [§349] The concept of a "private offering" also seems to imply that the offerees will be *few* in number.

    a) **Application:** The Supreme Court has stated that the number of offerees is not a major factor, but that the S.E.C. can adopt rules of thumb for purposes of administrative decisions. [S.E.C. v. Ralston Purina Co., *supra*]

    b) **But note:** Lower courts and the S.E.C. have emphasized the number of offerees in classifying the offer as public or private. Thus, when the number of offerees gets very large, the offering is likely to be deemed public and subject to registration—regardless of the other criteria discussed above (*i.e.*, no matter how sophisticated the investors might be, or how much information they are given). [Hill York Corp. v. American International Franchises, 448 F.2d 680 (5th Cir. 1971)]

    c) **And note:** It is the number of *offerees—not* the number of actual *purchasers*—that is determinative.

5) **Other relevant factors:** [§350] It is clear from the case law that the fact that all offerees are sophisticated investors, or that they are given the same information they would get in a registration statement, may not be sufficient to bring the offering within the section 4(2) exemption. There are several additional factors that may also be relevant in determining whether an offering is public or private.

    a) **Rationale:** Actual registration with the S.E.C. gives the S.E.C. an element of control over the offering, allowing more protection for investors, and it is felt that such control should be dispensed with only in very limited circumstances. [Woolf v. S.D. Cohn & Co., 515 F.2d 591 (5th Cir. 1975)]

    b) **Appearance of public offering:** [§351] Most of the additional factors considered by courts stem from the notion that if an offering *looks* public (*i.e.*, is large and dispersed), it should be treated as such under section 4(2).

        1/ **Dollar value of offering:** [§352] An offering of $4 million in securities looks more "public" than a $20,000 issue. [Hill York Corp. v. American International Franchises, *supra*]

    2/ **Marketability of the securities:** [§353]  Along the same lines, if the issuer has created a readily marketable security (*e.g.*, many units in small denominations such as $1 per share), there is more reason to find a distribution to the public. [Hill York Corp. v. American International Franchises, *supra*]

    3/ **"Diverse group" rule:** [§354]  Similarly, the more unrelated and diverse the offerees are, the more the offering appears to be public. [S.E.C. v. Continental Tobacco Co., *supra*]

    4/ **Manner of offering securities:** [§355]  And the *manner* in which the offering is made may also be important—*e.g.*, an offering made through the use of *public advertising* is likely to be considered "public" for purposes of registration. [Hill York Corp. v. American International Franchises, *supra*]

  c) **Combination of all the elements:** [§356]  Since various cases, S.E.C. releases, etc., tend to emphasize different important elements or tests, the careful securities lawyer tends to combine all of the various tests mentioned into one comprehensive checklist of elements.

(b) **Application of section 4(2) criteria:** [§357]  The following cases illustrate the application by the courts of section 4(2) criteria.

  1) **Example—public offering:** An issuer offered stock to its employees at the rate of 400 employees per year. The employees represented all income levels, occupational levels, lengths of service, sophistication, etc. A public offering was found since the employees were deemed to need the protection of the Act. [S.E.C. v. Ralston Purina Co., *supra*, §345]

  2) **Example—public offering:** An issuer under an injunction for a previous violation of the private offering rules made an offering to an undetermined number of people of diverse and generally unsophisticated backgrounds. The court held this to be a public offering, notwithstanding the fact that the issuer had prepared an investment memo for the offerees and allowed them access to other relevant corporate information. [S.E.C. v. Continental Tobacco Co., *supra*]

  3) **Compare—private offering:** On the other hand, an offering of the debt securities of a manufacturing firm to 80 institutional investors (banks, insurance companies, etc.) was held to be a private offering, as was an offering of an undivided interest in oil lease property to a single investor with experience in buying oil stocks. [Garfield v. T. C. Strain, 320 F.2d 116 (10th Cir. 1963)]

  4) **Private offering:** And the exchange by five shareholders of their stock in a close corporation for stock of another company

was held to be a private offering because they were in a position to obtain whatever information they wanted, and together had significant experience in running a manufacturing firm with nationwide sales distribution. [*Bowers v. Columbia General Corp.*, 336 F. Supp. 609 (D. Del. 1971)]

(3) **Integration of private offerings into public offerings:** [§358] If an issuer attempts to make two or more offerings under the private offering exemption, the S.E.C. may treat the several offerings as a single integrated offering. (*See supra*, §312.) It is difficult to be sure whether the several offerings will be deemed integrated under the S.E.C.'s general five-part test (*supra*, §313). Rule 506—the safe harbor provision for private offerings—contains its own, easier to predict integration provision, which, if followed assures that the S.E.C. will not challenge separate offerings on the basis that they should be integrated. (*See infra*, §370.)

    (a) **Rule 152—private placement followed by public offering:** [§359] SA rule 152 provides that the statutory private placement exemption (*i.e.*, offerings under section 4(2)) is not lost if the issuer later decides to make a public offering "and/or files a registration statement." This is potentially a very useful provision to issuers who might otherwise be deterred from conducting registered offerings because they had earlier done private placements and feared integration of the private and public offerings.

        1) **Rule 152 available for venture capital deals:** The express terms of rule 152 are limited to situations where the issuer "decides" to do a public offering only after completing the private placement. The S.E.C. staff, however, has accorded no-action status to a number of issuers who first sought venture capital (by private placements), but even at the time of the private placement contemplated that a public offering would eventually take place.

(4) **Exemption for offerings to "accredited investors":** [§360] Section 4(6) of the 1933 Act is related conceptually to section 4(2) (the "private offering" exemption). Section 4(6) provides an exemption from the Act's registration requirements for transactions involving offers and sales of securities by an issuer solely to one or more *accredited investors* if the aggregate offering price does not exceed the amount allowed under section 3(b) (currently $5 million, *see infra*, §362). No advertising or public solicitation is permitted in connection with such transactions.

    (a) **Exemption limited to "accredited investors":** [§361] Section 4(6) permits an offering only to "accredited investors." The term "accredited investors" is defined in SA section 2(15) and SA rule 215 and is similar to the term "accredited investor" under regulation D (*see infra*, §367).

    (b) **No mandatory disclosure:** Section 4(6) does not require the issuer to disclose information to accredited investors. However, the section does require any issuer relying on the exemption to file a notice of sale with the S.E.C.

e. **Small issue exemptions:** [§362]   In addition to the other security and security transaction exemptions set forth in the Act, section 3(b) of the 1933 Act permits the S.E.C. to exempt security offerings from registration if the protection of the Act is not required and less than $5 million in securities is involved in the offering. Pursuant to this section, the S.E.C. has formulated several additional exemptions. Although formulated under section 3 of the 1933 Act for *security* exemptions, these small business exemptions are really *transaction* exemptions.

(1) **Regulation D**

(a) **Introduction:** [§363]  In a major initiative aimed at facilitating the capital formation needs of small businesses, in 1982 the S.E.C. adopted regulation D, which contains rules 501 through 508.

(i) *Rules 501 through 503* set forth definitions, terms, and conditions that apply generally throughout the regulation;

(ii) *Rules 504 and 505* provide small issue exemptions from registration under section 3(b) of the 1933 Act;

(iii) *Rule 506*, which as indicated above is based on the section 4(2) private offering exemption rather than the section 3(b) small issue exemption, provides a private offering "safe harbor"—issuers complying with the provisions of rule 506 and regulation D will be deemed to have complied with all relevant provisions of section 4(2);

(iv) *Rule 507* bars issuers from using regulation D when the issuer (or any predecessor or affiliate) has been the subject of an injunction for failure to file required notices under regulation D; and

(v) *Rule 508* provides that an issuer that commits an *inadvertent and immaterial* violation of regulation D can, under some circumstances, still claim the regulation D exemption.

Regulation D *applies only to issuers*; control persons may not use regulation D.

1) **Purpose:** [§364]  Regulation D is designed to:

a) *Simplify and clarify* existing exemptions;

b) *Expand the availability* of existing exemptions; and

c) *Achieve uniformity* between federal and state exemptions.

2) **Derivation causes differences:** [§365]  As noted above, rule 506 is based on section 4(2) (the private offering exemption) of the 1933 Act, while rules 504 and 505 are based on section 3(b) (the small issue exemption). Perhaps the most immediate consequence of this difference is that offerings under rules 504 and 505 have specific dollar limitations (*see* below), but offerings

under rule 506 have no dollar limitation; in a rule 506 offering the emphasis is on the nonpublic nature of the offering.

(b) **Definitions and terms used in regulation D:** [§366] Rule 501 sets forth definitions that apply to all of regulation D.

1) **Accredited investor:** [§367] One of the key concepts in regulation D is the "accredited investor," defined in rule 501 to include the following eight categories:

a) *Institutional investors* such as banks, insurance companies, pension plans, etc. [Rule 501(a)(1)]

b) *Private business development companies* [SA Rule 501(a)(2)];

c) *Corporations, partnerships, tax-exempt charities,* and the like, in each case (i) *not* formed for the specific purpose of acquiring the securities in question and (ii) with total assets *exceeding $5 million* [SA Rule 501(a)(3)];

d) *Directors, executive officers, and general partners of the issuer* of the securities [SA Rule 501(a)(4)];

e) *Natural persons with $1 million in net worth* (individually, or jointly with spouse) [SA Rule 501(a)(5)];

f) *Natural persons with $200,000 in individual annual income;* (or $300,000 joint income with spouse) [SA Rule 501(a)(6)];

g) *Trusts, not formed for the specific purpose of acquiring the securities* in question, with total assets exceeding *$5 million,* if *directed by a "sophisticate"* as described in rule 506(b)(2)(ii) (as to the definition of "sophisticate," *see infra*, §386) [SA Rule 501(a)(7)]; and

h) Any *entity in which all the equity owners are accredited* investors [SA Rule 501(a)(8)].

2) **Purchasers:** [§368] As we will see, under rules 505 and 506 it is often important to determine how many "purchasers" there will be in a particular offering. Accredited investors are *not counted* in calculating the total number of purchasers in a regulation D offering. [SA Rule 501(e)(1)(iv)]

(c) **General conditions to be met:** [§369] There are several general conditions that apply to all offers and sales effected pursuant to rules 504 through 506 [*see* SA Rule 502]:

1) **Integration:** [§370] As noted above (*see supra*, §312), the concept of "integration" means that under certain circumstances, multiple offerings of securities may be deemed by the S.E.C. to

be a single offering. This is often devastating for the issuer because it usually means that section 5 of the 1933 Act was violated. In this regard, regulation D provides some help to issuers, by providing a safe harbor for all offers and sales that take place at least six months before the start of, or six months after the termination of, the regulation D offering, as long as there are no offers and sales (excluding those to employee benefit plans) of securities of the same or similar class within either of these six-month periods. [*See* SA Rule 502(a)]

2) **Information requirements:** [§371] Regulation D specifies *when* disclosure is required in a regulation D offering, and *what kind* of disclosure is required. [SA Rule 502(b)]

a) **When disclosure is required:** [§372] Regulation D requires the delivery of a written disclosure document when securities are sold *under rules 505 or 506 to anyone that is not an accredited investor.* In such a case, delivery of the information specified in rule 502(b)(2) (*see* below) is required to be made to those persons that are not accredited investors.

   1/ **Note:** When securities are sold under *rule 504, or only to accredited investors* under any provision of regulation D, there is *no mandatory disclosure.* However, in such a case, the issuer is still subject to the antifraud and civil liability provisions of the federal securities laws and *must comply with any applicable state disclosure requirements.*

b) **What kind of disclosure is required:** [§373] The nature of the required disclosure varies with the kind of issuer (*i.e.*, whether or not the issuer is a 1934 Act reporting company) and the dollar amount of the offering. [*See* SA Rule 502(b)]

   1/ **Issuers that are not 1934 Act reporting companies:** [§374] Issuers that are not reporting companies under the 1934 Act must provide disclosure based on regulation A (*see infra*, §406) for offerings up to $2 million. If the offering is for more than $2 million, disclosure is based on the 1933 Act registration forms. At $7.5 million, the requirements become somewhat more stringent, especially with respect to the financial statements that must be provided. [*See* SA Rule 502(b)(2)(i)]

   2/ **Issuers that are 1934 Act reporting companies:** [§375] Reporting companies in essence can use the information they are already filing with the S.E.C.: annual report, proxy statement, and the annual 10-K report. [*See* SA Rule 502(b)(2)(ii)]

   3/ **All issuers:** [§376] In addition to the foregoing, issuers in rule 505 or 506 offerings must give investors, prior to purchase, an opportunity to ask questions and to obtain additional information that the issuer can acquire without unreasonable effort or expense. [*See* SA Rule 502(b)(2)(v)] Issuers also must, prior to purchase, advise non-accredited investors of the limitations on resale applicable to the securities (*see* below). [SA Rule 502(b)(2)(vii)]

3) **Manner of the offering:** [§377] The use of general solicitation or general advertising in connection with rule 505 or 506 offerings is prohibited. [*See* SA Rule 502(c)]

4) **Limitations on resale:** [§378] As will be discussed *infra* (§§537 *et seq.*), resales of securities issued under most transaction exemptions, including rules 505 and 506, are restricted. Issuers must exercise reasonable care to assure that the purchasers are not "underwriters" as defined in 1933 Act section 2(11) (*see supra,* §93). Reasonable care may be demonstrated by:

   (i) *Reasonable inquiry* to determine if the purchaser is acquiring the securities for himself or for other persons;

   (ii) *Written disclosure* to each purchaser prior to sale that the securities are restricted and cannot be resold; and

   (iii) *Placement of a legend* on the security certificates, stating that the securities have not been registered and noting the existence of restrictions on transferability and sale of the securities.

   [*See* SA Rule 502(d)] Note that while these steps evidence reasonable care by the issuers, they are not the exclusive means to demonstrate such care.

(d) **Filing of notices of sales:** [§379] Within 15 days after the first sale of securities under regulation D, the seller must give the S.E.C. notice of the sale. There is a uniform notice of sales form for use in offerings under both regulation D and section 4(6) of the Act, called "form D." Issuers furnish information on form D mainly by checking appropriate boxes. [*See* SA Rule 503]

(e) **Specific conditions of rules 504, 505, and 506**

1) **Rule 504:** [§380] Rule 504 provides an exemption for offers and sales not exceeding an aggregate offering price of *$1 million* during any 12-month period. This exemption is not available to investment companies, 1934 Act reporting companies, or blank check companies (*see supra,* §296). Commissions or similar remuneration *may* be paid to those selling the securities in a rule 504 offering.

   a) **Calculating $1 million limit:** [§381] The aggregate offering price for an offering under rule 504 may not exceed $1 million, *less* the aggregate price for all securities sold (i) in the 12 months before the start of and during the rule 504 offering; (ii) in reliance on any exemption based on the 1933 Act section 3(b); or (iii) in violation of the 1933 Act section 5. [SA Rule 504(b)(2)]

2) **Rule 505:** [§382] Rule 505 provides an exemption to any issuer that is not an investment company for offers and sales to an *unlimited number of accredited* investors, and to no more than 35 *non-accredited* purchasers, where the aggregate offering price in any 12-month period does not exceed $5 million. [*See* SA Rule 505]

   a) **Calculating $5 million limit:** [§383] The maximum dollar amount under rule 505 is calculated in the same way that the $1 million limit is calculated under rule 504. [*See* SA Rule 505(b)(2)(i)]

   b) **"Unworthy offering" disqualification:** [§384] The rule 505 exemption is not available to issuers described in SA rule 262, the regulation A "unworthy offering" disqualification. (*See infra,* §393.)

3) **Rule 506:** [§385] Like rule 505, rule 506—the private offering safe-harbor provision—provides an exemption for offers and sales to an *unlimited number of accredited investors* and to no more than *35 non-accredited purchasers.* Unlike rule 505, there is *no dollar limitation* on rule 506 offerings (because of its origin under section 4(2) rather than section 3(b) and the corresponding emphasis on the non-public nature of the offering rather than its dollar amount; *see supra,* §365), and rule 506 has an additional requirement that the non-accredited purchasers be *sophisticated* in financial and business matters or employ a representative who is sophisticated.

   a) **"Sophisticate" defined:** [§386] To be a sophisticate, the purchaser or investment advisor must have "such knowledge and experience in financial and business matters that he is capable of evaluating the merits and risks of the prospective investment," or the issuer must reasonably believe that the purchaser meets that description. [SA Rule 506(b)(2)(ii)]

(2) **Regulation A exemption:** [§387] Regulation A, which had largely fallen into disuse in the 1980s, was extensively revised in 1992 by the S.E.C. as part of its "Small Business Initiative." Although it is presently too early to tell whether the revised regulation will be accepted by issuers, expectations for the "new" regulation A are high.

   (a) **Shortened registration:** [§388] Regulation A is *not a complete exemption* from registration. Instead, it provides a simplified form of registration which costs less to prepare and takes less time to complete than the standard registration (*see infra,* §§406-413). [SA Rules 251-263; Forms 1-A, 6-A]

(b) **Issuers covered by regulation A:** [§389] To use regulation A, an issuer must meet the following requirements:

    1) **Residence and principal place of business:** [§390] The issuer must be a resident of, and have its principal place of business in, the United States or Canada. [SA Rule 251(a)(1)]

    2) **No 1934 Act reporting companies:** [§391] The issuer must *not* be a 1934 Act reporting company immediately prior to the regulation A offering. [SA Rule 251(a)(2)]

    3) **No "blank check" companies:** [§392] The issuer must *not* be a blank check company (*see supra,* §296) for a discussion of "blank check" companies). [SA Rule 251(a)(3)]

        a) **Note:** The prohibition against blank check companies applies under regulation A whether or not the company proposes to issue penny stock (*see supra,* §298 for the definition of penny stock).

(c) **Limitations on availability of regulation A**

    1) **The "unworthy offering" rules:** [§393] Regulation A may not be used when persons involved in the offering (*e.g.,* underwriters, officers, and directors of the issuer) have engaged in conduct indicating that potential investors may need the protection of a full registration under section 5. Such offerings are deemed unworthy of the regulation A exemption. [*See* SA Rules 251(a)(6), 262]

        a) **Previous conduct by issuer:** [§394] Where the issuer, its predecessors (*i.e.,* entities whose assets have been acquired by the issuer) or any affiliated issuer has engaged in prohibited conduct within the past five years (*e.g.,* has been convicted of a crime involving the sale of securities) or has been the subject within that time of certain S.E.C. orders (such as a stop order issued in connection with the filing of a registration statement), the regulation A exemption is not available. [SA Rule 262(a)]

        b) **Previous conduct by control persons and promoters:** [§395] Similar disqualifications apply to control persons and promoters of the issuer. In addition, the regulation A exemption will *not* be available when any such person was *convicted within the previous 10 years of a securities-related offense.* [SA Rule 262(b)]

        c) **Previous conduct by underwriters:** [§396] The disqualifications relating to underwriters are similar to those for control persons and promoters. In addition, if an underwriter was named as an underwriter in previous offerings that resulted in certain S.E.C. sanctions (*e.g.,* pending investigations, refusal orders, or stop orders under section 8), the regulation A exemption will not be available. [SA Rule 262(b), (c)]

d) **Events occurring after filing:** [§397] If any prohibited conduct, above, occurs after a regulation A offering statement is filed, the S.E.C. may issue a suspension order terminating the exemption. [SA Rule 258]

e) **S.E.C. authorized exceptions:** [§398] However, the S.E.C. has the power to make exceptions to these rules of conduct upon the issuer's showing of "good cause," so that persons otherwise disqualified may use regulation A. [SA Rule 262]

2) **Limitation on type of securities offered:** [§399] Regulation A is not available when the securities being offered are fractional undivided interests in oil and gas rights or the securities of investment companies. [SA Rule 251(a)(4), (5)]

3) **Limitation on dollar amount of securities offered:** [§400] The regulation A exemption is limited to the offering of a small amount of securities by the issuer (and related persons).

a) **General rule:** [§401] As a general rule, securities offered pursuant to regulation A by the issuer may not amount to more than $5 million worth of securities during any one-year period. [SA Rule 251(b)]

1/ **Limitations on sales by security holders:** [§402] In addition, all security holders together may sell no more than $1.5 million worth of securities in any one-year period. The securities sold by security holders are counted against the issuer's $5 million limit, but the issuer can control how much is sold by security holders under regulation A. All sales of securities issued under regulation A require the filing of a form 1-A with the S.E.C. (*see infra*, §406), which must be signed by the issuer. Thus, the issuer can prevent an investor from selling by refusing to sign the form. [SA Rule 251(b); *see* SA Rule 251(d)(2)]

2/ **Further limitations on affiliate sales:** [§403] In addition to the above limitations on total sales and sales by security holders, sales by affiliates (control persons) are prohibited if the issuer has not had net income from continuing operations in at least one of its last two fiscal years. [SA Rule 251(b)]

b) **Calculation of offering price:** [§404] The $5 million/$1.5 million limitations apply to all securities offered under regulation A in the immediately preceding 12 months. The dollar amounts refer to the amount to be received by the issuer, including all non-cash consideration at its fair value. [SA Rule 251(b)]

c) **Limitation due to integration of issues:** [§405] Like regulation D (*see supra*, §§363-386), regulation A contains a safe harbor rule to protect issuers against the consequences of inadvertent integration of offerings. The integration safe harbor provides that sales made in reliance on regulation A will not be integrated with:

   (i) *Prior offers or sales of securities* (although regulation A seems to provide that no prior offers or sales will be integrated, the release proposing the 1992 revisions stated that a regulation A offering would not be integrated with "any previously completed registered or exempt offering"; the implication is that the S.E.C. will integrate previous offers or sales made in violation of the SA section 5 [SA Release No. 6924 (1992)]); or

   (ii) *Subsequent offers or sales* that are:

      i. Registered under SA section 5;

      ii. Made in reliance on SA rule 701 (relating to employee benefit plans) or otherwise under employee benefit plans;

      iii. Made in reliance on regulation S (concerning unregistered offers and sales made outside the United States); or

      iv. Made more than six months after the completion of the regulation A offering.

   [SA Rule 251(c)] Failure to meet the safe harbor provision requirements does not result in automatic integration; rather, the S.E.C. will apply its standard five-part test (set out in SA Release No. 4552; *see supra*, §313) to determine whether integration is appropriate.

(d) **Regulation A procedures**

1) **Offering statement:** [§406] The offering statement on Form 1-A consists of three parts and is the basic form to be used by issuers for regulation A offerings:

   a) **Part I:** Part I of the offering statement serves as a notification. It is filed with the S.E.C. and is publicly available, but it is not circulated by the issuer to investors.

b) **Part II:** Part II of the offering statement consists of the offering circular to be distributed to investors. A corporate issuer has a choice of three possible formats for the offering circular:

   1/ **Model A—50-question form U-7:** [§407] An issuer may use form U-7 (currently in widespread use for state "blue sky" disclosure). This form requires more extensive disclosure than the other two choices (below), but is a "fill in the blank," question and answer form that may be easier for inexperienced issuers to complete.

   2/ **Model B—previous regulation A format:** [§408] Model B provides a "pool" of disclosure items, ranging from basic disclosure, such as description of the business and management remuneration, to more specialized items, such as description of the investment policies of a real estate investment trust.

   3/ **Form SB-2—new form for "small business issuers":** [§409] Finally, if the issuer is a corporation, it may choose form SB-2 (*see infra*, §437) for the offering circular.

c) **Part III:** Part III of the offering statement specifies the exhibits that must be filed in a regulation A offering. They are filed with the S.E.C. and are publicly available, but are not circulated to investors.

d) **Note:** Issuers that are corporations must follow either Model B or form SB-2, above. [*See* SA Form 1-A]

2) **S.E.C. processing procedures:** [§410] A waiting period of at least 20 days must pass after filing of the offering statement before it is "qualified" by the S.E.C. and the selling of securities can begin. [SA Rule 252(g)(1)]

   a) **Initial response after filing:** [§411] When the offering statement is filed by the issuer, the S.E.C. comments on any matters requiring an amendment of the offering statement.

   b) **Acceleration:** [§412] As with a registered offering, the S.E.C. has a procedure whereby an issuer can obtain the S.E.C.'s reaction to a filing, make changes in response to S.E.C. comments, and obtain a green light from the S.E.C. when all comments have been addressed. Essentially, the procedure contemplates a kind of acceleration, similar to what usually takes place in a registered offering (*see supra*, §§189-190). [SA Rule 252(g)(2)]

   c) **Continuing responsibility of issuer:** [§413] Whenever there has been a material change in the information presented in the offering circular, or subsequent developments have made the information misleading or incomplete, the issuer must update the offering circular and file the updated version with the S.E.C. [SA Rule 253(e)] In any event, the issuer remains responsible for any misstatements or omissions in the offering statement.

3) **Reports of sales and use of proceeds:** [§414] An issuer relying on the regulation A exemption is required to file a report of sales and use of proceeds of the offering every six months after the S.E.C. has qualified the offering statement, and within 30 days after the offering is completed. [SA Rule 257]

4) **S.E.C. enforcement procedures—suspension of offering:** [§415] At any time after filing of the offering statement, the S.E.C. may order a "temporary suspension" of the regulation A offering if it has reason to believe that any of the below-enumerated grounds for suspension exist. If the temporary suspension is not lifted, the exemption is lost and the issuer, its affiliates, and any underwriters involved may not make a regulation A offering for a period of five years.

   a) **Grounds for suspension:** [§416] The following grounds will cause the S.E.C. to suspend a regulation A offering:

      1/ *Failure to meet the requirements for the exemption,* including failure to provide copies of, or to file, any materials required by the exemption. [SA Rule 258 (a)(1)]

      2/ *Misleading statements or omissions of material facts* in the offering statement or a solicitation of interest document (*see infra*). [SA Rule 258(a)(2)]

      3/ *Events after filing* which would have made the exemption unavailable had they occurred prior to filing. (Here, a temporary suspension may be ordered by the S.E.C. until the problem is corrected; *see supra,* §§393 *et seq.*). [SA Rule 258(a)(4)]

      4/ *Actions initiated against the issuer or its predecessors or affiliates* for offenses involving securities transactions (*see supra,* §§393 *et seq.*). [SA Rule 258(a)(5)]

      5/ *Actions against the directors, officers, principal security holders, present promoters, or underwriters* of the issuer for offenses involving securities transactions (*see supra,* §§393 *et seq.*). [SA Rule 258(a)(6)]

   b) **Suspension procedures:** [§417] If the issuer fails to request a hearing, and the S.E.C. does not order one within

30 days after issuance of a temporary suspension order, the order becomes permanent. Where a hearing *is* requested or ordered, the S.E.C. may either allow the necessary corrections to be made or make the suspension permanent. [SA Rule 258(c)] Normally, temporary suspensions will be lifted where it is shown that non-compliance was in good faith and is correctible.

5) **Substantial and good faith compliance:** [§418] Failure to comply with all of the requirements of regulation A will not result in the loss of the exemption with respect to an offer or sale to a particular person or entity, *if* the issuer can prove that:

(i) The failure did not pertain to a term or condition directly *intended to protect* the offeree or buyer;

(ii) The failure to comply was *insignificant* with respect to the offering as a whole; and

(iii) *A good faith and reasonable attempt* was made to comply with all applicable requirements of regulation A.

[SA Rule 260]

(e) **Offers and sales pursuant to regulation A**

1) **Solicitation of interest document:** [§419] In its 1992 regulation A overhaul, the S.E.C. added a provision permitting an issuer to "test the waters" before committing to an offering. Under the new rules, "[a]n issuer may publish or deliver to prospective purchasers a written document or make scripted radio or television broadcasts to determine whether there is any interest in a contemplated securities offering." The issuer is not, however, permitted to solicit or accept any consideration or commitment, nor may any sales be made, until the offering statement is qualified (*see supra*, §410). [SA Rule 254(a)]

a) **Copies to S.E.C. required:** [§420] The issuer must submit a copy of the solicitation of interest document or script to the S.E.C. on or before the date of the document's first use. The document must contain or be accompanied by the name and telephone number of a person able to answer questions concerning the submission. [SA Rule 254(b)(1)]

b) **Information required:** [§421] Every solicitation of interest document or script must:

(i) State that *no money or other consideration is being solicited,* and if sent, will not be accepted.

(ii) State that *no sales will be made, nor commitments accepted,* until delivery of an offering circular that includes complete information about the issuer and the offering;

    (iii) State that any indication of interest made by a prospective purchaser involves *no obligation or commitment* of any kind; and

    (iv) Identify the *chief executive officer* of the issuer and describe briefly and generally the issuer's business and products.

[SA Rule 254(b)(2)]

c) **Oral communications:** [§422] After submitting copies of the solicitation of interest document to the S.E.C., the issuer is permitted to communicate orally with prospective investors. [SA Rule 254(a)]

2) **Preliminary offering circular:** [§423] Recall that in a registered offering, written offers may be made during the waiting period, provided they are in the form of a red herring prospectus (*see supra*, §§181 *et seq.*). Similar provisions apply to regulation A: After the offering statement is filed, but before it is qualified by the S.E.C. (*see supra*, §410), the offering circular may be used in the form in which it was filed, provided that it contains a legend specified by the S.E.C. alerting potential investors that the document has not yet been qualified under regulation A. [SA Rule 255(a)]

a) **Oral offers permitted:** [§424] After the offering statement is filed, oral offers are permitted. [SA Rule 251(d)(1)(i)]

b) **No written offers except by preliminary offering circular:** [§425] Once the offering statement is filed with the S.E.C., the solicitation of interest document may no longer be used. [SA Rule 254(b)(3)] The only permissible written offers after filing but before qualification are those made by the preliminary offering circular. [*See* SA Rule 255(a)]

c) **Exception: "tombstone" advertisements:** [§426] Regulation A contains a counterpart to the tombstone ad rule for registered offerings (*see supra*, §179). Once the offering statement is filed, advertisements are permitted if they state from whom an offering circular may be obtained, and include no more than the following additional information:

    (i) *Issuer's name;*

    (ii) *Title of the security, amount* being offered, and per unit offering *price* to the public;

    (iii) General type of the *issuer's business;* and

(iv) A brief statement as to the general *location and character of the issuer's property*.

[SA Rule 251(d)(1)(ii)(C)]

3) **Final offering circular required after qualification**

a) **As to offers:** [§427]  After the offering statement is qualified by the S.E.C., written offers may be made by means of the final offering circular. In addition, other written materials may be used, provided they are accompanied or preceded by a copy of the final offering circular. [SA Rule 251(d)(1)(iii)] This requirement is analogous to the "free writing" privilege accorded issuers in registered offerings. (*See supra*, §§195-196.)

1/ **Tombstone ads permitted:** [§428]  Although generally after qualification, written materials must be preceded or accompanied by a final copy of the offering circular, tombstone ads may be used after qualification without such delivery. [SA Rule 251(d)(1)(ii)(C)]

b) **As to sales:** [§429]  No sale may be concluded unless an offering circular is furnished to the purchaser in accordance with the following rules:

1/ **"Forty-eight hour" rule:** [§430]  As a general rule, a purchaser must be furnished a preliminary or final offering circular at least 48 hours before any mailing of confirmation of sale. [SA Rule 251(d)(2)(i)(B)]

2/ **Delivery of final offering circular with confirmation:** [§431]  In addition, a copy of the final offering circular must be delivered to the purchaser at the time the confirmation of sale is delivered, unless it has been delivered earlier. [SA Rule 251(d)(2)(i)(C)]

3/ **"Ninety-day" rule:** [§432]  The regulation A exemption recognizes that the offering may continue after all securities in the offering have been sold for the first time, until the issue really comes to rest in the hands of more or less permanent investors. Therefore, the S.E.C. rules arbitrarily designate the length of the secondary trading period as 90 days after qualification of the offering statement. [SA Rule 251(d)(2)(ii)]

a/ **Effect of "ninety-day" rule:** [§433]  During this period, any dealer trading in the regulation A securities must furnish an offering circular to the purchaser no later than the time a confirmation of sale is delivered.

b/ **To whom rule applies:** [§434] These delivery requirements also apply to *underwriters* who have sold their allotments and are acting as dealers in the secondary trading markets. [SA Rule 251(d)(2)(ii)] However, if a dealer fails to comply with the 90-day rule, it does not destroy the regulation A exemption for *other persons* involved in the underwriting and distribution. [*See* SA Rule 260(a)(2)]

c) **Period of circular's use:** [§435] Unless used in connection with certain specific types of offerings (such as employee stock purchase plans), the original circular may be used only for a period of 12 months. After this time, a revised circular must be filed with the S.E.C. [SA Rule 253(e)(2)]

d) **Post-effective amendments:** [§436] The offering circular and sales material in a regulation A offering must continue to correctly represent all material facts throughout the period they are used. Hence, material changes in the issuer during the course of the offering may require suspension of the offering and an amendment to the circular. [SA Rule 253(e)]

(3) **Registrations on form SB-2:** [§437] In 1992, the S.E.C. adopted form SB-2, available to "small business issuers," as part of its Small Business Initiatives. The form, together with the other revisions made by the Small Business Initiatives, is designed to "facilitate capital raising by small businesses and reduce the costs of compliance with the federal securities laws." [SA Release No. 6949 (1992)]

(a) **Definition of "small business issuer":** [§438] Essentially, a small business issuer is a United States or Canadian entity that is not an investment company (under the 1940 Act), has annual revenues of less than $25 million, and, if it is a majority-owned subsidiary, its parent corporation is also a small business issuer. [SA Rule 405]

1) **Public float limitation:** [§439] In addition to the above requirements, a small business issuer must have less than $25 million in public float; *i.e.,* the aggregate market value of securities of the issuer, held by nonaffiliates of the issuer, must be less than $25 million. [SA Rule 405]

f. **Intrastate offering exemption:** [§440] Securities offered and sold only to persons residing within a single state, by an issuer that is also a resident of and doing business in that state, are exempt from registration under section 5. [SA §3(a)(11)]

(1) **Rationale for exemption:** [§441] The intrastate offering exemption is designed to facilitate the raising of local capital for local businesses. The exemption is permitted on the grounds that local investors will be adequately

protected both by their proximity to the issuer and by state regulations. [SA Release No. 5450 (1974)]

(2) **Transaction exemption:** [§442] Remember that the intrastate offering exemption is merely a transaction exemption, and securities sold under it may have to be registered when resold. [SA Release No. 5450 (1974)]

(3) **Antifraud provisions apply:** [§443] And even though an issuer qualifying for this exemption does not have to register its securities, the general antifraud provisions of the 1933 Act still apply to the offering (*see infra*, §699).

(4) **Qualifying for exemption under rule 147:** [§444] Over the years, considerable uncertainty surrounded the meaning of some terms of the intrastate exemption in section 3(a)(11). For this reason, the S.E.C. adopted rule 147, a safe harbor rule that provides specific criteria which, if followed, ensure that the issuer qualifies for the intrastate offering exemption. As with other safe harbors (for example, rule 506 under section 4(2)), if an issuance of securities does not qualify under rule 147, the issuer may still rely on the general terms of section 3(a)(11). (Both the general provisions of section 3(a)(11) and the specific requirements of rule 147 are set forth below.)

(5) **Requirements for statutory intrastate offering exemption—section 3(a)(11)**

    (a) **Entire issue must be intrastate:** [§445] Under section 3(a)(11), the entire issue of securities must be offered and sold to residents of one state. Thus, a single offer to a nonresident will destroy the exemption. [SA Release No. 4434 (1961)]

        1) **Integration with other offerings:** [§446] The issuer must be careful not to lose the exemption through integration of an attempted intrastate offering with other interstate offerings of securities. (*See supra*, §312.)

            a) **Example:** A company located in Texas wished to issue notes in Texas to finance Texas real estate developments, and to follow this with an offering of common stock to both residents and nonresidents. The S.E.C. staff refused to give the issuer a "no action" letter (assuring the issuer that it would take "no action" on the matter) with respect to the promissory notes. The S.E.C. in effect held that there might be an integration of the two offerings if the issuer proceeded as planned. [*In re* Property Investments, Inc., Fed. Sec. L. Rep. (CCH) ¶79,201 (1972)]

            b) **Example:** A company issued stock under section 3(a)(11) to residents of its own state. Thirty days later, these residents began distributing their stock to nonresidents, and the S.E.C. obtained an injunction. The company stopped the nonresident sales and began to issue stock with attached debt securities (notes) to these same residents in exchange for their original stock, and also sold this new issue of securities to additional residents of the state. [Hillsborough Investment Corp. v. S.E.C., 276 F.2d 665 (1st Cir. 1960)]

    1/    The S.E.C. again obtained an injunction, the court holding that when an issuer loses its exemption as to one issue of securities by a nonresident sale, it does not regain the exemption by halting nonresident sales and confining itself exclusively to sales to residents.

    2/    Here the exchange and further sale of the package of stock and debt securities was merely a continuation of the sale of the no longer exempt securities (*i.e.,* the two offerings were "integrated"), and hence was a violation of the Act.

2)    **Limitation on resales—"coming to rest" test:** [§447] Eventual resales to nonresidents are possible without destroying the intrastate offering exemption, but only after the original distribution to residents is complete—*i.e.,* only after the offering has "come to rest" in the hands of state residents.

    a)    **Intent of purchaser determinative:** [§448] Under section 3(a)(11), whether an issue of securities has "come to rest" depends on the intent of the original purchasers. If the securities were purchased with the intention of keeping them for investment, the issue is complete and resales to nonresidents may begin. But if the purchasers intend a further distribution or resale, the issue has not "come to rest" and any resale to nonresidents will destroy the exemption.

    b)    **Objective test of intent:** [§449] Whether the original purchasers intended to hold the securities for investment is a question of fact, to be determined by objective evidence. [SA Release No. 4434 (1961)]

        1/    **Examples:** A relatively long holding period of one year or more may be sufficient to prove the necessary investment intent. Conversely, a resident's resale within a short time to a nonresident supports an inference that the offering has not come to rest within the state, and may defeat the exemption. An even stronger inference is created when the original sale is to a broker-dealer, who resells within a short time to out-of-state residents. [SA Release No. 4434 (1961)]

(b)    **Issuer, offerees, and purchasers must reside within state:** [§450] The intrastate exemption requires that issuer, offerees, and purchasers *all* be residents of the same state.

1)    **Issuer:** [§451] The issuer must meet two requirements to establish "residence" under section 3(a)(11):

a) **Residence in state:** [§452] First, the issuer must reside in the state where the offering is made. For a corporation, the state of residence is the state of incorporation.

b) **Doing business in state:** [§453] Second, since the purpose of the intrastate exemption is to finance local business, the issuer must also be "doing business" in the state.

1/ **Test:** Under the statute, "doing business" is judged by: (i) whether the issuer is doing a majority of its business in the state; and (ii) whether the proceeds of the offering are used in the state.

2/ **Example:** A Minnesota corporation with its only office in Minnesota sold unsecured installment notes to Minnesota residents. However, the intrastate offering exemption was not available because the proceeds of the offering were for loans to land developers outside the state. [S.E.C. v. McDonald Investment Co., 343 F. Supp. 343 (D. Minn. 1972)]

2) **Offerees and purchasers:** [§454] With respect to offerees and purchasers, mere presence in the state is not sufficient to establish residence. Rather, the test is similar to that for "domicile." The purchaser must reside in the state *with an intent to remain.*

3) **Underwriters, dealers, and control persons not included:** [§455] Underwriters and dealers participating in the offering need *not* be from the same state as the issuer and offerees. And control persons may use the issuer's exemption, even though they are not residents of the state in which the offering is made.

(c) **No restrictions on use of facilities of interstate commerce:** [§456] The intrastate exemption is not lost because the mails or other instruments of interstate commerce are used in the offering. Thus, the securities in question may be:

1) *Offered and sold through the mails* or other interstate facilities;

2) *Offered through general newspaper advertising*, as long as the advertisement indicates that offers are being made only to residents of the state; or

3) *Delivered through the facilities of interstate commerce* and transportation.

(6) **Rule 147 criteria for intrastate offering exemption:** [§457] Because intrastate offerings need not be reported to the S.E.C., the S.E.C. has little control over such offerings. This fact, plus uncertainty over the meaning of certain broad terms and conditions in the general section 3(a)(11) exemption (such as the definition of "doing business"), gave rise to numerous violations of the intrastate offering exemption. Consequently, the S.E.C.

adopted rule 147, which provides the following specific, objective criteria for determining what is exempt under section 3(a)(11).

(a) **Integration of offerings:** [§458] All securities transactions that are part of an integrated offering must meet the requirements of rule 147, or no part of the offering will qualify for an exemption under the rule.

    1) **Safe harbor rule:** [§459] Rule 147 provides an integration safe harbor, so that transactions covered by other section 3 exemptions (*supra*, §§303 *et seq.*) or by the section 4(2) exemption (*supra*, §341), *and* which occur either six months or more before, or at least six months after the rule 147 transaction, will *not* be integrated with the intrastate offering, as long as there are no offers, offers to sell, or sales of securities of the same or similar class by or for the issuer during either of these six-month periods. [SA Rule 147(b)(2)]

        a) **Note:** Where there have been offers or sales during one of the six-month periods, so that rule 147's integration safe harbor is not available, reference must be made to the S.E.C.'s traditional five-factor test in determining whether issues will be integrated. [*See supra*, §313; *and see* SA Release No. 5450 (1974)]

(b) **Requirement of coming to rest:** [§460] Rule 147 also provides an objective standard for the "coming to rest" test (*see supra*, §447). The rule 147 offering has come to rest within the state if no sales are made to persons residing outside the state of issue during the time the securities are being offered and sold by the issuer *and* for an additional period of *nine months* following the last sale by the issuer. [SA Rule 147(e)]

    1) **Precautions against interstate resale:** [§461] To ensure that securities issued under the rule 147 exemption do not enter the interstate securities markets prior to the time stipulated under rule 147(e) (*i.e.,* nine months from last sale by issuer), the S.E.C. requires the issuer to take the following precautions [SA Rule 147(f)(1)]:

        a) **Restrictive legend:** [§462] The issuer must place a legend on each securities certificate, stating that the securities have not been registered under the 1933 Act and setting forth the limitations on resale contained in rule 147's "coming to rest" provisions, above.

        b) **Stop transfer instructions:** [§463] The issuer must also issue instructions to its transfer agent prohibiting transfer of the securities until the securities have "come to rest," as described above. (Such instructions are often referred to as "stop transfer instructions.") If the issuer does not use a transfer agent, it must make a notation in its own records that transfers require special action.

    c) **Written representation from each purchaser as to residence:** [§464] The issuer must also obtain a written representation from each purchaser as to the purchaser's residence.

(c) **Requirements of residence:** [§465] To qualify for an intrastate offering exemption under rule 147, the issuer, offerees, and purchasers must all be residents of the same state.

    1) **Issuers:** [§466] Rule 147 sets forth two requirements to establish an issuer's "residence":

        a) **Residence in a state:** [§467] State residence is defined in rule 147 as follows:

            (i) For a corporation, the *state of incorporation*;

            (ii) For a partnership, the state where the partnership has its *principal place of business*; and

            (iii) For an individual, the state in which the party has his *principal residence*.

        [SA Rule 147(c)(1)]

        b) **"Doing business" requirement:** [§468] Under rule 147, an issuer is deemed to be "doing business" in a state if it meets the "triple 80% plus principal office" test:

            (i) At least 80% of its consolidated *gross revenues* are derived from the operation of a business or property located in the state, or from the rendering of services within the state; *and*

            (ii) At least 80% of the issuer's consolidated *assets* are held in the state; *and*

            (iii) At least 80% of the *proceeds* from the securities transaction in question are to be used, and in fact are used, in the issuer's operations within the state; *and*

            (iv) The issuer's *principal office* is located within the state.

        [SA Rule 147(c)(2)] Rule 147 also indicates how to calculate the time for determining whether these criteria have been met. Basically, the tests have to be met at the time that any offers or sales in the offering are being made. [*See* SA Rule 147(c), 147(c)(2)]

        c) **Example:** XYZ Corp., whose business is selling products throughout the United States through mail order catalogues, is incorporated in State A and has its only warehouse and office there. All products are manufactured at XYZ's plant in A. Orders are accepted in A, and all products are shipped from XYZ's warehouse in A. Under these circumstances, XYZ is deriving at least 80% of its gross revenues from a business located in A and meets all of the other tests for application of rule 147 as well. [SA Release No. 5450 (1974)]

2) **Offerees and purchasers:** [§469] For purposes of establishing offerees' and purchasers' residence under rule 147, corporations and business organizations are deemed to be residents of the state in which their *principal business office* is located. Individuals are considered residents of the state in which their *principal residence* is located. [SA Rule 147(d)(1), (2)]

a) **Verification of residence:** [§470] Recall that rule 147 requires the issuer to obtain a written representation from each purchaser regarding his place of residence (*see supra*, §465). The value of such a representation is questionable, however, in light of the fact that rule 147 requires compliance as to offerees as well as purchasers, and the rule does not require any representations from offerees.

b) **Domicile vs. principal residence:** [§471] The residence of an individual offeree or purchaser frequently is crucial in an intrastate transaction. Under the statutory exemption, individuals are deemed resident in the state in which they are domiciled (*see supra*, §454). Under the safe harbor rule, however, an individual is resident in the state where she has her principal residence. This is significant, because domicile is established by the *individual's intentions*, and thus is determined subjectively, in contrast to the objective question of principal residence. For example, if securities offered in an intrastate offering decline in value, the individual purchasers may try to establish a violation of section 5, in order to rescind the transaction and get their money back. If the availability of the exemption depends on the plaintiff purchaser's domicile (and thus on the plaintiffs' intentions at the time of the purchase), the plaintiffs have an incentive to claim that they lacked the intention to be domiciliaries of the state, regardless of what their actual intentions were. Such testimony can be very difficult to rebut. Rule 147's test of principal residence of the purchaser avoids this problem by looking to residence, rather than domicile.

g. **Exemptions for reorganizations and recapitalizations:** [§472] If XYZ Corp. is incorporated in California and later forms a new corporation (ABC) in Delaware and transfers all of its assets and liabilities to ABC, there has been a *reorganization* of the enterprise. Or if XYZ exchanges a new issue of debt securities for its outstanding preferred stock, there has been a *recapitalization* (*i.e.,* a reordering of the capital structure of the corporation). This section explores the instances in which such reorganizations and recapitalizations are exempt from the section 5 registration requirements for new issues of securities.

(1) **Exemptions where no "offer or sale for value":** [§473] Several of the exemptions for reorganizations and recapitalizations are based on the fact that the registration requirements of section 5 apply only where a security is offered or sold. Thus, unless there is an "offer" (which includes "every attempt to dispose of a security for value") or a "sale" (including "every contract of sale or disposition of a security or interest in a security, for value"), the section 5 requirements do not apply to the transaction. [SA §2(3)]

(a) **"Rights" given to existing shareholders:** [§474] Where a corporation transfers "rights" to its shareholders to purchase additional stock (*e.g.,* a stock "warrant" such as a right to purchase one new share of common stock for each share already owned), these rights—even if issued without consideration—are still "securities." However, since there is *no sale for value*, registration of the rights is not required.

1) **Compare—exercise of rights:** [§475] But note that the underlying security, which is purchased upon exercise of the rights (*e.g.,* the common stock, above), *is* being offered for value, and if the right is immediately exercisable, then the underlying security must be immediately registered under the Act.

(b) **Stock dividends and stock splits:** [§476] Where a corporation issues a stock dividend (*e.g.,* one new share of common stock for each 10 shares of common stock already outstanding) or has a stock split (*e.g.,* splits each $10 par value common share into 10 $1 par value shares), there is no transfer for value, and the shares given in the dividend or stock split need not be registered.

1) **Option—stock or cash dividend:** [§477] Even where the corporation gives the shareholder a choice between the stock dividend and its cash equivalent, there is no "sale for value" if the shareholder takes the stock.

2) **Cash dividend:** [§478] But if the corporation declares a cash dividend and the shareholder is permitted to waive receipt of the cash, taking stock instead, there is a "sale for value." The shareholder received cash and then purchased the securities. [SA Release No. 929 (1936)]

(c) **Compare—"spin-off" transactions:** [§479] Issuers sometimes use spin-off transactions in attempts to exploit the theory of "no sale for value" to achieve a public distribution without registration.

1) **Conventional (legitimate) spin-offs:** [§480] In a conventional spin-off transaction, a parent corporation distributes the stock of a subsidiary to the parent's shareholders. Typically, no consideration is sought or received by the parent for the distributed stock. The parent's motivations for such a transaction may include antitrust concerns, "downsizing" issues, and the like.

2) **"Shell game" spin-offs:** [§481] Because a spin-off does not usually involve a sale for value, enterprising promoters in the

1960s conceived a technique for using a spin-off transaction to take a company public surreptitiously. One common variation involved a privately held company issuing a sizable amount of its (unregistered) stock to a publicly held "shell" corporation (*i.e.*, a corporation without assets).

a) **No registration:** The public shell would then distribute the unregistered stock of the privately held company to the shareholders of the public corporation. Registration was avoided on the theory that the stock in the spun-off private company was not being sold "for value."

b) **Effect:** With the stock of the private company now in the hands of a large number of the public company's shareholders (thereby permitting public trading and a public market), the promoters would begin to promote an active trading market in the private company stock so that they could sell their own shares to the public at a sizeable profit.

3) **S.E.C. reaction**

a) **Early position:** [§482] Recognizing that the shell game transaction amounted to a public distribution of the private company's securities without registration, the S.E.C. first warned that the public company helping to effect such a distribution could be considered an "underwriter" under the Act [SA Release Nos. 4982, 8638 (1969)], and this theory was upheld by the courts [S.E.C. v. Harwyn Industries Corp., 326 F. Supp. 943 (S.D.N.Y. 1971)—public company using such scheme several times held liable as an underwriter].

b) **Limitations on trading:** [§483] In 1971, the S.E.C. adopted a rule requiring that any broker-dealer quoting a security in a dealer stock quotation system (*e.g.,* NASDAQ; *see supra*, §6) have available certain comprehensive information about the issuer in order to trade in the issuer's securities. (A very few companies are exempted from this rule.) [SEA Rule 15c2-11]

1/ The rule works to thwart the active trading of securities normally associated with spin-off transactions, since it is difficult to create an active market in a stock that is not listed on a dealer quotation system where it can be traded by many securities firms.

4) **Judicial reaction:** [§484] The courts support the S.E.C. position by interpreting the statutory requirements of the 1933 Act in a way that prevents "spin-off" transactions (at least those which have no apparent business purpose other than to effect the distribution of securities of private companies to the public without registration).

a)   **Example:** D, a public company, bound itself contractually to a group of promoters to distribute the stock of several private companies to its shareholders as dividends. D retained a portion of the stock in each transaction for itself, making a profit when the stock subsequently went up as part of the promotional scheme. [S.E.C. v. Datronics Engineers, Inc., 490 F.2d 250 (4th Cir. 1973), *cert. denied*, 416 U.S. 937 (1974)]

1/   The court held that there were several violations of the 1933 Act in that:

a/   D could be considered to be the "issuer" of the securities. (The court distinguished the transaction here from that of an ordinary dividend, since D had a *contractual obligation* to make the dividend distribution.)

b/   There was a "sale" of the private companies' securities "for value" since D kept part of the stock that was distributed to its shareholders and, when subsequent trading began, D profited.

c/   And D could also be held liable as an underwriter since it took the stock of the private companies with the *intent* of distributing it to the public.

2/   The court was careful to distinguish transactions by companies having legitimate business purposes, even though the effect of such transactions could be substantially similar to the results in this case (*i.e.,* the distribution of the securities of a privately held company to the public without registration).

5)   **Present status of spin-offs:** [§485] The "shell game" phenomenon places issuers wishing to do legitimate spin-offs in an awkward position, because the S.E.C., reacting to the shell game problem, has taken the position that a spin-off involves a "sale." Typically, an issuer wishing to do a spin-off must provide public information about the company to be spun off (often by undertaking to register the spun-off company under the 1934 Act promptly after the spin-off is completed). If the issuer agrees to do this, the S.E.C. staff may provide a no-action letter for the transaction.

(2)   **Exemption for exchanges between issuer and existing shareholders:** [§486] Any security that the issuer exchanges voluntarily and exclusively for its outstanding securities—with no commission or other remuneration for soliciting the exchange—is exempt from registration under section 5. [SA §3(a)(9)]

(a) **Example:** XYZ Corp. exchanges a new issue of debt securities with a longer maturity date, but a lower interest rate, for an outstanding issue of shorter duration with a higher interest rate. XYZ pays no commission or other fee for initiating the exchange of securities. This exchange may be exempt from registration.

(b) **Exemption for initial transaction only:** [§487] Note that this is a transaction exemption; hence, later resales of the securities offered pursuant to this section (*e.g.,* sales by control persons) may ***not*** be exempt. [SA Release No. 646 (1936)]

(c) **Limitations on the exemption**

 1) **Must be in good faith:** [§488] To qualify for this exemption, an exchange offer must be made in good faith. An offer that is merely an attempt to evade the registration requirements of the 1933 Act will not be exempt under section 3(a)(9), even if it literally appears to comply with the requirements of the section. [SA Release No. 646 (1936)]

 a) **Factors considered:** In deciding whether an offer is merely an attempt to evade the registration requirements, the following factors are relevant: length of time the outstanding securities were outstanding; the number of holders of the outstanding securities; and whether the exchange is dictated by financial considerations of the issuer, as opposed to merely enabling one or a few security holders to distribute their shares to the public. [SA Release No. 646 (1936)]

 2) **Must be offered only to issuer's security holders:** [§489] The exchange may occur only between the issuer and its existing security holders. For example, the exemption would be destroyed if the issuer sold part of an issue to its security holders and the remainder to the public. [SA Release No. 2029 (1939)]

 a) **And note:** The issuer must guard against integration (*supra*, §312), so that securities issued at different times are not integrated into one issue and the section 3(a)(9) "exchange" exemption lost in the process.

 3) **No commission allowed:** [§490] As noted, no commission or other remuneration may be paid by the issuer for soliciting the exchange of the issuer's securities with its shareholders.

 4) **"Clean exchange" required:** [§491] As a rule, a transaction is exempt under section 3(a)(9) only if it involves a "clean exchange" of the issuer's old securities for its new securities, with no additional payments changing hands between the issuer and security holders.

 a) **Exception—certain payments from securities holders permitted:** [§492] Payments from securities holders to the issuer necessary to ensure that all holders of a class of securities receive the same treatment in an exchange transaction will not destroy the exemption. [SA Rule 149]

1/ **Example:** An issuer wishes to exchange an outstanding issue of debentures for new debentures. A dividend is payable on the old debentures to holders of record on June 30. As a condition of the offer, persons surrendering the old debentures are required to waive receipt of the dividend. A purchaser who purchases an old debenture after June 30, however, has no legal right to receive (or to waive) the dividend; moreover, the price this purchaser paid for the debenture will have been adjusted downward for the fact that it is "ex-dividend." Under these circumstances, it is fair to require the purchaser to pay the amount of the dividend to the issuer in order to participate in the exchange offer; otherwise, the purchaser gets to buy the debenture at a reduced price (ex-dividend) but gets the same consideration in the exchange as those who paid full price.

b) **Exception—certain payments from issuer permitted:** [§493] If the plan of exchange calls for cash payments to be made by the issuer to security holders (*e.g.,* because the securities surrendered are more valuable than the new securities distributed by the issuer), the exemption will still be available. [SA Rule 150]

(d) **Rationale for limitations:** [§494] The rationale for each of the foregoing restrictions is that the exemption is designed to apply only where the issuer is simply exchanging securities *as part of a corporate recapitalization*, and not where it is raising new capital (which requires that purchasers be protected by a registration statement and prospectus).

(3) **Exemption for approved reorganizations:** [§495] The 1933 Act also exempts those business reorganizations in which a new security is issued in exchange for outstanding securities, claims, or property interests (or partly in exchange for cash), and where the terms and conditions of the exchange are approved by a court or government agency. [SA §3(a)(10)]

(a) **Authorized agencies:** [§496] Agencies authorized to approve reorganizations (*i.e.,* after a hearing on the fairness of the transaction) include: (i) any court with jurisdiction over the parties and the transaction, (ii) any official or agency of the United States, and (iii) any state banking or insurance commission (or other state governmental authority) expressly authorized by state law to grant such approval. [SA §3(a)(10)]

1) **Example:** Huge Corp., incorporated under New York law, wishes to settle a class-action suit based on allegedly defective

products sold by Huge. Huge's settlement proposal involves the issue of its common stock to the class members in exchange for the release of their claims. This settlement may be approved by a court of general jurisdiction in New York State, and if the proper notice to class members was given, and an appropriate hearing on the fairness of the offer was held, the offering of securities will be exempt under section 3(a)(10).

(b) **State transactions:** [§497] For this exemption to apply to state-agency-authorized transactions, the governmental authority in question must be specifically authorized under state law to approve the transactions and the fairness of their terms. [*See* SA Release No. 312 (1935)]

1) **Example:** XYZ Insurance Co. wishes to form a financial services holding company. It organizes a new corporation (ABC) and, after a hearing conducted by the state insurance department on the terms and conditions of the proposed transaction, exchanges stock in the holding company for stock of the insurance company. As long as the state insurance department is specifically authorized by state law to approve such transactions, the transaction is exempted from registration by section 3(a)(10).

(c) **Comparison with section 3(a)(9) "exchange" exemption:** [§498] If Company A were to make an exchange offer for Company B stock, section 3(a)(9)—which applies only to exchanges by an issuer with its *own* security holders (*supra,* §486)—would not apply. However, the section 3(a)(10) government "approval" exemption would still be available.

1) **Note:** Similarly, the section 3(a)(9) exemption is generally lost where the issuer solicits cash from the security holders, but cash may be taken in a section 3(a)(10) transaction.

2) **And note:** While furnishing remuneration or commissions to brokers who participate in soliciting an exchange will destroy the exemption under section 3(a)(9), such payments may be made under the "approval" exemption of section 3(a)(10).

(4) **Exemption for selling or merging businesses—rule 145:** [§499] Technically, rule 145 provides not an exemption, but rather a clarification that certain corporate transactions (including mergers, consolidations, reclassifications, and asset acquisitions) involve "offers" and "sales" of securities, and therefore must be registered if no exemption is available.

(a) **Development of rule 145:** [§500] Former S.E.C. rule 133, a precursor to rule 145, provided that a "sale" of securities had to involve a volitional act on the part of the seller before registration was required. Therefore, in certain types of corporate reorganizations where this required volition was lacking, no registration was required.

1) **Sale of assets:** [§501] For example, suppose that A Corp. offered its common stock to B Corp. to buy B's assets. Although

the shareholders of B had to vote as a body (state law generally requiring a majority of the shareholders to approve a sale-of-assets transaction), and although there was a transfer for value (*i.e.,* shares of A for the assets of B), no registration was required under rule 133.

a) **Rationale:** Since no *single* shareholder could determine whether to make the investment in the offered securities, there was no "sale" involving a volitional act by the individual shareholder-seller.

2) **Stock-for-stock transactions:** [§502]  On the other hand, if A Corp. offered its common stock *directly* to the shareholders of B in exchange for their common stock, each shareholder of B *would* have to make up his own mind whether to sell. Accordingly, a "sale" would be involved and a registration of A's securities required—unless some other exemption were available.

(b) **Replacement of rule 133 by rule 145:** [§503]  Rule 133 was excessively formalistic—it focused on the final step in a corporate transaction and ignored the fact that each shareholder, when faced with a proposal for a transaction (such as a sale of assets), had to make an individual (and "volitional") decision as to whether the transaction was in her best interests. For this reason, the S.E.C., in a 180 degree reversal, *repealed* rule 133 and replaced it with rule 145.

1) **Provisions of rule 145:** [§504]  Rule 145 provides that securities issued in certain corporate reorganizations, previously exempted from section 5 by rule 133, must be registered, and that transfer limitations must be placed on the stock received by certain shareholders of the acquired company (*e.g.,* control persons). [*See* SA Release No. 5316 (1972); SEA Release No. 9804 (1972)]

(c) **Transactions covered by rule 145**

1) **In general:** [§505]  Rule 145 makes clear that proposals for certain business reorganization transactions that require the approval of shareholders of the selling company are "offers" under the 1933 Act, and that consummation of such transactions is a "sale" under that Act.

2) **Specific transactions covered**

a) **Reclassifications:** [§506]  Any reclassification of securities that involves the substitution or exchange of one security for another (other than simple stock splits) is subject to rule 145. [SA Rule 145(a)(1)]

1/ Thus, if XYZ Corp. issues a new debt security for an outstanding debt issue, this exchange is covered by rule 145 unless otherwise exempt.

b) **Mergers or consolidations:** [§507] Rule 145 also applies to a statutory merger, consolidation, or similar acquisition of one corporation (A) by another (B), in which shares held by A's security holders will become (or be exchanged for) securities of B.

    1/ The only exception to this aspect of the rule applies when the transaction is solely for the purpose of changing the issuer's domicile (*e.g.,* where A Corp. is incorporated in California and forms a new B Corp. in Delaware in order to merge into B and become a Delaware corporation). [SA Rule 145(a)(2)]

c) **Transfers of assets:** [§508] A transfer of assets by one person or corporation (A) to another (B) in exchange for securities issued by B is likewise subject to rule 145, *but only if:*

    (i) The plan or agreement of transfer provides for dissolution of the corporation whose security holders are voting (*i.e.,* A's security holders); *or*

    (ii) The plan or agreement of transfer provides for a pro rata distribution of the exchanged securities (of B) to the security holders that are voting (*i.e.,* A's shareholders); *or*

    (iii) The board of directors of A adopts resolutions with respect to the provisions in paragraphs (i) or (ii) above within one year after consent to the transaction has been given; *or*

    (iv) Notwithstanding paragraphs (i), (ii), or (iii), above, a subsequent dissolution or distribution is part of a preexisting plan for distribution of the securities in B.

*Note:* In each of the above four situations, registration under rule 145 is required because the securities of the purchasing entity (B) are being distributed from B to A and then to the public (*i.e.,* A's shareholders) within a short time after the purchase-of-assets transaction occurs. In effect, the transaction is a liquidating distribution to A's shareholders when A winds up its affairs and dissolves. [SA Release No. 5316 (1972)]

d) **Compare—stock-for-stock exchanges:** [§509] Rule 145 does not apply to stock-for-stock exchanges—*e.g.,* where X Co. seeks to acquire 80% of the outstanding common stock in Y Co. by offering its stock to Y shareholders in a stock-for-stock transaction. [SA Release No. 5463 (1974); SEA Release No. 10661 (1974)]

1/ **Rationale:** Recall that rule 145 mandates registration for transactions that previously (under former rule 133, discussed above) did not require registration. (*See supra*, §504.) Stock-for-stock exchanges, however, obviously involve a sale requiring registration, and they were treated as such even under rule 133. Rule 145 therefore does not address such exchanges.

3) **Note—relationship of rule 145 to exemptions:** [§510]  It is important to keep in mind that rule 145 is merely a provision clarifying that *certain transactions*, which were formerly exempted from SA section 5 by rule 133, *are no longer per se exempt*. If, however, such a transaction—*e.g.,* a merger—fits into the requirements of some *presently existing exemption*, then the transaction will be exempt. Nothing in rule 145 makes unavailable any current statutory- or rule-based exemption. Thus, a merger of A into B might be covered by rule 145, but exempt from section 5 under section 3(a)(10) (*i.e.,* as approved by a government agency).

(d) **Registration under rule 145:** [§511]  The S.E.C. has provided a form for registration of securities issued in business combination transactions (including transactions covered by rule 145).

1) **Form of registration:** [§512]  Form S-4 is the proper registration form to be used in rule 145 transactions. It requires detailed information about the proposed transaction. The form also requires information about the acquiring company and the acquired (or selling) company; the level of detail about the companies varies depending on whether each company would be permitted to register its securities on form S-3, S-2, or S-1. (*See supra*, §§217-223, for a discussion of these forms.)

a) **Proxy information:** [§513]  In addition, recognizing that many transactions registered on form S-4 are also subject to federal proxy regulation (because votes of shareholders are being solicited; *see infra*, §1131), form S-4 contemplates the inclusion of proxy disclosure, and when such information is included, it is deemed "filed" under the proxy rules. [SEA Rules 14a-6, 14c-5]

1/ **Note:** Since corporate acquisitions by companies whose securities are publicly traded generally require the filing of such proxy statements, those companies need not incur any additional work or expense because of rule 145. Generally, stockholders of the acquired corporation receive a combined proxy statement/prospectus on Form S-4, saving the time and expense of preparing separate disclosure documents.

2) **Delivery of prospectus:** [§514]  A prospectus must be given to all those who are security holders of record in the acquired (or

selling) company in a rule 145 transaction and who are entitled to vote on the proposed transaction. Delivery of the prospectus must be made prior to the time when a vote on the transaction is taken. [SA Rule 153A]

3) **Communications not subject to prospectus requirement:** [§515] Certain written communications made to shareholders of the selling company are *not* deemed to be a prospectus (under section 2(10) of the 1933 Act) or an "offer to sell" (under section 5), so that they may be distributed to shareholders without causing a "gun-jumping" violation of SA section 5. Such communications need not include all of the information that must be included in the section 10(a) final, or section 10(b) preliminary prospectus.

a) **Rationale—preventing delay:** [§516] From a business standpoint, this facilitates putting rule 145 transactions together without having to wait until the full registration process is completed.

b) **Preliminary proxy statement:** [§517] For example, a communication that meets the information standards of a "preliminary proxy statement" (discussed *infra,* §1155) may be sent to the shareholders after it is filed with the S.E.C. [SA Rule 145(b)(2)]

c) **"Bare bones" statement:** [§518] Or shareholders may be given a so-called "bare bones" statement containing only certain specific information: name of issuer, name of other parties to the transaction, brief description of the businesses of the parties, date, time, and place of meeting where a vote will be taken, description of the transaction involved, etc. [SA Rule 145(b)(1)]

(e) **"Underwriters" in rule 145 transactions:** [§519] Certain parties to the transactions covered by rule 145 are deemed to be "underwriters" and as such are restricted in subsequent transfers of the securities they receive in a rule 145 transaction. The idea is to prevent a control person (A) of a company (X), who could not otherwise distribute his X stock to the public without a registration, from merging X into Company Y under rule 145 in order to sell his newly acquired Y stock to the public without registration.

1) **"Underwriters" defined:** [§520] Any party (or affiliate of a party) to a rule 145 transaction, *except* the issuer, is considered to be an underwriter if he publicly sells or offers to sell the securities acquired in connection with the rule 145 transaction. [SA Rule 145(c)]

a) **Definition of "party":** [§521] "Parties" include any corporations or persons (other than the issuer of the securities) whose assets or capital structure are affected by the transaction. "Affiliate of a party" means a person who controls, is controlled by, or is under common control with a party.

> 1/ **Example:** If A Corp. sells its assets to B Corp. in return for common stock in B, A would be a party to the transaction, since its capital structure and assets are affected.

2) **Effect on control persons of acquired company:** [§522] The effect of these "underwriter" provisions is to limit the subsequent transfer of securities received by control persons of acquired companies ("affiliates of a party") in rule 145 transactions.

3) **Limited resales permitted:** [§523] "Underwriters" *may* make limited sales of their securities without further registration pursuant to the following rules:

a) **Sales pursuant to rule 144:** [§524] Resales by control persons may be made without further registration if the provisions of rule 144 relating to distribution of current public information, limitation on amount of securities sold, and manner of sale (*e.g.,* through a broker's transaction) are followed. (*See* discussion of rule 144, *infra*, §552.)

> 1/ **Note:** The two-year holding period of rule 144 does *not* apply to underwriter sales under rule 145.

b) **Registration alternative:** [§525] Alternatively, underwriters in rule 145 transactions may subsequently distribute their securities if the distribution by the underwriters is registered. The most convenient means of registering such a distribution is on the same form S-4 used to register the rule 145 transaction initially.

4) **Special exemption from underwriter status:** [§526] To further promote the free alienability of securities in circumstances that do not seem to require the application of the 1933 Act, rule 145 provides that persons who might otherwise have been considered "underwriters" (*see* above) will not be so considered if the following conditions are met. [SA Rule 145(d)(2)]:

a) *The person has held the securities* of the acquiring company (*i.e.,* B in the hypothetical at §521, *supra*) *for at least two years* after the business combination transaction; and

> 1/ *The person is not affiliated* (*i.e.,* a control person) *with the issuer* (*i.e.,* B) of the securities;

> 2/ *The issuer (B) is subject to the periodic reporting requirements* of sections 13 or 15(d) of the 1934 Act and has been so subject for at least 90 days; and

3/ ***The issuer (B) has filed all of the reports required*** under these sections during the past year (or such shorter period as the issuer was required to file the reports).

b) ***Alternatively,*** a person who is ***not an affiliate*** of the issuer (and has not been an affiliate for at least three months) and who has held securities acquired in a transaction subject to rule 145 for at least ***three years*** is not deemed an underwriter with respect to the sale of the securities, even if the issuer does not meet the information requirements. [SA Rule 145(d)(3)]

5) **Application of "underwriter" rules:** [§527] Suppose X Co. wants to acquire substantially all of the assets of Y Co. in exchange for X stock. If A, a control person of Y, will be a control person of X after the transaction, A cannot use rule 145 to resell her stock publicly. As a control person of X, A is governed by the resale terms of rule 144 (***including*** the two-year holding period). [*See* SEA Release No. 10661 (1974); *and see supra,* §524; *but see* SA Rule 145(d)(1)]

a) ***Assume instead*** that A is a control person of Y who will ***not*** be a control person of X after the transaction. Here, A ***can*** use rule 145 to resell her X stock publicly after the transaction—as long as she complies with the limited-sales provisions of rule 145(d) (*supra,* §§524-526).

b) ***Assume*** that B, who is not a control person of Y, has received Y stock in a private offering. B will be allowed to resell publicly the X stock he receives after a rule 145 transaction. [SEA Release No. 10661 (1974)]

h. **Bankruptcy exemptions:** [§528] Transaction exemptions can arise during bankruptcy proceedings. The main provision of the federal bankruptcy law involving exemptions to the registration requirements is chapter 11, which provides for the reorganization of bankrupt companies.

(1) **Appointment of examiners:** [§529] The basis for an acceptable reorganization plan (*i.e.,* where existing debtors may be asked to exchange their debts for new debt or equity securities, etc.) is left to be determined by the bankruptcy court on a case-by-case basis. However, where the debts exceed assets by $5 million or more, the court is required to appoint an examiner to investigate the debtor for fraud of insiders, etc. This provision is meant to protect public shareholders of large public companies. In addition, the S.E.C., or any other party having an interest in the outcome of the reorganization plan, may attend and be heard at all public hearings involving the plan.

(2) **Disclosure requirements:** [§530] Restructuring of the debtor's capital and debt structure usually involves an exchange of new debt and/or equity securities for the outstanding securities. The Bankruptcy Code provides for disclosure obligations in issuing these securities, which is done under the

supervision of the bankruptcy court. Thus, when the Bankruptcy Code applies, the issuer is exempt from the other federal and state securities laws. [*See* Bankruptcy Code §§1125, 1145]

(a) **Information required:** [§531] The Bankruptcy Code provides that the issuer must provide information that is adequate in light of the nature and history of the debtor and the condition of its accounting records so that the typical holder of claims or interests of the relevant class can make an informed judgment about the proposed exchange.

(b) **Timing:** [§532] This information must be given to creditors at or prior to the solicitation of acceptance of the reorganization plan.

(c) **S.E.C. or state disclosure requirements:** [§533] The S.E.C. and/or state securities commissioners may appear and contest whether the disclosure statement proposed by the bankruptcy court is adequate.

(3) **Debt securities:** [§534] The Bankruptcy Code does not allow the sale by the debtor of equity securities to raise new capital (equity securities may be issued only in exchange for old debts). It does, however, permit the trustee to issue debt securities to raise additional funds to operate the business. [*See* Bankruptcy Code §364] This is a transaction exemption. In addition, section 3(a)(7) of the 1933 Act appears to provide an exemption for debt securities issued under court approval in order to finance receivership, bankruptcy, or reorganization proceedings.

(4) **Resales, sales by control persons, and other provisions:** [§535] The Bankruptcy Code also sets forth standards under which a creditor or control person acquiring securities under the reorganization plan can resell the securities. [*See* Bankruptcy Code §1145(b)] A limited exemption for brokers selling such securities is also provided. [*See* Bankruptcy Code §1145(a)]

(5) **Inapplicability of section 3(a)(9) and (10) to bankruptcy proceedings:** [§536] The section 3(a)(9) (exchanges between the issuer and its existing shareholders) and 3(a)(10) (exemption for approved reorganizations) exemptions do not apply in corporate reorganizations undertaken under the Bankruptcy Code.

i. **Restrictions on resale of securities issued in transaction exemptions:** [§537] If an issuer (*e.g.*, XYZ Corp.) initially issues common stock to six sophisticated investors (a private offering under section 4(2)), but the six original investors immediately sell their stock to 90 new investors, should the "private offering" exemption apply, or has the XYZ offering now become a "public distribution" and so subject to registration?

(1) **Buyer's intent crucial:** [§538] In a normal securities distribution, dealers often sell to initial investors who intend to hold only for a short time and then take a profit by early sale once the newly issued securities move up in price (which often occurs in the first hours or days of a new offering). Since a "distribution" is complete only when the securities finally come to rest in the hands of those investors who intend to hold them for a *substantial* period of time (*see supra*, §73), the intent of the *original*

*purchasers* in buying the securities is very important in determining whether the private offering exemption should apply.

(a) **Purchasers as underwriters—registration required:** [§539] If the original purchasers from an issuer buy the securities with a *view toward distribution* (*i.e.,* resale to the public), they are "underwriters" (*see supra*, §93). And if a public distribution actually *does* take place without registration, there is a violation of the registration requirements of section 5 of the Act.

1) **Distributions by control persons:** [§540] For the purpose of determining those persons who are "underwriters" under the 1933 Act, control persons are considered "issuers" (*see supra*, §106). Thus, persons who purchase securities from a control person with the intent of making a public distribution thereof are "underwriters" if they in fact resell to numerous unsophisticated purchasers. If this occurs, the control person has conducted a transaction with an "underwriter," and therefore has lost the exemption in section 4(1). If no other exemption is available, the control person has violated section 5.

a) **Example:** W and his associate sold 25% of the issuer's shares through brokers without registration. Although not active in management, the two held 40% of the total stock and controlled the company "behind the scenes." They were therefore held to be control persons, and the brokers were "underwriters." As a result, the stock was sold in "transactions by underwriters," which are not within the exemption of section 4(1). Notice that the *seller need not be an underwriter* to lose the section 4(1) exemption; it is lost even if the seller sells to an underwriter. [United States v. Wolfson, 405 F.2d 779 (2d Cir. 1968), *cert. denied*, 394 U.S. 946 (1969)]

(b) **Purchasers with investment intent—private offering:** [§541] If, as opposed to buying for resale, the original purchasers take for "investment," *i.e.,* to keep or hold the securities for a significant period of time, and they otherwise satisfy the criteria for a private offering (*e.g.,* limited in number, sophisticated, etc.), no registration is required.

(2) **Traditional factors showing investment intent:** [§542] Whether the original purchaser bought for investment or for distribution is a *question of fact; i.e.,* what was the purchaser's intent at the time of purchase? In determining intent, the following factors have traditionally been held relevant by the courts:

(a) **Investment letters:** [§543] It is a common practice to require that the original purchasers give the issuer a letter indicating that they are buying for investment purposes rather than for resale. However, the purchaser's own statements on the matter are not conclusive; in particular, an investment letter will be given no weight if in fact the purchaser turns around and sells the securities shortly after purchasing them.

(b) **Length of holding period:** [§544] The longer the securities are held by the original purchasers before resale, the more likely it is that the original purchase was for investment and that the private offering exemption still applies. (At one time, the S.E.C. gave opinion letters on the subject—*i.e.,* that a one-year holding period was sufficient to show investment intent—but it no longer does so.) [SA Release No. 3825 (1957)]

1) **Note:** Here again, however, the length of time is not conclusive evidence of investment intent; the other factors must also be considered.

2) **Example:** Investment intent has been found where stock was purchased from a control person and then resold after a period of two years. [United States v. Sherwood, 175 F. Supp. 480 (S.D.N.Y. 1959)]

(c) **Restrictive legends on stock certificates:** [§545] To show that the issuer has made a reasonable investigation, and also to establish reasonable precautions by making unlawful secondary transfers more difficult, the issuer claiming a private offering exemption often places a legend on its stock certificates to the effect that the certificates cannot be transferred without the issuer's permission. Permission to transfer is then normally conditioned on the opinion of the issuer's counsel that a transfer will not violate the securities laws. [SEA Release No. 5121 (1970)]

(3) **"Change in circumstances" doctrine:** [§546] A change in circumstances was sometimes asserted by purchasers seeking to avoid underwriter status under the 1933 Act. They purchased with an intent to invest, the argument went, but a later change in circumstances necessitated sale of the securities. This argument was seldom successful.

(a) **Example:** G purchased convertible debentures directly from the issuer, in a private placement. Ten months later, G converted the debentures into stock and sold the stock on the stock exchange. The S.E.C. brought an enforcement proceeding, claiming a violation of SA section 5 because G was an underwriter who had publicly distributed stock in violation of SA section 5. G argued that the issuer was losing money, and that this constituted a changed circumstance justifying his sale. The court held that G failed to establish investment intent, and G therefore was an underwriter. [Gilligan, Will & Co. v. S.E.C., 267 F.2d 461 (2d Cir. 1959)]

(4) **Fungibility:** [§547] Another issue complicating the analysis of resales involves the fungibility of securities. If an investor bought 100 shares of ABC common stock in a private placement, and subsequently bought 100 more shares on the stock exchange, can she sell any of the 200 shares? Before the S.E.C.'s adoption of rule 144 (*see infra*), it was unclear whether any of the shares could be sold.

(5) **Importance to the investor:** [§548] Restriction of resales is an important issue because the ease or difficulty of resale is often crucial to an investor

and will affect the price an investor will be willing to pay. For example, if an investor perceives that he will be unable to sell when the price of the security is dropping or when he has an unforeseen need for cash, the investor will demand a substantial discount from the price of the security that he would otherwise pay.

(6) **Proof of "investment intent"—rule 144:** [§549]  Because of frequent confusion and ambiguity in determining whether an investor had "investment intent" (and therefore was not an underwriter), the S.E.C. adopted rule 144 specifying an objective set of criteria that will establish investment intent. If these criteria are satisfied, purchasers in a private offering of securities may *resell* the securities (referred to in rule 144 as "*restricted securities*") without violating the Act.

   (a) **Example:** A buys 100 shares from XYZ in a private offering by XYZ to sophisticated investors. After holding the shares for two years, A desires to sell but does not wish to violate any securities laws in doing so. If she complies with rule 144, A can rest assured that her sales are not unlawful (*i.e.,* she will not be deemed to be an underwriter, and her sales to the public will not turn the private offering into an unregistered public offering).

   (b) **Preference for rule 144 standard:** [§550]  While a seller of privately purchased securities can still rely on the traditional pre-rule 144 criteria (above) to establish investment intent, the seller bears a heavy burden of proof where the facts deviate from what is required by rule 144.

      1) **Note:** This suggests that lawyers should be very careful in advising clients that investment intent has been established where the requirements of rule 144 are not satisfied. [SA Release No. 5223 (1972)]

   (c) **Scope of rule 144**

      1) **"Restricted securities":** [§551]  Rule 144 applies to the sale of "restricted securities," which term is defined in rule 144 to encompass three types of securities:

         a) *Privately offered securities* acquired directly or indirectly from the issuer or a control person (discussed *supra*, §§341 *et seq.*);

         b) *Securities issued pursuant to rules 505 or 506, or* pursuant to *section 4(6)* of the Act (discussed *supra,* §§363 *et seq.*); and

         c) *Securities sold under Rule 144A* (discussed *infra*, §§589 *et seq.*).

      2) **Sales of securities by control persons:** [§552]  Rule 144 also applies to the sale of securities owned by control persons; *i.e.,* it states when (and how much stock) a control person may sell

without becoming an "issuer," and without making those that subsequently resell the stock "underwriters" (*see supra*, §106).

a) **Rule applicable to both restricted and nonrestricted securities:** [§553]  Where the securities of control persons are involved, rule 144 applies to sales of *both* restricted securities (*i.e.,* those purchased by the control person in a private offering) and nonrestricted securities acquired by the control person as part of a registered public offering of the issuer's securities.

b) **Example:** When XYZ Corp. was formed, A received 25% of the stock (restricted stock), and now serves on the board of directors; hence, A is a control person of XYZ. Over the next several years, A acquired additional stock in stock exchange purchases (nonrestricted stock). A now wishes to sell. If she does *not* comply with rule 144, she runs the risk of violating SA section 5 by selling either the restricted or unrestricted stock. Conversely, if she complies with rule 144, she will not violate section 5.

(d) **Requirements of rule 144:** [§554]  The following criteria must be met to qualify a sale under rule 144:

1) **Adequate public information about the issuer:** [§555]  Adequate information about the issuer (*i.e.,* information analogous to that contained in a registration statement) must be available to the public at the time of sale. [SA Rule 144(c)]

a) **1934 Act reporting companies:** [§556]  The information requirement is satisfied by all companies that are required to report—and have actually reported for at least 90 days before the rule 144 sale—under sections 13 or 15(d) of the 1934 Act. (*See infra*, §749.)

b) **Other companies:** [§557]  Issuers not required to report under the 1934 Act may choose to report voluntarily, in order to make rule 144 available to their security holders. Alternatively, they may make publicly available the information required under the 1934 Act to permit brokers to quote an over-the-counter security. [SA Rule 144(c)(2); *see* SEA Rule 15c2-11]

1/ **Meaning of "publicly available":** [§558]  The S.E.C. has stated that supplying the required information to the broker handling the sale for the seller is *not* sufficient to make information about the restricted securities publicly available. But supplying such information to the issuer's shareholders, brokers, marketmakers, and any other interested persons, plus the publication of financial information about the issuer in a recognized financial reporting service, are sufficient. [SA Release No. 6099 (1979)]

c) **Sales by noncontrol persons of restricted securities:** [§559] The public information requirements do not apply to sales of restricted securities by noncontrol persons (who have been such for at least three months) *if* at least three years have elapsed since the securities were acquired from the issuer or from a control person. [SA Rule 144(k)]

1/ **Note:** The three-year holding period for this purpose is calculated in the same way as, and is subject to the same tolling provisions applicable to, the general two-year holding period for restricted securities (*see* below).

2) **Two-year holding period for restricted securities:** [§560] Second, rule 144 provides that *restricted securities* cannot be resold until a period of two years has elapsed from the date of their acquisition from the issuer (or an affiliate of the issuer). The holding period is "tolled" (*i.e.,* it does not begin to run) until the initial buyer has fully paid for the securities. [SA Rule 144(d)(1)] (*Note:* The holding period/full payment rule *applies only to restricted securities;* thus, a control person (*i.e.,* an affiliate) selling nonrestricted securities need not comply with this provision.)

a) **Rationale:** This requirement ensures that the investor purchased the securities as an investment, rather than for public distribution.

b) **Determining full payment:** [§561] The original purchaser has fully paid for the securities if one of the following applies:

1/ *The purchaser has paid for them in cash.*

2/ *When a promissory note or installment contract was used*, the note or contract must have been a "full-recourse obligation"—*i.e.,* if the loan goes bad, the lender has recourse to *all* of the borrower's assets and not just to the stock that was purchased. Furthermore, the note or contract must be secured by collateral *other than* the securities themselves, having a fair market value at least equal to the amount of the note. The holding period is tolled for any period in which the market value of the collateral is inadequate. Finally, the promissory note must be paid in full before any securities can be sold, even if the holding period has run.

3/ *When the purchaser has borrowed* the money to pay the issuer from a third party (and the loan is not guaranteed by the issuer), the securities are deemed to be fully paid even if the purchaser only pledges the restricted stock as collateral for his full recourse loan from the third party.

    **4/**   ***When the securities issued are options***, they are not fully paid until the option is exercised and the option price is fully paid. Thus, if A had an option on 100 shares of XYZ common stock for one year, at the end of which time she exercised the option and paid the option price, the one-year option period could not be counted as part of the two-year holding period.

c) **Calculating the two-year holding period:** [§562] There are special rules for computing the two-year holding period in certain situations.

    **1/**   **Stock dividends or stock splits:** [§563] The holding period for securities acquired through stock dividends or splits relates back to the acquisition date of the original securities. Thus, where A buys 100 shares of XYZ common stock in 1994, and XYZ pays a dividend of one share for each 10 shares owned in 1995, the holding period for the 10 dividend shares would relate back to the 1995 date of purchase on the original securities. [SA Rule 144(d)(3)(i)]

    **2/**   **Pledged securities:** [§564] When securities are pledged (*i.e.,* put up as collateral), the pledgee can relate the start of its holding period back to the acquisition date of the pledgor *if* the pledge was made in connection with a full-recourse loan (*see supra*, §561).

        a/   **But note:** If the loan is not full recourse, the holding period begins to run on the date of the pledge. [SA Rule 144(d)(3)(iv)]

        b/   **Example:** A acquires stock in XYZ Corp. in 1993. In 1995, he pledges the stock to C under a full recourse loan agreement. If A then defaults and C takes the stock, C can use A's 1993 purchase date in calculating the two-year period for resale under rule 144.

    **3/**   **Gifts:** [§565] A donee's acquisition date relates back to the acquisition date of his donor. [SA Rule 144(d)(3)(v)]

    **4/**   **Trusts:** [§566] Similarly, the trustee or beneficiary of a trust may use the date on which the settlor of the trust acquired the securities in computing his holding period. [SA Rule 144(d)(3)(vi)]

    **5/**   **Estates:** [§567] And an estate wishing to sell securities pursuant to rule 144 may relate back its date of acquisition to the date the decedent acquired the securities. [SA Rule 144(d)(3)(vii)] a/ **Note:** *No holding period is required* if either (i) the *estate is not an affiliate* (control person) of the issuer or (ii) the securities are *sold by a beneficiary of the estate that is not an affiliate* of the issuer. [SA Rule 144(d)(3)(vii)]

3) **Limitation on amount of securities sold:** [§568] The volume of securities that may be resold under rule 144 is limited, so that during any three-month period only the following quantities may be sold:

a) **Sales by affiliates and sales of restricted securities:** [§569] Sales by control persons (or sales of restricted securities by non-control persons who cannot meet the qualifications to remove the volume limitations; *see infra,* §570) during the three-month period may not exceed the greater of:

(i) *One percent of the shares of the outstanding class of security;*

(ii) *If the security is traded on an exchange,* the average weekly reported volume of trading in such securities on all exchanges and/or reported through the automated quotations systems of a registered securities association for the four weeks prior to the filing of the notice of sale (*see infra,* §573); and

(iii) *The average weekly reported volume* of trading in such securities reported through the consolidated transaction reporting system that is contemplated by rule 11Aa3-1 of the 1934 Act during the four-week period preceding a filing of the notice of sale.

[SA Rule 144(e)]

b) **Exception for certain sales by noncontrol persons of restricted securities:** [§570] The volume limitations do not apply to sales of restricted securities by noncontrol persons (who have been such for at least three months) *if* at least ~~three~~ *Two* years have elapsed since the securities were acquired from the issuer or from a control person. [SA Rule 144(k)]

1/ **Note:** The holding period for these purposes is calculated in the same way, and is subject to the same tolling provisions, as apply to the ~~two~~ *one*-year holding period (*see supra,* §560).

c) **Securities otherwise acquired:** [§571] When restricted securities are pledged, given as a gift, placed in trust, or acquired in a decedent's estate, the respective sales by the pledgor, donor, settlor, or decedent (as the case may be) must be *combined* with the sales made by the pledgee, donee, trust, or estate within the relevant time period in calculating the total volume for the rule 144 limitation. Similar provisions apply in cases where convertible securities are sold together with securities of the class into which they are convertible, and where two or more persons act in concert in selling securities of the same issuer. [SA Rule 144(e)(3)]

4) **Limitation on manner of sale:** [§572] To preserve the "non-public" nature of rule 144 sales, the rule requires that sales thereunder be made in transactions directly with a "market maker" (as defined in section 3(a)(38) of the 1934 Act) or in "broker's transactions," within the meaning of section 4(4) of the 1933 Act (*see supra*, §§326 *et seq.*). [*See* SA Rule 144(f), (g)] Thus, the following limitations apply in a broker's transaction:

a) Except for sales by an estate or its beneficiary (if not a control person), *the person selling the securities may not:*

   (i) *Solicit orders* to buy the securities; or

   (ii) *Make any payment* in connection with the transaction to anyone other than the broker.

b) In addition, *the broker:*

   (i) May not do more than *execute the order* to sell and cannot receive more than the customary commission;

   (ii) May not *solicit the order* to buy, although he may contact other brokers who have expressed an interest within the previous 60 days, or customers expressing an interest within the previous 10 business days;

   (iii) May *publish bid and ask quotations* in an inter-dealer stock quotation system, as long as the broker has been "making a market" (*i.e.*, trading regularly) in the security to be sold; and

   (iv) Must *make a reasonable inquiry* to ensure that the person claiming the right to sell without registration is entitled to do so.

   Note that if seller is selling restricted securities and qualifies to avoid the volume limitations (*see supra*, §570), the manner of sale limitation does not apply.

5) **Notice of intent to sell:** [§573] The final requirement of rule 144 that a seller who intends to sell more than 500 shares, or any number of shares for an amount greater than $10,000, must file with the S.E.C. a notice of intention to sell the securities. [SA Rule 144(h)] This requirement does not apply where the seller of restricted securities qualifies to avoid the volume limitations. (*See supra*, §570.) The person filing this notice must have a

bona fide intention to sell the securities within a reasonable time. [SA Rule 144(i)]

6) **Nonexclusive rule:** [§574] Rule 144 is not exclusive. A nonaffiliate may effect sales of restricted stock, and an affiliate may effect sales of any stock, pursuant to a registration statement, another exemption, or a regulation A offering. [SA Rule 144(j)]

(7) **Alternatives to rule 144:** [§575] While rule 144 did make the criteria for selling restricted securities more definite in some respects, it also made them more stringent. Therefore, sellers may seek alternatives to rule 144, while still avoiding "underwriter" status.

(a) **Registered transactions:** [§576] One option that may be available to the would-be seller is to register the transaction. This is usually quite expensive, however, and requires extensive cooperation from the issuer. As a rule, this route is chosen only when the issuer was already planning a registered public offering, and the selling shareholders simply "piggyback" their offering on the issuer's offering.

(b) **Regulation A exemption:** [§577] In cases where a registered transaction is not readily available, sellers sometimes take advantage of regulation A, a shortened form of registration available to certain persons (*see supra*, §388). Under regulation A, a noncontrol person or a group of noncontrol persons can often sell restricted securities pursuant to the exemption without affecting the availability of regulation A to the issuer.

(c) **"Section 4(1½)"—private sales of restricted securities:** [§578] The discussion of resales so far has focused on *public* resales. The problem with these, as we have seen, is that the seller (when restricted securities are sold) or the seller's broker (when the seller is a control person selling *any* securities, restricted or not) are likely to be swept into the definition of "underwriter" contained in SA section 2(11). But what if the seller, rather than selling publicly, sells *privately?* This would avoid underwriter status, since an underwriter is one who is involved in a "distribution," *i.e.,* a sale to the public.

1) **No express exemption:** [§579] The first obstacle to such a sale is that SA section 4(2), the standard private offering exemption, is available only to an issuer. Even without an express exemption, however, a private sale is possible. The standards that the S.E.C. has required for such a transaction in order for the seller (and the seller's broker) to avoid underwriter status have come to be known as "section 4(1½)," because they resemble in some respects the requirements of SA section 4(2) (the issuer's private placement exemption) and result in the transaction's being exempt under SA section 4(1), the exemption for transactions not involving an issuer, underwriter, or dealer.

2) **Sales of restricted securities by noncontrol persons:** [§580] Suppose, for example, that A, a noncontrol person of XYZ

Corp., has purchased some of XYZ's common stock in a private offering by XYZ under section 4(2) of the 1933 Act. A desires to resell some of these restricted securities. He cannot appeal to section 4(2), since this section applies only to "issuers," and A is not an issuer. If A is also not an "underwriter" or "dealer," then presumably he can resell under section 4(1).

a) **Determining underwriter status:** [§581] *A is not an underwriter if* he does not purchase from, or sell for, or participate in a "distribution" for, the issuer (XYZ). [*See* SA §2(11); *and see supra,* §93] The S.E.C. and the courts have traditionally resorted to the concepts related to a "public offering" to determine the meaning of the word "distribution." What is necessary, then, is for A to avoid participating in a "public offering." This will be accomplished if A does not himself sell to the "public" *and* effectively prevents his purchasers from reselling to the public without an exemption (since if the purchasers resell to the public, the securities will have been "distributed," and A will thereby become an underwriter).

   1/ **Avoiding sales to the public:** [§582] Generally, the seller can avoid selling to the public by offering and selling only to those who can meet the SA section 4(2) requirements for offerees in a private placement.

      a/ **Note:** The S.E.C. staff has been less rigorous in enforcing some of the "private placement" requirements in the "section 4(1½)" context, compared to SA section 4(2). The staff has been unpredictable in this regard, however, and no-action treatment is usually sought for such a transaction.

   2/ **Restricting further resales:** [§583] The usual techniques for restricting sales apply here (*see supra,* §§543-545). A could require his purchasers to agree to contractual provisions limiting resales, place legends on the security certificates noting that the securities cannot be resold without registration or an exemption, give stop transfer instructions to the issuer's transfer agent, and so on.

3) **Sales by control persons:** [§584] Control persons may also rely on section 4(1) to resell their securities, whether or not restricted.

   a) **Restricted securities:** [§585] Control persons face no additional obstacles with respect to their sales of restricted securities than are faced by noncontrol persons. The key in either case is to *avoid becoming an underwriter by selling to the public*, and to *avoid selling to an underwriter* (by selling to someone who in turn sells to the public).

b) **Nonrestricted securities:** [§586] In sales by control persons of nonrestricted securities, the key is to *avoid selling to an underwriter.* The control person is not concerned with her personal underwriter status, because the securities were not acquired from the issuer or an affiliate (the securities are not restricted). However, if a purchaser from the control person sells to the public in a nonexempt transaction, the purchaser will be deemed to have acquired the securities from an affiliate of the issuer (*i.e.,* the control person) with a view to a distribution; *i.e.,* the purchaser will be deemed to be an underwriter.

1/ **Avoiding sales to an underwriter:** [§587] The most effective technique for avoiding sales to an underwriter is to extract from purchasers the same sorts of agreements limiting resales that are needed to exempt a sale of restricted securities (*see supra*). In addition, an investment letter should probably be obtained in which the purchaser states that she is purchasing for investment and not for resale.

(8) **Restrictions on resales of securities issued in reorganizations, recapitalizations, intrastate offerings, and rule 145 offerings:** [§588] As discussed above, sections 3(a)(9) (voluntary recapitalizations), 3(a)(10) (approved recapitalizations), 3(a)(11) (intrastate offerings), and rule 145 (certain mergers, etc.) are transaction exemptions. Thus, offerings pursuant to these sections, like those pursuant to section 4(2) (private offering), do not permit automatic resales of the securities without registration. Some exemption from the 1933 Act must be found for these subsequent transfers. Section 4(1) may provide this exemption for the ordinary investor, as it may for the purchaser in a private offering (the so-called section 4(1½) exemption; *see supra*, §578). The specific authorizations for resale given in connection with rule 147 offerings (*see supra,* §460) and rule 145 offerings (*see supra,* §524) have already been discussed.

(9) **Rule 144A—resales to "qualified institutional buyers" of privately placed securities:** [§589] The S.E.C. adopted rule 144A in 1990, reacting in part to the growth of overseas markets and to an increasing fear that United States capital markets were no longer able to compete effectively with their foreign counterparts. Rule 144A is designed to make the United States private placement market more attractive to investors, by making restricted securities (*i.e.,* securities purchased in a nonpublic transaction) easier to resell.

(a) **Policy:** [§590] The idea underlying rule 144A is that restrictions on resales are not needed as long as resales are made only to large and financially savvy institutions.

(b) **Implementation:** [§591] Like rule 144 (*see supra*, §§549-574), rule 144A provides that a person complying with its requirements will be deemed not to be engaged in a "distribution" and therefore will not be an "underwriter" under SA section 2(11).

(c) **Requirements:** [§592] Rule 144A is available for resales if the following requirements are met:

1) **Seller not an issuer:** [§593] The rule is *not available to offers or sales by issuers.* [SA Rule 144A(b)] The rule is not intended to provide an exemption for primary distributions.

2) **Offers and sales only to QIBs:** [§594] Offers and sales are permitted under rule 144A only to *qualified institutional buyers ("QIBs") or* persons whom the seller reasonably believes to be QIBs.

    a) **Definition of "QIB":** [§595] QIBs include any of the following entities *if* they own and have investment discretion for at least *$100 million in securities* of unaffiliated issuers:

        1/ *Insurance companies;*

        2/ *Investment companies, business development companies, and small business investment companies;*

        3/ *Retirement plans and trusts holding assets for retirement plans;*

        4/ *Charitable organizations;*

        5/ *Securities dealers registered under the 1934 Act* (note that dealers need only own and invest $10 million, rather than $100 million, in securities to be QIBs. [SA Rule 144A(a)(1)(ii)]);

        6/ *Investment advisers registered under the Investment Advisers Act;*

        7/ *Dealers acting as "middlemen" in so-called riskless principal transactions;*

        8/ *Members of a family of investment companies* (*e.g.,* a mutual fund in an affiliated group of funds); and

        9/ *Any bank or savings and loan institution,* if it meets the $100 million test (above) and in addition has an audited net worth of at least $25 million.

    b) **Establishing "reasonable belief" that buyer is a QIB:** [§596] Rule 144A specifies several nonexclusive means by which a seller may establish a reasonable belief that the buyer is a QIB, including examination of the buyer's publicly available financial information and written certifications from executive officers of the buyer attesting that the buyer owns and invests a sufficient dollar amount in securities.

3) **Notice to buyer:** [§597] The seller must take reasonable steps to notify the buyer that the seller may be relying on the exemption provided by rule 144A. "Reasonable steps" are neither defined nor illustrated in the rule, but presumably written disclosure of this fact will suffice.

4) **Securities sold are "non-fungible":** [§598] The securities sold under rule 144A must not be of the same class as securities listed on a United States stock exchange or quoted on NASDAQ. *Rationale:* Investors receive less disclosure—and potentially less protection—under Rule 144A than they would in a registered distribution. Therefore, securities sold under the rule should not be permitted to find their way into the hands of public investors without registration. Since rule 144A securities are of different classes than those traded publicly, the likelihood that rule 144A securities will find their way into the hands of the public is greatly diminished.

5) **Disclosure:** [§599] Rule 144A requires that some information about the issuer be made available to the buyer and seller.

   a) **Securities of 1934 Act reporting companies:** [§600] If the issuer of the securities is a 1934 Act reporting company (*see supra*, §43) or one of a limited number of foreign issuers, no information need be provided. The information already publicly available under the 1934 Act is sufficient for the purposes of the rule.

   b) **Securities of nonreporting companies:** [§601] If the issuer does not file reports under the 1934 Act, the issuer must provide certain basic information about itself. The information required includes a "very brief" statement of the nature of the issuer's business and the issuer's balance sheet, income statement, and retained earnings statement for the last three years (or shorter period that the issuer was in operation). The financial statements should be audited, if that is reasonably possible.

(d) **Resales do not destroy private placement exemptions:** [§602] Rule 144A includes an express provision that the fact that purchasers of securities from the issuer may purchase with a view to reselling under rule 144A does not affect the availability to the issuer of the section 4(2) and regulation D exemptions under the 1933 Act. [SA Rule 144A, preliminary note 7]

1) **Rationale:** Recall that one of the concerns faced by an issuer in a private placement transaction is that resales by the original buyers may cause the exemption to be lost, because a buyer who buys from the issuer "with a view to distribution" may be deemed to be an underwriter. If this were applied to rule 144A transactions, the purpose of the rule—to facilitate resales of privately placed securities and thereby to attract investors to those securities—would be defeated.

(e) **Securities sold under rule 144A are "restricted":** [§603] Finally, securities sold in accordance with rule 144A are not thereby transformed into unrestricted securities. Public distribution of such securities is conditioned on the availability of an exemption from registration.

(10) **Regulation S—unregistered offshore offers and sales:** [§604] Simultaneously with the adoption of rule 144A (*see supra*), the S.E.C. adopted regulation S. The major thrust of regulation S is to clarify that the registration requirements of the 1933 Act do not apply to offers and sales made outside the United States. The S.E.C.'s primary concern in drafting the complex provisions of regulation S is that securities distributed outside the United States might eventually end up in the hands of United States investors, and most of the regulation is designed to minimize the likelihood that an offering nominally conducted outside the United States is actually aimed at United States investors.

(a) **Structure:** [§605] Regulation S comprises rules 901-904 under the 1933 Act. *Rule 901* sets out the *general statement* of the regulation, namely that for the purposes of SA section 5, the terms "offer," "offer to sell," "sell," "sale," and "offer to buy" do not include offers and sales occurring outside the United States. *Rule 902* includes *definitions* applicable to the regulation. *Rule 903* sets forth a *safe harbor for issuers and distributors*; compliance with the regulation means the transaction will be deemed to occur outside the United States. *Rule 904* sets out a similar *safe harbor for resales* by persons other than issuers and distributors.

1) **Definition of "distributor":** [§606] "Distributor" is defined in regulation S as "any underwriter, dealer, or other person who participates, pursuant to a contractual arrangement, in the distribution of the securities" in question. [SA Rule 902(c)]

2) **Definition of "substantial United States market interest":** [§607] The conditions that must be met for the issuer safe harbor depend, in part, on whether there is a "substantial United States market interest" in the securities. Such an interest exists under the following conditions:

a) **Equity securities:** [§608] With respect to equity securities, (i) the United States public markets are the single largest market for the securities in the issuer's last fiscal year *or* (ii) 20% or more of the global trading in the securities took place in the United States public markets *and* less than 55% took place in the trading facilities of any single foreign country.

b) **Debt securities:** [§609] With respect to debt securities, (i) there are 300 or more United States holders of record of the securities *or* (ii) $1 billion or more of the issuer's debt securities is held of record by United States holders *and* 20% or more of the issuer's debt securities are held of record by United States holders.

(b) **General conditions:** [§610] To take advantage of the regulation S safe harbor, two conditions must be met:

1) **Offshore transaction:** [§611] The offer or sale must be made in an offshore transaction (defined in rule 902 essentially as a transaction in which the buyer is outside the United States at the time the buy order is placed, and the execution of the transaction and delivery of the securities takes place outside the United States).

2) **No directed selling efforts:** [§612] In addition, directed selling efforts in the United States are prohibited. Directed selling efforts are activities that are intended to, or could reasonably be expected to, result in conditioning the market in the United States for the securities offered. (*See supra*, §161, for a discussion of conditioning the market).

(c) **Issuer's and distributor's safe harbor:** [§613] The safe harbor for issuers and distributors is divided into three categories, depending on the nature of the securities offered, the issuer's status as a 1934 Act reporting company, and the degree of United States market interest in the securities offered. The category into which an offering falls determines which, if any, additional conditions must be met for the safe harbor to apply.

1) **Category 1—foreign issuers; no additional conditions:** [§614] If there is no substantial United States market interest in the securities, a foreign issuer need comply only with the two general conditions. Offerings by United States issuers are not eligible for Category 1 treatment.

2) **Category 2:** [§615] If there is a substantial United States market interest in the securities, issuers of equity securities that are 1934 Act reporting companies and issuers of debt securities must comply with a set of requirements under the regulation, including placing legends on the offering documents and compliance with a "restricted period" of 40 days, during which no offers or sales to United States persons are permitted.

3) **Category 3:** [§616] The final category applies to all other offerings. The requirements in this category are the most onerous, including a restricted period of 40 days for debt offerings and one year for equity offerings, stop-transfer procedures for equity offerings, and certifications from buyers that they are not buying for the account of a United States person.

(d) **Resale safe harbor:** [§617] The resale safe harbor is available to persons other than the issuer or a distributor of the securities. Affiliates and persons acting on behalf of the issuer or a distributor likewise cannot use the resale safe harbor, but affiliates who are such solely because they are officers or directors of the issuer may use the safe harbor as long as no compensation other than a normal broker's commission is paid in connection with the transaction. In most cases, only the two general regulation S requirements (*see* above) must be met in the case of resales.

(e) **Exemption only from registration requirement:** [§618] While regulation S exempts certain transactions from the registration requirements of SA section 5, the other provisions of the 1933 and 1934 Acts still apply. Thus, for example, while the amount of disclosure required under regulation S is small, the issuer remains potentially liable for violating the antifraud or other liability provisions of the Acts.

## G. LIABILITIES UNDER THE 1933 ACT

1. **Introduction:** [§619] The liability provisions of the 1933 Act are organized around the two basic objectives of the Act: providing full disclosure of material information to potential investors in newly issued securities and generally preventing fraud and/or misrepresentation in the interstate sale of securities.

   a. **Conduct resulting in liability:** [§620] Accordingly, the kinds of conduct that may result in liability under the 1933 Act may be sorted broadly into two categories:

      (1) **Liability for improper disclosure or violation of section 5 registration provisions:** [§621] Section 11 of the 1933 Act provides for liability where the issuer misrepresents or fails to state a material fact in the registration statement. In addition, liability may arise under section 12(1) of the Act where the issuer or the underwriter makes an improper offer to a potential purchaser in the pre-filing period (*see supra*, §158); where the issuer fails to deliver the required prospectus in the post-effective period (*see supra*, §208); or where the issuer or underwriter violates some other provision of section 5.

      (2) **Liability for fraud or misrepresentation in general:** [§622] In addition to the above, the 1933 Act includes liability provisions covering fraud or misrepresentation in the interstate sale of securities in general (*i.e.,* whether or not registration with the S.E.C. is involved). [SA §§12(2), 17; *and see* discussion *infra,* §§699, 721]

   b. **Remedies for 1933 Act violations:** [§623] A wide range of remedies is available in actions under the 1933 Act, depending in the first instance on the nature of the plaintiff. That is, there are different remedies available to the S.E.C. than are available to a private plaintiff (*e.g.,* an aggrieved investor).

      (1) **Private lawsuits:** [§624] When investors sue under the 1933 Act, they are typically looking to receive payment in compensation for what has turned out to be a bad investment. This may be accomplished in two ways:

         (a) **Damages:** [§625] A plaintiff entitled to receive damages does not receive the full amount invested in the securities, but rather receives the amount lost (subject to certain limitations). Section 11 of the 1933 Act, discussed below, gives purchasers the right to receive damages.

         (b) **Rescission:** [§626] A plaintiff receiving rescission gets back the full amount invested in the securities. In effect, the sale is reversed, the plaintiff receiving back her cash and returning the securities purchased. Sections 12(1) and (2) of the 1933 Act, discussed below, give purchasers the right to rescission.

(2) **S.E.C. lawsuits:** [§627] The S.E.C., as part of its enforcement responsibility, may sue persons alleged to have violated the 1933 Act. In such an action, the S.E.C. has three kinds of remedies available:

    (a) **Cease-and-desist orders:** [§628] Included in the Securities Enforcement Remedies and Penny Stock Reform Act of 1990 were provisions giving the S.E.C. a new remedy, the cease-and-desist order.

        1) **Compare—injunctions:** [§629] Cease-and-desist orders resemble injunctions, in that both direct the respondent to stop violating the Act. There are, however, some important differences between the two remedies, including the following:

            a) The cease-and-desist order is issued administratively, *i.e., by the S.E.C. itself,* while an injunction is issued by a federal district judge; and

            b) Violation of a cease-and-desist order may result in a *civil monetary penalty* under 1933 Act section 20(d), while violation of an injunction may lead to a contempt proceeding.

        2) **Types of orders:** [§630] There are two kinds of cease-and-desist orders: temporary and permanent.

            a) **Temporary orders:** [§631] Temporary cease-and-desist orders may be issued against *broker-dealers, investment advisers, investment companies,* and certain other regulated entities. [SA §8A(c)(2)]

                1/ **Note:** The temporary cease-and-desist order *may be issued ex parte—i.e.,* without notice to the respondent or a hearing—if the S.E.C. deems it appropriate.

            b) **Permanent order:** [§632] Permanent cease-and-desist orders may be issued against anyone violating the 1933 Act. Notice must be given to the respondent, who is also entitled to a hearing before an administrative law judge.

        3) **Order for an accounting and disgorgement:** [§633] In connection with a proceeding for a permanent cease-and-desist order, the S.E.C. may also order the respondent to furnish an accounting and to disgorge any monies received in violation of the 1933 Act, including reasonable interest. [SA §8A(e)]

    (b) **Injunctive relief:** [§634] Section 20(a) of the 1933 Act authorizes the S.E.C. to conduct investigations into possible violations of the Act. Section 20(b) gives the S.E.C. the power to seek injunctive relief from the federal courts whenever it appears that the Act or the rules thereunder have been or are about to be violated.

(c) **Criminal sanctions:** [§635]  Section 24 of the 1933 Act imposes criminal penalties upon conviction of a willful violation of any of the provisions of the Act, including violation of section 17(a), discussed *infra*, the general fraud provision of the 1933 Act. "Willful" means that the defendant had the intention to defraud or that he made representations without knowing whether or not they were true. It need not be shown that the defendant knew that a "security" (as defined by the 1933 Act) was being sold or that defendant knew he was violating some specific provision of the securities laws. [United States v. Brown, 578 F.2d 1280 (9th Cir. 1978)]

c. **Comparison of 1933 Act anti-fraud provisions with common law fraud remedies**

(1) **Elements of common law action:** [§636]  At common law, a defrauded purchaser of securities had to prove the same elements to recover as any other defrauded purchaser of goods:

(a) **Material fact:** [§637]  The plaintiff had to show that the defendant seller of the securities misstated, or failed to state, a *material fact* that the seller was under a duty to disclose.

(b) **Reliance:** [§638]  In addition, the plaintiff had to show that she relied on the misrepresentation.

(c) **Privity:** [§639]  The plaintiff also had to show that there was privity of contract between her and the defendant (*i.e.,* that plaintiff had purchased the security from the specific seller being sued).

(d) **Causation:** [§640]  And the plaintiff had to show that the defendant's misrepresentation was the actual and the proximate cause of the plaintiff's loss.

(e) **Scienter:** [§641]  Finally, the defendant had to have had actual knowledge of the misrepresentation or omission; *i.e.,* the defendant's misrepresentation must have been intentional.

(2) **Lesser burden under 1933 Act:** [§642]  In general, the liability provisions of the 1933 Act afford remedies to defrauded purchasers more liberal than those available at common law. These remedies were designed to make recovery easier for purchasers of securities by lightening the burden of proof they must carry with respect to the above elements (*see infra,* §§652 *et seq.*).

2. **Express Civil Liabilities**

a. **Introduction:** [§643]  The 1933 Act contains three express liability provisions. With the exception of section 11 (for material misstatements in an effective registration statement), none of these historically has been of major importance. The reason for this is that plaintiffs have preferred an action under rule 10b-5 of the 1934 Act (*see infra,* §§795 *et seq.*) or some other *implied* civil liability provision. Courts generally held that these implied civil liabilities were subject to fewer restrictions than the actions under one of the express liability sections. However, these express liability provisions have become more important recently because the Supreme Court increasingly has restricted the availability of causes of action under rule 10b-5 and has held that no implied civil liability will arise merely as the result of a violation of some section of the statutes or an S.E.C. rule. (*See infra,* §782.)

b. **Section 11—liability for misstatements or omissions in registration statement or prospectus:** [§644] Section 11 of the 1933 Act imposes liability on designated persons for material false or misleading statements or omissions in an effective registration statement or prospectus. [*See* SA §11(a)]

(1) **Persons subject to liability:** [§645] The following persons can be held liable under section 11 for material misstatements in the registration statement or prospectus:

(a) **Every person who signs the registration statement:** [§646] Every person who signs a registration statement can be held liable for material misstatements or omissions in the statement. The following persons *must* sign the registration statement:

(i) *The issuer;*

(ii) *The principal executive officers* of the issuer;

(iii) *The principal financial officer* of the issuer;

(iv) *The comptroller or principal accounting officer* of the issuer; and

(v) *A majority of the members of the board of directors* of the issuer.

[SA §6(a)]

(b) **Every director of the issuer:** [§647] Every person who was a director of the issuer at the time the registration statement became effective can also be held liable, even if the director did not sign the registration statement.

(c) **Every person named as "about to become" a director:** [§648] In addition, every person who is named in the registration statement (with his consent) as about to become a director of the issuer may be held liable.

(d) **Every "expert" who certifies preparation of registration statement:** [§649] All "experts" who consent to being named as having prepared or certified part of the registration statement may be held liable under section 11. For example, accountants are "experts" as to the certified financial statements included in the registration statement.

(e) **Every underwriter involved in the distribution:** [§650] Underwriters may also be held liable under section 11.

(f) **Control persons:** [§651] Finally, persons who "control" any person who is liable under section 11 may be held jointly and severally liable with the liable persons, unless the controlling person had no knowledge of nor reasonable grounds to believe in the existence of the facts on which the liability of the controlled person is alleged to rest. [*See* SA §15]

(2) **Elements of plaintiff's cause of action**

(a) **Material misstatements or omissions:** [§652] To recover damages under section 11, the plaintiff must prove that there has been a misstatement of, or a failure to state, a "material" fact. [*See* SA §11(a)]

1) **Definition of "material":** [§653] Material facts are defined in the 1933 Act as those matters to which there is a substantial likelihood that a reasonable investor would attach importance in deciding whether to purchase the registered security. [SA Rule 405]

2) **Judicial expansion of definition:** [§654] This definition has been elaborated on by the courts, which have held that a fact is material when it is *more probable than not* that a significant number of traders in the security would have wanted to know it before deciding to deal in the security. [Feit v. Leasco Data Processing Equipment Corp., 332 F. Supp. 544 (E.D.N.Y. 1971)]

3) **Example of material facts:** [§655] A Corp. decided to acquire B Corp. through an exchange of A's securities made directly with B's shareholders. However, A failed to disclose that a major reason for acquiring the target company (B) was the amount of surplus cash that could be drained from B into A. A's failure to make this disclosure and to estimate the amount of such cash (when estimates were known or could have been obtained from B's management) were held to be material omissions. [*See* Feit v. Leasco Data Processing Equipment Corp., *supra*]

(b) **Limited reliance requirement:** [§656] In general, the plaintiff need *not* prove that she purchased in reliance on the misstatement to recover.

1) **Exception—after-acquired securities:** [§657] However, if the issuer sends out an earnings statement covering the period of one year after the effective date of the registration statement, a person thereafter acquiring some of the registered securities must prove reliance on the misrepresentation or omission to recover. [SA §11(a)]

a) **But note:** The plaintiff need not actually have read the registration statement to prove reliance. It is sufficient that she relied on secondary sources that repeated the misstatement.

b) **And note:** The one-year period runs from the filing date of any post-effective amendments (where they are filed and the securities continue to be offered pursuant to the amendments).

(c) **Privity of contract not required:** [§658] Any person acquiring a security which was the subject of a defective registration statement may sue under section 11. Thus, the purchaser need *not* be in privity with the issuer.

1) **Example:** Where A purchases securities that are part of the registered offering from B (B having purchased them from the issuer), A may recover under section 11 even though she is not in privity of contract with the issuer.

   a) **And note:** A purchaser may sue any party listed as a potential defendant under section 11.

2) **Compare—tracing required:** [§659] However, there is a requirement that the plaintiff be able to trace her purchase of the issuer's securities back to the defective registration statement, *i.e.,* that she prove that the specific securities she purchased were *issued in the offering registered by that registration statement.* [*See* SA §11(a)] When an issuer has issued securities of the same class at different times, this tracing can be difficult, because securities of the same class are essentially indistinguishable from one another.

   a) **Example:** Thus, a plaintiff who read the registration statement and bought securities in the secondary trading market, but cannot trace the securities back to the actual securities offered in the registered offering, cannot recover.

   b) **Compare:** However, a plaintiff who did *not* read the registration statement, but purchased after the original offering (in the trading market) and before the statute of limitations has run, can recover if she is able to trace the securities to the registration statement. [Barnes v. Osofsky, 373 F.2d 269 (2d Cir. 1967)]

(d) **Causation of damages:** [§660] The plaintiff need *not* prove that her loss (*i.e.,* decline in value of the securities) was caused by the misrepresentation. (*Note:* This was an element of the plaintiff's cause of action at common law.)

1) **Reduction of damages:** [§661] However, the *defendant* may be able to reduce the damages by proving that all or some portion of the damages resulted from some cause other than the misrepresentation or omission of material fact in the registration statement.

   a) **Example:** A court has taken into account a general decline in stock market prices after the date plaintiff purchased the issuer's stock, and allowed the defendant issuer a discount in damages equal to the percentage decline in the Standard and Poor's index of stock market prices. [Feit v. Leasco Data Processing Equipment Corp., *supra*, §655]

### (3) Defenses

(a) **General affirmative defenses:** [§662] Any defendant (*including* the issuer) subject to liability under section 11 may claim the following defenses. [SA §11(a)]:

1) *That the alleged false statements were actually true;*

2) *That the misstatements or omissions were not of material facts;*

3) *That the plaintiff-purchaser knew* of the misleading statements or omissions and invested in the securities anyway; and

4) *That the statute of limitations has run.* Under section 11, the period of limitations is one year after discovery of the false statement, with an overall limitation of three years after the security is first bona fide offered to the public. [*See* SA §13] This means that if a portion of the issue remains unsold after three years, for example in a continuous offering, purchasers after that time are not protected by section 11 of the Act.

(b) **Due diligence defense—experts and nonexperts:** [§663] In addition to the above defenses, all defendants (*except* issuers) have a "due diligence" defense under section 11. In applying this "due diligence" defense, section 11 makes a distinction between "experts," *i.e.,* those who certify part of the registration statement as being true (such as certified public accountants who certify that the financial statements were prepared according to generally accepted accounting principles), and "nonexperts," or all others who may be held liable pursuant to section 11. (*See supra,* §§645-651.) Section 11 also draws a distinction between the standard of care (*i.e.,* what constitutes due diligence) required of nonexperts who review material prepared by other nonexperts, and that required of nonexperts reviewing statements of experts. [*See* SA §11(a)]

1) **Statements made by experts:** [§664] To avoid liability under section 11, experts may demonstrate that they have met the following test of "due diligence" as to representations they made in the registration statement:

   a) *That they actually believed that the statements they made were true;* and

   b) *That their belief was reasonable.*

      1/ *For their belief to be reasonable*, the experts must have made a *reasonable investigation* into the facts supporting the statements made. Normally, this means that they must at least have performed up to the standards of their profession (*e.g.,* accountants must make an investigation of the facts that would conform to the standards of their profession and must state the issuer's financial results according to the generally accepted accounting principles set forth by the S.E.C.). [*See* Escott v. BarChris Construction Corp., 283 F. Supp. 643 (S.D.N.Y. 1968)]

2) **Statements made by nonexperts:** [§665] "Nonexperts" who make statements that appear in the registration statement are held to the same standard of "due diligence" as experts. Thus, nonexperts must actually believe that the statements made were true and their belief must be reasonable—*i.e.,* based on a reasonable investigation of the facts.

    a) **Test for reasonable investigation by nonexperts:** [§666] Under section 11, the test for defining the scope of a "reasonable investigation" is *what a prudent person would do* in the management of his or her own affairs. [*See* SA §11(c)]

        1/ **Note:** As a practical matter, however, there is no single standard. The court looks at each individual defendant and, based on the person's position with the issuer, responsibilities relative to the issuer and the registration statement, and background, skills, training, and access to information, the court determines what the person should have done to fulfill the obligation of a "reasonable investigation."

        2/ **Comment:** In other words, the test is really what kind of investigation a prudent person *in the defendant's position*, with the same responsibilities, skills, etc., would have made. [Escott v. BarChris Construction Corp., *supra*]

    b) **Application—attorney drafting registration statement:** [§667] An attorney who is also a member of the issuer's board of directors and who drafts the issuer's registration statement (and collects facts from the issuer to do so) does not "certify" his work and thus is a "nonexpert" as to the registration statement in general. [Escott v. BarChris Construction Corp., *supra*]

        1/ **Reasonable investigation by attorney:** [§668] In *BarChris*, the court indicated that the attorney-director did not have to conduct an independent audit of the issuer, but that a reasonable investigation would go beyond merely trusting the opinions and responses of the issuer's officers as to material facts. Therefore, a reasonable investigation by the attorney would include:

       a/    Looking at original written records (*e.g.*, written contracts) to verify statements in the registration statement;

       b/    An examination of the issuer's facilities, operations, material contracts, corporate minutes and other documents, and major items important to its financial condition;

       c/    Use of a comprehensive questionnaire for directors and officers to elicit information required to be disclosed (such as whether they had any conflicting interests); and

       d/    Having an accountant check any suspicious items disclosed by the lawyer's investigation.

**2/**    **Compare—drafting attorney as corporate insider:** [§669] Note that if the lawyer drafting the registration statement becomes so involved with the issuer and the registration that he is held to be a "corporate insider" (like the other management officers), he will then be held to the same high standard of diligence as other officers (*see infra*, §674). [Feit v. Leasco Data Processing Equipment Corp., *supra*, §661]

**3/**    **Drafting attorney as expert:** [§670] It is also conceivable that an attorney might be requested to certify (as an expert) some portion of the registration statement. In this case, the attorney would be held to the due diligence standard of an expert (*supra*, §664).

**3)**    **Nonexperts reviewing statements by other nonexperts:** [§671] A nonexpert not involved in the actual drafting of the registration statement (such as a member of the issuer's board of directors) may also be potentially liable under the Act for statements made in the registration statement by other nonexperts. To avoid such liability, the nonexpert must show that she exercised due diligence appropriate to her position in reviewing the statements made by other nonexperts.

    **a)**    **Standard of diligence required:** [§672] The standard of diligence required for nonexpert reviewers is the same as for nonexperts concerning their own representations in the registration statement (*see supra*, §665).

    **b)**    **Application**

       **1/**    **Underwriters:** [§673] Underwriters qualify as nonexperts and so must make a reasonable investigation of the *nonexpert* portions of the registration statement. They cannot simply rely on assurances of accuracy from the issuer's management, attorneys, etc. [*See* Escott v. BarChris Construction Corp., *supra*, §667]

a/ Note that normally the "lead underwriter" (usually the underwriting firm that first established contact with the issuer, and which structures and manages the underwriting for all of the other underwriting firms) will conduct an investigation of the issuer for all members of the underwriting syndicate to satisfy the due diligence requirement. However, if the lead underwriter conducts a faulty investigation, this does *not* absolve the other underwriters.

b/ The S.E.C. has stated that a participating underwriter must be satisfied that the managing underwriter has made the kind of investigation that the participant would have performed if it had been the manager. [*See* SA Release No. 33-5275 (1972)]

2/ **Inside directors and executive officers:** [§674] The standard of diligence imposed on underwriters is high, but it is not as high (*i.e.,* the investigation need not be as extensive) as that imposed on directors who are also part of management (*i.e.,* officers of the issuer) and all of the principal executive officers of the issuer.

a/ Not all of the individuals in this category will be required to do the same things to show due diligence. What is required of each depends on the person's position, access to information about the issue, etc.

b/ However, it is clear that these persons are virtual **guarantors** of the accuracy of the registration statement, and it will be difficult for them to escape responsibility for material misstatements. [*See* Feit v. Leasco Data Processing Equipment Corp., *supra*, §669] For example, if there are misstatements made relating to the issuer's financial condition, the issuer's chief financial officer will have a hard time sustaining his burden of showing that he really did not know of the misrepresentations. [*See* BarChris, *supra*]

3/ **Outside directors:** [§675] Outside directors (those who are not employed by the issuer as part of management) must also meet the due diligence test for nonexperts. However, their position differs from inside directors in that although they must discharge the duty of a director, they cannot realistically be expected to do a great deal to check on the accuracy of the registration statement. Thus, the issue is how extensive is the duty of an outside director?

a/ It appears from the cases that outside directors will probably be expected to attend directors' meetings during the time registration is underway and will also be held responsible for reading directors' meeting minutes, reading the drafts of the registration statement before filing and, in a general way, questioning company management, accountants, and legal counsel. (And if this investigation turns up apparent misstatements, the directors must personally check into these matters and require company counsel to check into them.) [Escott v. BarChris Construction Corp., *supra*—holding liable two directors who failed to read the registration statement and one who gave it only a cursory review]

b/ Note again that what is actually expected of any specific director will depend in part on his background and familiarity with the registration process. For example, a lawyer-director might be expected to make a more extensive investigation than a doctor-director. [*See* BarChris, *supra*]

4) **Nonexperts reviewing statements made by experts:** [§676] Nonexperts (such as outside directors) are held to a lower standard of care when reviewing statements made by experts than when reviewing statements made by other nonexperts.

a) **No investigation required:** [§677] Because nonexperts are entitled to rely on statements made by experts, *no investigation need be made by the nonexpert.* Rather, the reviewing nonexpert need only show that he did not believe the statements made by the expert to be false and that he had no reasonable ground to believe they were false.

b) **Burden generally met:** [§678] In most cases, nonexpert defendants will be able to meet this burden of proof. For example, in the *BarChris* case, most of the nonexperts were held not liable for misrepresentations made by the issuer's expert accountants.

(4) **Measure of damages:** [§679] Where the plaintiff proves that there was a material misrepresentation or omission in the registration statement and that the securities purchased are traceable to the registered offering, the plaintiff can recover any damages suffered as a result of a decline in value of the securities. [*See* SA §11(e)]

(a) **If the stock is sold prior to filing suit:** [§680] If the stock is sold prior to the filing of a lawsuit, the plaintiff may recover the difference between the price she paid for the stock (but not exceeding the price at which the security was offered to the public) and the price at which it was sold prior to suit.

1) **Example:** X bought stock in a registered offering for $10; she sold it for $6 prior to filing suit and it was selling at $5 at the time of the suit. X can recover only $4 per share (the difference between the price paid and the price at which she sold).

(b) **If the stock has not been sold prior to suit:** [§681] If the stock has not been sold prior to the suit, the purchaser may recover either:

(i) *The difference* between the price she paid (not exceeding the offering price) and the value of the security *at the time of the suit;* or

(ii) *The price at which the stock was sold after the suit was instituted but before judgment*, if such damages are less than those that result from using the value at the time of the suit.

[SA §11(e)]

(c) **Determining value:** [§682] Where a court is required to determine the value of the issuer's securities at the time of the suit, it may consider various factors besides the actual market value. For example, it may adjust market value to account for "panic selling" then taking place, which may depreciate the securities beyond their normal investment value. [Beecher v. Able, 435 F. Supp. 397 (S.D.N.Y. 1975)]

(d) **Plaintiff not required to mitigate damages:** [§683] Where the plaintiff buys securities that decline in value due to misrepresentations made in the registration statement and then files suit, she need not sell the securities to mitigate damages just because the market price begins to rise.

1) **Example:** A buys debentures at $100 each. They decline to $75 at the time of the suit, rise to $100 while the suit is going on, but decline again to $70 just before judgment (at which time the plaintiff sells). The plaintiff's damages are measured by the difference in the price she paid ($100) and the value at the time of the suit ($75). [Beecher v. Able, *supra; and see* SA §11(e)(3)]

(e) **Limits on recovered amount**

1) **Offering price as ceiling:** [§684] In no case can the amount recovered exceed the price at which the security was offered to the public. [SA §11(g)]

2) **Liability of underwriter:** [§685] Also, the total liability of an underwriter cannot exceed the offering price of the securities that the underwriter sold to the public. [SA §11(e)]

(f) **Joint and several liability—contribution:** [§686] All persons who are liable under section 11(a) are jointly and severally liable, and every person who becomes liable to make any payment under section 11 may recover contribution from any person who, if had they been sued would have been liable, unless the person who has become liable was guilty of fraudulent misrepresentation and the person who has not become liable was not. [*See* SA §11(f)]

c. **Section 12(1)—liability for offers or sales in violation of section 5:** [§687] Section 12(1) provides that any person who offers or sells a security in violation of any of the provisions of section 5 of the 1933 Act shall be liable to the purchaser for: (i) the ***consideration paid*** (with interest) less the amount of any income received on the securities (*i.e.,* a suit for rescission); or (ii) for ***damages*** if the purchaser no longer owns the security.

(1) **Liability for any violation of section 5:** [§688] Liability under section 12(1) is absolute for any violation of any provision of section 5. Such violations include a sale of unregistered securities, failure to deliver the required prospectus, making an illegal offer in the pre-filing period, etc. (*See supra,* §§157 *et seq.*)

(a) **Control persons:** [§689] Persons who "control" any person liable under section 12(1) may be held jointly and severally liable with the controlled person, unless the controlling person had no knowledge of nor reasonable grounds to believe in the existence of the facts on which the liability of the controlled person is alleged to rest. [SA §15]

(b) **Participant liability:** [§690] Section 12(1) imposes liability on those who offer or sell a security in violation of section 5. But the 1933 Act nowhere delineates who may, for these purposes, be regarded as a statutory "seller" (or offeror). Clearly the person who passes title to the security is a seller, but may anyone else be regarded as a "seller" for purposes of section 12(1)? Courts were in conflict over this question until 1988, when the Supreme Court decided *Pinter v. Dahl,* 486 U.S. 622 (1988).

1) **Facts of *Pinter*:** Pinter, an oil and gas operator and securities broker, sold unregistered oil and gas interests to Dahl in an attempted private placement. Later, Dahl solicited some of his friends to purchase additional interests, because Dahl believed the interests were good investments. Pinter sold the interests to Dahl's friends on the strength of Dahl's representations that the friends qualified as private placement investors. It turned out that the friends were not qualified private placement investors, and when the investment became worthless, Dahl and his friends sued under section 12(1). Pinter counterclaimed, alleging, among other things, that Dahl was a "seller" under section 12(1) and therefore that Dahl was accountable to Pinter in contribution for the amounts awarded the other plaintiffs.

2) **Definition of "seller":** [§691] The Supreme Court held in *Pinter* that a "seller" for section 12(1) purposes includes:

    a)   The *person who actually passes title* to the security; and

    b)   *Persons who solicit the purchase* from the purchaser.

  3)  **Persons who are not sellers:** [§692] Under *Pinter*, however, the term "seller" does not include persons whose sole motivation in acting is to benefit the buyer.

## (2) Defenses to a section 12(1) cause of action

(a)  **No sale of a "security":** [§693] One defense to a section 12(1) cause of action is to prove that there was no offer or sale of a "security" as that term is defined in the 1933 Act. (*See* discussion *supra,* §§157 *et seq.*)

(b)  **No violation of section 5:** [§694] Another defense is that no violation of section 5 ever occurred (*i.e.,* the offering of securities was exempt from the registration provisions of section 5 of the Act).

(c)  **No privity:** [§695] Unlike section 11, section 12(1) imposes a condition of privity of contract between the plaintiff-purchaser and the seller-defendant. Therefore, a common defense to a section 12(1) action is that no privity of contract existed.

  1)  **Example:** Issuer sold to A, who resold to B, who resold to C (a broker), who resold to the plaintiff. Since the plaintiff has privity only with C, C is the only person against whom the plaintiff can bring a section 12(1) action. Consequently, if C were found not to have violated section 5 (even though A and B had committed violations), plaintiff could not sustain a section 12(1) action. [Winter v. D.J. & M. Investment & Construction Corp., 185 F. Supp. 943 (S.D. Cal. 1960)]

  2)  **Note:** Remember, however, that persons who solicit the plaintiff's purchase, although they do not actually pass title to the security, are nevertheless held to be "sellers." (*See supra,* §608.)

(d)  **Statute of limitations:** [§696] As under section 11, the period of limitations is one year after the violation, but in no event more than three years after the security was bona fide offered to the public. As above, if a portion of the issue is sold after three years from the first bona fide offer to the public, section 12(1) is unavailable.

(e)  **Laches:** [§697] One court has held that laches (an equitable counterpart to the statute of limitations that evaluates staleness of a claim in terms of the prejudice caused by a knowing delay in bringing a suit, rather than by the mere passage of time) is not a defense in a section 12(1) action where the period of limitations has not yet run. [Straley v. Universal Uranium & Milling Corp., 289 F.2d 370 (9th Cir. 1961)]

(f)  **No interstate commerce:** [§698] Section 12(1) incorporates the requirements of section 5. Section 5 is specific as to how the means of interstate commerce must be used for there to be a violation. Hence, this may preclude as broad an interpretation of interstate commerce as this term is given elsewhere in the securities laws. [*See* United States v. Robertson, 181 F. Supp. 158 (S.D.N.Y. 1959)]

d. **Section 12(2)—general civil liability under the Act:** [§699] The 1933 Act generally prohibits fraud in the interstate offer or sale of securities. Section 12(2) of the Act provides that any person:

(i) Who offers for sale a security (whether or not exempted from the registration requirements of section 5, except for certain government and bank securities) by the *use of any means of interstate commerce;*

(ii) By means of a prospectus or oral communication that contains an *untrue statement or omission of material fact* (the purchaser not knowing of such untruth or omission); and

(iii) Who *cannot sustain the burden of proof* that he did not know and in the exercise of reasonable care could not have known of the untruth

is liable to the purchaser of the security. [*See* SA §12(2)]

(1) **Scope of section 12(2) actions:** [§700] Except with respect to securities exempt under section 3(a)(2) (certain government and bank securities), section 12(2) applies whether or not the securities were registered pursuant to section 5 of the Act, whether or not they were offered under an exemption from the Act, and whether the securities were offered in writing or orally.

(a) **Example:** If XYZ Corp. makes an offering of its securities, section 12(2) applies to any misrepresentations made by XYZ, whether the offering is registered or unregistered (*i.e.,* even though XYZ uses an exemption from registration, such as the private offering exemption).

(2) **Plaintiff's cause of action:** [§701] A buyer bringing a section 12(2) action may sue for *rescission* to recover the consideration paid for the securities, plus interest, and less any income received; or for *damages*, if the securities have already been sold. In either case, the plaintiff must show the following:

(a) **Sale of a security:** [§702] The plaintiff must prove that there has been an offer or sale of a "security" as that term is defined in the Act (*see supra,* §158).

(b) **Use of jurisdictional means:** [§703] The cases have held that the language of section 12(2) requires that liability be limited to persons "who offer or sell securities by use of any means or instruments of transportation or communication in interstate commerce or the mails." [United States v. Robertson, *supra*]

1) **Note:** Most decisions have indicated that this requirement is satisfied where any part of the sale (including delivery after the sale) involves such means. [United States v. Robertson, *supra*]

2) **Application:** Thus, as long as any means of doing interstate commerce is used (*e.g.,* use of a phone or mail service), this is sufficient (even though the transaction itself does not involve more than one state). [Lennerth v. Mendenhall, 234 F. Supp. 59 (N.D. Ohio 1964)]

(c) **Sale by means of a prospectus or oral communication:** [§704] Section 12(2) also requires that the offer or sale of securities occur by means of a "prospectus or oral communication" that includes the misrepresentation or fails to disclose the material fact. Since section 12(2) does not have a reliance requirement, individual plaintiffs need not actually read the writing that contains the misrepresentation. [*See* Alton Box Board Co. v. Goldman, Sachs & Co., 560 F.2d 916 (8th Cir. 1977)]

(d) **Untrue statement or omission of material fact:** [§705] The plaintiff must also show that there was an untrue statement of, or an omission to state, a material fact.

1) **Example:** D was an exclusive dealer in Penn Central notes and sold a large note to P shortly before Penn Central went bankrupt. D knew P was required by law to purchase only highest quality paper, that Penn Central had large losses, and that other banking firms were removing Penn Central paper from their approved buying lists. D's opinion as to the quality of the security was a material fact under section 12(2). [*See* Franklin Savings Bank of New York v. Levy, 551 F.2d 521 (2d Cir. 1977)]

2) **Note:** The court in *Franklin* indicated that D's knowledge that P was required to purchase only the highest quality paper constituted a representation that the paper it sold to P was of the highest quality. Such a representation is a misrepresentation (if untrue) unless D makes a reasonable investigation of the financial facts and exercises reasonable care in arriving at a conclusion as to quality.

(e) **Defendant's knowledge of the untrue statement:** [§706] The plaintiff must *plead* that the defendant knew, or in the exercise of reasonable care should have known, of the untrue statement. However, the defendant then must bear the burden of proof on the issue (*i.e.,* that he did not know, and in the exercise of reasonable care could not have known, of the untrue statement).

(f) **No reliance or causation:** [§707] Note that the plaintiff need *not* prove reliance on the misrepresentation (*see supra,* §704). Section 12(2) requires, however, that the sale be accomplished *by means of* a prospectus (or oral communication) that contains a material misstatement or omission. One court has suggested that this language requires a showing of "some causal relationship between the misleading representation and the sale." [Alton Box Board Co., *supra*]

(3) **Defenses:** [§708] To avoid liability under section 12(2), a defendant may raise the following defenses:

(a) **Lack of knowledge:** [§709] The defendant may show that he did not know, and in the exercise of reasonable care could not have known, of the untrue statement. Note that this is basically a simple negligence standard.

    1) **Investigation requirement:** [§710] Whether an investigation is required depends on all the circumstances, but an underwriter probably has to make a reasonable investigation of an issuer. [Sanders v. John Nuveen & Co., 619 F.2d 1222 (7th Cir. 1980), *cert. denied,* 450 U.S. 1005 (1981)] According to the *Sanders* court, there is no substantive difference between the investigation required to establish reasonable care under section 12(2) and that required to prove due diligence for the nonexpert under section 11.

    2) **Standards:** [§711] And note that different standards have not been established with regard to statements made by experts and nonexperts (as they have under section 11; *see supra*, §§644 *et seq.*).

(b) **Waiver and estoppel:** [§712] The defendant may claim the defenses of waiver and estoppel if it can prove that the plaintiff has shown sufficient approval or acceptance of the defendant's misconduct.

(c) **Plaintiff's knowledge:** [§713] The defendant can also show that the plaintiff knew of the untrue statement.

(d) **Privity:** [§714] Under section 12(2) (as in section 12(1) above), there must be privity of contract between the plaintiff and the defendant.

(e) **Participant liability:** [§715] Like section 12(1), section 12(2) imposes liability on persons who "offer or sell" a security. The *Pinter* case (*supra,* §692) addressed the question of participant liability and who is deemed a "seller," but only with respect to section 12(1). The Court expressly reserved any decision on the parallel requirement in section 12(2). Lower courts addressing the issue since *Pinter*, however, have uniformly held that *Pinter* applies to section 12(2), as well as to section 12(1). [*See, e.g.,* Royal American Managers, Inc. v. IRC Holding Corp., 885 F.2d 1011 (2d Cir. 1989)] Consequently, the same rules presently apply to participant liability under sections 12(1) and 12(2). (*See supra*, §§687 *et seq.*)

(f) **Statute of limitations:** [§716] The period of limitations for a section 12(2) cause of action is one year after discovery of the false statement, but not more than three years after the sale.

    1) **Laches:** [§717] It is uncertain whether laches applies to section 12(2) actions.

## 3. Section 17—S.E.C. Anti-Fraud Enforcement

  a. **Criminal liability and injunctions:** [§718] As discussed above, sections 11, 12(1), and 12(2) of the 1933 Act provide plaintiffs with express causes of action based on specific types of misconduct in connection with the issuance of securities. These sections, however, are not available to the S.E.C., which is not a party to securities transactions. The Act therefore contains a provision—section 17—generally prohibiting fraud in connection with any offer or sale of securities. The S.E.C.'s 1933 Act antifraud enforcement is based on section 17, which makes it unlawful for any person in the *offer or sale* of securities by use of any means or instruments of transportation or communication in interstate commerce or by the use of the mails, directly or indirectly:

(i) *To employ any device, scheme, or artifice* to defraud [SA §17(a)(1)]; or

(ii) *To obtain money or property* by means of any *untrue statement of a material fact* or *any omission* to state a material fact [SA §17(a)(2)]; or

(iii) *To engage in any transaction, practice, or course of business* which operates or would operate as a fraud or deceit upon the *purchase* [SA §17(a)(3)].

(1) **Scope:** [§719] Note that section 17(a) is not limited to sales; it applies to *offers* as well.

(2) **Who is protected:** [§720] The Supreme Court has held that section 17(a)(1) prohibits fraud against brokers as well as against purchaser-investors. [United States v. Naftalin, 441 U.S. 768 (1979)]

    (a) **Rationale:** The Court held that although section 17(a)(3) specifically mentions "purchaser," this term should not be read into sections 17(a)(1) or (2), which are more general and cover fraud on brokers. The thrust of *Naftalin* is that sections 17(a)(1) and (2) apply to persons generally, in addition to purchasers of securities.

b. **Implied civil liability:** [§721] There is a long-standing split in the federal circuit courts over whether section 17(a) of the 1933 Act includes an "implied" civil cause of action permitting private persons to sue under the section and thereby, perhaps, avoiding some of the more onerous requirements of other sections of the 1933 and 1934 Acts (*e.g.,* 1933 Act section 12(2), *see supra*, §§699 *et seq.*; 1934 Act section 10(b) and rule 10b-5, *see infra*, §§795 *et seq.*) that create fraud remedies for private plaintiffs. The *trend is clearly away from an implied remedy under section 17(a)*. This is the better view, because an implied remedy would conflict with the express remedies contained in each Act. [*See* Landry v. All American Assurance Co., 688 F.2d 381 (5th Cir. 1982)]

c. **Conduct standard**

(1) **Causes of action for damages:** [§722] If a private cause of action is implied in section 17, the plaintiff would have to prove that the defendant acted intentionally or with actual knowledge. [Sanders v. John Nuveen & Co., 554 F.2d 790 (7th Cir. 1977)]

(2) **Injunctive actions brought by the S.E.C.:** [§723] However, the Supreme Court has held that in civil *injunctive* actions brought by the S.E.C., a distinction must be made between the various subsections of section 17(a). Subsection 17(a)(1) requires a showing of scienter, while the two

remaining subsections require only a showing of negligence. [Aaron v. S.E.C., 446 U.S. 680 (1980)]

4. **Liability Under the Securities Exchange Act of 1934:** [§724] A complete understanding of the liability provisions of the 1933 Act is impossible without also considering the provisions of the 1934 Act. The provisions of each statute overlap, and each has advantages and disadvantages in comparison with the other. (*See* discussion of 1934 Act provisions *infra*, §§795 *et seq.*)

5. **Indemnification**

    a. **Officers, directors, and control persons:** [§725] Officers, directors, and control persons of an issuer may be exposed to substantial liability under the securities laws and substantial litigation expenses in defense of securities actions. The laws of the various states vary as to whether and to what extent these persons (acting as representatives for the corporation) may be indemnified against such liability by the issuer.

        (1) **No judicial decision:** [§726] There is no direct judicial authority on the question whether indemnification of officers, directors, or control persons by the issuer against liabilities and expenses incurred in connection with the 1933 Act is unlawful. When such a decision comes, it will undoubtedly be based on the policy considerations underlying the 1933 Act.

        (2) **Policy of the S.E.C.:** [§727] It is currently the policy of the S.E.C. that before it will approve a registration statement, indemnification must either be *waived* by such persons *or* a statement must be made in the prospectus to the effect that the S.E.C. considers such indemnification against the policy of the 1933 Act (and therefore unenforceable) and that such persons promise to submit the question (if it arises) to a court of competent jurisdiction for a decision. [Regulation 5-K Item 512(h)]

            (a) **Sanction:** [§728] The S.E.C. will deny acceleration of the effective date of the registration statement unless this statement is made in the prospectus.

    b. **Underwriters:** [§729] Note that indemnification by the issuer of the ***underwriters*** is common. The S.E.C. has done nothing to discourage this, even though some scholars believe that there is no reason to make a distinction between officers and directors on one hand, and underwriters, on the other.

        (1) **Actual knowledge of misstatement:** [§730] One court, however, has held that at least where the underwriter has ***actual knowledge*** of materially misleading statements or omissions contained in the prospectus, the underwriter cannot rely on an indemnification agreement to escape liability. Rather, public policy requires that such underwriters be equally liable with the issuer to investors who have received the incorrect prospectus. [*See* Globus, Inc. v. Law Research Service, Inc., 418 F.2d 1276 (2d Cir. 1969), *cert. denied*, 397 U.S. 913 (1970)]

        (2) **Negligence:** [§731] It is still questionable what the result would be in a case where the underwriter was only ***negligent*** with respect to the inclusion of inaccurate information in the prospectus.

6. **Contribution:** [§732] A related question involves whether contribution is available in actions brought under sections of the 1933 Act that do not expressly provide for contribution (*i.e.,* sections other than section 11; *see supra* §686). The courts have been friendlier to the idea of contribution in these actions than they have been to claims for indemnification.

   a. **Distinguish indemnification:** [§733] While indemnification is the payment of all of a party's costs and expenses, contribution involves only the allocation of the damages among the defendants.

   b. **S.E.C. policy:** [§734] So far, the S.E.C. has not attempted to discourage claims for contribution.

      (1) **Rationale:** Contribution does not violate the policies underlying the 1933 Act; witness section 11(f), which expressly provides for contribution in a section 11 case. In fact, contribution furthers the policies of the Act, insofar as contribution tends to ensure that all defendants will bear some of the burden of the violation.

   c. **Compare—minority view under 1934 Act:** [§735] Notwithstanding some good reasons why contribution should be allowed in 1933 Act cases, some courts decline to permit actions for contribution under the *1934 Act*—where presumably the same policies apply. These minority cases usually stress that the question whether such an action should be implied in sections where it is not expressly provided turns on congressional intent, and in the absence of a clear expression of that intent, no action should be permitted. [*See, e.g.,* Chutich v. Green Tree Acceptance, Inc., 759 F. Supp. 1403 (D. Minn. 1991); *and see infra,* §910, for a discussion of contribution under the 1934 Act]

7. **Liability Insurance:** [§736] Another important issue in the area of liability is whether an issuer can purchase insurance to cover potential liabilities which could *not* be properly indemnified under state law.

   a. **Availability of insurance:** [§737] State law varies, but many states do allow such insurance, and commercial policies are available. Insurance policies are not uniform with respect to what conduct they insure against; however, most do not insure against willful misconduct.

   b. **S.E.C. policy:** [§738] Thus far, the S.E.C. has drawn a distinction between indemnification and insurance and has not discouraged insurance.

      (1) **Rationale:** The reasons for this distinction are:

         (a) If insurance were unavailable, the cost to the issuer's shareholders arising from liability could be extensive;

         (b) Underwriters might refrain from marketing securities; and

         (c) Directors and others might be unwilling to serve companies involved in the registration process.

8. **Stipulations Contrary to Liability Provisions Void:** [§739] Any condition, stipulation, or provision (as in a contract of sale) purporting to bind any person acquiring

any security to waive compliance by the seller with any of the provisions of the 1933 Act or its rules and regulations is *void*. [SA §14]

a. **Example:** A sold B stock in an unregistered public offering. Later, A offered to return the money for the stock and gave B 10 days in which to respond to the rescission offer. B did not respond. Still later, B sued for rescission under section 12(1) of the Act. The court held that B had not waived his rights under the 1933 Act by failing to respond to A's offer of rescission. [Meyers v. C & M Petroleum Producers, Inc., 476 F.2d 427 (5th Cir. 1973)]

# III. REGULATION OF SECURITIES TRADING— THE SECURITIES EXCHANGE ACT OF 1934

## *—chapter approach*

The previous section of this Summary dealt with the Securities Act of 1933 and its regulation of the original distribution of securities. This section will cover the Securities Exchange Act of 1934 and its regulation of the trading of securities *subsequent* to their original distribution. For example, if XYZ Corp. issues 100,000 shares of its common stock to the public and thereafter registers this stock for trading on the New York Stock Exchange, the 1934 Act will regulate many aspects of the trading of XYZ's common stock.

This chapter covers a lot of important information. For exam purposes, the most important topics for you to study are:

1. **Rule 10b-5:** Rule 10b-5 is one of the most important remedy provisions of the 1934 Act; therefore, it is almost inevitable that it will appear in a question on your exam. The key approach is to memorize all of the many elements of the cause of action and then to sift through the facts of your question to determine if each element is present. Remember to consider rule 10b-5 whenever you see trading by insiders.

2. **Tender Offers and Repurchases of Stock:** This is an important area of securities regulation law. Be sure you discuss the requirements for making a tender offer (*e.g.,* disclosure of information) and what a corporation might do in defense of tender offers by corporate raiders (*e.g.,* buy its own shares).

3. **Proxy Solicitation:** Although this topic is generally covered in a Corporations class, the S.E.C. promulgated extensive revisions to the proxy rules (contained in Regulation 14A) in October 1992. That, and the increasing attention paid to the proxy contest as a potential takeover technique in times of scarce capital, suggest that at least a brief review of the information on proxy contests and remedies for violation of the proxy rules would be worthwhile.

4. **Short-Swing Profits on Insider Transactions:** This is sometimes the subject of an exam question. If your professor has stressed this area of law, the best approach is to study the rules carefully until you know them exactly, because section 16 is a highly technical area of securities law. Also consider rule 10b-5 if there has been any misrepresentation or nondisclosure of significant information.

5. **Participants and Advisors to Securities Transactions:** This material is important to know to practice law capably and ethically. However, this area is also in tremendous turmoil. Because the law changes rapidly, some professors skip the subject altogether; others place great emphasis on this topic because the law is on the "cutting edge." Consider the coverage of the topic in your class, and adjust your studying accordingly.

## A. OVERVIEW OF THE 1934 ACT

1. **Purpose of the Act:** [§740] The purpose of the Securities Exchange Act of 1934 ("SEA") is to protect interstate commerce and the national credit, and to ensure a fair and honest market for the trading of securities. [SEA §2]

2. **Registration and Reporting Requirements—Section 12:** [§741] Section 12 of the 1934 Act requires that certain securities be registered with the S.E.C. Once a company has registered its securities, it thereafter must file reports with the S.E.C. on a periodic basis. In addition, many of the company's other activities are subject to regulation under other provisions of the 1934 Act.

a. **Corporations required to register their securities:** [§742] Companies whose securities must be registered with the S.E.C. may be divided into two categories: *listed companies* and *over-the-counter (or "OTC") companies*. (*See supra*, §§3 *et seq.* for a discussion of stock exchanges and over-the-counter trading.) Companies of either kind that have triggered the 1934 Act registration requirements and begun to comply with the 1934 Act are typically referred to as "*registered*" or "*reporting*" companies.

(1) **Listed companies:** [§743] All companies whose securities are traded on a national stock exchange must register the securities so traded. [*See* SEA §12(a), (b)]

(a) **Example:** If the common stock of XYZ Corp. is traded on a national securities exchange (such as the New York Stock Exchange), XYZ must register the stock with the S.E.C. under section 12 of the 1934 Act.

(2) **Over-the-counter companies:** [§744] In addition to listed companies, the 1934 Act requires registration of securities of *all companies that have reached a certain size*, even if their stock is not traded on a securities exchange. "Size" is measured by reference to the company's total assets, and the number of shareholders it has: A company that has *more than $5 million in assets* must register *each class of equity security that is held by 500 or more shareholders*. [SEA §12(g); SEA Rule 12g-1]

(a) **Example:** If no securities of XYZ are traded on a national exchange, but XYZ has in excess of $5 million in assets and at least 500 shareholders who own its common stock, XYZ must register the stock with the S.E.C. under section 12.

b. **Information required with registration:** [§745] Section 12 requires that the registering company supply the S.E.C. with information similar to that submitted with an S-1 registration statement under the 1933 Act—*i.e.*, information concerning its organization, financial structure, and the nature of its business; its securities outstanding; the names of directors, officers, underwriters, and principal shareholders, and their remuneration and material contracts with the issuer; bonus and profit-sharing arrangements; management and service contracts; options outstanding with respect to the issuer's securities; and all other material contracts and important financial statements (duly certified by public accountants). [SEA §12(b)(1); *see* SEA Form 10]

c. **Exemptions from registration requirements:** [§746] There are numerous exemptions from the registration requirements of the 1934 Act. The following securities are among those that need not be registered with the S.E.C.:

(i) *The securities of investment companies* (*i.e.*, "mutual funds") which are registered under the Investment Company Act of 1940;

(ii) *The securities of savings and loan companies,* where the companies are supervised by state or federal agencies; and

(iii) *The securities of organizations operated exclusively for religious, educational, or charitable purposes.*

[SEA §12]

d. **S.E.C. exemptive power:** [§747] In addition to the statutory exemptions, the S.E.C. has the power to exempt securities from registration if such an exemption is in the public interest and does not endanger investors. [SEA §3(a)(12)(A)(v)]

e. **Reporting requirements of registered companies:** [§748] All companies that have securities registered with the S.E.C. pursuant to SEA section 12 must make periodic (annual and quarterly) reports to the S.E.C. to keep the information in the registration statement "reasonably current." In addition, if a significant event takes place, the issuer is required to file a "current report." [SEA §13(a); Forms 10-K, 10-Q, 8-K] SEA section 13 contains the substantive reporting requirements. Form 10-K is the annual report of the issuer and requires virtually the same information that is required of an issuer registering an offering of securities on form S-1 under the 1933 Act (*see supra,* §223). The principal executive officer, financial officer, and accounting officer, as well as a majority of the members of the board of directors must sign the 10-K report filed with the S.E.C. [SEA Form 10-K Gen. Instr. D(2)] This signature requirement may affect their liability for any misstatements made in the report (*i.e.,* create a duty of "due diligence" similar to section 11 of the 1933 Act). (*See infra,* §781, for a statutory basis for imposing such a duty.)

f. **Reports required of companies offering their securities to the public:** [§749] Every issuer of a security registered under the 1933 Act must also file periodic reports with the S.E.C. Like the section 12 registration requirements above, the periodic report provisions refer to SEA section 13 for the content and nature of the reports that must be filed with the S.E.C. Reporting may be discontinued when the issuer has fewer than (i) 300 holders of the class of security so registered *or* (ii) 500 holders of the class of security so registered and has had total assets under $5 million at the end of each of its three most recent fiscal years. [SEA §15(d); SEA Rule 12h-3]

g. **Effect is registration of the issuer:** [§750] Note that technically what is registered under section 12 of the 1934 Act is a class of securities, but the net effect, under the associated reporting requirements, is to register the issuer and subject the issuer to periodic reporting requirements of the 1934 Act.

(1) **Reporting requirements are the same, whether triggered by size, listing, or 1933 Act registration:** [§751] Notice that we have discussed several events that may trigger the reporting requirements of 1934 Act section 13. (*See supra,* §§748-749.) It is important to realize that, regardless of which event triggers the reporting requirements, the obligation to report is essentially the same. [*See* SEA §§13, 15(d); SEA Rules 13a-1, 13a-11, 13a-13, 15d-1, 15d-11, 15d-13]

h. **Integration of the disclosure requirements:** [§752] In 1980, the S.E.C. began a shift toward reliance on the 1934 Act and continuous reporting through that Act's monthly, quarterly, and annual reports to keep disclosure about issuers current. Since then, the requirements for disclosure under the 1933 and 1934 Acts have largely been integrated. [*See, e.g.,* 1933 Act Form S-3]

3. **Registration of Securities Professionals Under the 1934 Act:** [§753] In addition to the registration requirements of section 12, other provisions of the 1934 Act require the registration of national securities exchanges, broker-dealers, information processors, and clearing agencies.

a. **Registration of national securities exchanges:** [§754] The 1934 Act defines an "exchange" [SEA §3(a)(1); *and see infra,* §§1602 *et seq.*], and requires such an exchange to register with the S.E.C. unless exempt [SEA §6].

(1) **Effect of registration requirement:** [§755] It is unlawful for any broker, dealer, or other securities exchange to employ any means of interstate commerce for the purpose of using the facilities of a national exchange unless the national exchange is registered (or exempt from registration) under the Act.

(2) **Agreement to comply:** [§756] National exchanges must also agree to comply with the 1934 Act and to enact rules governing the conduct of exchange members. [SEA §6]

(3) **Regulation of transactions:** [§757] The 1934 Act also regulates various types of transactions entered into by stock exchange members. For example, the S.E.C. tries to avoid any conflicts of interest, particularly where a member of the exchange is acting as a broker (agent) *and* as a dealer (buying or selling from his own inventory) at the same time. [SEA §11; *and see infra,* §1660]

b. **Registration of broker-dealers:** [§758] The 1934 Act provides for the registration with the S.E.C. of all brokers and dealers who transact securities business in interstate commerce. [SEA §15(b); *and see infra,* §1695]

(1) **Standards of conduct:** [§759] The 1934 Act authorizes the S.E.C. to adopt and enforce rules for broker-dealers with respect to training, qualifications, and financial responsibility. [SEA §15(b)]

(2) **Censure, suspension, revocation, or denial of registration:** [§760] As a means of enforcing its standards of conduct, the S.E.C. is authorized under the 1934 Act (after a hearing) to censure a broker-dealer, or to deny, suspend, or revoke its registration for various types of prohibited conduct (*e.g.,* a willful violation of the securities laws). [SEA §15(b)(4)]

(3) **Indirect regulation:** [§761] Not only does the S.E.C. regulate the conduct of brokers and dealers directly, but it also oversees the regulation of their conduct by regulating the organizations of which they are members. Section 15A of the 1934 Act, for example, permits self-regulatory organizations of over-the-counter brokers and dealers to register with the S.E.C. (one organization, the National Association of Securities Dealers or "NASD," has done so). All brokers and dealers doing an interstate

securities business in the over-the-counter market must belong to the NASD, which regulates their conduct. Also, broker-dealers that belong to the national securities exchanges are regulated directly by the exchanges, which in turn are regulated by the S.E.C.

c. **Registration of information processors:** [§762] "Securities information processors" (*i.e.,* persons who distribute information about securities, price quotations, or transactions) are required to register with the S.E.C. and make periodic reports. [SEA §11A(b)]

d. **Registration of back-office agencies:** [§763] Transfer agents, clearing houses, and others involved in the mechanical completion of securities trades are also required to register and make periodic reports. [SEA §17A]

   (1) **Transfer agents:** [§764] Banks often have stock transfer departments, and public corporations usually appoint outside transfer agents, who are responsible for keeping track of all shareholders and stock certificates, and seeing that all transfers are completed properly.

   (2) **Clearing houses:** [§765] The exchanges normally have clearing houses, through which all certificates that are part of exchange transactions pass, so that proper deliveries will be made.

4. **Additional Reporting Requirements Under the 1934 Act:** [§766] In addition to the reports required of registered companies and 1933 Act issuers under section 13 of the Act (*see supra*, §§748-749), other persons and entities are also required to file reports which the Commission uses to administer the provisions of the Act.

a. **Reports by five percent owners of registered securities:** [§767] The 1934 Act requires that the purchaser of 5% or more of a class of equity security registered under the Act must file certain information with the S.E.C., the issuer of the security, and the securities exchange (if the securities are traded on a national exchange). [SEA §13(d); *see* SEA Rule 13d-1]

   (1) **Information to be included:** The report must contain information concerning the purchaser, the source of the funds used to purchase the securities, any plans the purchaser may have to acquire more of the same securities, and any plans it may have to attempt to change the issuer's business or corporate structure.

   (2) **Purpose:** This provision is aimed at regulating "tender offers," *i.e.,* situations where Company A makes an offer to buy the shares of Company B from Company B's shareholders directly. (For a discussion of tender offers, *see infra*, §§978 *et seq.*)

b. **Reports by officers, directors, and ten percent security holders:** [§768] Officers and directors of the issuing corporation, and 10% owners of a class of security registered under section 12 must file a report with the S.E.C. listing their holdings, and must also file a monthly update of any changes therein. This report helps the S.E.C. enforce section 16(b) of the Act (which prevents insiders from making profits on short-term purchases and sales of registered securities). [SEA §16(a); *and see infra*, §§1282 *et seq.*]

c. **Reports by national securities exchanges and associations:** [§769] National securities exchanges and securities associations are required to file many reports concerning changes in their rules, discipline of their members, etc. [SEA §§6, 15]

d. **Reports by institutional investors:** [§770] In 1975, Congress added section 13(f) to the 1934 Act. This statute authorizes the S.E.C. to adopt rules creating an institutional disclosure system. The S.E.C. has since adopted rule 13f-1 and form 13F. Rule 13f-1 applies to institutional (banks, etc.) investment managers who exercise investment discretion over accounts having $100 million or more in exchange-traded or over-the-counter-quoted equity securities. The managers must file form 13F annually with the S.E.C., reporting the number of shares of each security held, the aggregate fair market value of the shares, and information about the nature of their investment discretion and voting authority.

e. **Liability for filing false reports:** [§771] Filing materially false reports with the S.E.C. under the 1934 Act can result in civil and criminal liability. [*See, e.g., infra*, §780; *and see* S.E.C. v. Jos. Schlitz Brewing Co., 452 F. Supp. 824 (E.D. Wis. 1978)]

5. **Regulation of Practices Relating to Stock Ownership:** [§772] The 1934 Act also regulates the following matters relating to stock ownership:

   a. **Proxy solicitation:** [§773] The Act governs the manner in which voting proxies are solicited from the shareholders of companies whose securities are registered under section 12 of the Act. [SEA §14; *and see infra*, §§1128 *et seq.*]

   b. **Tender offers:** [§774] Sections 13 and 14 of the Act govern the practices used in making a tender offer (*see infra*, §978).

6. **Regulation of Accounting Records and Internal Controls:** [§775] The 1934 Act also requires that reporting companies (i) make and keep books, records, and accounts which, in reasonable detail, accurately and fairly reflect the financial transactions of the issuer, and (ii) devise and maintain a system of internal accounting controls sufficient to provide reasonable assurances that proper recording of transactions and control of assets is achieved. [SEA §13(b)(2)] Although the terminology of this section is very general and broad, the S.E.C. has indicated that it will not second-guess reasonable methods or reasonable business decisions of issuers, and that the objective of this provision is to reach knowing or reckless conduct.

7. **A National Securities Market:** [§776] The 1934 Act also establishes the goal of a "national market system" and directs the creation of a National Market Advisory Board to move the securities markets in that direction. [SEA §11A]

8. **Role of the S.E.C. in Administering the 1934 Act:** [§777] The Act grants specific powers to the S.E.C. for the purpose of administering its provisions. The S.E.C. has investigatory and study powers [SEA §§19, 21, 22], rule making powers [SEA §23], enforcement powers [SEA §§15, 19], and injunctive powers [SEA §21]. In addition, the S.E.C. has the power to control certain practices designed to manipulate securities market prices. [SEA §§9, 10; *and see infra*, §1720]

a. **Good faith reliance on S.E.C. rules:** [§778] The 1934 Act provides that good faith reliance on a rule adopted by the S.E.C. is a complete defense to liability under the Act. Even though an S.E.C. rule is amended or rescinded, or declared by the courts to be invalid, one who has relied thereon in good faith will not be liable under the Act. However, once a rule has been judicially declared invalid, it may no longer be relied upon. [B.T. Babbitt, Inc. v. Lachner, 332 F.2d 225 (2d Cir. 1964)]

9. **Role of Other Regulatory Agencies:** [§779] The 1934 Act also grants power to the Board of Governors of the Federal Reserve System over "margin requirements"—*i.e.,* requirements applicable to customer loans from banks, broker-dealers, and other lending sources to purchase securities, and broker-dealer borrowings from regulated banks. In addition, the Federal Reserve System, the Controller of the Currency, and the Federal Deposit Insurance Corporation have power under the Act to regulate the issuance and exchange of bank securities. [SEA §12(i)]

10. **Liability Provisions of the 1934 Act:** [§780] Several provisions of the Securities Exchange Act provide—either expressly or by implication—for a private cause of action for damages resulting from a violation of its provisions.

    a. **Express provision for damages:** [§781] Some of these liability provisions *expressly* provide for private damage actions. For example, section 18 of the 1934 Act provides for the liability of anyone making false or misleading statements in any document filed pursuant to the SEA or any rule or regulation adopted thereunder (such as misstatements made in a filing pursuant to sections 12(b) or (g)). Recovery is allowed to any person who purchased or sold a security in reliance on such false statements at a price which was affected by the statement.

        (1) **Note:** Additional provisions for express liability include section 16(b) of the Securities Exchange Act, regulating short-swing trading (*see infra,* §1282) and section 9 of the same Act, regulating market manipulation (*see infra,* §1709).

    b. **Implied provision for damages:** [§782] Although other regulatory provisions do not expressly provide for private damage actions, in many instances a private right of action has been implied by the courts. [*See, e.g.,* SEA §10(b); SEA Rule 10b-5, *infra,* §§795 *et seq.*] The trend of decisions, however, is definitely away from implying private causes of action. This trend is based on the Supreme Court's strict interpretation of statutory language, the supposed intent of Congress to avoid overlap of the federal securities laws, and the concern that in the past it has been too easy to recover under the securities laws, resulting in the filing of unwarranted suits in order to recover their settlement value. Also, the Court appears willing to leave more regulation to the states, and to free the marketplace from undue regulation in general.

        (1) *Cort v. Ash* **test:** [§783] In *Cort v. Ash,* 422 U.S. 66 (1975), the Supreme Court established a four-prong test to determine whether a private right of action would be implied from a federal statute:

            (i) Is the plaintiff one of the *class for whose benefit the statute was enacted?*

(ii) Is there any indication of *legislative intent*, explicit or implicit, *to create or deny such a remedy?*

(iii) Is implication of a private cause of action *consistent with the underlying purposes* of the legislative scheme?

(iv) Is the cause of action one *traditionally relegated to state law?*

In more recent cases, the Supreme Court seemed to emphasize the first three prongs of the test. Ultimately then the issue is whether Congress intended to create a private right of action. [*See* Transamerica Mortgage Advisors, Inc. v. Lewis, 444 U.S. 11 (1979)]

(a) **Example:** An accounting firm was sued for filing false financial reports with the S.E.C. for a bankrupt broker-dealer. The suit was pursuant to section 17(a) of the 1934 Act, which does not expressly provide for a private right of action. In considering whether to find an implied right, the Court looked primarily at the intent of Congress. The Court stated that where Congress intended a private remedy, it usually said so. Also, the Court found that: there was no indication that Congress intended a private right of action; there was an express remedy for filing false reports under section 18 of the 1934 Act; and section 17(a) was not passed specifically to protect persons such as plaintiff (*i.e.,* section 17(a) was passed *primarily* to see that the S.E.C. received needed regulatory information). Thus, the Court found no implied right of action. [*See* Touche Ross & Co. v. Redington, 442 U.S. 560 (1979)]

(b) **Compare:** Other situations occur where the courts have recognized implied private actions, such as for the failure to register as a reporting company when required to do so pursuant to section 12(g) of the 1934 Act. [*See* Kerber v. Kakos, 382 F. Supp. 625 (N.D. Ill. 1974)]

(2) **Express remedy:** [§784] Where the Act provides an express remedy for a specific situation, it is unlikely that the courts will also imply an additional remedy under some other provision of the 1934 Act. [*See, e.g.,* Cramer v. General Telephone & Electronics, 443 F. Supp. 516, *aff'd,* 582 F.2d 259 (3d Cir. 1978)]

(3) **Conclusion:** [§785] In the past, questions concerning the liability sections of the securities laws were fairly easy because the courts tended to construe the provisions broadly and expansively to grant causes of action in order to accomplish the regulatory purposes of the acts. Now these questions are more complex, requiring careful analysis to determine whether a cause of action exists and, if so, under which sections of the securities laws.

c. **Defenses:** [§786] There are a number of possible defenses to causes of action brought under the various sections of the 1934 Act. For the most part, these defenses are discussed in connection with the various liability provisions to which they relate. In addition, *Burks v. Lasker,* 441 U.S. 471 (1979), approved the application of a state-law defense to shareholder derivative actions based on violations of the federal securities laws. (Shareholder derivative actions are discussed at length in the Corporations Summary.) Specifically, *Burks* recognized as a valid defense a motion by the corporation to have the action dismissed because there has been a determination by a committee of the board consisting of "independent" directors to the effect that the continuation of the litigation is not "in the best interests" of the corporation.

(1) **Applicable state law:** [§787] Under *Burks*, the federal court must first determine whether the board has the power under applicable state law to dismiss a derivative action on this basis. If it does, the court must determine whether the directors who purported to make the decision were, in fact, independent and acted in good faith, after making a reasonable investigation. It is not clear whether these questions are themselves to be determined according to state or federal law.

   (a) **Note:** There are many interests that might disqualify directors from being independent: *e.g.,* a direct pecuniary interest of the director in the transaction at issue; the interest of a director in retaining her position as a director; the interest of a director arising from any business relationships with the corporation (which presumably could be terminated by the officers), etc.

(2) **Conflict with federal securities laws:** [§788] The second question is whether permitting termination of the derivative suit would conflict with the policy of the particular federal securities laws involved. The Court in *Burks* found that this type of decision by the board did not conflict with the policy of either the Investment Company Act of 1940 or the Investment Advisors Act. Of course, these two acts rely heavily on the concept of independent, outside directors of investment companies to protect shareholders (*compare* this policy with that of rule 10b-5, discussed *infra*).

   (a) **But note:** There are many types of transactions where derivative suits are brought. The type of action may have a bearing on the outcome of the cases. *Burks* involved an allegation of simple negligence on the part of certain of the officer-directors, in which other outside directors were not involved.

(3) **Compare—class actions:** [§789] In many instances, the federal courts do not make a careful distinction between the types of cases that may be brought as derivative actions and those that must be class actions. Where this is the case, this defense may be obviated by the plaintiff bringing the action as a class action rather than as a derivative suit.

(4) **Alternative standard:** [§790] In *Burks*, the Court indicated that it was a question of state law as to whether a shareholder's derivative suit could be dismissed by an independent committee of directors. Under state law in that case, the standard of review of the committee's decision by the courts was simply whether the committee acted independently, thoroughly, and in good faith. State laws are not uniform on the standard of review, however, and thus in *Joy v. North*, 692 F.2d 880 (2d Cir. 1982), the court held that Connecticut state law required the reviewing court to make an independent determination of the balance of probabilities as to a

likely future benefit to the corporation from continuing the litiga-tion. If the court determines that the likely recoverable damages, dis-counted by the probability of finding liability, are less than the costs to the corporation in continuing the action, it should dismiss the case. The costs that may be properly taken into account are attorneys' fees, other out-of-pocket expenses related to the litigation, time spent on the case by corporate personnel, and indemnification expenses. Where the court finds a likely net return but one which is insubstantial in relationship to shareholder equity in the corporation, it may then con-sider the impact of two indirect expenses—distraction of key per-sonnel and potential lost profits that may result from the publicity of a trial.

## 11. Role of the Courts

a. **Jurisdiction:** [§791] The district courts of the United States have *exclusive* original jurisdiction over violations of the 1934 Act or its regulations and over actions brought to enforce liabilities or duties thereunder. Nationwide service of process is available. [SEA §27]

b. **Court powers**

(1) **Powers of subpoena and contempt:** [§792] The district courts have the power to issue orders to appear, to give testimony, and to produce evi-dence. In addition, a district court can cite persons in contempt for any violations of its orders. [SEA §21]

(2) **Mandamus:** [§793] Upon application by the S.E.C., the district courts may issue writs of mandamus to compel various corporate acts.

c. **Judicial review:** [§794] Appeal from decisions of the S.E.C. is to the District of Columbia Circuit, or to the circuit in which the appellant resides or has its principal place of business. [SEA §25] S.E.C. decisions must be based on a record, and the S.E.C.'s decision on factual issues is conclusive if based on "substantial evidence." Appeal from district court decisions is also to the cir-cuit courts, then by certiorari to the United States Supreme Court.

## B. CIVIL LIABILITY UNDER RULE 10b-5 OF THE 1934 ACT [§795]

Rule 10b-5 is one of the most significant remedy provisions of the 1934 Act. It was adopted by the S.E.C. to strengthen the remedies provided in the 1933 Act against fraud in the purchase and sale of securities. (*See supra*, §699.) A discussion of rule 10b-5 fol-lows and will give substantive meaning to the many references to the rule throughout the remaining sections of this Summary.

1. **Statement of Rule 10b-5:** [§796] Rule 10b-5, which was enacted by the S.E.C. pursuant to section 10(b) of the 1934 Act, makes it unlawful, in connection with the *purchase or sale of any security*, for any person, directly or indirectly, by the use of *any means or instrumentality of interstate commerce*, or of the mails, or of any facility of any national securities exchange:

a. *To employ any device, scheme, or artifice to defraud;*

b. *To make any untrue statement of a material fact, or to omit to state a material fact* necessary in order to make the statements made, in light of the circumstances under which they were made, not misleading; or

c. *To engage in any act, practice, or course of business which operates or would operate as a fraud or deceit* upon any person.

2. **Securities and Transactions Covered**

a. **Securities covered:** [§797] Rule 10b-5 is very broad in its application to securities transactions; however, a "security" must be involved before the rule will apply. The term "security" is broadly defined (about the same as under the 1933 Act; *see supra,* §§123 *et seq.; and see* section 3(a)(10) and (11) of the 1934 Act). However, the trend of the Supreme Court is to limit the scope of the federal securities laws to the regulation of public trading markets and large, interstate investment promotions. One way to do this is to narrow the definition of "security." [*See, e.g.,* Marine Bank v. Weaver, *supra,* §139—a certificate of deposit is not a security]

b. **Transactions covered:** [§798] The courts have indicated that all securities transactions are covered under rule 10b-5, whether on exchanges, over-the-counter transactions, or private transactions to purchase or sell. [Fratt v. Robinson, 203 F.2d 627 (9th Cir. 1953)]

   (1) **Rule applies to purchases and sales:** [§799] The antifraud provisions of the 1933 Act apply only to fraud committed *by the seller* against purchasers (*see supra,* §§619 *et seq.*). Thus, prior to the adoption of rule 10b-5, there was no general prohibition against fraud committed by a purchaser in inducing a seller to sell.

      (a) *Section 9 of the 1934 Act* applies to both purchases and sales, but only in the context of securities listed on a national exchange (*see infra,* §1721); *section 15* also applies to both, but only in securities transactions in which broker-dealers are involved (*see infra,* §1867).

      (b) *Rule 10b-5* applies to both purchases and sales in *all contexts.*

c. **Interstate commerce requirement:** [§800] Before rule 10b-5 will apply to a transaction, some means of interstate commerce, or the mails, or a national securities exchange must be used "in connection with" the purchase or sale of securities.

   (1) **Note:** The courts have held that the misrepresentation itself need not be transmitted by these jurisdictional means; it is sufficient if *any part* of the securities transaction occurs in interstate commerce (*e.g.,* delivery of the securities). [Fratt v. Robinson, *supra*]

   (2) **And note:** *Any use* of the interstate means is sufficient; the transaction itself need not involve more than one state. Thus, most courts have held that an intrastate telephone call is sufficient to establish jurisdiction since the phone lines also carry interstate messages. [*See, e.g.,* Dupuy v. Dupuy, 511 F.2d 641 (5th Cir. 1975)]

3. **Jurisdiction, Venue, and Service of Process:** [§801] One of the reasons that rule 10b-5 has been used so frequently is its broad procedural provisions.

    a. **Jurisdiction:** [§802] The federal courts have exclusive jurisdiction over all civil actions arising under rule 10b-5, regardless of the amount in controversy.

    b. **Venue:** [§803] Suit may be brought in the district court of any district in which any act or transaction in violation of the rule occurred; or in any district where the defendant is found, resides, or transacts business.

    c. **Service of process:** [§804] Process may be served anywhere in the world.

    d. **Supplemental jurisdiction:** [§805] In addition, supplemental jurisdiction (*see* Civil Procedure Summary), state actions for common law fraud can be joined in federal court with the rule 10b-5 action.

4. **Elements of Cause of Action:** [§806] A plaintiff must prove each of the following elements to establish a cause of action under rule 10b-5.

    a. **Fraud, misrepresentation, or deception:** [§807] Rule 10b-5 requires that there be some misrepresentation, omission, deception, or fraud in connection with the purchase or sale of securities. Issues may arise in several contexts as to whether the requisite "deception" has actually occurred.

        (1) **Situations where no one is deceived:** [§808] Where fraudulent conduct has occurred but has not deceived anyone, the question arises whether there has been any "deceit" within the meaning of rule 10b-5.

            (a) **Fraud committed by all corporate directors:** [§809] The cases have held that even where all the directors of a corporation are involved in perpetrating the deception (*e.g.,* issuing stock for spurious assets), there may still be a "fraud" on the corporation and its shareholders. [Hooper v. Mountain States Securities Corp., 282 F.2d 105 (5th Cir. 1960); *and see* Pappas v. Moss, 393 F.2d 865 (3d Cir. 1968)—corporation and minority shareholders were defrauded when directors-majority shareholders issued themselves stock at below-market prices]

            (b) **Fraud committed by all directors and shareholders:** [§810] There is even authority for a corporate recovery when all the directors *and* all the shareholders of the corporation are involved in the fraud. This type of situation may occur at the time a corporation is being formed, if all parties dealing with the corporation are part of the fraudulent scheme.

                1) **Example:** All of the officers, directors, and shareholders of American Southern Publishing Co. participated in a plan to issue 412,000 shares of $1 par value stock to buy a bankrupt company that they personally controlled. The plan then called for an issuance of additional stock to the public for $2 per share. The trustee in bankruptcy of American was granted a cause of action under rule 10b-5 against the promoter-shareholders on the basis of their plan to defraud *future*

*shareholders and creditors.* [Bailes v. Colonial Press, Inc., 444 F.2d 1241 (5th Cir. 1971)]

(c) **Noninterested directors approve transaction:** [§811] Even where only noninterested directors vote to authorize the sale of a corporation's stock for inadequate consideration, such action may constitute a "deception" under rule 10b-5.

1) **Example:** A corporation and its joint venture partner (the controlling shareholder) discovered oil. The discovery was not publicly disclosed and was not reflected in the market value of the corporation's stock. A sale of stock at market prices to the controlling shareholder was held to have defrauded the corporation. *Rationale:* The controlling shareholder had "caused" the directors to issue the stock for inadequate consideration and without full disclosure of all material facts to all of the company's shareholders. [Schoenbaum v. Firstbrook, 405 F.2d 215 (2d Cir. 1968)]

2) **Compare:** Where disinterested directors approved a favorable change in a stock option plan for certain officers and other directors immediately before the corporation publicly announced it was repurchasing its own shares at a price substantially above the prevailing market price, the court held that approval of a transaction by a disinterested majority of the board possessing authority to act and fully informed of all relevant facts sufficed to bar a rule 10b-5 claim that the corporation or its shareholders were deceived, provided that the board is not controlled or dominated by the officer-beneficiaries. [Maldonado v. Flynn, 597 F.2d 789 (2d Cir. 1979)]

(2) **Breach of fiduciary duties as "fraud":** [§812] Federal courts have split on the question of whether a breach of duty under state corporate law (*e.g.,* breach of the directors' fiduciary duty or duty of care) is a sufficient "fraud" for 10b-5 purposes. But the trend is clearly *against* finding a rule 10b-5 cause of action in these circumstances.

(a) **Cause of action permitted:** [§813] Some decisions can be read as permitting a 10b-5 cause of action even though a state cause of action (and an adequate state remedy) for breach of fiduciary duty is available. For example, a 10b-5 cause of action has been allowed in situations where a corporation (and its directors) issued stock for inadequate consideration—a breach of fiduciary duty under state law. [Hooper v. Mountain States Securities Corp., *supra;* Pappas v. Moss, *supra;* Schoenbaum v. Firstbrook, *supra*]

(b) **Cause of action denied:** [§814] Other decisions have held that no cause of action is available under 10b-5 where state law provides an adequate remedy. The cases typically read the *Schoenbaum* decision, above, as granting the 10b-5 cause of action *not* on the basis of the breach of fiduciary duty (*i.e.,* issuance of stock for inadequate consideration), but because the directors of the company failed to disclose all material information to the minority shareholders—a traditional basis for a 10b-5 cause of action.

1) **Example:** No 10b-5 cause of action was allowed where a corporation merged its 52%-owned subsidiary into itself on unfair terms. The transaction was held not "deceptive" within rule 10b-5 because the corporation had disclosed all of the material facts concerning the transaction to the minority shareholders of the subsidiary. [Popkin v. Bishop, 464 F.2d 714 (2d Cir. 1972)]

2) **Example:** When a 90%-owned subsidiary (A) was merged into its parent corporation (B) under a state short-form merger statute (*i.e.,* a statute allowing mergers without a vote of the shareholders of the surviving corporation), the minority shareholders of A alleged a breach of rule 10b-5 by B in that (i) the cash terms of the merger were unfair, and (ii) there was no business purpose for the merger except to freeze out the minority shareholders. The Court held that because all material facts concerning the transaction were disclosed and the transaction was permitted by state law, rule 10b-5 did not provide a cause of action for breach of fiduciary duty. [Santa Fe Industries, Inc. v. Green, 430 U.S. 462 (1977)]

    a) The Court in *Santa Fe* indicated that the state should be free to regulate the conduct of corporate officials—except for the specific areas regulated by federal statute—and that expansion of rule 10b-5 to cover this form of activity (*i.e.,* an alleged breach of duty by corporate fiduciaries) would be an unnecessary intrusion into the powers of the states.

    b) There were two bases stated for the *Santa Fe* decision:

        1/ Rule 10b-5 was intended to deal only with deception and manipulation in connection with the sale of securities. Conduct not constituting fraud is outside of the scope of the rule.

        2/ A private right of action under rule 10b-5 exists only for misrepresentations or omissions (*i.e.,* fraud) and when the cause of action is not one typically relegated to the states. Here the conduct was traditionally regulated by the states, and there was an adequate state remedy. Rule 10b-5 was not meant to regulate corporate mismanagement in general.

    c) After *Santa Fe*, plaintiffs who wish to state a rule 10b-5 cause of action will attempt to show that there has been a material misrepresentation or omission of fact, whatever other fraud or deception might be present. [*See, e.g.,* Goldberg v. Meridor, 567 F.2d 209 (2d Cir. 1977)] In *Goldberg*, the court stated that the plaintiff could maintain a rule 10b-5 cause of action as a minority shareholder objecting to the terms of the merger of the company into its parent corporation. The court found the needed "deception" on the basis that (although applicable law did not require a shareholder vote) the parent corporation had failed to state all material facts to the subsidiary's shareholders and had printed affirmative misrepresentations in a laudatory press release. State law did not provide for dissenter's appraisal rights as in *Santa Fe*, but state law did provide for an injunction. Also the misrepresentations and omission would have been relevant to obtaining such an injunction (whereas *Sante Fe* held that advance notice to the shareholder of the merger made no difference and was not a misrepresentation since there was no action available under state law for an injunction).

d) *Santa Fe* can be read to bar a rule 10b-5 action in the absence of misstatements or omissions, *or* in the ***presence*** of the availability of adequate state remedies. [*See* Healey v. Catalyst Recovery of Pennsylvania Inc., 616 F.2d 641 (3d Cir. 1980)—a rule 10b-5 cause of action exists if there has been a material misstatement or omission of fact, even if there was an adequate state remedy; dissent argued that the rationale of *Santa Fe* is that there is no rule 10b-5 cause of action for a material omission as long as there is an adequate state remedy for the breach of a fiduciary duty]

e) In a later case, arising under 1934 Act section 14(e) (prohibiting fraud in tender offers), the Court held that misrepresentation or nondisclosure is required. The Court pointed out, in this connection, that rule 10b-5 contains language similar to section 14(e). One possible inference from this is that rule 10b-5 actions must be based on allegations of misrepresentation or nondisclosure; other kinds of "fraud" might not be sufficient. [Schreiber v. Burlington Northern, Inc., 472 U.S. 1 (1985)]

b. **Misrepresentation or deceptive omission of a fact:** [§815] Rule 10b-5 requires that the misrepresentation or omission must be of a "fact."

(1) **Fact vs. opinion:** [§816] In many areas of the law, a distinction is made between "fact" and "opinion"; however, this distinction is not always clear-cut in securities cases. Although the S.E.C. has traditionally taken the position that only "historical facts" need be disclosed (*see supra*, §246), this view is not always appropriate nor followed in rule 10b-5 cases.

(a) **Prediction of earnings:** [§817] If XYZ Corp. predicts that its net income for the coming year will be $1 per share, this is an "opinion" or a "prediction" and not a "historical fact." But since it is clearly an important factor for any investor to consider, courts in securities cases may find that such a prediction is a "fact" if it is disclosed. [*See, e.g.,* Beecher v. Able, 374 F. Supp. 341 (S.D.N.Y. 1974)]

1) **Actions based on inaccurate predictions:** [§818] Outside the context of registration statements covering new issues (regulated by the Securities Act of 1933), companies have issued earnings projections for many years, but there have been few actions under rule 10b-5 for inaccurate forecasts.

   a) **Example:** Where a company had substantial earnings in the previous year but projected that its earnings for the coming year would be "nominal," and it actually sustained a $52 million loss, it was held that the company was *not* liable under rule 10b-5 since the forecast was not "intentionally" or "recklessly" made (*i.e.,* there was some basis in fact for the forecast). [Beecher v. Able, Fed. Sec. L. Rep (CCH) ¶95,303 (1975) (second opinion); *and see* discussion of scienter, *infra,* §880]

   b) **Compare:** Where a company's prediction of its earnings for the year ending in three months was in error by more than 50%, the court held that it was a triable issue whether the "fact" of the company's earnings had been misrepresented. [Marx v. Computer Sciences Corp., 507 F.2d 485 (9th Cir. 1974)]

2) **Disclosure of facts underlying prediction:** [§819] At present, there is no requirement that an issuer predict what its earnings will be. However, if it chooses to do so, the issuer must have a reasonable basis for its forecast. The disclosures accompanying the projections should help an investor to understand the basis for the projections, and should also include a discussion of the assumptions underlying the projections. [Regulation S-K item 10(b); *see supra,* §246]

   a) **Note:** While there is no requirement to disclose earnings projections, issuers are encouraged to do so. [*See* SA Release No. 6084 (1979); *and see supra,* §246]

(b) **Balance sheet figures:** [§820] A similar problem exists with respect to financial figures in the balance sheet of a company. For example, XYZ may have purchased real estate for $100,000 and carried this cost figure on its balance sheet. However, the *market value* of the property may now be $200,000. The problem with disclosing market value is that this value is often uncertain, and hence such information is in the nature of an "opinion."

1) **Disclosure of replacement cost:** [§821] Traditional accounting principles dictate that cost (or market value, if it is lower) be used to record assets. But it is relevant to an investor's decision to know the "real" value of the company's assets. Therefore, the S.E.C. now requires that certain large companies registering securities under the 1933 Act disclose in their financial statements the *replacement cost* of fixed assets and inventories. [S.E.C. Accounting Series Release No. 190 (1976)]

2) **Example—failure to disclose market value:** [§822] Where the controlling shareholder of a company bought additional shares from other shareholders without disclosing that the market value of the company's tobacco inventory was substantially higher than the book value reflected in the company's financial statements, the court sustained a cause of action based on material nondisclosure. [Speed v. Transamerica Corp., 235 F.2d 369 (3d Cir. 1956)]

   a) **Note:** In this case, market price was easily determined, and the information was in the possession of a corporate "insider" who was taking advantage of other shareholders.

   b) **Compare:** Consider the result in *Speed* to a later case—*Gerstle*—involving an alleged violation of the proxy rules. There the court held that a company (A) had no obligation to disclose in its proxy statement, seeking approval of merger with another company (B), opinions about the market value of B's properties. However, the court did say that if A had any firm offers to buy the properties of B, it would have to disclose this "fact." [Gerstle v. Gamble-Skogmo, Inc., 478 F.2d 1281 (2d Cir. 1973)]

(c) **"Fair" price statements:** [§823] When one company attempts to acquire another, some form of proposal is often made to the target company's shareholders. For example, in a tender offer, the proposal is made directly to the shareholders; in a classic merger, the target's shareholders vote to approve the proposal (*i.e.,* the merger agreement). When such a proposal is made, the target's board of directors is usually called upon to recommend voting for or against the proposal. In making this recommendation, the board must take into account the fairness of the price proposed to be paid, and the recommendation will include the board's opinion as to the price. If the board states that it believes the price is "high," and in hindsight the price proves to be low, is the board's statement actionable as a misrepresentation of fact?

   1) **Truth of belief distinguished from truth of subject matter:** [§824] Statements of belief are factual in two senses:

      a) **Truth of the belief:** [§825] A statement that "the Board believes that $42 per share is a fair price for your stock" is false if, in fact, the board does not believe that the price is fair. [*See* Virginia Bankshares, Inc. v. Sandberg, 501 U.S. 1083 (1991)]

      b) **Truth of the underlying subject matter:** [§826] A statement that "the Board believes that $42 per share is a fair price" is also an *endorsement* of the price, and may be taken to mean that there is sufficient extrinsic evidence to support a price of $42. Thus, the statement may be false if in fact $42 is *not* a fair price; *i.e.,* if there is no reasonable basis to conclude that $42 is a fair price. [*Virginia Bankshares, Inc. v. Sandberg, supra*]

2) **Lawsuit must be based on untruth of both belief and subject matter:** [§827] In the *Virginia Bankshares* case, *supra*, the Supreme Court held that under SEA rule 14a-9 (a provision of the proxy rules analogous to rule 10b-5), it is not sufficient for the plaintiff merely to prove that the belief stated was not actually held; in addition the plaintiff must show that the ***statement was false as to its subject matter*** (*e.g.*, in the example above, that $42 was not a fair price).

   a) **Rationale:** [§828] To find liability on mere disbelief, with out any proof that the statement was false as to its subject matter, would rest "an otherwise nonexistent section 14(a) liability on psychological enquiry alone." [*Virginia Bankshares, Inc. v. Sandberg, supra*] This, in turn, could produce frivolous litigation instituted in the hope of achieving a quick settlement; the alternative for the board, in such a case, would be to undergo lengthy discovery aimed at determining what each board member believed at the time of the statement.

3) **Note:** While the holding in *Virginia Bankshares* might seem surprising to some, because it appears to immunize the board from liability for false statements about their own beliefs, the Court pointed out that it would be "rare to find a case with evidence solely of disbelief . . . without further proof that the statement was defective as to its subject matter."

(2) **Omission of fact:** [§829] In some cases, it may be clear that a material fact (*i.e.*, one that would be important to an investor's decision) is left out of the disclosure document. For example, in soliciting proxies for a vote on a merger, management does not disclose that it has received an additional offer to merge with a different company at a higher price. But the question of ***how much*** must be disclosed—in order to disclose all that is important—is always difficult to answer.

   (a) **Standards for disclosure:** [§830] Various decisions have indicated that the "average investor" must be able to understand the disclosures made and the essential features of the transaction. The information must also be concise and relevant; *i.e.*, not everything that is arguably related need be disclosed. [*Feit v. Leasco Data Processing Equipment Corp.*, *supra*, §674; *and see infra*, §833—materiality]

      1) **"Fairness" as standard:** [§831] It may be that what the courts are really doing is reviewing transactions for their substantive "fairness," and determining what should have been disclosed on the basis of whether the transaction seems to have been fair or unfair.

   (b) **Failure to disclose importance of facts:** [§832] There have been a few cases in which the courts have found liability for an omission of material fact where the party failed to state the importance of facts that were disclosed. [*See, e.g.,* Robinson v. Penn Central Co., Fed. Sec. L. Rep. (CCH) ¶93,334 (E.D. Penn. 1971)]

c. **Materiality:** [§833] The misrepresented or undisclosed fact must be "material" to the investor's decision. A number of tests of "materiality" have been applied by the courts.

(1) **Substantial likelihood of significance:** [§834] In the context of a proxy statement, the Supreme Court has held that the test for materiality is whether there is a *substantial likelihood* that a reasonable shareholder would consider the fact of significance in determining how to vote. The Court did not require proof of a substantial likelihood that disclosure would have caused the reasonable shareholder to change his vote, but only that the omitted fact would have assumed *actual significance.* [TSC Industries, Inc. v. Northway, Inc., 426 U.S. 438 (1976)] This "substantial likelihood" standard has also been adopted for rule 10b-5 cases. [Basic, Inc. v. Levinson, 485 U.S. 224 (1988)]

(2) **Probability vs. magnitude:** [§835] When it is uncertain whether an event will or will not occur, the question whether there is a substantial likelihood that a reasonable shareholder would consider the event significant is difficult to answer. The Supreme Court has adopted a test for such circumstances that balances two issues: First, *how likely* is the occurrence of the event? Second, if the event occurs, *how significant* would it be to the issuer (and, thus, to the investor in the issuer's securities)? [Basic, Inc. v. Levinson, *supra*]

(a) **Example:** The stock of Company B began to trade heavily, due to rumors that B was engaged in preliminary merger negotiations with C. Officers of B were asked on several occasions whether merger negotiations were underway; each time, they denied the rumors. Eventually C made a tender offer for B, and B revealed that negotiations had in fact been underway for some time. The Court held that the proper test for materiality would balance, at the time of each denial, the likelihood that the negotiations would bear fruit against the significance (to B) of the merger if it were to take place. Thus, a very low probability (approaching zero) of success in the merger discussions would justify nondisclosure. Because the merger unquestionably would be very significant to B, however, even a small increase in the likelihood of success would make the fact of the negotiations material. [Basic, Inc. v. Levinson, *supra*]

(3) **Materiality in a nondisclosure context:** [§836] Some courts also draw a distinction between the test for materiality in a misrepresentation case and in a case in which there was a failure to disclose a material fact, holding that in a failure to disclose case, the test for materiality is more stringent. [*See, e.g.,* S.E.C. v. Texas Gulf Sulphur Co., 401 F.2d 833 (2d Cir. 1968)] In other words, courts confronting a failure to disclose may require more of the plaintiff than they would in a misrepresentation case. This makes sense in cases based on transactions occurring over the stock exchange, since it is really impossible for those with inside information

to disclose everything to the market before trading. To do this, they would have to write and deliver a registration statement before trading, which obviously is not feasible.

d. **Reliance and transaction causation:** [§837] The plaintiff must show that he *actually relied* on the material fact that was misrepresented. There are essentially two elements of reliance that must be proved in a rule 10b-5 case: (i) The plaintiff must have actually *believed* the misrepresentations and (ii) the belief must have been the *cause* of (*i.e.,* a "substantial factor" in) the plaintiff's entering the transaction ("transaction causation"). [List v. Fashion Park, Inc., 340 F.2d 457 (2d Cir. 1965)] In addition, reliance is treated differently in cases arising from face-to-face transactions than in those arising from impersonal transactions on a securities exchange. Both kinds of cases are discussed below.

(1) **Substantial factor test:** [§838] In showing transaction causation (*i.e.,* reliance), the plaintiff must be able to show that his belief in the misrepresentation was a "substantial factor" in his having entered the transaction. [List v. Fashion Park, Inc., *supra*]

(a) **Relationship to causation:** Reliance in the "substantial factor" sense is closely related to causation, because this kind of reliance requires the plaintiff to show that the misrepresentation or omission caused the plaintiff to enter into the transaction. (For a complete discussion of the causation requirement, *see infra,* §§891-897.)

(2) **Relationship to materiality:** [§839] When a fact is shown to be material, this is a strong indication that it was a substantial factor in causing the plaintiff to enter the transaction. On this basis, reliance would seem to flow as a logical assumption from a showing of materiality; however, one does not necessarily follow the other. For example, the defendant might be able to prove that the plaintiff knew that a material fact was misrepresented, but entered the securities transaction anyway. [List v. Fashion Park, Inc., *supra*]

(3) **Face-to-face security transactions:** [§840] The role of reliance in face-to-face transactions differs according to whether the plaintiff claims that an *affirmative misrepresentation* was made by the defendant, or that the defendant *failed to disclose a material fact.*

(a) **Affirmative misrepresentations:** [§841] Cases involving material misrepresentations (rather than omissions) and a personal, face-to-face relationship between plaintiff and defendant usually require the plaintiff to show that he *actually relied* on defendant's material misrepresentation. [*See, e.g.,* Reeder v. Mastercraft Electronics Corp., 363 F. Supp. 574 (S.D.N.Y. 1973)]

(b) **Nondisclosure cases:** [§842] If, on the other hand, the defendant failed to disclose a material fact, then in a case involving a face-to-face relationship between the plaintiff and the defendant *reliance by the plaintiff is generally presumed.* This is so in part because of the difficulty of proving that the plaintiff "relied" on something that was not said. The presumption of reliance can be rebutted by showing that the plaintiff did *not* rely. Note, however, that in many cases such a showing will amount to a demonstration that the particular undisclosed facts or circumstances were not "material" to this plaintiff. [*See, e.g.,* Affiliated Ute Citizens v. United States, 406 U.S. 128 (1972); Barnes v. Resource Royalties, Inc., 795 F.2d 1359 (8th Cir. 1986); Shores v. Sklar, 610 F.2d 235 (5th Cir. 1980)]

(4) **Open-market (impersonal) transactions:** [§843] Most securities transactions now occur over an exchange or in the over-the-counter market; the buyer and seller remain unaware of each other's identities, and the transactions, in that sense, are impersonal. These transactions pose their own set of problems regarding "reliance." First, in an impersonal market, "reliance" in the conventional sense seldom, if ever, exists—because the plaintiff does not know who the defendant is, she is also ignorant of the other's misrepresentations (and certainly of any omissions), at least until after the transaction is consummated. In addition, cases arising out of market transactions are usually brought by large classes of plaintiffs. To require proof of reliance, in the conventional sense, would make such class actions difficult or impossible to maintain: the individualized element of reliance would overwhelm the common elements of the case, and therefore no class could be certified. Such cases would have to be brought individually, and as a result, many smaller investors (who lack the resources to bring such a suit) would have no remedy at all. Various doctrines have evolved as the courts struggle with these difficulties, but the law in this area has not yet jelled. To clarify the issues, it is again useful to sort the cases into those involving affirmative misrepresentations and those involving nondisclosure.

(a) **Affirmative misrepresentations**

1) **Types of cases:** [§844] When defendants make affirmative misrepresentations, and plaintiffs purchase or sell securities on the *open market*, two types of cases arise:

a) **Actual reliance:** [§845] It is possible that the plaintiff actually read and relied on fraudulent statements made by the defendant. This would fulfill even a strict reliance requirement.

b) **"Fraud on the market":** [§846] Alternatively, the plaintiff may allege that the defendant's statements were material and affected the market price and that the plaintiff relied on the integrity of the market price in purchasing or selling securities. Note that such an allegation does not show whether the plaintiff actually relied on the misrepresented fact; rather, this method is used when either plaintiff cannot establish that he personally read or relied on the defendant's statements or when a class of plaintiffs is suing and wishes to avoid the individual issue of reliance (*see supra*, §843). [Basic, Inc. v. Levinson, *supra*, §834]

2) **Lack of reliance as a defense:** [§847] Note that even where the plaintiff is permitted to recover without proving actual

reliance, the defendant can prevent recovery by proving that the plaintiff did *not* rely. Thus, as with face-to-face transactions involving nondisclosure (*see supra*, §842) the "fraud on the market" doctrine provides only a rebuttable presumption of reliance from a showing of misrepresentation of a material fact. [*See* Basic, Inc. v. Levinson, *supra*; Blackie v. Barrack, 524 F.2d 891 (9th Cir. 1975)]

(b) **Nondisclosure of material facts:** [§848] In cases where the defendant fails to disclose material facts, and the plaintiff purchases or sells securities on the open market, the reliance issue must be phrased somewhat differently. Here, the question is whether the plaintiff would have acted differently had he known of the undisclosed facts; in other words, did the plaintiff rely on the absence, or nonoccurrence, of the material facts?

1) **Using materiality to infer reliance:** [§849] To answer this hypothetical question, courts have understandably permitted an inference of reliance to be raised from the fact of materiality. That is, if the plaintiff can show that a *reasonable investor* would have considered the fact important in making a decision (materiality), then no reliance need be shown. [*See* Schlick v. Penn-Dixie Cement Corp., 507 F.2d 374 (2d Cir. 1974)]

2) **Class actions:** [§850] As with affirmative misrepresentations, courts in nondisclosure class actions have tended to dispense with the reliance requirement. [*See, e.g.,* Blackie v. Barrack, *supra*]

3) **Nonreliance as a defense:** [§851] Since it is extremely unlikely that actual reliance could be shown in a nondisclosure case—or that the defendant could show the plaintiff's nonreliance—these opinions seem to dispense with the reliance requirement altogether. However, if by some remarkable set of circumstances the defendant *could* prove that the plaintiff would not have relied on the omission, then the plaintiff could *not* recover. [Basic, Inc. v. Levinson, *supra*]

e. **Purchase or sale requirement:** [§852] The deceptive transactions must occur in connection with the "purchase or sale" of a security by the plaintiff.

(1) **Definition of "purchase or sale":** [§853] "Purchase" and "sale" are defined to include "any contract to purchase or sell." [SEA §3(a)(13), (14)]

(a) **More than mere offer:** [§854] Thus, something *beyond a mere offer* to purchase or an offer to sell must be involved before rule 10b-5 will apply. [Blue Chip Stamps v. Manor Drug Stores, 421 U.S. 723 (1975)]

(b) **Contract to purchase or sell:** [§855] But at the same time, an actual completed purchase or sale need not be involved since the Act indicates that "any contract" to purchase or sell is sufficient. So, for example, it has been held that a pledge of securities as collateral in a loan transaction constitutes a "sale" of the securities to the pledgee, so that the pledgor is a "seller" and the pledgee a "purchaser." [Rubin v. United States, 449 U.S. 424 (1981)]

1) **Oral contracts:** [§856] Some doubt exists as to whether an oral contract makes the parties purchasers or sellers so as to give them standing under rule 10b-5. Some courts hold that an oral contract is sufficient. [*See, e.g.,* Threadgill v. Black, Fed. Sec. L. Rep. (CCH) (Transfer Binder) ¶91,402 (D.C. Cir. 1984)] Other courts hold that an oral contract is not enough, at least when it is not enforceable under the Statute of Frauds. [*See, e.g.,* Kagan v. Edison Bros. Stores, Inc., 907 F.2d 690 (7th Cir. 1990); Pelletier v. Stuart-James Co., 863 F.2d 1550 (11th Cir. 1989)]

(c) **Merger:** [§857] A merger transaction is an example of a purchase and sale transaction; *i.e.,* A, a shareholder in X Corp., exchanges his shares for shares in Y Corp. when X and Y are merged. [S.E.C. v. National Securities, 393 U.S. 453 (1969)]

(2) **Purchase or sale by the plaintiff:** [§858] The *plaintiff* must either be an actual "purchaser" or an actual "seller" of securities to have standing to maintain a 10b-5 cause of action. [Blue Chip Stamps v. Manor Drug Stores, *supra*]

(a) **Example:** Plaintiff, a shareholder of Newport Steel Corp., brought a shareholder derivative suit alleging a rule 10b-5 violation against the president of Newport. The president had caused Newport to reject a merger proposal (which would have benefited all Newport shareholders), and then sold his own 40% controlling interest for double the market price to the same interested purchaser. The court held that the plaintiff had no standing to sue, since *neither* the corporation nor the plaintiff was a purchaser or seller as required by rule 10b-5. [*See* Birnbaum v. Newport Steel Corp., 193 F.2d 461 (2d Cir.), *cert. denied,* 343 U.S. 956 (1952)]

(b) **Purpose of requirement:** [§859] The purpose of the "purchase or sale" requirement is to prevent vexatious litigation, since plaintiffs might otherwise bring 10b-5 actions simply to extract a settlement from the defendant, by threatening to use the liberal federal discovery rules to disrupt the defendant's business. [Blue Chip Stamps v. Manor Drug Stores, *supra*]

(c) **Contexts in which the issue arises**

1) **Depreciation in value:** [§860] The "purchase or sale" issue may arise when the plaintiff has not actually sold his stock, but argues that the stock has depreciated in value due to the misrepresentations made by the defendant. [*See, e.g.,* Greenstein v. Paul, 400 F.2d 580 (2d Cir. 1968)—plaintiff had no standing since there was no purchase or sale]

    2) **Transaction prevented:** [§861]  The issue may also arise when the plaintiff claims he would have purchased stock but for the negative statements made by the defendant. [*Blue Chip Stamps v. Manor Drug Stores, supra*—no rule 10b-5 cause of action because no actual purchase or sale]

  (d) **Exceptions to requirement of purchase or sale by plaintiff**

    1) **Derivative suits:** [§862]  Normally, a plaintiff who brings a rule 10b-5 action to enforce a fiduciary responsibility of corporate management will sue in a representative capacity on behalf of the corporation (*i.e.,* a shareholder derivative suit). In such a suit, the courts have held that the individual plaintiff shareholder need *not* be an actual purchaser or seller; it is sufficient if there is a purchase or sale *by the corporation.* [Superintendent of Insurance v. Bankers Life & Casualty Co., 404 U.S. 6 (1971)]

    2) **Action for injunction:** [§863]  Another exception to the purchase or sale requirement exists where the plaintiff seeks an injunction against the defendant's continued market manipulation in violation of rule 10b-5. Here, status as a *shareholder* (without an actual purchase or sale in connection with the defendant's activity) may be sufficient for standing to bring the injunctive action. [Mutual Shares Corp. v. Genesco, Inc., 384 F.2d 540 (2d Cir. 1967)]

      a) **But note:** The view that an injunction plaintiff under rule 10b-5 need not be a purchaser or seller may be diminishing in influence—the federal circuit court most recently addressing the issue held that an *injunction plaintiff was not entitled to an exception* to the *Blue Chip* rule (that only a purchaser or seller has standing to bring a rule 10b-5 action). [Cowin v. Bresler, 741 F.2d 410 (D.C. Cir. 1984)]

    3) **Forced sale:** [§864]  Where the plaintiff in effect is forced to sell his stock, the purchase-sale requirement will be held to have been met. [Alley v. Miramon, 614 F.2d 1372 (5th Cir. 1980)]

      a) **Example:** Through a series of deceptions, the defendant liquidated the corporation, and the plaintiff shareholder received none of the liquidation proceeds. The liquidation was held to be a "forced sale." Since it was an objectively verifiable event, the court found that there was no chance that the basic rationale of the *Blue Chip Stamps* case would be offended by this decision. [Alley v. Miramon, *supra*]

  f. **"In connection with" requirement:** [§865]  The language of rule 10b-5 requires that the defendant's misrepresentation or deception be "in connection with" the purchase or sale of a security by the plaintiff.

(1) **Defendant need not be an actual purchaser or seller:** [§866] Formerly, the defendant was required to be directly involved in the purchase or sale transaction, either in a face-to-face transaction with the plaintiff-buyer or by trading in the market. This was known as the requirement of *privity*. (*See infra*, §§874 *et seq.*) But subsequent decisions have indicated that a defendant can also be held liable—without actually purchasing or selling the securities—as long as his fraudulent activity is "in connection with" the purchase or sale of a security by the plaintiff.

   (a) **Example:** [§867] The defendant corporation was held liable for a misleading press release that might have caused reasonable investors to rely thereon in the purchase or sale of the company's securities. [S.E.C. v. Texas Gulf Sulphur Co., *supra*, §836]

(2) **Relationship to other rule 10b-5 requirements:** [§868] The "in connection with" requirement is conceptually related to the other rule 10b-5 requirements of reliance and causation.

   (a) **The reliance requirement:** [§869] One of the requirements for application of rule 10b-5 is that the plaintiff must have relied on the defendant's material misrepresentation or omission. A showing of such reliance would *tend* to establish the necessary connection or "nexus" between the defendant's misrepresentation and the purchase or sale by the plaintiff by proving "transaction causation"—*i.e.*, that the misrepresentation was the cause of the plaintiff entering the securities transaction. (*See* discussion of reliance, *supra*, §§837 *et seq.*)

      1) **But note:** A showing of reliance does not necessarily satisfy the "in connection with" requirement. The plaintiff could have actually relied on the defendant's fraudulent conduct, and yet the court might still find that the nexus was not sufficiently close to meet the requirement. Or the connection might be sufficiently close with no reliance by the plaintiff on the misrepresentation.

   (b) **The causation requirement:** [§870] Another rule 10b-5 requirement is that of causation—*i.e.*, that the plaintiff's economic loss was caused by the defendant's wrongful conduct. If the plaintiff is able to show that the defendant's wrongful conduct "caused" such a loss, this will tend to establish the "in connection with" requirement between the defendant's conduct and the plaintiff's purchase or sale of securities. (*See* discussion of causation *infra*, §§891 *et seq.*) However, the courts conceivably could interpret the "in connection with" requirement more narrowly, so that causation of loss might exist without satisfying the requirement.

(3) **Problem of remoteness:** [§871] The most common issue in this area is whether the fraud or deception is so remote from the plaintiff's purchase or sale transaction as to sever the requisite "connection."

   (a) **Fraud as part of the securities sales transaction:** [§872] Where the defendant's fraud occurs as part of the securities transaction itself, it is clear that a sufficient connection exists. For example, A sells securities to B, without disclosing material inside information: Assuming fraud, the necessary connection with B's purchase exists.

(b) **Fraud separate from the sales transaction:** [§873] The more difficult cases are those where the defendant's fraud is not directly related to and does not involve the terms of the securities transaction itself. For example, where a corporation's articles provided that terminated employees could not continue to own stock, and the defendants, through a series of deceptive steps, induced the board of directors to remove plaintiffs (who owned 45% of the close corporation) as officers and employees, the court held that the repurchase of the securities (a sale by the plaintiffs) was not "in connection with" the deceptive acts by the defendants. [Ketchum v. Green, 557 F.2d 1022 (3d Cir.), *cert. denied*, 434 U.S. 940 (1977)] The court reasoned that (i) the connection between the series of deceptive acts and the final sale of securities was too indirect and remote; (ii) the real purpose of the deceptive acts was to remove plaintiffs as officers and employees, not to get their stock back, and so the issue was really one concerning a struggle for management control; and (iii) the dismissal of the rule 10b-5 cause of action was consistent with the trend in the Supreme Court to leave most corporate management issues to regulation by state law. (*See supra*, §§812-814.)

g. **Privity requirement**

(1) **Early view:** [§874] As stated above (*supra*, §866), the early view required the plaintiff to be in a direct privity relationship with the defendant to maintain a rule 10b-5 action.

(a) **Face-to-face transactions:** [§875] This view was developed in cases where the plaintiff had dealt face-to-face with the defendant in a securities transaction. Thus, A (the seller) would have negotiated personally with B (the purchaser) in the sale of securities owned by A.

(b) **Transactions in the securities market:** [§876] Rule 10b-5 actions later began to be brought in securities transactions consummated on the securities exchanges and in the over-the-counter market, where the buyer normally does not know who the seller is. At first the courts held that—due to lack of privity—a rule 10b-5 action could **not** be sustained in these circumstances. [*See, e.g.,* Joseph v. Farnsworth Radio & Television Corp., 99 F. Supp. 701 (S.D.N.Y. 1951)]

1) **Example:** In *Joseph*, corporate officers sold stock over the exchange without releasing adverse financial information about their company. In two purchases made 13 and 44 days later, respectively, plaintiffs bought company stock in transactions over the exchange. The court denied recovery, holding that there must be a "semblance of privity" to recover under rule 10b-5. [*Aff'd in* Joseph v. Farnsworth Radio & Television Corp., 198 F.2d 883 (2d Cir. 1952)]

(2) **Current view:** [§877] The more recent decisions have moved away from requiring privity.

(a) **Situations involving affirmative misrepresentations:** [§878] Where the defendant has made affirmative misrepresentations, rule 10b-5 has been applied even though there is *no privity* of contract between buyer and seller.

1) **Example:** Rule 10b-5 was held to apply where the defendant corporation and some of its officers released false financial information, on which plaintiffs relied in buying the company's securities over an exchange. Even though there was no contemporaneous selling of the company's securities by the company or any of its officers, the plaintiff's lack of privity with those who made the affirmative misrepresentations was no bar to the action. [Heit v. Weitzen, 402 F.2d 909 (2d Cir. 1968)]

2) **Note:** *Heit v. Weitzen* in effect overruled *Joseph, supra.*

(b) **Situations involving nondisclosure:** [§879] Some courts distinguish cases in which material facts are never disclosed at all, and require some semblance of privity between the plaintiff and the defendant; others, however, have thus far *not* imposed such a restraint on recovery.

1) **Example—privity required:** Defendant received inside information concerning a merger. In April, he purchased stock in the target company. He sold the stock two months later, realizing a profit of $13,000. Plaintiffs purchased and sold stock in the target company between May and June, realizing a profit, but lacking the inside information that defendant had and therefore failing to realize the full profit that would have been theirs had they known the information. Plaintiffs sued defendant for $361,000 (the amount of profit they would have earned had they known the inside information). The court denied recovery, holding that there must be some causal connection between the defendant's trading and the plaintiff's loss; *i.e.,* there must be at least some privity between the parties. [Fridrich v. Bradford, 542 F.2d 307 (6th Cir. 1976), *cert. denied,* 429 U.S. 1053 (1977)]

2) **Example—no privity required:** An underwriter of a proposed new issue of debentures discovered revised, lower company profit projections and passed this information on to its customers, who sold their company securities before any public disclosure of the projections was made. The plaintiffs were contemporaneous purchasers of company securities. The plaintiffs could not trace their shares to the defendants; thus, no actual privity was established. Nevertheless, the court held that this was *not* a bar to a rule 10b-5 cause of action. [Shapiro v. Merrill Lynch, Pierce, Fenner & Smith, Inc., 495 F.2d 228 (2d Cir. 1974)]

h. **Scienter:** [§880] A major issue in actions brought under rule 10b-5 concerns the degree of culpable intent required of the defendant.

(1) **Analysis of rule 10b-5 language:** [§881] Rules 10b-5(1) and 10b-5(3) expressly prohibit fraudulent conduct. But the language of rule 10b-5(2) does not speak in terms of intentional fraud or deception; it simply makes it unlawful to "make any untrue statement of a material fact or omit to state a material fact necessary in order to make the statements made . . . not misleading."

   (a) **Comment:** Thus, it is arguable that actions brought under subsections (1) and (3) must meet a common law fraud standard (*i.e.,* actual knowledge or intentional action); while subsection (2) may establish ***absolute liability*** for a misstatement or omission, regardless of the defendant's care.

(2) **Actual knowledge requirement:** [§882] For a long time there was a split of authority as to whether the plaintiff was required to show actual knowledge of the fraud by the defendant in order to recover.

   (a) **Second Circuit—actual knowledge required:** [§883] The Second Circuit has consistently maintained that in private actions for damages there must be a showing of the defendant's ***actual knowledge*** of the misrepresentation, or such reckless disregard of the truth as to amount to actual knowledge. [Fischman v. Raytheon Manufacturing Co., 188 F.2d 783 (2d Cir. 1951); Lanza v. Drexel & Co., 479 F.2d 1277 (2d Cir. 1973)—corporate director not liable without actual knowledge of misrepresentations made by others, and director did not have affirmative duty to investigate what representations had been made]

   (b) **Ninth Circuit—case-by-case approach:** [§884] In contrast, the Ninth Circuit held that the fact situations dealt with under rule 10b-5 are so complex that no one standard is sufficient to decide all cases. Thus, it held that the proper approach was to analyze the defendant's duty to the plaintiff and to closely examine the facts of their relationship in each case. In some instances, negligence would be sufficient to find liability; in other instances, actual knowledge would be required. [White v. Abrams, 495 F.2d 724 (9th Cir. 1974)]

   (c) **Resolution by the Supreme Court—scienter required:** [§885] The proper standard to be applied in private actions has now been mostly resolved by the Supreme Court. For liability to exist under rule 10b-5, it must be shown that the defendant had "*scienter*," *i.e.,* actual intent to deceive, manipulate, or defraud. [Ernst & Ernst v. Hochfelder, 425 U.S. 185 (1976)]

      1) **Facts of *Hochfelder*:** In *Hochfelder*, the defendant (an accounting firm) audited the books of a small securities firm and prepared its financial statements filed with the S.E.C. and the Midwestern Stock Exchange. Plaintiffs were customers of the firm who had given the firm's president money to be invested in "escrow accounts." The president, however, embezzled the

money, and, to prevent detection of his fraud, had a firm rule that no mail addressed to him could be opened by any other person. Plaintiffs claimed that if the defendant had not been negligent in its audit, it would have discovered the rule against opening the president's mail, would have investigated, and ultimately would have discovered the fraud. As it was, no reports of the escrow accounts ever showed up in the financial statements prepared by the defendant.

   2) **Holding:** The issue in *Hochfelder* was whether rule 10b-5 applies where the defendant has been ***negligently*** nonfeasant in performing its duties, thus aiding and abetting the perpetration of a fraud. The Supreme Court held that defendant was ***not*** liable unless plaintiff could prove that the defendant acted with scienter (which, said the Supreme Court, includes ***intentionally*** fraudulent conduct).

(3) **Reckless conduct:** [§886] The Supreme Court in *Hochfelder* reserved the question whether a defendant who lacked actual knowledge of a fraud, but acted recklessly, might be liable under rule 10b-5. Circuit courts addressing the issue after *Hochfelder*, however, have uniformly held ***that recklessness is enough*** to establish liability under rule 10b-5.

   (a) **Definition:** [§887] Reckless conduct has been defined as "highly unreasonable [conduct], involving not merely simple, or even inexcusable negligence, but an extreme departure from the standards of ordinary care, and which presents a danger of misleading buyers or sellers that is either known to the defendant or is so obvious that the actor must have been aware of it." [Sundstrand Corp. v. Sun Chemical Corp., 553 F.2d 1033 (7th Cir.), *cert. denied*, 434 U.S. 875 (1977)]

   (b) **Defense of lack of "due diligence":** [§888] At common law, plaintiffs in fraud cases were sometimes stymied by the "lack of due diligence" defense; the essence of which was that the plaintiff's reliance on the defendant's omissions or misrepresentations was not justified, and would have been prevented had the plaintiff exercised "due diligence." The trend in rule 10b-5 cases, however, is to limit the availability of this defense, as described below.

      1) ***Prior to Hochfelder***, the approach of the federal courts had varied somewhat; but essentially, the courts had adopted a standard of ***negligence*** in determining whether a plaintiff had exercised due diligence in purchasing securities. [*See* Dupuy v. Dupuy, *supra*, §800]

      2) ***Following Hochfelder***, the courts have reexamined the due diligence defense and have held that mere negligence on the plaintiff's part may not be enough to preclude a rule 10b-5 action. If the contributory fault of the plaintiff overrides the defendant's fraud, the plaintiff's action may have to reach the level of gross conduct as compared to the action of the

defendant. In other words, the plaintiff must have *justifiably relied* on the defendant's misrepresentation. [*See, e.g.,* Holdsworth v. Strong, 545 F.2d 687 (10th Cir. 1976)—plaintiff was not denied a cause of action under rule 10b-5 for failing to ascertain the corporation's financial status, since there was a basis for plaintiff to have trusted defendant's representations; plaintiff's conduct may have been negligent, but was not reckless; *and see* Dupuy v. Dupuy, *supra*]

a) **Defense applicable to face-to-face transactions only:** [§889] Note that to the extent the rule 10b-5 due diligence defense survives *Hochfelder*, it is properly applied only to face-to-face transactions. It would be manifestly unreasonable to require a purchaser on the exchange to investigate independently the condition of the company whose securities she is purchasing.

(4) **Standard of culpability for S.E.C. injunctions:** [§890] This portion of this summary generally deals with *private* (*i.e.,* nongovernment) litigation. However, the standard of culpability that must be proved by the S.E.C. to obtain an injunction has developed along lines similar to those applicable to private plaintiffs. For a long time, there was confusion among the lower courts concerning the degree of culpability to be applied in S.E.C. civil enforcement actions for an injunction pursuant to section 10(b) and rule 10b-5 of the 1934 Act. The confusion was resolved when the Supreme Court held that civil injunction actions brought under section 21(d) for violations of rule 10b-5 could be successful only on a showing of scienter by the defendant. [Aaron v. S.E.C., *supra*, §723] *Compare* the standard required of the S.E.C. in actions brought under *1933 Act section 17(a)*, *supra*, §783.

i. **Causation and causation-in-fact:** [§891] Courts have consistently stated that "causation" is a necessary element in a private action for damages under rule 10b-5. That is, the defendant's action must have "caused" the plaintiff's injury.

(1) **Standard for causation:** [§892] To show causation, the plaintiff must be able to show that the defendant's deception was a substantial factor in causing the loss. Note that this test is also applied to the reliance requirement, which is closely related to causation. (*See supra,* §§837-851.)

(2) **Types of situations in which causation questions arise:** [§893] Causation may become an issue in many different situations, for example:

(i) *Situations involving defendant's mismanagement* (*e.g.,* stealing of corporation assets);

(ii) *Affirmative misrepresentations* made by the defendant about the issuer (*e.g.,* that conditions are better or worse than they really are);

(iii) *Nondisclosures of material information* about the issuer (*e.g.,* withholding important positive or negative information); or

(iv) *Situations where the corporation itself is the seller or buyer* (e.g., where the corporation sells or repurchases its stock at a price that is too high or too low).

Each of these situations must be carefully examined to determine whether the violation of rule 10b-5 is the **actual cause** of the plaintiff's loss. Thus, where directors of a corporation authorize a sale of stock for inadequate consideration, it is clear that their action has caused a loss to the corporation and its shareholders. But where management of the corporation breaches some fiduciary duty (such as engaging in a transaction in which they have a conflict of interest), this may or may not be the cause of a drop in the price of stock bought by the plaintiff.

(3) **Relationship to other elements of a rule 10b-5 cause of action:** [§894] The causation requirement is conceptually related to other elements of a rule 10b-5 cause of action—specifically, materiality (*supra,* §§833 *et seq.*) and reliance (*supra,* §§837 *et seq.*).

(a) **The materiality requirement:** [§895] It seems almost inevitable that a court would find that causation has been shown once materiality has been proved (*i.e.,* that a reasonable investor would have considered the fact important in making a decision). In cases arising from nondisclosure in face-to-face transactions, the Supreme Court has held that causation (and reliance) may be presumed when material facts are withheld in violation of an obligation to disclose them. [*See* Affiliated Ute Citizens of Utah v. United States, *supra,* §842]

1) **Note:** It is also conceivable, however, that a fact could be material but not the cause of loss. For example, it may be material to know that management engages in transactions in which their interest and the corporation's conflict, but this may not be the cause of the plaintiff's loss (*i.e.,* the price of the stock that the plaintiff bought might have gone down due to general market factors).

(b) **The reliance requirement:** [§896] The plaintiff establishes reliance on a material fact by showing that it was (or, in nondisclosure cases, would have been) a substantial factor in causing him to **enter the transaction** in which he experienced a loss. (*See supra,* §§837-851.) The factors of reliance and causation are so interrelated that sometimes the courts appear not to make a distinction between them (*i.e.,* transaction causation—reliance—is equated with loss causation), and, in fact, sometimes it is difficult or impossible to make an adequate distinction.

1) **Example:** Suppose that the earnings of XYZ Corp. have gone down, and this information is disclosed by XYZ to A (a shareholder who then sells his stock), but not to B. B then buys XYZ stock without the benefit of the material information; on disclosure of the drop in earnings, the market price of XYZ stock declines and B loses money on his investment. B may be able to recover from XYZ, and perhaps from A as well. [Shapiro v. Merrill Lynch, Pierce, Fenner & Smith, Inc., *supra,* §879]

2) **Analysis:** It is clear in the above situation that the fact of XYZ's lower earnings was material. It is also clear that a reasonable investor (and the plaintiff here) probably would have relied on the fact had he known about it; thus, there is also reliance (transaction causation). But was it the nondisclosure that *actually caused* the loss?

    a) The answer must be "no," at least in the sense of the nondisclosure actually causing the drop in stock price. The stock price dropped simply as a result of XYZ's lower earnings.

    b) However, the subject of the nondisclosure was a material fact (*i.e.,* the lower earnings), the disclosure of which caused a drop in the market price of the stock. And the nondisclosure was the cause of the plaintiff entering the transaction (*i.e.,* had the plaintiff known the about the lower earnings, he would not have entered the transaction). Thus, since the nondisclosure was of a material fact, disclosure of which caused the loss, there is causation.

    c) In this case, a finding of reliance and causation amounts to essentially the same thing—*i.e.,* that the nondisclosure was the cause of the plaintiff entering the transaction.

    d) On the other hand, if the drop in the market price of XYZ stock had been due to a general economic decline, then loss causation might not exist. Even though there was a material nondisclosure that caused the plaintiff to enter the transaction, the undisclosed fact would not have actually caused the drop in market price of the XYZ stock (which, by hypothesis, was due instead to a general economic decline).

(4) **Causation in nondisclosure situations:** [§897] As seen above, the most difficult causation questions arise from an omission to disclose material facts. In these situations, the courts have at times proved willing to infer causation (and even reliance) upon a showing of materiality.

    (a) **Example:** Bank officers who were "making a market" (*i.e.,* buying and selling as principals) in restricted securities of the Ute Tribal Development Corporation failed to disclose to sellers of the securities that the price defendants were paying was less than could be obtained in the trading market (which the defendants were helping to create). The Court held that both *reliance and causation* of loss would be established if the facts withheld were found to be material. [Affiliated Ute Citizens of Utah v. United States, *supra*]

    1) **Note:** In the *Affiliated Ute* case, there was privity of relationship between the plaintiffs and defendants. Thus, although the language of the opinion is very broad in indicating that reliance and causation may be proved from the existence of an

undisclosed material fact, the Supreme Court could later decide to narrow this language by pointing out that the facts here presented a particularly appropriate case in which to infer the existence of reliance and causation.

(b) **Example:** Tippees, who had received inside information about XYZ Corp.'s poor earnings, sold their stock in XYZ at about the same time that plaintiffs (without such information) had bought XYZ stock. The court held that, despite a lack of privity, causation could be established if "the plaintiff would have been influenced to act differently than he did act if the defendant had disclosed to him the undisclosed fact." Note that, again, this is the test for materiality. [Shapiro v. Merrill Lynch, Pierce, Fenner & Smith, Inc., *supra*]

(c) **And note:** Consider the discussion of the "market causation" theory in *Fridrich v. Bradford, supra,* §879. (*See infra*, §908.)

j. **Burden of proof:** [§898] In private civil causes of action for damages, the burden or proof is on the plaintiff to prove the rule 10b-5 cause of action by a *preponderance of the evidence.* [Herman & MacLean v. Huddleston, 459 U.S. 375 (1983)]

## 5. Remedies

a. **Implied private cause of action:** [§899] Although rule 10b-5 says nothing about a private right of action (the rule merely makes certain conduct unlawful), the courts have *implied* private causes of action for both rescission and damages. [Kardon v. National Gypsum Co., 69 F. Supp. 512 (E.D. Pa. 1946)]

b. **Action for rescission:** [§900] A seller suing under rule 10b-5 can recover her securities and a buyer can recover the amount paid for the securities. There are equitable limitations applicable to rescission, however, such as waiver, laches, estoppel, and impracticality (as in unwinding the merger of two publicly traded companies or if the defendant-purchaser has sold the securities purchased from the plaintiff).

c. **Damages:** [§901] There are several basic formulas for awarding damages in private actions: (i) plaintiff may be awarded *restitution, i.e.,* the difference between the value of what she gave up and the value of what she received in the transaction (out-of-pocket losses); (ii) plaintiff may recover damages based on the *defendant's profits*; or (iii) plaintiff may recover the "benefit of her bargain."

(1) **Restitution:** [§902] Most courts grant the plaintiff damages based on restitution (what she has lost), but the restitution formula is applied differently by different courts.

(a) **Value measured after "reasonable time":** [§903] Some courts have placed a time limitation on measuring the plaintiff's damages. Thus, the plaintiff would recover the difference between the value of what she gave up—as of a reasonable period of time after the discovery of the fraud—and the value of what she received. [Mitchell v. Texas Gulf Sulphur Co., 446 F.2d 90 (10th Cir. 1971)]

1) **Example—plaintiff as seller:** XYZ Corp. knows, but does not disclose, very favorable news about its ore exploration activity. During this time, A sells 100 shares of XYZ stock for $10 per share. Shortly thereafter, XYZ discloses the news and its stock quickly goes to $20 per share. A discovers the fraud soon after the news is disclosed. Her damages will be measured as of a reasonable time after the discovery of the fraud, when a reasonable person would have sought to mitigate damages by repurchasing the shares she had sold (*e.g.,* at the time the stock reached $20 per share). Her damages will thus be $1,000 ($20 minus $10 equals $10 per share x 100 shares). Even though the stock may continue to appreciate to $30, A cannot measure her damages at this amount.

2) **Plaintiff as buyer:** If the plaintiff is a defrauded buyer, damages are then calculated on the basis of what would have been a reasonable time for the plaintiff to mitigate damages by selling the stock after discovery of the fraud.

(b) **Value measured at time of trial:** [§904] Some courts are more lenient, giving the plaintiff damages based on the difference between the value of the securities at the time of the trial and the value of consideration paid by or to the plaintiff. [Myzel v. Fields, 386 F.2d 718 (8th Cir. 1967), *cert. denied*, 390 U.S. 951 (1968)]

(2) **Defendant's profits:** [§905] Some courts prefer a "disgorgement of profits" rule to mere restitution. In such a court, a defrauded seller would sue for the profit the buyer had made on the transaction. [Ohio Drill & Tool Co. v. Johnson, 498 F.2d 186 (6th Cir. 1974)]

(3) **Benefit of the bargain:** [§906] Alternatively, the plaintiff may request damages in the amount she expected to receive compared to what she actually received (*e.g.,* the acquiring company promised to pay shareholders of the acquired company $62.50 per share of common stock and only paid $59 per share). Plaintiff may bring an action to recover the difference of $3.50 per share. [Osofsky v. Zipf, 645 F.2d 107 (2d Cir. 1981)]

d. **Unlimited liability:** [§907] An unresolved issue is whether a defendant can be held liable for the total amount of damages suffered by all plaintiffs in a rule 10b-5 case—despite the fact that this amount would far exceed the profit made by the defendant. There is authority that apparently would permit such unlimited damages.

(1) **Example:** In an affirmative misrepresentation case, the defendant was a corporate officer who had bought his company's stock on the basis of inside information. He was held liable to the plaintiffs who sued, with no apparent allowance for the fact that he also might later be sued by others who had also sold their stock on the exchange during the same period. If such others did sue, the defendant's liability could exceed his trading profits many times over. [Mitchell v. Texas Gulf Sulphur Co., *supra*]

(2) **Example:** In a nondisclosure case, the Second Circuit did not limit the possible extent of the defendant's liability; although in remanding the

case to the district court, it noted that the lower court should inquire into factors that could possibly circumscribe unlimited damages. [Shapiro v. Merrill Lynch, Pierce, Fenner & Smith, Inc., *supra*]

(3) **Attempts to limit liability:** [§908] A few courts have attempted to find a rationale for limiting a defendant's liability in a rule 10b-5 action. For example, one court held that for rule 10b-5 liability to exist, there must be *"trading causation"* between the plaintiff's losses and the defendant's trading on the basis of the undisclosed inside information. [Fridrich v. Bradford, *supra*]

   (a) **Facts of *Fridrich*:** Defendant, a broker, received inside information in April that Company Y was to merge with Company Z. Later that month, defendant purchased shares of Y in the over-the-counter market, and sold the stock in June, after the merger was announced, at a profit of $13,000. Plaintiffs, who had purchased and sold shares between May and June at a slight profit but without the benefit of the inside information, then sued defendant for damages of $361,000 (the additional profit they would have made had they known of the inside information and retained their stock until after the merger announcement). There was no privity between plaintiffs and defendant; plaintiffs' sales and defendant's purchases were not contemporaneous in time; and defendant had in no way "caused" plaintiff's trading (for example, there was no evidence that defendant's trading on the inside information had caused any fluctuation in the market price of Company Y's stock). The S.E.C., in a previous action, had already forced defendant to disgorge his $13,000 profit. [Fridrich v. Bradford, *supra*]

      1) **Holding:** The court held that merely possessing inside information does not result in liability. There must be some *causal connection* between the defendant's trading and the plaintiff's losses (a type of reliance requirement).

      2) **Comment:** Obviously, the court was trying to find some way to limit the defendant's damages, but the rationale of the case does not resolve many of the conceptual problems related to affirmative misrepresentations or nondisclosure of material information. For example, some affirmative misrepresentation cases have held that liability will be imposed even if the defendant does *not* trade in the issuer's stock—and such a rule may be necessary to force issuers to disclose material information to those trading in their stock. [Heit v. Weitzen, *supra,* §878]

   (b) **Example:** A corporation disclosed material inside information to a financial analyst in advance of general disclosure to the public, and the analyst used the information to trade in the company's shares (without, of course, disclosing the information). The court held that in a nondisclosure case the proper measure of damages is the postpurchase decline in market value for a reasonable time after public disclosure of the material information. There is a limit on the amount of recovery, however, to the amount gained by the tippee as a result of selling at the earlier date (rather than delaying sale until after the disclosure). [*See* Elkind v. Liggett & Myers, Inc., 635 F.2d 156 (2d Cir. 1980)] In *Elkind,* the evidence showed that the plaintiffs purchased and the defendant sold stock over the exchange when the information was undisclosed (at $55 per share); the disclosure was made and the stock dropped to $52, and a day later was at $46 per share. The defendant tippee's maximum liability is the price realized on sale ($55) minus the price of the stock within a reasonable time after disclosure (here $46 per share). If the total damages of plaintiffs exceed the total liability of the defendants, then the amount paid to each plaintiff is a pro rata share of the defendant's total liability amount.

e. **Punitive damages:** [§909]  Punitive damages are *not* available under rule 10b-5.

f. **Right to contribution:** [§910]  In 1993, the Supreme Court confirmed that a defendant in a case brought by a private plaintiff under rule 10b-5 has a right of contribution against other defendants found liable in the case. [Musick, Peeler & Garrett v. Employers Insurance Co., 113 S. Ct. 2085 (1993)]

g. **S.E.C. actions:** [§911]  This portion of the summary is concerned with *private* (*i.e.,* nongovernment) litigation. However, it is useful at this point briefly to note the remedies available to the S.E.C. in litigation under rule 10b-5. The S.E.C. may recommend a criminal action to the Justice Department under rule 10b-5 or an action for injunction, or may sue to recover trading profits made by the defendants. [S.E.C. v. Texas Gulf Sulphur Co., 312 F. Supp. 77 (S.D.N.Y. 1970), *aff'd,* 446 F.2d 1301 (2d Cir. 1971)] Where the S.E.C. sues a defendant that purchased securities based on inside information, the proper measure of damages is the difference between the price paid (*e.g.,* $5/share) and the price at which the security traded within a short time after the material information was disclosed to the public (*e.g.,* $10/share). [*See* S.E.C. v. MacDonald, 699 F.2d 47 (1st Cir. 1983)]

6. **Defenses:** [§912]  The following defenses are available to a defendant in a rule 10b-5 action.

a. **On the merits:** [§913]  The defendant may be able to defend on the merits of the case: *e.g.,* that full disclosure of the facts was made, that the statements made were true, that the untruthful statements were not material or did not cause the plaintiff's loss, or that the defendant lacked scienter.

b. **Other defenses:** [§914]  Other, procedural, defenses may also be available to the plaintiff.

(1) **Statute of limitations:** [§915]  Although there is no express statute of limitations applicable to rule 10b-5, the Supreme Court held in 1991 that actions brought under the rule would be subject to the same limitations period applicable to most other litigation under the 1933 and 1934 Acts: suit must be brought *within one year after discovery* of the facts constituting the violation, and in no event later than *three years after the violation took place.* The Court "borrowed" the period from 1934 Act section

9(e), noting that the same period applies to almost all actions expressly created under that Act (with the exception of section 16; *see infra*, §1393). [Lampf, Pleva, Lipkind, Prupis & Petigrow v. Gilbertson, 501 U.S. 350 (1991)]

(a) **Retroactivity:** [§916] Probably the most controversial feature of the *Lampf* case, *supra*, resulted from a different decision, announced the same day by the court. Under *James Beam Distilling Co. v. Georgia*, 501 U.S. 329 (1991), when a new rule is announced and then applied to the litigants in the case before the Court—which is precisely what happened in *Lampf*—that rule must be applied to litigants in all pending cases. Based on *Beam*, most federal courts applied the *Lampf* period retroactively and dismissed large portions of their rule 10b-5 dockets, including cases against some of the better-known securities fraud defendants of the 1980s, such as Michael Milken and Charles Keating.

(b) **Congressional response:** [§917] Congress, reacting to the possibility that billions of dollars in damages might become unrecoverable, adopted 1934 Act section 27A. The effect of section 27A is that rule 10b-5 cases pending on June 19, 1991 (the date of the Supreme Court's *Lampf* decision), are subject to the statute of limitations that would have applied in the absence of *Lampf*. Cases already dismissed pursuant to *Lampf* were to be reinstated upon motion made by the plaintiff within 60 days of the enactment of section 27A.

(c) **Pre-*Lampf* statute of limitations:** [§918] Because section 27A reinstates pre-*Lampf* law for cases pending at the time *Lampf* was decided, some familiarity with the pre-*Lampf* law is necessary. Briefly, before *Lampf*, there was a good deal of uncertainty surrounding the question of which statute of limitations applied to rule 10b-5 cases. Most courts applied a relevant state statute, for example, the state's statute of limitations for fraud, or the statute of limitations in its blue sky law. When the fraud statute was applied, it generally did not begin to run until discovery of the fraud; when the blue sky law was applied, the principle of **equitable tolling** generally was applied, under which the statute of limitations was tolled as long as the plaintiff remained ignorant of the fraud without any fault or lack of diligence on her part.

(2) **Laches:** [§919] A rule 10b-5 action can be brought either at law (for damages) or in equity (for rescission). When rescission is requested, the defendant has the equitable defense of laches (unfair delay by plaintiff). [Tobacco & Allied Stocks, Inc. v. Transamerica Corp., 143 F. Supp. 323 (D. Del. 1956), *aff'd*, 244 F.2d 902 (3d Cir. 1957)]

(3) **Other common law defenses:** [§920] Other common law defenses, such as in pari delicto (*i.e.,* equal fault), may be applicable to rule 10b-5 actions. However, courts are careful to subordinate such defenses to the primary objective of seeing that the purposes and policies of the securities acts are carried out. [*See* Bateman Eichler, Hill Richards, Inc. v. Berner, 472 U.S. 299 (1985)]

(a) **Example:** In *Bateman*, the Court held that the defense of in pari delicto did ***not*** prevent a tippee (who had been given false information) from suing the corporate insiders who passed on the false information. The court reasoned that barring such private actions would result in fraudulent schemes going undetected by the S.E.C., because there would be no incentive for plaintiff-tippees to bring such actions.

(4) **Lack of plaintiff's "due diligence":** *See* discussion *supra*, §888.

7. **Scope of Rule 10b-5 Actions**

a. **Where other 1934 Act provisions apply:** [§921] It is clear that rule 10b-5 applies to many situations where other provisions of the 1934 Act also apply. [Jordan Building Corp. v. Doyle, O'Connor & Co., 401 F.2d 47 (7th Cir. 1968)]

(1) **Example:** In *Jordan*, defrauded purchasers of securities brought a rule 10b-5 action against broker-dealers and the individual partners owning the broker-dealers for misrepresentations in connection with an issuer's registered offering of securities. The court held that rule 10b-5 applied to defrauded purchasers as well as to sellers, and that the remedies of the securities acts were ***cumulative*** and not mutually exclusive.

(2) **Example:** Rule 10b-5, an implied private remedy, has also been applied by some courts when an express statutory remedy (section 18) under the 1934 Act also applied to the transaction. [*See* Ross v. A. H. Robins Co., 607 F.2d 545 (2d Cir. 1979)] Section 18 creates a private remedy for false or misleading statements contained in any report filed with the S.E.C. under the 1934 Act. Its requirements for a cause of action are more stringent than for a rule 10b-5 action. Nevertheless, the *Ross* court permitted application of rule 10b-5 because ***false reports had been filed with the S.E.C.*** and had affected the price of the company's stock on the open market. [*See also* Wachovia Bank & Trust Co. v. National Student Marketing Corp., 650 F.2d 342 (D.C. Cir. 1980)—section 18 does ***not*** prohibit an implied action pursuant to rule 10b-5; the sections are different in that rule 10b-5's broader provisions are designed to apply to complex market manipulation schemes that the restrictive terms of section 18 do not cover]

b. **Buyers' actions against sellers:** [§922] Before the adoption of rule 10b-5, there were no provisions for actions brought by defrauded ***sellers*** against buyers. When the rule was adopted, it was thought to apply only to this situation. But the courts soon began to apply rule 10b-5 to situations involving defrauded buyers as well, which raised possible conflicts with the express liability provisions set forth in sections 11 and 12(1) of the 1933 Act (since the 1933 Act also applies to defrauded buyers). [*See* Fischman v. Raytheon Manufacturing Co., *supra*, §883] One rationale for providing cumulative remedies is that rule 10b-5 requires that the plaintiff prove scienter, whereas the private damages provisions of the 1933 Act do not require such a high degree of culpability. Hence, if the plaintiff can carry this higher burden of rule 10b-5, she should be freed from the restrictions of the 1933 Act liability sections.

c. **Where section 11 of the 1933 Act conflicts:** [§923] An action under section 11 applies specifically to a registration statement filed in connection with a securities offering. (*See supra*, §644.) Nevertheless, based on the rationale stated in the paragraph above, the Supreme Court has held that the availability of a section 11 action does not preclude resort to rule 10b-5. [Herman & MacLean v. Huddleston, *supra*, §898]

d. **Where section 12(2) of the 1933 Act conflicts:** [§924] There are also cases that have held that rule 10b-5 may be used where otherwise the plaintiff would have a cause of action under section 12(2) of the 1933 Act (*see supra*, §699). [*See, e.g.,* Ellis v. Carter, 291 F.2d 270 (9th Cir. 1961)] Thus, the plaintiff may choose between these sections on the basis of which cause of action is easier to prove. The following factors may prove relevant to her decision.

  (1) *Section 12(2)* is subject to the defendant's "due care" defense and has more stringent venue provisions.

  (2) *Rule 10b-5* requires that the plaintiff prove scienter—*i.e.,* an intentional (or perhaps reckless) misstatement or omission by the defendant.

e. **Where section 17(a) of the 1933 Act and rule 10b-5 both apply:** [§925] The language of section 17(a) of the 1933 Act (*see supra*, §718) and rule 10b-5 are almost identical; however, section 17(a)(3) applies only to fraud against purchasers while sections 17(a)(1) and (2) are broader in scope. Also, section 17(a) contains the word "offer," so that it applies to fraud not only in connection with sales, but also with offers to sell (while rule 10b-5 requires an actual purchase or sale; *see supra*, §§852-857). Furthermore, the Supreme Court has held that in *injunction* actions pursuant to section 17(a)(2) and (3), the culpability standard is only negligence, while in rule 10b-5 actions, scienter must be shown. If the Supreme Court were to uphold private damage actions under section 17(a), then negligence may also be the applicable standard in these situations. [*See* Aaron v. S.E.C., *supra*, §723]

  (1) **Civil remedy under section 17(a):** Thus, the question whether there is an implied civil remedy under section 17(a) is an important one since, if there is, it may afford a remedy in some situations not covered by rule 10b-5. At this point, however, the issue has not been decided by the Supreme Court, and the trend in the lower courts is away from an implied remedy under section 17(a). (*See supra*, §721.)

8. **Insider Trading and the Duty to Disclose:** [§926] Trading on inside information has been found by the courts to be a "fraud." Rule 10b-5 does *not* specifically mention "insiders," nor does it specifically require that a person having information not known by another disclose this information in a securities transaction. Nevertheless, the S.E.C. and the courts have applied rule 10b-5 to such transactions.

a. **Elements of rule 10b-5 in insider trading cases:** [§927] One would suppose that the elements of a cause of action for insider trading under rule 10b-5 would be the same as in other rule 10b-5 cases. (*See supra*, §§795 *et seq.*) The courts, however, have followed a different analytical path in disposing of insider trading cases under the rule (and remember that the rule does not expressly address the problem of insider trading). For these reasons, it is helpful to frame an analysis of insider trading situations a little differently. Basically, two relevant questions must be answered:

(i) Was the defendant an *insider, or a tippee*?

(ii) Did the defendant, directly or derivatively, *breach a duty* by trading or tipping?

(1) **Persons who may be liable for insider trading:** [§928] The persons who may be liable for insider trading under rule 10b-5 may be sorted into two categories: insiders and tippees.

   (a) **Insiders:** [§929] An "insider" is someone in possession of material information concerning securities that is not possessed by others who are trading in the issuer's securities. As a rule, the insider has this information by virtue of her relationship to the issuer. There are two key elements of insider status:

      (i) *The person must have a relationship that gives access*—directly or indirectly—to information about the issuer's securities intended only for business purposes and not for personal benefit; and

      (ii) *There must be an inherent unfairness* resulting from the insider taking advantage of the information, knowing that it is unavailable to those with whom the insider is dealing.

   Thus, for example, controlling shareholders, directors, officers, and corporate employees have all been held to be insiders when trading on material inside information.

   (b) **Tippees:** [§930] Tippees are persons who receive a tip from insiders and subsequently trade securities related to the tipped information. [*In re* Investors Management Co., SEA Release No. 9267 (1971); *In re* Cady, Roberts & Co., 40 S.E.C. 907 (1961); *and see* Dirks v. S.E.C., 463 U.S. 646 (1983)]

(2) **Breach of "fiduciary" duty:** [§931] The typical insider trading case consists of a purchase or sale by the insider or her tippee over an exchange without disclosing inside information. In such cases, the Supreme Court has held that *no violation of rule 10b-5 occurs unless the insider (or tippee) breaches a duty* in so trading. [*See* Chiarella v. United States, 445 U.S. 222 (1980)] This duty may be a duty of the insider to disclose all material information before trading in securities (the so-called disclose or abstain rule), or, in the case of persons not subject to the disclose or abstain rule, it may be a duty owed to an employer, or to the issuer, to use the information only for the issuer's benefit. The key is that some identifiable duty must be breached. The duty breached by insider trading is often found in fiduciary relationships, such as the principal-agent relationship or the employer-employee relationship. Consequently, it has become common to speak of the requirement of a breach of fiduciary duty in an insider trading case, although actually the required duty need not be

a fiduciary duty in a technical sense; rather, the term "fiduciary" is given a broader meaning here than in other contexts.

(a) **Who is a "fiduciary"?** [§932] *Texas Gulf Sulphur, supra,* §911, held that officers, directors, and key employees were all "fiduciaries" for purposes of rule 10b-5. As such, they all owed a duty to disclose all material information to shareholders before trading, or abstain from trading altogether. That the court included corporate officers and directors is not surprising, because these are commonly said to owe fiduciary duties to the corporation's shareholders. Including the other employees was somewhat more controversial; it is not clear that they would have fiduciary duties to Texas Gulf Sulphur's shareholders in cases not involving rule 10b-5.

(b) **Insiders' duty to disclose to purchasers:** [§933] When an insider sells to someone not already a shareholder, the insider technically does not owe the purchaser any fiduciary duty. Can rule 10b-5 be violated in such a case, even though technically no fiduciary duty exists between the buyer and seller at the time of the transaction?

   1) **Same duty applies:** [§934] The courts have held that *the same fiduciary duty applies to the insider* in such a case. A sale that would violate the insider's fiduciary duty if carried out with an existing shareholder may not be carried out with a person who, by that sale, becomes a shareholder. [*See* Dirks v. S.E.C., *supra*; Chiarella v. United States, *supra*; Gratz v. Claughton, 187 F.2d 46 (2d Cir.), *cert. denied*, 341 U.S. 920 (1951)]

(c) **Materiality:** [§935] For this duty of disclosure to arise, the information held by the insider must be "material" (*i.e.,* there must be a substantial likelihood that the information would have actual significance to a person buying or selling the issuer's securities).

   1) **But note:** The materiality and disclosure requirements in the rule 10b-5 insider trading context must mean something different than they do in the registration statement context under the 1933 Act (*see supra*, §571) and in the context of a proxy statement (*infra*, §999). To hold otherwise would prevent insiders from ever buying or selling the corporation's stock (both because they could not afford preparation of such a complete disclosure document and because in many cases they could not secure the issuer's cooperation in doing so).

(d) **Tippees and the duty to disclose:** [§936] The breadth of the duty to disclose is most significant in the context of *tippee liability* for insider trading. Because tippees usually are not insiders, they need not follow fiduciary standards in trading with shareholders of the issuer. Nevertheless, it is clear that rule 10b-5 prohibits at least some cases of trading by tippees. [*See* Dirks v. S.E.C., *supra*] Tippee liability under rule 10b-5 is discussed *infra*, §§945 *et seq.*

(3) **Application:** [§937] The principles above have been applied to various parties as follows:

(a) **Trading insiders:** [§938] Insiders who trade on confidential, non-public information are liable under rule 10b-5 to the persons with whom they trade.

    1) **Controlling shareholders, directors, and officers:** [§939] Shareholders with a controlling interest, directors, and officers of a corporation are all insiders who can be held liable for trading on inside information with respect to the securities of their corporation. [S.E.C. v. Texas Gulf Sulphur Co., *supra*, §911]

    2) **Corporate employees:** [§940] A group of corporate employees who accepted stock options knowing material facts about the company unknown to the company were held liable under rule 10b-5. [S.E.C. v. Texas Gulf Sulphur Co., *supra*]

    3) **Tippees can sue insiders:** [§941] Note that tippees who are given supposedly inside information by corporate officer-insiders that turns out to be false and misleading can sue the insiders for recovery of their losses. [Bateman Eichler, Hill Richards, Inc. v. Berner, *supra*, §920]

        a) **Note:** The common law defense of in pari delicto (*i.e.,* equal fault) does not bar a private damage action under the federal securities laws against corporate insiders and broker-dealers who fraudulently induce investors to purchase securities by misrepresenting that they are conveying material, nonpublic information about the issuer. A private cause of action by such tippees will be barred only when the tippee's culpability for the violation is at least substantially as great as that of the insiders against whom recovery is sought.

(b) **Issuers:** [§942] Technically, the issuer is not an insider with respect to its own information. However, an issuer may be held liable if material information is not properly disclosed to shareholders and the public before trading in the corporation's securities begins.

    1) **Example:** In *Texas Gulf Sulphur, supra*, the S.E.C. sought an injunction against the corporation to prevent further violations of rule 10b-5. At issue was the corporation's failure to make complete and accurate disclosure in a news release with respect to its ore exploration activities. The court held that the news release was misleading concerning material facts, and that the corporation (through its officers and directors) had not displayed due diligence in finding the truth and disclosing it. This case stands for the proposition that *if the issuer does disclose material facts,* the disclosures must be accurate. Furthermore, the disclosure must be timely. [*See* Financial Industrial Fund, Inc. v. McDonnell Douglas Corp., 474 F.2d 514 (10th Cir. 1973)]

2) **Defense of a valid "corporate purpose":** [§943] There is some indication that if the corporation itself does not trade in its securities on the basis of the inside information (even though other insiders may have done so) and there is a valid corporate purpose for not disclosing the information, the corporation itself may not be held liable in a private damage action for the *nondisclosure.* [Astor v. Texas Gulf Sulphur Co., 306 F. Supp. 1333 (S.D.N.Y. 1969)]

a) **Example:** In *Astor*, the corporation's desire to buy up the land surrounding its rich ore discovery was held to be a valid corporate purpose for the nondisclosure.

b) **Note:** No case has yet held that there is any rule 10b-5 liability for withholding (*i.e.*, not disclosing) material, inside information—even where there is *no corporate purpose* for doing so—when no one (corporation, officers, tippers, tippees, etc.) used the information to trade in the stock. [*See* Elkind v. Liggett & Meyers, Inc., *supra*, §908] But if the corporation discloses the inside information to anyone who might make use of it, it must disclose the information to the market before trading by the initial recipient of disclosure will be permitted. [*See* Elkind v. Liggett & Myers, Inc., *supra*—corporation disclosed its earnings statement to a financial analyst who traded in the information before a public disclosure was made]

(c) **Tippers:** [§944] "Tippers" (*i.e.*, insiders who provide material information to others, who then trade on that information) *are liable* under rule 10b-5, *even if they do not themselves trade on the information.*

1) **Example:** In *Texas Gulf Sulphur, supra*, one of the defendants tipped his friends, who traded on the information. The defendant was held liable for the profits made by his friends.

2) **Example:** A brokerage firm, participating as an underwriter in a public offering of securities, learned adverse information about the issuer. Before this information became public, the brokerage firm disclosed the adverse information to certain of its clients, who then sold securities of the issuer and thereby avoided substantial losses. The brokerage firm was held liable to contemporaneous buyers of the issuer's securities. [Shapiro v. Merrill Lynch, Pierce, Fenner & Smith, Inc., *supra*, §907]

(d) **Tippees:** [§945] Those who receive inside information from tippers—"tippees"—and subsequently trade on it are liable to the persons selling to, or buying from, the tippee. At present, the courts are split as to whether the tippee is liable for the full amount of the loss suffered by the other parties, or only for the tippee's illicit gains (or avoided losses).

1) **Example:** In *Shapiro, supra*, the tippee-defendants who traded in the issuer's securities were found liable for the losses of the persons buying on the New York Stock Exchange contemporaneously with the defendant's sales. The court noted that the resulting liability might be "draconian," because there was no necessary relationship between what the defendants gained and what the plaintiffs lost, but it did not reduce the defendants' liability.

2) **Example:** In *Fridrich v. Bradford, supra* §908, the court declined to hold the tippee-defendant liable for the full amount lost by the plaintiffs, electing instead to limit liability to the amount gained unlawfully by the defendant by making the illegal trades.

3) **"Breach of duty"—*Dirks*:** [§946] Recall that liability under rule 10b-5 for insider trading is premised on a breach of a duty owed to the person with whom the defendant trades or to some other person found to have enforceable rights in, or expectations regarding, the information. (*See supra*, §931.) Clearly an insider breaches such a duty by trading with a shareholder of the issuer, but in most cases a *tippee, as an unrelated party, is not bound by such duties.* What, then, supports a tippee's liability for insider trading? The Supreme Court answered this question in *Dirks v. S.E.C., supra.*

   a) **Facts of *Dirks*:** [§947] Dirks, a stock analyst, was given material information by a corporate insider that the assets of the issuer were vastly overstated. The insider was not motivated by any personal gain but sought only to reveal the corporate fraud. Dirks gave this information to his clients, who then sold the issuer's stock to unknowing purchasers.

   b) **Result:** [§948] The Supreme Court held that neither the insider (the tipper) nor Dirks (the tippee) violated rule 10b-5. A tippee is liable for acting (either trading, or tipping others) on a tip only if, in giving the tip:

      1/ The insider-tipper has **breached her fiduciary duties to the shareholders; and**

      2/ The insider-tipper has **acted from a motive of "personal benefit."**

   c) **The "personal benefit" requirement**

      1/ **Gifts:** [§949] The requirement that the insider act to receive a "personal benefit" is satisfied if the insider receives a pecuniary gain or a reputational benefit that translates into future earnings. The Supreme Court in *Dirks,* however, stated that this requirement is also met when an insider makes a *gift of confidential information to a trading relative or a friend.*

    a/ **Rationale:** According to the Supreme Court, such a "tip and trade resemble trading by the insider himself followed by a gift of the profits to the recipient." Note that while the Court's statement is true, it is difficult in this situation to see the requisite "benefit" to the insider.

  2/ **Commissions:** [§950] In another case, a tippee who passed information to others but who bought no stock himself (but nevertheless benefited from the trading by receipt of broker's commissions) was held liable for insider trading. [Shapiro v. Merrill Lynch, Pierce, Fenner & Smith, Inc., *supra*]

(e) **Corporate outsiders and inside information:** [§951] Corporate insiders (officers, directors, or employers) almost by definition possess a relationship to the corporation and its shareholders that makes them culpable if they trade on inside information. Corporate "outsiders" however, may stand on a different footing since they acquire information in a variety of situations.

1) **Rumors:** [§952] An outsider may hear rumors from several sources concerning a company, invest based on this information, and be held not liable for abuse of inside information. [*See* S.E.C. v. Monarch Fund, Fed. Sec. L. Rep. (CCH) ¶97,148 (2d Cir. 1979)]

  a) **Example:** In *Monarch Fund*, the defendant was an attorney responsible for advising two investment funds. He heard that a company in which the funds owned shares was receiving additional financing. He confirmed the rumors with a partner in the firm providing the financing. The court held this was not improper "inside" information because the information lacked "specificity" (defendant did not know the specific facts of what was going to happen); it was not clear that the information actually was confidential and nonpublic; and defendant's inquiries were reasonable under the circumstances. (Compare this with the type of information acquired by outsiders in *Texas Gulf Sulphur, supra*.)

2) **"Outsider" has no fiduciary duty:** [§953] In *Chiarella v. United States, supra*, §934, the Supreme Court significantly limited the concept of who is an "insider." *Chiarella* involved an employee of a financial printing firm who discovered information about pending tender offers from materials left to be printed by the bidders; he invested in the target companies based on this information. The Court held that no

criminal action could be brought against the employee since he was not an "insider" of the target companies; *i.e.,* there was no relationship of trust and confidence between the defendant and the target companies or their shareholders, as there would be between management of a company and its shareholders. Furthermore, the defendant had not received the information directly from one of those insiders (*i.e.,* he was not a "tippee").

3) **Outsiders and "market information":** [§954]  At issue in *Chiarella, supra,* was information about the supply and demand for stock of the target companies, rather than "inside information" about the companies. This kind of information is called "market information," and it is often very valuable, particularly in the period immediately preceding a big change in demand.

    a) **Difficulties in applying rule 10b-5 to market information:** [§955]  Rule 10b-5 is difficult to apply to cases involving corporate outsiders trading on market information. Such outsiders are not bound by any fiduciary duties to the issuer's shareholders. Thus, for example, an investor who plans to acquire control of an issuer need not disclose those plans to the market before beginning to purchase the issuer's securities (within the limitations of the tender offer rules—*see infra,* §§978 *et seq.*). In the same way, the printer's employee in the *Chiarella* case was not liable. However, as a policy matter, it may be unsatisfactory to permit someone like the employee in *Chiarella* to escape liability under rule 10b-5: after all, he used information he had come by illicitly to benefit at the expense of shareholders who lacked that information.

        1/ **Note:** In *Chiarella,* the government attempted to argue that the printer's employee "misappropriated" the employer's confidential information, and that he was liable under rule 10b-5 by virtue of *that* breach of duty, rather than the more traditional breach of fiduciary duty to the shareholders. This argument had not been made at trial, however, and for that reason it was rejected by a majority of the Supreme Court.

    b) **The "misappropriation theory" of liability:** [§956]  After the *Chiarella* case, the S.E.C. has attempted to deal with the problem of corporate outsiders using market information by emphasizing the misappropriation of confidential information. Under this so-called "misappropriation theory," a person who *takes information not intended for her* or who *misuses information lawfully in her possession,* and subsequently trades on that information, *violates rule 10b-5.* The misappropriation of information "substitutes" conceptually for the breach of fiduciary duty normally invoked to support rule 10b-5.

1/ **Note:** The Supreme Court's *Chiarella/Dirks* theory of insider trading emphasizes the defendant's breach of fiduciary duty, owed (albeit only derivatively in the case of a tippee) to her trading partner(s). The misappropriation theory, on the other hand, is applied by the S.E.C. in cases where the defendant has not breached any duty to her trading partners at all; instead, the duty breached relates to the manner in which she obtained or used the nonpublic information.

c) **Supreme Court has not addressed misappropriation theory:** [§957] In 1987, the Supreme Court deadlocked, in a 4-4 vote, on a case in which the defendant was convicted of criminal violations of rule 10b-5 based on the misuse of confidential information. [Carpenter v. United States, 484 U.S. 19 (1987)]

1/ **Facts of *Carpenter:*** In *Carpenter*, a reporter for the *Wall Street Journal*, traded (and tipped others, who also traded) on information taken from columns he had written, but which had not yet been published. The columns in question (from a daily series called "Heard on the Street") were widely acknowledged to be influential; a favorable report on a company in that column frequently was followed by a rise in the company's stock price.

2/ **Result:** The tie vote by the Supreme Court resulted in an affirmance of the reporter's conviction under rule 10b-5. The Justices wrote no opinions on that issue. However, the Court affirmed by opinion the reporter's convictions under the federal mail and wire fraud statutes, based on the same conduct.

d) **Misappropriation theory in the circuit courts:** [§958] In the circuit courts, the misappropriation theory has been *applied to actions by the government, but not to actions by private plaintiffs.*

1/ **Injunctions:** [§959] The misappropriation theory will support an action under by the S.E.C. for an injunction. [*See, e.g.,* S.E.C. v. Clark, 915 F.2d 439 (9th Cir. 1990); S.E.C. v. Materia, 745 F.2d 197 (2d Cir. 1984), *cert. denied*, 471 U.S. 1053 (1985)]

2/ **Criminal prosecutions:** [§960] Likewise, the misappropriation theory supports a criminal case brought under rule 10b-5. [*See, e.g.,* United States v. Newman, 664 F.2d 12 (2d Cir. 1981), *cert. denied*, 464 U.S. 863 (1983)]

3/ **Private damages actions:** [§961] Private plaintiffs, however, ***cannot*** rely on the misappropriation theory—they must show breach of a duty owed to them, rather than breach of a duty owed, for example, to the defendant's employer. [Moss v. Morgan Stanley, Inc., 719 F.2d 5 (2d Cir. 1983)]

4) **Outsider can become fiduciary:** [§962] In certain circumstances, such as where corporate information is revealed legitimately to an underwriter, accountant, lawyer, or consultant working for the corporation, these outsiders may become fiduciaries of the shareholders because they have entered into a confidential relationship in the conduct of the business of the corporation and are given access to information solely for corporate purposes. [Dirks v. S.E.C., *supra*]

b. **Insider trading legislation in the 1980s:** [§963] The turbulent securities markets of the 1980s produced two significant statutes dealing with insider trading: the Insider Trading Sanctions Act of 1984 and the Insider Trading and Securities Fraud Enforcement Act of 1988.

(1) **Insider Trading Sanctions Act:** [§964] In 1984, Congress gave the S.E.C. additional enforcement powers against insider trading by enacting the Insider Trading Sanctions Act of 1984. Under this statute, the S.E.C. can seek a civil penalty of up to ***three times*** the amount of the insider's ill-gotten profits (or avoided losses). There are many unanswered questions under this Act, for example: Would successive actions under the Act and for criminal violations violate the constitutional prohibition against double jeopardy? In view of the Act's provisions establishing the possibility of penalties at three times the insider's trading profits, would a nontrading tipper be covered by the Act? [*See* SEA §21A]

(2) **Insider Trading and Securities Fraud Enforcement Act of 1988:** [§965] In 1988, Congress adopted the Insider Trading and Securities Fraud Enforcement Act. This statute, which added section 20A to the 1934 Act, provides a cause of action to persons who sold or purchased a security in the market at the time that the defendant purchased or sold a security of the same class, if the defendant's transaction violated "any provision of [the 1934 Act and the rules thereunder]."

(a) **Note:** The 1988 Act does not "adopt" the misappropriation theory; instead, it relies on the existing provisions of the 1934 Act to establish a violation. Once a violation is established, however, the 1988 Act establishes a cause of action in favor of contemporaneous traders in the market.

(b) **But note:** The *Moss* case, *supra,* held that private plaintiffs seeking damages lack standing to sue under the misappropriation theory, because private plaintiffs are required to show the breach of a duty owed to them before they can recover. The 1988 Act may overrule *Moss*, because it grants standing to sue to precisely those persons who were held to lack standing in *Moss*.

(c) **Remedies under the 1988 Act:** [§966] Although the 1988 Act seems to expand greatly the class of potential plaintiffs in rule 10b-5 cases, it limits the amount recoverable to the *defendant's profit gained or loss avoided*. This amount is then further reduced by the amount of any profits the defendant has already disgorged relating to the same securities transactions. [SEA §20A(b)(1), (2)]

c. **Liability of insiders under state law:** [§967] Although state courts originally rejected the idea of corporate recovery of profits made on insider trading, several courts have developed theories upon which to hold insiders liable.

(1) **Breach of fiduciary duty:** [§968] For example, a state court has upheld a common law shareholder derivative suit for profits made by corporate officers in selling their corporation's securities based on inside information concerning a possible drop in corporate earnings. The court held that the insiders had breached their fiduciary duty to the corporation; and that even though the corporation had not been injured by the insider trading, the defendants should not be unjustly enriched. [Diamond v. Oreamuno, 24 N.Y.2d 494 (1969); *but see* Freeman v. Decio, 584 F.2d 186 (7th Cir. 1978)—no cause of action on similar facts]

(a) **Note:** The reviewing court emphasized that the federal securities laws were not exclusive remedies, and that even where a cause of action is available under rule 10b-5, or under section 16(a) of the 1934 Act, a common law claim can be brought in state court.

(b) **But note:** In this same situation, a *derivative action* would not lie under rule 10b-5, since presumably neither the corporation nor the shareholder suing on behalf of the corporation is a purchaser or seller of the securities. [Davidge v. White, 377 F. Supp. 1084 (S.D.N.Y. 1974); *and see supra*, §862] However, the buyers who bought without the material information might sue the inside sellers who traded on the inside information under rule 10b-5.

9. **Class Actions Under Rule 10b-5:** [§969] Rule 10b-5 actions are frequently brought as class actions, since many shareholders may be similarly injured by the same rule 10b-5 violation.

a. **"Class action" defined:** [§970] The class action is a suit in which a representative plaintiff presses her own claim and the claims of others similarly situated in a single action to establish the liability of the defendant and the gross amount of damages. It is in some respects an ideal method for enforcement of private rule 10b-5 rights, since it contributes to the efficient use of limited judicial resources, yet ensures that the interests of all plaintiffs (which may otherwise be too small to be asserted economically in individual actions) are given vindication in the courts, and thereby contributes to the effective enforcement of the federal securities laws.

b. **Federal court jurisdiction:** [§971] The 1934 Act vests "exclusive jurisdiction in the federal district courts over violation of the securities acts, and over all suits to enforce any liability or duty created by the securities acts or the rules and regulations thereunder. [SEA §27]

(1) **Federal Rules of Civil Procedure applied:** The federal courts must apply the Federal Rules of Civil Procedure in all procedural matters; therefore, the Federal Rules apply to class actions brought under the federal securities laws.

c. **Preconditions to the existence of a class:** [§972] Federal Rule 23(a) lists four mandatory preconditions to the existence of a class of plaintiffs:

(i) *The class must be so numerous* that joinder of all members is impracticable.

(ii) *There must be questions of law or fact common to the entire class* of plaintiffs.

(iii) *The claims or defenses of the representative parties must be typical* of the claims or defenses of the entire class.

(iv) *The representative parties must fairly and adequately protect* the interests of the entire class.

*Even assuming that the above preconditions* to the existence of a class are met, Federal Rule 23(b) imposes an *additional* requirement that the class representative (plaintiff) plead and show the existence of one of the following *special circumstances:*

(1) *That inconsistent, varying, or disadvantageous judgments are likely* if a class action is not permitted;

(2) *That final injunctive or declaratory relief is appropriate; or*

(3) That a *class action is superior to other available methods* for the fair and efficient adjudication of the controversy.

d. **Exclusion from the class:** [§973] Under Federal Rule 23(c)(2), potential class members can avoid being bound by any judgment rendered in a class action by requesting exclusion from the class.

e. **Application in rule 10b-5 case:** [§974] *Cannon v. Texas Gulf Sulphur* provides a good example of the application of the class action provisions to a rule 10b-5b situation. Over 364,000 shares had been sold during a five-day period following a misleading press release, and 26 actions involving 250 plaintiffs had already been filed. Although each plaintiff's reliance on the press release might have to be determined individually, the number of common questions predominated over those that had to be tried separately. The court concluded that a class action was appropriate on behalf of all shareholders who had sold their stock in the five-day period. [Cannon v. Texas Gulf Sulphur Co., Fed. Sec. L. Rep. (CCH) ¶92,372 (1969)]

10. **Using Rule 10b-5 to Enforce Fiduciary Duties of Insiders**

a. **Fiduciary duties at common law:** [§975] There is a long history of state common law actions to enforce fiduciary duties owed by corporate insiders (officers, directors, and majority shareholders) to the corporation and its shareholders. Often, these actions are brought by the shareholders in the form of derivative suits on behalf of the corporation.

(1) **Nature of fiduciary duties:** [§976] Under state law, corporate insiders were held to have the duties of acting with due care, in "good faith," and with fairness. More specifically, these duties required:

(a) That insiders have *no conflicts of interest*;

(b) That there be *no competition with the corporation*;

(c) That there be *no seizing of a corporate opportunity*;

(d) That there be *no oppression of minority shareholder interests*; and

(e) That there be *full and fair disclosure of all transactions with the corporation*.

b. **Fiduciary duties under rule 10b-5:** [§977] Until approximately the mid-1970s, rule 10b-5 was seen as a desirable means to enforce the fiduciary duties of corporate management. Many breaches of officers' and directors' fiduciary duties were accompanies by transactions in securities, and prospective plaintiffs often were able to make out the other elements of the rule 10b-5 private cause of action. The *Blue Chip Stamps* case, *supra, §854,* signaled the beginning of the end of this era, however, and two years later, the *Santa Fe Industries* case, *supra,* §814, marked the end of rule 10b-5's role as a significant arrow in the quiver of corporate plaintiffs.

## C. TENDER OFFERS AND REPURCHASES OF STOCK [§978]

A "tender offer" is an offer by a person (the "bidder") to purchase the securities of a corporation (the "target"), made directly to the shareholders of the target. This offer may be made either *in cash* or (if the bidder is a corporation) *in the stock* of the bidder. The offer may be made with (a "friendly" offer) or without (a "hostile" offer) the cooperation of the target's management.

1. **Inadequacies of Earlier Regulation:** [§979] Several provisions of the securities laws applied to tender offers prior to 1968, but there were gaps in the coverage of these provisions.

a. **Securities Act of 1933:** [§980] If the bidder made a cash offer to purchase, then the 1933 Act would not be applicable (since it was an offer to purchase rather than an offer to sell securities) and there would be no affirmative disclosure requirement imposed on the bidder. Also, the antifraud sections of the 1933 Act [SA §§11, 12, 17] would not apply, since they apply only to defrauded *purchasers* of securities (*see supra,* §619).

b. **Securities Exchange Act of 1934**

(1) **Rule 10b-5:** [§981] The antifraud provisions of rule 10b-5 are available to plaintiff-sellers who sell their stock where there has been a material misrepresentation or omission by the bidder (*see supra,* §795). However, since rule 10b-5 requires the plaintiff to be an actual purchaser or seller

of securities, it was questionable whether the target itself—or its shareholders who did not sell—could bring an action. Therefore, this section did not adequately cover the tender offer area.

(2) **Proxy rules:** [§982] The proxy rules of section 14 of the 1934 Act are of limited applicability, because as a rule tender offers do not require a shareholder vote, and therefore do not require any solicitation of proxies (*see infra*, §1128).

(3) **Market manipulation:** [§983] If the bidder or the target engage in market manipulation (*see infra*, §1709), the other might have recourse to section 9 or rule 10b-5 of the 1934 Act. But the problems of proof and the limited coverage of section 9 (*see infra*, §1724) make this section inadequate for most of the problems that typically arise in tender offers.

2. **Federal Regulation of Tender Offers:** [§984] Due to the limitations in the coverage of other provisions of the federal securities laws, in 1968 Congress passed the Williams Act (named after Senator Harrison Williams of New Jersey) specifically to regulate tender offers. The Williams Act added to the 1934 Act section 13(d) and (e), and section 14(d), (e), and (f).

a. **Jurisdiction to regulate:** [§985] Jurisdiction of the federal government over tender offers is based on their effect on interstate commerce and on the use of the mails or other means of interstate commerce to effect the transaction.

b. **Overview of SEA regulation of tender offers:** [§986] The following sections of the 1934 Act apply to tender offers:

(1) **Reporting requirement:** [§987] Section 13(d) requires any party who acquires 5% or more of an equity security registered under section 12 of the 1934 Act (*see supra*, §§742-744) to report such acquisition and his intentions with respect to the issuer of the security. [*See also* Schedule 13D—sets forth the reporting requirements of section 13(d) in more detail]

(2) **Disclosure requirements:** [§988] Section 14(d) is the basic section that regulates the making of tender offers. Under this section, the bidder must make an appropriate disclosure prior to commencing the tender offer. [*See also* Schedule 14D-1] In addition, section 14(d)(4) requires disclosure by anyone making a "solicitation or recommendation to the holders of [the target's securities] to accept or reject a tender offer." [*See also* Schedule 14D-9] Rule 14e-2 requires the target's management to disclose its position on the tender offer; this disclosure in turn triggers the target's obligation to file a Schedule 14D-9.

(3) **Antifraud provision:** [§989] Section 14(e) is an antifraud provision that makes it unlawful for any party making a tender offer—or defending against one—to make untrue statements of material fact (or to omit to state material facts), or to engage in any fraudulent, deceptive, or manipulative act or practice in connection with any tender offer.

(a) **Note:** Although the language of section 14(e) is essentially the same as that of rule 10b-5, the two sections have been construed differently by the courts. [*See, e.g.,* United States v. Chestman, 947 F.2d 551 (1991), *cert. denied,* 503 U.S. 1004 (1992); *and see infra,* §§1051 *et seq.*]

    (b) **And note:** While section 14(e) applies only in the context of tender offers, it is *not* limited to tender offers made for securities registered under the 1934 Act.

c. **Remedies for violation of tender offer rules:** [§990] Although the 1934 Act says nothing about remedies for violation of the tender offer rules, the courts have filled in some of the gaps in the statutory provisions by *implying* remedies to enforce the provisions of the Act. However, since the mid-1970s the trend in the courts has been to limit implied private rights of action (*see* discussion *supra,* §782); thus the law with respect to each section of the Williams Act [SEA §§13(d), (e); 14(d), (e)] must be checked carefully.

3. **Preliminary Reporting Requirement—Section 13(d):** [§991] The preliminary reporting requirements of section 13(d) are calibrated so that anyone making significant acquisitions of registered equity securities must disclose her plans with respect to the issuer of those securities at a very early stage. Schedule 13D of the 1934 Act specifically requires disclosure of certain information. Note that some persons may use section 13(g) reporting, which requires less disclosure, when there is no intention to make any change in the control of the issuer. [*See* SEA Schedule 13G]

a. **Ownership criteria:** [§992] Any person who has acquired beneficial ownership in excess of 2% of a class of equity security registered under SEA section 12 within a 12-month period *and* who thereby or otherwise owns more than 5% of the class must, within 10 days after the acquisition, file an information statement with the S.E.C., sending copies to the issuer of the security and to any exchanges on which the security is traded. [SEA §13(d)(1), (6)(B)]

    (1) **Updating:** [§993] Section 13(d) requires the updating of this statement if any material changes of fact subsequently occur.

    (2) **Percentage requirement:** [§994] Section 13(d) applies to the acquisition of any class of registered equity security, and the 5% ownership requirement applies to *each class separately.*

        (a) **Example:** If A acquires 5% of the convertible debentures of XYZ Corp., the reporting requirements apply even though—if the debentures were converted into common stock—A would not own 5% of the underlying common stock. [GAF Corp. v. Milstein, 453 F.2d 709 (2d Cir. 1971)]

        (b) **Note:** In determining whether 5% of an underlying security is owned, the general rule is that all exercisable warrants, options, or conversion rights to the underlying security must be considered to have been exercised. [SEA Rule 13d-3(d)(1)(i)]

    (3) **Groups of persons:** [§995] Moreover, when two or more persons act as a partnership, limited partnership, syndicate, or other group for the purpose of acquiring, holding, or disposing of the securities of an issuer,

such a group is deemed a "person" for purposes of section 13(d) (as well as section 14(d)). [SEA §§13(d)(3), 14(d)(2)]

(a) **Formation of a group—five percent requirement:** [§996] A critical issue in group situations is the determination of when the group is "formed." The Second Circuit has held that the mere formation of a group of persons for the purpose of attempting to obtain control of an issuer triggers the section 13(d) filing requirement if the members of the group collectively own enough securities to trigger the filing requirement. There need be no additional stock purchases made by the group *as a group.* [GAF Corp. v. Milstein, *supra*]

   1) **Example:** In *GAF Corp.*, the defendants were members of a family who each individually owned stock in GAF and collectively had the required percentage of shares prior to passage of section 13(d). After the Act was passed, and without purchasing additional stock, they formed a group with the intention to gain control of GAF and oust its management. Although section 13(d) requires a "person" to file only if acquiring more than 2% of a class of stock within a 12-month period after passage of the Act, the group was held to have "acquired" a beneficial interest in the prior, individual holdings of its members.

(b) **Necessity of showing group "purpose":** [§997] The burden of proof is on the plaintiff to show that the defendant "group" has been formed for a "common objective" covered by section 13(d) (*e.g.*, gaining control or ousting current management). Moreover, plaintiff is normally required to show such purpose by *objective acts*. [Bath Industries, Inc. v. Blot, 427 F.2d 97 (7th Cir. 1970)]

   1) **Note:** The *Bath* court, contrary to *Milstein*, required *additional purchases* of shares *after* formation of the group, and pursuant to group agreement, in order to trigger the reporting requirements of section 13(d).

b. **Information required:** [§998] The following data must be disclosed in a section 13(d) information statement [*see* Schedule 13D]:

   (1) **Information about the purchasers:** [§999] The purchaser must disclose the background and identity of the persons involved in the purchase of securities.

   (2) **Information about consideration:** [§1000] The sources and amounts of consideration used in the purchases must be disclosed.

   (3) **Information about the purpose of the purchases:** [§1001] The purchaser must disclose whether or not the purpose of the purchases is to acquire control of the issuer and any plans or proposals that relate to (or would result in) liquidation of the issuer, sale of its assets, merger with any other entity, or any other major change in its business or corporate structure.

(4) **Information about ownership:** [§1002] The purchaser must disclose the number of shares she owns beneficially and the existence of any rights to purchase additional shares.

(5) **Information about contracts, etc.:** [§1003] The purchaser must disclose the existence of any contracts, arrangements, or other understandings relating to the issuer or its securities.

c. **Exemptions from section 13(d):** [§1004] The following transactions are exempt from the reporting requirements of section 13(d).

(1) *Offers for and acquisitions of shares made by means of a 1933 Act registration statement*, since presumably the filing of the registration statement gives ample notice of the potential change in control. However, acquisitions made pursuant to any exemptions under the 1933 Act, or by means of a regulation A offering under the 1933 Act, are *not* exempt from section 13(d).

(2) *Acquisitions where less than 2% of the tendered class of security are purchased* within a 12-month period, or where less than a 5% total is owned.

  (a) **Example:** Thus, if 2.1% is acquired within 12 months, but total ownership is only 4.9%, the reporting requirement is *not* triggered.

  (b) **Example:** Similarly, if only 1.9% is acquired in a period of 12 months, the reporting requirement is *not* triggered even though a total of 5.1% is owned.

(3) *Acquisitions made by the issuer of its own equity securities*—such acquisitions are governed by section 13(e), which includes similar, detailed disclosure requirements (*see infra,* §1088).

(4) *Acquisitions otherwise exempted* by rule or regulation of the S.E.C.

d. **Relationship to section 16(a) of the 1934 Act:** [§1005] The provisions of sections 13(d) and 16(a) of the 1934 Act overlap somewhat. Section 13(d) requires that ownership of 5% or more of a registered equity security be reported, whereas section 16(a) requires the reporting of purchases by officers, directors, or persons owning 10%, including a purchase by a person who thereby becomes the owner of 10%. [*See* SEA §16(a); *and see infra,* §1287]

e. **Implied private rights of action**

(1) **By the target company:** [§1006] Courts generally agree that a target company has an implied private right of action against the bidder for a violation of section 13(d) (*e.g.,* for filing a false statement). [*See, e.g.,* Gearhart Industries, Inc. v. Smith International, Inc., 741 F.2d 707 (5th Cir. 1984)]

  (a) **Target's remedies under section 13(d):** [§1007] Target companies suing under section 13(d) typically obtain a temporary injunction against the bidder, pending corrective disclosure. [*See, e.g.,*

Florida Commercial Banks v. Culverhouse, 772 F.2d 1513 (11th Cir. 1985); Gearhart Industries, Inc., *supra*] Although the target usually would prefer an order directing the bidder's divestment of target stock, or "sterilization" of the bidder's target stock (*i.e.*, a prohibition on voting that stock), those remedies are rarely if ever granted. [*See, e.g.,* Rondeau v. Mosinee Paper Corp., 422 U.S. 49 (1975); Gearhart Industries, Inc., *supra*]

(2) **By the shareholders of the target company:** [§1008] It has also been held that the shareholders of the target company do have standing pursuant to section 13(d), but damages are not available. [*See, e.g.,* Kamerman v. Steinberg, 891 F.2d 424 (2d Cir. 1989); Sanders v. Thrall Car Manufacturing Co., 582 F. Supp. 945 (S.D.N.Y. 1983), *aff'd*, 730 F.2d 910 (2d Cir. 1984)]

4. **Basic Tender Offer Rules—Section 14(d):** [§1009] Section 14(d) contains the basic regulatory provisions concerning the making of tender offers.

a. **"Tender offer" within meaning of section 14(d):** [§1010] A "tender offer" is generally thought to be an offer to purchase that is made "publicly," to all or substantially all of the shareholders of a corporation. However, it is not defined in the 1934 Act.

(1) **Broad interpretation by the courts:** [§1011] The courts define the term tender offer on a case-by-case basis, and a broad definition will be used so as to effectuate the purposes of the 1934 Act and its tender offer provisions (*i.e.*, protection of the public and of investors). [Hanson Trust PLC v. SCM Corp., 774 F.2d 47 (2d Cir. 1985)]

(2) **Consideration of all relevant facts:** [§1012] In short, all of the relevant facts must be considered in determining whether a tender offer exists.

(a) **Eight-factor test:** [§1013] Most courts refer to the eight-factor test given in *Wellman v. Dickinson*, 475 F. Supp. 783 (S.D.N.Y. 1979). Note that *not all eight factors need be present* for the court to find a tender offer.

1) Was there an active and widespread solicitation of shares by the offeror?

2) Was the solicitation for a substantial percentage of the outstanding stock?

3) Was a premium price offered over the market price before the offer?

4) Were the terms of the offer firm and fixed?

5) Was the offer contingent on the tender by shareholders of a fixed minimum number of shares?

6) Was the offer to shareholders open for only a limited time?

7) Was there pressure put on the shareholders to sell?

8) Were there public announcements accompanying the offer?

(b) ***Hanson Trust* "totality of the circumstances" test:** [§1014] In the *Hanson Trust* case, *supra*, the Second Circuit declined to elevate *Wellman* to a "litmus test," and stated that the question "whether a solicitation constitutes a 'tender offer' within the meaning of section 14(d) turns on whether, viewing the transaction in the light of the totality of the circumstances, there appears to be a likelihood that unless the pre-acquisition filing strictures of section 14(d) are followed there will be a substantial risk that solicitees will lack information needed to make a carefully considered appraisal of the proposal put before them."

1) **Note:** Although the court stated that it would not follow *Wellman*, its opinion relying on the totality of the circumstances actually enumerates almost all of the *Wellman* factors.

(c) **Acquisitions over a stock exchange:** [§1015] Normally, acquisitions made over a stock exchange in normal market transactions would not be a tender offer. However, under appropriate circumstances (for example, if the eight-factor test of *Wellman* were met), open-market purchases could amount to a tender offer. [*See, e.g.,* Hanson Trust PLC v. SCM Corp., *supra*; S.E.C. v. Carter Hawley Hale Stores, Inc., 760 F.2d 945 (9th Cir. 1985)]

(d) **Negotiated purchases:** [§1016] Similarly, although privately negotiated purchases ordinarily do not constitute tender offers, under appropriate circumstances (for example, when enough of the *Wellman* factors are present, or when the "totality of the circumstances" so dictates) negotiated purchases may amount to a tender offer. [*See, e.g.,* Hanson Trust PLC v. SCM Corp., *supra*; Hoover Co. v. Fuqua Industries, Inc., Fed. Sec. L. Rep. (CCH) ¶97,107 (N.D. Ohio 1979)]

(e) **Alternative test for open-market and negotiated purchases—*S-G Securities*:** [§1017] Still another test, broader than the eight-factor test of *Wellman, supra*, and designed to apply to open-market and negotiated purchases, was applied by the court in *S-G Securities, Inc. v. Fuqua Investment Co.*, 466 F. Supp. 1114 (D. Mass. 1978). Under the *S-G Securities* test, a tender offer is present if there is:

1) ***A publicly announced intention*** by the bidder to acquire a block of the target's stock, for the purpose of acquiring control of the target; and

2) ***A subsequent rapid acquisition*** by the bidder of large blocks of stock through open market and privately negotiated purchases.

b. **Tender offers must satisfy conditions of section 14(d):** [§1018] It is unlawful for any person to make use of the means of interstate commerce to make a tender offer for any class of equity security registered under section 12 if, at the consummation of the tender offer, the bidder would be the beneficial owner of more than 5% of the class of securities tendered, *unless* the following conditions required by section 14(d) are met.

(1) **Disclosure of information:** [§1019] The bidder must make the following disclosures in connection with the tender offer:

(a) **Schedule 14D-1:** [§1020] Pursuant to its authority under section 14(d), the S.E.C. has promulgated Schedule 14D-1, which a bidder must file with the S.E.C. (with copies to the target and all stock exchanges on which the target's stock is traded) *at or before the commencement of a tender offer.* The disclosures required by Schedule 14D-1 resemble those required by Schedule 13D (*see supra*, §§998 *et seq.*), but Schedule 14D-1 requires some additional disclosure as well. For example, Schedule 14D-1 requires disclosure of:

1) Past contacts, transactions, or negotiations with the subject company (*i.e.,* the target);

2) Persons retained, employed, or to be compensated in connection with the offer;

3) If material to a decision by a potential tendering shareholder, financial statements of the bidder(s); and

4) If material to a decision by a potential tendering shareholder, certain additional information about: the relationships between the bidder, the target, and their respective officers and directors; regulatory and antitrust issues affecting the transaction; applicability of the margin regulations (governing the use of securities as collateral for loans); pending litigation affecting the offer; and other information material to the tendering shareholders.

(b) **Identity of "bidder" and financial statement disclosure:** [§1021] The requirement in schedule 14D-1 that the bidder(s) provide material financial disclosure was litigated in the late 1980s, in cases brought by targets seeking to enjoin the offer. Rule 14d-1(c)(1) defines a bidder as one who makes a tender offer, or in whose behalf a tender offer is made. Thus, the entity making the actual bid for the target's stock clearly is a bidder, but other participants might also be considered to be bidders.

1) **Securities firms as bidders:** [§1022] Investment banks are often heavily involved in tender offers, by providing the financing for the offer (through, for example, the sale of "high-yield" (junk) bonds), and providing financial and business advice in connection with the offer. In addition, it is common for an investment bank to own some of the equity in the company making the bid. If the investment bank is "central to the offer," and is "one of the principal planners and players," then it may be deemed a "bidder" required to furnish financial statements.

[MAI Basic Four, Inc. v. Prime Computer, Inc., 871 F.2d 212 (1st Cir. 1989)—investment bank that played a central advisory and fund-raising role, and which owned 14% of the bidder directly plus additional indirect interests, deemed a "bidder"]

a) **Minority interests in the bidder:** [§1023] Courts are presently split as to whether an entity that owns only a minority position in the bidder may itself be deemed a "bidder" required to furnish financial statements. [*Compare* MAI Basic Four v. Prime Computer, Inc., *supra*—minority position not a bar to a finding that an entity is a bidder; Koopers Co. v. American Express Co., 689 F. Supp. 1371 (W.D. Pa. 1988)—same, *with* City Capital Associates, Ltd. v. Interco, Inc., 860 F.2d 60 (3d Cir. 1988)—"bidder" means the entity that will actually acquire the target's stock, and those who control it]

2) **Other activities of securities firms:** [§1024] Securities firms also play a significant role by advising their customers whether or not to tender.

(c) **Disclosure and publication of tender offer documents:** [§1025] In addition to filing the Schedule 14D-1, the bidder must (as both a practical and a legal matter) take steps to inform the public of the offer. [*See* SEA Rule 14d-6] In addition to satisfying a disclosure requirement, the offer is generally deemed to commence on the date it is first published. (*See infra*, §§1037 *et seq.*) This will happen in one of two ways: long-form publication or summary publication.

1) **Long-form publication:** [§1026] Long-form publication essentially requires the bidder to publish the offer (which must include or summarize the Schedule 14D-1) in a newspaper of general circulation. [SEA Rule 14d-6(e)(1)] Because this produces a rather lengthy (and expensive) advertisement, it is rarely used.

2) **Summary publication:** [§1027] Summary publication consists of a short advertisement, similar to a "tombstone" ad (discussed *supra*, §179) that gives the essential terms of the offer and states where copies of the complete offer materials may be obtained. [SEA Rule 14d-6(e)(2)]

(2) **Substantive requirements:** [§1028] In addition to requiring disclosure, section 14(d) also imposes substantive requirements on tender offers, intended to ensure minimum standards of fairness and to curb abuses. Section 14(d) also gives the S.E.C. authority to modify its requirements through rules, and the S.E.C. exercised this authority in the mid-1980s to protect offerees further.

(a) **Withdrawal right:** [§1029] The offeree may change her mind and withdraw the securities that she tendered and deposited with the offeror at any time while the offer remains open. [SEA §14(d)(5); SEA Rule 14d-7(a)]

(b) **Pro rata purchases:** [§1030]  Where the bidder seeks to purchase less than all of the issuer's outstanding stock, and a greater number of shares are offered than the bidder intends to purchase, she must purchase pro rata from each person who tenders shares. [SEA §14(d)(6); SEA Rule 14d-8]

(c) **Equal treatment of security holders:** [§1031]  A tender offer must be open to all holders of the securities for which the offer is made, and the consideration paid to any security holder in the offer must be the highest consideration paid to any other holder during the offer. [SEA §14(d)(7); SEA Rule 14d-10]

(d) **No purchases outside the offer:** [§1032]  The bidder is also prohibited from purchasing any securities of the class tendered outside the tender offer. The objective of this provision is to prevent the bidder from manipulating the market price during the offer or from giving a person selling outside the offer a different deal than one tendering shares into the offer. [SEA Rule 10b-13; SEA Release No. 8712 (1969)]

(e) **Target company recommendations:** [§1033]  No later than 10 business days from the date a tender offer commences, the target company must disseminate to its shareholders a statement on Schedule 14D-9 disclosing that it: (i) recommends acceptance or rejection of the bid; (ii) expresses no opinion and is remaining neutral; or (iii) is unable to take a position. The reasons for the position taken must also be stated. [SEA Rule 14e-2]

(f) **Disclose or abstain from trading:** [§1034]  Any person who obtains information about a tender offer from either the bidder, the target, or officers, directors, or employees of either must disclose the information to the public *or* abstain from trading in the securities of the target. Bidders or those acting on their behalf are exempt. In addition, one may not "tip" such information to a tippee where it is "reasonably foreseeable" that the tippee will act in violation of this disclosure rule. [*See* SEA Rule 14e-3—passed by the S.E.C. in reaction to the Supreme Court's opinion in the *Chiarella* case; *and see supra*, §953]

(3) **Offers requiring registration under 1933 Act:** [§1035]  Where a tender offer involves the public offer of the bidder's securities to the target's shareholders, the bidder must also register the securities in question under the 1933 Act (unless an exemption applies). In such a case, the bidder must file both Schedule 14D-1 *and* the appropriate 1933 Act registration form with the S.E.C., and must distribute both the tender offer documents *and* the prospectus for the securities offered to the shareholders of the target.

(a) **Note:** [§1036]  All of the rules that apply to an announcement of an offer of securities (*e.g.*, rule 135) and to solicitations of interest prior to the effective date of the registration statement (*see supra*, §160) also apply in the tender offer situation.

(b) **And note:** What must be disclosed about the bidder in the registration statement under the 1933 Act goes far beyond the requirements of section 14(d). [*See, e.g.,* Feit v. Leasco Data Processing Equipment Corp., *supra*, §654]

(4) **When a tender offer begins:** [§1037] A tender offer begins when a bid is first "published or sent or given to security holders." [SEA Rule 14d-2] This is true even if there is no current offer by the bidder to purchase securities. Any announcement relative to the following items is considered a "publication": the identity of the bidder; the identity of the target company; and the amount, class, and price of the stock sought.

(a) **Five-day grace period for cash offers:** [§1038] If the tender offer is for cash, or for securities that are exempt from registration under the 1933 Act, the bidder is permitted to announce the offer publicly without causing the offer to "commence," as long as within five business days, the bidder either makes the required disclosure to the holders of the target's securities or withdraws the offer. [SEA Rule 14d-2(b)]

1) **Significance of the grace period:** [§1039] Recall that the bidder is required to file a Schedule 14D-1 at or before the "commencement" of the offer. (*See supra*, §1020.) The grace period thus permits the bidder in a cash offer (or one using exempt securities) to announce the bid without having already prepared the Schedule 14D-1. This permits the bidder to act very quickly. In addition, if the market reacts poorly to the announcement, the bidder can withdraw the offer without incurring the expense of preparing the Schedule 14D-1.

c. **Standards for complete disclosure:** [§1040] Even when some disclosure has already been made, a court may require that the bidder provide *more complete disclosure*. For example, a court might require a person filing a section 13(d) or section 14(d) report to augment or more fully disclose his intention in the required report. But the issue of just how much of the bidder's plans must be disclosed is a difficult one.

(1) **Excessive disclosure may incur liability:** [§1041] The problem with disclosing "anything and everything" is that the offerees and public investors might unjustifiably rely on some statements, raising other liability problems (*e.g.,* for misrepresentation) if the plans of the offeror change.

(2) **Criteria for full disclosure:** [§1042] In *Susquehanna Corp. v. Pan American Sulfur Co.,* 423 F.2d 1075 (5th Cir. 1970), involving a violation of section 14(d), the court indicated some criteria for determining whether full disclosure was made:

(a) *The offeror must be "precise and forthright"* in his statements;

(b) *The offeror must make full and fair disclosure as to all material facts* called for by the various items of schedule 13D; and

(c) *The offeror must not "delineate extravagantly"* or "enlarge beyond reasonable bounds."

(3) **Disclosure of present intentions:** [§1043] The court in *Susquehanna* also noted that the offeror could not lull officers and shareholders of the target company into believing that it would retain the incumbent directors and officers if its intention was to do otherwise. Its *present intention* in this matter was a "fact" that had to be disclosed.

(a) **Note:** In addition, the plaintiff charged that disclosure should have been made of discussions between the defendant and a third company about a possible merger affecting the plaintiff. However, the court ruled that such discussions were "speculative" and not actual "plans," and therefore were not present *facts* required to be disclosed.

(b) **And note:** The defendant had simply disclosed as part of the offer for the plaintiff's shares that it had *no present intentions* of engaging in any of the changes required to be disclosed by section 13(d), but that if it decided that any such changes were in the best interests of shareholders in the future, it would propose such a course of action. The court upheld this statement as an adequate disclosure of the offeror's present intentions.

d. **Exemptions:** [§1044] The tender offer rules of section 14(d) do *not* apply to the following situations:

(1) **Five percent limitation:** [§1045] Section 14(d)(1) is *not* applicable if, after consummation of the offer, the person making the offer is not the owner of at least 5% or more of the class of equity security tendered.

(a) **Acquiring five percent:** [§1046] Because a "person" for section 14(d) purposes includes a group of persons acting together (*see supra*, §995), the 5% threshold can sometimes be exceeded in ways that are not obvious.

1) **Example:** Three people, each of whom owns 2% of the equity in Target Corp., band together to make a tender offer for Target. A *Schedule 13D report is due immediately*. The rationale for this result is that the group "acquired" 5% at the moment it was formed. The section 13(d) report, in turn, must disclose the group's intention to make a tender offer for Target. [GAF Corp. v. Milstein, *supra*, §996]

(b) **Note:** Only *beneficial* ownership is counted toward the 5% ownership requirement; beneficial ownership is determined by whether the shareholder controls the voting of the shares.

(2) **Equity securities:** [§1047] Only equity securities registered under section 12 are covered by section 14(d)(1)—*i.e.,* registered common stock as opposed to debt securities, such as bonds.

(3) **Offers made by issuer for its own securities:** [§1048] Offers made by the issuer for its *own* securities are not covered by section 14(d). These

offers are governed by section 13(e), which includes similar, detailed disclosure requirements. (*See infra,* §1088.)

(4) **Limited purchases:** [§1049] Also excluded are acquisitions by offerors where the actual purchases made, together with all purchases during the previous 12 months, do not exceed 2% of the class outstanding.

(5) **Other exempted transactions:** [§1050] The S.E.C. may exempt by rules or regulations other securities transactions that would normally be regulated by the tender offer rules.

5. **Actions for Misstatements or Insufficient Disclosure—Section 14(e):** [§1051] Under section 14(e) it is unlawful for any person to make untrue statements or to omit to state material facts, *or* to engage in any scheme of deception or fraud in connection with any tender offer or in opposition thereto. (Note the similarity of language between section 14(e) and section 10(b) and rule 10b-5, discussed *supra,* §795.)

a. **Private remedies for violation of section 14(e):** [§1052] Section 14(e) may be enforced by private persons (for example, shareholders of the target denied the opportunity to tender their stock by management's actions, or the bidder, denied the opportunity to take over the target) or by the S.E.C. Private plaintiffs have three possible remedies: *damages, a temporary injunction* (usually seeking to force corrective disclosure) *or a permanent injunction* (which may be sought by the target to prevent the bidder from going forward with the offer). Each remedy requires the plaintiff to prove different elements, and each is considered below.

b. **Private action for damages:** [§1053] A private plaintiff seeking damages for violation of section 14(e) must prove: standing to sue; misstatements, nondisclosure or some other species of fraudulent act; materiality; (maybe) reliance; (maybe) causation; and (maybe) scienter.

(1) **Standing:** [§1054] In *Piper v. Chris-Craft Industries, Inc.,* 430 U.S. 1 (1977), the Supreme Court held that a defeated bidder does not have an implied damages remedy under section 14(e).

(a) *Piper:* [§1055] In *Piper,* Chris-Craft had sought control of Piper Aircraft through several tender offers. It eventually gained 42% of Piper's stock, partly as the result of exchanging some of its shares for Piper shares in a tender offer. But a rival bidder, Bangor Punta, eventually gained control (slightly over 50%) of Piper. Chris-Craft alleged (and two lower courts agreed) that Piper, Bangor Punta, and Bangor Punta's underwriter had made material misstatements or omissions in connection with the tender offer. Nevertheless, the Court held that Chris-Craft had no cause of action for damages. The Court reasoned that Congress's intent in passing the Williams Act was *to protect shareholders of the target*, who prior to the Williams Act had been essentially at the mercy of "corporate raiders"; there was no evidence of intent to protect the defeated bidder. Further, the Court held that application of the principles announced in *Cort v. Ash* (*see supra,* §§783 *et seq.*) suggested that a private damages remedy was inappropriate for a defeated bidder.

(b) **Note:** In *Piper,* the Court suggested in dictum that, in light of the avowed purpose of Congress to protect the target's shareholders, shareholders *would* have standing to seek damages—perhaps even in a case in which the shareholder did not tender, based on false statements made by the target's management. Of course, very likely only a nontendering target shareholder would sue. A tendering shareholder would, as a rule, have little cause to complain, because shareholders who tender typically receive a substantial premium over the market price.

(c) **Bidder *and* shareholder:** [§1056] Many bidders are already shareholders of the target at the time they launch the tender offer. The *Piper* case left open the possibility that such a bidder would have standing, but one circuit court has held that a bidder that was also a shareholder would be considered merely a bidder for standing purposes, and hence would be barred from a damages action, under *Piper.* [Kalmanovitz v. G. Heileman Brewing Co., 769 F.2d 152 (3d Cir. 1985)]

(d) **Rule 10b-5 as an alternative:** [§1057] In the wake of *Piper,* one court has held that bidders do not have standing to sue for damages under section 9(e), 10(b), or rule 10b-5 of the 1934 Act for injury allegedly incurred in a tender offer contest. [Crane Co. v. American Standard, Inc., 603 F.2d 244 (2d Cir. 1979)]

(e) **Comment:** *Piper* is another case from the period in which the Supreme Court made it clear that the seemingly limitless expansion of antifraud securities law was at an end. Other cases establishing this point include *Blue Chip Stamps* (*supra*, §854) and *Hochfelder* (*supra*, §885).

(2) **Misstatements, nondisclosure, or fraudulent acts:** [§1058] For a cause of action to exist under section 14(e), there must be a misstatement of a material fact, a failure to disclose a material fact, or some other scheme of fraud or deception. The Supreme Court has stated that the purpose of section 14(e) is to see that shareholders receive full disclosure, not to allow the courts to oversee the substantive fairness of tender offers. [Schreiber v. Burlington Northern, Inc., 472 U.S. 1 (1985); *and see* the discussion of rule 10b-5, *supra*, §§807, 812-814]

(3) **Materiality:** [§1059] The misrepresented or undisclosed fact must be material. The test for materiality is whether there is a *substantial likelihood that a reasonable shareholder would consider the information important* in deciding whether to accept the tender offer. [Seaboard World Airlines, Inc. v. Tiger International, Inc., 600 F.2d 355 (2d Cir. 1979)] *See also* the definitions of materiality in rule 10b-5 cases, *supra*, §§833 *et seq.,* and in proxy cases, *infra*, §§1135 *et seq.* This is the same standard as set for proxy cases in *TSC Industries, Inc. v. Northway, Inc., infra,* §1254.

(a) **Application:** In applying this standard, the courts have indicated that the marketplace conditions under which a tender offer takes place must be considered in testing materiality. The essential objective of the tender offer rules is to assure fair and honest dealing, not to impose an unrealistic requirement of "laboratory conditions." [Electronic Specialty Co. v. International Controls Corp., 409 F.2d 937 (2d Cir. 1969)]

1) **Example:** Parties to a tender offer often act quickly, impulsively, and in angry response to the actions of the opposing party. They are not required to follow through on all statements of intent or preference (as long as such statements are truthful at the time given), nor are they required to correct erroneous reports in the news media. [Electronic Specialty Co. v. International Controls Corp., *supra*]

(4) **Reliance:** [§1060] At present, courts are split as to whether the plaintiffs must show their individual reliance on a misrepresentation or omission. [*See, e.g.,* Plaine v. McCabe, 797 F.2d 713 (9th Cir. 1986)—reliance in a §14(e) case may be inferred from a sufficient showing of causation; Lewis v. McGraw, 619 F.2d 192 (2d Cir. 1980)—§14(e) cause of action fails absent a showing of reliance] In the future, it is likely that reliance will be handled in much the same way as it now is under rule 10b-5; *i.e.,* on a case-by-case basis, with certain presumptions that apply in cases where a reliance requirement seems incongruous (for example, in cases of fraudulent omission). (*See supra*, §§837 *et seq.*)

(5) **Causation:** [§1061] As with reliance, the status of the law on causation in section 14(e) cases is uncertain.

(a) *Piper***:** [§1062] The *Piper v. Chris-Craft* case, *supra*, was decided by the majority on the issue of standing. Justice Blackmun, concurring, would have decided the case against the plaintiffs, because in his view they had not shown causation. A court might follow Justice Blackmun and hold that causation is a requirement in section 14(e) cases.

(b) **Rule 10b-5 analogy:** [§1063] On the other hand, it is possible that a court today will follow the cases under rule 10b-5 and hold that causation may, in an appropriate case, be presumed from a finding that a material fact was misrepresented or omitted. The best analogy is to a rule 10b-5 face-to-face transaction case, because in a tender offer situation, the bidder's and target's statements are made with the intention of encouraging or discouraging the tendering (or withholding) of the securities, much like similar statements made in a face-to-face securities purchase and sale transaction.

(6) **Standard of culpability:** [§1064] The Supreme Court has not addressed the question whether section 14(e) requires a showing of scienter. There are two analogous provisions that could influence a court deciding this question: 1933 Act section 17(a) and rule 10b-5 under the 1934 Act.

(a) **Language in sections 17(a) and 14(e) and rule 10b-5:** [§1065] The language used in section 17(a) of the 1933 Act is very similar to that used in 1934 Act section 14(e) and, for that matter, in rule 10b-5 under the 1934 Act. In other words, all three provisions are drafted in essentially the same way (although the paragraph structure varies among them).

(b) **Significance:** [§1066]  The Supreme Court has held that 1933 Act section *17(a)(1) requires a showing of scienter,* while subsections *(a)(2) and (a)(3) do not.* [Aaron v. S.E.C., *see supra,* §723] On the other hand, the Court has held that *all three parts of rule 10b-5 require a showing of scienter.* [Ernst & Ernst v. Hochfelder, *see supra,* §885] A court confronting the question whether section 14(e) requires a showing of scienter might follow *Aaron,* and hold that some parts of section 14(e) require scienter while others do not; or the court might follow *Hochfelder,* and hold that section 14(e) always requires scienter.

(c) **Majority view:** [§1067]  Most courts adopt the analogy to rule 10b-5, and require a showing of scienter in all section 14(e) cases. [*See, e.g.,* Connecticut National Bank v. Fluor Corp., 808 F.2d 957 (2d Cir. 1987)]

(7) **Damages:** [§1068]  *See* the discussion of the measure of damages in connection with rule 10b-5 (*supra,* §901).

6. **Private Action for Injunction:** [§1069]  A plaintiff who is injured by a violation of the tender offer rules may, as an alternative to an action for damages, also sue for an injunction.

a. **Relevant distinctions:** [§1070]  The cases that deal with injunctions under the tender offer rules must be carefully distinguished in two respects. First, as to their factual circumstances—*i.e.,* whether they relate to the preliminary filing requirement of section 13(d), section 14(d) disclosure requirement for tender offers, or the section 14(e) antifraud provision (this is relevant since there are standing questions with respect to each section). Second, the cases differ significantly when a *preliminary*—as opposed to a *permanent*—injunction is sought.

b. **Permanent injunctions:** [§1071]  Before the court will permanently enjoin the making or consummation of a tender offer, the plaintiff must show that it will suffer *irreparable injury* as a result of the defendant's violation of the tender offer rules.

(1) **Example:** An action was brought under section 13(d) for the defendant's failure to file the required report after acquiring 5% of the plaintiff's stock. Although the defendant had intended to make a tender offer, it had not actually done so at the time the plaintiff's action was brought. The Supreme Court found that the violation was not willful and that no irreparable injury resulted. [Rondeau v. Mosinee Paper Corp., *supra,* §1007] Under these circumstances, the Court held that a permanent injunction would not issue against a mere *technical violation* of the tender offer rules. The Court stated that the plaintiff (the potential target company) would have to show that it would suffer an irreparable injury that could not be remedied at law, before an injunction would issue to bar the defendant from voting the shares it had acquired and from acquiring any more shares for a period of five years.

(a) **Note:** The *Rondeau* case probably sets the standard for permanent injunctions in section 14(d) and 14(e) cases as well.

c. **Preliminary injunctions:** [§1072] A plaintiff seeking a preliminary injunction must meet the burden of showing either (i) probable success if the case were to go to trial on the merits *and* the possibility of irreparable injury, *or* (ii) the existence of serious questions going to the merits *and* a balance of hardships in the plaintiff's favor. [Stark v. New York Stock Exchange, Inc., 466 F.2d 743 (2d Cir. 1972)]

(1) **Example:** The plaintiff (the target company) was granted an injunction upon a showing that the defendant had failed to disclose its intentions regarding the disposition of the plaintiff's assets if the tender offer were successful, and that the defendant had also failed to disclose that the English government had the statutory power to control the disposition of the plaintiff's assets. [General Host Corp. v. Triumph American, Inc., 359 F. Supp. 749 (E.D. Wis. 1973)]

d. **Standing to seek injunctions:** [§1073] The question of who has standing to seek an injunction is somewhat unresolved at present, at least with respect to tender offerors.

(1) **Recap—action for damages:** Recall that the bidder in a tender offer has *no* standing under section 14(e) to bring a private cause of action for damages. [Piper v. Chris-Craft Industries, Inc., *supra*, §1054]

(2) **Injunctive relief:** While *Piper* did not specifically address injunctions, there is language in the opinion that would seem to indicate that the Court's holding would not disturb the bidder's right to seek injunctive relief. A lower court has so held. [*See* A & K Railroad Materials, Inc. v. Green Bay & Western Railroad, 437 F. Supp. 636 (E.D. Wis. 1977)—bidder has standing to sue for an injunction, but mere negligence is insufficient to support the action; *and see* Humana, Inc. v. American Medicorp, Inc., 445 F. Supp. 613 (S.D.N.Y. 1977)]

7. **Enforcement by the S.E.C.:** [§1074] The S.E.C. may use several means to enforce the tender offer rules:

(i) *Injunctions;*

(ii) *Criminal prosecutions;*

(iii) *Cease-and-desist proceedings;* or

(iv) *Orders for compliance* with section 13 or 14.

Each of these is explored in more detail in the materials on S.E.C. enforcement actions, *infra*, §§1481 *et seq.*

8. **Tactics in Opposing a Tender Offer:** [§1075] The target company's managers will usually attempt to fight (under threat of losing their jobs) the takeover attempt. While in most cases such a fight can be justified by sound business reasons, there is always some price at which fighting the tender offer can no longer be justified,

because the shareholders' interests are best served by recommending acceptance of the tender. For managers to resist in these circumstances amounts to placing their self-interest (in their jobs) above the well-being of the shareholders, and may lead to liability under state law for breach of fiduciary duty. Generally, the question which defensive tactics are permissible is governed by the law of the state of the target's incorporation. (*See* Corporations Summary.) Some defensive techniques, however, raise federal securities law issues.

a. **Advance provisions:** [§1076] Corporations often take measures in advance of any tender offer to prepare for one. These measures, referred to as "shark repellents," are aimed at making it more difficult for a potential bidder to gain control of the company.

   (1) **Staggered Board:** [§1077] For example, the company might stagger the election of its board of directors (*i.e.,* elect them serially over a period of several years) so that it is more difficult for the bidder to control the target company's board of directors.

   (2) **Dual-class recapitalizations:** [§1078] Another, and sometimes controversial, advance defensive tactic involves the issuance of "supervoting" stock to management, which thereby gains control of the target. Such a recapitalization may be accomplished by an exchange offer in which the target offers new, supervoting common stock to all its existing shareholders. The "catch" is that the new stock pays lower dividends than the existing common stock. In the usual case, relatively few shareholders want to exchange dividend rights for enhanced voting rights, and thus few of the shareholder-offerees will accept the offer. Management, however, will exchange its shares, and thereby take control. Alternatively, the target may issue a stock dividend, in the form of a new class of stock, to all shareholders. The dividend stock carries supervoting rights which, however, are lost upon any transfer of the stock. Most stocks have a fairly high turnover rate, and thus, before long most public shareholders will transfer their shares, causing them to lose the supervoting rights carried by the dividend stock. Management, however, will retain its shares, and will thereby gain control.

      (a) **Obstacles to the dual-class recapitalization:** At present, only the AMEX permits a listed company to have classes of voting stock with unequal voting rights; the NYSE and NASDAQ both have a "one share, one vote" rule.

b. **Persuasion of the shareholders:** [§1079] Management of the target may attempt to persuade the shareholders not to tender their shares to the bidder. However, any solicitation or recommendation to the target's shareholders must be made in accordance with the rules and regulations contained in section 14(d)(4) and rule 14d-9. Also, any recommendation that is made is subject to the antifraud provisions of section 14(e). (*See supra,* §1051.)

   (1) **Target's management must disclose its position:** [§1080] In fact, quite apart from considerations of defense, the target's *management is required to make a statement to the target's shareholders* concerning management's position with respect to the offer. [SEA Rule 14e-2]

(2) **Schedule 14D-9:** [§1081] Schedule 14D-9 sets forth the information that management must send to the S.E.C. as soon as practicable on the date such information is first published, sent, or given to security holders.

(3) **Stop-look-and-listen communications:** [§1082] As soon as the offer is made, and while determining what it will recommend to shareholders, the target may transmit (without any filing with the S.E.C.) a communication to its shareholders which states that management is studying the proposal and will (before a specified date not later than 10 business days after commencement of the offer) give its recommendation. [SEA Rule 14d-9(e)]

c. **Litigation:** [§1083] Management may choose to bring an immediate action against the bidder, alleging that there have been misrepresentations or omissions of material facts in the tender offer.

(1) **Suit for injunction:** [§1084] If management is successful in obtaining a preliminary injunction, the tender offer may well be dropped; the bidder may be reluctant to spend large sums of money in litigation, with no assurance that conditions will be suitable for continuing the offer when the litigation is concluded. (*See supra*, §§1069 *et seq.*)

(2) **Suit for rescission:** [§1085] Rescission of a successful tender offer has never been granted and would be highly impractical. Many, if not most, of the former target shareholders (who may number in the thousands, or even tens of thousands) will have spent the money received in the offer by the time the suit is brought. Understandably, courts are extremely reluctant to attempt to "unwind" such transactions.

d. **Merger with a "white knight":** [§1086] When a tender offer is attempted, the target often looks for another company with which to merge, that will promise to employ the target's management. Management's rationale for such a merger is typically that the merger is a "better deal" for shareholders than the tender offer.

e. **Purchase of its own shares:** [§1087] The target may attempt, directly or through its pension fund, to purchase enough of its own shares to prevent control from going to the bidder. Such a purchase could take place on the open market, or in a self-tender by the target. Where the result of such a stock purchase is to remove a company's stock from public ownership and trading, the transaction is known as "going private." Although issuer repurchases are not prohibited by the securities laws, they are extensively regulated.

(1) **Self-tender offers:** [§1088] If the issuer's purchase program amounts to a tender offer (*see supra*, §§1009 *et seq.*), then the issuer must comply with 1934 Act rule 13e-4. This rule requires the issuer to file an Issuer Tender Offer Statement on Schedule 13E-4 with the S.E.C.; the disclosure required by this form and the related rules is substantially similar to that required of the bidder in a conventional tender offer (*see supra*, §§1020 *et seq.*).

(2) **Open-market purchases and "market manipulation":** [§1089] If the target's open-market purchases cause the price of its securities to rise, the

purchases may be deemed "manipulative" by the S.E.C., under 1934 Act section 9(a)(2). (*See infra*, §§1721 *et seq.*) The S.E.C. has promulgated a safe harbor rule, 1934 Act rule 10b-18, which restricts the manner, time, price, and volume of issuer repurchases on the open market.

(a) **Note:** 1934 Act rule 10b-18 is a safe harbor; compliance with the rule prevents the inference that the repurchases were manipulative under 1934 Act section 9(a)(2), but noncompliance does not raise any presumption that the repurchases *were* manipulative. [1934 Act Rule 10b-18(c)]

(b) **Requirements of rule 10b-18:** [§1090] To take advantage of the rule 10b-18 safe harbor, an issuer (and its affiliated purchasers) must comply with the rule's purchasing conditions:

1) **Single broker-dealer:** [§1091] All rule 10b-18 purchases must be made from or through a single broker or dealer on any one trading day.

2) **Time of purchases:** [§1092] A rule 10b-18 purchase is not permitted to be (i) the opening purchase (*i.e.*, the first purchase) on any trading day or (ii) made within one-half hour of the end of trading on any day. An exception exists for NASDAQ-quoted securities, which may be the subject of a rule 10b-18 purchase at any time during which a current independent bid quotation is reported in NASDAQ.

3) **Price of purchases:** [§1093] Rule 10b-18 purchases must not be made at a price higher than the market price. (This is designed to limit the purchaser's ability to cause the market price to rise.)

4) **Volume of purchases:** [§1094] The daily volume of rule 10b-18 purchases may not exceed 25% of the average daily trading volume for the security over the preceding four weeks. For securities that are not publicly traded, rule 10b-18 provides that the volume over a six-day period may not exceed 1/20th of 1% of the outstanding shares (excluding shares held by affiliates) of the security.

(3) **Rule 10b-6 and issuer repurchases:** [§1095] Issuers repurchasing their own securities must also take note of 1934 Act rule 10b-6, which prohibits an issuer from buying stock that is the subject of a distribution. This could cause problems, for example, when an issuer has outstanding both common stock and preferred stock convertible into common. In such cases, the issuer is deemed to be involved in an ongoing distribution of the common stock. Rule 10b-6(f), however, exempts from this prohibition securities being distributed only "technically," for example, because the issuer has outstanding a class of securities that is convertible into the securities being purchased.

(4) **"Going private" transactions:** [§1096] When a purchase of securities will cause a publicly held company to become private, or the de-listing of

a class of the company's equity securities, then the transaction is called a "going private" transaction. Issuer repurchases may result in going private; when they do, they are subject to 1934 Act rule 13e-3. The rule requires extensive disclosure, prohibits fraud or untrue statements, and requires compliance with specific administrative procedures.

(a) **Fairness concerns in going private transactions:** [§1097] Even with extensive regulation, many market observers are concerned about the possibilities for unfairness to shareholders inherent in issuers' going private transactions (often called "management buyouts," or "MBOs"). The chief concerns result from the superior access to information possessed by management, as well as the fact that the timing and price of the transaction are largely under management's control. There is an obvious conflict of interest between the purchasing managers and the selling shareholders in such a transaction.

(5) **When a tender offer has been commenced:** [§1098] If a bidder has already commenced a tender offer for the target, then in addition to complying with the above rules, *the target must comply with 1934 Act rule 13e-1* before purchasing its own securities. Rule 13e-1 requires the target to file a statement with the S.E.C. disclosing certain information about the planned repurchase, including the securities to be repurchased, the markets in which the repurchase will take place, and the source of the funds to be used to make the repurchase.

f. **"Poison pills":** [§1099] A "shareholder rights plan" (so called by its proponents; more commonly called a "poison pill") is a technique whereby the shareholders of a potential target are given the right either to purchase securities or to force a successful bidder to buy securities, in either case at a price highly favorable to the target's shareholders. As a rule, the price is so favorable that a takeover transaction is impossible for as long as the shareholders retain the rights. The target's board of directors, however, is given the power to redeem the rights; thus, poison pills are useful in forcing a bidder to negotiate with the target's board. Poison pills are typically structured in one of two ways:

(1) **"Call plans":** [§1100] A call plan gives target shareholders the right to acquire additional securities of the target (or the survivor of a merger involving the target), at a greatly reduced price. The right is triggered by the happening of any one of several specified events, for example, the merger of the target and another company. The effect is to make a merger of the target prohibitively expensive for the bidder.

(a) **Flip-over pills:** [§1101] The pill discussed immediately above is an example of a "flip-over" pill, because the shareholders' rights "flip over" and become exercisable against the bidder in the event of a merger.

(b) **Flip-in pills:** [§1102] So-called "flip-in" pills are triggered by the bidder exceeding some specified limit, usually expressed in terms of percentage ownership of the target's stock. Thus, for example, a flip-in pill might be triggered when the bidder acquires more than

20% of the target's common stock, and the pill would then give the target's shareholders—other than the bidder—the right to acquire additional shares of the target at a greatly reduced price.

(2) **"Put plans":** [§1103] A put plan gives the target shareholders the right to force the target (or the survivor of a merger involving the target) to buy stock of the target at a price specified by the plan. These are attractive mostly to smaller investors and to targets whose securities are held largely by smaller holders, because such shareholders may have difficulty raising enough money to buy significant quantities of securities in a call plan, even at the discounted prices call plans feature.

g. **"Greenmail":** [§1104] So-called "greenmail" is a payment from the target to the bidder in order to persuade the bidder to abandon its takeover plans. In the typical scenario, the target pays the bidder, in exchange for which the bidder executes a "standstill" agreement under which it agrees not to acquire additional shares in, or otherwise seek control of, the target for a specified period (often five or 10 years). The legal issues surrounding greenmail arise primarily under state law, and involve conflicts of interest and the fiduciary duties of the target's management and board. Target shareholders are often understandably distressed by the thought of management using corporate assets to dissuade a bidder who, after all, might have offered the shareholders an attractive price for their stock.

(1) **Tax consequences:** [§1105] In 1987, Congress enacted Internal Revenue Code section 5881, imposing a 50%, nondeductible excise tax on profit received in a greenmail transaction. Section 5881 is relatively easy to avoid, however, because "greenmail" as defined under the statute includes only payments made to a person who has made or threatened to make a tender offer (and who meets certain additional criteria). Avoidance, then, is simply a matter of not explicitly threatening a tender offer, leaving the possibilities to the imagination of the target's management.

h. **Employee stock ownership plans ("ESOPS"):** [§1106] Originally intended as an employee benefit, ESOPS are sometimes used to thwart the takeover plans of a bidder. An ESOP can be structured so as to make it difficult or impossible for a bidder to gain control of the target's board of directors.

(1) **Techniques for defensive use:** [§1107] The following are examples of ESOP techniques that have been employed in efforts to defeat takeover attempts:

(a) **Reset provisions:** [§1108] Reset provisions provide target employees with economic incentives to vote against a takeover attempt. Reset provisions permit the conversion price of target company preferred stock, issued to the ESOP, to be reset if the price of the target's common stock falls (for example, if a tender offer were to be withdrawn). Because employees are protected against this "downside risk," they have every reason to perpetuate the existing target management in office, especially since the ESOP would probably not survive if the bidder succeeds in obtaining control.

(b) **Mirrored voting:** [§1109] The trustees of an ESOP may be contractually required to vote unallocated shares held by the plan in the same proportion as shares allocated to (and therefore voted by) participants. Because the target's employees generally do not favor takeover attempts, this tactic usually produces a large, block vote against the bidder.

(c) **"Heavy" voting:** [§1110] An ESOP often holds senior securities (for example, preferred stock) that are convertible into common shares. When the senior securities are convertible into fewer shares of common stock than they carry votes, the voting power of the senior securities is said to be "heavy."

　　1) **Example:** An ESOP holds preferred stock, each share of which is convertible into 8/10 of a share of common stock of the target. Each unconverted preferred share, however, carries one full vote, and as far as voting power is concerned, is the equivalent of a full common share. Voting is "heavy." [NCR Corp. v. American Telephone & Telegraph Co., 761 F. Supp. 475 (S.D. Ohio 1991)]

(d) **Leverage:** [§1111] An ESOP is said to be "leveraged" when all shares allocated to the plan are issued at once, whether or not any participants have purchased or are likely to purchase them. An unleveraged ESOP, by contrast, receives shares incrementally, according to the plan's needs. Leveraged plans are more effective as takeover defenses, because they enable the target's management to reap the maximum benefit from mirrored and "heavy" voting.

(2) **Enforceability of defensive ESOPS:** [§1112] Although the techniques discussed above can be effective, ESOPS employing these techniques may be held to be unenforceable under state law or applicable stock exchange rules.

(a) **Breach of fiduciary duty:** [§1113] An ESOP must have a legitimate business purpose. In the absence of a legitimate purpose, an ESOP that consolidates control, or entrenches management, is a breach of fiduciary duty because it places the interests of management above those of the shareholders. [*See, e.g.,* NCR Corp. v. American Telephone & Telegraph Co., *supra*]

(b) **Stock exchange regulations:** [§1114] The defensive issuance of shares to an ESOP may violate stock exchange rules prohibiting the issuance of large amounts of stock without shareholder approval. [*See* Norlin Corp. v. Rooney, Pace, Inc., 744 F.2d 255 (2d Cir. 1984)]

i. **Stock lockups:** [§1115] Rather than issue shares to an ESOP, the target may issue shares to a "white knight"—that is, to a bidder whose offer the target views more favorably than the first bidder's. The ultimate goal of such a transaction might be to induce the white knight to make a tender offer at a price higher than the first bidder's. Alternatively, a stock lockup may be designed to force the first bidder to comply with state anti-takeover statutes (discussed *infra*), or to prevent the first bidder from obtaining enough shares to oust the incumbent board of directors.

j. **"Crown jewel" lockups:** [§1116] Takeover attempts are frequently launched in an effort to acquire control of the target's most desirable assets—its "crown jewels." Therefore, a target may grant an option on the crown jewels as a defense against the takeover attempt. These lockups typically are granted to white knights—that is, to potential bidders whose bids are viewed more favorably than the hostile bidder's.

9. **State Anti-Takeover Legislation:** [§1117] In *CTS Corp. v. Dynamics Corp.*, 481 U.S. 69 (1987), the Supreme Court upheld an Indiana statute imposing certain restrictions on bidders seeking to acquire Indiana targets. In the wake of *CTS*, many other states passed anti-takeover legislation. Although strictly speaking these statutes are not part of the field of securities regulation, belonging rather to the realm of state corporation law, they have a significant impact on the work of securities lawyers dealing with takeovers. For this reason, they are briefly discussed below.

a. **Shareholder protection statutes:** [§1118] The most common form of state anti-takeover legislation is the shareholder protection statute. Such statutes purport to protect the target's shareholders. Shareholder protection statutes may be grouped roughly into three groups, according to the approximate date of their passage and the manner in which the "protection" of the target's shareholders is implemented. [*See* Amanda Acquisition Corp. v. Universal Foods Corp., 877 F.2d 496 (7th Cir. 1989)]

(1) **First-generation statutes:** [§1119] Before *CTS*, Illinois had attempted to limit takeovers of corporations with substantial assets in Illinois, by requiring approval of a public official before such an acquisition could be consummated. The Illinois statute was held unconstitutional under the Commerce Clause. [Edgar v. MITE Corp., 457 U.S. 624 (1982)]

(2) **Second-generation statutes:** [§1120] Second-generation statutes do not impose any restrictions on the bidder's ability to buy the target's shares. Instead, they restrict the voting power of shares acquired by a hostile bidder. The voting power limitations can be eliminated by action of the target's management or by a vote of the target shareholders (excluding management and the hostile bidder). Second-generation statutes are fairly common today. Whether they effectively restrict takeovers, however, is debatable. Although few data are available, it would seem that if the number of shareholders wishing to tender is enough to give the hostile bidder control, those same shareholders would vote to restore the voting power of that bidder's shares. The chief restriction imposed by second-generation statutes is the delay resulting from the shareholder meeting necessary to conduct the required ballot, and equivalent delays are in any case achievable by means of a "poison pill" device.

(a) **Example:** The *CTS* case involved a second-generation statute, which applied only to Indiana corporations, and provided that upon the acquisition of a threshold percentage of target shares, the acquired shares would lose their voting power unless the share acquisition was approved by either the target's board of directors or a majority of disinterested shareholders (*i.e.,* those not affiliated with the bidder or target management). The statute was held constitutional, and not preempted by the Williams Act. [CTS Corp. v. Dynamics Corp., *supra*]

(3) **Third-generation statutes:** [§1121] Most recently, state shareholder protection statutes have attempted to limit the ability of an "interested shareholder" (as defined by the statute) to effect a business combination with the target. Because most takeover attempts have as a goal a merger, liquidation or partial liquidation, or other similar transaction, all of which are usually included among the prohibited business combinations, such statutes have the effect of making hostile takeovers less common. These statutes have been held constitutional and not preempted. [*See, e.g.,* Amanda Acquisition Corp. v. Universal Foods Corp., *supra*]

b. **Challenges to state shareholder protection statutes:** [§1122] Federal-law challenges to state anti-takeover statutes have proceeded on two theories: that the state law is preempted by the Williams Act, and that the state law is unconstitutional under the Commerce Clause.

(1) **Williams Act challenges:** [§1123] In general, the Williams Act will preempt a state law only if the law is in conflict with the Act. [*See* SEA §28(a); CTS Corp. v. Dynamics Corp., *supra*] Precisely when a state anti-takeover law conflicts with the Williams Act remains unsettled. In the *MITE* case, *supra*, the Supreme Court decided—by a plurality—that the Illinois statute at issue was preempted, because the Illinois statute at issue favored management over the shareholders. Whether the Williams Act mandates state-law neutrality between these groups, however, remains questionable.

(2) **Commerce Clause challenges:** [§1124] Even if not preempted by the Williams Act, a state anti-takeover statute may be unconstitutional under the Commerce Clause. The circumstances under which a statute violates the Commerce Clause, however, are not entirely clear at this point. Certainly, a statute that overtly discriminates against bidders from other states would be unconstitutional. Also, states may not enact laws creating a significant risk that an activity will become subject to different, and inconsistent, regulation. Beyond this, however, it is difficult to predict in what direction the Supreme Court's Commerce Clause analysis will turn. The most recent cases on this point are the *MITE* and *CTS* cases, discussed *supra*.

c. **Other state anti-takeover statutes:** [§1125] In addition to the shareholder protection statutes discussed above, many states have enacted other kinds of legislation designed to protect domestic corporations from takeover attempts. These may be loosely grouped into two categories: "constituency" statutes, and "disgorgement" statutes.

(1) **Constituency statutes:** [§1126] Constituency statutes permit a corporation's board of directors to consider the welfare of persons other than the shareholders. For the most part, however, the statutes are unclear as to whether such interests may be treated as superior to those of the shareholders, or whether they merely codify the common law rule that such

interests may be considered when they are not in conflict with those of the shareholders.

(2) **Disgorgement statutes:** [§1127] Disgorgement statutes (to date, only Pennsylvania has adopted such a law) provide that investors must disgorge to the target profits received from shares acquired before the investors obtained control, if those shares are sold within some period of time after obtaining control. (Pennsylvania's law is similar in some respects to the "short-swing" disgorgement requirement by SEA section 16; *see infra,* §§1282 *et seq.*)

## D. REGULATION OF PROXY SOLICITATIONS

1. **"Proxy" Defined:** [§1128] A proxy is a power of attorney to vote shares owned by someone else. At common law, proxies were illegal, but today they are permitted and regulated both by state statutes and by the Securities Exchange Act.

   a. **Power to revoke:** [§1129] A proxy establishes an agency relationship that is revocable at any time, except under certain limited conditions.

      (1) **Irrevocable proxies:** [§1130] Under state law, a proxy that is expressly made irrevocable *and* is "coupled with an interest" generally is irrevocable.

         (a) **Definition:** "Coupled with an interest" means that some consideration was received by the shareholder for granting the proxy. For example, when a shareholder borrows money and pledges her stock as security, granting the lender an irrevocable proxy to vote the pledged shares, the proxy is coupled with an interest and is therefore irrevocable.

         (b) **But note:** State statutes usually limit the duration for which even an irrevocable proxy coupled with an interest may be given (*e.g.,* to a period of five years).

   b. **What constitutes a proxy solicitation:** [§1131] Under federal law, a "solicitation" is any communication to the shareholders reasonably calculated to result in the granting, withholding, or revocation of a proxy. [SEA Rule 14a-1]

      (1) **Note:** The federal proxy rules may apply even though the party sending the communication is not soliciting a proxy for the purpose of voting.

         (a) **Example:** X may send a communication attempting to influence the shareholders of ABC Corp. not to give their proxies to management. The common stock of ABC Corp. is listed on the NYSE. This communication is covered by the federal proxy rules (although delivery of a proxy statement may not be required; *see infra,* §1159).

2. **Regulation by the States:** [§1132] The regulation of shareholder proxies is a central part of state corporate law. In addition to regulating the revocability of proxies, the states regulate many aspects of proxy solicitation, including the extent to which the expenses of a proxy contest can be paid by the corporation and how

the shareholders' meeting is conducted (including permissible methods for counting the proxies, etc.).

a. **State remedies:** [§1133]  State-law remedies for fraud in the solicitation of proxies are usually available.

b. **Federal jurisdiction over proxy rules exclusive:** [§1134]  However, the federal courts have exclusive jurisdiction over application of the federal proxy rules.

3. **Federal Proxy Rules—An Introduction:** [§1135]  Because it favors the solicitation of proxies by corporate management, the proxy system is an effective tool for maintaining control over a large, public corporation. Because of the tremendous number of shares such a corporation will have outstanding, purchasing a majority of the outstanding voting stock—*e.g.,* in a tender offer—is often prohibitively expensive. Soliciting proxies from the many individual shareholders whose aggregate votes constitute the needed majority is not cheap, either—but it is far less expensive than purchasing a majority of the outstanding voting stock. Also, in most cases, state law permits management to use *corporate funds* to pay for the solicitation. To prevent abuses in the proxy solicitation process, authority to regulate proxies relating to securities registered under the 1934 Act has been given to the S.E.C. in section 14(a) of that 1934 Act.

a. **Objectives of the S.E.C. rules:** [§1136]  Pursuant to its authority under section 14(a), the S.E.C. has adopted rules for the regulation of proxy solicitations. [*See* SEA Regulation 14A] These rules are designed to accomplish three objectives:

(1) **To encourage full disclosure:** [§1137]  Those who solicit proxies (or attempt to dissuade shareholders from granting them) must fully disclose all material facts to the shareholders being solicited. [SEA Rules 14a-3 - 14a-6]

(2) **To prevent fraud:** [§1138]  The federal rules specifically prohibit the use of fraud in the solicitation of proxies. [SEA Rule 14a-9]

(3) **To provide for shareholder proposals:** [§1139]  Shareholders (other than management) may also solicit proxies from other shareholders, and the S.E.C. rules require management to include in its proxy statement proper proposals made by these shareholders. [SEA Rule 14a-8]

b. **Scope of coverage of proxy rules**

(1) **Companies covered:** [§1140]  The federal proxy rules apply to all companies with securities registered under section 12 (*i.e.,* all "registered companies"). (*See supra*, §§742-744.)

(2) **Securities covered:** [§1141]  Similarly, the proxy rules apply to all securities registered under section 12.

(a) **Over-the-counter companies:** [§1142]  The proxy regulations apply only to the *registered equity securities* of the companies registered under section 12(g) (*i.e.,* "over-the-counter" companies).

"Equity" securities are broadly defined under the Act and include, for example, convertible debentures.

(b) **Listed companies:** [§1143] Companies with securities listed for trading on a national securities exchange must register the securities with the S.E.C. under section 12(b). Therefore, the proxy rules apply to *any* such listed security, including listed *debt* securities.

    1) **Debt securities:** [§1144] Although debt securities do not normally vote, any corporate action requiring the consent of debt security holders would be subject to the proxy regulations.

        a) **Example:** A solicitation of the vote of debenture holders, requesting them to waive a provision in the trust indenture covering the debentures, would require compliance with the proxy rules.

(3) **Transactions and matters covered:** [§1145] Whenever a corporation has a matter that calls for a shareholder vote, it is subject to the proxy rules. For example, the approval of a merger or the amendment of the articles of incorporation are subject to shareholder vote, and thus the proxy rules apply to these matters.

(4) **Communications covered:** [§1146] In the normal course of a corporation's affairs, management and others related to the corporation (*e.g.*, securities firms) may wish to distribute information to shareholders concerning the corporation. If such material is distributed immediately prior to or during a proxy solicitation, an issue may arise as to whether such material is distributed with the intent of influencing the proxy solicitation, and therefore, whether it is actually part of the proxy solicitation.

(a) **Note:** It is clear that the issuer may distribute its regular annual, semi-annual, or quarterly financial report and not have it deemed a "proxy solicitation." Indeed, the proxy rules *require* most issuers subject to the 1934 Act to send the annual report to their shareholders. [SEA Rule 14a-3]

(b) **Statement of intended vote is not a "solicitation":** [§1147] The proxy rules exclude from the definition of "solicitation" a communication by a security holder, who does not otherwise engage in a non-exempt solicitation, stating how the security holder intends to vote and the reasons therefor. [SEA Rule 14a-1(l)]

4. **Proxy Disclosure Requirements:** [§1148] There are two kinds of required disclosure under the proxy rules: the proxy statement and the annual report. Each is discussed below.

    a. **The proxy statement:** [§1149] The proxy rules set forth what information must be disclosed in the proxy statement, essentially: all material facts regarding matters to be voted on by the security holders and identification of the participants in the solicitation. [*See* SEA Schedule 14A; *see infra*, §1169]

(1) **If proxies are not solicited—the information statement:** [§1150] What if the issuer is not soliciting proxies? For example, there might be insiders of the issuer who control enough votes to constitute a quorum (and, perhaps, a majority of the votes present at any shareholder meeting). Can the issuer avoid the disclosure otherwise required under the proxy rules? The answer is no, because SEA section 14(c) requires the issuer to "file with the [SEC] and transmit to [the security holders] information substantially equivalent to the information which would be required to be transmitted if a solicitation were made. . . ." [*See* SEA Schedule 14C]

b. **The annual report:** [§1151] The second component of required proxy disclosure is the issuer's annual report. If directors are to be elected, then before the annual meeting (or special meeting in lieu of the annual meeting) at which the election is to take place, the registrant must provide shareholders with an annual report. The contents of the annual report are specified in the proxy rules. [*See* SEA Rule 14a-3]

(1) **Note:** Shareholders of 1934 Act reporting companies are familiar with the glossy annual report, typically distributed each spring. These reports are required by SEA rule 14a-3.

c. **Antifraud provisions:** [§1152] The proxy rules contain antifraud provisions in SEA rule 14a-9. These provisions apply to all proxy "solicitations" as defined in rule 14a-1, whether or not the particular solicitation is exempt from the delivery or filing requirements. If the activity in question is part of a solicitation, the antifraud rules apply to all materials used and statements made by the parties. [*See* SEA Rule 14a-9; *see infra*, §1249]

5. **Proxy Statement Delivery Requirements:** [§1153] In addition to specifying what information must be disclosed to shareholders when their proxies are solicited, the proxy rules specify the manner in which the information must be disclosed: by delivery of a preliminary or definitive proxy statement and, if directors are to be elected, an annual report.

a. **Solicitation prohibited without delivery of proxy statement:** [§1154] A solicitation subject to the proxy rules is not permitted to begin unless *each person solicited* has been furnished with a *written proxy statement containing the information required by Schedule 14A.* [SEA Rule 14a-3]

(1) **Proxy statement may be preliminary:** [§1155] Note, however, that the written proxy statement required before a solicitation can begin *need not be in definitive form*—a preliminary proxy statement will meet the S.E.C.'s requirements, as long as it contains the information required by Schedule 14A. [*See* SEA Rules 14a-3(a), 14a-4(f)]

(2) **Proxy card prohibited until definitive proxy statement delivered:** [§1156] Even though the proxy solicitation can begin before the definitive proxy statement is delivered, *the person soliciting* proxies may *not* deliver a proxy card (called the "form of proxy"—*i.e.,* the actual form on which the shareholders grant authority to vote their shares and specify how the shares are to be voted) *until a definitive proxy statement has been delivered* to the shareholders. [SEA Rule 14a-4(f)]

(3) **Exceptions to delivery requirements:** [§1157] The proxy statement delivery requirements do not apply to certain solicitations.

(a) **Public solicitation:** [§1158] Solicitations made by public broadcast, speech, advertisement, etc., need not be preceded or accompanied by delivery of a written proxy statement.

(b) **Soliciting person not seeking proxy authority:** [§1159] Similarly, when the person soliciting is not actually seeking a proxy from the shareholders, no written proxy statement need be delivered.

(c) **Proxy contests:** [§1160] In addition to the above exceptions, there is an exception to the delivery requirement for defensive solicitations in proxy contests. Although a proxy statement ultimately must be delivered, the S.E.C. recognizes the practical need to respond quickly in a proxy contest, and permits a defensive solicitation to begin before the proxy statement is completed. (*See infra,* §1176.)

6. **Proxy Statement Filing Requirements:** [§1161] All written materials used in a solicitation must be filed with the S.E.C. [SEA Rule 14a-6] Some materials must be filed in preliminary, "draft" form before definitive copies are disseminated to the shareholders. Other materials need not be filed with the S.E.C. until final, definitive versions have been prepared and are actually disseminated.

a. **Varieties of written proxy materials:** [§1162] Written materials distributed to shareholders in connection with a proxy solicitation may be loosely grouped into three categories: the proxy statement, the form of proxy, and other soliciting materials.

b. **Advance filing requirements:** [§1163] The S.E.C. requires the following materials to be *filed in advance of their use,* to give the S.E.C. an opportunity to review and comment on them.

(1) **Proxy statement and form of proxy:** [§1164] Both the proxy statement and the form of proxy itself must be filed with the S.E.C. *at least 10 days before the definitive versions are disseminated* to shareholders.

(a) **Exception:** [§1165] The issuer need not file preliminary copies of the proxy statement or the form of proxy if the solicitation relates to any meeting of security holders at which the only matters to be acted upon are:

(i) The *election of directors*;

(ii) Election, approval or ratification of *accountants*;

(iii) A proposal by a security holder pursuant to *SEA Rule 14a-8* (*see infra*, §1186);

(iv) The approval or ratification of a plan of *executive compensation*; or

(v) ***Certain matters affecting investment companies*** registered under the Investment Company Act of 1940.

[SEA Rule 14a-6(a)]

(2) **Other soliciting materials:** [§1166]  Materials other than the proxy statement and the form of proxy need not be filed in advance of their dissemination to shareholders.

c. **Filing requirements for definitive versions:** [§1167]  All materials used in a solicitation must be filed (or mailed for filing) with the S.E.C. and with each national securities exchange on which securities of the registrant trade ***no later than the day on which they are first used.*** When the materials have been filed in preliminary form, the final versions are prepared with a view to the S.E.C.'s comments on the previously filed versions.

(1) **Note:** If preliminary versions of proxy materials have been disseminated, the above rule applies also to those; *i.e.*, copies must be filed with the S.E.C. no later than the day on which they are first used.

d. **Antifraud provisions applicable:** [§1168]  Note that whether or not the S.E.C. requires advance filing of particular solicitation documents, the antifraud provisions of the 1934 Act apply to all materials used and statements made by the parties. [*See* SEA Rule 14a-9; *see infra*, §1249]

7. **The Proxy Statement:** [§1169]  The following information must be included in the proxy statement (or the information statement, if proxies are not solicited):

a. **Details about solicitation:** [§1170]  A statement identifying for whom the solicitation is being made, the means (mail, etc.) being used, who bears the cost, the amount already spent, and an estimate of the total amount to be spent in the proxy solicitation. [Schedule 14A]

b. **Details about director election:** [§1171]  In addition, if directors are to be elected at the shareholders' meeting, the proxy statement must name and give detailed information about (i) the nominees of the party that is soliciting the proxy, (ii) other directors whose terms of office continue beyond the meeting, and (iii) the officers of the registrant. The statement must include such information as transactions during the past year between the specified persons and the corporation. [Schedule 14A]

c. **Details about specific matters:** [§1172]  Detailed information must be disclosed relating to the specific matters for which the proxy is being solicited. [Schedule 14A]

(1) **Example:** Specific rules cover the information required in situations of merger, sale of corporate assets, liquidation or dissolution, or the purchase of another company.

(a) With respect to mergers and other reorganization transactions, cross-reference here the requirements of SA rule 145 (*supra*, §499). In rule 145 transactions, a registration statement on Form S-4 is usually filed, and serves as both the Schedule 14A proxy statement and as a 1933 Act prospectus.

(2) **And note:** Financial statements must also be filed in connection with certain transactions, such as mergers and authorizations to issue new securities.

d. **Details about executive compensation:** [§1173]  If the solicitation is made in behalf of the registrant, the proxy statement must also disclose details about the registrant's compensation of its executive officers. Information is required about the person serving as chief executive officer, the four most highly compensated officers other than the CEO, and up to two persons for whom disclosure would have been provided but for the fact that they were no longer serving as executive officers at the end of the most recent fiscal year. [Schedule 14A; Regulation S-K Item 402(a)(3)]

e. **Details about general matters:** [§1174]  There are some general matters that must also be disclosed, including significant changes in control, the fact that securities owned by control persons have been pledged as collateral for loans, the vote required on each issue, the shares entitled to vote, and the record date for voting. [Schedule 14A]

8. **Proxy Contests:** [§1175]  A proxy contest typically results from a fight between management and other shareholders for control of the company. Most often, the insurgent shareholders will have acquired a substantial position in the company and either (i) want to control the company through election of a majority of the directors or (ii) will have proposed a merger or made a tender offer for the shares of the company, and management seeks to avoid a loss of control by merging with another company. In the first situation, the insurgents will solicit shareholder proxies in order to elect their slate of directors; while in the second situation, a so-called "defensive merger," management will solicit proxies in support of the merger.

a. **Defensive solicitation of proxies:** [§1176]  Either management or the insurgents may make certain defensive solicitations prior to distribution of the proxy statement. Any such solicitation must identify the person on behalf of whom the solicitation is made and give a description of that person's interest in the issuer. [SEA Rules 14a-11, 14a-12]

(1) **Requirements for pre-delivery defensive solicitations:** [§1177]  To make a solicitation prior to delivering a written proxy statement, the following requirements must be met:

(a) **Prior opposing solicitation:** [§1178]  There must be a prior opposing proxy solicitation which either (i) might have the effect of defeating a proposal to be made at a shareholders' meeting [SEA Rule 14a-12] or (ii) contests the election of directors [SEA Rule 14a-11].

1) **Example:** An insurgent group of shareholders wishes to elect its own slate of directors to the board of Acme Co. After management has begun to solicit proxies for management's slate of directors, the insurgents can begin to solicit proxies for their opposing slate, even prior to delivering a written proxy statement.

2) **Example:** An insurgent group of shareholders makes a solicitation concerning a matter to be proposed at the next shareholders' meeting. Management may then send out its own materials, even before delivering to the shareholders a written proxy statement.

(b) **Form of proxy prohibited without written proxy statement:** [§1179] Although a solicitation may begin prior to delivering a written proxy statement, *no form of proxy may be delivered until the written proxy statement is delivered.* [SEA Rules 14a-11(b)(1), 14a-12(a)(2)]

(c) **Timing of delivery:** [§1180] Following a predelivery defensive solicitation, written proxy statements must be delivered to shareholders at the earliest practicable date. [SEA Rules 14a-11(b)(3), 14a-12(a)(4)]

b. **Shareholder lists:** [§1181] Normally, the question of a shareholder's access to the registrant's shareholder list is governed by state law. For 1934 Act reporting companies, however, the S.E.C.'s involvement in proxy regulation means that *federal law plays a part in the issue.*

(1) **General rule:** [§1182] If management is soliciting proxies, then a shareholder who wants to send proxy soliciting material (usually in opposition to management) must either (i) be given *access to the registrant's shareholder list,* or (ii) the *registrant must mail the materials to its shareholders on behalf of the requesting shareholder.* The choice belongs to the *registrant,* which will most often choose to send the materials rather than to give the shareholder access to the shareholder list. [SEA Rule 14a-7; *see infra,* §1225]

(2) **Special rule for "going private" and "roll-up" transactions:** [§1183] When management proposes a "going private" or "roll-up" transaction, the option of having the registrant send the materials or having access to the registrant's shareholder list *belongs to the requesting shareholder, not to the registrant.* [SEA Rule 14a-7(b)]

(a) **"Going private" transaction defined:** [§1184] Going private transactions are transactions in which a publicly held company becomes closely held, usually by means of a tender offer. (*See supra,* §§1096-1097.)

(b) **"Roll-up" transaction defined:** [§1185] A roll-up transaction is one in which limited partnerships are either combined or reorganized; usually, the interests of the limited partners are purchased by a successor entity which then either sells securities or is itself acquired by the former general partner.

(c) **Rationale:** Going private and roll-up transactions involve the purchase of investors' interests, frequently by the managers of the enterprise. When the buyers are the managers, they have access to substantially more information about the business than do the investors. These transactions thus pose a greater risk of abuse than do run-of-the-mill transactions. The S.E.C., therefore, has given the choice to the requesting shareholders—they decide whether to demand a shareholder list, and to mail directly to shareholders, or alternatively to permit the registrant to do the mailing.

9. **Shareholder Proposals:** [§1186]  As an alternative to an independent proxy solicitation, a shareholder may serve notice on management of her intention to propose action at the shareholders' meeting. Then, in order to put the matter before the shareholders at the meeting, the shareholder may, under certain circumstances, compel management to include the proposal in the registrant's proxy statement. [SEA Rule 14a-8] Management, however, will in almost every case attempt to exclude the proposal (usually to avoid the expense of including it) from the proxy statement, relying on SEA rule 14a-8(c), which provides a list of permissible reasons for not including an otherwise proper shareholder proposal.

a. **Requirements:** [§1187]  To be included in the registrant's proxy statement, a shareholder proposal must meet the requirements of SEA rule 14a-8(a) and (b), which are briefly outlined below.

(1) **Eligible shareholders:** [§1188]  The proponent of the proposal must meet the following requirements:

(a) **Holds at least one percent or $1,000 market value:** [§1189]  The proponent must be the record or beneficial owner of at least 1% or $1,000 in market value (whichever is less) of the registrant's securities entitled to be voted at the meeting. Co-proponents of a proposal may aggregate their shares to meet this requirement.

(b) **Holding period of at least one year:** [§1190]  The proponent (or co-proponents) must have held no less than the minimum quantity of securities for at least one year.

(c) **Holds at time of meeting:** [§1191]  The proponent (or co-proponents) must continue to hold no less than the minimum quantity of securities through the time of the meeting.

(2) **Procedural requirements:** [§1192]  Shareholder proposals must be submitted in accordance with the following procedures.

(a) **Length; number of proposals:** [§1193]  A proponent may submit only one proposal, together with an accompanying statement in support. The proposal together with the supporting statement may not exceed 500 words.

(b) **Shareholder information:** [§1194]  Together with the proposal, the proponent must provide her name, address, the number of voting securities she holds of record or beneficially, the dates on which she acquired the securities, and documentary evidence of beneficial ownership.

(c) **Attendance at meeting:** [§1195]  Either the proponent or her representative (if allowed to present the proposal under state law) must attend the meeting and present the proposal.

1) **Failure to attend or to present proposal:** [§1196] If the proposal is not presented at the meeting and the failure is not excused by good cause, the registrant is not required to include in its proxy statement any proposals submitted by the shareholder for the next two years.

(d) **Timeliness:** [§1197] The proponent must submit the proposal far enough in advance to permit the registrant to consider it, and potentially to include it in the printed proxy statement sent to the shareholders.

1) **Annual meetings:** [§1198] Proposals that are to be presented at the registrant's annual meeting of shareholders must be received by the registrant 120 days before the date corresponding to the day and month on which the proxy statement was delivered to shareholders for last year's annual meeting.

a) **If there was no annual meeting in the last year:** [§1199] If the registrant had no annual meeting in the previous year, or if this year's meeting date was changed by more than 30 days from last year's, the proponent of the proposal must deliver the proposal to the registrant a reasonable time before the solicitation is made.

2) **Other meetings:** [§1200] Proposals to be presented to shareholders at meetings other than annual meetings must be delivered to the registrant a reasonable time before the solicitation is made.

b. **Management's omission of shareholder proposals:** [§1201] Where management opposes the shareholder proposal, it must file the proposal and the reasons for opposing it with the S.E.C. [SEA Rule 14a-8(d)] The S.E.C. staff will review the proposal and give an indication of whether it agrees or disagrees with management (*i.e.,* whether it would issue a "no action letter" if management omits the proposal from its proxy solicitation). Note, however, that the "no action" position expressed in the staff's letter is not binding on the proponent of the proposal, who remains free to litigate the propriety of excluding the proposal in federal court. Management may properly omit shareholder proposals in the following situations [SEA Rule 14a-8(c)]:

(1) **Proposal not a "proper subject":** [§1202] If the shareholder's proposal is not a "proper subject" for action by the shareholders, it may be omitted from management's proxy solicitation. The state law of the issuer's domicile applies to determine what is a "proper subject."

(2) **Proposal illegal:** [§1203] Management need not include a proposal that, if implemented, would require the registrant to violate any state or federal law or the law of any foreign jurisdiction to which the registrant is subject.

(a) **Note:** If compliance with a foreign law would cause the registrant to violate United States law, this basis for exclusion does not apply.

(3) **Proposal contrary to S.E.C. rules or regulations:** [§1204] If the proposal or its supporting statement violates any of the proxy rules (including rule 14a-9, prohibiting false or misleading statements), it need not be included in the registrant's proxy statement.

(4) **Proposal relates to redress of personal claim:** [§1205] Management need not include proposals that are designed primarily to further some personal interest of the proponent not shared with other shareholders in general, *e.g.,* redressing a grievance against the registrant.

(5) **Proposal relates to insignificant operations of the registrant:** [§1206] Management need not include a proposal that relates to insignificant operations. To establish that the shareholder proposal relates to operations that are not significantly related to the registrant's business, two elements must be shown:

   (a) **No economic significance:** [§1207] The operations in question must account for *less than 5%* of the registrant's *total assets* at the end of its most recent fiscal year, and less than 5% of its *net earnings* and *gross sales* for its most recent fiscal year; *and*

   (b) **No other significance:** [§1208] The operations *must not be significant in some other way* to the registrant's business.

   1) **Example:** Acme Corp. had revenues last year of $141 million, and profits of $6 million. One Acme line of business is the importation and sale of paté de foie gras. Its paté sales last year grossed $79,000, with a net loss of $3,126. A shareholder sought to include in Acme's proxy statement a proposal that Acme form a committee to study the methods by which its French supplier produced paté, and to determine whether the geese used in production were mistreated. Acme attempted to exclude the proposal on the ground that it was insignificant to its business. When the dispute arrived in court, the court held that Acme could not exclude the proposal; although the *economic* insignificance of the paté business to Acme was clear, the court ruled that the proposal might raise *policy questions* important enough to be considered "significantly related" to Acme's business. The court held that the rule evaluates, but is not limited to, economic significance—the absence of policy significance must be shown before a proposal can be excluded. [Lovenheim v. Iroquois Brands, Ltd., 618 F. Supp. 554 (D.D.C. 1985)]

(6) **Proposal deals with matter beyond registrant's power:** [§1209] Management need not include proposals relating to issues or situations over which the registrant has no control.

(7) **Proposal deals with ordinary business operations of registrant:** [§1210] Management may exclude proposals relating to the conduct of the ordinary business operations of the registrant. [SEA Rule 14a-8(c)(7)]

   (a) **Rationale:** Matters related to the ordinary business operations of the registrant are within the bailiwick of either the registrant's board of directors or its management; they are not matters over which shareholders have authority.

(b) **Exception:** [§1211] Even if a proposal arguably relates to the conduct of the registrant's ordinary business operations, it may not be excluded from the proxy statement if it also involves important political or social issues.

   1) **Example:** In 1969, shareholders proposed to Dow Chemical Corporation that the board of directors should consider adopting a policy that the corporation would not manufacture napalm. Although this could be called an ordinary business decision involving the company's product line (and the S.E.C. staff issued a no-action letter permitting the proposal's exclusion on that basis), the shareholders brought an action in federal district court to force the company to include the proposal. The court ruled that the proposal must be included, because of its political and social significance. [Medical Committee for Human Rights v. S.E.C., 432 F.2d 659 (D.C. Cir. 1970)]

(c) **S.E.C. adopts _Medical Committee_:** [§1212] After the decision in _Medical Committee, supra_, the S.E.C. announced that it would adopt the policy of that case and that henceforth, rule 14a-8(c)(7) would be interpreted so as to exclude shareholder proposals only if the proposals "do not involve any substantial policy or other considerations." [S.E.C. Release No. 34-12999 (1976)]

(d) **Recent developments:** [§1213] In early 1993, the S.E.C. staff attempted to retreat from the _Medical Committee_ interpretation of rule 14a-8(c)(7). Two corporations sought to exclude shareholder proposals relating to equal opportunity employment (in one case) and nondiscrimination against homosexuals (in the other). The staff permitted each registrant to exclude the proposal, stating that it no longer considered employment policies to have sufficient political or social importance to mandate inclusion. (Under _Medical Committee,_ there is no doubt that the proposals would have to be included.) The shareholder proponents sued the registrants in federal district court, seeking injunctions against the exclusion of their proposals. [NYCERS v. S.E.C., 843 F. Supp. 858 (S.D.N.Y. 1994), _rev'd,_ 45 F.3d 7 (2d Cir. 1995); ACTWU v. Wal-Mart Stores, Inc., 821 F. Supp. 877 (S.D.N.Y. 1993)]

   1) **District court:** [§1214] In each case, the district court required the registrant to include the shareholder proposal. The district judge reasoned that an S.E.C. staff position that contradicts a position taken earlier by the S.E.C. is not entitled to deference from the court. Moreover, the court held, the issuance of a no-action letter that differs from earlier Commission policy amounts to an administrative rulemaking in violation of the procedural requirements of the Administrative Procedures Act.

   2) **Second Circuit:** [§1215] The S.E.C. appealed the decisions in the _NYCERS_ and _Wal-Mart_ cases, _supra,_ arguing that the

district court's ruling would in effect hamstring the S.E.C. staff. In early 1995, the Second Circuit reversed both cases.

(8) **Proposal relates to election to office:** [§1216] Management may exclude proposals relating to an election to office; shareholders have a say in such matters simply by voting for or against the candidate.

(9) **Proposal counter to proposal to be submitted by registrant at the meeting:** [§1217] Similarly, when the proposal runs counter to a proposal to be submitted by the registrant, the shareholders initially will have their say by voting for or against management's proposal. In such a case, it generally adds little to put a second proposal on the agenda, and management is permitted to exclude such proposals.

(10) **Proposal moot:** [§1218] Moot proposals, for obvious reasons, need not be included in the proxy statement.

(11) **Proposal duplicative:** [§1219] If the proposal would substantially duplicate another proposal previously submitted by another proponent, and the earlier proposal will be included in the registrant's proxy materials, the later proposal need not be included.

(12) **Proposal previously rejected:** [§1220] If the proposal deals with substantially the same subject matter as a proposal submitted at any shareholder meeting (regular or special) in the preceding five years, it may be omitted from the proxy materials for any shareholder meeting held within three years after the latest such submission, *if*:

  (a) The proposal was submitted at only *one such prior meeting* and it received *less than 3%* of the vote;

  (b) The proposal was submitted at *two such prior meetings*, and at the time of its second submission, it received *less than 6%* of the vote; *or*

  (c) The proposal was submitted at *three or more* such prior meetings, and at the time of its latest submission, it received *less than 10%* of the vote.

(13) **Proposal relates to specific amounts of cash or stock dividends:** [§1221] State corporation law provides that dividends are within the board's discretion. Dividends are also of particular interest to shareholders. To avoid inundation by proposals to censure the board for slashing the dividend, or demanding that the board consider raising the dividend, such proposals are not required to be included in the registrant's proxy materials.

## 10. Participation of Broker-Dealers in Proxy Contests

  a. **Stock held in "street name":** [§1222] A substantial majority of corporate stock in the United States is held in "street name," *i.e.,* registered on the books of the corporation in the name of a bank or brokerage firm, rather than of the beneficial owner. S.E.C. rules require that the corporation take certain steps to see that proxy solicitation material is forwarded by banks and brokers to these beneficial owners. [SEA Rule 14a-13]

(1) **Broker-dealer rules:** [§1223] The S.E.C. has also adopted rules regulating the solicitation of proxies by banks and broker-dealers holding securities in street name. [SEA §14(b); SEA Rule 14b-1]

(2) **Exchange rules:** [§1224] The national exchanges (and the National Association of Securities Dealers ["NASD"] with respect to its member firms that trade over-the-counter securities) have also adopted solicitation rules pertaining to securities held in street name.

   (a) *Where stock is held by the broker-dealer in a fiduciary capacity* (*e.g.,* as trustee) the broker-dealer can give the proxy without soliciting the consent of the beneficial owner.

   (b) *However, if the stock is held in street name merely for safekeeping* on behalf of the beneficial owner, the broker-dealer must transmit all solicitation material to the beneficial owner and secure the beneficial owner's direction as to giving the proxy. For example, the rules of the New York Stock Exchange provide that if there is a proxy contest involving a security listed on the exchange, in no event may the broker-dealer vote shares held in its name; it must get appropriate instructions from the beneficial owner.

(3) **Direct communication between registrant and beneficial owners:** [§1225] Until 1986, direct communications between the registrant and the beneficial owners of its securities were not possible. There existed no mechanism by which the registrant could determine the identities of the beneficial owners. In 1986, however, the S.E.C. adopted rules that permit registrants to request and receive, from the record holders, lists of the names, addresses, and the number of shares beneficially owned of those beneficial owners who do not object to the disclosure of this information. [SEA Rules 14b-1(b)(3); 14b-2(b)(4)(ii), (iii)] (Such owners are usually referred to as "NOBOs," for "non-objecting beneficial owners.") The availability of NOBO lists makes communications between the registrant and its shareholders much easier, and thereby eases the burden of proxy compliance, at least a little bit.

   (a) **Insurgent shareholders need not be given access to NOBO lists:** [§1226] Access to NOBO lists is available to registrants only. No other party has a legal right to obtain a NOBO list from the record holder of the securities. This gives management a sizable advantage in a proxy contest, because management has the ability to communicate directly with the NOBOs, while the insurgent group has only the right to request that management either provide a list of owners, or mail the insurgent group's materials on behalf of the insurgents. Management generally chooses to mail the insurgents' materials to avoid disclosing its NOBO information. [*See* SEA Rule 14a-7]

(4) **State law:** [§1227] If no federal laws apply, proxy solicitation of securities held in street name is governed by state law. The laws of most states

provide that the beneficial owner may require the record owner to give her a proxy to vote the shares.

b. **Solicitations by broker-dealers:** [§1228] The broker-dealer must be careful in communicating with shareholders during a proxy contest because the broker-dealer risks becoming involved as a "participant" in a solicitation. If the broker-dealer is a participant, the proxy statement used by the registrant will be defective, since it will not disclose the broker-dealer's status as a participant or the information required by SEA Schedule 14A about the broker-dealer.

(1) **"Participant" in a solicitation:** [§1229] The term "participant" is defined in Schedule 14A, Item 4, Instruction 3. The definition *includes the registrant and anyone who solicits proxies, or finances their solicitation,* but it *excludes persons who merely transmit soliciting materials.* Thus, it is especially risky for a broker-dealer to contribute anything to the text of materials that are sent, because to do so might make the "merely transmits" exclusion unavailable.

(2) **Note:** The broker-dealer does not violate this rule by asking instructions of the beneficial owner on how to give the proxy. [SEA Rule 14a-2(a)(1)(iii)] But if the broker-dealer were to give favorable treatment to one soliciting party (for example, by delaying sending the materials of another), there would be a violation of the proxy rules (and also of the national exchange and NASD rules).

(3) **But note:** The broker-dealer may advise its customers how to respond to a proxy solicitation if there has been an unsolicited request for such advice. [SEA Release No. 7208 (1964)] And rule 14a-2(b)(3) exempts *financial advisers*, who furnish unsolicited proxy voting advice from the informational and filing requirements of rules 14a-3 through 14a-6, 14a-8 and 14a-10 through 14a-14. However, advisers must disclose to the recipient of any advice: (i) any significant relationship with the registrant, an affiliate, or shareholder proponent; and (ii) any material interest of the adviser in the matter to which the advice relates. In addition, the adviser may not receive remuneration for providing the advice, except from the recipient. This exemption does not apply where there is an election contest for directors under rule 14a-11.

11. **Exemptions from the Proxy Rules:** [§1230] SEA Rule 14a-2 contains a number of exemptions from regulation under the proxy rules. The more commonly encountered exemptions include the following:

a. **Solicitation of ten persons or fewer:** [§1231] Anyone (other than management) may solicit proxies from fewer than 11 persons without having to comply with the proxy rules. [SEA Rule 14a-2(b)(2)] This provision may be helpful to an insurgent group that must, under state law, own or control by proxy a certain percentage ownership of stock to obtain a shareholder list.

b. **Solicitation by beneficial owners:** [§1232] The *beneficial* owner of securities may solicit a proxy from the *registered* owner without having to comply with the proxy rules. [SEA Rule 14a-2(a)(2)] This is important if an insurgent is purchasing shares to gain control of the target company and needs to be able to vote the shares against management.

(1) **Example:** A may purchase 100 shares of XYZ Corp. from B and become the beneficial owner thereof after the date set by XYZ for determination of stock ownership on its record books (the "record date"). Thus, B would appear on the corporate records as the registered owner as of the record date. Under rule 14a-2(a)(2), A may solicit a proxy from B without complying with the proxy rules.

c. **"Tombstone ads":** [§1233] The proxy rules do *not* apply to a "tombstone" newspaper ad, if the ad indicates only where copies of the proxy statement may be obtained, the name of the registrant, the reason for the ad, and the proposals to be voted on by the shareholders. [SEA Rule 14a-2(a)(6); *see supra*, §179]

d. **Broker-dealer exemptions:** [§1234] "Impartial transmission" of solicitation materials by broker-dealers is also exempted from the proxy rules (*see supra*, §1028).

e. **1992 amendments to the proxy rules:** [§1235] Until 1992, any exchange of views or opinions among shareholders about their company was potentially a "proxy solicitation" under the 1934 Act. One effect of this was to chill communications regarding corporate matters among shareholders, particularly large, institutional shareholders who were most likely to attract the attention of the S.E.C. In 1992, however, the S.E.C. adopted far-reaching amendments to the proxy rules. Under the 1992 amendments, many communications among shareholders that formerly were regulated are now permitted without regulation.

(1) **Statement of intended vote not a "solicitation":** [§1236] The 1992 amendments exclude from the definition of "solicitation" certain communications by a security holder, who does not otherwise engage in a non-exempt solicitation, *stating how the security holder intends to vote and the reasons therefor.* [SEA Rule 14a-1(l)]

(a) **Requirements:** [§1237] To be excluded from the definition of "solicitation," at least one of the following must be true:

1) **Communication made in public medium:** [§1238] The communication will be excluded if it is made in a public medium; *i.e.,* the communication is made by means of speeches in a public forum, press releases, published or broadcast opinions, statements or advertisements appearing in a broadcast medium, newspaper, magazine, or other bona fide publication disseminated on a regular basis.

2) **Communication made by a fiduciary to beneficiary:** [§1239] A communication directed to persons to whom the security holder owes a fiduciary duty in connection with the voting of securities of the registrant held by the security holder is excluded.

3) **Communication made in response to unsolicited request:** [§1240] A communication made in response to unsolicited requests for additional information with respect to a prior exempt communication made under 1) or 2), above, is exempt.

(b) **Persons eligible:** [§1241] The exclusion from the definition of "solicitation" is available to all shareholders, including officers and directors of the registrant, as long as they do not otherwise engage in a regulated solicitation.

(c) **Note: antifraud provisions may not be applicable:** [§1242] One interesting effect of excluding these communications from the definition of "solicitation" is that the antifraud provisions of the proxy rules [SEA Rule 14a-9; *see infra*, §§1249 *et seq.*] are apparently *not* applicable to such communications. Rule 14a-9, by its terms, applies only to "solicitations subject to this regulation" (*i.e.*, Regulation 14A).

(2) **Exempt solicitations:** [§1243] The following activities are considered to be "solicitations" under the rules, but nevertheless are exempt from some or all of the provisions of the proxy rules:

(a) **Exemption from delivery and disclosure rules—soliciting person not seeking proxy authority:** [§1244] Under SEA Rule 14a-2(b), as amended in 1992, a solicitation by a person who, during the solicitation period (i) *does not seek the power to act as a proxy* for a security holder and (ii) *does not furnish or request a form* of revocation, abstention, consent or authorization is exempt from the proxy statement delivery and disclosure rules. [SEA Rule 14a-2(b)(1)]

1) **Ineligible persons:** [§1245] Certain persons are specifically excluded from eligibility for the rule 14a-2(b) exemption:

a) *The registrant, or any affiliate or associate* (meaning generally a 10% or more shareholder, or a relative or affiliate of such a person);

b) *An officer or director of the registrant engaging in a solicitation financed by the registrant;*

c) *A nominee for whose election as director proxies are solicited;*

d) *Anyone soliciting in opposition to certain transactions* (*e.g.*, a merger, recapitalization, reorganization) recommended or approved by the board of directors of the registrant, if the soliciting person is proposing an alternative transaction to which it or an affiliate is to be a party;

e) *Anyone who is required to report beneficial ownership of the registrant's securities on Schedule 13D (see supra,*

§992), unless that person has filed the schedule and neither disclosed an intent nor reserved the right to attempt to take over the registrant;

f) *Anyone who would receive a special benefit* from a successful solicitation, not shared by all shareholders pro rata; and

g) *Others* listed in SEA Rule 14a-2(b)(1)(i)-(x).

2) **Irrevocable election:** [§1246] To remain eligible for this exemption, the person claiming the exemption must refrain from all non-exempt solicitation throughout the relevant solicitation period. Thus, once a person has availed herself of this exemption, she is *deemed to have made an irrevocable election* to maintain exempt status throughout the solicitation period. [S.E.C. Release No. 34-31326 (1992)] In other words, such a person will be barred from conducting any non-exempt solicitations during that period.

3) **Note—required notice to S.E.C. for $5 million holders:** [§1247] Any person who at the beginning of a solicitation owns beneficially securities of the solicited class with a market value of over $5 million, and who avails herself of this exemption, must file a notice with the S.E.C. *not later than three days* after the written solicitation is first given to any security holder. [SEA Rule 14a-6(g)]

(b) **Exemption from delivery rules—solicitations by public broadcast speech, advertisement, etc.:** [§1248] A solicitation that is made by public speech, press release, published or broadcast opinion, statement or advertisement appearing in a broadcast medium, newspaper, magazine, or other bona fide publication disseminated on a regular basis, *is exempt* from the proxy statement delivery rules. [SEA Rule 14a-3(f)] That is, such solicitations can be made regardless of whether the persons solicited have received a copy of the proxy statement, *if:*

1) *No form of proxy, consent, or authorization or means to execute such documents is provided* to a security holder in connection with the communication; *and*

2) *A definitive proxy statement is on file with the S.E.C.*

12. **Enforcement Provisions:** [§1249] An action may be brought for any violation of the proxy rules, and the courts will fashion whatever relief is appropriate under the circumstances. Normally, however, actions claiming violation of the proxy rules are brought under the antifraud provisions relating to the solicitation of proxies. [SEA Rule 14a-9]

a. **Antifraud provisions:** [§1250] The purpose of the antifraud provisions is to ensure complete disclosure to shareholders of all material facts necessary to support an intelligent decision on matters in which proxies are solicited, thus protecting the shareholders and the integrity of the shareholder voting process. To establish a cause of action for fraud under these provisions, each of the following elements must be proved.

(1) **Misrepresentations or omissions of fact:** [§1251] Solicitations that are made by any proxy statement, form of proxy, notice of meeting, or other communication, either written or oral, and which contain any affirmative misrepresentation or omission of a material fact, are prohibited. Compare the broader prohibition of rule 10b-5 (*supra,* §878) and section 14(e) (tender offers, discussed *supra,* §1051).

(a) **Requirement of a "fact":** [§1252] As to what constitutes a "fact," *see* the discussion of rule 10b-5, *supra,* §816.

1) **Examples:** The following are examples of the type of fact that may prove to be a material misrepresentation:

(i) Predictions of specific future market prices for the issuer's shares;

(ii) Statements that impugn character, integrity, or personal reputation, or makes charges concerning illegal, immoral, or improper conduct, without factual foundation;

(iii) Failure to identify a proxy statement, form of proxy, or other soliciting material so as to distinguish it clearly from the soliciting material of others soliciting for the same meeting or subject matter; and

(iv) Claims made prior to a shareholders' meeting concerning the results of the proxy solicitation.

[SEA Rule 14a-9]

(b) **Proxy contests:** [§1253] Many of the fraud cases involve a proxy contest, where two parties (management and insurgents) are fighting for control of the corporation. To some degree, the courts take this into account and do not require an exhaustive disclosure or even a perfectly balanced presentation of the facts by the soliciting parties. [Abramson v. Nytronics, Inc., 312 F. Supp. 519 (S.D.N.Y. 1970)]

(2) **Materiality:** [§1254] The misrepresentation or omission must be of a *material* fact.

(a) **Test for materiality:** The Supreme Court has stated that the test for materiality is whether there is a *substantial likelihood* that a reasonable shareholder would consider the fact of significance in determining how to vote. [TSC Industries, Inc. v. Northway, Inc., 426 U.S. 438 (1976)] The Court stated that this did *not* require proof of a substantial likelihood that disclosure would have caused the reasonable shareholder to change her vote, but only that the omitted fact would have had *actual significance* to the voter.

(b) **Examples of material statements**

1) X Corp., the majority shareholder of Y Corp. and which controlled a majority of the positions on Y's board of directors, solicited proxies from Y shareholders for the purpose of merging Y into X. However, X failed to disclose in its solicitation the appraised value of various unsold advertising plants owned by Y, and its intention to sell these plants after the merger was completed. [Gerstle v. Gamble-Skogmo, Inc., *supra*, §822] The court indicated that X's failure to disclose the market value of the unsold plants was not a material omission, since this was not a "fact," but rather a guess or an estimate—and at the time the S.E.C. discouraged the disclosure of such information. However, the court did find a material omission in that X failed to disclose its ***intentions*** (a fact) to liquidate the unsold Y plants after the merger.

2) It has also been held that defendants could be held liable where material facts, although disclosed, were not sufficiently highlighted in the proxy statement so that their significance could be understood. [Kohn v. American Metal Climax, Inc., 322 F. Supp. 1331 (E.D. Pa. 1971)]

3) One case even found a violation of the proxy rules where the defendant did not reveal the ***probable interpretation*** of the material facts so that a reasonable shareholder could understand their implication. [Robinson v. Penn Central Co., *supra*, §832]

4) *Compare:* Where A Corp. bought 34% of the stock of B Corp. and put five persons on B's board of directors, the following omissions were held ***not*** to be material in its proxy solicitation to buy the remainder of B in a stock-for-stock exchange.

   (i) That the president of A was also the chairman of the board of B;

   (ii) That A was effectively "in control" of B; and

   (iii) That A had made substantial purchases of its own stock in the two-year period preceding the solicitation, without further proof that the purchases were for the purpose of manipulating the stock price of A.

   [TSC Industries, Inc. v. Northway, Inc., *supra*]

(3) **Causation:** [§1255] To establish a cause of action under the antifraud provisions, the plaintiff must prove that the misrepresentation or omission of material fact was the cause of her loss.

(a) **Question of fact:** [§1256] The courts have held that the issue of causation is one of fact, to be determined at trial.

(b) **Defined in terms of materiality:** [§1257] Initially, plaintiffs were required to prove that the misleading facts or omissions had actually caused their damages. This requirement, however, posed complex problems of proof for the plaintiffs (who typically sue in a class action). To require each member of the class to establish causation specific to that member is to make class certification impossible, because the individual question of causation will dominate the common questions. The problem is much the same as that raised by the requirement that the plaintiffs establish reliance in an action under rule 10b-5 (as to which, *see supra*, §§837 *et seq.*). In 1970, the Supreme Court held that the causation required in an action under rule 14a-9 is defined in terms of *materiality.* [Mills v. Electric Auto-Lite Co., 396 U.S. 375 (1970)]

1) **Solicitation an "essential link":** [§1258] Once materiality is shown, the plaintiff can prove causation simply by showing that the proxy solicitation itself was an essential link in effecting the transaction. In other words, the plaintiff need only show that the party soliciting the proxies needed the votes represented by the proxies to carry the proposition.

a) **Example:** In *Mills v. Electric Auto-Lite Co.,* defendant, which owned 54% of the stock of A Corp., solicited proxies to get the two-thirds vote of the A shareholders required to effect a merger (*i.e.,* solicitation was necessary to accomplish the transaction). However, defendant failed to disclose to A's shareholders that it controlled 54% of A's stock. The Court held that causation was established by proof of (i) the materiality of the omission and (ii) that the solicitation was an essential link in the transaction.

2) **Where solicitation not required for transaction:** [§1259] Suppose that the party soliciting the proxies has enough votes by itself to approve the transaction, but nevertheless conducts a proxy solicitation, and there is a material misrepresentation or omission in the proxy statement. In 1991, the Supreme Court addressed this question in *Virginia Bankshares, Inc. v. Sandberg*, 501 U.S. 1083 (1991). The Court took a relatively strict view of causation, holding that the causation required in a rule 14a-9 case *had not been established* when the plaintiffs' (minority shareholders') votes were not needed, under state law or corporate bylaw, to approve a merger.

a) **Facts of *Virginia Bankshares*:** [§1260] In *Virginia Bankshares,* proxies were solicited in connection with a proposed merger of First American Bank of Virginia ("the Bank") into Virginia Bankshares, Inc. ("VBI"). VBI owned about 85% of the voting stock of the Bank, making the merger a "freeze-out" merger in which the votes of the minority shareholders were not required by state law or by the corporate charter or bylaws. Nevertheless, the directors of the Bank solicited the proxies of the minority shareholders. The proxy solicitation materials contained the statement that "The Plan of Merger has been approved by the Board of Directors because it provides an opportunity for the Bank's public shareholders to achieve a high value for their shares." The materials also contained the statement that the merger plan was "fair" to the minority shareholders.

b) **Plaintiff's claim:** [§1261] Plaintiff claimed that the statements by the Bank's directors were false, because the directors believed neither that the $42 price was high nor that the merger terms were fair to the minority shareholders. To satisfy the "essential link" portion of the test set out in *Mills, supra*, the plaintiff made two arguments:

1/ **Public relations:** First, the plaintiff argued that although the votes of the minority shareholders were not legally required to effectuate the merger, the defendants would not be willing to proceed without them, because of the bad publicity and bad shareholder relations that would result.

2/ **Deprivation of state remedy:** Second, the plaintiff claimed that the transaction itself would have been potentially voidable because of a director's conflict of interest, and that to protect the transaction, the Bank's directors needed the affirmative vote of the "untainted" minority shareholders. By approving the merger based on the board's misleading statements, the plaintiff argued, the Bank's minority shareholders had been deprived of the state law remedy for the conflicting interest.

c) **Supreme Court's holding:** [§1262] The Supreme Court held that neither of the plaintiff's theories of causation satisfied the *Mills* "essential link" requirement.

1/ **The "public relations" argument:** [§1263] The Court rejected the public relations argument, reasoning that *such a claim could be made after almost any corporate action* and would be *difficult to disprove*, requiring a trial in virtually every case. "A subsequently dissatisfied minority shareholder would have virtual license to allege that managerial timidity would have doomed corporate action but for the ostensible approval induced by a misleading statement . . . The issues would be hazy, their litigation protracted, and their resolution unreliable."

2/ **The "deprivation of state remedy" argument:** [§1264] The Court rejected the deprivation argument because under relevant state law, the allegedly defective disclosure resulted in defective approval by the minority shareholders. In other words, *no state remedy was lost*, because no minority approval valid under state law had been given.

d) **Fraudulent statements of opinion:** [§1265] Another issue raised by the *Virginia Bankshares* case was whether a statement of opinion—for instance, that $42 is a high value for the Bank's shares—is actionable under rule 14a-9.

    1/ **When actionable:** [§1266] The Supreme Court held that a statement of opinion (or of reasons for a particular board action) can be actionable if:

        (i) The board *did not in fact hold the opinion* stated; *and*

        (ii) The *fact underlying the opinion is also misrepresented*.

        a/ **Example:** The statement, "The Plan of Merger has been approved by the Board of Directors because it provides an opportunity for the Bank's public shareholders to achieve a high value for their shares," is actionable on a showing that:

            1] The board did not approve the plan because they believed it provided a high price to minority shareholders, but rather they approved the plan because they wanted to keep their jobs; and

            2] In fact, $42 is not a high price for the Bank's shares.

    2/ **Falsity of belief alone not enough:** [§1267] The Court specifically held that it is not enough to prove that a board member did not believe the statement in the soliciting materials. If the facts underlying the statement of opinion or belief are correctly stated, no cause of action will lie.

(4) **Standard of culpability:** [§1268] Section 14(a) of the 1934 Act offers no explicit standard of liability for proxy fraud. The courts that have considered the issue have come to different conclusions.

(a) **Corporation—negligence suffices:** [§1269] Courts have indicated that a corporation conducting a proxy solicitation can be held to have violated the proxy rules on a finding of negligence. [Gerstle v. Gamble-Skogmo, Inc., *supra*]

(b) **Officers, directors, and employees—negligence may suffice:** [§1270] Officers, directors, and employees may be liable for a proxy violation as principals or agents, as participants, or as aiders and abetters; and there are dicta that liability may be incurred upon a finding of negligence. [*See* Gerstle v. Gamble-Skogmo, Inc., *supra*]

1) **Distinguish rule 10b-5:** [§1271]  Although the language of rule 14a-9 is similar to that of rule 10b-5, it may be appropriate to require scienter in rule 10b-5 cases but not in rule 14a-9 cases. The S.E.C.'s authority under SEA section 10(b) is limited to regulating "manipulative or deceptive devices," which implies fraud. The S.E.C.'s authority under SEA section 14(a), by contrast, extends to all proxy regulation "necessary or appropriate in the public interest or for the protection of investors." This is substantially broader than the language of section 10(b), and can provide the basis for a broader reading of the regulations adopted pursuant to the respective sections of the Exchange Act. [Gerstle v. Gamble-Skogmo, Inc., *supra*]

(c) **Outside accountants—scienter required:** [§1272]  A court has also held that in a private (*i.e.*, nongovernment) lawsuit brought against the outside accounting firm responsible for putting false financial statements in the proxy statement, liability could only be found if scienter was present. [Adams v. Standard Knitting Mills, Fed. Sec. L. Rep. (CCH) ¶97,382 (6th Cir. 1980)]

b. **Remedies for violation of the proxy rules**

(1) **Actions by the S.E.C.:** [§1273]  The S.E.C. does *not* have the same administrative remedies available under the proxy rules as it does under the 1933 Act (*see supra*, §§619 *et seq.*). However, the S.E.C. may bring an action for an *injunction* to prevent the solicitation of proxies, to prevent the voting of proxies obtained through improper solicitation, to require resolicitation of proxies, etc.

(2) **Implied private actions:** [§1274]  The courts have also held that a private cause of action is *implied* in section 14(a).

(a) **Appropriate relief granted:** [§1275]  The courts will fashion whatever relief is appropriate to remedy the loss caused by the proxy violation, *e.g.*, damages, rescission of the transaction, etc. [J.I. Case Co. v. Borak, 377 U.S. 426 (1964)]

(b) **Derivative and class actions:** [§1276]  A shareholder may bring a direct cause of action or join with others to bring a class action; or, alternatively, the shareholder may bring a derivative suit on behalf of the corporation. [J.I. Case Co. v. Borak, *supra*]

(c) **Merger cases:** [§1277]  In *J.I. Case Co. v. Borak*, which involved a merger, the Court indicated that an appropriate remedy might be to *unwind* the merger. One factor to be considered in the decision whether to rescind a merger is the "fairness" of the terms of the transaction. However, practically speaking, rescission is seldom if ever feasible in merger cases.

1) For example, if the merger involved public companies, it would be difficult or impossible to trace back and return all of the shares traded at the time of the merger, since trading of the stock would inevitably have taken place since the time of the merger.

2) A case subsequent to *Borak* indicated that, at least in that case, it was not feasible to unwind the merger. Hence, the plaintiffs were allowed to recover their share in the profits realized after their company was merged into the defendant and the assets of their company sold at a substantial profit. [Gerstle v. Gamble-Skogmo, Inc., *supra*]

(d) **Reimbursement of costs:** [§1278]   The successful plaintiff in an action alleging violation of section 14(a) is entitled to reimbursement of reasonable costs and attorneys' fees if the action is brought on behalf of a class of shareholders and benefits all members of the class. [Mills v. Electric Auto-Lite Co., *supra*]

c. **Reimbursement of proxy contest expenses:** [§1279]   The extent to which expenses incurred in the solicitation of proxies may be reimbursed by the corporation is primarily a matter of state law.

(1) **Reimbursement of management:** [§1280]  Where its expenses are "reasonable" in amount, management may be reimbursed for the solicitation of proxies whether it wins or loses. However, some courts limit reimbursement to situations where the proxy solicitation is concerned with a matter of "corporate policy," excluding expenses incurred in a personal contest for *control* of the corporation. [Rosenfeld v. Fairchild Engine & Airplane Corp., 309 N.Y. 168 (1955)]

(a) **Note:** It is often difficult to distinguish what is a matter of corporate policy from what is merely a contest for control—since the contesting parties will always frame a contest for control in terms of a dispute over policy.

(2) **Reimbursement of insurgents:** [§1281]   Where the insurgents in a proxy contest are successful, they may be reimbursed for *reasonable* amounts expended in soliciting proxies. The *Rosenfeld* case, *supra*, held that for reimbursement to be proper it had to be *ratified by the shareholders*, and that the contest had to be for the *benefit of the corporation*. Unsuccessful insurgents receive no reimbursement.

## E.   INSIDER LIABILITY FOR SHORT-SWING PROFITS

1. **Introduction:** [§1282]  Section 16 is designed to prevent corporate insiders from using inside information about their companies to make short-swing profits by buying and then selling or selling and then buying securities of their corporation within a six-month period. To accomplish this, section 16 requires insiders to file periodic reports of their holdings of the issuer's securities [SEA §16(a)] and requires insiders to disgorge any "profits" resulting from short-swing trading [SEA §16(b)].

a. **Makes short sales by insiders unlawful:** [§1283] In addition, section 16(c) makes it unlawful for insiders to engage in short sales of their company's equity securities.

   (1) **"Short sale" defined:** [§1284] A "short sale" is a sale of securities that the seller does not yet own, but plans to purchase just in time to cover the obligations of the sale. This strategy can be thought of as a "bet against the company"—the short seller sells at today's price, hoping that later, when she has to cover the sale by delivering the securities, she will be able to purchase the securities more cheaply. (*See infra*, §1217.)

b. **Distinguish rule 10b-5 "insider trading":** [§1285] Although both rule 10b-5 and section 16 are sometimes said to prohibit "insider trading," the provisions operate entirely differently. A rule 10b-5 case is based on a misrepresentation or failure to disclose (*see supra*, §§926 *et seq.*). Section 16, on the other hand, is based on the amount of time elapsed between a purchase and sale (or a sale and purchase) of the issuer's securities by an insider. If the amount of time is too short, the insider must give up her "profits," regardless of whether information was misrepresented or withheld. The presence or absence of fraud is irrelevant to a section 16 case.

c. **Limitations of section 16:** [§1286] Section 16 is not intended to be a comprehensive solution to the problem of insider trading. In fact, its narrow focus on short-swing trades makes it oblivious to even the most outrageous intentional frauds, as long as there are no purchases and sales within six months of one another.

   (1) **Example:** A, a director of X Corp., has owned 100 shares of X Corp. stock for three years. At a board meeting A becomes aware that X Corp. is about to suffer a large loss of business. A sells her X Corp. shares, based on her inside information. A has not incurred any liability under section 16 (although she may be liable under rule 10b-5; *see supra*, §§926 *et seq.*).

   (2) **But note:** Rule 10b-5 and section 16(b) *can* apply to the same transaction. In the example above, had A owned the X Corp. stock for only three weeks, she could be liable to X Corp. under section 16(b) for her short-swing profits and concurrently liable under rule 10b-5 in an action by the S.E.C.

2. **Nature of a Section 16 Cause of Action:** [§1287] Sections 16(a) and 16(c) are enforceable by the S.E.C. and not by private plaintiffs. However, any shareholder of the issuer can bring a lawsuit under section 16(b) to recover for the issuer an insider's profit from short-swing trading. Section 16(b) provides that:

   (i) Any officer, director, or 10% owner of any class of an equity security registered under section 12;

   (ii) Who realizes any profit;

   (iii) From a purchase and sale, or sale and purchase, of;

   (iv) Any nonexempt equity security of the issuer;

(v) Within any period of less than six months;

(vi) Shall be liable to the corporation for the profits made from the trading.

These elements are discussed in detail below.

3. **All Equity Security Transactions Regulated:** [§1288] To qualify as an "insider" by virtue of stock ownership, a person must beneficially own more than 10% of some class of *registered* equity security. But once qualified as an "insider" (either by owning more than 10% of a registered equity security, or by being an officer or director of a company with a class of registered equity security), purchases and sales of *any equity security of the issuer*—whether or not it also is registered—may give rise to liability.

    a. **Note:** This differs from other provisions of the 1934 Act (*e.g.,* the tender offer rule, *supra,* §978), which apply only to transactions involving the *registered* equity securities themselves.

4. **"Insiders" Defined:** [§1289] "Insiders" covered under section 16 are officers and directors of a corporation with a class of equity securities registered under section 12 of the Act, *and* all persons who beneficially own more than 10% of any class of the corporation's equity securities registered under section 12. Courts have generally refused to expand the class of potential defendants beyond the persons described in section 16 (*e.g.,* to other persons who possess the same inside information as officers and directors).

    a. **Officers and directors:** [§1290] Whether a potential defendant was an officer or director at a particular point in time is in most cases readily established through the corporate minute book.

        (1) **"Officer" defined:** [§1291] An officer is defined as an issuer's president, principal financial officer, principal accounting officer (or, if there is no such accounting officer, the controller), any vicepresident of the issuer in charge of a principal business unit, division or function (such as sales, administration or finance), any other officer who performs a policy-making function, or "any other person who performs similar policy-making functions for the issuer." [SEA Rule 16a-1(f)]

            (a) **Officers of subsidiary and parent corporations:** [§1292] Officers of subsidiary or parent corporations of the issuer may be deemed to be officers of the issuer, but only if they perform policy-making functions for the issuer.

            (b) **Honorary titles:** [§1293] Merely holding an officer's title is not enough to cause section 16(b) liability to attach; the person in question must in fact perform the functions of an officer. It is the duties, rather than the title, that determine whether an employee is an officer under section 16(b). [C.R.A. Realty Corp. v. Crotty, 878 F.2d 562 (2d Cir. 1989); Merrill Lynch, Pierce, Fenner & Smith, Inc. v. Livingston, 566 F.2d 1119 (9th Cir. 1978)]

        (2) **Timing issues:** [§1294] Section 16 raises two timing issues with respect to officers and directors: what happens if a person was not an officer or

director at the time of the purchase, but becomes one by the time of the sale? And what is the result in the reverse situation; that is, the person was an officer or director at the time of the purchase, but is no longer one at the time of the sale?

(a) **Transaction before person becomes an officer or director:** [§1295] When a transaction takes place before the person becomes an officer or director of a covered company, then the policy underlying section 16 does not apply: that is, such a person generally has no access to inside information. The S.E.C. adopted this view in 1991, in SEA rule 16a-2(a): transactions carried out in the six months prior to the person's becoming an officer or director are not subject to section 16.

1) **Exception—transaction shortly before going public:** [§1296] There is one case, however, in which the rule stated immediately above does not apply. The exception is intended to trap transactions by persons who trade shortly before their company goes public. The S.E.C. believes that in general, insiders of companies that are about to go public know about those plans far enough in advance to plan for section 16; in addition, the possibilities for abuse just before the company goes public are greater than they are later on, when a market price has been established for the company's securities. Therefore, if an officer or director has become subject to section 16 *solely as the result of the issuer's registering a series of securities under section 12,* the officer or director *is* subject to both section 16(a) reporting and section 16(b) liability.

(b) **Transaction after person ceases being officer or director:** [§1297] A transaction that takes place after the person ceases to be an officer or director is subject to section 16 *only if it takes place within six months of a transaction that happened while the person was an officer or director.*

(3) **Deputization issue:** [§1298] Despite its general limitation to named insiders, section 16 may also apply to situations where an officer or director of A Corp. has been appointed by A to an inside position (such as director) in B Corp. While the person might not engage in any prohibited purchases or sales in B stock for himself, the entity with which he is affiliated (A) may.

(a) **Deputizing corporation may be liable:** [§1299] Thus, A Corp. may be found to have "deputized" one of its own insiders to serve on the board or as an officer of B—and if A subsequently purchases and sells B's stock, a section 16 plaintiff may seek to hold A Corp. itself liable as a director or officer of B (rather than the individual appointed by A).

(b) **Rationale:** The rationale behind deputization lies in agency law. An individual officer or director of A Corp. who is appointed to the board of another corporation, B Corp., with a view to representing A Corp.'s interests, is in a practical sense a surrogate for A Corp., and legally is A Corp.'s agent. It is not unreasonable, then, that A Corp. should be considered as though it itself were represented on the board of B Corp., as indeed, under agency law, it is.

(c) **Question of fact:** Whether a deputization has actually occurred is always a question of fact.

(d) **Example:** Martin-Marietta Corp. purchased a substantial number of shares of Sperry Rand. Rand then asked Bunker (president of Martin-Marietta) to join its board, which he did. While Bunker served on the board of Rand, Martin-Marietta continued to purchase additional shares of Rand stock; while this was going on, Bunker received reports on Rand's progress and discussed this information with other personnel at Martin-Marietta. After Bunker resigned from the board of Rand, Martin-Marietta sold all of its Rand stock at a profit. [Feder v. Martin-Marietta Corp., 406 F.2d 260 (2d Cir. 1969)]

    1) Even though Rand had initiated Bunker's appointment to its board, the court found that he had been deputized by Martin-Marietta to represent its interests in Rand. Therefore, the profits made by Martin-Marietta on its purchases and sales of Rand stock were recoverable under section 16(b) in a suit brought by a Rand shareholder.

    2) However, the Court has refused to find a deputization where A Corp.'s investment in and sale of B Corp.'s stock was made *independently* and *without the specific knowledge* of A's representative sitting on B's board of directors. [Blau v. Lehman, 368 U.S. 403 (1962)]

b. **More-than-ten-percent shareholder:** [§1300] Every person who directly or indirectly is the "beneficial owner" of more than 10% of any class of registered equity security is subject to the provisions of section 16.

(1) **Beneficial ownership:** [§1301] In calculating 10% ownership, it is "beneficial ownership" that counts—*i.e.,* whether a person receives the benefit of owning the stock, even if he does not hold record title. Note that the question of beneficial ownership is significant beyond the case of 10% holders: it is equally important in analyzing questions involving officers and directors. For example, if an officer of a covered company is claimed to be required to disgorge profits under section 16(b), then the plaintiff must establish that equity securities of the company *beneficially owned by the officer* were involved in the challenged transactions.

(2) **Timing of ownership:** [§1302] Although officers and directors need *not* occupy their positions at the time of both purchase and sale (*see supra,* §§1294-1297), the language of the statute indicates that 10% shareholders can only be liable where such ownership exists both at the time of purchase and at the time of sale.

(a) **Example:** A owns no stock in X Corporation. On March 3, A buys X Corporation common shares (which are registered under the 1934

Act) in an amount sufficient to make A an 11% shareholder. On May 1 (less than six months later), A sells all the X Corporation common shares. *Result:* Although A must report the May 1 sale under section 16(a), A is *not* liable to disgorge any profit under section 16(b). The purchase by which A became a more-than-10% shareholder is not counted for section 16(b) purposes, because at the time of that purchase, A was not a more-than-10% shareholder. [Foremost-McKesson, Inc. v. Provident Securities Co., 423 U.S. 232 (1976)]

(b) **Example:** A owns 12% of a registered equity security, sells 3% on Monday, and sells the remaining 9% on Tuesday. A can be held liable for his profits from the sale of only the first 3%, since at this point he owned more than 10%; thereafter, at the time he sold the remaining 9%, he did not own more than 10%. [Reliance Electric Co. v. Emerson Electric Co., 404 U.S. 418 (1972)]

(c) **Limited applicability of section 16(b):** Thus, if a 10% owner is careful, he may structure his purchases and sales so as to limit the applicability of section 16(b). For example, a person could buy over 10% in a series of separate purchases and only those acquired *after* he reached 10% could be matched with subsequent sales under section 16(b).

(3) **Family ownership:** [§1303]  As part of a complete overhaul of its rules relating to section 16, the S.E.C. in 1991 provided that an insider is *presumed* to be the "beneficial owner" of securities held by *virtually all relatives, including in-laws and adopted relatives* (all of whom are considered to be members of the insider's "immediate family")—but only if the relative "shares the same household" as the insider. [SEA Rules 16a-1(a)(2)(ii)(A), 16a-1(e)] The presumption may be rebutted by the insider. [*Id.*]

(a) **Note:** The S.E.C. may technically lack the power to pass such a rule. Section 16 gives the S.E.C. the power to *exempt* classes of persons from the section, not to *include* persons within the section. The validity of this rule, as a matter of administrative law, will probably be litigated.

(4) **Securities held in trust:** [§1304]  The existence of securities held in trust has the potential to complicate vastly the otherwise fairly routine application of section 16 to fact situations. Although the S.E.C.'s rules relating to section 16 treatment of securities held in trust were revised in 1991, the revisions did not simplify matters much. They did, however, improve the consistency and fairness of the requirements applicable to trustees and beneficiaries. Below are some highlights of the new rules.

(a) **"Beneficial owner" status—section 16(a) reporting:** [§1305]  A person is subject to section 16(a) reporting as a 10% holder if she *has sole or shared voting power* for more than 10% of the securities of a registered class.

1) **Trustee as beneficial owner:** [§1306] Merely being a trustee of a trust does not make the trustee a beneficial owner of the assets of the trust. However, if the trustee or any member of her immediate family (*see supra*, §1303) is a beneficiary of the trust, then the trustee is a beneficial owner of the trust's securities.

2) **No reporting requirement without investment control:** [§1307] Neither a trustee nor a trust beneficiary is required to report *transactions over which they lacked investment control*, even if they are considered to be beneficial owners of the securities. [SEA Rule 16a-8]

   a) **Note:** This means that, under section 16, a beneficial owner of securities is not be required to report transactions in those securities, as long as the person lacks investment power with respect to the transactions in question.

(b) **Liability under section 16(b):** [§1308] To be liable for transactions in the issuer's securities, a beneficial owner of more than 10% must also have a direct or indirect pecuniary interest in the securities involved in the transaction. [SEA Rule 16a-1]

1) **Trustee's liability for trust transactions:** [§1309] A trustee who is compensated for trust services may have a "pecuniary interest" in the securities involved in trust transactions. In addition, if the trustee has *voting power* over the securities, she is considered to be their beneficial owner. Nevertheless, if the trustee lacks investment power over a trust transaction—that is, lacks the power to cause or prevent the transaction—then the trustee is not financially liable for the transaction under section 16(b). (This might be the case, for instance, when the trustee stewards the trust assets but is required to invest according to instructions of an investment adviser.)

2) **Beneficiary's liability for trust transactions:** [§1310] Just as with trustees, even though a trust beneficiary has a pecuniary interest in a transaction, the beneficiary is not liable under section 16(b) unless she also had investment control over the transaction producing the profit. [SEA Rule 16a-8]

(c) **Examples:** Here are some examples of possible complications.

1) **Director is beneficiary:** Assume that D is a director of C Corporation. D is also the sole beneficiary of a trust that holds 5% of the outstanding common stock of C (which has been registered under the 1934 Act). D, however, has no investment control over any trust asset. If the trust buys C stock in January, and sells C stock in March, making a profit, must D report the January and March transactions under section 16(a)? Is D liable for that profit under section 16(b)?

a) **Answer:** No, to both questions. Under rule 16a-1, D is the beneficial owner of the C stock if she has the right to *vote* the stock. Normally, this would trigger D's reporting requirement, as a director who beneficially owns C stock. Likewise, as the sole beneficiary of the trust, D has the requisite pecuniary interest for section 16(b) liability to attach. However, because D lacks investment control (which is, in fact, the most common state of affairs for trust beneficiaries), rule 16a-8 *exempts D both from reporting and from disgorgement*. Finally, the fact that D is a director of C does not change this result: D owns no C stock directly, so any section 16 reporting or disgorgement liability arises only because of the trust's ownership, as to which the exemptions provided in rule 16a-8 are available.

2) **Variation one—trustee is related to beneficiary:** Suppose the facts are the same as stated immediately above, *but* the trustee is the spouse of the director. Is D liable for the profit under section 16(b)?

   a) **Answer:** Again, D has neither reporting nor disgorgement liability under section 16. If D has actually given her spouse inside information, and the spouse-trustee has traded on that information, then rule 10b-5 has been violated. (*See supra,* §§926 *et seq.*)

3) **Variation two—trust is 11% holder:** Suppose that the same facts as in a), above, *except* that the trust holds 11% of the C common stock.

   a) **Answer:** As before, D has neither reporting nor disgorgement liability under section 16. The *trust*, however, is liable, both to report the January and March transactions, and to disgorge the profit to C.

(5) **Securities owned by corporation:** [§1311] Another possibility complicating the question of beneficial ownership under section 16 involves corporate ownership of securities (rather than direct ownership, or ownership by a trust). The principal question may be stated thus: When is an officer, director, or 10% holder the beneficial owner of securities owned of record by a corporation of which the individual is a shareholder?

(a) **S.E.C. General Counsel opinion:** [§1312] In 1938, the General Counsel of the S.E.C. opined that a shareholder of a corporation is considered the beneficial owner of securities held of record by the corporation only if the corporation "merely provides a medium through which [the shareholder] invest[s], or trade[s] in securities." [S.E.C. Release No. 34-1965 (1938)]

   1) **Opinion not always followed:** [§1313] The General Counsel's opinion, *supra,* has not always been followed by the courts. Thus, in a case in which A, a more-than-10% owner of M, a family corporation, also owned a large block of shares in

B, another corporation, A was held individually liable to disgorge 19% of B's profits from short-swing trades in M stock. [Marquette Cement Manufacturing Co. v. Andreas, 239 F. Supp. 962 (S.D.N.Y. 1965)]

a) **Note:** The result in *Andreas, supra,* is controversial, and the case has been rejected by other courts. [*See, e.g.,* Popkin v. Dingman, 366 F. Supp. 534 (S.D.N.Y. 1973)]

(b) **Rule 14a-8 safe harbor:** [§1314] Finally, with respect to corporations, the S.E.C. has provided a safe harbor rule that states that a shareholder is not liable for transactions by the corporation if:

(i) The shareholder is not a controlling shareholder; *and*

(ii) The shareholder neither shares nor has sole investment control over the corporation's transaction.

This safe harbor is nonexclusive, and so a shareholder not meeting its requirements remains free to argue against liability purely on the basis of the S.E.C.'s General Counsel opinion, *supra.*

5. **"Equity Security" Defined:** [§1315] Section 16 applies to transactions in equity securities. The 1934 Act defines "equity security" as "any stock or similar security; or any security convertible, with or without consideration, into such security"; as well as certain "acquisition rights" to such securities; and "any other security which the Commission shall deem to be of a similar nature and consider necessary or appropriate . . . to treat as an equity security." [SEA §3(a)(11)]

a. **Convertible securities:** [§1316] A security convertible into an equity security (*e.g.,* a debenture convertible into common stock) is an equity security for the purposes of section 12. Thus, the 10% holder of such a security is an "insider" and therefore subject to the reporting requirements of section 16(a).

(1) **Calculating ten percent of convertible securities:** [§1317] However, for purposes of determining whether the holder of convertible securities is a more-than-10% shareholder under section 16(b), the court will consider the relative amount of the ***underlying security*** (that is, of the security into which the convertible security can be converted) owned by the shareholder, ***not*** the relative amount of the convertible security itself. [SEA Rule 16a-4(a); *see* Chemical Fund, Inc. v. Xerox Corp., 377 F.2d 107 (2d Cir. 1967)]

(a) **Example:** In *Chemical Fund, Inc. v. Xerox, supra,* an investment company held more than 10% of the corporation's convertible debentures. These debentures, however, if converted into common stock and added to the already outstanding common, would equal less than 3% of the corporation's common stock. The court held that the investment company was not a beneficial owner of more than 10% within the meaning of section 16.

1) **Rationale:** The rationale of the decision is that section 16(b) is aimed only at those shareholders who exercise control of the

corporation through voting. Thus, the court reasoned, it makes sense to consider the position of the shareholder after conversion and to disregard percentage ownership of unconverted, nonvoting securities. This reasoning has now been adopted by the S.E.C. [S.E.C. Release No. 28869 n.36 (1991)]

(2) **Example:** Corporation C has a registered class of common stock, and a registered class of preferred stock (which also has voting rights). A owns 12% of the C preferred stock, which is convertible into 4% of the C common stock. A buys and sells C common stock within a period of less than six months.

    (a) **Result:** A is a "10% holder" and is subject to section 16(a) reporting *and* to section 16(b) liability for her transactions in *any* equity security of C, including transactions in C common stock.

    (b) **Rationale:** The C preferred stock is an equity security in its own right, and it carries voting rights. Hence, ownership of more than 10% of this class of stock triggers the application of section 16. [S.E.C. Release No. 34-28869 n.36 (1991)]

    (c) **Note:** If the C preferred stock did *not* have voting rights, the result would be different—only securities that *have* voting rights are considered in deciding percentage ownership of a class of equity securities. The reasoning, per *Chemical Fund, supra*, is that the statute is aimed at abuses made possible by voting control, and this is manifestly not possible when the securities in question do not have voting rights. [*Id.*]

6. **Purchase and Sale Requirement:** [§1318] To establish liability under section 16(b), there must be a matching purchase and sale, or sale and purchase. The general rule is that for the purposes of section 16(b), a "purchase" occurs when the purchaser incurs an irrevocable liability to take and pay for the stock; and a "sale" occurs when the seller incurs an irrevocable liability to deliver and accept payment for the stock. Although these rules are easily stated, there are several types of stock transactions where it may not be clear if a "purchase" or "sale" has actually occurred. Many of these transactions involve the exchange of stock either for property or for other stock.

a. **Security conversions:** [§1319] There are various types of security conversions (*e.g.*, conversion of preferred stock or debentures into common stock), and the cases are split as to whether a "purchase" and/or a "sale" is involved in these transactions.

    (1) **Traditional approach:** [§1320] Earlier judicial decisions seemed to take a simplistic approach to the question, defining all exchanges of stock as "purchases" or "sales."

        (a) **Example:** Where a call (option to buy) was issued by the company for conversion of preferred stock into common, the court held that the conversion was a "purchase" of the common stock. Similarly, the giving up of the convertible preferred stock would be a "sale."

[Park & Tilford, Inc. v. Schulte, 160 F.2d 984 (2d Cir.), *cert. denied*, 332 U.S. 761 (1947)]

(b) **Example:** Another court followed the *Park & Tilford* approach in a later case, holding that the conversion of convertible debentures into common stock involved a "sale" of the debentures and the "purchase" of the common. Here, the debentures had been purchased less than six months prior to the conversion, and some of the common stock was sold less than six months after the conversion. [Heli-Coil Corp. v. Webster, 352 F.2d 156 (3d Cir. 1965)]

(2) **Involuntary conversions:** [§1321] Some courts have held that a conversion of preferred into common is not a purchase of the common, at least if the conversion is "involuntary." If the holder is forced to convert or lose a large part of his investment, and has no control over the decision to call the convertible securities for redemption, such courts may find that the conversion does not constitute a purchase or sale. [Petteys v. Butler, 367 F.2d 528 (8th Cir. 1966), *cert. denied*, 385 U.S. 1006 (1967); Ferraiolo v. Newman, 259 F.2d 342 (6th Cir. 1958), *cert. denied*, 359 U.S. 927 (1959)]

(3) **Policy approach:** [§1322] Still other courts have looked at the rationale of section 16(b) in determining whether a conversion transaction involves a "purchase" or "sale." For example, the Second Circuit essentially overruled its earlier *Park & Tilford* case, *supra*, 19 years later, when it proposed a test for determining whether conversion transactions are within the scope of section 16(b): If the transaction is one that could support the speculative, short-term profit-taking by insiders that section 16(b) was designed to prevent, it will be deemed a "purchase" or "sale" within the meaning of the Act. [Blau v. Lamb, 363 F.2d 507 (2d Cir. 1967), *cert. denied*, 385 U.S. 1002 (1967)]

b. **Stock options:** [§1323] Before 1991, the case law on "purchase" and "sale" transactions involving stock options and other so-called derivative securities was confused, largely because many courts treated the *exercise* of the option, rather than its acquisition, as the significant event for section 16 purposes. In 1991, however, as part of its comprehensive revision of the section 16 rules, the S.E.C. announced that henceforth, the *acquisition* of a stock option (or other derivative security) would be deemed the significant event. *Exercise* of an option is now viewed by the S.E.C. as merely a *change from indirect to direct beneficial ownership*, with no particular significance under section 16. [S.E.C. Release No. 34-23369 (1991)]

(1) **Rationale:** [§1324] The S.E.C.'s position is based on the long-overdue recognition that derivative securities (for instance, stock options) are functionally equivalent to the underlying equity securities. Contrary to the general rule regarding "purchases" and "sales" (*see supra*, §1318), the S.E.C.'s position with respect to stock options is that the significant event is *not* a person's irrevocable liability to take and pay, or deliver and accept payment. Rather, the critical event—the one providing the opportunity to profit from inside information—occurs when the person has the legal *right* to receive (or to deliver) the underlying equity security at a fixed price. This point is illustrated in the following examples.

(a) **Example 1—Purchase stock/sell stock:** [§1325] "If an insider of IBM purchased 1,000 shares of IBM common stock on February 23, 1990 ($102-5/8 per share NYSE), he would have paid $102,625. If the insider sold the 1,000 shares on April 16, 1990, for $110,750 ($110-3/4 per share NYSE), a profit of $8,125 would have been made." [S.E.C. Release No. 34-28869 (1991) (footnote omitted)]

(b) **Example 2—Purchase option/exercise option/sell stock:** [§1326] "Similarly, the same insider could have bought 10 IBM call option contracts (covering 1,000 IBM common shares) on February 23, 1990, for $9,875 ($9-7/8 per share), exercisable on or before October 19, 1990, at $100 per share. If on April 16, 1990, the insider exercised the option and purchased the stock for $100,000 and sold the stock for $110,750 ($110-3/4 per share), the profit would be $875." [*Id.*]

(c) **Example 3—Purchase option/sell stock:** [§1327] "If the insider purchased the same 10 IBM call option contracts (covering 1,000 IBM common shares) on February 23, 1990, for $9,875 ($9-7/8 per share), exercisable on or before October 19, 1990, but, instead of exercising the option and selling the underlying stock, he sold 1,000 shares of IBM common stock otherwise held on April 16, 1990, for $110,750 ($110-3/4 per share), the insider would lock in the ability to earn a profit of $875." [*Id.* (footnote omitted)]

(d) **Example 4—Purchase option/sell option:** [§1328] "Suppose the same insider purchased 10 IBM call option contracts (covering 1,000 IBM shares) on February 23, 1990, for $9,875 ($9-7/8 per share), exercisable at $100 before October 19. On April 16, the insider sold the call options for $13,625 ($13-5/8 per share). The profit would have been $3,750." [*Id.*]

(e) **Example 5—Purchase stock/purchase put option:** [§1329] "The same insider also could have bought 1,000 shares of IBM stock on February 23, 1990, for $102,625, and on April 16, 1990, bought 10 put option contracts (covering 1,000 IBM shares) expiring October 19 with an exercise price of $115, at a price of $7-1/2 per share, or $7,500. By purchasing the put options, the insider locked in the ability to earn a profit of $4,875, when the insider could receive $115,000 for the 1,000 shares under the put options." [*Id.*]

(f) **Comment:** Although an opportunity to profit from inside information arises from ownership of stock options as certainly as from ownership of stock, owning options in most cases does not provide *access* to inside information. In this respect, perhaps, the S.E.C.'s new rules may go too far, for they treat options as though they were stock.

(2) **Employee stock options:** [§1330] Previously, the S.E.C.'s scheme for addressing the problems posed by stock options distinguished between options purchased from third parties (*e.g.,* market-traded options) and those granted to the individual by the issuer, for example, employee stock options issued as part of an incentive plan. Under the 1991 revised rules, ***all options, including employee stock options,*** are treated in the

same way. Since employee stock options present precisely the same profit opportunities as other options, the S.E.C. determined that different treatment for employee options could no longer be justified. [S.E.C. Release No. 34-28869, *supra*]

(3) **Effect of revised rules:** [§1331] The practical effect of the 1991 revised rules is that a purchase of an option is treated as the purchase (or sale, as appropriate) of the underlying security, and will be matched against any counterpart transaction—in the underlying security *or* in a derivative of the underlying security—to create a "profit" recoverable under section 16.

    (a) **Purchase of call option:** [§1332] The purchase of a call option gives the option holder the right to buy the underlying security at a fixed price and for a fixed duration. This transaction is treated as a purchase of the underlying security, and can be matched against a sale of the underlying security, a sale of a call option, or a purchase of a put option.

    (b) **Purchase of put option:** [§1333] A put option is essentially the reverse of a call option—it gives the option holder the right to sell the underlying security, again at a fixed price and for a fixed duration. This transaction is treated as a sale of the underlying security, and can be matched against a purchase of the underlying security, a purchase of a call option, or a sale of a put option.

    (c) **Exercise of an option:** [§1334] Consistent with the S.E.C.'s rationale for its treatment of options under the 1991 revised rules (*see supra*, §1323), the exercise of an option in most cases amounts to neither a purchase nor a sale under section 16. The opportunity for profit is created when the option is acquired, and its exercise, because it does not create a new opportunity for profit, is exempt.

        1) **Exception—exercise of "out-of-the-money" options:** [§1335] In its 1991 release announcing the new section 16 rules, however, the S.E.C. reserved an exception to the rule that the exercise of an option is exempt: exercise by an insider of an out-of-the-money call option may constitute a purchase of the underlying security.

            a) **Definitions:** [§1336] Understanding the scope of this exception requires us to understand three key terms relating to an option's exercise price.

                1/ **"In-the-money":** [§1337] An option is in the money if its exercise price represents a profit opportunity for the option holder. Thus, a call option is in the money if its exercise price is less than the current market price of the underlying security.

                2/ **"At-the-money":** [§1338] An option is at the money if its exercise price is the same as the current market price. (These are treated as in-the-money by the S.E.C.)

3/ **"Out-of-the-money":** [§1339] An option is out of the money when its exercise would produce a loss to the option holder. (Options that are out-of-the money are also sometimes referred to as "under water.")

b) **Rationale:** The S.E.C.'s reluctance to treat the exercise of an out-of-the-money option as exempt from section 16 appears to be based on a general suspicion of such transactions, rather than on a specific perception of danger. In support of its decision, the S.E.C. noted merely that "there appears to be little economic justification for an insider to exercise an out-of-the-money option" and referred to unspecified "concerns as to the reasons that an insider would" do so. [S.E.C. Release No. 34-23369, *supra*]

(4) **Stock appreciation rights:** [§1340] "Stock appreciation rights" ("S.A.R.s") usually give officers the right to receive the increase in value of the optioned shares from the date of grant of the option to the date of exercise of such rights. Whether there is section 16(b) liability depends on whether the S.A.R. is paid out in cash or stock, and whether or not the form of payment is under the control of the S.A.R.-holder.

(a) **S.A.R.s that can be settled only for cash:** [§1341] An S.A.R. that can be settled only for cash (*i.e.,* where the holder does *not* have an option to settle for cash or stock) is *exempt* from section 16 *if* it meets the following conditions:

1) **Award satisfies conditions of rule 16b-3(c):** [§1342] Rule 16b-3 sets out a detailed set of conditions that a plan must meet in order for awards to be exempt from section 16(b); *or*

2) **S.A.R. may be exercised only on limited conditions:** [§1343] Alternatively, a cash-only S.A.R. is exempt from section 16 if it can be exercised only under one of the following conditions:

a) The occurrence of a *fixed date* of redemption at least six months after award; or

b) *Death* of the holder; or

c) *Retirement* of the holder; or

d) *Disability* of the holder; or

e) *Termination* of the holder's employment.

(b) **S.A.R.s settled for stock:** [§1344] S.A.R.s settled for stock are derivative securities, and are treated the same as options.

(c) **S.A.R.s settled in cash *or* stock:** [§1345] An S.A.R. that can be settled either in cash or stock, at the option of the holder, can be treated in one of three ways.

    1) **Settled for stock:** [§1346] An S.A.R. giving the holder the option as to form of settlement, and which is settled for stock, is treated as an S.A.R. that can only be settled for stock—that is, as an *option*.

        a) **Note:** Such an S.A.R. would be reported at *grant*, with the amount of any liability calculated later.

    2) **Settled for cash—not eligible for exemption:** [§1347] An S.A.R. settled at the holder's option for cash and that does not meet the exemptive requirement of rule 16b-3 (*see supra*, §1342) is treated as the exercise of an option (which is normally exempt) and the simultaneous sale of the underlying stock.

    3) **Settled for cash—eligible for exemption:** [§1348] An S.A.R. settled at the holder's option for cash, and the award of which is eligible for exemption under rule 16b-3 (*see supra*, §1342) is exempt, just as is an S.A.R. that must be settled in cash.

c. **Recapitalizations:** [§1349] Most recapitalizations (*i.e.,* transactions in which a corporation exchanges a new security for one of its already outstanding securities) do *not* involve a purchase or sale of the new stock. Insiders are generally unable to take advantage of inside information in recapitalizations since (i) all similarly situated shareholders are treated the same way, (ii) shareholder approval of the recapitalization is normally required, and (iii) each shareholder simply continues his investment in the corporation in a different form. [Roberts v. Eaton, 212 F.2d 82 (2d Cir.), *cert. denied*, 348 U.S. 827 (1954)]

    (1) **Leveraged recapitalizations:** [§1350] Note, however, that *Roberts, supra*, did not deal with a "leveraged recapitalization." In such transactions, popular in the 1980s, shares of the corporation's old stock are exchanged, usually for a package including a share of newer common stock, cash, and perhaps a debt security. The shareholder's incentive to participate is that the package offered by the corporation is worth considerably more than the market price of the old stock, just before the recap is announced. Such transactions pose obvious dangers of insider abuse, and a court confronting an insider who used her knowledge of a proposed leveraged recap to purchase and sell the company's stock at a profit might decline to follow *Roberts, supra*.

d. **Stock dividends and gifts:** [§1351] A corporation may issue additional shares of common stock pro rata to its shareholders. Such a transaction may be effected by issuing "rights" to acquire additional shares, or warrants, or by simply issuing additional shares in the form of a stock dividend. These transactions have been held *not* to involve a "purchase" by the shareholder recipients. [Shaw v. Dreyfus, 172 F.2d 140 (2d Cir.), *cert. denied*, 337 U.S. 907 (1949); *see* SEA Rule 16a-9(b)]

(1) **Exercise of rights is a purchase:** [§1352] Note, however, that the *exercise* of such a right (or warrant) by a shareholder *is* a "purchase" of the securities received upon exercise. [Shaw v. Dreyfus, *supra*; *see* SEA Rule 16a-9, note]

(2) **Gifts:** [§1353] A bona fide gift of stock is *not* a purchase by the donee under section 16. [Shaw v. Dreyfus, *supra*; Truncale v. Blumberg, 80 F. Supp. 387, 83 F. Supp. 628 (S.D.N.Y. 1948); *see* SEA Rule 16b-5] Note that this is consistent with the treatment of gifts under the 1933 Act, *see supra*, §157.

e. **Reorganizations:** [§1354] Corporate reorganizations often fall within section 16(b). Generally, when a corporation is merged or sold in exchange for stock, a "sale" of the securities surrendered and a "purchase" of the securities received takes place. [*See* SEA Rule 16b-7—exempting certain mergers, and thus implying other mergers are covered by section 16]

(1) **Opportunity for abuse:** [§1355] The typical merger case presents opportunities for abuse, since those parties involved in the merger possess inside information that outsiders do not, and stock prices of target companies typically rise.

(2) **Tender offers and defensive mergers:** [§1356] A tender offer involves the direct purchase of the shares of the target company by the bidder.

(a) **Typical situation:** [§1357] The bidder (B) may begin by purchasing a minority interest in the target (A) and may then attempt to negotiate a merger of the two companies. Frequently, the target (A) will seek a defensive merger with a "white knight" (C). The bidder (B) may then find itself in a difficult situation with respect to section 16(b), as to its ownership of some of A's shares. This would be the case if B acquires 10% or more of a class of registered equity security, thus becoming an "insider" for section 16(b) purposes.

1) If B should fail in its tender offer and sell its A shares, B may be liable under section 16(b) if its purchase and sale of A's shares have occurred within less than six months.

2) Likewise, if C gains control and merges A into C, and B is then forced to exchange its A shares for C shares, B may be liable under section 16(b).

a) However, it has been held that where B loses in its tender offer bid through a successful defensive merger of A into C, B's exchange of its A shares for C shares is *not* a "sale" within section 16(b). [American Standard, Inc. v. Crane Co., 510 F.2d 1043 (2d Cir. 1974), *cert. denied*, 421 U.S. 1000 (1975)]

(b) **"Unorthodox transactions" not within section 16:** [§1358] In 1973 the Supreme Court, departing from the normally strict interpretation of "purchase" and "sale" under section 16, held that certain merger transactions were "unorthodox" and, if such a transaction did not present the dangers of abuse of inside information that section 16 was designed to combat, the transaction would not be covered by section 16. [Kern County Land Co. v. Occidental Petroleum Corp., 411 U.S. 582 (1973)]

1) **Facts of *Kern County Land*:** [§1359]  Occidental Petroleum made a tender offer on May 8 for Kern County Land ("Kern") stock, acquiring by June 8 more than 10% of Kern common stock for $85 per share. Meanwhile, Kern successfully negotiated a defensive merger with Tenneco, pursuant to which Kern shareholders would receive one share of Tenneco preferred stock for each share of Kern stock they owned. Occidental (seeing that it was going to lose the battle) entered into an option agreement with Tenneco giving Tenneco the right to purchase all the Tenneco preferred stock that Occidental was to receive in the merger, for $105 per share. This option agreement was entered into within six months of the date Occidental had first acquired the 10% Kern interest. The option could not be exercised by Tenneco before December 9, 1967, a date six months and one day after the expiration of Occidental's tender offer. The option price paid by Tenneco to Occidental was $10 per share, to be part of the purchase price if Tenneco exercised the option. The Tenneco-Kern merger plan closed on August 30. On December 11, Tenneco exercised its option to buy Occidental's Tenneco preferred stock, which resulted in a profit to Occidental of more than $15 million. However, Tenneco then sued Occidental for this profit under section 16(b), alleging that both the execution of the option and the exchange of shares upon consummation of the merger were "sales" by Occidental, occurring within six months of its purchase of Kern shares.

a) The Court held that neither the execution of the option agreement nor the merger of Tenneco and Kern constituted a "sale" of the Kern stock by Occidental under section 16(b). The Court stated that the option price was not so large as to ***compel*** the exercise of the option by Tenneco. Furthermore, the merger-sale was involuntary as to Occidental (*i.e.,* once the merger was approved by Kern's shareholders, Occidental had no way to prevent its consummation), and was not motivated or caused by any abuse of inside information. In other words, the Court found no possibility of the kind of harm section 16(b) was intended to remedy.

b) To have held otherwise in this situation would have provided a powerful incentive for target companies to enter defensive mergers: if such mergers were concluded within six months of the time the tendering company bought its shares, the defensive merger company (after gaining control) would be able to collect damages against the tendering company for a violation of section 16(b). [*See* American Standard, Inc. v. Crane Co., *supra*]

(c) **Comment:** [§1360] *Kern County Land* opened up a defense to potential defendants that previously appeared to be closed. At least in the context of "unorthodox" corporate combinations, the Supreme Court has approved a "subjective" approach—leading to a case-by-case determination of whether, in the factual context of the case, there has been a violation of the policy of section 16(b) against the speculative abuse of inside information.

(d) **Exemption relating to certain combinations:** [§1361] Where Company A owns 85% or more of the equity securities of Subsidiary B (or 85% or more of the assets of B or a group of companies including B), and A is merged into B (or the group is consolidated into one company) and the shareholders of A receive a new security in exchange for their shares in A (*i.e.,* A is not the surviving company), the shareholders of A do *not* have a "purchase" or "sale" as part of the transaction. [SEA Rule 16b-7]

    1) **Rationale:** This rule is designed to exempt shareholders of a controlling corporation which, for legal purposes, exchanges its shares for the shares of a controlled subsidiary.

    2) **But note:** Not included within this exemption is an insider shareholder of A who purchases a security of one of the corporations involved in the merger and then sells the securities of another of these companies within a six-month period during which the merger occurs. However, the securities involved in the combination transaction itself do not count as a purchase or sale. [*Id.*]

7. **"Within a Period of Less Than Six Months":** [§1362] For section 16(b) to apply, the matching purchase and sale must occur within a period of *less than* six months.

a. **Less than six months:** [§1363] "The law does not take account of fractions of days." This maxim of equity applies to section 16, as it does to most legal calculations of elapsed time. Application of this rule can, however, produce some confusion, especially if it is not clear whether to "not take account of fractions" means to disregard them altogether, or to count them as *full days* rather than as fractional days.

(1) **Rule:** [§1364] For section 16 purposes, *a fractional day counts as a full day.* Because a fractional day counts as a full day, the section 16 "period of less than six months" can be generically defined as a period that begins at any time on day 1 and *ends at midnight on the day that is two days before the corresponding date six months later.* [*See* Morales v. Reading & Bates Offshore Drilling Co., 392 F. Supp. 41 (N.D. Okla. 1975)] This result follows because if the period were to extend to the following day, then that *entire* day would be counted, and therefore the period would be *exactly* six months, rather than "less than six months" as the statute requires. In other words, because any fraction of a day counts as a full day, the statutory term "less than six months" amounts to "six months less at least one full day."

(2) **Example:** D, a director of X corporation, purchased 1,000 shares of X Corporation common stock (registered under section 12 of the 1934 Act) at 9:15 a.m. on January 20. At 3:15 p.m. on July 19, D sold all 1,000 shares. D's sale is *exactly six months* after her purchase, because January 20 is counted as a full day (the purchase at 9:15 a.m. is treated as though it took place immediately after midnight) and so is July 19 (the 3:15 p.m. sale is treated as though it took place precisely at the instant that the "six-month point" was reached).

b. **Special problems in determining time of transaction:** [§1365]  Although the specific date on which a purchase or sale occurred is generally a matter of record, for some transactions it is occasionally difficult to determine the date of occurrence.

(1) **Shares to be determined on contingent events:** [§1366]  For example, in some instances, shares are to be delivered as part of a purchase price based on future contingent events.

(a) **Example:** Company A purchases Company B, and promises to pay additional shares of A stock to B in the event that the market price of A stock declines over a certain period of time. If the price of A stock does go down, A must pay more of its shares to B. When are these contingent shares of A "purchased" by B? Courts have split on this question.

(b) **Date of delivery:** [§1367]  One possibility is that contingent shares are purchased on the date of their *delivery* (not the contract date, although the parties were committed as of this date). [Booth v. Varian Associates, 334 F.2d 1 (1st Cir. 1964), *cert. denied*, 379 U.S. 961 (1965)]

(c) **Date of commitment:** [§1368]  Another possibility is that contingent shares are purchased on the date that the commitment to purchase (or sell, as the case may be) becomes complete. For example, in a case in which the purchase price for a closely held corporation was expressed in shares to be paid by the buyer over a number of years, the price of the additional shares was set at the outset but the *number* of additional shares to be delivered was contingent on future earnings. The court held that the purchase of the final installment of shares was made at the time the sale of the company closed, three years earlier. [Prager v. Sylvestri, 449 F. Supp. 425 (S.D.N.Y. 1978)]

(2) **Option agreements:** [§1369]  Recall that under the S.E.C.'s 1991 revised rules, an option to buy or sell stock is treated as a purchase or sale of the underlying stock, which can be matched against counterpart transactions either in options or in the underlying stock. (*See supra*, §§1330 *et seq.*) The *time* at which a transaction takes place in a derivative security, such as a stock option, then, is the *time of grant* of the option. Neither the time the option becomes exercisable nor the time it is actually exercised has any significance for section 16 purposes, because the grant of the option is viewed as the purchase (or sale, as the case may be) of the underlying stock.

(a) **Effect:** [§1370] The effect of this rule is that a matching transaction must be found within a period of less than six months before or after the date of grant or no liability will result from the grant.

(b) **Grant of employee stock option is usually exempt:** [§1371] Options granted under an employee stock option plan are typically exempt from section 16, pursuant to rule 16b-3 (*see supra*, §1342). As a result, there normally is no section 16 liability resulting from the grant of an employee stock option.

8. **"Profit" Under Section 16(b):** [§1372] The profit of the defendant under section 16(b) is calculated according to the statute, and is unrelated to any "real-world" notion of buying low and selling high.

a. **Any purchase or sale may be matched:** [§1373] Section 16(b) may be applied to any matched "purchase" and "sale" (or "sale" and "purchase"), if the matched transactions occur within a period of *less than* six months.

(1) **Example:** A, a director, buys 100 shares of XYZ stock on June 1 for $10 per share. On July 1, A sells the stock for $9 per share. On August 1, A buys 100 shares for $8 per share. Finally, on September 1, A sells the stock for $7 per share. In three months A has lost a total of $200, but is still liable under section 16(b), since the $9 sale can be matched with the $8 purchase (providing a $100 profit).

(a) **Note:** If the matched purchase and sale transactions occur exactly six months apart, or extend beyond six months, there is no liability.

b. **Profit maximized:** [§1374] The matching of purchase and sale transactions that will produce the maximum profit is used, and there is no attempt made to trace particular securities bought and sold. For example, if 100 shares are purchased at $1 per share and 100 at $2 per share, and five months later 100 shares are sold at $10 per share, the recoverable profit is $9 per share.

(1) **Loss transactions:** [§1375] Any transactions in the six-month period that produce losses are ignored.

c. **"Profit" from a sale followed by a purchase:** [§1376] Section 16 profit can be earned not only from a purchase followed by a sale, but also from a sale followed by a purchase.

(1) **Example:** B, a director of G Corp. (which has its common stock registered under section 12), sells 100 shares of G common stock on June 1, at $10 per share. Two months later, on August 1, B purchases 100 shares of G common stock at $5 per share. B is liable to G Corp. for her profit of $5 per share.

(a) **Rationale:** Students are often puzzled that section 16(b) covers transactions like this one. The rationale for the $5 per share profit is that after making the August 1 purchase, B is in precisely the position she was in before the June 1 sale, except that she has $500 in cash that she didn't have before. In other words, had she not engaged in the two stock transactions, she would have had 100 shares of G common stock on August 2. Having engaged in the transactions, she has 100 shares of G common stock, *and* $500 in cash, which represents her profit on the transactions (and which is forfeitable to G Corp. under section 16(b)).

d. **Strict liability:** [§1377]  The general rule is that there are no defenses to a section 16(b) action if all elements of the cause of action are present (*i.e.,* an "insider," registered equity securities, and a matching purchase and sale within the required time period). Thus, it makes no difference that the insider cannot be shown to have had access to any inside information, or to have used any inside information in effectuating the matching purchase and sale. [Smolowe v. Delendo Corp., 136 F.2d 231 (2d Cir. 1943)]

(1) **Exception—"unorthodox" transactions:** [§1378]  There is a narrow category of cases, involving what the Supreme Court has called "unorthodox" transactions, in which even though arguably a purchase and sale have taken place within six months, section 16(b) does not apply. These transactions typically involve mergers and acquisitions (they are discussed in more detail *supra*, §§1358 *et seq.*).

e. **Matching transactions in derivative securities:** [§1379]  Recall that the S.E.C. treats transactions in derivative securities as equivalent to transactions in the underlying security. (*See supra*, §1324.) For the purpose of calculating the "profit" on matching transactions in derivative securities, the S.E.C. has adopted special rules. [SEA Rule 16b-6(c)]

(1) **Derivative securities with identical characteristics:** [§1380]  "Profit" on the sale and purchase, or purchase and sale, of derivative securities with identical characteristics is calculated in the same way it is for equivalent transactions in the underlying securities.

(a) **Example:** D, a director of X Corporation, purchased and sold call options for X Corporation stock (which was registered under 1934 Act section 12). On February 1, D purchased 10 options for $10 each; on March 1, she sold 10 options for $9 each; on April 1, she purchased 10 options for $8 each; and on May 1, she sold 10 options for $7 each. D has made a "profit" of $10 under section 16, because the April 1 purchase (at $8) will be matched with the February 1 sale (at $9).

(2) **Derivative securities with different characteristics, relating to the same underlying security:** [§1381]  Consistent with the idea that derivative securities are for most purposes equivalent to their underlying securities, the S.E.C. has limited the profits recoverable under section 16(b) in the case where the derivatives are based on the same security, but have different characteristics. In such a case, the maximum profit recoverable is the difference in price of the *underlying security* on the date of purchase or sale and the date of sale or purchase.

(a) **Example:** D, a director of X Corporation, on June 3 purchased 10 call options, each immediately exercisable for 100 shares of X Corporation common stock (which is registered under section 12 of the 1934 Act). On June 3, the price of X Corporation common stock is 46½. On July 1, D sold X Corporation convertible debentures, which in the aggregate could be immediately converted into 1,000 shares of X Corporation common stock at an effective conversion price of $25 per share. The market price of X Corporation common stock on July 1 was 51½. D's profit under section 16(b) is limited to the difference between the price of X common on the sale date, 51½, and the purchase date, 46½—that is, $5 per share—for a total of $5,000.

(3) **Insiders who write options:** [§1382] What happens when an insider does not just *sell* an option, but *writes* an option? In other words, an insider, D, might sell to someone the right to demand stock of an issuer *from D* at any time in the next three months (for example). An insider who writes a call option is considered to have sold the stock on the date the option is granted. Similarly, a put option written by an insider is treated as if the insider purchased the underlying stock on the date the option was written.

   (a) **Options expire without exercise:** [§1383] But what happens if, as is often the case, an option written by an insider expires without being exercised? In such a case, the S.E.C. limits the section 16 profit recoverable to the amount of the fee, or premium, the insider received for writing the option. If upon the expiration of the option the insider receives no value, then no profit is recoverable under section 16. [SEA Rule 16b-6(d)]

      1) **Example:** D, a director of X Corporation, wrote a call option under which G could purchase from D 100 shares of X Corporation stock (which is registered under section 12 of the 1934 Act) at $100 per share. The option was exercisable on any date beginning January 1, 1994, through March 31, 1994. On January 1, D received $10 from G for writing the option. The option expired without exercise. On April 10, D purchased 100 shares of X common stock.

      2) **Analysis:** The writing of the call option is *treated as a sale of the underlying stock.* (*See supra*, §1332.) This transaction could then be matched with a purchase of the stock in the next six months to produce liability, with a profit calculated by reference to the price of the stock on the relevant dates. However, the S.E.C. rule is that D is liable only for the option premium received on the option expiring unexercised. [SEA Rule 16b-6(d)]

9. **Other Elements of Damages Under Section 16(b):** [§1384] In addition to the defendant's profits, a section 16(b) plaintiff can also recover additional sums related to the case.

   a. **Interest:** [§1385] Interest on the profit may be awarded in the discretion of the court, based on considerations of "fairness." [Blau v. Lehman, *supra,* §1322]

b. **Dividends:** [§1386]  Dividends paid on securities that are held during the six-month period may be part of the "profit" realized, depending on the circumstances.

(1) **Dividends not included:** [§1387]  Dividends are not included in the following situations [Adler v. Klawans, 267 F.2d 840 (2d Cir. 1959)]:

(a) Where they are declared *on stock prior to purchase by the insider;*

(b) Where they are declared *prior to the stockholder becoming an insider;* and

(c) Where they are declared *on specific certificates which were not sold at a profit*. However, there is authority to the contrary on this point. [Western Auto Supply Co. v. Gamble-Skogmo, Inc., 348 F.2d 736 (8th Cir. 1965)—dividends paid on a number of shares equivalent to the number sold were held part of profit]

(2) **Dividends included:** [§1388]  Dividends declared on the actual shares sold while the owner is an insider are held by all courts to be part of the "profit."

c. **Attorney's fees:** [§1389]  Attorney's fees are recoverable in a section 16 action as part of the plaintiff's judgment.

(1) **Note:** The provision for attorney's fees often provides the main motivation for bringing a section 16(b) action. Lawyers often look for section 16 situations and then find a shareholder on whose behalf they can sue.

10. **Procedural Aspects of Actions Under Section 16**

a. **Jurisdiction:** [§1390]  Federal courts have exclusive jurisdiction over section 16 actions.

b. **Service:** [§1391]  Nationwide service of process is available.

c. **Venue:** [§1392]  The plaintiff may sue under section 16 in the district where any act or transaction constituting the violation occurred, or in the district where the defendant is found or transacts business, or if the transaction was consummated on a securities exchange, the action may be brought in the district in which the exchange is located.

d. **Statute of limitations:** [§1393]  Section 16(b) provides for a statute of limitations of two years from the date when the profit is realized by the insider. The statute is tolled, however, if the insider has not filed the reports required by section 16(a), until such time as the profits are discovered or with reasonable diligence should have been discovered.

e. **Law or equity:** [§1394]  The plaintiff may elect either a jury or a court trial.

f. **Proper plaintiff:** [§1395]  The corporation may sue under section 16 for the profit made by its insider *or*, if the corporation declines to proceed, any security holder of the corporation may bring a *derivative action on behalf of the* *corporation.* Note that the S.E.C. has no authority to seek injunctive or other relief for the violation of section 16(b).

(1) **No contemporaneous ownership requirement:** [§1396] Section 16 lawsuits are easily brought because of the fact that *any* security holder is a proper plaintiff. The plaintiff need not be the owner of equity securities, nor must he have owned the securities at the time the wrong occurred. Thus, plaintiff can purchase securities subsequent to the date of the wrong and still bring an action. [Blau v. Mission Corp., 212 F.2d 77 (2d Cir. 1954), *cert. denied*, 347 U.S. 1016 (1954)]

(2) **Sixty-day notice and demand:** [§1397] A security holder may sue under section 16(b) only "if the issuer shall fail or refuse to bring such suit within 60 days after request or shall fail diligently to prosecute the same thereafter."

(3) **Circumstances excusing sixty-day notice:** [§1398] The 60-day notice period under section 16(b) has been excused in the following situations:

(a) **Defendant dominates the corporation:** [§1399] Notice is not required if the individual defendant dominates the corporation, so that a demand on the corporation to sue the individual would be futile. [Weisman v. Spector, 158 F. Supp. 789 (S.D.N.Y. 1958); Netter v. Ashland Paper Mills, Inc., 19 F.R.D. 529 (S.D.N.Y. 1956)]

(b) **Statute of limitations will run:** [§1400] Likewise, the plaintiff-shareholder need not wait for 60 days to elapse after making demand on the corporation if the two-year statute of limitations applicable to actions under section 16(b) would run out during that time. [Benisch v. Cameron, 81 F. Supp. 882 (S.D.N.Y. 1948); Grossman v. Young, 72 F. Supp. 375 (S.D.N.Y. 1947)]

11. **Exemptions:** [§1401] The S.E.C. has provided a number of exemptions from section 16(b) liability.

a. **Securities received in foreclosure on a debt:** [§1402] Section 16(b) exempts a security acquired in good faith in connection with a debt previously contracted. Thus, the receipt of securities in connection with a foreclosure is not a "purchase" within the meaning of section 16(b).

b. **Gifts and inheritance:** [§1403] By rule, the S.E.C. has exempted bona fide gifts and transfers of securities by will or intestate descent. [SEA Rule 16b-5]

c. **Exemption for dealers:** [§1404] A problem might arise where a securities firm acts as a dealer in a registered equity security of a company and becomes an insider of that company (*e.g.,* by acquiring 10% of the security). In this event, the firm's trading activity in the company's securities could violate section 16(b).

(1) **Exemption from section 16(b):** [§1405] The Act provides an exemption for dealers—with respect to securities *not* held in their investment accounts—to the extent that transactions are engaged in pursuant to maintaining a primary or secondary market in the security. [SEA §16(d)]

Note, however, that such securities are *not* exempt from the reporting requirement of section 16(a).

    (a) **"Securities in an investment account":** [§1406] These are securities identified as such in the broker-dealer's records and for I.R.S. purposes. Those are held as permanent capital by the broker-dealer, rather than being purchased as part of market-making activity.

## F. LIABILITY OF PARTICIPANTS IN AND ADVISERS TO SECURITIES TRANSACTIONS [§1407]

This section of the Summary discusses the potential liability of persons who aid, abet, participate in, or render advice in connection with a transaction that violates the 1933 or 1934 Acts.

1. **Liability of Collateral Participants:** [§1408] "Collateral participants" are those who are involved in the securities transaction in some way, but are not directly responsible for the transaction.

    a. **Liability under 1933 Act**

        (1) **Section 11:** [§1409] One court has held that a person may be liable as an aider or abettor under Securities Act section 11. [*In re* Caesar's Palace Securities Litigation, 360 F. Supp. 366 (S.D.N.Y. 1973)] This position appears to be unsound, however, because section 11 specifically lists the persons who may be liable under its provisions, and the list does not include aiders and abettors.

        (2) **Section 12(1):** [§1410] Securities Act section 12(1) provides a rescission remedy to purchasers of securities that were required to be registered under section 5, but were not registered. The action may be brought only against the "seller" of the securities. (*See supra*, §§687 *et seq.*) The question then becomes, who is a "seller" under the statute? For a time, the courts were split. The Supreme Court case of *Pinter v. Dahl, supra*, §690, resolved the question to some extent by holding that under section 12(1), a *"seller" includes persons who solicit the purchase.* "Sellers" do not include persons whose sole motivation in acting is to benefit the buyer. [Pinter v. Dahl, *see supra*, §§692 *et seq.*] It remains to be seen how much "solicitation" of a purchaser is necessary to meet the standard of *Pinter.*

            (a) **Defenses:** [§1411] Collateral participants in section 12(1) cases have available essentially the same defenses that direct participants have: no sale of a "security," no violation of section 5, no privity, statute of limitations, and the jurisdictional defense (no activity in interstate commerce). (*See supra*, §§693 *et seq.*)

        (3) **Section 12(2):** [§1412] Securities Act section 12(2) provides a rescission remedy to purchasers of securities sold by means of a prospectus or oral communication that contained a materially misleading statement or omission. (*See supra*, §§699 *et seq.*) As with section 12(1), the action may be brought only against the "seller" of the securities, and again the question arises as to who may be considered a "seller" within the statute. The

*Pinter* case, *supra*, arose under section 12(1), and the Supreme Court noted that it was not expressing any view about the scope of the term as used in section 12(2). However, because the language is identical to that of section 12(1)—in fact, most of it is literally *the same language*—one would expect the term "seller" to have the same meaning under each section. The circuit courts have so held. [*See, e.g.,* Cyrak v. Lemon, 919 F.2d 320 (5th Cir. 1990); *In re* Craftmatic Securities Litigation, 890 F.2d 628 (3d Cir. 1989); Royal American Managers, Inc. v. IRC Holding Corp., 885 F.2d 1011 (2d Cir. 1989); Moore v. Kayport Package Express, Inc., 885 F.2d 531 (9th Cir. 1989); Schlifke v. Seafirst Corp., 866 F.2d 935 (7th Cir. 1989)]

(a) **Defenses:** [§1413] Again, collateral participants have available the same defenses as the direct participants: lack of knowledge of the misleading statement or omission (and the exercise of reasonable care would not have revealed the misleading statement or omission), plaintiff's knowledge of the true facts, lack of privity, the statute of limitations, lack of materiality, statute of limitations, and the jurisdictional defense (no activity in interstate commerce). (*See supra,* §§708 *et seq.*)

(4) **Section 17:** [§1414] It is highly unlikely that a private civil cause of action is available under Securities Act section 17. (*See supra,* §721.)

b. **Liability under rule 10b-5 of the 1934 Act:** [§1415] For many years, the courts and the S.E.C. upheld aider and abettor liability under rule 10b-5. In 1994, however, all this changed, when the Supreme Court decided the case of *Central Bank v. First Interstate Bank*, 114 S. Ct. 1439 (1994). *Central Bank* squarely held (albeit by a 5-4 vote) that *there is no implied private right of action against one who aids or abets a rule 10b-5 violation.*

(1) **Facts of *Central Bank*:** [§1416] Central Bank was the trustee on a bond issue. Before the bond issue closed, Central received information suggesting that the value of the land securing the bonds had declined significantly. Central's in-house appraiser recommended obtaining an independent appraisal of the land, but the bank failed to do so before the closing. Before the independent appraisal had been finished, the issuer defaulted on the bonds. Central Bank was sued as an aider and abettor of rule 10b-5 violations allegedly committed by the issuer and others.

(2) **Supreme Court's analysis:** [§1417] The Supreme Court began its analysis by observing that the text of the statute controlled its decision and that a private plaintiff may not bring suit under rule 10b-5 for conduct not prohibited by SEA section 10(b). Pointing out that Congress knew how to impose liability for aiding and abetting (*i.e.,* by using the words "aid and abet"), the Court held that because section 10(b) does not include such language, aiding and abetting liability does not exist under rule 10b-5.

(3) **Significance of *Central Bank*:** [§1418] It is too early to assess fully the ultimate impact of *Central Bank*. However, it is clear that the decision continues and extends on the restrictive interpretation of rule 10b-5 that began with *Blue Chip Stamp* (*see supra,* §§854 *et seq.*) and continued

with *Ernst & Ernst v. Hochfelder* (*see supra,* §§885 *et seq.*). Likewise, it is clear that the decision means that fewer actions will be maintainable against lawyers, accountants, and other professionals whose involvement in securities transactions is extensive but who seldom are primary violators of rule 10b-5. Among the most important questions raised by the case are the following:

(a) **S.E.C. civil actions:** [§1419] Although *Central Bank* involved private plaintiffs, the Court's reasoning is clearly broad enough to extend to actions brought by the S.E.C.

    1) **Note:** *Central Bank* does **not** raise problems for criminal aiding and abetting prosecutions because a criminal action proceeds under a different statute [18 U.S.C. §2] from the action against the primary violator.

    2) **And note:** *Central Bank's* impact on the S.E.C. may be less than one would at first expect, even if it means that the Commission can no longer bring actions against aiders and abettors. Under the Securities Enforcement and Penny Stock Reform Act of 1990, the S.E.C. can obtain an accounting and disgorgement of profits from any person who "is, was or would be a cause of [a] violation" of the 1934 Act. [SEA §21C(a)] This administrative remedy probably will function as at least a partial replacement for what the S.E.C. may have lost under *Central Bank.*

(b) **Effect on aiding and abetting actions under other provisions:** [§1420] *Central Bank* has left unclear the scope of private actions against aiders and abettors under other provisions of the securities laws, the 1934 Act, at least when the statute does not expressly provide for such an action. The Court's reasoning in *Central Bank* was extremely broad, and there is no apparent reason to confine it to SEA section 10(b) and rule 10b-5. The next few years will likely reveal in more detail the precise contours of aiding and abetting liability under the federal securities laws.

2. **Liability of Controlling Persons:** [§1421] Both the 1933 Act and the 1934 Act contain provisions making "controlling persons" liable for the securities law violations of persons they control. (*See supra,* §689.)

    a. **Liability under 1933 Act:** [§1422] The 1933 Act provides that any person who controls another person found liable under sections 11 or 12 is jointly and severally liable along with the controlled party—**unless** the controlling person had no knowledge of, nor reasonable grounds to believe in, the existence of the facts that form the basis of the controlled person's liability. [SA §15]

    b. **Liability under 1934 Act:** [§1423] The 1934 Act provides that controlling persons are liable for the securities violations of persons they control, unless they acted in "good faith" and did not directly or indirectly induce the acts that are the basis of the controlled person's liability. [SEA §20(a)]

c. **Compare—"good faith" as a defense:** [§1424] Ignorance (*i.e.,* no knowledge) is a clear defense to an action brought under section 15 of the 1933 Act, whereas section 20(a) of the 1934 Act requires the defendant to establish both that she did not induce the offense by the controlled party, and that she acted in "good faith." Although the 1934 Act states these as independent requirements, it is questionable whether a party can act in good faith, but nevertheless induce violations by the controlled party. Arguably, good faith at least requires ignorance of the controlled party's actions. In that respect, it is parallel to the "ignorance" requirement of 1933 Act section 15. Good faith, however, might require more than merely ignorance of the activities of the controlled party—but just how much more remains unclear.

(1) **Affirmative action to prevent fraud:** [§1425] Some courts have held that to satisfy section 20(a)'s "good faith" requirement, a defendant must demonstrate that she took affirmative steps to prevent the primary wrongdoer's activities. Other courts disagree.

(a) **Example:** It has been held that to show "good faith" under section 20(a) of the 1934 Act, a broker-dealer in a controlling position must prove that it had taken affirmative acts to prevent the misconduct of its registered representatives." [S.E.C. v. First Securities Co., 507 F.2d 417 (7th Cir. 1974)]

(b) **Compare:** However, a court has held that a newspaper was not liable as a controlling person under section 20(a) for a 10b-5 violation committed by its financial columnist, even though it had not taken affirmative steps to ensure that its columnists reported facts fairly and accurately. [Zweig v. Hearst Corp., 521 F.2d 1129 (9th Cir.), *cert. denied,* 423 U.S. 1025 (1975)]

1) **Rationale:** The court concluded that the "good faith" requirement had been satisfied, based on the following facts: the columnist had a long history of employment, with no previous instances of misconduct; the stories did not, on their faces, reveal any impropriety; and it would be impractical, to say the least, for a major metropolitan newspaper to check every story it runs for impropriety.

d. **Application of agency principles:** [§1426] A major issue in determining the liability of controlling persons is whether principles of agency apply in addition to liability under section 15 of the 1933 Act or section 20(a) of the 1934 Act. For example, may an employer of a person who violates the securities laws while acting within the scope of his employment be held liable on the basis of respondeat superior, even though the employer might not be liable under sections 15 or 20(a)?

(1) **No tort liability:** [§1427] Some courts hold that there can be no liability under respondeat superior; the only basis for an employer's liability for a violation by the employee is found in the specific provisions of the securities laws. [*See* Carpenter v. Harris, Upham & Co., 594 F.2d 388 (4th Cir.), *cert. denied,* 444 U.S. 868 (1979)—"culpable participation" required before respondeat superior applies; Rochez Bros., Inc. v. Rhoades,

527 F.2d 880 (3d Cir. 1975)—respondeat superior not applicable to securities law violations]

(2) **Respondeat superior applies:** [§1428] However, other courts have held that an employer *can* be liable, on the basis of traditional agency principles, for acts of employees that constitute a violation of the securities laws. [S.E.C. v. Management Dynamics, Inc., 515 F.2d 801 (2d Cir. 1975); *see* Marbury Management, Inc. v. Kohn, 629 F.2d 705 (2d Cir.), *cert. denied,* 449 U.S. 1011 (1980); Fey v. Walston & Co., 493 F.2d 1036 (7th Cir. 1974)]

3. **Liability of "Outside" Directors:** [§1429] An "outside" director is a member of the board of directors who is not otherwise employed by the corporation. A frequent issue is to what extent outside directors may be held liable as collateral participants when the corporation participates in a transaction that violates the securities laws.

a. **Liability under 1933 Act:** [§1430] The subject of outside director liability under section 11 has been discussed *supra,* §675. In addition, a director might be held liable as a "controlling person" under section 15 on the theory that the director is responsible for management of the corporation. (*See supra,* §1421.)

b. **Liability under 1934 Act:** [§1431] An outside director could be held liable under the 1934 Act in a number of different situations.

(1) **Liability as an aider or abettor:** [§1432] An outside director might be liable in an action by the S.E.C. if she knowingly aids or abets others in the corporation in committing a violation of the securities laws, but this is unclear after *Central Bank v. First Interstate Bank.* (*See supra,* §§1415, 1419.)

(2) **Liability as a controlling person:** [§1433] In addition, an outside director may be found liable as a "controlling person" under section 20(a). (*See supra,* §1421.) Here, too, however, the courts have split over the extent of the director's involvement that is required before an outside director will become liable as a controlling person. [*Compare* Burgess v. Premier Corp., 727 F.2d 826 (9th Cir. 1984), *with* San Francisco-Oklahoma Petroleum Exploration Corp. v. Carstan Oil Co., 765 F.2d 962 (10th Cir. 1985)]

(3) **Liability for negligence:** [§1434] Even though an outside director has not knowingly aided or abetted a securities violation and is not liable as a controlling person, the issue remains as to whether she can be held liable for negligently failing to discover a violation of the securities laws committed by others in the corporation.

(a) **In rule 10b-5 cases:** [§1435] In a case that specifically raised this question, a circuit court held that, absent actual knowledge of the misrepresentations or omissions made by company officers, there was no duty under rule 10b-5 for an outside director to investigate what information was communicated or omitted by company officers in the sale of the company's securities to another company. [Lanza v. Drexel & Co., *supra,* §883]

1) **Example:** In *Lanza*, officers of Company A had misrepresented A's financial condition to the owners of Company B, which was purchased for stock. An outside director of A knew of some material adverse information about the company, but did not know that A's officers had not communicated this information to B in the course of negotiations.

(b) **In proxy cases:** [§1436] Although negligence does not establish an outside director's liability under rule 10b-5, it may be sufficient in proxy cases. However, there is authority going both ways (*i.e.,* actual knowledge of the violation by an outside director must be shown vs. negligent failure to discover violation is sufficient). (*See supra*, §1414.)

4. **Liability of Underwriters:** [§1437] Underwriters generally act in the role of advisers and agents for the issuer in distributing the issuer's securities to the public and are a key link in the securities marketing chain.

a. **Liability under 1933 Act:** [§1438] Section 11 makes underwriters specifically liable for material misstatements or omissions in the registration statement. (*See supra*, §650.) This liability is subject, however, to the "due diligence" defense. (*See* defenses to section 11 liability *supra*, §§662 *et seq.*) The underwriter in a firm commitment underwriting might also be liable under section 12(1) or (2) of the 1933 Act (*i.e.,* as the "seller").

b. **Liability under 1934 Act:** [§1439] The most commonly invoked liability provisions of the 1934 Act do not specifically mention underwriters as defendants, taking a broader approach instead. For instance, rule 10b-5 makes it unlawful for "any person" to do the prohibited acts. Because underwriters are "persons," they may be liable under the 1934 Act either as principals (underwriters, among other things, sell securities), as controlling persons, or, possibly, as aiders and abettors but (after *Central Bank, supra*, §1419), only in an action by the government, if at all.

(1) **Liability as a principal:** [§1440] It is possible that an underwriter may be liable as a principal in a securities law violation when the underwriter is a joint principal with the issuer and not merely acting as the underwriter. Or the underwriter may make a separate, independent false representation (not made by the issuer) in connection with the sale of the issuer's securities that violates the provisions of the Act. [Sanders v. John Nuveen & Co., *supra,* §710]

(2) **Liability as an aider or abettor:** [§1441] After *Central Bank* (*see supra*, §1419), private citizens cannot sue an aider and abettor of a rule 10b-5 violation. In fact, whether even the S.E.C. can bring an action against such an aider and abettor is in doubt. [*Id.*]

5. **Liability of Accountants:** [§1442] Accountants carry out two primary functions relating to disclosure under the securities laws: gathering information about the issuer (***the audit function***) and presenting that information in financial statements, which they certify and which become a part of the registration statement (***the accounting function***).

a. **Professional standards for accountants:** [§1443]  Liability can arise when an accountant fails to carry out either the audit or the accounting function properly. In addition, accountants are no less interested in maintaining their professional reputations than are lawyers, and they have developed standards and guidelines relating to the manner in which they carry out their professional duties.

(1) **Manner of conducting the audit of the issuer:** [§1444]  Accountants gather information about the issuer, which is ultimately presented in the issuer's financial statements. The accounting profession has developed standards of good practice that apply to the process of gathering this information, called *"GAAS"* (for Generally Accepted Auditing Standards). GAAS standards are based on Statements of Auditing Standards ("SAS") promulgated by the American Institute of Certified Public Accountants. Although courts have resisted making GAAS a legal standard for liability under the securities laws, GAAS frequently is cited in support of the argument that accountants, on the facts, did all that could be expected of them. [*See, e.g.,* S.E.C. v. Arthur Young & Co., 590 F.2d 785 (9th Cir. 1979)]

(2) **Manner of presentation of the information:** [§1445]  Accountants have also developed practice standards governing the process by which the transactions and events of a business entity are measured, recorded, and classified. These standards are referred to as *"GAAP"* (for Generally Accepted Accounting Principles), which are based on Statements of Financial Accounting Standards ("SFAS") promulgated by the  Financial Accounting Standards Board. As with GAAS, an accountant's compliance with GAAP will not immunize her from liability under the securities laws. [*See, e.g.,* United States v. Simon, 425 F.2d 796 (2d Cir. 1969), *cert. denied,* 397 U.S. 1006 (1970)] Just as with GAAS, however, in most cases compliance with the professional standard is significant in establishing a defense. [*See* S.E.C. v. Arthur Young & Co., *supra*]

b. **Liability under 1933 Act:** [§1446]  A 1933 Act registration statement must contain certified financial statements. The accountants that certify the statements are subject to liability under section 11 as "experts." (*See supra*, §664.)

(1) **Standard of negligence:** [§1447]  To avoid liability, the accountants must have reasonable grounds to believe (after a reasonable investigation) and must actually believe (at the time the registration statement becomes effective) that the statements made by them are true and that there is no omission of a material fact. This holds the accountants to a standard of simple negligence ("reasonableness") with respect to both the audit function and the accounting function.

c. **Liability under 1934 Act:** [§1448]  The cases that have been brought against accountants have primarily been rule 10b-5 cases.

(1) **Standard of culpability:** [§1449]  It is important to remember that in an action under rule 10b-5, the plaintiff (or the government) must prove *scienter*, defined by the Supreme Court as an intention to commit fraud or deceit. [*See* Ernst & Ernst v. Hochfelder, *supra*, §885; Aaron v. S.E.C., *supra*, §723]

(a) **Recklessness:** [§1450] It remains unclear whether recklessness can constitute scienter under rule 10b-5, although every circuit court to address the question has held that it can.

(2) **Liability for material omissions:** [§1451] A related question involves liability for omissions—that is, assuming that scienter can be established, must the plaintiff also prove a duty to speak (as is required, for example, in cases alleging insider trading violations of rule 10b-5)? (*See supra,* §§931 *et seq.*) Courts typically hold that the plaintiff must establish such a duty, but differ as to whether the duty can arise simply from participation in a fraudulent scheme, or whether it must be established outside the securities laws. [*Compare* Robin v. Arthur Young & Co., 915 F.2d 1120 (7th Cir. 1990), *with* Roberts v. Peat, Marwick, Mitchell & Co., 857 F.2d 646 (9th Cir. 1988)]

(3) **Scope of accountant's responsibility:** [§1452] The financial statements prepared by the accountants may be used to sell securities (in a registration statement or in a document used as part of a private offering) or may be filed with the S.E.C. pursuant to the filing requirements under the securities acts. In either case, the question arises as to the persons to whom an accountant may become liable as the result of a breach of duty.

(a) **Duty to those who read financial statements:** [§1453] Where the accountant could reasonably expect that the financial statement would be used in making investment decisions, and where persons actually did read the statement, there is actual reliance and the accountant will be held liable if he has breached the required standard of care. [Ernst & Ernst v. Hochfelder, *supra*]

(b) **Duty to those who have not read financial statements:** [§1454] Some cases have gone even further, holding an accountant liable where he could *reasonably expect* that the financial statement would be used in making investment decisions, but where the persons dealing with the issuer did *not* actually read the financial statements (*i.e.,* there was no actual reliance). [Competitive Associates, Inc. v. Laventhol, Krekstein, Horwath & Horwath, 516 F.2d 811 (2d Cir. 1975)]

1) **Example:** Where accountants intentionally falsified financial reports of an investment advisor, which were then filed with the S.E.C., customers of the investment advisor—who had not actually read the reports—were allowed to recover against the accountants.

(c) **Duty owed where no expectation of reliance:** [§1455] The courts have exculpated accountants in cases where they could have had no reasonable expectation that the financial statements would be relied on by anyone other than the members of the firm for which it was prepared. [Landy v. Federal Deposit Insurance Corp., 486 F.2d 139 (3d Cir. 1973), *cert. denied,* 416 U.S. 960 (1974)]

d. **Implied causes of action:** [§1456] Of great importance to accountants and other professionals has been the recent trend of court opinions that have refused to imply private causes of action for violations of various sections of the securities acts that do not explicitly provide for causes of action. For example, section 17(a) of the 1934 Act requires broker-dealers to file certain financial reports with the S.E.C. and the national exchange. [*See* Touche Ross & Co. v. Redington, *supra*, §783—court refused to imply a private cause of action against defendant accounting firm for improper auditing procedures leading to filing of false financial statements on behalf of D's broker-dealer client]

e. **Disclosure of accountant-client relationship:** [§1457] The S.E.C. requires disclosure of the relationship between companies and their public accountants. [SA Release No. 5550; SEA Release No. 11147; Accounting Series Release No. 165 (1974)]

(1) *In monthly reports* required by the 1934 Act of registered companies, changes in a company's accounting firms (*e.g.*, resignation of a firm) and major disputes over accounting issues must all be disclosed.

(2) *In financial statements*, accountants must disclose any material disagreements with management, all events that gave rise to the disagreement, any matters accounted for differently than by a previous accounting firm's methods, how the result would come out under the previous accountants' methods, etc.

(3) *In proxy statements,* issuers must disclose the accounting firm to be used by the company, the name of any previous accountant, the existence and composition of any audit committee of the board of directors, etc.

6. **Liability of Lawyers:** [§1458] In the traditional view of the lawyer's role, lawyers are responsible chiefly to their *clients*. In contrast, the S.E.C. occasionally suggests that securities lawyers ought to assume a "watchdog" function. Such a lawyer would normally resolve ambiguities (*e.g.*, whether a fact is "material") against her client, and would be expected to inform the government if the client declined to follow her advice. This view emphasizes the lawyer's responsibilities to the *public*. It is a response to the role that some lawyers have played in securities fraud—many complex fraudulent schemes would not have been possible without the diligent efforts of counsel. At present, neither view has prevailed, but it is certain that the legal profession can no longer avoid the issue.

a. **Liability to clients for malpractice:** [§1459] Lawyers have always had the responsibility of performing competently for their clients; consequently, they may be liable to their clients for a knowing or negligent failure to do so. *Third parties* affected by the lawyer's malpractice may also have a cause of action against the lawyer.

b. **Liability as principals:** [§1460] A lawyer may also be liable for a violation of the securities laws as a principal in a business transaction. For example, a lawyer may own securities and make a material misrepresentation in connection with their sale, or become a partner with someone else who violates the securities laws.

c. **Liability to those affected by securities transactions:** [§1461] In addition, a lawyer may in some situations be liable to parties affected by a securities transaction. When such liability is alleged, it is important to determine whether it is claimed to result from the lawyer's involvement as a participant or as an aider and abettor.

(1) **Liability as participant:** [§1462] Often, lawyers participate in securities transactions in roles that go beyond simply counseling their client. In such cases, the additional roles played by the lawyer may become a source of liability under the securities laws.

   (a) **Liability as a director:** [§1463] For instance, when the lawyer who drafted the issuer's registration statement is also a director of the issuer, the lawyer may be liable to purchasers of the issuer's securities under 1933 Act section 11. [*See* Escott v. BarChris Construction Co., *supra*, §667]

   (b) **Liability as an expert:** [§1464] Similarly, lawyers participate in some transactions not as advisers to a party, but instead as experts with respect to a particular subject matter. For instance, a lawyer might render an opinion that title to real property has been passed to the issuer, and this opinion might be referred to in the registration statement. This can result in the lawyer's liability, not as a lawyer per se, but as an expert whose certification was material to the transaction. [SA §11; *see supra*, §664]

   (c) **Liability as a "seller":** [§1465] Occasionally, lawyers are alleged to be liable under 1933 Act section 12 as "sellers" of securities; this usually occurs when the issuer has encountered serious trouble and is unable to repay the investors. To sustain such a claim, the lawyers would have to be heavily involved in the solicitation process. [*See* Pinter v. Dahl, *supra*, §690] As a rule, such claims against lawyers fail. [*See, e.g.,* Abell v. Potomac Insurance Co., 858 F.2d 1104 (5th Cir. 1988)—whatever the role of counsel, none of the investors can claim to have "bought bonds from" the law firm]

(2) **Aiding and abetting liability:** [§1466] Historically, aiding and abetting liability has been the most important source of lawyers' liability under the securities laws.

   (a) **Under the 1933 Act:** [§1467] Most of the 1933 Act's remedial provisions specifically state who the proper defendants are; thus, they may not be useful for a person seeking to assert aiding and abetting liability. The government, however, may assert that a lawyer aided and abetted her client's violation of section 17(a) (the 1933 Act's general fraud provision). Especially after the recent *Central Bank* case (*supra,* §1419), the S.E.C. may increase its use of this theory in cases against lawyers.

      1) **Note:** It remains unclear whether a private citizen can bring an action under section 17(a), but the better view is that she *cannot.* (*See supra*, §§721 *et seq.*)

   (b) **Under the 1934 Act:** [§1468] For many years, probably the most common securities law claim made against lawyers was aiding and abetting the client's violation of 1934 Act rule 10b-5. [*See, e.g.,* S.E.C. v. National Student Marketing Corp., 457 F. Supp. 682 (D.D.C. 1978)] In 1994, however, the Supreme Court in *Central Bank, supra,* §1441, held that *private* actions under rule 10b-5 could not be asserted against an aider and abettor, and it is uncertain whether even the S.E.C. can bring an action for aiding and abetting a rule 10b-5 violation. The precise significance of *Central Bank* is not yet clear, but the decision will sharply reduce the potential liability of lawyers and other secondary parties in securities matters.

(3) **Legal opinion letters:** [§1469] Regardless which Act is claimed to be violated, the most common factual basis for a lawyer's liability as an aider and abettor is the delivery of a legal opinion letter. Because the delivery of such letters is usually made a condition to closing a securities transaction, it is relatively easy to point to the delivery of the letter as a *sine qua non* of the transaction, and with hindsight, to find that the lawyer "must have" known her client's (fraudulent) intentions. [*See, e.g.,* S.E.C. v. Spectrum Ltd., 489 F.2d 535 (2d Cir. 1973)—S.E.C. action for an injunction against lawyer who delivered opinion letter to the effect that a securities transaction did not require 1933 Act registration]

d. **S.E.C. injunctions against lawyers:** [§1470] The S.E.C. has traditionally used injunctions as a form of punishment (*i.e.,* public advertisement that a lawyer has engaged in wrongdoing), as well as a means of preventing future violations of the securities laws.

(1) **Basis for injunction:** [§1471] Although injunctions have traditionally issued on a showing of a negligent violation, after *Aaron v. S.E.C.* (*supra,* §723), the S.E.C. now has to show in rule 10b-5 actions that the lawyer *knowingly* violated the securities laws. Possibly this might mean at the minimum reckless conduct. [*See* McLean v. Alexander, 599 F.2d 1190 (3d Cir. 1979)] On the other hand, negligence is a sufficient basis for an injunction in an S.E.C. action under section 17(a)(2) or (3) of the 1933 Act (although scienter must be shown under section 17(a)(1)). [Aaron v. S.E.C., *supra,* §1449; *and see supra,* §723]

e. **A.B.A. Model Rules of Professional Conduct:** [§1472] The American Bar Association has set out general guidelines for the lawyer's relationship with clients. In some aspects, the Rules are in sharp contrast with positions taken by the S.E.C. The main controversy with the S.E.C. arises over the lawyer's duty under the Code of Professional Responsibility to protect the confidences and secrets of the client.

(1) **Attorney-client relationship:** [§1473] In general, the attorney has a relationship of confidentiality with the client; his duty is to protect this relationship and the interests of the client. The principle of confidentiality is given effect in two related bodies of law: the *attorney-client privilege* in the law of evidence and the *rule of confidentiality* established in the A.B.A. rules on professional ethics. [A.B.A. Model Rule 1.6] The attorney-client privilege applies in judicial and other proceedings in which a client's communications with his lawyer are sought as evidence. The rule on confidentiality applies in situations other than those where evidence is sought from the lawyer through compulsion of law. Based on these rules,

a lawyer should not act as an investigator for the S.E.C. with respect to the lawyer's clients. However, the lawyer cannot go beyond certain bounds in protecting the client's interests; a lawyer does have certain duties to the public. [*See* A.B.A. Model Rule 1.2(d)—lawyer may not assist the client in unlawful conduct]

(2) **Disclosure of confidential information**

   (a) **A.B.A. Model Rules approach:** [§1474]  Under the A.B.A. Model Rules, the lawyer is not required to, but *may* reveal the client's confidences or secrets when:

   (i) *The client consents;*

   (ii) *Necessary to establish a claim or defense on behalf of the lawyer* in a controversy between the lawyer and the client or to respond to allegations in any proceeding concerning the lawyer's representation of the client; or

   (iii) *The lawyer knows* that the client clearly *intends to commit a crime that the lawyer believes is likely to result in imminent death or substantial bodily harm*.

   1) **Example:** Thus, if a lawyer knows that the client is going to violate the securities laws and he continues to aid the client in doing so, he may be liable as an aider and abettor. [A.B.A. Model Rule 1.2(d)] But the lawyer is not required to report this possible future crime to anyone. The Rules clearly indicate that the lawyer *may* do so, if he chooses, only when the violation is likely to result in imminent death or serious bodily harm. Note that the S.E.C. has argued [*see* S.E.C. v. National Student Marketing Corp., *supra,* §1468]  that the lawyer should reveal *to the S.E.C.* the client's intended violations of the securities laws.

   2) **Frauds:** [§1475] *When the attorney knows that* in the course of representation the client has *committed a crime or fraud* on anyone, he should ask the client to rectify the act, but if the client does not, the attorney may not reveal the crime or fraud to affected persons. [A.B.A. Model Rule 1.6]

(3) **When attorney believes client's conduct is illegal:** [§1476]  The attorney should resolve all doubts in favor of the client, and as long as it appears that the client will not knowingly engage in illegal conduct, the attorney may continue representation.

   (a) **Discontinuance of representation:** However, if the lawyer knows that the conduct is illegal even after resolving all doubts in the client's favor, he may *not* continue to represent the client. [A.B.A. Model Rule 1.16(a)(1)] And even if there is doubt as to the law, the lawyer *may* discontinue the relationship if the client refuses to take the lawyer's advice. [A.B.A. Model Code EC 7-8]

(4) **The entity is the client:** [§1477] The Rules also provide that in the case of a corporation, the lawyer's client is the entity and not management. [A.B.A. Model Rule 1.13] This means that in certain circumstances if management intends to violate the securities laws, or has in the past violated the securities laws, the lawyer ought to report this to the corporation's board of directors and in some cases, to the shareholders. [*See* S.E.C. v. National Student Marketing Corp., *supra*]

(5) **Compare—S.E.C. position:** [§1478] There are clear differences in the positions taken by the S.E.C. and the A.B.A. concerning the lawyer's duty in cases involving securities law violations.

(a) **Permissive vs. mandatory disclosure:** [§1479] The A.B.A. position is that the lawyer cannot reveal known, past fraud by a client if this knowledge was gained as a result of privileged communications with the client. And even if the lawyer knows that the client intends to commit a crime, disclosure is still a matter of choice with the lawyer. [A.B.A. Model Rule 1.6] The S.E.C.'s position would be that the lawyer has a duty to disclose these matters to the S.E.C.

(b) **Investigation of facts vs. belief of client:** [§1480] The S.E.C. requires the attorney to make a reasonable investigation of facts given her by her client for use in preparation of documents such as registration statements, opinion letters, etc. The A.B.A. permits the lawyer to take the word of her client, unless the lawyer knows or is reckless in not knowing of misrepresentations or omissions of material fact by the client.

## G. S.E.C. ENFORCEMENT ACTIONS

### 1. S.E.C. Investigations

a. **Introduction:** [§1481] Section 21(a) of the 1934 Act provides the S.E.C. with the power to conduct investigations regarding violations of the 1934 Act and the rules and regulations thereunder.

b. **Stages of investigation:** [§1482] Investigations typically go through two stages:

(1) **Informal inquiry:** [§1483] Initially, the S.E.C. begins an informal inquiry into a possible violation. Witnesses are interviewed but no one is required to talk with the S.E.C. if he does not wish to do so.

(2) **Formal investigation:** [§1484] The second stage is a formal investigation. The staff of the S.E.C. asks the Commission for an order based on a showing of the likelihood of a violation of the securities laws. A formal order then permits the staff to issue subpoenas and to examine witnesses under oath. At this stage, there is no punishment for failure to respond; the S.E.C.'s only recourse is to initiate a proceeding in court to enforce compliance.

(a) **Right to counsel:** [§1485] A person who is subpoenaed to testify in a formal investigation has the right to be represented by counsel during his own testimony. He has no right, however, to have counsel present during the taking of testimony from other witnesses. [S.E.C. v. Meek, Fed. Sec. L. Rep. (CCH) ¶97,323 (10th Cir. 1980)]

(b) **Proper purpose:** [§1486] The target of a formal S.E.C. investigation may believe that the Commission staff is acting with an improper motive (for example, that it was influenced by political pressure, or motivated by a personal conflict between the target's management and an S.E.C. Commissioner or staff member). In such a case, recourse is to the federal district court.

    1) **Example:** W, the target of an S.E.C. investigation into proxy disclosure, believed that the investigation was the result of political pressure applied by a Senator, S, who was sympathetic to one of W's competitors. S had introduced legislation seeking to make ineligible for certain federal loans any person who was under S.E.C. investigation, and then contacted the S.E.C., urging an investigation of W. W brought an action in federal district court, seeking an order of protection against the S.E.C., which was refused. On appeal, the Court of Appeals ruled that while an informal investigation may be begun at any time, and for any reason, a formal investigation must be the result of the S.E.C.'s own, independent judgment, and may not be influenced by outside forces (such as the Senator). [S.E.C. v. Wheeling-Pittsburgh Steel Corp., 648 F.2d 118 (3d Cir. 1981)]

(c) **Confidentiality:** [§1487] The S.E.C. takes the position that its investigations are secret, and witnesses are often warned that they may not disclose their testimony to anyone else. [*See* SA Rule 122]

(d) **Wells submissions:** [§1488] After the investigation is complete, the S.E.C. staff evaluates the information it has obtained and determines whether to seek the Commission's approval to commence an enforcement action. If the staff decides that enforcement is appropriate, the Commission considers the staff's recommendation in a closed session. Although the target of the investigation (and of any ensuing enforcement action) has no right to be heard at this stage, the S.E.C. has an informal practice of giving targets the opportunity to submit a written statement (a "Wells submission") to the Commission. But there is no legal right to make such a submission, and to do so can occasionally be perilous: Statements made in the Wells submission may later become evidence in court proceedings.

(e) **Notice to target not required:** [§1489] The target of an S.E.C. investigation has essentially no rights with respect to the investigation until administrative or court proceedings are begun. Thus, the target has no right to be advised of the identities of third parties from whom the S.E.C. is seeking to subpoena information, nor even a right to be informed that she is a target of the investigation at all. [S.E.C. v. O'Brien, 467 U.S. 735 (1984)]

c. **Parallel proceedings:** [§1490] S.E.C. investigations are "parallel proceedings" from the time they are initiated since the end result of an investigation may be either a recommendation to file an injunctive action or a reference to the Justice Department with a recommendation that it initiate a criminal prosecution by bringing the matter before a federal grand jury.

(1) **Right to refuse to testify:** [§1491]  The witnesses in the investigation have the right to refuse to testify on the basis that their answers may tend to incriminate them. Exercise of this right, however, may come at a price, because in the civil proceeding, the factfinder (that is, the court or administrative law judge) is permitted to draw adverse inferences from the defendant's refusal to testify. The defendant thus has the choice to answer the questions, and risk the consequences in the criminal proceeding, or not to answer, and risk losing the civil case.

(2) **Parallel investigations:** [§1492]  It may also happen that the S.E.C. is conducting an investigation at the same time that the Justice Department is conducting a grand jury investigation into the same matter, either as a result of referral by the S.E.C. or otherwise.

   (a) **I.R.S. proceedings:** [§1493]  In *United States v. LaSalle National Bank*, 437 U.S. 298 (1978), the Supreme Court held that a summons issued by the Internal Revenue Service after a recommendation for criminal prosecution had been made to the Department of Justice would not be enforced, since this might broaden the Justice Department's right of criminal litigation discovery or interfere with the role of the grand jury.

   (b) **S.E.C. proceedings:** [§1494]  On the other hand, the court in *S.E.C. v. Dresser Industries, Inc.,* 628 F.2d 1368 (D.C. Cir.), *cert. denied,* 449 U.S. 953 (1981), decided that the S.E.C.'s order for Dresser to comply with a subpoena of its corporate records in connection with an S.E.C. investigation into illegal payments to government officials should be enforced even though the Justice Department was pursuing the same matter before a federal grand jury. Perhaps the *Dresser* case is distinguished from the *LaSalle* case in that the court held that at least in the early stage of both proceedings, before any infringement of the defendant's rights in connection with the criminal proceeding, dual investigations should be permitted and cooperative sharing of discovered information is possible. When specific rights were threatened, the defendant could then seek relief from the courts.

d. **Section 21(a) reports:** [§1495]  Section 21(a) of the 1934 Act allows the S.E.C., in its discretion, to publish information concerning violations of the securities laws. The S.E.C. has followed a policy of referring to this section as a basis for issuing reports which document probable violations of the securities laws, without any formal administrative proceedings. Many of these reports concern persons (such as directors of corporations) over which the S.E.C. has no formal administrative authority to impose disciplinary actions (as the S.E.C. does over broker-dealers, etc.). In addition, the S.E.C. has negotiated with such persons the terms of written statements which amount to confessions of wrongdoing and which also frequently contain "undertakings" as to certain remedial action which the wrongdoer agrees to implement at the price of the S.E.C.'s not instituting formal investigation or an injunctive action. [*See* SEA Release No. 15664 (1979)] These actions by the S.E.C. have been criticized as the creation of an unauthorized form of administrative remedy having no statutory basis, and generally the S.E.C. is unwilling to conclude an investigation with only a section 21(a) report unless the target's conduct is not clearly wrongful under established law. [*See, e.g., In re* Carnation Co., SEA Release No. 22214 (1985)—disclosure of preliminary merger negotiations; *and see In re* Spartek, Inc., SEA Release No. 15567 (1979)—statements of corporate officer to stock exchange official]

2. **S.E.C. Administrative Proceedings**

a. **Overview:** [§1496] An S.E.C. administrative proceeding is a quasi-judicial procedure that takes place before an administrative law judge, who is the S.E.C.'s employee. In these proceedings, the S.E.C. can impose a wide variety of sanctions, ranging from the relatively innocuous to the severe. (*See supra,* §§627-632.) In 1990, Congress added to the available administrative sanctions in the Securities Enforcement Remedies and Penny Stock Reform Act. This Act gave the S.E.C. a new cease-and-desist remedy, similar to an injunction, as well as civil fines and disgorgement, all available without the need to convince a federal district judge of the merits of the case (because all of these are administrative remedies). Because administrative proceedings involve the S.E.C. acting as legislature (pursuant to its rulemaking authority), prosecutor (because the Enforcement Division initiates the proceeding), and judge (its administrative law judge "tries" the case), concerns arise about fairness and due process-type protections for the target of the proceedings.

b. **Notice and hearing:** [§1497] In general the S.E.C. may take action against a company or a person only after notice and an opportunity for a hearing. Furthermore, the proceedings must be conducted pursuant to the requirements of the Administrative Procedure Act (similar to a court trial, but with essentially no right of discovery for the "defendant" and greatly expanded admissibility of evidence).

c. **Ex parte proceedings:** [§1498] In addition, the S.E.C. may suspend trading in nonexempt securities, without any notice or hearing to the company involved, for a period of 10 days. [SEA §12(k)] Renewals of this period must be based on new circumstances arising after the original suspension notice. [S.E.C. v. Sloan, 436 U.S. 103 (1978)]

d. **Burden of proof:** [§1499] Most of the formal administrative proceedings conducted by the S.E.C. are disciplinary proceedings to punish alleged violations of the securities laws by persons required to be registered with the S.E.C. and expressly subjected by these laws to such administrative sanctions by the statutes (*e.g.,* registered broker-dealers, investment advisers, etc.).

   (1) **Hearings:** [§1500] Hearings are conducted before an administrative law judge; the decision is then reviewed by the full S.E.C., and an appeal is available to the circuit courts.

   (2) **Preponderance of the evidence:** [§1501] In a disciplinary proceeding before the S.E.C., the standard of proof to prove fraud is a "preponderance of the evidence." [Steadman v. S.E.C., 450 U.S. 91 (1981)] The

basis for this decision is the Court's interpretation of section 7(c) of the Administrative Procedure Act, which governs all agency hearings.

### 3. S.E.C. Injunctive Actions

a. **Introduction:** [§1502] When the S.E.C. files a lawsuit, it most often seeks an injunction in federal district court, enjoining those who have allegedly violated or are about to violate the securities laws. Injunctions may be either **temporary** or **permanent.** [*See* SEA §§21(d), 27—giving federal courts jurisdiction; *and see* SA §20(a)]

    (1) **Temporary injunction:** [§1503] A temporary injunction is issued pending a final decision on the merits, usually because the defendant poses a danger to the public in the interim between the time the complaint is filed and the time final judgment is rendered. (*See infra,* §1511.)

    (2) **Permanent injunction:** [§1504] A permanent injunction, on the other hand, is issued after the case has been determined on the merits. The focus, however, remains on the future. Thus, to obtain a permanent injunction the S.E.C. must show not only that the defendant has committed violations of the securities laws in the past, but also that she is likely to do so in the future. (*See infra,* §1511.)

b. **Consents:** [§1505] Usually defendants do not litigate; instead they agree to a "consent injunction," which is entered in court at the same time the complaint is filed.

c. **Consequences:** [§1506] An injunction can be a severe punishment. Many provisions of the securities laws disqualify a person from engaging in the securities business if the person has been enjoined in an S.E.C. action. Also, as a result of the injunction, private civil actions may be filed against the injunction defendant.

    (1) **Collateral estoppel:** [§1507] If the S.E.C. injunction action is litigated, then all of the factual issues that are litigated and decided by the court may not be litigated again in a separate action against the defendant. To avoid this possibility in subsequent civil actions by private plaintiffs based on the S.E.C.'s injunction action, defendants are highly motivated to settle actions with the S.E.C. without going to trial. Of course, in settlements, where defendants admit facts and these admissions become part of a consent injunction, the collateral estoppel effect is still present.

d. **Culpability standard:** [§1508] *See* the discussion of the *Aaron* case, *supra,* §890.

e. **Basis for injunction:** [§1509] The purpose of an injunction, temporary or permanent, is to prevent future harm, and not to punish past misconduct. For many years, however, the S.E.C. was able to obtain injunctions with little evidence that future harm was likely to result. Courts did not consider an injunction to be a severe sanction, and so were not too concerned about its propriety in a particular case. Often the court would reason that an injunction, after all, was merely a command not to break the law again. Today, however, the severe consequences of an injunction to the defendant are more widely recognized, and the standards for imposing an injunction have become more important. [*See* Aaron v. S.E.C., *supra*] Courts increasingly require the S.E.C. to produce substantial evidence of the likelihood that future violations will occur if an injunction is not issued.

(1) **Distinguish private injunctions:** [§1510] An action by the S.E.C. to obtain an injunction is different from an action by a private citizen to do so, because the S.E.C.'s action is statutory while the private citizen's is equitable. Thus, to obtain an injunction, the S.E.C. needs to show only what the statute requires, *i.e.,* that the defendant is presently committing a violation or is about to commit one, while a private citizen must show irreparable harm and the inadequacy of any remedy at law. [*See* S.E.C. v. Caterinicchia, 613 F.2d 102 (5th Cir. 1980)]

(2) **Standards for temporary injunction:** [§1511] One court has held that the standard the S.E.C. must meet to obtain a temporary injunction *varies according to the conduct that the Commission seeks to enjoin.* A broad injunction against any future violations of the securities laws requires the S.E.C. to "make a substantial showing of likelihood of success as to both a current violation and the risk of repetition," but a lesser amount of evidence is needed to sustain a freeze order intended to preserve the defendants' funds to pay any judgment that might ultimately be rendered. [S.E.C. v. Unifund SAL, 910 F.2d 1028 (2d Cir. 1990)]

   (a) **Example:** In *Unifund SAL, supra,* there was evidence that the defendants had received information about a pending takeover. The court pointed out that while the evidence suggested that the defendants knew about the takeover discussions, the S.E.C. had not introduced any evidence establishing the *source* of the information. The identity of the source is crucial—an insider trading case rests on the breach of duty committed by the source, and the recipient's knowledge of that breach. (*See supra*, §§926 *et seq.*) Therefore, the court concluded that the S.E.C. had not provided enough evidence that a violation had actually been committed, and refused to issue a broad injunction against future violations. However, the court continued, there was some basis to infer that insider trading had occurred, and therefore the S.E.C. was granted a freeze order for a limited period, requiring the defendant to maintain funds in their trading accounts adequate to cover a judgment in the event the S.E.C. prevailed.

(3) **Permanent injunction:** [§1512] When a permanent injunction is sought, the fact of past misconduct has already been adjudicated and the availability of the remedy turns on the likelihood that the defendant will violate the securities laws again. The S.E.C. must convince the court that the defendant's past conduct indicates *there is a reasonable likelihood of further violations* in the future. The decision whether to issue an injunction rests in the *sound discretion of the trial court.* [S.E.C. v. Caterinicchia, *supra*]

(4) **Current trend of decisions:** [§1513] Some courts consistent with the view of injunctions as punishment for past wrongs, have found a "likelihood of future violations" (the basis for issuing an injunction) based on the defendant's one past violation. More recent decisions,

however, indicate that courts now require the S.E.C. to demonstrate a realistic likelihood of recurrence of wrongdoing to get an injunction. [*See* S.E.C. v. Commonwealth Chemical Securities, Inc., 574 F.2d 90 (2d Cir. 1978)]

(5) **Factors considered in evaluating likelihood of future violations:** [§1514] The following factors are looked at: the degree of scienter involved; the isolated or recurrent nature of the defendant's conduct; the sincerity of the defendant's assurances; and the defendant's recognition of wrongdoing. [S.E.C. v. Universal Major Industries Corp., 546 F.2d 1044 (2d Cir. 1976), *cert. denied*, 434 U.S. 834 (1977)]

f. **Ancillary relief:** [§1515] The S.E.C., when it settles an investigative action with a defendant, often asks for and gets a variety of ancillary remedies designed to remedy both the consequences of past wrongs and to prevent future ones:

(1) **Appoint receiver:** [§1516] If the defendant is a corporation and its affairs are in bad condition, a receiver may be appointed to run the corporation.

(2) **Disgorge profits:** [§1517] The defendant may be required to disgorge profits made in connection with securities law violations (such as the use of inside information).

(3) **Appoint special counsel:** [§1518] The defendant may be required to appoint "special counsel" to investigate and report on all past securities law violations.

(4) **Resignations:** [§1519] Certain officers and directors may be required to resign.

(5) **Appoint independent directors:** [§1520] The defendant may be required to appoint independent persons, approved by the S.E.C., to the board of directors. [*See In re* Occidental Petroleum Corp., SEA Release No. 16950 (1980)]

(6) **Civil fines:** [§1521] In the Securities Enforcement and Penny Stock Reform Act of 1990, the S.E.C. was given the ability to seek, in addition to disgorgement, a civil monetary penalty in specified amounts. (*See infra*, §§1547-1554, for further discussion of these provisions.)

(7) **Officer and director bars:** [§1522] Another remedy introduced by the Securities Enforcement and Penny Stock Reform Act of 1990 is the power to ban or suspend a person from serving as officer or director of a 1934 Act reporting company. (*See infra*, §§1547-1554, for further discussion of these provisions.)

4. **Administrative Proceedings Against Professionals Pursuant to Rule 2(e):** [§1523] Any person compelled to appear before any administrative agency of the United States has the right to be represented by counsel. Furthermore, any member of the bar of the highest court of any state may represent others before any agency (except the Patent Office) on filing a written declaration that he is currently

qualified and is authorized to represent the particular party. Additionally, the S.E.C. has enacted the "S.E.C. Rules of Practice" to provide for efficient and expeditious conduct of its own administrative proceedings. Rule 2 thereof sets out the requirements for persons who may appear and practice before the S.E.C., and subsection 2(e) thereof gives the S.E.C. the power to suspend or disbar persons practicing before it. This power, as exercised by the S.E.C., is the subject of substantial controversy.

a. **Bases for disbarment or suspension:** [§1524] There are several bases under rule 2(e) for denial of the privilege of practicing before the S.E.C. Those most commonly referred to are stated in rule 2(e)(1), which sets forth several bases for action against a lawyer.

   (1) **Qualifications:** [§1525] The S.E.C. may bar the lawyer from practicing before it because the lawyer lacks the "requisite qualifications" to represent others.

   (2) **Personal character:** [§1526] The lawyer may be barred because she lacks the necessary "character or integrity."

   (3) **Conduct:** [§1527] If the lawyer has engaged in "unethical or improper professional conduct," she may be barred.

   (4) **Violation of securities laws:** [§1528] Finally, the lawyer may be barred if she has willfully violated or willfully aided and abetted the violation of the federal securities laws. No definition of the key word "willfully" is given in the rule.

      (a) **Aiding and abetting:** [§1529] Note that rule 2(e) includes, as a basis for suspending a lawyer, "aiding and abetting" a violation of the securities laws by another person. It is unclear whether this provision survives the Supreme Court's decision in the *Central Bank* case, *supra,* §1419. While *Central Bank* involved aiding and abetting claims brought by private citizens, the language of the opinion appears broad enough to encompass actions brought by the government as well. If the S.E.C. indeed lacks the power to bring an action against an aider and abettor, it may also lack the ability to suspend that person from practice.

b. **Prohibition of practice before the S.E.C.:** [§1530] If there is a sufficient basis under rule 2(e), pursuant to the terms of rule 2(e)(1), the S.E.C. may deny a professional, either temporarily or permanently, the privilege of appearing or practicing before it "in any way." Rule 2(g) defines "practicing before" the S.E.C. as including: (i) transacting any business before the S.E.C.; and (ii) the preparation of any statement, opinion, or other paper by any attorney, accountant, engineer, or other expert, filed with the S.E.C. in any registration statement, notification, application, report, or other document with the consent of the attorney, accountant, engineer, or other expert.

   (1) **Note:** This provision clearly prohibits a disbarred or suspended attorney from representing a client in a formal or informal administrative proceeding before the S.E.C. It also specifically provides that participation in any way in preparing documents to be filed with the S.E.C. is prohibited. And

the S.E.C. staff has also taken the position that it even encompasses the giving of any advice relating to any of the federal securities laws. [*In re Stephen Joel Sitomer,* SEA Release No. 12501 (1976)]

c. **History of the use of rule 2(e):** [§1531]  The ethical conduct of lawyers has always been supervised by the general disciplinary system maintained by the courts and the state bar associations. Additionally, since 1935, rule 2(e) has been used by the S.E.C. to regulate the conduct of lawyers involved in securities transactions.

   (1) **Early S.E.C. action:** [§1532]  Regulation initially policed and disciplined unethical lawyer conduct occurring in face-to-face contact with S.E.C. members and employees, such as might occur in an administrative hearing. Most of the early proceedings were ones where the lawyer could be said to have attempted to subvert the integrity of the S.E.C.'s regulatory processes by intentionally filing false information in required S.E.C. reports.

   (2) **Present S.E.C. position:** [§1533]  In 1970, rule 2(e) was amended to proscribe conduct that was a willful violation or a willful aiding and abetting of a violation of the securities laws (if such was established after a hearing before the S.E.C.). Shortly thereafter, the S.E.C. began to assert its present position that, in effect, it may discipline any lawyer who fails to perform what the S.E.C. deems to be a duty to the S.E.C., even if the lawyer's conduct occurs in a securities transaction to which the federal securities laws apply generally and the conduct occurs in the privacy of the lawyer's office. In effect, the S.E.C. launched the beginning of its attempt to conscript lawyers in private practice as an extended enforcement arm of the S.E.C. This has caused controversy since this kind of role for the attorney conflicts with the traditional paradigm of the lawyer-client relationship.

d. **Statutory basis for rule 2(e):** [§1534]  The S.E.C. has never claimed that it has express statutory authority to discipline lawyers who appear before it. Rather, the S.E.C. bases its authority on its general rulemaking powers under the separate federal securities acts and on its inherent authority under the securities laws in general. There has not been a lot of judicial review of the S.E.C.'s position, but what there is has been generally supportive of the S.E.C. [*See, e.g.,* Touche Ross & Co. v. S.E.C., 609 F.2d 570 (2d Cir. 1979)]

e. **Applications**

   (1) **Example:** [§1535]  In an action against a law firm pursuant to rule 2(e), where many of the firm's lawyers did work for a corporate client and its subsidiaries, and where one or more of the firm's partners served on the client's boards of directors and were personally involved financially in transactions with the client, and where material facts about the client were either omitted or misstated in reports filed with the S.E.C. (the partners failing to report accurate facts to the lawyers drafting the reports and the drafting lawyers failing independently to investigate the facts given by the client, although they knew of the personal interests of the firm's partners), the S.E.C. affirmed its authority to bring rule 2(e) proceedings to discipline lawyers involved in securities transactions. In a dissenting

opinion, Commissioner Karmel argued that there was no statutory basis on which to imply the S.E.C.'s power to discipline professionals and that it was dangerous and perhaps unconstitutional (as against the right to counsel) for a federal agency to have regulatory power, enforcement power, and the right to discipline lawyers who might be involved as advocates for their clients. [*See In re* Keating, Muething & Klekamp, SEA Release No. 15982 (1979)]

(2) **Example:** [§1536] In an action against two lawyers under rule 2(e) arising out of their representation of a corporate client that persistently failed to disclose material adverse financial information (to correct previously issued favorable and unrealistic reports), the S.E.C. indicated that the provision of rule 2(e) permitting discipline of professionals who *knowingly* violate or aid and abet a violation of the securities laws requires a showing of scienter (or at least reckless conduct) to prove a violation. The S.E.C. also found that the entity was the client and that when management failed to make the required disclosures, it was a violation of the required ethical standards of rule 2(e) for the lawyers to fail to take steps to end the noncompliance (this effort might involve approaching the board of directors and taking other reasonable steps under the circumstances). [*In re* William R. Carter and Charles J. Johnson, Jr., SEA Release No. 17597, Fed. Sec. L. Rep. (CCH) (Transfer Binder) ¶82,847 (1981)]

5. **Liability Under SEA Section 15(c)(4):** [§1537] Section 15(c)(4) of the 1934 Act gives the S.E.C. a sanction for persons who do not make required filings, or who make filings that are late or incomplete.

a. **Persons subject to section 15(c)(4):** [§1538] Section 15(c)(4), as it was amended in the 1980s, applies to any person who is subject to section 12, 13, 14, or 15(d) of the 1934 Act, and who fails to comply, and any person who knowingly is the *cause* of such a failure to comply.

b. **Remedies:** [§1539] Under section 15(c)(4), the S.E.C. may "publish its findings and issue an order requiring such person . . . to comply, or to take steps to effect compliance, with such rule or regulation. . . ."

(1) **Scope:** [§1540] The S.E.C. has held that it does not have the power to issue general, prospective orders directing future compliance with the law. Instead, section 15(c)(4) gives the S.E.C. the power to address specific violations by ordering the violators (and those who were the "causes" of the violation) to comply with respect to specific instances of violation. [*In re* George C. Kern, Jr., S.E.C. Release No. 34-29,356 (1991)]

c. **Persons "causing" a failure to comply:** [§1541] The standard of culpability for a person alleged to have "caused" another person not to comply remains unclear. The S.E.C. at one time noted that scienter should be a requirement for a finding that a person has violated this provision. Later, however, the S.E.C.'s Enforcement Division abandoned that view, asserting that simple negligence by such a person would suffice if a failure to comply was the result. [*See In re* George C. Kern, Jr., *supra*]

d.   **Application:** [§1542]  K, an experienced mergers and acquisitions lawyer, served on the board of a corporation that was also a client. When the corporation received an unwanted merger inquiry, K coordinated the defense and was responsible for making the necessary filings with the S.E.C. Part of the defense strategy involved soliciting other bidders ("white knights") for the corporation, and the corporation's intention to pursue that possibility was disclosed in its first filing on form 14D-9. Over the next two weeks, numerous parties were contacted and discussions were begun with one party. Several different options for a transaction between the corporation and the white knight were considered, but only one was ultimately pursued. The discussions with the white knight were not disclosed in subsequent Schedules 14D-9. The S.E.C. brought an action against the lawyer, alleging that he was the "cause" of the corporation's (his client's) failure to file complete Schedules 14D-9. The administrative law judge agreed with the staff, but denied relief on the grounds, *inter alia*, that the S.E.C. lacks the power to issue general, injunction-like orders to comply with the law under section 15(c)(4). The S.E.C., on its own initiative, decided to review the administrative law judge's decision, but did not release its decision for three years. Ultimately, the S.E.C. affirmed the administrative law judge's ruling that it lacks the power to issue general, prospective compliance orders under section 15(c)(4). [*In re* George C. Kern, Jr. (Allied Stores Corp.), Admin. Proc. File No. 3-6869 (Nov. 14, 1988) (Opinion of Chief Admin. Law Judge Blair), [1988-1989 Transfer Binder]  Fed. Sec. L. Rep. (CCH) ¶ 84,832 (1988), *aff'd in part, vacated in part*, S.E.C. Release No. 34-29,356 (1991)]

(1)   **Note:** The decision in *Kern, supra,* has been widely criticized. In *Kern,* the S.E.C. may have abandoned scienter as a requirement for a "cause" violation of the section. Additionally, the S.E.C. seems to be demanding that lawyers provide daily, "motion-picture" updates of discussions occurring at a frenetic pace in a supercharged atmosphere, where nothing is certain and everything is subject to change at a moment's notice. Unlike *Carter and Johnson, supra,* the events that took place in *Kern* were not unusual, and the parties were otherwise not lawbreakers.

6.   **Self-Regulatory Enforcement:** [§1543]  Enforcement by the self-regulatory organizations ("SROs") has become increasingly important as the S.E.C.'s resources become more and more overcommitted. With much of the S.E.C.'s attention diverted to major investigations and enforcement proceedings, the SROs have become the parties primarily responsible for redressing more common, and more minor, infractions, such as account churning by brokers.

a.   **Scope:** [§1544]  The SROs enforce both the S.E.C.'s rules and regulations relating to the conduct of brokers, dealers, and other members, and their own rules and regulations, which in some cases are much more vague than the S.E.C.'s rules and correspondingly more flexible.

(1)   **Example:** Both the New York Stock Exchange and the National Association of Securities Dealers require their members to comply with "just and equitable principles of trade." Such a rule would be too vague to be enforceable by the S.E.C. [*See* Colonial Realty Corp. v. Bache & Co., 358 F.2d 178 (2d Cir.), *cert. denied*, 385 U.S. 817 (1966)]

b. **Appeal to the S.E.C.:** [§1545] Rule 19d-1 under the 1934 Act provides that the S.E.C. must be notified whenever final disciplinary action has been taken by an SRO, and section 19(e) of the Act provides that final disciplinary action taken by an SRO can be appealed to the S.E.C.

c. **Exclusivity:** [§1546] Although the SROs can enforce the rules and regulations of the S.E.C., the S.E.C. has only a limited ability to enforce the rules of the SROs. Essentially, the S.E.C. must find that an SRO is "unwilling or unable" to act to remedy the situation, or that the S.E.C.'s intervention is otherwise required in the public interest.

7. **The Securities Enforcement Remedies and Penny Stock Reform Act of 1990:** [§1547] In 1990, Congress passed a significant new statute that provided the S.E.C. with some enhancement to old remedies, and some brand-new administrative remedies that are likely to be used extensively in the future.

   a. **Enhancements:** [§1548] The S.E.C. has typically sought disgorgement of profits as an ancillary remedy in cases in which it obtains an injunction against the defendant. (*See supra*, §1517.) Pursuant to the 1990 Remedies Act, the S.E.C. now has the ability to seek, in addition to disgorgement, a civil monetary penalty, and to bar an individual from serving as an officer or director of a 1934 Act reporting company.

      (1) **Civil monetary penalties:** [§1549] Section 20 of the 1933 Act and section 21 of the 1934 Act, as amended by the 1990 Remedies Act, provide that the S.E.C. may seek civil monetary penalties in amounts:

         (a) Up to $5,000 for a natural person, and $50,000 for a corporation, per violation; or

         (b) If the violation involved fraud, deceit, manipulation, or deliberate or reckless disregard of a regulatory requirement, up to $50,000 for a natural person, and $250,000 for a corporation, per violation; or

         (c) If the violation meets the requirements of (b) above (*i.e.*, it involved fraud, etc.), and in addition directly or indirectly resulted in either substantial losses or created the risk of substantial losses to other persons, or substantial monetary gain to the respondents, up to $100,000 for a natural person, and $500,000 for a corporation; and

         (d) In any case above, if the gross amount of monetary gain accruing to the person as a result of the violation is greater than the amount of the penalty set forth, the penalty imposed can be up to the amount of the monetary gain.

      (2) **Officer and director bars:** [§1550] In addition to imposing civil fines on the defendants, the S.E.C. can seek to bar or suspend a person from serving as an officer or director of a 1934 Act reporting company. The Senate Report on the 1990 Remedies Act stated that these provisions were not intended to establish federal law qualifications for directors and officers (an area that has historically been reserved to the states), but noted that in some cases, the public interest requires that certain individuals be prevented from holding positions of trust with publicly held corporations.

b. **New remedies—administrative cease-and-desist order:** [§1551] S.E.C. cease-and-desist orders, authorized by section 8 of the 1933 Act and section 21C of the 1934 Act, resemble injunctions but are issued administratively. Because of their convenience for the S.E.C., they may become the most frequently used remedies under either Act. Like an injunction, the cease-and-desist order may be temporary or permanent. Unlike an injunction, the S.E.C. need not petition a court to obtain a case-and-desist order; as an administrative remedy, it can be imposed by an administrative law judge, or in some cases by the S.E.C. itself, without a hearing and without notice to the respondent. (*See supra*, §§1502-1520.)

(1) **Due process protections:** [§1552] The defendant is entitled to a certain amount of due process in such a proceeding; just how much depends on the nature of the defendant and the nature of the order.

(a) **Temporary cease-and-desist order:** [§1553] Temporary cease-and-desist orders are available only against regulated entities, *e.g.,* broker-dealers and others over whom the S.E.C. and the SROs have oversight authority. A temporary cease-and-desist order can be issued ex parte, without a hearing and without notice to the defendant, if the Commission deems it in the public interest (or if notice and a hearing would be impracticable). The respondent can, however, appeal the order to the S.E.C., and from there to a federal district court.

(b) **Permanent cease-and-desist order:** [§1554] A permanent cease-and-desist order may be issued against anyone (not just persons regulated by the S.E.C.) violating the 1933 or 1934 Acts. The order directs the respondent to refrain from future violations, and can also order disgorgement and take other steps to ensure compliance. Notice must be given to the respondent, who is entitled to a hearing before an administrative law judge. The judge's decision can be appealed to the S.E.C., and from there to a federal court of appeals.

## H. CRIMINAL ENFORCEMENT AND RICO

1. **Overview:** [§1555] Perhaps because of the events of the late 1980s, when most people think of criminal conduct under the securities laws, they think of insider trading or complex stock frauds. In fact, the criminal provisions of the 1933 and 1934 Act cover much more than fraud and insider trading. Willful violation of any provision of either statute, or of any rule or regulation promulgated under either statute, is a *felony*. In addition, a "knowing and willful" false statement in a filing under the 1934 Act is also a criminal offense. Each violation of the 1933 Act is potentially punishable by five years' imprisonment, and the penalty for violating the 1934 Act is even more severe: each infraction can result in up to 10 years in prison.

a. **Other statutes:** [§1556] Charges arising from securities transactions are often brought under provisions other than the securities laws. Sometimes this is done to avoid difficult issues that have cropped up under the securities laws.

(1) **Mail and wire fraud:** [§1557] Thus, for example, in *United States v. Carpenter, supra,* §957, the prosecution charged violations of SEA section 10(b) and rule 10b-5, and also of the federal mail and wire fraud

statutes. Ultimately, the securities law convictions were affirmed by an equally divided Court, but the mail and wire fraud convictions were affirmed unanimously.

(2) **RICO:** [§1558] The Racketeer-Influenced and Corrupt Organizations statute ("RICO") [18 U.S.C. §§1961-68] is also frequently used in securities prosecutions. Its advantages include a pre-trial asset freeze, treble damages, and longer prison sentences. RICO is also available in civil actions, and RICO claims are usually added to securities law claims in private actions for damages. (*See also* §§1579 *et seq.*)

2. **Commencing a Criminal Action:** [§1559] The S.E.C. does not have the authority to bring a criminal action, which can be done only by the United States Attorney's office in the relevant jurisdiction(s). Nevertheless, the S.E.C. is obviously heavily involved in, and very knowledgeable about, illegal securities activities, and securities prosecutions are usually the result of an informal referral from the S.E.C.'s Enforcement Division. A formal referral under 1934 Act section 21(d) is also possible, although such referrals (which require a vote of the Commission) are relatively rare.

   a. **Parallel proceedings:** [§1560] There is a good deal of cooperation between the Justice Department and the S.E.C., and frequently both agencies pursue a defendant at the same time. Such parallel proceedings may raise troublesome procedural issues, as when the S.E.C. seeks discovery in its civil action and the defendant resists, claiming that the Justice Department (which will have access to everything the S.E.C. discovers) is improperly broadening the scope of its criminal discovery by "hiding behind" the S.E.C.'s civil discovery request. This argument, however, has not succeeded for defendants in securities cases. [*See, e.g.,* S.E.C. v. Dresser Industries, Inc., *supra*, §1494]

   b. **Fifth Amendment:** [§1561] Defendants in parallel proceedings may exercise their Fifth Amendment privilege and refuse to testify. In a civil proceeding, however, the factfinder is allowed to draw an adverse inference from the refusal to testify, and asserting this right might cost the defendant the case. On the other hand, if the defendant testifies, a transcript of the testimony will be made available to the Justice Department and can be used to impeach the defendant in later criminal proceedings.

3. **Standard of Culpability:** [§1562] Both the 1933 Act and the 1934 Act make it a criminal offense "willfully" to violate a provision of the statute, or of an S.E.C. rule or regulation thereunder. [SA §24; SEA §32(a)] The 1934 Act, however, goes on to provide that a false statement made in a 1934 Act filing is criminal when it is made "willfully and knowingly." Finally, the 1934 Act provides that if the defendant can prove lack of knowledge of the statute or rule allegedly violated, no prison term can be imposed.

   a. **Culpability under the 1933 Act:** [§1563] The provisions of the 1933 Act relating to criminal intent are relatively straightforward: a "willful" violation is a crime. "Willful" under the Act means only the intent to do the act charged, together with knowledge that the act is wrongful. It does not mean that the defendant knew the act violated any particular provision of a statute, nor even that the act was unlawful. In a fraud case in which scienter is required, "willfulness" includes the intent to deceive, but not necessarily the intent to violate the securities laws.

(1) **Example:** The defendant was charged with violating Securities Act section 17(a) by fraudulently selling securities. On appeal, he argued that the government had not met its burden of proving that he knew the items sold were "securities" under the Act. The court held that the government did not need to prove that the defendant knew the items were securities; it was enough to show that the items were in fact securities, and that the defendant intended to deceive the buyers in connection with the sales. [United States v. Brown, *supra, §635*]

b. **Culpability under the 1934 Act:** [§1564] The 1934 Act sets up two possible standards of culpability: "willfulness," relevant to any violation of the statute or rule under the statute; and "willful and knowing," relating to false statements made in filings under the statute or rules.

(1) **"Willful" violation of the 1934 Act or rules:** [§1565] "Willfulness" under the 1934 Act means much the same thing as it does under the 1933 Act; *i.e.,* intentional conduct and knowledge that the act is wrongful, but not necessarily that it is unlawful, nor that it violates any particular rule or regulation. [United States v. Dixon, 536 F.2d 1388 (2d Cir. 1976)]

(2) **"Willful and knowing" false statements in filings under the 1934 Act:** [§1566] The courts have not reached a consensus on what the addition of the word "knowing" means in prosecutions for false filings under the 1934 Act. It might signify an intent to deceive, or perhaps specific knowledge of the provision of law that was violated. However, the former has not appeared in the cases, and courts have rejected the latter. [*See, e.g.,* United States v. Dixon, *supra*] Professors Loss and Seligman, eminent commentators, have concluded that the word "knowingly" in section 32(a) is redundant [10 Louis Loss & Joel Seligman, Securities Regulation 4692 (3d ed. 1993)]

c. **The 1934 Act "lack of knowledge" defense:** [§1567] The 1934 Act also includes a provision that a defendant who proves that he did not know of the rule or regulation violated shall not be sentenced to prison. The courts have construed this provision restrictively, holding that it is satisfied only if the defendant establishes that he had what amounts to a good faith belief that his conduct was lawful. The provision will not apply in a fraud case, in which proof of scienter forecloses the possibility of the innocence required the "no knowledge" defense. [*See* United States v. Lilley, 291 F. Supp. 989 (S.D. Tex. 1968)]

d. **Statute of limitations:** [§1568] The relevant statute of limitations for criminal prosecutions under the securities laws is five years; it is not contained in the securities statutes, but rather appears in the criminal code. [*See* 18 U.S.C. §3282]

4. **Illegal Trading in Securities Under the 1934 Act:** [§1569] In addition to fraud and the sale of unregistered, nonexempt securities, the securities laws are violated by selling or buying securities without complying with more technical, regulatory

requirements of the 1934 Act. In the 1980s, the government began numerous criminal prosecutions for such violations, most in the Southern District of New York.

a. **"Stock parking":** [§1570] "Stock parking" refers to an arrangement whereby one person holds title to securities on behalf of another person, who does not wish her ownership of the securities to be known. The arrangement can be implemented in numerous ways: for instance, the "true owner" may sell the securities to the counterparty, subject to a (usually secret) agreement to repurchase them at a fixed price. Or the counterparty may purchase the securities, subject to an agreement by the "true owner" to purchase them in turn at the counterparty's cost, plus commissions. Stock parking is itself not a crime, but the agreements that the various parties enter into to effectuate the scheme are seldom disclosed (secrecy being the whole point of "parking" the stock), and the securities business is so heavily regulated that the failure to disclose an arrangement of this sort inevitably causes a breach of a disclosure requirement at some point. [*See, e.g.,* United States v. Bilzerian, 926 F.2d 1285 (2d Cir. 1991)]

b. **Price manipulation and rule 10b-5:** [§1571] "Manipulation" in the 1934 Act means "manipulation of the price of securities," and in section 9(e) the Act contains an explicit prohibition against doing so. (*See infra,* §1721.) The government has argued, however, that in addition to section 9(e), rule 10b-5 can be violated by price manipulation: specifically, when a person buys or sells a large block of securities with an intent to affect the price of that class of securities. The argument goes that the alleged manipulator should have disclosed her intention to affect the price, and by failing to do so, she violated rule 10b-5. While no court has expressly accepted this theory, the Second Circuit has held that to prove it, the government would have to prove that the defendant's sole intention was to affect the price of the class of security. A transaction effected with an investment intent is *not manipulative* under rule 10b-5, *even if the price is affected by the transaction.* [United States v. Mulheren, 938 F.2d 364 (2d Cir. 1991)]

5. **Mail Fraud and Wire Fraud:** [§1572] The mail fraud and wire fraud statutes [18 U.S.C. §§1341, 1343] are often used to prosecute persons for securities transactions, because they are relatively uncomplicated and the elements are conceptually simple (and often easy to prove).

a. **Elements of mail or wire fraud:** [§1573] To make out a case of mail fraud or wire fraud, the prosecution must prove:

(i) A *scheme to defraud;*

(ii) *Specific intent to defraud* (*i.e.,* scienter—but sometimes a reckless disregard for the truth will suffice); and

(iii) The *mailing of a letter, or sending a wire,* in furtherance of the scheme.

(1) **Person mailing need not be defendant:** [§1574] Note that while it is a requirement that a letter (or wire) be sent, *it is not required that the defendant be the one sending the letter.* A scheme in which the defendant, in face-to-face meetings, fraudulently convinces others to send him money through the mail is mail fraud, even though all the mailings were done innocently.

(2) **Defendant need not have specific intent to use mail:** [§1575] The government does not need to establish the defendant's specific intent to use the mail (or cause the mail to be used); it is enough if the *use of the mail was reasonably foreseeable.*

b. **"Intangible business property" and the "intangible right of honest services":** [§1576] When a securities transaction is prosecuted as mail fraud, a problem may arise in identifying just what the victim was defrauded of. Insider trading cases, for instance, raise this issue. Prosecutors can make one of two arguments:

(1) **Intangible business property:** [§1577] This idea is closely linked to the "misappropriation" theory of insider trading (discussed *supra*, §§956-961). Essentially, the argument is that the tipper deprived the source of the exclusive use of the information. [*See* Carpenter v. United States, *supra*, §1557]

(2) **Intangible right of honest services:** [§1578] Alternatively, the prosecution can argue that the tipper (and the tippee) schemed to deprive the source of the information of her "intangible right of honest services." In 1988, Congress amended the criminal code specifically to add this possibility to the prosecutors' arsenal, by defining "scheme or artifice to defraud" to include "a scheme or artifice to deprive another of the intangible right of honest services." This appears to mean that a breach of fiduciary duty, if part of a fraudulent scheme, suffices as the basis for mail fraud. [*See* 18 U.S.C. §1346]

6. **Racketeer-Influenced and Corrupt Organizations Act ("RICO"):** [§1579] Finally, RICO has been important in both the criminal and civil enforcement of the securities laws. RICO was adopted in 1970 as a deterrent to the infiltration of legitimate business by organized crime. Beginning in 1980, however, prosecutors and private plaintiffs discovered its usefulness in many cases of simple fraud, unconnected to any organized crime activity. The result was a massive increase in the number of RICO claims.

a. **RICO sanctions:** [§1580] RICO's sudden increase in popularity may be accounted for in large part by the severe sanctions it imposes on violators. Under RICO, both the criminal penalties and the civil damages remedy are unusually harsh.

(1) **Criminal RICO:** [§1581] The penalties for a RICO violation include 20-year prison terms, heavy fines, forfeiture (not only of the profits from the illicit activity but also of the defendant's interest in the entire enterprise), and a pre-trial freeze of the defendant's assets.

(a) **Pre-trial asset freeze:** [§1582] RICO's pre-trial asset freeze, in particular, has been sharply criticized. While its stated purpose is to ensure that the defendant does not conceal or liquidate his assets before the government can levy on them, it is often used by the prosecution to intimidate the defendant. A successful freeze essentially renders the defendant indigent pending the outcome of the trial. Consequently, the prospect of a pre-trial freeze makes most defendants amenable to a negotiated plea.

(b) **Constitutionality of the pre-trial asset freeze:** [§1583] The asset freeze has been challenged, on the grounds that it renders the defendant unable to retain private counsel. But in *United States v. Monsanto*, 491 U.S. 600 (1989), the Supreme Court upheld the freeze, reasoning that the Constitution does not provide the right to counsel of the defendant's choice.

(2) **Civil RICO:** [§1584] RICO also includes a civil cause of action, for anyone "injured in his business or property by reason of a [RICO violation]." Its importance to private plaintiffs in securities cases lies in the remedies it provides: A successful claim entitles the plaintiff to *treble damages and attorney's fees.* [18 U.S.C. §1964(c)]

b. **Establishing violation of RICO:** [§1585] Establishing a RICO violation, whether civil or criminal, is a two-stage process.

(1) **Pattern of racketeering activity:** [§1586] The prosecution (or the plaintiff) must prove that the defendant engaged in a "pattern of racketeering activity," defined to mean at least "two acts of racketeering activity, one of which occurred after October 15, 1970 and the last of which occurred within 10 years (excluding any period of imprisonment) after the commission of a prior act of racketeering activity." [18 U.S.C. §1961(5)]

(a) **Acts of racketeering activity:** [§1587] The acts of racketeering activity (sometimes referred to as the "predicate acts") are set forth in section 1961(1). They are all crimes under state or federal law, including the stereotypical "racketeering" acts or threats of murder, kidnapping, gambling, arson, robbery, bribery, extortion, and narcotics offenses, but also include fraud in the sale of securities, mail fraud, and wire fraud.

(b) **Criminal conviction not required:** [§1588] Note that while the acts of racketeering activity are all acts for which the defendant could be convicted, RICO does not require that the defendant actually be convicted of—or even charged with—any of them. [Sedima, S.P.R.L. v. Imrex Co., 473 U.S. 479 (1985)]

(c) **"Pattern" requires *relationship* plus *continuity*:** [§1589] RICO requires *at least two predicate acts* to find a "pattern of racketeering activity." But merely proving two predicate acts will not suffice to establish a pattern. The prosecutor or plaintiff must in addition show that the *predicate acts* are *related to one another*, and that the predicate acts *amount to, or constitute a threat of, continuing racketeering activity—i.e.,* continued commission of predicate acts. [H.J. Inc. v. Northwestern Bell Telephone Co., 492 U.S. 229 (1989)]

1) **Example:** In *H.J. Inc., supra*, the plaintiffs alleged that the defendants repeatedly bribed members of the Minnesota Public Utilities Commission with cash, promises of future employment, tickets to sporting events, and the like, to influence the commissioners to approve unfairly high rates for the telephone company. The Supreme Court held that the predicate acts (of bribery) were related to each other by their

common purpose, and that the allegation that the acts occurred frequently over a six-year period could suffice to establish continuity. The Court stated further that continuity could also be established at trial by showing that the alleged bribes were a regular way of conducting Northwestern Bell's business, or a regular way of conducting the business of the RICO "enterprise" (*i.e.,* the Minnesota Public Utilities Commission).

2) **Note:** The Supreme Court's formulation of the pattern requirement is vague and provides little guidance to lower courts or potential defendants. Justice Scalia, concurring in *H.J. Inc., supra,* stated that the majority opinion is "about as helpful to the conduct of [the lower courts'] affairs as 'life is a fountain.'" Since *H.J. Inc.,* the lower courts have divided over what the proper test is for determining whether acts form a "pattern," and virtually every circuit has developed its own, distinctive approach to the problem.

(d) **Single fraudulent scheme can violate RICO:** [§1590]  The "pattern" requirement of RICO requires multiple predicate acts, not multiple schemes that are furthered by the predicate acts. Thus, even a single fraudulent scheme, if it is supported by a pattern of racketeering activity, can be the basis for a RICO claim. [H.J. Inc. v. Northwestern Bell Telephone Co., *supra*]

(2) **Violative acts:** [§1591]  RICO is violated when the defendant engages in one or more of four expressly prohibited activities, each of which depends on the existence of a "pattern of racketeering activity." The RICO prohibitions are in a sense, the "value added" (or perhaps "danger added") to a RICO offense. That is, the "pattern of racketeering activity" amounts simply to two felonies, and, standing alone, does not constitute a RICO offense. To prove a RICO offense, it must be proven that the defendant:

(i) *Invested income* from a pattern of racketeering activity in an "enterprise"; *or*

(ii) *Acquired or maintained an interest* in an "enterprise" through a pattern of racketeering activity;

(iii) *Conducted or participated in the affairs* of an "enterprise" through a pattern of racketeering activity; *or*

(iv) *Conspired to violate (a), (b), or (c), above.*

[18 U.S.C. §1962 (a)-(d)]

(3) **The "enterprise" requirement:** [§1592]  RICO defines the term "enterprise" to include any "individual, partnership, corporation, association or other legal entity, and any union or group of individuals associated in fact although not a legal entity." [18 U.S.C. §1961(4)]

(a) **Defendant and enterprise cannot be the same person:** [§1593] Most courts hold that the enterprise and the defendant must be different persons. [*See, e.g.,* Bennett v. United States Trust Co., 770 F.2d 308 (2d Cir. 1985); Haroco, Inc. v. American National Bank & Trust Co., 747 F.2d 384 (7th Cir. 1984); *but see* United States v. Hartley, 678 F.2d 961 (11th Cir. 1982)]

   1) **Rationale:** Section 1962(c) prohibits "conduct[ing] or participat[ing] in the conduct of [an] enterprise's affairs through a pattern of racketeering activity." If the defendant and the enterprise were the same person, section 1962(c) would make it illegal to conduct or participate in one's own affairs. Because this interpretation would be senseless, most courts have rejected it.

   2) **Group associated in fact:** [§1594] The practical effect of the distinction between the defendant and the enterprise is that plaintiffs and prosecutors search for an "enterprise" separate from the deepest pocket defending the case. Here, the statute is accommodating. Usually the "enterprise" is identified as a "group of individuals associated in fact," which although at first appearing to exclude corporations (which are not usually considered to be individuals), has been held to be broad enough to include virtually any entity as a group member.

(b) **"Pattern" and "enterprise" are not the same:** [§1595] Another complexity arises from the Supreme Court's description of a RICO enterprise as "an entity separate and apart from the pattern of activity in which it engages." [United States v. Turkette, 452 U.S. 576 (1981)] Disagreement over the meaning of this statement and the nature and amount of proof required to establish such a separate enterprise continues.

(c) **"Conduct" or "participate":** [§1596] In 1993, the Supreme Court held that to be liable under section 1962(c), the defendant must have participated in the operation or management of the enterprise. This does not imply upper management responsibilities; an ordinary day-to-day employee "participates in the operation" of the enterprise, in the Court's view. But it excludes liability for an accounting firm, whose involvement in the enterprise extended only to preparing financial statements based on the client's accounting system. [Reves v. Ernst & Young, 113 S. Ct. 1163 (1993)]

(d) **"Through a pattern":** [§1597] Similarly, section 1962(c) requires the plaintiff or prosecutor to prove that the defendant conduct or participate in the affairs of the enterprise "*through* a pattern of racketeering activity." Some courts have held that this requires that the affairs of the enterprise be furthered by or related to the predicate acts; others have held that it suffices if the defendant was enabled to commit the predicate acts by virtue of her position in the enterprise. [*Compare* United States v. Kovic, 684 F.2d 512 (7th Cir. 1982), *with* United States v. Cauble, 706 F.2d 1322 (5th Cir. 1983)] The D.C. Circuit has held that the defendant must exercise managerial control over the enterprise. [Yellow Bus Lines, Inc. v. Drivers Local Union 639, 913 F.2d 948 (D.C. Cir. 1990)]

c. **Respondeat superior:** [§1598]  So far, courts have not been receptive to efforts to impose the RICO liability of an employee upon the employer on an agency theory. Thus, in a case in which defrauded brokerage customers sought to recover against the broker's firm, the court held that the enterprise itself is not liable (and, in dictum, continued that this would be true even if the enterprise were "wholly illegitimate"). [Schofield v. First Commodity Corp., 793 F.2d 28 (1st Cir. 1986)]

d. **Purchasers of securities:** [§1599]  RICO includes as a predicate offense "fraud in the sale of securities." Does this language exclude fraud in the purchase of securities? Most courts have held that *fraudulent purchasers are liable under RICO.*

e. **Concurrent jurisdiction:** [§1600]  The federal and state courts share jurisdiction over RICO cases. [Tafflin v. Levitt, 493 U.S. 455 (1990)]

# IV. REGULATION OF THE SECURITIES MARKETS

## ___chapter approach___

The regulation of the national securities exchanges is very important to the well-being of the securities markets, but it is seldom tested on law school exams. However, you should learn the material in this chapter so that you have a basic understanding of how the securities markets work.

The only topic likely to appear on an exam concerns the regulation of trading activities of broker-dealers. In this area, you should watch for possible conflicts of interest between the brokers and their clients, and also be familiar with the rules that brokers must follow in working with clients.

## A. REGULATION OF THE NATIONAL SECURITIES EXCHANGES

1. **Introduction:** [§1601] As part of its purpose of regulating interstate trading of securities subsequent to their original distribution, the Securities Exchange Act of 1934 includes provisions regulating the "national securities exchanges" where many such securities are traded.

   a. **"Exchange" defined:** [§1602] An "exchange" is any organization, association, or group of persons providing a marketplace or facilities for bringing together purchasers and sellers of securities. [SEA §3(a)]

      (1) **Requirement of registration:** [§1603] It is unlawful for a broker or dealer to make use of any means of interstate commerce for the purpose of trading or reporting the trade of a security on an exchange unless the exchange is registered with the S.E.C. as a "national securities exchange" or exempted from registration. An exchange is exempt from registration if the volume of transactions on the exchange is so small that regulation is not necessary for the protection of the public interest or investors. [SEA §5]

         (a) **Section 6:** [§1604] The terms and conditions that must be complied with to register as a national securities exchange are set forth in section 6 of the 1934 Act (*e.g.*, the rules of the exchange must be designed to prevent fraudulent and manipulative practices).

   b. **Listing securities for trading:** [§1605] To trade its securities on an exchange, an issuer must "list" the security with the exchange. The exchanges have set up rules by which an issuer can qualify its securities for trading (*e.g.*, requisite size of the firm in terms of sales and assets, net worth, etc.).

      (1) **Registration with the S.E.C.:** [§1606] Once the issuer has listed a security with a national securities exchange, the security must then be registered with the S.E.C. under section 12 of the 1934 Act. (*See supra*, §743.)

   c. **Exchange membership:** [§1607] Each national securities exchange sells memberships to securities firms or individuals in the securities business.

Membership carries with it the privilege of executing transactions over the exchange.

d. **Exchange disseminates price information:** [§1608] Each exchange has developed an information system for disseminating information to the public about the prices at which various securities have been bought and sold over the exchange.

e. **Exchange defines broker and dealer functions:** [§1609] Also, to make the exchange work effectively, various broker and dealer functions have been developed for those members and their agents who participate in trading on the exchange. For example, the function of a "specialist" (*infra,* §1647) is to ensure a continuous market (*i.e.,* that purchase or a sale in a listed security can always be made, at some price) in the securities for which he is responsible.

2. **Competition of Markets for Trading of Securities**

a. **Competing markets:** [§1610] Many markets compete for the trading of securities.

(1) **NYSE and regional exchanges:** [§1611] For example, a security may be listed for trading on the New York Stock Exchange ("NYSE") and on one or more of the regional exchanges, such as the Pacific Coast Stock Exchange.

(2) **Over-the-counter markets:** [§1612] In addition, broker-dealers who are not members of an exchange may engage in buying and selling securities that are listed on an exchange in "over-the-counter" (*i.e.,* nonexchange) transactions.

(3) **Institutional trading:** [§1613] The institutions that own large amounts of securities may also engage in buying and selling securities directly with other such institutions.

(a) **Proprietary trading systems:** [§1614] Institutional investors may trade on an exchange through the National Association of Securities Dealers Automated Quotations ("NASDAQ") system, or on a proprietary trading system, which is simply a computerized facility for bringing together buyers and sellers and disseminating information about price and availability. These trading systems compete to some extent with the more-established exchanges. The exchanges, therefore, have paid close attention to the development of trading systems. Generally, the S.E.C. has been willing to permit trading systems to operate, provided they register as broker-dealers. On occasion, markets have sued to overturn the S.E.C.'s decision to permit a trading system to compete with the markets, but the markets have not been successful to date. [*See, e.g.,* Board of Trade v. S.E.C., 923 F.2d 1270 (7th Cir. 1991)]

b. **Impact of communications technology:** [§1615] As the technology for information processing has grown, the securities markets have become increasingly competitive. Computers and other communications equipment have made it possible to collect, classify, and communicate large amounts of data about securities transactions very rapidly.

(1) **Example:** The NASDAQ system (which uses computers to list all firms making a market in over-the-counter stocks) provides over-the-counter firms with much better information than was formerly available concerning transactions in specific over-the-counter stocks.

(2) **Comment:** This technology has now made it possible to combine all of the competing markets into what is, in effect, one large national securities market. This is the direction contemplated by the 1934 Act and by the actions of the S.E.C. [*See* SEA §11A]

c. **Development of national market system:** [§1616] Congress has directed that the S.E.C. use its authority under the 1934 Act to facilitate the establishment of a "national market system" for securities. [SEA §11A]

(1) **Specific mandate:** [§1617] In this regard, the S.E.C. has been directed specifically to:

(a) *Conduct studies and make recommendations* to Congress;

(b) *Require the exchanges and other organizations* regulating the over-the-counter market *to act jointly* in working toward the eventual establishment of a national securities market; and

(c) *Establish a National Market Advisory Board* to assist in the development of a unified national market system.

(2) **Motivation to encourage competition:** [§1618] The S.E.C. is clearly encouraging a breakdown of those factors that restrain competition between security markets in order to move toward a national securities market.

(3) **Broad scope of regulation:** [§1619] In addition, activities that relate to the securities markets are regulated under the 1934 Act so that the S.E.C. has sufficiently broad power to move in the direction of a national market system. For example:

(a) **Information processors:** [§1620] Those who make use of the means of interstate commerce in the business of processing and communicating information about securities and securities markets are subject to registration with the S.E.C. [SEA §11A(b)(1)]

(b) **Clearing agencies:** [§1621] In addition, transfer agents, clearing houses, and others involved in the mechanical completion of securities trades are also subject to registration and regulation by the S.E.C. [SEA §17A]

(4) **Projected elements of the national market system:** [§1622] The following items have been suggested by Congress and the S.E.C. as important aspects of the future national market system:

(a) *A nationwide system for disclosure* of market information so that price and volume information is available in all markets.

(b) *Elimination of artificial impediments to dealing* in the best available markets created by exchange rules or otherwise.

(c) *Establishment of terms and conditions* under which qualified broker-dealers could negotiate access to all exchanges.

(d) *An auction trading market* which would provide price and time priority protection for all public orders.

(e) *The type of securities to be included in the system* would be dependent on their characteristics (trading volume, etc.) and not on where they are traded (*i.e.*, which exchange, etc.). [*See* SEA Release No. 14416 (1978)]

3. **Institutional Trading on the Exchanges:** [§1623] The stock exchanges originally functioned as markets where *individuals* could buy and sell the listed securities of issuers. However, over the years the savings of individuals have accumulated in financial institutions (*e.g.,* insurance companies, banks, pension plans), which tend to invest large sums of money in correspondingly large blocks of stock. As a result, the economic importance of the individual investor has diminished.

   a. **Impact of institutional investment on exchanges:** [§1624] The financial institutions invest almost exclusively in the larger, better known companies, and therefore invest predominantly in securities listed on the NYSE. Many of the problems affecting the national exchanges in recent years have arisen as a result of the effect of institutional investing.

     (1) **Maintaining a continuous market:** [§1625] For example, it is much more difficult to maintain a continuous trading market at relatively even prices when huge blocks of stock are being traded relatively infrequently than when small amounts of stock are being traded continuously by many small investors.

     (2) **Impact on competition:** [§1626] The institutions that do a lot of business on the exchanges have increasingly sought ways to save the expenses (such as commissions) involved in their securities transactions. On the other hand, the exchanges (particularly the NYSE) have attempted to preserve the economic position of their members by rules which are anticompetitive (*e.g.,* prohibiting trading transactions by exchange member firms in listed securities from occurring off the exchange). These opposing pressures (institutions pushing for a more competitive market and the exchanges seeking to preserve their existing economic position) have over the years resulted in many changes in the laws that affect the national exchanges. The Securities Exchange Act of 1934 regulates the national exchanges, but extensive power of self-regulation (with S.E.C. overview) is vested in the exchanges themselves.

4. **Self-Regulation of Exchanges vs. S.E.C. Supervision:** [§1627] The stock exchanges are self-regulatory organizations ("SROs") under the 1934 Act. [SEA §3(a)(26)] As such, they have substantial responsibility for the content of their

policy, and they are permitted to operate on what amounts to a presumption that they will exercise their power appropriately to ensure that their members treat the public fairly. [*See, e.g.,* SEA §§6, 15A] Nevertheless, the S.E.C. retains supervisory authority over the exchanges.

a.  **Registration with the S.E.C.:** [§1628]  A broker-dealer is prohibited from effecting transactions on a securities exchange unless such exchange has registered with the S.E.C. according to the provisions of section 6 of the 1934 Act, or is exempted from registration by other provisions of the Act. [SEA §5]

b.  **Self-regulation of exchanges:** [§1629]  The 1934 Act also provides for extensive self-regulation of members' activities and business practices by a national securities exchange. [SEA §6]

   (1)  **Rules, policies, and procedures:** [§1630]  The exchange may propose rules, and adopt policies and procedures for implementing its rules.

   (2)  **S.E.C. review:** [§1631]  Any proposed rule or change to an existing rule must be filed with the S.E.C., which then goes through an administrative notice and comment procedure, giving the public the right to comment on the proposal. [SEA §19(b)] In addition, the S.E.C. can, by its own rulemaking procedures, abrogate, add to, and delete rules from the rules of a self-regulatory organization. [SEA §19(c)]

   (3)  **Disciplinary action:** [§1632]  If the exchange imposes any disciplinary sanction on an exchange member, or denies membership to a firm, the exchange must notify the S.E.C., which may then review (either on its own motion or on the motion of the aggrieved party) the actions taken by the exchange. [SEA §19(d)]

   (4)  **S.E.C.'s power to sanction:** [§1633]  Finally, the 1934 Act empowers the S.E.C. to impose sanctions on the exchanges, exchange members, and persons associated with exchange members for violation of the federal securities laws. [SEA §19(h)]

5.  **Accommodation of Exchange Rules to the Antitrust Laws:** [§1634]  One of the principal "problem" areas concerning national exchanges concerns the application of the federal antitrust laws to exchange rules that restrain competition. Historically, exchanges have shown a tendency to protect the economic position of member firms from outside competition. Through the exercise of its self-regulatory power, the exchange may allow, or permit its member firms to engage in, conduct that violates the antitrust laws.

   a.  **Rules in restraint of competition:** [§1635]  Historically, the anticompetitive impulse of exchanges has been expressed in three major ways:

   (1)  *Setting fixed commission rates;*

   (2)  *Restricting membership on the exchange* and restricting the opportunity to transact business on the exchange exclusively to members; and

   (3)  *Prohibiting exchange members from executing orders off the exchange* in securities that are listed on the exchange.

b. **Securities laws do not preempt field:** [§1636]  The federal antitrust laws have been one of the tools used by those who wish to make the securities exchanges more competitive. The courts have indicated that the Securities Exchange Act does **not** exclusively occupy the field of securities regulation, and that the 1934 Act must be reconciled or accommodated with the antitrust laws.

(1) **Example:** An over-the-counter securities firm in Texas sued the NYSE for requiring (without notice to plaintiff) some of its member firms to disconnect direct telephone lines between their firms in New York and plaintiff's offices in Texas. The Supreme Court held that the NYSE rules violated the Sherman Act because they permitted collective anti-competitive action without according fair procedures of notice and hearing to those affected. [Silver d/b/a Municipal Securities Co. v. New York Stock Exchange, 373 U.S. 341 (1963)]

   (a) **Note:** Although regulation of relationships between exchange member firms and over-the-counter firms was held to be a proper subject of exchange rules, the Court indicated that the antitrust laws are repealed vis-a-vis exchange rules only to the **minimum extent necessary** to accommodate the purposes of the Securities Exchange Act of 1934.

   (b) **And note:** While the S.E.C. had power under section 19(b) to disapprove the NYSE rules, it had no actual power under the Act to regulate any specific application of the rules. Hence, the antitrust laws were required to help establish appropriate procedures for administration of the NYSE rules, and were not preempted by the regulatory scheme established by the S.E.C. under the 1934 Act.

(2) **Rationale extended:** [§1637]  A lower court has gone beyond the rationale of *Silver* (*i.e.,* that the antitrust laws apply where the S.E.C. has **no** direct supervisory power over application of exchange rules) to hold that even where the S.E.C. **has** direct supervisory power, the antitrust laws may still apply. [Thill Securities Corp. v. New York Stock Exchange, 433 F.2d 264 (7th Cir. 1970), *cert. denied*, 401 U.S. 994 (1971)]

   (a) **Example:** In *Thill*, plaintiff contested an NYSE rule prohibiting a member firm from giving up part of its commissions to nonmember firms with respect to trades in which the firms cooperated. (For example, a mutual fund might direct that the securities firm trading the fund's portfolio give part of the commission on a trade to another firm that had provided services for the fund; *see infra*, §1642.)

   (b) **Holding:** Even though the S.E.C. had **direct supervisory power** over the NYSE rule on commissions (under section 19(b)(9)), the court stated that this did not in itself cloak the NYSE rule with antitrust immunity. However, in a later opinion, the holding in *Thill* was limited to its specific factual context. [Gordon v. New York Stock Exchange, 422 U.S. 659 (1975)]

(3) **Antitrust laws inapplicable to rules fixing commissions:** [§1638]  Finally, however, the Supreme Court has decided that the antitrust laws

are *inapplicable* to exchange rules that fix commission rates to be charged by member firms. Since section 19(b) specifically gives the S.E.C. power to supervise exchanges in establishing commission rates, and the S.E.C. has a long history of actually exercising this power, the antitrust laws are preempted from limiting the exchange's self-regulatory power in this respect. [Gordon v. New York Stock Exchange, *supra*] One major factor in the decision must have been that the S.E.C. (just before the case was decided) had adopted rule 19b-3, which abolished fixed commission rates.

(4) **Application to over-the-counter market:** [§1639] Antitrust laws are applicable to the over-the-counter market (*infra*, §§1688 *et seq.*) to the same extent as they are to the national securities exchanges.

c. **Fixed commission rates as limiting competition:** [§1640] As noted above, one of the classic anticompetitive strategies of the exchanges has been to fix the commission rates that its members must charge for transacting trades on the exchange.

(1) **Minimum rates:** [§1641] For a long time, the NYSE set *minimum* commission rates that its member firms could charge their customers. With pressure from the "third market" (*i.e.,* the trading of listed securities in the over-the-counter market), exchange members began to look for ways to avoid these minimum rates in order to offer their customers lower rates and thus preserve their business.

(2) **"Give-up" of commission:** [§1642] Under one method of avoiding the minimum rates, a customer would pay the exchange member the full commission on the trade, but would then direct the member firm to "give-up" part of the commission to a specified third party (regardless of any involvement of this third party in the transaction). In either a direct or indirect way, the customer of the member firm would have an interest in the "give-up" (*i.e.,* the customer might have received other services from the party receiving the "give-up").

(3) **Negotiated commissions:** [§1643] Finally, the NYSE prohibited customer-director "give-ups," and the 1934 Act was amended with the intention of abolishing fixed commission rates. The 1934 Act now provides that no national securities exchange may impose any schedule or otherwise fix the rates of commission charged by its members. [SEA §6(e)]

   (a) **Application:** By rule, the S.E.C. has now abolished fixed commission rates pursuant to section 6(e). *See also* SEA Rule 19b-3, which prohibits the *exchanges* from fixing the rates that member firms must charge. [SEA Release No. 11203 (1975)]

   (b) **Exceptions:** [§1644] However, the S.E.C. may permit exceptions if it finds:

      (i) *That such fixed rates are reasonable* in relation to the costs of services; and

(ii) *That the rates do not impose any unnecessary or inappropriate burden* on competition.

[SEA §6(e)]

d. **Exchange membership as limiting competition:** [§1645] A second anti-competitive strategy of the exchanges has been to restrict membership on the exchange and to limit the opportunity to transact business on the exchange to its members.

(1) **Institutional membership:** [§1646] The financial institutions, which control the bulk of the trading on national exchanges, for a long time desired to have membership on the NYSE either directly or to acquire as subsidiary corporations broker-dealers who had such membership. In this way, a financial institution that was constantly trading in securities listed on an exchange could save the commission expenses it would otherwise have to pay exchange members.

(a) **But note:** With the abolition of fixed minimum commission rates, however, the demand for institutional membership was almost completely extinguished. In addition, in 1975 Congress amended SEA section 11(a) to provide that a member of an exchange cannot effect a trade on the exchange for its own account or the account of an affiliate or person for whom the member exercises investment discretion (subject to limited exceptions, for example where a member is acting as a specialist; *see infra*, §§1647 *et seq.*). This abolishes the principal benefit sought by the financial institutions seeking memberships.

6. **The Specialist System**

a. **"Specialist" defined:** [§1647] A specialist is a member of a stock exchange who engages in the buying and selling of one or more specific securities listed on the exchange. He may act either as a broker (buying and selling for other brokers on the exchange) or as a dealer (buying or selling for his own account).

b. **Function of the specialist:** [§1648] The function of a specialist is to buy when stock is offered for sale but other bids for the purchase of the security are not available, and to sell when there are offers to buy but other offers to sell are not available. In other words, the specialist is supposed to see that there is a *continuous trading market* in the specific securities for which he is responsible, *i.e.,* to see that a security may *always* be bought or sold. In addition, as auctioneers, specialists set the opening price and establish the "bid" and "asked" spread within which others trade.

(1) **Note:** At least one specialist is responsible for each security listed on a national exchange.

(2) **Effect of specialists:** The specialists obviously occupy a key position in the functioning of the stock exchanges; they purchase and sell a substantial portion of all the securities sold on the exchanges.

c. **Types of orders executed:** [§1649] Typically, the specialist executes the following types of orders:

(1) **Limited price orders:** [§1650] A limited price order is an order to buy or sell a stated amount of security at a *specified price*, or at a better price if obtainable. For example, the specialist may receive an order to buy 100 shares of XYZ when the price drops to $10 per share or less.

(2) **Stop-loss orders:** [§1651] A stop-loss order is an order to buy or sell a stated amount of a security at the *market price*, if and when a transaction occurs at a designated price. For example, the specialist may receive an order to sell 100 shares of XYZ if the price ever drops below $10 per share (and the specialist may then sell at the market price).

(3) **Market orders:** [§1652] Specialists execute very few orders to buy or sell at the current market price (market orders), since these orders are normally executed between brokers at the "post" (the location on the exchange where the particular stock is traded). But where the order is at a price different from the current market price, the order is typically given to the specialist (who remains permanently at one post) to execute.

(4) **Recording of orders:** [§1653] The specialist records each buy or sell order to be executed at a price above or below the current market price. As the market moves up or down, the specialist executes these orders.

d. **Objections to the specialist system:** [§1654] Most objections to the specialist system arise in connection with specialists trading for their own accounts (*i.e.,* acting as principals in stock transactions).

(1) **Advantage of position as specialist:** [§1655] The specialist has the advantage of special knowledge and superior bargaining power in buying and selling for her own account. For example, knowing what the limited orders to sell are above the market price may tell the specialist whether or not a stock can advance in price.

(a) **Example:** If there are a lot of sell orders at $5 per share, just above the market price of $4 per share, the specialist would probably not buy for her own account. As soon as a price advance begins, it will run into all of the sell orders at $5 per share and the stock will probably retreat back to the $4 price.

(b) **Access to inside information:** [§1656] In addition to the information specialists obtain from actually trading in the stock, many specialists have access to "inside information" through relationships developed with insiders in the companies whose stock they trade.

(2) **Potential for market manipulation:** [§1657] By personal trading, the specialist is able to stimulate public interest and encourage market speculation. There is no question that the specialists are in a position to manipulate the market.

(a) **"Churning" to create commissions:** [§1658] Specialists make income from commissions on buying and selling; the more trading activity in a stock, therefore, the more income they make. Specialists may thus be motivated to create interest in a stock by stimulating the trading volume. Knowing when all of the buy orders are below the market price, the specialist might begin to "churn" (*i.e.,* buy and then immediately resell) the stock to create interest in a security.

(b) **Specialist trading may accentuate price trend:** [§1659] Rather than stabilizing the market, the specialist who trades excessively for her own account may actually accentuate an existing price trend.

e. **Arguments supporting the specialist system:** [§1660] There are also some strong arguments in favor of the specialist system:

(1) *Specialist trading contributes to price continuity and increases liquidity* of stock ownership; and

(2) *Acting as a dealer* (and profiting thereby) enables the specialist to assume substantial risks to *ensure an orderly market.*

f. **Regulating the activities of specialists:** [§1661] Because the position of specialist carries a significant potential for abuse, the 1934 Act regulates the trading activities of specialists. [SEA §11(a)]

(1) **Trading limitations:** [§1662] Specialists function both as brokers and as dealers. However, a specialist must restrict her activities as a dealer to those "reasonably necessary" to permit her to "maintain a fair and orderly market." [SEA Rule 11b-1]

(2) **NYSE rules governing specialists:** [§1663] Numerous rules have been adopted by the NYSE to implement the basic objective to be achieved by specialists, *i.e.,* maintaining an orderly market.

(a) **Registration:** [§1664] Specialists are required by the NYSE to be registered with the exchange.

(b) **Orderly market:** [§1665] A specialist cannot exercise a trade in which she is personally interested unless the objective is to maintain an orderly market. Moreover, if a specialist is found to have engaged in "continued dealings" for her own account, and not for the objective of maintaining an orderly market, she can be suspended. [NYSE Rules 103, 104]

1) **Specialists in market crashes:** [§1666] Market crashes provide perhaps the ultimate test of the specialist system. Specialists who are solely or primarily self-interested would use their knowledge of the imbalance of buy and sell orders (in a crash, everyone wants to sell and no one is buying) to sell off their own securities. By and large, however, specialists performed well in the October 1987 market crash. That is, specialists purchased large quantities of securities on October 19, in a market that was heading down quickly. Then, on October 20, when the market rebounded upward, specialists sold large quantities of securities. These purchases and sales were clearly not done in

the short-term financial interest of the specialists, but rather in discharge of their obligation to maintain a fair and orderly market.

(c) **Capital requirements:** [§1667] In addition, NYSE rules seek to establish fiscal responsibility of specialists by requiring that specialists be able to assume positions of a certain amount in each stock for which they are responsible, and that specialists have net liquid assets of a certain amount. These requirements are a necessity if specialists are to adequately perform their assigned functions.

　　1) **Capital requirements after the 1987 crash:** [§1668] Since the October 1987 market crash, the capital adequacy requirements have become stricter. In a significant stock market crash, specialists may be called on to buy huge quantities of securities, and the capital requirements at the time of the 1987 crash were not strict enough to ensure that all specialists were ready to meet those needs. As a result, several specialists were bankrupted by the 1987 crash, further contributing to the panic and hysteria that gripped the market as it crashed.

(d) **Dealer transactions on the exchange:** [§1669] The 1934 Act has been amended to prohibit any member of a national securities exchange (including a specialist) from effecting transactions on the exchange for its own account (*i.e.*, acting as a principal), the account of an associated person, or an account with respect to which it or an associated person has investment discretion (so-called "covered accounts"). [SEA §11(a)]

　　1) **Note:** In addition to certain specified exceptions to this regulation (*see infra,* §1670), the S.E.C. has been given authority to exempt other transactions as well. [SEA §11(a)(1)(I)]

　　2) **And note:** The S.E.C. may also regulate or prohibit:

　　　　a) *Exchange transactions by members for covered accounts* (*i.e.*, those that are otherwise permitted by section 11(a));

　　　　b) *Over-the-counter transactions for covered accounts;* and

　　　　c) *Exchange transactions by nonmembers of the exchange for covered accounts.*

　　　[SEA §11(a)(2); *see* SEA Rule 11a-1]

　　3) **Dealer transactions exempted from prohibition:** [§1670] The 1934 Act provides for specific exemptions from the prohibition against dealer transactions by members of the exchange. [SEA §11(a)]

　　　　a) **Market-maker transactions:** [§1671] A specific exemption is given in the Act for transactions by a dealer acting in the capacity of a "market-maker." [SEA §11(a)(1)(A)]

A "market-maker" is any specialist or any dealer who holds himself out as willing to buy and sell a particular security on a regular or continuous basis. [SEA §3(a)(38)]

b) **When outside orders are given priority:** [§1672] The Act also provides that transactions may be effected for the account of exchange members, if: (i) the member is primarily engaged in the securities business, and its principal income is derived from the securities business, and (ii) the transaction is effected in such a way as to yield "priority, parity and precedence" to orders of persons who are neither members nor associated with members. [SEA §11(a)(1)(G)]

7. **Regulation of Off-the-Exchange Transactions:** [§1673] In addition to regulating trading on the national securities exchanges by exchange members, the S.E.C. and the national exchanges also regulate the trading in listed securities by exchange members *off the exchange*.

a. **Background:** [§1674] Historically, the stock exchanges sharply limited trading in listed securities elsewhere than on the exchange floor. The reason for this was simple: if a security was available only on the exchange floor, from an exchange member, a customer who wanted to buy or sell the security had no choice but to pay the usual commission on the transaction. In the 1970s, however, large customers (*e.g.,* financial institutions like banks, trusts, and insurance companies) began to apply pressure to exchange members to participate in off-exchange transactions.

(1) **The birth of the "third market":** [§1675] As long as the exchanges were unwilling to permit member firms to participate in off-exchange transactions, financial institutions that wanted to avoid paying broker's commissions had to deal directly with one another and with nonmember firms. As the number of participants in this market grew, it became known as the "third market."

(2) **The third market today:** [§1676] The elimination of fixed minimum commissions (*see supra,* §1643) nearly eliminated the third market, which declined and, for a time, almost ceased to exist. In the late 1980s, however, the third market was reborn. In its new incarnation, it does not comprise exchange-member firms, but rather nonmembers trading in exchange-listed securities.

b. **Block transactions:** [§1677] Many exchange member firms also found that they were unable to handle in normal exchange transactions the purchase or sale of the large blocks of securities being traded by financial institutions. These firms found that to facilitate such transactions for their customers, they often had to negotiate the transaction off the exchange—either by finding off-the-exchange brokers or dealers willing to participate, or by finding other institutions in the third market that wished to participate.

c. **NYSE Rule 390:** [§1678] The New York Stock Exchange eventually responded to the pressure from members and their customers, and on the recommendation of the S.E.C., the Exchange amended its rule 309 to permit member firms to engage in off-exchange transactions. Such transactions, however, were subject to some strict requirements, discussed immediately below.

(1) **Permission required:** [§1679] Member firms were required by rule 390 to first obtain permission from the Exchange before engaging in an off-the-exchange transaction involving a listed security.

(2) **Solicitation of nonmember market-makers:** [§1680] Once permission was granted, an exchange member firm could, under certain conditions, approach a nonexchange broker-dealer making a market in the listed security (provided the market-maker was a broker-dealer registered with the S.E.C.) to participate in an off-the-exchange transaction. However, efforts had to first be made to fill the order or make the sale over the exchange, and the relevant specialists also had to be given a chance to participate at the same price as those participating in the off-the-exchange transaction.

d. **S.E.C. permission to trade off the exchange:** [§1681] The S.E.C. viewed the amended rule 309 as merely an interim measure, and in the late 1970s adopted rules 19c-1 and 19c-3. These rules preempted rule 309 of the New York Stock Exchange as it then existed, and eliminated many of the remaining restrictions on off-exchange trading by member firms.

(1) **Where member firm acts as broker:** [§1682] When acting as a broker (*i.e.,* agent), a member firm may effect a transaction in securities listed on a national exchange on other exchanges than that on which the security is listed or with a market-maker in the third market.

(a) **But note:** The exchange rules may still require that members effecting such transactions first satisfy orders, at the same or better price, that are listed with the exchange specialist.

(b) **And note:** The exchanges may also still adopt rules which would prohibit member firms from effecting transactions "in house" (*i.e.,* acting as agent for both the buyer and the seller).

(2) **Where member firm acts as principal:** [§1683] Where, however, the member firm acts as a *principal* in the transaction (*e.g.,* by selling securities it owns in its investment account), the member firm must comply with exchange rules regulating off-the-exchange sales.

(3) **Newly listed securities:** [§1684] The S.E.C. has also adopted a rule removing off-exchange trading restrictions on securities that are newly or recently listed on an exchange. [SEA Rule 19c-3] This allows exchange-member brokerage firms to compete directly with exchange specialists on transactions involving these stocks. The rule applies to securities first listed on an exchange after April 26, 1979.

8. **Civil Liability for Violations of Exchange or NASD Rules:** [§1685] In a number of cases, a plaintiff has brought a *private action* against an exchange or a member firm, alleging an implied federal cause of action based on violation of a stock exchange or NASD rule.

a. **Pre-*Blue Chip* view:** [§1686] The older cases hold that under limited circumstances, such an action is possible. [*See, e.g.,* Landy v. Federal Deposit Insurance Corp., *supra,* §1455; Buttrey v. Merrill Lynch, Pierce, Fenner & Smith, Inc., 410 F.2d 135 (7th Cir.), *cert. denied*, 396 U.S. 838 (1969); Colonial Realty Corp. v. Bache & Co., *supra,* §1544]

b. **Modern view:** [§1687] After the Supreme Court decided the *Blue Chip* case (cutting back implied liability under the securities laws; *see supra,* §854) the lower courts have refused to recognize implied actions based on violations of stock exchange or NASD rules. [*See, e.g.,* Carrott v. Shearson Hayden Stone, Inc., 724 F.2d 821 (9th Cir. 1984); Thompson v. Smith Barney, Harris Upham & Co., 709 F.2d 1413 (11th Cir. 1983); Sacks v. Reynolds Securities Inc., 593 F.2d 1234 (D.C. Cir. 1978)]

## B. REGULATION OF THE OVER-THE-COUNTER MARKET

1. **In General:** [§1688] Securities that are traded outside the exchanges are said to be traded "over-the-counter." This trading, like that which occurs on the national securities exchanges, is also subject to regulation under the 1934 Act.

2. **Role of Securities Firms:** [§1689] Securities firms act as the agents (*i.e.,* as brokers) of the buyer and seller in over-the-counter securities transactions. And sometimes the securities firms may act as principals (*i.e.,* as dealers) as well, owning the security and acting as either buyer or seller in the transaction.

3. **Transaction Information Systems:** [§1690] There are several systems that disseminate information about the prices at which over-the-counter securities are bought and sold.

   a. **Local newspapers:** [§1691] For example, local newspapers may collect information on local over-the-counter stocks and publish this information daily.

   b. **NASDAQ system:** [§1692] One of the most important information systems for the over-the-counter market is the NASDAQ system. This is a national, computer-oriented information network, which lists certain over-the-counter securities and the firms that are making a market in these securities (*i.e.,* firms that have indicated a willingness to buy or sell the security at a quoted price).

   c. **"Pink sheets":** [§1693] Another important source of price information about over-the-counter securities are the so-called "pink sheets," published by the National Daily Quotations Bureau. The pink sheets contain quotations for securities that are not carried in the NASDAQ system.

   d. **OTC Bulletin Board:** [§1694] The OTC Bulletin Board is a computer bulletin board system ("BBS") operated by the NASD as an electronic interdealer quotation system. Securities not quoted in the NASDAQ system may be quoted on the OTC BBS, which makes price information more current and more accessible. Eventually the OTC BBS will replace the pink sheets altogether, although it has not yet done so.

4. **Regulation of Broker-Dealers:** [§1695] The 1934 Act provides for the registration with the S.E.C. of all broker-dealers transacting a securities business in interstate commerce. [SEA §15] This requirement applies to essentially all

broker-dealers, including those in the over-the-counter market, because it is difficult for a broker to avoid using instrumentalities of interstate commerce.

a. **Self-regulation required:** [§1696] In addition to registering with the S.E.C., broker-dealers must be members of a national securities association which is itself registered with the S.E.C. Only one such association exists today; that association is the National Association of Securities Dealers ("NASD").

b. **Authority of the NASD:** [§1697] The NASD is authorized by the Act to adopt and enforce rules for member broker-dealers addressing a wide variety of matters including training, broker qualifications, and capital requirements. [SEA §15(b)] The S.E.C., however, continues to exercise authority over both the NASD itself, and over NASD members. [SEA §15A]

(1) *The NASD's proposed rule additions, deletions, or changes must first be approved by the S.E.C.* [SEA §19(b)]

(2) *In addition, the S.E.C. may exercise its power to abrogate, add to, delete, or amend the rules* of the NASD when necessary to ensure its fair administration and to accomplish the purposes of the Act. [SEA §19(c)]

(3) *If the NASD imposes any disciplinary sanction on any member, or denies membership* to a broker-dealer, the NASD must inform the S.E.C. The S.E.C. may then review the actions taken by the NASD, either on its own motion or on the motion of an aggrieved party. [SEA §19(d)]

(4) *Finally, the S.E.C. has the power to sanction NASD members* and persons associated with members. [SEA §19(h)]

5. **Regulation of the "Penny Stock" Market:** [§1698] A significant segment of the OTC market is composed of "penny stocks," low-priced (under $5 per share) stocks of small, new companies with little or no operating history, but supposedly glowing futures. Congress reacted to widespread fraud and abuse in the penny stock market by passing the Securities Enforcement Remedies and Penny Stock Reform Act of 1990.

a. **Administrative sanctions and registration provisions:** [§1699] The 1990 Act added several administrative remedies to those previously available to the S.E.C. (*see supra*, §§1481 *et seq.*) and added new and stringent regulations governing the distribution of securities issued by "blank check" companies (*see supra*, §§296-301).

b. **Broker-dealer regulation under the 1990 Act:** [§1700] The 1990 Act also provides for extensive regulation of brokers and dealers who deal heavily in penny stocks, and authorizes the S.E.C. to make rules regulating participants in the penny stock market. [SEA §15(g)]

(1) **Suspensions and bars:** [§1701] Under the 1990 Act, the S.E.C. may suspend or bar persons from "being associated with any broker or dealer, or from participating in an offering of penny stock," if they have violated the 1933 or 1934 Acts in connection with a penny stock offering. [SEA §15(b)(6)(A)] It is illegal for such persons to work for a broker or dealer,

or participate in a penny stock offering, in violation of the bar. [SEA §15(b)(6)(B)(i)] Likewise, it is illegal for a broker or dealer to hire such persons. [SEA §15(b)(6)(B)(ii)]

(2) **Risk disclosure document:** [§1702] A broker or dealer selling penny stock to a retail customer is required to deliver a document containing the information in Schedule 15G, which sets out in detail many of the risks and dangers associated with an investment in penny stocks. Perhaps anticipating the response of penny-stock dealers, Schedule 15G includes as an instruction the statement that "No material may be given to a customer that is intended in any way to detract from, rebut or contradict the Schedule." [SEA Rule 15g-2]

(3) **Written purchase agreement:** [§1703] The dealer must obtain from the customer a written agreement to purchase the stock, setting forth the identity and quantity of the penny stock to be purchased. [SEA Rule 15g-9(a)(2)(ii)]

(4) **Price information:** [§1704] Penny-stock dealers must also disclose to the customer available "inside" price information (the *wholesale* bid and asked prices) for the security sold. If the inside price is not available (*e.g.,* because the dealer has not consistently traded the security with other dealers), that fact and the reasons therefor must be disclosed. [SEA Rule 15g-3]

(5) **Dealer compensation disclosure:** [§1705] Penny-stock dealers must disclose to the customer the aggregate amount of all compensation received in connection with the penny stock transaction. [SEA Rule 15g-4]

(6) **Salesperson compensation disclosure:** [§1706] In addition to disclosing the dealer's compensation, *supra*, the individual salesperson must disclose to the customer the total amount of compensation that she will receive from all sources (including the issuer or other promoters) and *that is determined* (*i.e.,* that can be calculated) *at the time of the transaction.* [SEA Rule 15g-5]

(7) **Account statements:** [§1707] Penny-stock dealers must provide their customers with a monthly account statement setting out price information for each penny stock owned by the customer. [SEA Rule 15g-6]

(8) **Customer suitability:** [§1708] Finally, before a broker-dealer is permitted to engage in any penny stock transaction with a customer, the *dealer must approve the customer's account.* This requires that the dealer obtain from the customer *information about the customer's financial situation, investment experience, and investment objectives.* Once that information is obtained, the dealer must determine, based on the information, that penny-stock investments are suitable for the customer, and that the customer is capable of evaluating the risks of such an investment. Finally, the customer's financial information must be summarized in a written document, and presented to the customer for signature, along with the statement that the broker-dealer is required by law to do so. [SEA Rule 15g-9]

## C. REGULATION OF MARKET MANIPULATION AND STABILIZATION
[§1709]

The previous two sections of this Summary discussed the general regulations relating to the two principal markets for the trading of securities—the national stock exchanges and the over-the-counter market. This section concerns the prohibitions in the 1934 Act against manipulation of the trading that occurs in these markets.

1. **Regulation of Short Sales:** [§1710] Short sales are one of the more controversial kinds of trading activities taking place in the securities markets. Although an outright ban on short sales was considered in 1934, ultimately Congress decided to let the S.E.C. determine what kinds of short-selling practices to forbid.

   a. **Short sale defined:** [§1711] A short sale is a sale of securities that the seller does not own, or any sale consummated by the delivery of a security borrowed by or for the seller. [SEA Rule 3b-3]

   b. **Why sell short:** [§1712] Traders sell securities short because they believe that the price of the security will drop. Thus, a short sale is a "bet" that the market price of the securities will fall, and is sometimes cited as one way in which a sophisticated trader can make money even in a falling market.

      (1) **Example:** Cathy does not own any Acme Corp. stock, but she believes that Acme stock will fall in price. Her trading strategy, then, might be to sell short Acme stock. She will sell, say, 1,000 shares of Acme stock today. Under normal market practice, her sale will not "settle" (and Cathy will not have to deliver the Acme stock) until three business days after the contract date. If Cathy is correct, and the price of Acme stock falls, she can "cover" her sale of three days ago with cheaper stock purchased today.

         (a) **Note:** An alert reader may wonder how Cathy can obtain Acme stock for delivery the same day in order to cover her earlier short sale. The answer lies in the ability of traders to borrow stock from one another: In order to implement her short-sale strategy, Cathy will borrow enough shares of Acme stock to cover the short sale. This borrowed stock is available to her when she needs it, at the then-current market price.

   c. **Dangers of short sales:** [§1713] Short sales increase the volatility of market prices. That is, it is relatively easy and cheap to sell short a large quantity of an issuer's shares, and if the sales are accompanied by rumor-mongering, it is probable that other investors, hearing of the sales and the rumors, will choose to sell their shares. The effect of all this is to drive down the price, which of course fits the short-seller's strategy perfectly—the lower the price goes, the more easily and cheaply the short sales can be covered.

      (1) **"Bear raids":** [§1714] A bear raid is a concerted effort to drive down the price of a security, using techniques similar to those described immediately above.

      (2) **Dangers to short sellers:** [§1715] Selling short may be an appropriate strategy for a sophisticated investor, but it is seldom the best choice for

others. The chief danger is that the short seller is exposed to liability that increases every time the price of the security goes up, until the sale is covered. Unlike an investor with a "long" position, whose risk is limited to the amount invested, the short seller's risk is hard to measure and is limited only by the potential increases in the price of the security.

d. **Regulation of short selling:** [§1716]  To mitigate somewhat the potential dangers of unlimited short selling, the S.E.C. has promulgated several rules governing the practice.

(1) **Short sales must be identified:** [§1717]  First, all sales of exchange-traded securities (whether or not taking place on the exchange) must be identified as "long" or "short." [SEA Rule 10a-1(c)]

(2) **Short sales prohibited on downtick:** [§1718]  Next, short sales are not permitted to be made at a price lower than the last reported sale price. In addition, short sales are not permitted to be made at the last sale price, *unless* that price is higher than the immediately preceding reported sale price.

(a) **Example:** At 11:15 a.m., Acme stock sold for 11-3/4. At 11:20, Acme stock sold for 11-5/8. At this point, no short sales are permitted, because the last reported sale price (11-5/8) is lower than the immediately preceding price (11-3/4). (This is called a "downtick" or "minus tick.")

(b) **Example:** Same facts as above, but at 11:25, Acme stock sold for 11-5/8 (again). At this point, short sales are still not permitted, because the last reported sale price (11-5/8) was the same as the preceding price, and that price was lower than the next preceding price (11-3/4). (This is called a "zero-minus tick.")

(c) **Example:** Same facts as above, but at 11:30, Acme stock sold for 11-3/4. At this point, short sales are permitted, because the price for the sale (11-3/4) is higher than the immediately preceding price (11-5/8). (This is called an "uptick" or "plus tick.")

(d) **Example:** Same facts as above, but at 11:35, Acme stock sold for 11-3/4 (again). At this point, short sales are permitted, because the price for the sale (11-3/4) is the same as the immediately preceding price, and that price is higher than the next preceding price (11-5/8). (This is called a "zero-plus tick.")

(3) **Short sales prohibited during distributions:** [§1719]  During a distribution of securities (*see supra*, §§67 *et seq.*) the influx of new securities into the market tends to depress the price. Because the price is likely to decline at least a little, the short-seller's risk is reduced. Short sales were thus more likely to occur during a distribution. On the other hand, short sales during a distribution may make it impossible for the issuer to complete the distribution. In response to the NASD's request, the S.E.C. adopted rule 10b-21. The rule applies after the filing of a registration statement or notification under regulation A relating to the class of

securities sold short, and prohibits covering a short sale with securities purchased from an underwriter or broker participating in an offering.

e. **Comment:** The short sale regulations may discourage abuses, but they cannot prevent them. Virtually anything that can be accomplished by selling short can also be accomplished by using derivative securities, such as options, which do not carry similar restrictions. Nevertheless, the short-sale regulations may be valuable if only because they tend to inhibit short sales by investors who lack the financial sophistication to understand and manage the risks that short sales entail.

2. **Prohibition of Market Manipulation:** [§1720] Market manipulation is an attempt to set stock prices—or other important criteria of stock market performance, such as the volume of shares traded—by entering into transactions for the specific purpose of such manipulation. There is a series of provisions in the 1934 Act aimed at prohibiting market manipulation.

   a. **Manipulation of listed securities prohibited—section 9:** [§1721] Section 9(a) of the 1934 Act prohibits "any person" from using the instrumentalities of interstate commerce or the facilities of "any national securities exchange" to engage in certain specified manipulative activities with respect to securities listed on a national securities exchange. Although SEA section 9 applies only to listed securities, its prohibitions are incorporated into sections 10(b) and 15(c), and thus the substance of the Act's anti-manipulation provisions applies to both listed and unlisted securities. [*See* S.E.C. v. Resch-Cassin & Co., 362 F. Supp. 964 (S.D.N.Y. 1973)]

      (1) **Per se violations:** [§1722] A series of "per se violations" are listed in section 9. These include activities such as attempting to create a misleading appearance of active trading; effecting a series of transactions on the exchange creating the appearance of active trading, to induce a purchase or sale of a security by others; or disseminating misleading information with respect to the listed security. [SEA §9(a)(1)-(5)]

      (2) **Violation of S.E.C. rules:** [§1723] Other types of market transactions may also violate the 1934 Act if effected in contravention of rules adopted by the S.E.C. [SEA §9(a)(6), (b), (c)]

         (a) **Section 9(a)(6):** Section 9(a)(6) relates to "market stabilization," and makes it unlawful to engage in transactions in a listed stock for the purpose of "pegging, fixing, or stabilizing the price of such security" in contravention of such rules as may be adopted by the S.E.C.

         (b) **Note:** Rather than adopt rules regulating stabilization pursuant to section 9, the S.E.C. regulates stabilization in rules 10b-6, 10b-7, and 10b-8. (*See infra,* §1734.)

      (3) **Limited use of section 9:** [§1724] Section 9 has received only limited use by the S.E.C., due to several factors.

         (a) **Applies only to listed securities:** [§1725] One reason for its limited use is that section 9 applies only to securities listed on a national securities exchange. Other sections that are used because of their broader coverage are rule 10b-5, which applies to both listed and over-the-counter securities, and rule 15c1-2 (which is limited, however, to broker-dealer transactions).

(b) **Must show "intent" or "willfulness":** [§1726] Under section 9, the S.E.C. must prove the defendant's "intent" or "purpose" to engage in an unlawful act before it can obtain injunctive relief. And a plaintiff in a private damage action must be able to show defendant's "willfulness." [SEA §9(e)]

b. **General prohibition against market manipulation—rule 10b-5:** [§1727] As noted above, rule 10b-5—a general prohibition against fraud in the purchase and sale of securities—applies to both listed and over-the-counter securities. Because of this, and the burdensome requirement of proving intent or willfulness under section 9, rule 10b-5 has had broad application in market manipulation cases.

(1) **And note:** The specific prohibitions of section 9 with respect to listed securities have been held incorporated under rule 10b-5. [S.E.C. v. Resch-Cassin & Co., *supra*]

(2) **But note:** Since the *Hochfelder* decision now requires at least reckless conduct to prove a 10b-5 case, section 9 may be used more frequently in market manipulation cases in the future. (*See supra*, §885.)

c. **Liability provisions applicable to broker-dealers—section 15(c):** [§1728] Section 15(c) is a general fraud provision worded similarly to section 9 and rule 10b-5, but specifically applicable to transactions involving broker-dealers in the over-the-counter market. (*See supra*, §1720.)

(1) **S.E.C. rules:** [§1729] Pursuant to section 15(c), the S.E.C. has adopted rules prohibiting certain manipulative and deceptive practices in securities trading. [SEA Rules 15c1-2 - 15c1-9]

(2) **No "willfulness" element:** [§1730] Note that the specific element of "willfulness" (required in a private damage action brought under section 9) is *not* present in a section 15(c) action. [*See* SEA §15(c); *infra*, §§1777 *et seq*.]

(3) **S.E.C. enforcement powers:** [§1731] In addition to private damage actions that may be brought under section 15(c), the S.E.C. has specific enforcement powers against broker-dealers for any violations of its rules adopted pursuant to section 15(c). In addition, it may review disciplinary proceedings brought by the NASD against any of its broker-dealer members. (*See supra*, §1632.)

d. **Application of anti-manipulation provisions:** [§1732] Cases arising out of stock market manipulation usually involve people who have ready access to the market mechanism (such as broker-dealers). Such persons are in a position to run the price of a security up (*e.g.*, by devices such as false market quotes) while at the same time refusing to accept sell orders from customers owning the security. The broker-dealers can then sell their own positions in the security at a very substantial profit, thereafter allowing the market for the security to collapse.

(1) **Methods of attack:** [§1733]  In these situations, the S.E.C. might attempt to attack the manipulation scheme directly under one of the many antifraud provisions discussed above. More often, an action will be brought for some technical violation of the securities acts (due to the less demanding requirements of proof), and the offending broker-dealer will be disciplined.

(a) **Example—section 9:** Defendant, a brokerage firm, ran the price of a stock up by 75% in 20 days by putting successively higher bids in the quotation sheets, giving the public false indications of trading activity. After defendant sold its interest, the price of the stock collapsed. The court found defendant liable for a violation of section 9(a)(2). [S.E.C. v. Resch-Cassin & Co., *supra*]

(b) **Example—section 15:** Company X sold $300,000 of its common stock to the public in a regulation A offering. The underwriter of the securities issue was the defendant broker-dealer and its branch office manager (who was also on the board of directors of Company X). Personnel of the defendant purchased a significant number of X shares, gave out false information about the prospects of X to the defendant's customers, and arbitrarily raised the daily quotation price. Furthermore, no sale orders were accepted from customers unless orders to buy an equal amount of shares were available at the time (thus permitting an artificial market price to exist). Finally, defendant's personnel sold all their own shares in preference to sell orders of other customers, and then allowed the market for X stock to collapse. [*In re* Shearson, Hammill & Co., SEA Release No. 7743 (1964)]

1) The S.E.C. found numerous violations of the securities acts, including section 5 of the 1933 Act and SEA Rule 15c1-2. The agency brought an action for suspension of the offending brokers associated with the defendant under sections 15(b), 15A, and 19(a)(3) of the 1934 Act.

2) In addition, members of the defendant's executive committee were suspended for a substantial period of time. This sanction was imposed, rather than a general broker-dealer suspension or revocation, because the offending sales personnel had already been terminated by the firm, the firm was either involved in lawsuits or had settled the claims of customers who had been hurt, and the firm had instituted closer supervision practices. Nevertheless, the S.E.C. believed that the public interest still demanded the sanction imposed as a penalty for the lax supervision methods employed by the firm.

3. **Regulation of Market Stabilization:** [§1734]  Market stabilization is a specific form of market manipulation and, as such, is regulated under the 1934 Act. [*See* SEA §9(a)(6)]

a. **"Stabilization" defined:** [§1735] "Stabilization" is an attempt to maintain a fixed market price for a security by purchasing all of the shares that are offered at a price lower than the desired price.

(1) **Occurs in original public distributions:** [§1736] Market stabilization usually occurs in connection with an original public distribution of shares, where the underwriters stabilize the price until the entire issue is sold. It is critical to maintain the market for a new issue at the offering price until the entire issue is sold out, particularly in situations where securities of the same class are already outstanding.

(2) **May determine success of public offering:** [§1737] Stabilization can be extremely important to a successful public offering of securities, which ultimately depends on whether the underwriter is able to sell the securities to the public at the offering price.

 (a) **Note:** Even when the underwriter is able to quickly sell the entire issue, there is *always* some immediate reselling by purchasers before the entire issue is sold out. The early purchasers may change their minds about owning the stock, or they may have bought purely for speculation, with the hope of selling immediately for a profit in the case of an early price rise.

 (b) **And note:** If such reselling is not absorbed through public buying pressure, the market price of the remaining stock will drop below the initial offering price and the entire issue will not be sold at the price originally set. For this reason, the ability of the underwriters to purchase the resold shares as they come to the market, thereby stabilizing the market at the initial offering price, is of critical importance to a successful public offering.

b. **Arguments against stabilization:** [§1738] The argument against stabilization is that it is a form of manipulation, and when the manipulable activity ceases, the price returns to its natural level.

(1) **Example:** The classic manipulation case involves a defendant who artificially raises the price of a security, gets people to purchase it at this price, and then withdraws from the market by selling her shares of the manipulated security. As soon as the defendant withdraws, the price goes down.

(2) **And note:** In the public distribution context, stabilizing can result in losses to purchasers, just as classic manipulation does. [*See* SEA Release No. 34-2446 (1940)]

c. **Regulation of stabilization in public distributions:** [§1739] The 1934 Act prohibits transactions for the purpose of pegging or stabilizing the price of a security *only* when such transactions are in violation of the rules and regulations adopted by the S.E.C. [SEA §9(a)(6)] The S.E.C. has adopted several rules that apply specifically to stabilization in distribution situations. [SEA Rules 10b-6, -7, -8]

(1) **Trading generally prohibited:** [§1740] Regulation of stabilization begins with a fundamental rule: Any issuer, underwriter, prospective

underwriter, or dealer who is a participant in a distribution is prohibited from bidding for or purchasing (i) any security that is the subject of the distribution, (ii) any security of the same class and series, or (iii) any right to purchase any such security, *except* in conformity with the stabilization rules set forth in SEA Rules 10b-7 or 10b-8. [SEA Rule 10b-6] The remaining details of this prohibition on trading are discussed below.

(2) **When prohibition becomes effective**

    (a) **Purchases on an exchange:** [§1741] All persons who have *agreed to become dealers,* and *all prospective underwriters*, are prohibited from trading in the securities described in the paragraph above (*i.e.*, the securities being distributed, securities of the same class and series, or rights to purchase such securities), beginning:

        1) **Penny stock:** [§1742] If the securities being distributed have a price of less than $5 per share, or a public float of less than 400,000 shares:

            (i) *Unsolicited purchases* are permitted at any time before the later of the date the distribution begins or the date the person becomes a participant in the distribution.

            (ii) *Solicited purchases* are permitted up to nine days before the later of the date the distribution begins or the date the person becomes a participant in the distribution.

              a) **Note:** While the securities subject to this rule are often referred to as "penny stock," they do not necessarily meet the 1934 Act's definition of penny stock, which does not specify minimum public float. (For a discussion of penny stocks and broker-dealer regulation, *see supra,* §§1700-1708.)

        2) **Other stock:** [§1743] If the securities being distributed have a price of $5 or more per share, *and* a public float of more than 400,000 shares:

            a) *Unsolicited purchases* are permitted at any time before the later of the date the distribution begins or the date the person becomes a participant in the distribution.

            b) *Solicited purchases* are permitted up to two days before the later of the date the distribution begins or the date the person becomes a participant in the distribution.

    (b) **Purchases over-the-counter:** [§1744] The rules for purchases on an exchange apply also to purchases on NASDAQ. However, an additional exception to the prohibition may benefit underwriters of NASDAQ securities that are also NASDAQ market makers for those securities. Under the exchange-trading rules, an underwriter would have to withdraw from the NASDAQ market in the security two or nine days before the distribution commences. SEA rule

10b-6A, however, provides that a NASDAQ market maker may continue to make a market in the security even though it is also an underwriter. It must, however, deal at the prices set by other market makers, and it is limited in the amount traded per day to 30% of its average daily volume for the security in question. [SEA Rule 10b-6A]

    (c) **Stabilizing purchases:** [§1745]  Recall that these rules collectively compose the *general* prohibition against participants in a distribution purchasing securities of the kind distributed. ***None of the foregoing applies to purchases made to stabilize prices.*** Stabilizing purchases must be made under rules 10b-7 and 10b-8, and are legal if made in accordance with those rules.

  (3) **Termination of general trading prohibition:** [§1746]  The prohibition against unregulated bids and purchases continues as to each underwriter or dealer until he has completed his participation in the distribution. [SEA Rule 10b-6(a)]

    (a) **Issuer:** [§1747]  The restrictions on the issuer continue until the distribution is completed.

    (b) **Underwriters:** [§1748]  The restrictions apply to the underwriter until it has distributed its participation, including all other securities of the same class acquired in connection with the participation, and until any stabilization or trading agreements with respect to the distribution are terminated. [SEA Rule 10b-6(c)(3)]

    (c) **Participating dealers:** [§1749]  Also, although the prohibition normally terminates with respect to participating dealers when they finish distributing their allotment, a dealer is still prohibited from making a market in the security distributed if it is acting at the instigation of the underwriter, knowing that the underwriter is having trouble distributing the entire issue. [S.E.C. v. Resch-Cassin & Co., *supra*, §1733]

  (4) **Stabilization permitted to prevent price decline:** [§1750]  Stabilization in support of a public distribution is permitted "for the purpose of preventing or retarding a decline in the open market price of the security being distributed." [SEA Rule 10b-7]

    (a) **Stabilizing price level:** [§1751]  Stabilization may not be commenced at a price higher than the highest current independent bid price. If no bona fide market for the security exists, stabilizing may commence at the price at which the security is initially offered to the public. [SEA Rule 10b-7]

      1) **Stabilizing bid may not be raised:** [§1752]  In addition, the stabilizer is not permitted to raise the price at which the security is stabilized. The stabilizer can follow the market down (attempting to stabilize it), but he cannot follow the market up, attempting to support it at higher and higher levels. [SEA Rule 10b-7(j)]

2) **Stabilizing "at the market" prohibited:** [§1753]  Similarly, stabilizing at the "market price" is illegal. For a buyer to represent that its stabilizing bid is "at the market" is misleading, since the market price is itself (at least in part) the result of the stabilized bid. Thus, stabilizing bids are only appropriate when made for specific amounts (*e.g.*, for $12 per share). [SEA Rule 10b-7(g)]

(b) **Disclosure of stabilizing:** [§1754]  The fact that the underwriters may be stabilizing the price of an issued security must be disclosed to a purchaser at or before the completion of the transaction. In addition, if stabilization is contemplated, a specific disclosure of that fact must be made in the prospectus. The stabilizer must also report all actual stabilizing transactions to the S.E.C. [SEA Rules 10b-7(k), 17a-2; Regulation S-K, Item 502]

(5) **Stabilization problem situations:** [§1755]  Interpreting S.E.C. rules in a manner consistent with legitimate stabilization has caused problems in several contexts:

(a) **Offerings of warrants or convertible issues:** [§1756]  Where warrants to purchase another security are issued, or where securities convertible into another security are issued, the offering technically continues as to the underlying stock as long as the warrants or convertible securities are outstanding (*i.e.*, unconverted). Because the offering is deemed to continue, the purchase prohibitions of rule 10b-6 remain in effect until all the warrants are exercised or until all the convertible securities are converted.

1) **Exemption for "technical" offerings:** [§1757]  SEA rule 10b-6(f), however, contains an exemption that permits purchases during the time that a distribution continues, if the distribution would exist *"solely because the issuer . . . has outstanding securities which are . . . convertible into, or exchangeable or exercisable for,"* the security being distributed. The net result is that, although an offering is technically under way as long as convertible securities or warrants are outstanding, the exemption protects purchasers, underwriters, and others who are prohibited from buying during a distribution.

(b) **"Shelf registrations":** [§1758]  The same problem exists with "shelf registrations" where the securities to be sold are offered over a significant period of time.

1) **Example:** Certain shareholders of Company S stock registered a secondary offering of their stock, to be sold at *various times* (thus making the offering a "shelf registration") at the "market price" by a specific broker-dealer, Jaffee & Co. The broker began to sell the stock, and while the offering was in progress, Jaffee himself (as an individual) made purchases of the stock. Likewise, other shelf shareholders made market purchases at times when they personally were not selling, but when the shelf shareholders as a group were still engaged in distributing the

stock. The court held that Jaffee's activities violated rule 10b-6, and noted that as long as the selling group was engaged in the distribution, the danger of manipulation existed.

    a) **Note:** Since the offering was at the market, no stabilizing was permissible. [SEA Rule 10b-7(g); *see supra,* §1753]

    b) **Coordination among shelf shareholders:** [§1759] Probably the biggest problem raised by *Jaffee* was the suggestion that to avoid the prohibition on purchases during a distribution, the activities of the shelf shareholders had to be highly coordinated. That is, as long as *any* shelf shareholder was selling, the distribution was not over and it was unlawful for any other shelf shareholder to purchase.

2) **Modern S.E.C. view:** [§1760] In 1986 the S.E.C. revised its interpretation of rule 10b-6 so that the time periods specified in the rule (two days/nine days; *see supra,* §§1742-1743) apply only to the individual activities of that shareholder. The same is true for the time the distribution is considered to end—for each shareholder, it ends when she has distributed all *her* shares.

    a) **Exception for affiliated shareholders:** [§1761] The revised interpretation, however, does not apply to shareholders who are "affiliated purchasers" with the issuer or with other shareholders. "Affiliated purchasers" are defined as purchasers who either are acting in concert with the specified party, or are in a normal affiliate relationship with the party.

d. **Stabilization in nonpublic distributions:** [§1762] Section 9(a)(6) indicates that stabilization is prohibited only when the S.E.C. has adopted rules prohibiting it, and the S.E.C. rules as to stabilizations (SEA Rules 10b-6 through 10b-8) all concern stabilization in connection with a public distribution. It is therefore unclear whether stabilizing for purposes other than public distribution is unlawful.

    (1) **Example:** A person who pledges stock for a loan might want to purchase additional shares on the market to maintain the price of the stock she had pledged so that she will not have to put up additional collateral.

    (2) **General fraud provisions:** [§1763] Even if SEA Rules 10b-6 through 10b-8 do not apply to nondistribution stabilizing transactions, the S.E.C. might penalize stabilization with the more general fraud provisions of the 1934 Act, such as section 15(c) or rule 10b-5, on the theory that stabilization is merely a special case of manipulation.

4. **The "Hot Issue" Problem**

a. **"Hot issue" defined:** [§1764] A "hot issue" is a security offered through a public distribution for which there is tremendous demand. Thus, a "hot issue" will typically be over-subscribed; *i.e.,* there will be more initial offers to purchase than there are shares available.

b. **"Hot issue" problems:** [§1765] Normally, a "hot issue" rises immediately to a premium price over the initial offering price at which it comes to the market. Underwriters and dealers may attempt to profit from this situation, to the detriment of the public, by:

(1) *Holding back a portion of the initial issue* to be sold, so that it can be sold later at higher prices;

(2) *Allocating part of the issue to employees, relatives,* etc., for later sale; or

(3) *Allocating part of the issue to other broker-dealers*—who will immediately put quotes in the quotation services raising the price of the issue—and then, as demand rises, all parties (*i.e.,* the underwriters and cooperating broker-dealers) will sell to the public at a substantial premium over the stated offering price.

c. **Violation of the securities acts:** [§1766] The S.E.C. considers all of the above practices to be violations of the securities acts. [SEA Release No. 6097 (1959)]

(1) **Note:** Possible violations include violation of sections 11 and 12(2) of the 1933 Act for misrepresenting that the offering will be made *to the public*, at the offering price, and for not identifying the trading firms as underwriters; and the antifraud provisions of the 1934 Act, including rules 10b-5, 10b-6, and 15c1-8.

(2) **Compare:** It is not a violation of the "hot issue" rules for the dealers to sell the issue to relatives and friends where the stock (which appreciated rapidly) was held for investment (at least six months) and maintained or increased in price even after the original purchasers sold (*i.e.,* no one was left "holding the bag"). [*See In re* Institutional Securities of Colorado, S.E.C. Admin. Proc. File No. 3-5104 (1978)]

d. **"Free-riding" prohibited:** [§1767] "Free riders" are another of the problems associated with hot issues. Free riding broadly refers to several different types of broker-dealer misconduct, all of which involve "riding" the market upward as the price of a hot issue rises. The NASD has adopted rules prohibiting free riding. [*See* NASD Manual (CCH) ¶2151.06] The NASD rules describe free riding as, among other things, holding back part of the allotment of the securities, selling the securities (at the offering price) to a person affiliated with the broker-dealer, or selling to others upon whom the broker-dealer wishes to bestow a favor. [*See id.*]

## D. REGULATION OF TRADING ACTIVITIES OF BROKER-DEALERS

1. **Registration of Broker-Dealers with the S.E.C.:** [§1768] The 1934 Act provides for registration with the S.E.C. of all broker-dealers who undertake to effect security transactions in interstate commerce (unless they deal exclusively in exempt securities).

   a. **Definition of broker and dealer:** [§1769] Section 3 of the 1934 Act defines "broker" and "dealer."

(1) *A broker* is a person engaged "in the business of" effecting transactions in securities for the account of others. [SEA §3(a)(4)]

(2) *A dealer* is a person engaged "in the business of" buying *and* selling securities for his own account, but does not include such persons when they are not doing so as part of "a regular business." [SEA §3(a)(5)]

(3) *What is a "regular business"* is a fact question, but the buying and selling would have to be fairly regular to qualify. Thus, a single, isolated transaction does not qualify. [De Bruin v. Andromeda Broadcasting Systems Inc., 465 F. Supp. 1276 (D. Nev. 1979)]

b. **A "security" must be sold:** [§1770]  For the provisions of the 1934 Act relating to brokers and dealers to apply, a "security," as defined in the 1934 Act, must be involved. The definition in the 1934 Act is only slightly different from that of the 1933 Act. [*See* SEA §3(a)(10)]

c. **Requirement of registration:** [§1771]  Section 15(a) of the 1934 Act forbids a broker or dealer who does any interstate business to use the mails or any means or instrumentality of interstate commerce to effect any transaction in, or to induce or attempt to induce the purchase or sale of, securities (other than securities exempted under the 1934 Act), unless the broker or dealer is registered with the S.E.C. under section 15(a) of the Act.

(1) **Note:** This section exempts broker-dealers *whose business is exclusively* intrastate. The interpretation of what is intrastate turns principally on the location of the broker-dealer's customers. [SEA §15(a)(1)]

d. **Regulation by the S.E.C.:** [§1772]  Under section 15(b) of the 1934 Act, the S.E.C. has established qualification standards for registration of all brokers and dealers and any persons associated with them. Registration subjects the registrant to certain standards of operational capability, training, experience, and competence. It also subjects the broker-dealer to the requirement of passing certain examinations relating to the securities business and to maintaining certain financial stability standards. Registered broker-dealers must also file periodic reports with the S.E.C. Finally, the S.E.C. may, on notice and after a hearing, censure, suspend, or revoke the registration of any broker or dealer for statutory violations.

2. **Sources of Authority to Regulate:** [§1773]  Besides direct regulation by the S.E.C., broker-dealers may also be subject to indirect regulation through the regulation of organizations of which the broker-dealers are members.

a. **Self-regulation:** [§1774]  The 1934 Act provides for the self-regulation of registered broker-dealers through a registered national securities association, the National Association of Securities Dealers ("NASD"), subject to supervision and review by the S.E.C. [SEA §15(a); *and see supra,* §§1695 *et seq.*]

b. **Regulation by national stock exchanges:** [§1775]  As noted above (*see supra,* §1627), the 1934 Act requires national securities exchanges to regulate their members, and the S.E.C. exercises supervisory power over such regulation.

c. **Regulation of investment advisors:** [§1776] An "investment adviser" is one who engages in the business of advising others whether to invest in, purchase, or sell securities. While investment advisers do not perform the same functions as broker-dealers, they do occupy an important position in the securities business where they are trusted by, and able to take advantage of, those purchasing and selling securities. For this reason, the S.E.C. regulates the activities of such advisers pursuant to the Investment Advisers Act of 1940.

3. **Regulation Under General Antifraud Provisions:** [§1777] The 1934 Act contains several general antifraud provisions (*e.g.,* rules 10b-5 and 15c1-2) that regulate the activities of broker-dealers. Section 17(a) of the 1933 Act (*see supra,* §718) is similar to these antifraud provisions; its language is essentially the language used in rules 10b-5 and 15c1-2.

a. **Comparison of antifraud provisions:** [§1778] The differences between the three antifraud provisions are as follows:

| Provision | Applicable to Sales of Securities? | Applicable to Purchases? | Applicable to Broker-Dealers? | Applicable to Any Person? |
|---|---|---|---|---|
| SA §17(a) | Yes | No | Yes | Yes |
| SEA Rule 10b-5 | Yes | Yes | Yes | Yes |
| SEA Rule 15c1-2 | Yes | Yes | Yes | No (only to broker dealers) |

b. **Requirement of intent:** [§1779] The language of the above provisions seems to require that actions brought thereunder be based on a showing of actual fraud by the defendant (*i.e.,* intentional fraudulent conduct or misrepresentations) for plaintiff to recover. However, the Supreme Court has held that in S.E.C. civil injunctive actions, a cause of action may be proved only by showing scienter under section 17(a)(1), but that negligence is sufficient under section 17(a)(2), and (3). (*See* the discussion *supra,* §723.) Also, there is considerable doubt as to whether a private cause of action will be implied pursuant to section 17(a) (*see supra,* §721).

(1) **"Shingle theory":** [§1780] Also, the courts have held that when a broker-dealer goes into business (*i.e.,* "hangs out its shingle"), it impliedly represents that it will deal fairly and competently with its customers, and that there will be an adequate basis for any statement (*e.g.,* as to a security's value) or recommendations it makes to its customers. This "shingle theory" sometimes allows a court to find a cause of action against a broker-dealer under one of the three statutes mentioned above where an intentional misstatement or omission by the broker-dealer might not otherwise be proved. [Charles Hughes & Co. v. S.E.C., 139 F.2d 434 (2d Cir. 1943)] In effect, the "intent" is proved by showing that defendant intentionally *did an act* that was unlawful, not that defendant intentionally committed fraud.

(a) **Example:** Where a broker-dealer made optimistic statements to its customers about a security without having any actual basis for doing so, the broker-dealer was held liable. [*In re* Alexander Reid & Co., SEA Release No. 6727 (1962)]

    (b) **Example:** Likewise where a broker-dealer sold securities to a customer at a price far in excess of their market value, without disclosing the actual market value, it was held liable. [Charles Hughes & Co. v. S.E.C., *supra*]

    (c) **Compare:** A broker-dealer's implied representation about the value of a security probably does not amount to an absolute warranty, giving rise to liability if the security turns out to be worth less than the price the customer paid for it. Thus, the broker-dealer is probably not liable for unavoidable errors of fact. However, the broker-dealer must act "reasonably" and in "good faith"—*i.e.,* the broker-dealer must at least not be negligent in recommending the security to the client. [*See* S.E.C. v. Capital Gains Research Bureau, 375 U.S. 180 (1963)—action under the Investment Advisers Act of 1940; Charles Hughes & Co. v. S.E.C., *supra*]

  (2) **Not as rigidly applied in private actions:** [§1781] The "shingle theory" is probably not as rigidly applied in private actions against defendant broker-dealers; *i.e.,* in private actions, the plaintiff may have to prove actual fraudulent intent. However, in disciplinary actions brought by the S.E.C., the "shingle theory" is usually vigorously enforced. [Hanly v. S.E.C., 415 F.2d 589 (2d Cir. 1969)]

4. **Regulating Conflicts of Interest:** [§1782] The S.E.C. has focused on several basic areas in its supervision of broker-dealers: situations where there is a conflict of interest between the broker-dealer and the client's financial interest; situations where the broker-dealer makes a recommendation to a client without adequate information; and situations where the broker-dealer has failed to adequately supervise the activities of those involved in his firm. This section discusses common conflict of interest problems.

  a. **Commissions and markup policies:** [§1783] One conflict of interest inherent in the relationship between the broker-dealer and its client is that the broker-dealer naturally wants to charge as high a commission as possible on security transactions and the client of course wants to pay as low a commission as possible.

    (1) **NASD policy regarding markups:** [§1784] The NASD has adopted a policy that its members may neither effect securities transactions at a price "not reasonably related to the current market price of the security" nor charge an unreasonable commission. [NASD Rules, art. III, §§1, 4]

      (a) **Five percent markup policy:** [§1785] The NASD has indicated that a markup (*i.e.,* an increase over the market price to dealers or over the dealer's actual cost) of 5% (10% in the case of low-priced securities) would probably not violate sections 1 and 4 of the NASD rules. The following factors, however, are to be considered in determining whether a markup is "reasonable":

        (i) *The type of* security involved;

(ii) *The availability* of the security in the market generally;

(iii) *The unit price* of the security;

(iv) *The total amount of dollars involved* in the transaction;

(v) *Whether disclosure of the markup is made* to the customer;

(vi) *The pattern of the broker-dealer's markups*; and

(vii) *The types of services and facilities* offered by the broker-dealer.

[*See generally* NASD Notice to Members 92-16 (1992); Kevin B. Waide, 51 S.E.C. 252 (1992); LSCO Securities., Inc., SEA Release No. 34-28,994 (1991); Alstead Dempsey & Co., 47 S.E.C. 1034 (1984)]

(b) **Markup base:** [§1786]  The NASD rules indicate that the markup is to be based on the "market price" *or,* where evidence of market price is not available, on the broker-dealer's own contemporaneous cost.

1) **Example:** Appropriate markup bases include (i) the broker-dealer's cost for security purchases and sales occurring on the same day, and (ii) the "ask quotations" published in the quotation sheets of the National Daily Quotations Bureau, where the broker-dealer did not make any purchases and sales on the same day. The court stated that although the "ask quotations" were not firm offers to sell, they were prima facie evidence of market value. [Merritt, Vickers, Inc. v. S.E.C., 353 F.2d 293 (2d Cir. 1965)]

2) **Cost used as base:** [§1787]  If the base used for markups is the broker-dealer's cost, the markup rule might limit the broker's ability to earn profits on his dealer transactions. For this reason, the court in *Merritt, Vickers, Inc.* used cost as a basis only for a transaction where the broker-dealer bought the stock (*e.g.,* at $5 per share) and sold it on the same day (where a selling price of $5.25 would represent a 5% markup). In other transactions, the courts approved a referral to quotes on market prices as a basis for markups.

   a) **Example:** If a broker-dealer bought the stock of XYZ Corp. on January 1 at $5 per share, and held it until March 1 when its "market price" was quoted at $10 per share, it could base its selling price on a markup of 5%—*i.e.,* a sales price of $10.50 per share—without violating the rules.

3) **Market price used as base:** [§1788]  For securities traded on NASDAQ, determining the market price is simply a matter of surveying the NASDAQ quoted prices, much as would be done

for exchange-traded securities. But for securities traded neither on an exchange nor on NASDAQ, it can be more difficult to determine what the market price is.

a) **NASD requirements:** [§1789] Since 1988, the NASD requires broker-dealers to mark customer order tickets for each transaction in a non-NASDAQ, non-exchange-traded security, to show the name of each dealer contacted and the price quotation received, in order to determine the prevailing market price. [NASD Notice to Members 88-33 (1988)]

b) **Determining market price:** [§1790] In a 1988 interpretation restating its "5% rule" (*see supra,* §1785), the NASD set out four factors for determining the market price for a security:

1/ **Competitive market:** [§1791] If the securities trade in a competitive market, the prices paid by other dealers to the market maker whose markup is being reviewed should be the basis for the markup.

2/ **Broker-dealers trading as principals with clients:** [§1792] A market maker dealing with a client as a principal is entitled only to the "inside spread"; that is, the best available price (to another dealer) is used to calculate the markup. If the dealer is not making a market in the security, its cost is used as the basis for the markup.

3/ **No independent market for the security:** [§1793] If the market maker dominates the market, or there is otherwise no independent market for the security, the market maker's contemporaneous cost should be used as the basis for calculating the markup.

4/ **Price quotes:** [§1794] A dominant market maker should never use its own quoted price as the basis for a markup, but instead should use its actual contemporaneous cost.

4) **Burden of proof:** [§1795] The burden of proof is on the broker-dealer to show special circumstances justifying an "excessive" markup. [Merritt, Vickers, Inc. v. S.E.C., *supra*]

(2) **S.E.C. policy:** [§1796] There are no specific S.E.C. rules against excessive markups, but the S.E.C. has regulated markups via the general anti-fraud provisions of the 1934 Act.

(a) **Example:** A dealer who sold securities at a price substantially higher than the prevailing market price was held to violate rule 10b-5, because the dealer made a false "implied representation" that its price bore a reasonable relationship to the market price. [Charles Hughes & Co. v. S.E.C., *supra,* §1780]

    (b) **Fraud per se:** [§1797] The S.E.C. considers a markup of more than 10% of the prevailing market price to be fraud per se. [*See, e.g.,* Alstead Dempsey & Co., SEA Release No. 34-20825 (1984)]

    (c) **Offer quotations from other dealers:** [§1798] Although the NASD relies to some extent on price quotes from other dealers to establish the prevailing market price (*see supra*), the S.E.C. considers such quotations unreliable and whenever possible uses the dealer's contemporaneous cost. [Alstead Dempsey & Co., *supra*]

    (d) **Rule 10b-10:** [§1799] Rule 10b-10 requires broker-dealers to disclose price-related information to the customer on the order ticket. In some cases, the markup must be disclosed; in other cases, the dealer must disclose whom it contacted and what prices were quoted in order to inform the customer about the basis for the asserted market price. [SEA Rule 10b-10; *and see infra*, §1807]

b. **Underwriter's compensation:** [§1800] Many states have securities laws limiting the amount and type of compensation that an underwriter may receive in an original distribution of securities. The NASD also has undertaken to regulate underwriter compensation and requires that such compensation be fair and consistent with just and equitable principles of trade. [NASD Rules, art. III, §1]

    (1) **Standard:** [§1801] Compensation received by the underwriter must be "fair and reasonable" under all of the circumstances (taking into consideration the size of the offering, the type of security, the type of underwriting, etc.). [NASD underwriting guidelines, NASD Manual (CCH) ¶2151.02]

    (2) **Advance review:** [§1802] Underwriting agreements for "unseasoned" companies (new companies or those without an established earnings record) must be reviewed by the NASD in advance of the underwriting.

    (3) **Compensation factors and guidelines**

        (a) **Excessive compensation:** [§1803] Compensation that exceeds 18 to 20% of the gross dollar amount received by the issuer in the offering will probably be held to be excessive.

        (b) **"Compensation":** [§1804] All types of the issuer's securities received or purchased (prior to, at the time of, or subsequent to the underwriting) by the underwriter may be considered part of the underwriter's compensation. The rule of thumb is that securities amounting to no more than 10% of the total number of shares offered by the issuer may be received by the underwriter as compensation.

        (c) **Other factors:** [§1805] Other factors involved in underwriter compensation are expenses payable by the issuer, cash commissions received, consulting and advisory fees, options and warrants granted to the underwriter, etc.

(4) **Resale price maintenance:** [§1806] The typical underwriting agreement requires all underwriters and members of the selling group to adhere to the public offering price as stated in the prospectus. Of course, any sales below the stated price would make the prospectus false, and so courts have recognized that such a resale price maintenance agreement does not violate the antitrust laws. [United States v. Morgan, 118 F. Supp. 621 (S.D.N.Y. 1953)] Furthermore, the NASD has rules that prohibit various forms of price discounting in underwritings (such as by having a purchaser swap securities above their market value for securities being offered in the underwriting). [SEA Release No. 15807 (1979)] The S.E.C. has upheld the right of the NASD to enforce such administrative rules. [SEA Release No. 16956 (1980)]

c. **Duty to disclose nature of relationship:** [§1807] Broker-dealers may also be in a position of conflict with their customers' interests where they are representing their own or others' interests in the same transaction. Therefore, under SEA Rule 10b-10, broker-dealers are required to furnish their customers with written confirmation of securities transactions entered into on behalf of the customer, and these confirmations must disclose the nature of the broker-dealer's relationship to the customer—*i.e.,* whether it is acting as broker for the customer, as dealer for its own account, as broker for some other person or as broker for both the customer and some other person. Where the broker-dealer is acting as an agent, it must also disclose the source and amount of any commission received. [SEA Rules 10b-10, *and see* NASD art. III, §12]

(1) **Example—acting in dual capacity:** A broker-dealer who failed to disclose to customers that it was acting as agent for **both** the seller and the buyer of the same securities, and receiving a double commission therefor, was held to have violated article III, section 12 of the NASD rules. [Merritt, Vickers, Inc. v. S.E.C., *supra,* §1795]

d. **Duty to disclose role as market maker:** [§1808] Failure by a broker-dealer to disclose the fact that it is making a market in stocks it has recommended to a customer may also be in violation of the 1934 Act.

(1) **Function of a market maker:** [§1809] A "market maker" is a broker-dealer who publishes (either in the NASDAQ or other quotation service) bona fide "two-way" quotations with respect to any other over-the-counter security. This means that the broker-dealer is quoting both a bid price (what it will buy the security at) and an ask price (what it is willing to sell the security for).

(a) **Note:** Functioning as a market maker also implies that the broker-dealer stands ready to either buy or sell a given security in reasonable quantities. Usually the broker-dealer is carrying an inventory of the security for its own account as well.

(b) **And note:** The market maker may also engage in simultaneous transactions, where it buys from one customer and sells to another.

Such transactions are subject to the NASD "mark-up" policy discussed *supra*, §1784.

(2) **Representations as to price:** [§1810] A broker-dealer may not represent to a customer that a transaction is occurring at the "market price" unless it has reasonable grounds to believe that a trading market in the security in fact exists (other than the market made by the broker-dealer). [SEA Rule 15c1-8]

(a) **And note:** Under the general antifraud provisions, every sale by a broker-dealer carries with it the implied representation that the price is reasonably related to that prevailing in the open market. (*See* "shingle theory," *supra,* §1780.)

(3) **Single market makers:** [§1811] Where a broker-dealer is the only firm making a market in a security (*i.e.*, the only firm regularly quoted as willing to buy and sell the security), there will be no market for the security other than that created by the broker-dealer. A single market maker may not represent to its customers that transactions in the security are made at the market price.

(a) **Close scrutiny:** [§1812] This situation often occurs in the over-the-counter market, and any price representations made to customers will be closely scrutinized.

(4) **Multiple market makers:** [§1813] Even when there are several firms making a market, it is still necessary for a broker-dealer to disclose its position as a market maker to its customers in order to avoid liability. Under rule 10b-5, for example, this is a *material fact* that must be disclosed. [Chasins v. Smith, Barney & Co., 438 F.2d 1167 (2d Cir. 1971)]

(a) **Note:** In *Chasins,* the defendant broker-dealer *had* disclosed its role as principal in the transaction. Nevertheless, the court held that defendant's failure to disclose its position as a market maker violated the securities laws.

(b) **Comment:** Since there is normally a competitive market where there are several market makers, and the purchaser usually gets the best price by buying from the market maker, the *Chasins* decision may not be followed in the future (at least where the broker-dealer discloses that it is acting as a principal).

e. **Duty to fulfill expected role as agent:** [§1814] Where a broker-dealer has implied in its dealings with customers that it is acting as an agent for them, it is a violation for the broker-dealer to trade with its customers as a principal, even if this fact is disclosed in the written confirmations. [*In re* Norris & Hirshberg, Inc., 177 F.2d 228 (D.C. Cir. 1949)—broker-dealer traded as principal with its customers' discretionary accounts, without disclosing that it was acting as a dealer]

f. **Prohibition against causing sales:** [§1815] It is also unlawful for a broker-dealer to cause, or attempt to cause, a customer to enter into a transaction not actually agreed upon, *e.g.*, by sending a written confirmation of a sale that the customer did not agree to. [NASD Manual (CCH) ¶2152]

(1) **Regulatory provisions:** [§1816] "False confirmations" are prohibited by article III, sections 1 and 18 of the NASD rules. Such conduct also violates the general antifraud sections of the 1934 Act.

(2) **Example:** Approximately 5% of the confirmations sent by a broker-dealer were canceled. The sales had been solicited by telephone calls. The S.E.C. found these facts to constitute a violation. [*In re* Palombi Securities Co., SEA Release No. 6961 (1962)]

g. **Prohibition against "churning":** [§1817] The 1934 Act also prohibits "churning," *i.e.,* excessive trading by a broker-dealer in a customer's account, for the primary purpose of generating commission income. Churning is facilitated when the broker-dealer has discretionary accounts for which it may effect trades without prior approval of the customer. [SEA Rule 15c1-7]

(1) **Question of fact:** [§1818] Whether the broker-dealer is guilty of churning is a question of fact. The key issue is whether the trading has been so excessive as to indicate that the primary purpose of the trading was to generate commissions for the broker. [Hecht v. Harris, Upham & Co., 430 F.2d 1202 (9th Cir. 1970)]

(a) **Elements of churning:** [§1819] The decision whether churning has occurred must be based on consideration of all the relevant facts; no set turnover rate, commission ratio, etc., constitutes churning as a matter of law. [Nesbit v. McNeil, 896 F.2d 380 (9th Cir. 1990)] To establish a claim of churning, the customer must show that: (i) the trading in her account was excessive in light of her investment objectives; (ii) the broker exercised control over the trading in the account; and (iii) the broker acted with the intent to defraud or with willful and reckless disregard for the interests of the client. [Nesbit v. McNeil, *supra*]

(b) **Example:** Where the account in question represented less than one-tenth of 1% of the original dollar volume in the broker-dealer's office, but generated 5% of the total commissions, the court found the broker-dealer guilty of churning. [Hecht v. Harris, Upham & Co., *supra*]

(c) **Example:** Churning was found when trades over an 11-year period increased the value of an account by almost $183,000, but commissions on the numerous transactions aggregated $250,000. [Nesbit v. McNeil, *supra*]

(d) **But note:** Where the investor's purpose was "short-term" profits, and all investments were closely supervised, the court concluded that the broker-dealer could *not* be held liable for churning. [Marshak v. Blyth, Eastman, Dillon & Co., 413 F. Supp. 377 (N.D. Okla. 1975)]

(2) **Duty of the customer:** [§1820] The plaintiff in a rule 10b-5 cause of action for churning will recover if churning occurred unless (considering all of the facts) plaintiff was guilty of recklessness or worse in not discovering or terminating the broker's activity. [Petrites v. J.C. Bradford & Co., 696 F.2d 1033 (5th Cir. 1981)]

(3) **Scope of doctrine:** [§1821] Churning is not limited merely to accounts over which the broker-dealer has been given discretionary authority. It may be found in any appropriate situation where a broker, by virtue of the trust and reliance placed in her by the customer, is able to determine the volume and frequency of sales. [*In re* Norris & Hirshberg, Inc., *supra*, §1814]

(4) **Liability of broker-dealer:** [§1822] If a salesperson is guilty of churning, the broker-dealer may also be liable for failure to exercise adequate control (pursuant to SEA section 20). [*See* Kravitz v. Pressman, Frohlich & Frost, Inc., 447 F. Supp. 203 (D. Mass. 1978)]

(5) **Damages:** [§1823] Normally, the plaintiff customer may recover the total amount of commission paid on the securities transactions in question. The older cases held that no damages could be recovered for losses in the market value of the securities purchased. [*See, e.g.,* Hecht v. Harris, Upham & Co., *supra*] The better view (and the current trend) is that a customer who can demonstrate harm to the value of her portfolio can recover damages for that harm, as well as the excessive commissions paid to the broker. [Nesbit v. McNeil, *supra*]

5. **Broker-Dealers' Duty to Disclose Adequate Information:** [§1824] One of the major regulatory purposes of the federal securities laws is requiring full disclosure of relevant information to potential investors. The 1933 Act requires issuers of publicly issued securities to make full disclosure to investors. The 1934 Act requires issuers, and others trading in securities registered under the Act, to provide full disclosure in certain situations; it also requires broker-dealers to ascertain and disclose relevant information in making recommendations to clients.

   a. **"Boiler room" operations:** [§1825] A "boiler room" operation is a high-pressure securities sales operation (*e.g.,* by unsolicited telephone calls) in which the broker-dealer typically provides inadequate or false information to its sales people concerning the security being sold. Normally the securities of only a single issuer are involved.

      (1) **Proceeding against broker-dealer:** [§1826] The 1934 Act authorizes the S.E.C. to shut down a boiler room operation by revoking the broker-dealer's license. To be successful, the S.E.C. must be able to prove that the broker-dealer *willfully* violated the securities laws. [SEA §15(b)]

      (2) **Proceeding against individual salespeople:** [§1827] Prior to 1964, statutory law provided that broker-dealers registered with the NASD could not hire (without prior approval of the S.E.C.) any sales representative who had been found to "cause" the revocation of a broker-dealer's registration. This was a form of "indirect control" of the individual salesperson responsible for violating the securities acts, since nothing in the law authorized the S.E.C. to proceed directly against him.

         (a) **Private cause of action:** [§1828] However, those customers who were damaged by the purchase of misrepresented securities could bring a private suit for damages or rescission against the salesperson under rule 10b-5.

(b) **Example:** [§1829] Berko, a salesman, participated in a high pressure telephone campaign to sell 100,000 shares of a company's securities. A brochure sent out to potential customers contained substantial misrepresentations about the company's financial condition. The S.E.C. found that rules 10b-5 and 15c1-2 as well as section 17(a) of the 1933 Act had been violated, and revoked the registration of the broker-dealer that employed Berko. Besides using the misleading sales information provided by the broker-dealer, Berko made additional representations that the stock would double in price in a year, without having adequate information as to the financial condition of the company. The court approved the S.E.C.'s finding that Berko caused the revocation of the broker-dealer's registration, and therefore no other registered securities firm could hire Berko without the S.E.C.'s approval. [Berko v. S.E.C., 316 F.2d 137 (2d Cir. 1963)]

    1) **Note:** In selling securities of an unknown issuer, a salesperson cannot rely without independent verification on information given him by the broker-dealer (as he might do in a different type of sales operation dealing with an established company's securities).

    2) **And note:** It makes no difference in such a nondisclosure case that some of the salesperson's customers may have actually profited by his recommendations. (The price of the stock in *Berko* actually did double in a year and only later plummeted.)

(c) **Direct action against salesperson:** [§1830] In 1964, the 1934 Act was amended to allow the S.E.C. to proceed directly against "any person" (including the broker-dealer's individual salesperson), and to censure or bar him from associating with *any* broker-dealer if he has willfully violated the securities acts. [SEA §15(b)(6)]

    1) **Note:** The S.E.C. can also proceed for revocation against the employer broker-dealer in a boiler room operation under section 15(b)(4)(E), on a charge that the employer has "wilfully aided, abetted, counseled, commanded, induced or procured the violation" by the employee.

b. **"Know thy customer" rules:** [§1831] In an effort to control "boiler room" operations, both the NASD and the New York Stock Exchange have adopted rules that prohibit a broker from recommending securities to a customer unless the broker has reasonable grounds to believe that the securities are appropriate for the customer in light of the customer's other securities holdings, her financial situation, and other relevant data. [Art. III, §2, NASD Manual (CCH) ¶2152; NYSE Rule 405, NYSE Manual (CCH) ¶2405]

(1) **Duty applies to salespeople:** [§1832] The cases have made it clear that this rule applies independently to all individual salespeople employed by a broker-dealer, as well as the broker-dealer itself. [Hanly v. S.E.C., *supra*, §1781, *and see supra*, §1780]

(2) **Duty to investigate:** [§1833] In light of the "know your customer" rules, what investigation, if any, must a broker make in order to discover information about the customer?

 (a) **NASD rules do not require investigation:** [§1834] The NASD "know your customer" rule does not expressly require a broker to investigate the customer's financial situation. [*See* Art. III, §2, NASD Manual (CCH) ¶2152]

 (b) **NYSE rules require investigation:** [§1835] The New York Stock Exchange rules, however, require the broker to investigate "the essential facts relative to every customer." The broker's recommendations to the customer must be reasonable in light of these "essential facts." [*See* NYSE Rule 405, NYSE Manual (CCH) ¶2405]

(3) **Violations of the rules:** [§1836] The following actions are typical violations of the S.E.C. or NASD rules:

 (a) *Recommending a speculative security to someone seeking a "safe" investment.*

 (b) *Inducing a customer to withdraw interest-bearing funds prior to the interest date* in order to buy a misrepresented and speculative security. [*In re* Boren & Co., SEA Release No. 6367 (1960)]

 (c) *Failing to instruct sales employees about the "suitability" requirement,* and failing to adequately supervise its application. [*In re* Boren & Co., *supra*]

 (d) *Making optimistic statements or absolute representations* about the prospects of a company, *without any adequate basis in fact,* to convince the customer that the security involved fits her needs. [Kahn v. S.E.C., 297 F.2d 112 (2d Cir. 1961)]

 (e) *Making recommendations reflecting an undue acceptance of management's statements and financial projections without investigation,* failing to investigate "red flags" and "warning signals," and failing to disclose known adverse information. [*See* Merrill Lynch, Pierce, Fenner & Smith, Inc., SEA Release No. 14149 (1977)]

(4) **Scope of duty:** [§1837] Difficult questions may arise concerning the scope of the broker-dealer's duty to ascertain suitability, especially concerning speculative securities and in situations where there is little or no reliance on the broker-dealer's recommendations.

 (a) **Speculative securities:** [§1838] Speculative securities involve a greater degree of risk; they are not suitable for all investors. And because the customer is more likely to lose money in speculative securities than in more conservative securities, speculative securities are more likely to generate litigation. Courts are thus often confronted with customers who invest in speculative securities, lose money, and then sue the broker, claiming that speculative securities were an inappropriate investment. Often, the broker's defense is that (i) the customer's instructions were to invest in the speculative securities, and (ii) that the customer is seeking the best of both worlds: potentially large gains from speculation, **and** recourse to the broker's pocket if the investment loses money.

(b) **Lack of reliance:** [§1839] Does the scope of the broker-dealer's duty to ascertain suitability change, depending on the type of relationship that exists between the broker and the customer? In other words, do factors such as the duration of the relationship, sophistication of the customer, etc.—which tend to indicate whether the customer relied on the broker's judgment—affect the scope of the broker's duty?

   1) **Example:** In applying the "shingle theory" (*supra,* §1780) to a security salesperson, one court indicated that the fact that the investor was sophisticated or did not actually rely on the salesperson's statements was *irrelevant*.

   (i) The court went on to hold that even in situations where the customer does not rely on the broker, a salesperson may not make statements without adequate information. Furthermore, the salesperson is required to disclose any lack of essential information and the risks that arise therefrom.

   (ii) The salesperson is also required to undertake a reasonable investigation and reveal what information is reasonably ascertainable. A recommendation implies that a reasonable investigation has been made and that the recommendation is based on the results thereof.

   [Hanly v. S.E.C., *supra,* §1832]

   2) **Caveat:** [§1840] However, other courts have been reluctant to award damages unless the customer has been able to prove *reasonable reliance* on the broker-dealer's recommendation. [Phillips v. Reynolds & Co., 294 F. Supp. 1249 (E.D. Pa. 1969)]

(5) **Duty where customer has investment advisor:** [§1841] Brokers often execute trades suggested by investment advisers. The broker can still be liable in these situations for improper recommendations. [*See* Rolf v. Blyth, Eastman, Dillon & Co., 570 F.2d 38 (2d Cir. 1978)—broker suggested adviser who made recommendations (with discretionary power) which were executed by the broker; portfolio dropped from $1.4 million to $225,000 in a very short time]

(a) **But note:** *Rolf* should not be seen as establishing a duty of the broker to inquire about suitability in all situations. In *Rolf*, the broker was charged by the customer with supervising the investment adviser (not merely executing orders); the broker was aware that the adviser was buying "junk"; and the broker advised the client that the adviser's suggestions were consistent with the client's investment goals (when they were not).

c. **Duty of broker-dealers in submitting quotations:** [§1842] The S.E.C. has imposed a duty of care on broker-dealers in the submission of quotations on over-the-counter securities to any interdealer quotation system or in any other publication of such quotations. [SEA Rule 15c2-11]

   (1) **Permissible quotes:** [§1843]  A broker-dealer may not give a quote on over-the-counter securities that are not quoted on NASDAQ unless:

      (a) *The issuer has registered its securities* under the 1933 or 1934 Acts and is current in filing the required reports under the 1934 Act; *or*

      (b) *The broker-dealer has obtained, and makes available* to any person on request, *certain financial information* relating to the issuer.

         1) When the broker-dealer is permitted to give a quote on this latter basis, it must have no reasonable basis for believing that the information is not true and correct. In addition, the information must be obtained from sources that the broker-dealer has a reasonable basis for believing to be reliable.

         2) This obligation does *not* impose a duty on the broker-dealer to investigate the accuracy of information (other than to believe in the reliability of the source), but the threat of liability tends to make broker-dealers more conservative as to the types of securities in which they deal.

6. **Broker-Dealer's Duty to Supervise:** [§1844]  The 1934 Act provides for the censure, denial of, suspension, or revocation of a broker-dealer's registration for failure adequately to supervise its associates (*i.e.,* salespeople and employees), where the result is a violation of the securities acts. [SEA §15(b)(4)(E)]

   a. **NASD rules:** [§1845]  The NASD rules also require the registered principal (*i.e.,* the person in charge of the broker-dealer organization) to supervise all transactions and correspondence of its employees. [NASD Rules, art. II, §27] The following have been found to be violations of the duty to supervise:

      (1) *Failure to properly instruct employees about the difference between principal and agency transactions;*

      (2) *Failure to instruct employees about the "suitability of customer recommendations" rule* (*i.e.,* that the security sold to a customer must be suitable to the customer's needs);

      (3) *Failure to adequately explain sales literature;* and

      (4) *Failure of the principal to approve correspondence* by employees. [*In re* Boren & Co., SEA Release No. 6367 (1960)—the above were found to be violations of both NASD Supervision Rules and 1934 Act as inconsistent with "just and equitable principles of trade"]

b. **Stock exchange rules:** [§1846] The national stock exchanges have similar rules, as required under section 6 of the 1934 Act. [*See In re* Shearson, Hammill & Co., *supra,* §1733]

c. **Liability of controlling persons:** [§1847] In addition to actions brought for a broker-dealer's failure to adequately supervise, the broker-dealer may also be held liable as a "control person" for the securities law violations of persons they control. (*See supra,* §107.)

7. **Margin Requirements:** [§1848] To generate greater sales volume, broker-dealers often encourage their customers to buy securities on credit (*i.e.,* on "margin"). The regulations developed in this area under section 7 of the 1934 Act are the province of the Federal Reserve Board, but the S.E.C. brings enforcement actions for violations by broker-dealers.

a. **Federal Reserve Board regulations:** [§1849] Below are the margin regulations:

(i) *Regulation T* governs the extension of credit by market intermediaries (such as broker-dealers) in securities transactions.

(ii) *Regulation U* governs extension of credit by commercial banks for the purpose of buying securities.

(iii) *Regulation G* governs lending by persons other than broker-dealers and banks, where the credit extended is secured by the stock purchased.

(iv) *Regulation X* governs borrowing from domestic or foreign lenders.

Under these regulations, credit may only be extended to buy specific exchange and over-the-counter securities. That is, if a security is not approved as collateral under the above regulations, no loan may be made by the regulated organizations on such a security.

b. **Margin amount:** [§1850] Under Federal Reserve Board Regulation T, a "margin amount" may be set. Thus, if the margin is 50%, a broker-dealer may not loan a customer more than 50% of the market value of the securities.

c. **Implied action for margin rule violations:** [§1851] Neither section 7 nor regulation T expressly provide for a private civil cause of action to enforce their provisions or to compensate for damages caused by a violation of the rules. Generally, most courts that have considered the issue in recent years have ruled that there is no implied private right of action under section 7. However, a few courts have recognized an implied civil action against broker-dealers for such violations.

8. **Civil Liability for Violations of NASD, Stock Exchange, or S.E.C. Rules:** [§1852] There have been a number of instances where a plaintiff has brought a cause of action against a defendant broker-dealer for the defendant's violation of an NASD, national stock exchange, or S.E.C. rule. The recent trend of court opinions, however, has been to limit sharply the implication of private remedies under various sections of the securities laws as well as pursuant to NASD or stock exchange rules. (*See supra,* §1685.)

# V. APPLICATION OF FEDERAL SECURITIES LAWS TO MULTINATIONAL TRANSACTIONS

## _chapter approach_

The material covered in this chapter is included for the sake of completeness. Unless your professor has covered this material during your course, it is doubtful that an exam question will be taken from the information in this chapter.

## A. IN GENERAL [§1853]

Many securities transactions involve investors and firms in foreign countries as well as in the United States. Therefore, questions often arise as to the applicability of the federal securities laws to these multinational transactions (subject matter jurisdiction) and as to the capability of the court to obtain personal jurisdiction over the parties involved in the transaction. (The question of subject matter jurisdiction is discussed below; _see_ the Conflict of Laws Summary for discussion of personal jurisdiction over foreign defendants.)

## B. REGISTRATION UNDER THE 1933 ACT [§1854]

The 1933 Act confers jurisdiction over multinational transactions whenever United States facilities of interstate commerce are used to effect a securities transaction. The 1933 Act defines "interstate commerce" to include commerce between any foreign country and the United States. [SA §2(7)]

1. **Territoriality as Basis for Application of 1933 Act:** [§1855] The registration requirements of the 1933 Act are limited by geography: Offerings taking place within the United States must comply with the 1933 Act, regardless of the nationality of the issuer. Offerings outside the United States need not be registered under the 1933 Act, again irrespective of the issuer's nationality.

   a. **Offshore offerings:** [§1856] The foregoing leaves open the question whether a particular offering in fact is outside the United States. It is easy to imagine an offering in which all the initial buyers are located overseas, but those buyers promptly resell to United States persons. To clarify some of the questions relating to offshore offerings, the S.E.C. adopted Regulation S in 1990.

      (1) **Regulation S:** [§1857] Regulation S, discussed _supra,_ §§604 _et seq.,_ was in part intended to clarify that the registration requirements of the 1933 Act do not apply to offers and sales made outside the United States.

      (2) **Rule 144A and resale of Regulation S securities:** [§1858] Simultaneously with the adoption of Regulation S, the S.E.C. adopted rule 144A. In conjunction with Regulation S, rule 144A makes it possible for a foreign issuer in two steps to effect a distribution to "qualified institutional buyers" (defined _supra,_ §595) in the United States. In the first step, the foreign issuer sells its securities abroad. In the second step, the overseas buyers resell under rule 144A to "qualified institutional buyers" in the United States. For a discussion of both of these provisions, _see supra,_ §§589 _et seq._

b. **United States offerings:** [§1859]   With what regulations must a foreign issuer comply to conduct a registered offering in the United States? At one time, the United States capital markets were seen as so desirable that the S.E.C. did not concern itself much with the convenience of foreign issuers. The increasingly competitive nature of the global economy, however, makes it essential that the United States accommodate foreign capital to the extent consistent with the protection of United States investors. This is gradually being accomplished by efforts to streamline and harmonize domestic regulation with regulation in other countries.

(1) **Registration forms:** [§1860]   There are two principal kinds of foreign issuers: sovereign issuers (*i.e.,* foreign governments) and private issuers (foreign corporations and other business entities).

(a) **Foreign sovereign issuers:** [§1861]   Schedule B to the 1933 Act specifies the information required to be included in a 1933 Act registration statement by a foreign sovereign. Note that the S.E.C. has never adopted a form for use by foreign sovereign issuers.

(b) **Foreign private issuers:** [§1862]   The S.E.C. has adopted forms F-1, F-2, F-3, and F-4 for foreign private issuers. These forms are intended to parallel those used by American domestic issuers, and in most cases are comparable to forms S-1, S-2, S-3, and S-4, used by domestic issuers.

(2) **Financial disclosure by foreign issuers:** [§1863]   Probably the most difficult hurdle that a foreign issuer needs to clear before conducting an offering in the United States is the requirement that its financial statements be reconciled to United States generally accepted accounting practices ("GAAP") and the S.E.C.'s Regulation S-X. Often, foreign accounting practices vary substantially from those prevalent in the United States, and reconciliation is a lengthy (and expensive) task. To mitigate the burden somewhat, the S.E.C. recognizes two methods of reconciliation:

(a) **Full reconciliation:** [§1864]   Full reconciliation requires that essentially all data (including geographic and industry segment data) be reconciled to GAAP and Regulation S-X. Although full reconciliation is not required for periodic reports under the 1934 Act, it is required for 1933 Act registration statements.

(b) **Measurement item reconciliation:** [§1865]   In cases where full reconciliation is not required, the S.E.C. accepts reconciliation of measurement items only—that is, of income statement and balance sheet data. While this is considerably less burdensome than full reconciliation, it nevertheless entails significant expense and potential delay.

2. **American Depositary Receipts ("ADRs"):** [§1866]   One technique has been used since the 1920s to attempt to avoid extensive regulation under the 1933 Act. Under this approach, an American bank purchases (in exempt secondary-market transactions) shares of foreign issuers. The shares are held in a trust or other custodial arrangement by the bank, which then issues receipts evidencing beneficial ownership of a stated number of shares. ADRs are popular with investors—in 1990

the dollar volume of ADRs traded, $125 billion, was almost 70 times what it had been only seven years earlier. But the regulatory status of ADRs at present is unclear.

a. **Regulation of ADRs:** [§1867]  In 1983, the S.E.C. promulgated form F-6, a registration form for ADRs. If the foreign issuer arranges for the ADR in the United States, the issuer must sign the form. The bank will sign the form in any case. In addition, the foreign issuer must comply with the periodic reporting requirements of the 1934 Act. Existing ADR arrangements were "grandfathered," and those issuers do not have to file 1934 Act reports. At present, then, some foreign issuers using ADRs must file 1934 Act reports, and some do not. The S.E.C. is currently studying ADRs and their regulatory environment.

3. **Multi-Jurisdictional Disclosure:** [§1868]  In recent years, the S.E.C. has proposed a number of possibilities for multi-jurisdictional disclosure; *i.e.,* a system of registration and disclosure that would satisfy the regulatory requirements of two or more nations at the same time. To date, however, only Canada and the United States have agreed to a system of multi-jurisdictional disclosure. [*See* SA Release No. 33-6902 (1991)]

## C.  APPLICATION OF THE 1934 ACT [§1869]

Like the 1933 Act, the 1934 Act defines "interstate commerce" to include commerce between any foreign country and the United States. [*See* SEA §3(a)(17)]

1. **Regulation Under the 1934 Act:** [§1870]  The registration requirements of the 1934 Act [SEA §12(b), (g)] do not distinguish between foreign and domestic registrants. On its face, therefore, the Act seems to require registration and periodic reporting if a foreign issuer has securities listed on a United States exchange [SEA §12(b)] or has at least 500 shareholders and more than $5 million in assets [SEA §12(g)].

a. **Exemption:** [§1871]  Under rule 12g3-2(b), however, all such foreign issuers are exempt from registration *if* they file with the S.E.C. all information that they make public abroad (*e.g.,* stock exchange reports, filings required by the laws of their domicile, voluntary statements released to shareholders, etc.) and if their securities are neither traded on any United States exchange nor listed on NASDAQ. [SEA Rule 12g3-2(b)]

(1) **"Grandfather" provision:** [§1872]  Until 1983, it was possible for a foreign issuer to have securities traded on NASDAQ and still be exempt from the 1934 Act's registration and reporting requirements under rule 12g3-2(b). When the S.E.C. modified the exemption to require NASDAQ-listed issuers to register and report, they "grandfathered" foreign issuers that were listed on NASDAQ at the time the rule changed. Consequently, there are still a number of foreign issuers listed on NASDAQ who have not registered under the 1934 Act and who do not report on United States forms.

(2) **Reporting for non-exempt foreign issuers:** [§1873]  Issuers whose securities trade on an exchange or NASDAQ, and who are not grandfathered under rule 12g3-2(b), must file an annual form 20-F. The form is

generally similar to a domestic form 10-K, but requires substantially less disclosure of self-dealing transactions and of management compensation than its United States counterpart. Financial statements filed with form 20-F need not be reconciled to GAAP (*see supra*, §1863).

(a) **But note:** If the form 20-F will be incorporated by reference into a 1933 Act registration statement (*see supra*, §61), the financial statements must be reconciled to GAAP (*see supra*, §1445).

(b) **Other reports:** [§1874] Foreign registrants are not required to file quarterly reports, because these are not common outside the United States. When material information becomes public abroad, however, a foreign registrant must file a form 6-K disclosing that information.

b. **Foreign Corrupt Practices Act:** [§1875] Finally, if a foreign issuer registers a class of securities under the 1934 Act, the issuer becomes subject to the Foreign Corrupt Practices Act ("FCPA"). The FCPA imposes criminal penalties for certain corrupt practices (bribery of government officials and the like) and also requires the issuer to keep accurate and fair books and records and to devise a system of internal accounting controls to ensure that such payments are not being concealed.

2. **International Securities Fraud:** [§1876] The preceding section focused on regulation of foreign entities and their securities transactions. Other international issues arising under the securities laws involve misconduct and the extent to which United States authorities can pursue (or prosecute) those responsible. Often the potential defendant first raises a defense based on jurisdiction, under SEA section 30(b).

a. **Interpretation of section 30(b) of the 1934 Act:** [§1877] Section 30(b) provides that neither the 1934 Act nor its rules apply to any person insofar as he transacts "a business in securities without the jurisdiction of the United States." This section has been referred to on several occasions when the courts have considered the extraterritorial application of the 1934 Act. At issue is the meaning of the phrases "transacts a business in securities," and "without the jurisdiction of the United States."

(1) **General rule:** [§1878] United States courts appear willing to apply the provisions of the 1934 Act to securities transactions involving foreign nationals and foreign transactions when there are (i) substantial United States contacts with the transaction, and (ii) substantial United States interests to be protected. [Schoenbaum v. Firstbrook, 405 F.2d 200 (2d Cir. 1968)]

(a) **Example:** Acquitaine (a Canadian corporation) purchased additional shares of its subsidiary Banff Oil (also a Canadian corporation) at an unfair price, based on inside information about an oil discovery. An American shareholder of Banff sued Acquitaine under rule 10b-5. Although all of the events took place in Canada, the court found jurisdiction under the 1934 Act because Banff was listed and traded on the American Stock Exchange and application of United States law *was necessary to protect American investors*. [Schoenbaum v. Firstbrook, *supra*]

1) **Note:** Section 30(b) was held to exempt *only* transactions by foreign securities professionals (*i.e.,* those in the securities business), and even then, only where the transactions were outside the jurisdiction of the United States under the above rationale.

(b) **Example:** A United States corporation sued, under section 16(b), a foreign corporation that held 10% of its common stock where the foreign corporation purchased and sold the stock within a period of six months. The cause of action was *not* barred by section 30(b) since the foreign corporation was a mutual fund and not a broker-dealer (*i.e.,* not a "securities professional"). Also, the court found that since the transactions were executed on the NYSE, the business was not "without the jurisdiction" of the United States. [Roth v. Fund of Funds, Ltd., 405 F.2d 421 (2d Cir. 1968), *cert. denied,* 394 U.S. 975 (1969)]

1) **Note:** Section 16(b) of the 1934 Act might have been applied in this case even if the trading *had* occurred abroad, rather than on a United States exchange; jurisdiction under section 16 depends on whether the issuer's securities are registered under section 12, and not on the use of facilities of interstate commerce.

(c) **Example:** A French bidder planned a tender offer for R, an American corporation. After the bidder leaked information about the transaction, foreign investors purchased R shares and options to buy R shares. The orders to buy were placed in Europe and the Middle East, but ultimately were executed in the United States, over the NYSE and the Philadelphia Options Exchange. The Second Circuit Court of Appeals held that the S.E.C's action for an injunction could proceed, even though the misconduct took place outside the United States, because the *trading* took place inside the United States. "The [misconduct] created the near certainty that United States shareholders, who could reasonably be expected to hold [R] securities, would be adversely affected." [S.E.C. v. Unifund SAL, *supra,* §1511]

(2) **Interpretation by the S.E.C.:** [§1879] In the view of the S.E.C., the 1934 Act applies to extraterritorial transactions whenever its application is necessary for the protection of American investors and markets. But the S.E.C. is also aware that Congress also built into each provision of the 1934 Act certain jurisdictional requirements that may limit its application.

(a) **Factors considered:** [§1880] In determining whether a particular section of the 1934 Act applies to extraterritorial transactions, the S.E.C. considers all provisions of the section as to use of jurisdictional means, involvement of a registered security, and whether the provisions seem to apply only to persons in the securities business.

b. **Application of SEA rule 10b-5:** [§1881] Most of the cases involving extraterritorial application of the provisions of the 1934 Act have concerned rule 10b-5. The rationale for applying rule 10b-5 to securities transactions involving foreign nationals and foreign transactions is that (i) substantial United States contacts exist with respect to the transaction, and (ii) substantial United States interests need to be protected. (*See supra,* §1878.)

(1) **Suits against nonresidents:** [§1882] Rule 10b-5 applies to purchases by United States investors of foreign securities in a foreign country, at least when *substantial acts of fraud* in connection with the purchase were practiced in this country. [Leasco Data Processing Equipment Corp. v. Maxwell, 468 F.2d 1326 (2d Cir. 1972)]

(2) **Suits against United States residents:** [§1883] However, antifraud provisions of the 1933 and 1934 Acts were held *not* to apply in a suit brought by foreign plaintiffs against United States firms involved in a fraudulent sale of stock. The court held that all of "the basic misrepresentations" had occurred abroad, and that whatever took place in the United States was "merely preparatory and of small consequence to what happened abroad." [Bersch v. Drexel Firestone, Inc., 519 F.2d 974 (2d Cir. 1975), *cert. denied,* 423 U.S. 1018 (1975)]

(3) **Test used:** [§1884] The Second Circuit Court of Appeals (which has had the most extensive experience in questions of extraterritorial securities fraud) has created a twofold test for resolving transnational jurisdictional questions:

    (a) **Substantial effects test:** [§1885] Under the substantial effects test, jurisdiction is premised on foreseeable and substantial effects from the transnational transaction within the United States, regardless of where the activity in question occurred.

    (b) **Conduct test:** [§1886] Under the conduct test, jurisdiction is based on the fact that some significant activity occurred within American territorial limits. [*See* Continental Grain, Ltd. v. Pacific Oilseeds, Inc., Fed. Sec. L. Rep. (CCH) ¶96,767 (8th Cir. 1979)]

3. **International Tender Offers:** [§1887] Corporate takeovers sometimes raise difficult and sensitive issues concerning the extraterritorial reach of the United States securities laws. Often cases are brought in the United States federal courts, even though the bidder expressly excluded United States citizens from the tender offer (to avoid the application of United States securities law).

    a. **Example:** GEC, a British corporation, made a tender offer for Plessey, another British corporation, to all Plessey shareholders except those resident in the United States. Plessey ADRs trade in the United States and are listed on the New York Stock Exchange. After the bid was announced, the price of Plessey ADRs on the NYSE rose dramatically. Plessey sued GEC in Delaware federal court, seeking an injunction compelling GEC to file tender offer documents under the Williams Act. The Delaware district court held that, *inter alia,* GEC did not use jurisdictional means to carry out a securities transaction in the United States, all its actions were taken outside the United States, imposition of United States requirements was not necessary to protect United States interests in the bid, and interfering in a transaction of immense magnitude to British interests would violate international norms and could hinder comity. [Plessey Co., PLC v. General Electric Co., PLC, 628 F. Supp. 477 (D. Del. 1986)]

b. **But note:** *Plessey, supra,* did not involve any allegations of fraud. When fraud is alleged, the court may be more willing to assert jurisdiction, perhaps on the theory that a foreign government will be less protective of one of its citizens if that person has committed fraud. On the other hand, allegations of fraud are merely allegations, and in the typical tender offer contest, allegations of fraud are commonplace, although most are never proved.

(1) **Example:** M, a Luxembourg corporation, made a tender offer for the stock of C, a British corporation. Only 2.5% of C's shares were held in the United States, but C owned half of N, a Delaware corporation that controlled the largest gold producer in the United States. Defending itself against M's takeover attempt, C sued M in federal court in New York. The Second Circuit Court of Appeals held that the United States courts had jurisdiction over the bid, and remanded the case to the district court with a suggestion that if the plaintiff should prevail, an injunction might be an appropriate remedy. [Consolidated Gold Fields PLC v. Minorco, S.A., 871 F.2d 252 (2d Cir. 1989)]

# VI. REGULATION OF SECURITIES TRANSACTIONS BY THE STATES

## chapter approach

This chapter summarizes the state laws regulating securities and explains how federal and state securities laws interface to provide a complete regulatory system. In answering exam questions, don't overlook issues that ask you to consider the applicability of state law.

## A. IN GENERAL [§1888]

Both the Securities Act of 1933 and the Securities Exchange Act of 1934 preserve the power of the states to regulate securities transactions. [SA §18; SEA §28(a)] Every state has adopted some form of securities regulation, and every securities transaction may, therefore, be subject to the law of one or more of the states having contact with the transaction, as well as to federal law.

## B. UNIFORM SECURITIES ACT

1. **Structure of Act:** [§1889]  The Commissioners on Uniform State Laws have adopted the Uniform Securities Act, divided into sections addressing (i) fraud in general, (ii) broker-dealer registration, (iii) registration of new securities offerings, and (iv) remedies.

2. **Adoptions by the States:** [§1890]  In drafting their own securities laws, most of the states have adopted some part of the Uniform Securities Act, have used some of the concepts found in the federal acts, and have added some provisions of their own choosing. Yet despite their wide diversity, nearly all the states regulate both the original distribution of securities and their subsequent trading (including the registration of broker-dealers).

3. **Revised Uniform Securities Act:** [§1891]  In 1985, the National Conference of Commissioners on Uniform State Laws promulgated the Revised Uniform Securities Act. The Revised Act was amended in 1988 and, as amended, was recommended for adoption by the states.

## C. ORIGINAL DISTRIBUTION OF SECURITIES [§1892]

Since most states have securities laws regulating the original distribution of securities within their borders, an issuer making an original distribution within a state must usually comply with **both** the Securities Act of 1933 and the relevant state law.

1. **Blue Sky Laws:** [§1893]  The state statutes that regulate the original distribution of securities are called "blue sky laws." There are basically four different types of regulatory systems that may be set up by these state statutes:

   a. **Prohibition of fraud:** [§1894]  Some states simply prohibit fraud or misrepresentation in the purchase and sale of securities, and provide civil and criminal sanctions for violations. [*See* N.Y. Gen. Bus. Law §359-e(3), (8) (McKinney 1984), 2 Blue Sky L. Rep. (CCH) ¶42,111; People v. Concord Fabrics, Inc., 83 Misc. 2d 120 (1975)]

b. **Registration by notification:** [§1895]   Other states require that issuers file with state authorities certain material information about themselves and the securities to be issued. After the passage of a stated period of time, the registered securities may then be issued. Civil and criminal sanctions for violations are provided in these statutes as well.

c. **Registration by qualification:** [§1896]   Some blue sky laws require the filing of comprehensive information (similar to a registration statement under the 1933 Act) and review of the offered securities by state officials prior to issuance. A typical standard used in such a review is whether the securities are being offered on a "fair, just, and equitable" basis. [*See, e.g.,* Opinion of Attorney General of Alaska, 2 Blue Sky L. Rep. (CCH) ¶70,555 (1961)]

d. **Registration by coordination:** [§1897]   Other states permit securities registered under the federal laws to be issued without further processing by the state. [*See* Data Access Systems, Inc. v. Bureau of Securities, 305 A.2d 427 (N.J. 1973)—state securities agency prohibited from substantively reviewing a distribution of securities in New Jersey which had been registered with S.E.C. under the 1933 Act]

2. **Exemptions from State Regulation:** [§1898]   State laws normally provide for a number of exemptions from the registration or other qualification requirements. The exemption may be based either on the type of transaction or on the type of securities.

a. **Limited offering exemption:** [§1899]   Many states recognize an exemption from registration if the securities are offered in a transaction that is "limited" in one of several ways:

(1) **Isolated transaction:** [§1900]   Some states exempt securities that are offered in a single, isolated transaction, to a limited number of purchasers. [Tarsia v. Nick's Laundry & Linen Co., 399 P.2d 28 (Or. 1965)]

(2) **Limited persons and time:** [§1901]   States may also recognize an exemption for securities offered to a limited number of persons during a specific period of time. [Cann v. M & B Drilling Co., 480 S.W.2d 81 (Mo. 1972)] At present, this is the most common form of limited offering exemption used by the states.

(3) **Private offerings:** [§1902]   Some states have an exemption similar to the exemption in 1933 Act for private offerings. [People v. Humphreys, 4 Cal. App. 3d 693 (1970)]

(4) **Limited number of shareholders:** [§1903]   An exemption may also exist for a sale of securities if the shareholders of the corporation after the sale do not exceed a specified number.

(5) **Sales restricted to accredited investors:** [§1904]   Some states provide exemptions similar to those contained in 1933 Act Regulation D, for sales to accredited investors.

(6) **Uniform Limited Offering Exemption:** [§1905]   An exemption may be modeled on the Uniform Limited Offering Exemption ("ULOE"),

promulgated in 1980 by the National Association of Securities Administrators. The ULOE was designed to coordinate with Regulation D's provisions for limited offerings.

    (7) **Combinations:** [§1906] Finally, a state's limited offering exemption may consist of some combination of the above.

  b. **Other transaction exemptions:** [§1907] States may provide for other types of transaction exemptions as well; *e.g.,* some states recognize an exemption for preincorporation subscription agreements in certain situations.

  c. **Security exemptions:** [§1908] In addition, the blue sky laws typically provide for a number of exemptions based on the type of security offered. For example, many states exempt:

    (1) *Government securities;*

    (2) *Short-term commercial paper;* or

    (3) *Securities issued by certain types of corporations regulated by government entities,* such as public utilities, insurance companies, and banks.

  d. **Exemption for secondary distributions:** [§1909] Many states regulate "secondary," as well as original, distributions (*i.e.,* transfers of securities by shareholders after the original distribution is completed). (*See infra,* §§1911 *et seq.*) Where this is the case, exemptions are provided to allow "ordinary trading transactions" to occur without impediment. Typically, the following transactions are exempted:

    (1) *Isolated or limited offerings by nonissuers;* and

    (2) *Securities listed on stock exchanges or in certain financial manuals.*

3. **Regulatory Authority of State Agencies:** [§1910] The grant of authority to agencies that regulate the distribution of securities differs in each state. Some simply administer a general "fraud" standard, while others regulate under a "fair, just, and equitable" standard. The latter standard, often referred to as "merit" regulation, gives state agencies greater latitude in approving or disapproving a securities issue.

4. **Civil Liability Under Blue Sky Laws:** [§1911] State statutes usually provide specific remedies for violation of their blue sky laws. In the absence of (or in addition to) such a provision, the courts may apply appropriate common law remedies.

  a. **Violation of registration requirement:** [§1912] Most states that require registration of new securities offerings also provide liability for any violation of the registration requirement (similar to SA section 12(1)). [Weidner v. Engelhart, 176 N.W.2d 509 (N.D. 1970)]

  b. **General liability provisions:** [§1913] In addition, many states that have adopted modified versions of the Uniform Securities Act have included liability provisions similar to section 12(2) of the 1933 Act. [Shermer v. Baker, 472 P.2d 589 (Wash. 1970)]

c. **Liability of officers and directors:** [§1914] Some state laws expressly provide for the liability of directors and officers of a corporation that sells securities in violation of the state statute. Even where the statute does not so provide, state courts generally hold that any officer or director who "participates" or "aids" in such sale is jointly and severally liable with the corporation. [Adams v. American Western Securities, Inc., 510 P.2d 838 (Or. 1973)]

d. **Common law:** [§1915] Even where there is no blue sky law, state courts have developed a common law to cover securities transactions. In some cases, this common law provides results similar to those reached under the federal securities acts. [Diamond v. Oreamuno, *supra,* §968—state court used common law to uphold shareholder action against corporate management for abuse of inside information in selling corporate stock]

5. **Constitutional Law Problems:** [§1916] Because the states and the federal government both regulate the distribution of securities, and each has its separate legal system set up to do so, problems may arise when securities transactions have contacts with more than one of these jurisdictional units. The court in which a securities action is brought must determine *whether it has jurisdiction* over the securities transaction in question and, if it does, *which law it should apply.*

a. **Two basic problems:** [§1917] Basically, the situation of multiple jurisdictional units creates two problems:

(1) **Jurisdiction question:** What courts can entertain litigation when a problem has contacts with more than one state?

(2) **Conflict of laws question:** What law will be applied to settle the issues that are raised?

b. **Jurisdiction**

(1) **State jurisdiction statute:** [§1918] In deciding whether a state court has jurisdiction over a securities action, the first question is whether the state's jurisdiction statute purports to cover the transaction. This is a matter of statutory interpretation.

(a) **Domestic corporations:** [§1919] In almost every instance, a state's law will give jurisdiction to its courts over security transactions by domestic corporations (*i.e.,* those incorporated in the state). However, some statutes do not purport to cover sales of securities by resident corporations to out-of-state residents, on the basis that the buyer's state of residence will assume jurisdiction over such transactions. [*See, e.g.,* Cal. Admin. Code, title 10, rule 260.105.2]

(b) **Foreign corporations:** [§1920] The difficult questions, therefore, arise with respect to security transactions by foreign (*i.e.,* out-of-state) corporations—*e.g.,* where XYZ, incorporated in State A, attempts to sell securities to residents of State B. The securities laws of most states govern such transactions if an "offer" or "sale" is made "within the state." [Kreis v. Mates Investment Fund, Inc., 473 F.2d 1308 (8th Cir. 1973); B.C. Turf & Country Club v. Daugherty, 94 Cal. App. 2d 320 (1949)]

(2) **Constitutionality of statute:** [§1921] After the applicability of the state statute is determined, the constitutionality of the state's jurisdiction must be decided as well. For example, suppose that a foreign issuer offers to sell securities to a resident of State X by use of the mails, telephone, or other means of interstate commerce that do not require the offeror to be present in the state. If the state's statute purports to cover this situation, is the state statute constitutional?

    (a) **"Significant contacts":** [§1922] Most state statutes do cover these types of situations. If the transaction has "significant contacts" with the state, this is sufficient to sustain the constitutionality of such a statute. [Travelers Health Association v. Virginia *ex rel*. State Corporation Commission, 339 U.S. 643 (1950)—regulation by Virginia of mail order sales of insurance policies by Nebraska company as "securities" upheld]

    (b) **Service of process:** [§1923] Most states require a foreign corporation that enters its borders to issue securities to file a "consent" to service of process within the state.

        1) **Substituted service:** [§1924] Where a foreign corporation does not physically enter the state, but solicits purchasers by using the means of interstate commerce (*e.g.,* the mails), the state may rely on substituted service of process. [McGee v. International Life Insurance Co., 355 U.S. 220 (1967)—such service is constitutional]

c. **Conflict of laws:** [§1925] A number of conflict of laws issues can arise when a securities transaction involves a company with contacts in more than one state.

(1) **Constitutional question:** [§1926] The first conflicts issue involves a constitutional question: When can a state court constitutionally apply its own law to a case having contacts with more than one state? The answer is basically the same as noted above with respect to jurisdiction—*i.e.,* when the local forum has "substantial contacts" with the transaction.

(2) **Policy question:** [§1927] Assuming the forum state has substantial contacts with the securities transaction, the second issue is: When will the state court apply its own law and when will it apply the law of another state having substantial contacts?

    (a) **Note:** Resolution of cases involving substantial contacts with more than one state can be very difficult, since they involve many competing considerations. Ultimately, the question can be resolved only by making a decision as to which state's law should apply—a policy question that forms part of the subject matter of Conflict of Laws. (*See* Conflict of Laws Summary.)

        1) **Example:** To achieve a desired result, a California court applied California law to require cumulative voting of a Delaware corporation which had its principal office and business in California. However, the decision leaves unexplored many

important questions, *e.g.,* the full faith and credit to be given the corporate laws of other states, and the burden on interstate commerce when one state in effect regulates the corporate charters of out-of-state corporations. [Western Airlines v. Sobieski, 191 Cal. App. 2d 399 (1961)]

    (b) **And note:** Various formulas are often used to rationalize such a determination of policy—*e.g.,* in a contract formation case, apply the law of the state where the contract was formed; or in a tort case apply the law of the state where the injury occurred.

  (3) **Federal law vs. state law:** [§1928] Significant issues also arise with respect to conflicts between federal and state law. (*See* the Conflict of Laws and Constitutional Law Summaries.) Where the basic cause of action is based on federal securities laws, then state legal rules that impact significantly on the effectuation of federal rights, or that are inconsistent with federal policy underlying the federal cause of action, will also be treated as raising federal questions.

## D. SECONDARY DISTRIBUTION OF SECURITIES [§1929]

Many states have statutory provisions that regulate the trading of securities subsequent to their original distribution, as does the Securities Exchange Act of 1934.

1. **General Fraud Provisions:** [§1930] Nearly every state has some general provision against fraud, and a few states have provisions similar to rule 10b-5 of the 1934 Act. [Shermer v. Baker, *supra,* §1913]

2. **Registration of Broker-Dealers:** [§1931] Many states also have provisions requiring the qualification and registration of persons involved in the securities business as broker-dealers. [Uniform Securities Act §204]

3. **Tender Offer Statutes:** [§1932] In addition, many states have adopted special provisions governing the regulation of tender offers made on companies domiciled within the state's borders. Where the state statute is in too great a conflict with the purposes and manner of regulation of the federal laws, state law may be held preempted by federal law. Alternatively, the state law may also be held to impose an undue burden on interstate commerce and thus be invalid on this basis.

    a. **Undue burden on interstate commerce:** [§1933] A state tender offer statute may be found to be invalid under the Commerce Clause of the Constitution where it imposes an undue burden on interstate commerce. [Edgar v. MITE Corp., *supra,* §1119]

      (1) **Example:** In *Edgar,* Illinois state law provided that any tender offer for the shares of a target company must be registered with the Illinois Secretary of State. A "target company" was defined as a corporation that had shareholders located in Illinois owning 10% or more of the class of equity securities subject to the offer, *or* that met any two of the three following conditions:

        (i) The corporation had its *principal office* in Illinois;

        (ii) The corporation was *organized* under Illinois law; or

(iii) At least 10% *of the corporation's stated capital and paid-in-surplus* were represented within the state.

Offers filed with the secretary of state became registered 20 days after a registration statement was filed, unless the secretary called a hearing. During this time, either the secretary, or a majority of the target company's outside directors, or Illinois shareholders owning 10% or more of the class of securities subject to the offer could require a hearing. If the hearing was held, state law required the secretary to deny registration if a full disclosure of all relevant information on the offer had not been made, or if the "tender offer is inequitable." The Court found that allowing the Illinois Secretary of State to block a nationwide tender offer on this basis had a substantial effect on interstate commerce.

b. **Preemption of state law:** [§1934] In *Edgar*, the Supreme Court held that the Illinois takeover law was unconstitutional under the Commerce Clause of the Constitution. However, a majority of the Court could not agree that the Illinois law was also preempted by the Williams Act. Thus, *Edgar* left open the question of how far states could go in regulating takeovers. For a discussion of the post-*Edgar* trend, *see supra*, §§1117 *et seq.*

1.  XYZ Corp. has issued 100,000 shares of common stock. This stock is listed for trading on the New York Stock Exchange. XYZ's articles of incorporation authorize 200,000 shares, and so XYZ now wishes to issue an additional 50,000 shares in a public offering. Will the 50,000 new shares be offered in the primary market?

    *Y*

2.  The two basic purposes of the Securities Act of 1933 are (i) to ensure disclosure of all material facts concerning issuers in new offerings and (ii) to prevent fraud in the interstate sale of securities. True or false?

    *T*

3.  A buys and sells securities for his customers on a commission basis. Would A generally be designated as a "dealer" under the securities acts?

    *X no-broker*

4.  XYZ Corp. offers a $5 million issue of debt securities to the public. Does XYZ have to comply with both the Securities Act of 1933 and the Trust Indenture Act of 1939?

    *N/a*

5.  XYZ Corp. has $3 million in assets and 496 stockholders owning its common stock. Its stock is traded on the New York Stock Exchange. Must XYZ register and report to the S.E.C. under the SEA of 1934?

    *X yes*

6.  In a "firm commitment" underwriting, does the issuer initially sell its own securities to the public?

    *no-uw*

7.  ABC Corp. sells a new issue of its securities to the public without registration under the 1933 Act. ABC does not use the facilities of interstate commerce to make the offering. Does the 1933 Act nevertheless apply to this transaction?

    *not enough info but prob*

8.  X owns 2,500 of the 100,000 shares of XYZ Corp. She is not an issuer, underwriter, or dealer, as those terms are defined in the 1933 Act. X purchased the shares over the New York Stock Exchange. When X goes to sell these shares to the public, must X register them under the 1933 Act?

    *no*

9.  A has a position on the board of directors of XYZ Corp. and owns 25% of its outstanding common stock. A originally formed the corporation, although he no longer is an officer or active in its day-to-day management. A proposes to sell his 25% interest to the public through a brokerage firm. The stock is traded over the New York Stock Exchange. Must A register his stock under the 1933 Act?

    *yes-control*

10. X purchases 100,000 shares of ABC Corp.'s common stock from ABC, with the intent of reselling these shares immediately to the public. Is X an underwriter?

    *yes*

11. Suppose that A hears that XYZ Corp. is selling 100,000 shares of its common stock in a public offering. The offering, although made to the public, is not registered with the S.E.C. A buys 10,000 shares. At a dinner party, A is talking with B about his investments and describes his investment in XYZ. The next day B buys 100 shares from XYZ. Is A an underwriter?

    *No-NO view to resell*

12. A purchased a large section of land, then subdivided it into very small parcels and leased it to many investors. The leases included an obligation by A to drill test wells for oil. Is it likely that a court would find that A had marketed a "security" to the lessees?

13. Would a subdivision of lots, where most purchasers are buying the lots for speculation later to resell them for a profit, be an offering of a "security" under the 1933 Act?

14. Are general partnership interests usually securities under the 1933 Act?

15. XYZ Corp. is incorporated in Delaware, with its offices in California. Its common stock is listed on the New York Stock Exchange and is selling at $10 per share. It has 500,000 shares outstanding. XYZ now proposes to sell an additional 500,000 shares to the public. XYZ has registered with the S.E.C. under section 12 of the 1934 Act and is current in filing all required reports. It has not yet filed its registration statement with the S.E.C. XYZ and ABC Corp. (an underwriter) sign a letter of intent for the underwriting. ABC is incorporated in New York and has its principal offices there. Negotiations are conducted by long-distance telephone and through the mails. Has XYZ or ABC violated section 5 of the 1933 Act?

16. Assume that in the above question, XYZ publishes a notice in the newspaper announcing that it will distribute 500,000 shares of its common stock to the public at the market price and that the underwriter of the issue will be ABC. Is this a violation of section 5?

17. Assume that ABC, as the lead underwriter for XYZ, uses the telephone to call securities dealers in several states to invite them to become members of the retail selling group in the marketing of the XYZ public offering. Has ABC violated section 5 of the 1933 Act?

18. Under section 5 of the 1933 Act, may actual sales be made during the waiting period (after filing but before the registration statement has become effective)?

19. Assume that XYZ Corp. (questions 15-17) has filed its registration with the S.E.C. but that it has not yet become effective. Darling Dealer Corp., a securities dealer in Seattle, Washington, intends to accept an invitation from ABC to become a dealer in XYZ's offering. Darling Dealer lists XYZ in its monthly list of recommended securities (which it mails to customers). It has never before listed XYZ. Is this a violation of section 5?

20. ABC mails a copy of the preliminary prospectus on XYZ to dealers throughout the United States, enclosing a form inviting these dealers to indicate if and to what extent they are interested in purchasing some of XYZ's stock from the underwriting group and offering it at a markup to the public as soon as the registration statement becomes effective. Is this a violation of section 5?

21. Darling Dealer, having indicated that it will take 100,000 of the XYZ shares when the registration statement becomes effective, then calls one of its customers in Oregon and offers to sell 1,000 shares at the proposed offering price (as it will be set in the final prospectus), and the customer accepts the offer. Does this violate section 5?

22. Assume that XYZ's registration statement has become effective. Suppose that Darling Dealer now calls one of its customers in Oregon and offers to sell 1,000 shares, which the customer accepts. Does this violate section 5?

*No — Sales after ED are ok*

23. Suppose that in the above example, Darling Dealer then mails the stock and a confirmation of sale to the customer, but no statutory prospectus is enclosed. Is this a violation of section 5?

*Yes — Pros. must be delivered when securities are*

24. Darling Dealer, a member of the selling group, mails a prospectus to a potential customer, including with it a separate written report compiled by the Darling research department, which gives XYZ a highly enthusiastic recommendation. This material has never been filed with the S.E.C. Is this a violation of section 5?

*depends when not if after effective*

25. What is the general registration form to be used by commercial and industrial companies in registration under the 1933 Act where another form does not specifically apply?

*S-I*

26. The financial statements of an issuer used in a registration statement under the 1933 Act must be certified by an independent accountant. X is an accountant. Is X "independent" under the 1933 Act in the following circumstances?

   a. X is a member of the board of directors of B Corp., the issuer's subsidiary corporation. _____

   b. X was formerly an employee of the issuing corporation. _____

   c. X owns shares of the common stock of the issuer. _____

27. Must the following facts about XYZ Corp. be disclosed in its registration statements under the 1933 Act?

   a. The recent earnings history of the company (its net profits). _____

   b. A five-year projection of its net earnings made by the company's vice president of finance. _____

   c. All significant personal financial dealings of each member of XYZ's key management with XYZ. _____

   d. The fact that the president of XYZ is seeing a psychiatrist. _____

28. Registration with the S.E.C. of a new issue under the Securities Act of 1933 guarantees the accuracy of the facts represented in the registration statement or the prospectus. True or false? _____

29. If the S.E.C. has already instituted stop order proceedings under the 1933 Act in a preeffective registration statement matter, may the issuer still withdraw the registration statement without the approval of the S.E.C.? _____

30. Technically speaking, the S.E.C. does not require the registration statement to be amended to account for changes that occur after its effective date, at least where a period of less than nine months has transpired. True or false? _____

31. XYZ Corp. issues its stock to the public through a registration statement and prospectus under the 1933 Act. At the time the registration statement is declared effective by the S.E.C., there are no material misstatements or omissions therein. But subsequent events, which occur while the offering is still going on, make some of the material statements in the prospectus misleading. May A, an investor in the XYZ securities, bring an action under section 11 for these misstatements? _____

32. A stop order proceeding is not available under the 1933 Act once the registration statement has been declared effective. True or false? _____

33. Does an amendment filed by the issuer to a registration statement under the 1933 Act normally start the 20-day waiting period for effectiveness running again? _____

34. XYZ Corp. wishes to register all of the securities it will issue in the future at one time, in order to avoid the expense of drafting and filing multiple registration statements under the 1933 Act. Is it true that such a registration procedure will probably not be permitted by the S.E.C.? _____

35. If a security is exempted from registration under the 1933 Act, it may be sold and resold and never have to be registered, even if resold by a control person. True or false? _____

36. Generally speaking, after the expiration of 40 days from the date on which securities are first offered to the public, dealers are exempt from the prospectus delivery requirements of the 1933 Act even if the public offering involved was illegal because the securities were not registered. True or false? _____

37. Under the 1933 Act, may dealers who are still selling the securities originally allotted to them as part of the distribution dispense with the prospectus delivery requirements after 40 days from the date the securities are first offered to the public? _____

38. May a broker-dealer rely on either the dealer exemption (section 4(3)) or the broker exemption (section 4(4)) of the 1933 Act? _____

39. The broker's exemption covers not only the broker but also the selling customer. True or false? _____

40. Suppose that A, a broker-dealer, has purchased some of XYZ's securities for its own account and has been trading these securities during the 40-day period after the new offering of XYZ's securities was declared effective. During this period, the S.E.C. enters a stop order suspending the distribution of the offering. C, a customer, approaches A and asks to buy some of the XYZ securities that A has in inventory. May A use the broker exemption to sell to C without violating section 5 of the Act? _____

41. There are no hard and fast rules for determining whether an issuance of securities is a private offering. True or false? _____

42. One of the tests the S.E.C. uses for determining whether a security is being offered to the "public" is whether the purchasers thereof need the protection of the 1933 Act. True or false? _____

43. XYZ Corp. contemplates a private offering of its securities under section 4(2). It offers and ultimately sells its securities to 11 persons. Is the offering certain to be a private offering? _____

44. XYZ Corp. makes a private offering of its common stock on January 1 and additional offerings on March 1, August 1, and November 1. Are these offerings in danger of losing their non-public offering exemption? _____

45. Regulation A is not a total exemption from registration under the 1933 Act; rather, it provides the opportunity for a shortened form of registration for offerings under a certain amount. True or false? _____

46. XYZ Corp. has 100,000 common stockholders. It issues "rights" to these stockholders to buy additional shares of common stock (ownership of 10 shares allows the stockholder to buy one additional share at a 5% discount from the then prevailing market price). No consideration is paid for the rights which are good for six months. Must XYZ register the rights with the S.E.C.? _____

47. XYZ amends its corporate charter to provide that dividends that are in arrears on its cumulative preferred stock will be canceled and that dividends will no longer be cumulative. XYZ does not issue new stock certificates to the preferred stockholders. Is this a "sale" for "value" of new securities that, absent an exemption, must be registered under the 1933 Act? _____

48. XYZ Corp. has outstanding class A bonds. It proposes to issue a new class B bond in exchange for the A bonds, exchanging the bonds at equal face value. The B bonds have different maturity dates, interest rates, default provisions, etc. XYZ will pay the A bondholders a cash amount to account for the interest differential in the two bonds. May XYZ rely on the section 3(a)(9) exemption in making the exchange? _____

49. X Corp. proposes to issue common stock in exchange for the assets of Y Corp. Y will first obtain the approval of its shareholders, as required by state law, to an agreement setting forth the terms and conditions of the exchange and providing for a distribution of the X common stock to the Y shareholders. X has determined that the private offering exemption of section 4(2) of the SA would be available. Alternatively, may X use rule 145 and the S-4 registration procedure? _____

50. XYZ Corp. issues 100,000 shares of its common stock pursuant to rule 147. A buys 50,000 of these and holds for two years. He then wishes to resell his shares in a public distribution. Since he has met his investment intent pursuant to the rule, although he is a control person, may he sell without registration under the Act? _____

51. XYZ Corp. makes an intrastate offering pursuant to rule 147. All purchasers are residents of the same state as XYZ, but one of the offerees is not. Is the exemption therefore lost? _____

52. There is no violation of the private offering exemption under the 1933 Act even though investors took with a view toward distribution of the securities, if in fact there was no actual public distribution of the securities. True or false? _____

53. XYZ Corp. sells to A, B, and C in a private offering. A and B (although representing that they are taking for investment) violate their representations and A sells to D through G, and B sells to H through L. May A and B be held as underwriters under the 1933 Act if the total offering amounts to a public offering? _____

54. X issues stock to A in a private offering. A is a control person who establishes his investment intent with respect to the offering. A then sells all of his control stock over the stock exchange without registration, to many purchasers. Has A violated the 1933 Act as an "issuer" making a public distribution without registration? _____

55. If XYZ Corp. sells to P in a private offering, and P holds the securities until she has satisfied investment intent under section 4(2) of the Act, and P then sells to P2, may P2 (if he is not a control person) then resell immediately in a public distribution? _____

56. A is the owner of 25% of the common stock of Z Corp. In addition, A sits on the board of directors of Z and is a good friend of the president. None of the stock that A owns is restricted stock. A has held the stock for one year and now desires to sell it. May A use rule 144? _____

57. X Corp. is not subject to the reporting requirements of sections 13 or 15(d) of the SEA of 1934. Y owns restricted securities of X and wants to sell them. He has held them for two years, and X has furnished the information called for under rule 15c 2-11 of the 1934 Act to the broker for Y. Can Y use rule 144 to sell the stock? _____

58. C got her stock as a gift from her father. Her father got the stock in a private placement from X Corp. and held it for one year. C has now held for 18 months. She is not a control person. C meets all of the other requirements of rule 144. May she sell under the rule? _____

59. XYZ Corp. has registered a public offering of its stock. A buys some stock and resells to B within a two-month period of the offering. There are material misrepresentations in the registration statement. B does not read the registration statement and knows nothing of the misrepresentations. However, when the misrepresentations are made public, XYZ stock goes down. B discovers the fraud and sues XYZ. Can B recover under section 11 of the 1933 Act? _____

60. XYZ offers securities under a materially defective registration statement. A buys and then resells to B in an over-the-counter transaction. B has read the registration statement and other materials on XYZ. The stock is bought by B three months after the offering and held in the broker's house account. XYZ has had previous public offerings. B discovers the fraud six months after purchase and brings a lawsuit against the issuer. The broker transfers shares out of the house account to B, which B cannot trace back to the registration statement. Can B recover under SA section 11? _____

61. XYZ sells stock to the public pursuant to a registration statement; the offering price is $10 per share. An hour after the offering begins, all of the stock has been sold for the first time, and the stock is trading at $15 per share. A buys 100 shares at $15. There is a material misstatement in the prospectus. A month later,

when the stock has fallen to $10 per share, A sells. Discovering the misstatement, A sues XYZ. What amount per share can A recover? _____

62. XYZ sells stock directly to the public in a public distribution without registration. A is one of the purchasers. XYZ has never heard of section 5 of the 1933 Act; neither has A. A becomes disenchanted with the stock and sues under section 12(1) of the Act to rescind the transaction. Will A win? _____

63. XYZ recruits an advisory board of influential business and civic leaders to advise the company about new marketing plans and ideas. XYZ raises money through an intended private offering, which turns out to be a public offering. In the offering memorandum, the name, background, and experience of each member of the advisory board appear, and the indication is given that offerees may call these people for recommendations about the company. Several offerees do so and receive assurances that the company is sound, as well as invitations to purchase XYZ securities. The memorandum contains several material misstatements in its financial statements, and, in fact, the company is broke. May the purchasers sue the members of the advisory board under section 12(2)? _____

64. XYZ Corp. has assets of $5 million and 450 shareholders. It also has its common stock listed for trading on the New York Stock Exchange. Must it register with the S.E.C. under section 12 of the 1934 Act? _____

65. XYZ Corp. is not registered with the S.E.C. under section 12 of the 1934 Act since it has neither securities that are listed on a national exchange nor over $5 million in assets and 500 or more shareholders of a class of its equity securities. XYZ engages in a fraudulent securities transaction. May it be sued under rule 10b-5 of the 1934 Act? _____

66. The statute of limitations for rule 10b-5 actions is three years from the date the misrepresentation or omission is discovered. True or false? _____

67. XYZ Corp. chooses to predict its future earnings for the coming year. Is there a possibility that if this prediction is inaccurate and carelessly made, XYZ could be subject to a rule 10b-5 suit on the basis of having misrepresented a material fact? _____

68. XYZ Corp. declares a cash dividend on its common stock but does not disclose this to the public. Hence, trading in XYZ's stock is continued without awareness on the part of buyers and sellers that a dividend has been declared. Is this an omission of a material fact by the corporation? _____

69. The board of directors of XYZ Corp. unanimously agrees to issue stock of the corporation to themselves at prices substantially below the current fair market value of the stock. Since the directors are responsible for management and have approved the sale, is it true that no one connected with the corporation has a cause of action under rule 10b-5? _____

70. In the example above, is there a substantial possibility that a federal court would find no rule 10b-5 cause of action since there is already an established state cause of action for breach of directors' fiduciary duties to shareholders? _____

71. P is a shareholder of XYZ Corp. She claims that her stock has depreciated in value in the market due to a series of misrepresentations made by the management of XYZ to the public. P has not actually bought or sold any XYZ stock during the period of these misrepresentations. P sues XYZ under rule 10b-5. Does P have standing to bring the suit? _____

72. For rule 10b-5 to apply, there must be a sufficient connection between the activity complained of (*i.e.,* a misrepresentation, etc.) and the purchase or sale of securities. True or false? _____

73. In the audit of XYZ Corp., the auditing firm (ABC) fails to accurately account for the corporation's liabilities from outstanding warranties given on XYZ products. As a result, XYZ's published financial statements are substantially inaccurate. A shareholder who bought XYZ stock in the market at $100 per share sues when the stock drops to $50 per share after the true facts are published. One of the named defendants in the rule 10b-5 suit is ABC. At trial it is shown that ABC's omission of the material fact was the result of negligence. May the shareholder recover under rule 10b-5 against ABC? _____

74. Although in some transactions (such as face-to-face buy-sell transactions) the courts still seem to require that there be privity in order to bring a 10b-5 action, in most situations involving transactions over a stock exchange, the courts seem to have dispensed with the privity requirement. True or false? _____

75. XYZ Corp. issues a materially false press release concerning its financial condition. A buys XYZ stock over the stock exchange at $10 per share. Later, when XYZ corrects the press release and discloses its true financial condition, the stock drops to $7 per share. Shortly thereafter, XYZ announces that merger discussions it has been carrying on with another corporation have terminated, at least for the present time. A then sues XYZ under rule 10b-5 on the basis of the false press release. At trial, A does not prove reliance on the false press release, but simply proves that XYZ's financial condition was a material fact. XYZ proves that, in fact, A did not rely on the financial condition of the corporation, but would have bought the stock anyway (since A had inside information about the merger discussions which were being conducted, in which $25 per share sale by XYZ Corp. of its stock was being considered). Is this a successful defense to A's lawsuit? _____

76. Reliance and causation mean the same thing in a rule 10b-5 cause of action. True or false? _____

77. Where a defendant violated rule 10b-5 by trading on inside information over an exchange, it is clear that the courts would allow unlimited recovery by all injured plaintiffs no matter what their total damages, even when defendant's total profits were substantially less than plaintiff's damages. True or false? _____

78. Indicate whether the following persons are "insiders" of XYZ Corp., as the term insiders has been defined by the courts:

   a. Controlling shareholder of XYZ who is briefed on all major developments of the corporation. _____

   b. Directors of XYZ. _____

c.      Officers of XYZ. _____

d.      Other high-ranking corporate executives, although not officers. _____

e.      Tippers with inside information received from the corporate officers. _____

f.      Tippees receiving inside information from inside tippers. _____

79.   May XYZ Corp. itself be held liable for damages under rule 10b-5 for failure to disclose a material fact to the investing public? _____

80.   A Corp. makes a direct offer to the shareholders of B Corp. of cash and/or its stock for their common stock in B. If the common stock of B Corp. is registered under section 12 of the 1934 Act, would this be a tender offer for the purposes of section 14(d) of the 1934 Act? _____

81.   ABC Corp. acquires more than 5% of the registered common stock of XYZ Corp. It is ABC's present intention to attempt to gain control of XYZ Corp. through a tender offer. Must ABC disclose this information to the management of XYZ? _____

82.   ABC Corp. makes a tender offer for the common stock of XYZ Corp. XYZ sends out a letter to its shareholders which misrepresents the financial condition and the experience of ABC's management. Does ABC have standing in federal court to bring a damage action against XYZ under section 14(e) of the SEA? _____

83.   In the above hypothetical, could ABC Corp. get an injunction against the mailing of such a letter? _____

84.   For the federal proxy rules to apply, must a company have a class of its equity securities registered under section 12 of the 1934 Act? _____

85.   XYZ Corp. has a class of its equity securities registered under section 12 of the SEA of 1934. It schedules its annual meeting of shareholders, where one issue to be voted on is the merger of XYZ into ABC Corp. No proxies are solicited. Under the federal proxy rules, must XYZ Corp. file with the S.E.C. and distribute to its shareholders prior to the shareholders' meeting the same information that would have been included in a proxy statement had proxies been solicited? _____

86.   The antifraud provision of the federal proxy rules of the 1934 Act does not apply to oral representations made in the course of a proxy solicitation. True or false? _____

87.   Under the antifraud provisions of the federal proxy rules, in cases where proxies are needed to secure affirmative action on a matter proposed to the shareholders, the plaintiff in a private damage action need only show that a misstatement or omission was "material" in order substantially to meet the requirement that the proxy materials be shown to have caused the damage for which the complaint seeks relief. True or false? _____

88.   As a general rule, for an insider to be liable under section 16(b) of the 1934 Act, she must be shown to have actually received and unfairly used "inside" information. True or false? _____

89. X owns 15% of the common stock of ABC Corp. The common stock is registered under section 12 of the 1934 Act. X also owns 15% of the convertible preferred stock of ABC, which is not registered under section 12. X buys and then sells shares of the convertible preferred stock within six months at a profit. May a shareholder of ABC sue X in a derivative action for the profit under section 16(b)?   _____

90. X owns 8% of the registered common stock of ABC Corp. He buys an additional 4% at $10 per share on March 1. On April 1, he sells 4% at $20 per share. Is X liable as an "insider" under section 16(b) of the 1934 Act for his profit in the sale on April 1st?   _____

91. Directors and officers may be held liable under section 16(b) as "insiders" even though they were not such both at the beginning and the end of the matched purchase and sale (or sale and purchase), as long as they held office at either time of the purchase or sale (or sale and purchase). True or false?   _____

92. Generally, when a corporation is merged or sold in exchange for stock there is a "sale" of the securities surrendered by the selling company's shareholders and a "purchase" of the securities received from the buying company. Thus, section 16(b) would apply to such transactions. True or false?   _____

93. A is a lawyer. She does not represent XYZ Corp., but she is a good friend of XYZ's president, B. XYZ is having trouble selling a private offering of its securities. B asks if A will help him market the issue, and A agrees. A takes no compensation for her services. A calls several of her clients and suggests that they buy some of the XYZ stock. They do so. In fact, the XYZ investment memorandum contained material misrepresentations concerning XYZ's financial position. May the clients of A successfully sue A as an aider and abettor under rule 10b-5?   _____

94. It has been clearly established by the courts that any employer can be held liable on the basis of traditional agency principles for the acts of employees that constitute a violation of either the 1933 or 1934 Acts. True or false?   _____

95. X, an accountant, assists ABC Corp., X's largest client, in the publication of materially false financial statements. (X, knowing that ABC has not stated its income according to generally accepted accounting principles, nevertheless certifies the financial statements as having been prepared correctly.) The financial statements are then used as part of an offering memorandum in a private placement of securities. Y buys some of the stock without having read the financial statements. When the fraud is disclosed, may Y bring suit for his losses against X under rule 10b-5?   _____

96. A is a lawyer representing XYZ Corp. in a registration under the 1933 Act. In conferences with the president of the corporation, it is disclosed to A that the backlog of orders which XYZ has stated that it has is really not as large as indicated. A considers this a material misstatement of fact in the draft of the registration statement. He asks the president to correct it, and the president declines, feeling that the sale of the stock issue depends on showing favorable prospects for the future. A resigns as counsel for the corporation. XYZ goes ahead with the issue, using the material misrepresentation. When the fraud is disclosed, might the S.E.C. take the position that A has also violated the securities laws?   _____

97. A "financial institution" is any institution (usually relatively large in assets) that accumulates money from others for investment. True or false? _____

98. XYZ Corp. has its common stock listed for trading on the New York Stock Exchange. May XYZ's stock be traded at the same time on other regional exchanges, over-the-counter, and directly between financial institutions? _____

99. The SEA of 1934 completely precludes regulation of the national exchanges by the federal antitrust laws. True or false? _____

100. The basic function of a "specialist" on the floor of a national securities exchange is to see that a continuous trading market exists for buying and selling specific securities listed on the exchange. True or false? _____

101. Under specific and limited circumstances, the courts will imply a private remedy for damages for violation of one of the rules of a national securities exchange (such as by a broker-dealer member). True or false? _____

102. A is a broker-dealer doing a securities business in interstate commerce. She is not a member of any national securities exchange.

    a.    Must A register with the S.E.C. (unless dealing in exempt securities)? _____

    b.    Must A belong to and be regulated by the National Association of Securities Dealers ("NASD")? _____

103. Stock market manipulation is any attempt to set prices or other criteria of stock market performance through transactions entered into with that specific purpose. True or false? _____

104. Market stabilization is one form of market manipulation which is specifically prohibited by the 1934 Act only when the S.E.C. adopts rules to prohibit it. True or false? _____

105. A is an underwriting firm selling a new issue of XYZ Corp. to the public in a registered offering. It plans to hold back 50,000 of the 500,000 shares being offered in the hopes that demand will lift the stock almost immediately above its $5 per share offering price. Once the price rises above $5, A will begin selling the 50,000 shares for its own account. Are such sales by A an unlawful manipulation of the market for XYZ's stock? _____

106. The "shingle theory" holds that a broker-dealer subject to one of several anti-fraud provisions of the securities acts may be held liable under one of these sections even though the broker-dealer's conduct does not amount to the statutorily required intentional wrongdoing. True or false? _____

107. X, a broker-dealer, buys 100 shares of XYZ Corp. on March 1 for $5 per share and sells the same day for $10 per share. Could this be a conflict of interest with X's relationship with its customers in violation of NASD and S.E.C. rules? _____

108. NASD and S.E.C. rules require that registered broker-dealers disclose their relationship with their customers where the broker-dealer is making a market in a security which the broker-dealer buys or sells to the customer. True or false? _____

109. In a "boiler room" operation, the crux of the 1934 Act violation is that the broker-dealer and its salespeople normally fail to comply with NASD and S.E.C. rules requiring that broker-dealers know the facts concerning any recommended security and give full disclosure of such facts to the customer. True or false?

_____

110. May X, a broker-dealer, be held liable under the NASD or S.E.C. rules where it fails to exercise reasonable supervision over its sales personnel in the recommendations that such personnel give their customers?

_____

111. The Federal Reserve Board, and not the S.E.C., is responsible for developing the margin rules pursuant to section 7 of the SEA of 1934. True or false?

_____

112. Rule 10b-5 of the 1934 Act will be applied to foreign nationals and foreign securities transactions as long as there is some substantial U.S. contact and a substantial U.S. interest to be protected. True or false?

_____

113. XYZ Corp. wishes to sell a public offering of its stock to residents of seven states. If XYZ registers its stock under the 1933 Act, will it be required to register in any of the seven states?

_____

# ANSWERS TO REVIEW QUESTIONS

1. **YES**    The primary markets are the facilities for the first issuance of securities to the public. [§2]

2. **TRUE**   Material disclosures are to be given in the registration statement and prospectus (liability provisions of sections 11 and 12(1) relate thereto), and section 12(2) of the SA is a general liability provision relating to fraud in the interstate sale of securities. [§§40-41, 85-89]

3. **NO**     The securities acts define the terms "broker" and "dealer" in specific contexts. But, in general (in functional terms), a *broker* is one who buys or sells securities as an agent, for a commission. [§§10-11]

4. **YES**    The 1933 Act applies to public offerings of securities, and the Trust Indenture Act applies to specified large issues of debt securities. [§§40, 55]

5. **YES**    Where a company has a class of its equity securities listed on a national stock exchange, it must register with the S.E.C. under section 12 of the 1934 Act. [§43]

6. **NO**     A firm commitment underwriting is one where the underwriter buys the issuer's securities, marks them up, and sells them to the public. [§76]

7. **NO**     Interstate commerce must be involved. However, it is extremely unlikely that a public offering could be made without using some means of interstate commerce. [§§62, 66]

8. **NO**     Section 4(1) of the Act indicates that registration applies only to issuers, underwriters, or dealers. X is none of these. And she is not a control person, which would make her an issuer by the terms of the 1933 Act. [§§90, 107]

9. **YES**    He is probably a "control person" and hence an issuer by the terms of the Act. [§101]

10. **YES**   This is one of the specific definitions given for underwriters in the 1933 Act. [§93]

11. **NO**    The theory for finding A an underwriter would be that he "participated" in the public offering. However, it is doubtful that there is sufficient participation here to warrant such a finding. [§§96-97]

12. **YES**   Under the *Howey* test, it appears to be an investment contract, with management provided by A. [§142]

13. **DEPENDS**   Such a plan, although dealing with a commodity (real estate) that is not normally thought of as a security, has the elements associated with a security—profit-making and services by central management (subdivision). However, if resales are totally the responsibility of the buyers, then perhaps there is no security since there is substantial involvement in management by the investors. [§§134-139]

| 14. | **NO** | They generally require that the investor participate actively in management. [§143] |
|---|---|---|
| 15. | **NO** | The Act allows the issuer and the underwriter to conduct negotiations and enter agreements in the pre-filing period [§159] |
| 16. | **YES** | Rule 135 forbids mention by the issuer of the underwriter in the pre-filing period. [§167] |
| 17. | **YES** | The telephone calls are unlawful "offers" in the pre-filing period. There is an exemption for negotiations between the issuer and the underwriter, but here negotiations are being conducted with possible dealers. [§159] |
| 18. | **NO** | However, certain *offers* are permissible in this period. [§§176-177] |
| 19. | **YES** | It is an unlawful offer. [§179; *and see* SA Rule 139(b)] |
| 20. | **NO** | It is using a prescribed written method to solicit offers. [§181] |
| 21. | **YES** | It is a sale under the 1933 Act. Sales are not permitted in the waiting period. [§176] |
| 22. | **NO** | Oral offers may be made in the waiting or post-effective period, and sales may be made in the post-effective period. There is no written offer involved and no securities have been delivered, so no prospectus need be delivered at this point. [§§193-195] |
| 23. | **YES** | A written confirmation is considered a prospectus under the terms of the Act so that it must be accompanied by an approved statutory prospectus. Also, sections 5(a) and 5(b) of the Act require that a prospectus accompany or precede delivery after sale. [§§198-199] |
| 24. | **NO** | Additional sales literature may be used in the effective period, as long as the statutory prospectus either accompanies or precedes it. But Darling should be careful that it has not made any material misrepresentations in such literature or it may be liable under section 12(2) of the 1933 Act. [§197] |
| 25. | **Form S-1** | The SA provides a number of forms for use by particular types of companies or for special types of securities offerings. S-1 is the general form. [§§218-223] |
| 26. | **NO in all three cases** | In a. and b., X has too close a relationship with the issuer. In c., there is too much potential for a conflict of interest between the duty as an accountant and X's desire to see a successful public offering of the issuer's stock so that X might benefit financially. [§234] |
| 27. a. | **YES** | As part of the financial statements. [§234] |
| b. | **NO** | However, the S.E.C. now takes the position that projections of earnings are to be encouraged. [§245] |
| c. | **YES** | This is material since it may disclose a conflict of interest between the key management and the issuer, which is relevant information to an investor. [§239; *and see* Regulation S-K *item* 404] |

d. **NO**      Not expressly required by any directive related to the 1933 Act, and yet it is potentially very important to investors since the performance of the company is dependent on the emotional stability of the president and other key officers. [§239] If the omission of this fact would make the registration statement, as a whole, misleading, then the psychiatric care must be disclosed. [*See* SA Rule 408]

28. **FALSE**      The S.E.C. does not make such a guarantee. The issuer and specified persons involved with the offering must take responsibility for any material inaccuracies. [§261]

29. **NO**      Withdrawal at this stage is at the discretion of the S.E.C. staff. [§281]

30. **TRUE**      However, since section 12(2) of the 1933 Act covers any misrepresentation in the sale of securities, an issuer would probably want to update the registration statement and prospectus if subsequent events made anything stated therein at the time of use a material misrepresentation. [§294]

31. **NO**      Section 11 applies only to errors in the registration statement or prospectus at the time they are declared effective. [§§293-294]

32. **FALSE**      A stop order proceeding is available at any time. [§§276-277] There are limitations, however, on the issuance of a refusal order.

33. **YES**      But the S.E.C. may, on request, shorten this period and declare the statement effective. [§267]

34. **YES**      Except in limited circumstances. This is a "shelf registration," or a registration of securities that are not presently being offered. The problem is that there is no way to provide accurate information on XYZ to potential investors in such a registration procedure. [§§283-286]

35. **TRUE**      However, with a transaction exemption only the specific transaction is exempt; later resales (as by a control person) may have to be registered. [§§303, 311]

36. **TRUE**      The Act gives dealers a limited prospectus delivery exemption, which begins after the end of the statutorily defined "distribution" period. [§§323-324]

37. **NO**      The delivery requirement continues as long as the dealer is selling part of its original allotment. [§325]

38. **YES**      Of course, where the dealer exemption applies, the dealer will have no need for the broker exemption. [§305]

39. **FALSE**      The selling customer must find its own exemption. [§310]

40. **NO**      The transaction does not come under a broker's exemption since it is a dealer sale (out of inventory). [§311]

41. **IN GENERAL, TRUE**      Under section 4(2) of the Act, the S.E.C. and the courts look at a number of variables in making the private offering determination. [§§343-346] There are, however, specific "safe harbor" rules with objective criteria for determining whether an offering is a private one. (*See, e.g.*, Rules 504-506.) [§§362-386]

42. **TRUE**      This is a basic consideration underlying the S.E.C.'s application of the section 4(2) exemption for offerings not made to the public. [§345]

43. **NO**      The S.E.C. and the courts consider several variables in deciding whether an offering is private and, therefore, exempt under SA section 4(2). While the number of offerees and the number of purchasers are both relevant, neither figure is determinative. An offering could be public, notwithstanding that it was made only to 11 offerees and purchasers. [§§341-356]

44. **YES**      Where possible, the S.E.C. will argue that apparently separate private offerings should be integrated into one public offering, in order to prevent issuers from avoiding the registration provisions of the 1933 Act. [§§312-313, 358]

45. **TRUE**      Section 3(b) of the Act permits the S.E.C. to provide for exemptions in certain small offerings. The S.E.C. has allowed for a shortened registration procedure in the case of regulation A offerings. [§§387-388]

46. **NO**      There is no sale for "value." [§474]

47. **YES**      Here there has been a change in the rights of the security holders. It is not a mere exchange of paper with no increase or lessening of the substantive rights of the preferred stockholders. [§486]

48. **YES**      But if XYZ required the class A bondholders to pay money to it on the exchange, the exemption might not apply. [§498]

49. **YES**      The transaction is the type covered by rule 145—sale of assets. [§508]

50. **NO**      A control person must always find an exemption for his sales. Rule 147 is a transaction exemption and does not cover secondary sales by control persons. [§442]

51. **YES**      All offerees and purchasers must be residents of the same state. [§462]

52. **TRUE**      There must actually be a public distribution or no violation of the Act has occurred. [§538]

53. **YES**      The distribution continues until it comes to rest in the hands of those taking for investment. A and B could be held to have participated in a public distribution. [§539]

54. **YES**      It makes no difference that A established investment intent. Control persons become issuers when making a public distribution whether the stock they distribute is control stock or restricted stock. [§540]

55. **YES**      Once P has held the securities and satisfied investment intent, the private distribution has been completed. Subsequent purchasers who are not control persons may then buy and resell the securities as they wish, using section 4(1) of the Act as their exemption. [§549]

56. **YES**      The two-year holding period of rule 144 applies only to sales of restricted stock. [§560]

| 57. | **NO** | This is not sufficient disclosure of information concerning X to apply rule 144. The S.E.C. requires that information about the issuer be supplied to the issuer's shareholders, brokers, marketmakers, and any other interested persons. In addition, financial information about the issuer must be published in a recognized financial reporting service. [§559] |
|---|---|---|
| 58. | **YES** | Rule 144 provides that restricted securities cannot be resold until at least two years have passed since the date the securities were acquired from the issuer. In this case, 30 months have passed, and so rule 144 will apply to C's sale. [§§560, 565] |
| 59. | **YES** | As long as B can trace the securities to the registration statement, he may recover even though he can show no reliance on the misrepresentation. [§§656, 659] |
| 60. | **NO** | Although she relied on the misrepresentation, she cannot trace her securities to the registration statement. [§659] |
| 61. | **$0** | Measure of recovery is the price paid less what it is sold for; but the price paid cannot exceed the offering price. [§680] |
| 62. | **YES** | It is a violation of section 5 to make a public offering without registration absent an exemption. Section 12(1) relates to any violation of section 5. It makes no difference that XYZ did not intentionally violate the Act. [§§687-692] |
| 63. | **YES** | Section 12(2) is a general fraud provision for purchasers. Here, the issue is whether the advisory board members "participated" to the extent necessary to become sellers under section 12(2). Because the advisory board members solicited the purchasers, the board members here become sellers. [§§714-715] |
| 64. | **YES** | The registration provisions of the 1934 Act apply to all companies registered on a national securities exchange and/or those with assets of more than $5 million and having a class of equity security with 500 or more shareholders. [§§742-744] |
| 65. | **YES** | Rule 10b-5 applies to all types of securities and securities transactions, not just those securities registered under the 1934 Act. There is, however, an interstate commerce requirement; that is, in order for the rule to apply, the means of interstate commerce, or the mails or a national securities exchange must be used in connection with the purchase or sale of securities. [§§798-800] |
| 66. | **FALSE** | Since the 1991 Supreme Court decision in the *Lampf* case, the statute of limitations for rule 10b-5 actions provides that actions must be brought within one year after discovery of the facts constituting the rule 10b-5 violation, and in no event more than three years after the violation took place. [§915] |
| 67. | **PROBABLY** | Although the registrant is not a guarantor of earnings predictions made by its management, the facts state that the prediction was made "carelessly." The question, then, is whether the registrant's carelessness amounts to scienter, so that a rule 10b-5 action is available. While we could wish for more facts, management is in a unique position to know and understand the data supporting the |

prediction. Management carelessness may well rise to the level of "reckless-ness," which has been accepted as equivalent to scienter in rule 10b-5 cases by every appellate court to consider the issue. [§886]

68. **YES**  Clearly, a reasonable investor would want to know that the company had declared a dividend. Hence, the fact of a dividend is a *material* fact, and it must be announced by the corporation to avoid liability under rule 10b-5. [§834]

69. **NO**  The shareholders have a rule 10b-5 cause of action. [§809]

70. **YES**  The current trend is to find that rule 10b-5 was not meant to cover this type of transaction. [§814]

71. **NO**  For a plaintiff to bring a 10b-5 cause of action, she must be an actual purchaser or seller of securities. [§858]

72. **TRUE**  Otherwise, nearly any fraud could somehow be connected with a purchase or sale of securities, and there would be no limitation on rule 10b-5 causes of action. [§865]

73. **NO**  The shareholder must prove actual intentional wrongdoing by ABC (or possibly recklessness). Negligence is not sufficient. [§885]

74. **TRUE**  By and large this is true, although some courts still appear to be trying to use privity as a means of limiting the scope of 10b-5 actions. [§877]

75. **PROBABLY**  In most exchange transaction situations, the courts seem to find reliance from a showing of materiality. However, it is probably left open for defendant to prove that plaintiff did not rely on the misrepresentation or omission of material fact by defendant. [§839]

76. **FALSE**  Sometimes they appear to be the same thing (*i.e.*, transaction causation). But courts always state both elements separately, as independent requirements. [§896]

77. **FALSE**  It is not clear at all. This area of rule 10b-5 is very much up in the air, with courts struggling with the problem of coming up with a reasonable solution to the question of who should bear what risk of loss in this situation. [§§907-908]

78. **YES as to all**  But only when they actually are in possession of inside information. They may be in a position to have inside information (such as a director) but not actually possess it (*e.g.*, absent from the board meeting when the information was presented). [§§928-930, 938-945]

79. **MAYBE**  In certain circumstances; *see* discussion of the *Texas Gulf Sulphur* case. [§942]

80. **YES**  A tender offer is an offer directly to a company's shareholders for their stock. Section 14(d) is the basic section that regulates the making of tender offers. [§§978, 988]

81. **YES**  When a person acquires more than 2% in one year and has a total of more than 5% of the registered equity securities of a company, then that person must

disclose her intentions with regard to the company to the management of that company. *See* discussion of section 13(d) of the 1934 Act. [§§992-994]

82. **NO**　　　The Supreme Court recently held that a defeated bidder has no standing to bring a damages action in this circumstance. [§1054]

83. **PROBABLY**　　　This area is somewhat uncertain at present, but lower federal court opinions indicate that ABC would have standing here. [§1073]

84. **YES**　　　The proxy rules apply only to registered companies. [§1140]

85. **YES**　　　Where a matter requires shareholder vote, even if proxies are not solicited, an information statement must be filed and distributed. [§1150]

86. **FALSE**　　　Oral misrepresentations made by one soliciting proxies in the course of such solicitation are covered by rule 14a-9 of the proxy rules. [§1251]

87. **TRUE**　　　The Supreme Court has indicated in the *Mills* case that causation is proved by showing materiality in a case where the proxy solicitation was an essential link in the accomplishment of the transaction. [§§1257-1258]

88. **FALSE**　　　Section 16(b) applies if its specific requirements are met, whether or not inside information was actually used in the trading of securities by an insider. [§1377]

89. **YES**　　　X qualifies as an "insider" under section 16 by virtue of his 15% ownership of a registered class of equity securities. Thereafter, purchases and sales of any equity security (*i.e.*, the convertible preferred stock), even if not registered, are covered by section 16. [§1288]

90. **NO**　　　Section 16(b) requires that an insider for stock ownership must be a 10% owner at the time of a "purchase" *and* at the time of a "sale," if the purchase and sale are to be matched for section 16(b) purposes. Here, the purchase on March 1 does not qualify since X did not own 10% on that date. [§1302]

91. **TRUE**　　　The provision is different for officers and directors than it is for 10% owners. [§§1294-1297]

92. **TRUE**　　　But an exception has been made for certain defensive merger situations where the 10% owners must make such an exchange involuntarily. [§§1354-1359]

93. **NO**　　　Before the 1994 Supreme Court decision in *Central Bank*, the answer to this question would have turned on whether A met the *Hochfelder* requirements of scienter (or, perhaps, recklessness). After *Central Bank*, however, it is clear that there is no implied private right of action against one who aids or abets a violation of rule 10b-5. [§1415] However, if A meets the *Hochfelder* requirement of scienter, A might be liable as a primary violator. Aiding and abetting, and other secondary liability theories, might be unnecessary.

94. **FALSE**　　　There is a split of authority on this point. Some courts indicate that the specific provisions of the securities acts control (*i.e.*, those which relate to the liability of "control" persons) and that traditional agency principles do not apply. Other courts are contra. [§§1426-1428]

| 95. | **YES** | X has intentionally participated in a violation of rule 10b-5. [§1449] |
|---|---|---|
| 96. | **YES** | The S.E.C. position might be that A must protect the public interest, and not just the interests of XYZ. Here, XYZ appears to have disclosed to A its intention to commit a crime under the securities laws. Under the A.B.A. Code of Professional Responsibility, A has the option of whether or not to disclose this (including disclosure to the S.E.C.). But the S.E.C. position might be that A has participated in the violation if he does not disclose such an intention by XYZ. [§§1474, 1478-1480] |
| 97. | **TRUE** | This is a general definition of a "financial institution." Institutions have an enormous influence on the national exchanges. [§1623] |
| 98. | **YES** | A company's securities may be traded in many markets simultaneously. [§§1610-1614] |
| 99. | **FALSE** | The Supreme Court has indicated that the SEA of 1934 must accommodate the federal antitrust laws. It is only where the two directly conflict, and the S.E.C. has the power to regulate and actually has exercised it, that the antitrust laws are precluded. [§§1636, 1639] |
| 100. | **TRUE** | The specialist is in charge of specific securities and has the responsibility of seeing that whenever a buyer or seller wishes to place an order on the exchange for that security, that the security can always be bought or sold. [§1648] |
| 101. | **TRUE** | Courts are reluctant to do so, but in appropriate circumstances they have implied such private damage actions. However, the trend of recent United States Supreme Court decisions is against the implication of such private remedies. [§§1685-1687] |
| 102. | **YES to both** | Broker-dealers transacting an interstate business must be registered with the S.E.C. and must be members of the NASD (or, in theory, any other comparable body itself registered with the S.E.C.). As a practical matter, NASD membership is required because there are no other organizations comparable to the NASD that are registered with the S.E.C. [§§1695-1696] |
| 103. | **TRUE** | Such manipulation is regulated by specific provisions of the 1934 Act and by the general liability provisions of the Act (*see* rule 10b-5). [§§1720-1727] |
| 104. | **TRUE** | Currently, the S.E.C. has rules in effect with respect to stabilizing transactions in connection with the marketing of new issues of securities. However, if other stabilization transactions were to appear manipulative to the S.E.C., it would undoubtedly use the general liability provisions of the Act (10b-5) to attack the transaction. [§1739] |
| 105. | **YES** | The S.E.C. regulates such "hot issues" and prohibits A's conduct and similar conduct which gives the appearance that a stock is being offered at a specific price when in fact part of the offering is not really being sold to the public at the offering price at all. [§§1764-1766] |
| 106. | **TRUE** | The courts have indicated that such broker-dealers make certain implied representations simply by entering the securities business (hanging out a shingle); these representations act as implied warranties, so that violation may be found |

under one of the antifraud provisions without proving actual intentional fraud. [§1780]

107. **YES** In a general policy statement, the NASD has indicated that its broker-dealers may not charge unreasonable commissions or markups. A markup limit of 5% has been set for same day transactions. However, X could try to prove that 100% was not unreasonable if the actual market for the stock had moved up that much from the time it purchased the stock. [§1785]

108. **TRUE** To avoid conflicts of interest with customers, the rules require such disclosures to those with whom the broker-dealer is doing business. [§1808]

109. **TRUE** In a boiler room operation, a single security is promoted by high pressure tactics. There is little or no concern for the rules requiring the broker-dealer to know the security and recommend it only where suitable to the client's needs. [§§1825, 1830]

110. **YES** The registered broker-dealer is held responsible for all the transactions entered into by personnel registered under the broker-dealer. [§§1844-1847]

111. **TRUE** But the S.E.C. has the responsibility of enforcement. [§1848]

112. **TRUE** The position of the courts on this issue is about the same as it is with respect to application of any other United States law to foreign transactions. [§1881]

113. **DEPENDS** Most states regulate the public distribution of securities within their borders. Some grant an exemption from state registration when the issue is registered under the 1933 Act. XYZ will have to examine and comply with the law of each of the seven states in making its distribution. [§§1893-1897]

## SAMPLE EXAM QUESTION I

A, who owns 25% of the stock of XYZ Corp., is a director and an officer of XYZ, active in daily management. She pledges her stock in XYZ to a bank, as collateral for a loan to buy some real estate. The stock of XYZ is publicly traded. Immediately after receiving the loan proceeds, A resigns as an officer of XYZ, knowing that the company is entering a period of financial difficulty. A enters the real estate business. As soon as the 90-day period of the loan is up, the bank calls the loan, and A refuses to pay. The bank resorts to the security (the XYZ stock), which it sells to pay off A's loan. Shortly thereafter, the news breaks that XYZ is in financial trouble, and the stock drops substantially in price. Applying only the law of the Securities Act of 1933, is the bank an underwriter unlawfully engaged in a public distribution without registration?

## SAMPLE EXAM QUESTION II

Without complying with any of the registration requirements under the Securities Act of 1933, XYZ Co. advertises in newspapers and over radio and television to find distributors for its product, a line of cosmetics. The distributors come from all walks of life, having had a great variety of former jobs, income levels, and educational backgrounds. Each distributor pays a fee of $5,000 for his "franchise," for which he receives an inventory of products which may be resold at a suggested retail price of $7,500. Also, the distributors receive the right to find other distributors, for which a finder's fee of $1,000 will be paid. Each distributor signs a contract with XYZ, which provides that the distributor is an "independent contractor." The company agrees to provide each new distributor with a one-week training course on how to recruit other distributors and for a fee will provide brochures, inspirational tape recordings, etc., which can be used in the recruiting meetings. But XYZ holds no meetings to assist its franchisees to recruit new distributors. All of XYZ's written materials and advertising allude to the tremendous profits that can be made under its program. But orally, before having the distributor sign a contract, the company warns potential distributors that selling the product and recruiting distributors is very hard work. The company acknowledges that the product line is really nothing special, and that the real money is to be made in recruiting other distributors. Actual results by distributors to date indicate that most have not earned their investment back; but a few have made substantial profits, mostly by selling other distributorships. One of the disgruntled distributors seeks advice as to whether he can get his $5,000 investment back if he returns the inventory unused. Consider only whether a "security" is involved under the 1933 Act.

## SAMPLE EXAM QUESTION III

QRS Corp. registers an offering of its stock for public distribution through an underwriter. In the prospectus it indicates that its earnings for the coming year will be "nominal." The stock is sold at $20 per share, which is the market price at the time of the offering. At the end of the year, the company announces that it has a loss of $25 million, or about one-third of its net worth. Immediately, the stock's price drops to $5 per share and remains there. Those who purchased QRS stock in the public offering bring a lawsuit to recover for material misstatements in the prospectus. At trial it is shown that the projection of earnings was done by the company's vice president of finance and accounting and that it was based on an "optimistic" outlook for the company's performance on existing government contracts which were behind schedule and experiencing cost overruns at the time the projection was made. Considering only section 11 of the 1933 Act, can the purchasers recover from QRS? (Do not consider the amount of damages.)

# SAMPLE EXAM QUESTION IV

A is a successful promoter. She has a number of very wealthy friends who invest in the deals she puts together. She gets ideas, finds management, raises the money, puts the corporation together, and then, after several years of operation, merges the companies into larger companies.

A has a new idea for the manufacture of rotating widgets. She finds B (president), C (vice president of finance), D (vice president of marketing), E (vice president of manufacturing), and hires F as her attorney. F incorporates X Co., and for 10 cents per share, F issues common stock as follows:

A = 50% or 50,000 shares
B = 20% or 20,000 shares
C =  9% or 9,000 shares
D =  9% or 9,000 shares
E =  9% or 9,000 shares
F =  3% or 3,000 shares

Prior to the issuance of the stock, A explains to B, C, D, E, and F the basic idea, showing some feasibility studies concerning the development of the product, hands out some articles on the industrial applications involved, and talks about the plan for issuing stock and financing the company. B, C, D, and E are all experienced executives who have participated in forming companies before; they ask no more questions, simply trusting in A's track record. A has hired F because F's fees are cheap; this is F's first incorporation, and being impressed with the 3,000 shares offered, F asks no more questions. Also, A gives the impression that she does not want to hear any questions—the investors can simply take the deal or leave it. The group discusses the financing plans; all agree that this should be covered in the business plan which is to be written. All persons taking the common stock sign investment letters; F sees that a restrictive legend is placed on the shares and issues instructions to the transfer agent that no shares are to be transferred without an opinion from F. All shareholders become members of the board of directors.

State and resolve all issues raised by the above facts under section 4(2) of the Securities Act of 1933.

# SAMPLE EXAM QUESTION V

X purchases 100,000 shares of privately offered (*i.e.*, restricted) securities from Y Co., giving Y a promissory note for the purchase price. The note is secured by collateral in the form of the restricted securities of Y that X purchased, the securities having a fair market value at least equal to the purchase price. The note is a nonrecourse note, meaning that in the event of default, the seller (Y) can look only to the collateral for payment; Y does not have recourse to X's other assets. Two years later X, who is not a control person of Y, wants to sell these restricted securities over an exchange. The note has not been paid.

1.   X does not want to become an underwriter and have to register the Y shares under the 1933 Act. Is rule 144 available to X for sale of his restricted securities?

2.   Assume that the facts are the same except that X gives Y securities other than the Y stock as collateral. A month after the purchase of the Y stock, the value of the collateral

decreases to $50,000 less than the outstanding obligation on the note. X does not put up additional collateral. This condition continues for a period of six months, after which the market price of the collateral rises to a point above the amount owing on the note. Also, this time the note is a full-recourse note, and it is paid off prior to X wanting to sell the securities. Two years after the purchase date, X wants to use rule 144 for sale of the restricted securities. Is it available?

3. Assume that X buys the shares and pays Y cash, getting the money from a bank loan, for which he pledges the restricted securities. The securities drop in value below the amount of the bank note, and after two years they are still below the amount owed on the note. Finally, the bank's examiners require that the bank collect the under-secured loan, and so they ask X to sell the stock and pay off the loan. Can X use rule 144 to sell the restricted securities?

## SAMPLE EXAM QUESTION VI

XYZ is a drug manufacturer. It is a public company, traded on the New York Stock Exchange. A, the head of research, has been working on a cure for cancer for 15 years. The company has spent $5 million on this research. The only other person in the company that knows about all of the ramifications of the project is B, the company president. On January 1, A mentions to B while they are having lunch together, that he has made an interesting but puzzling breakthrough. Using an extract from cancerous cells of cattle, he had injected various cancerous animals and found that in some cases he has cured them. B becomes very excited. The stock of the company has been doing very poorly in the market, and B is under fire from some shareholders and the board of directors for better performance. A, however, has been down many blind alleys before, and he succeeds in calming B down, indicating that there are so many variables involved that it may be as long as five years before he knows whether they have really discovered anything. B goes away depressed, but he continues to think about the matter. Recalling vaguely the *Texas Gulf Sulphur* case, and thinking that his own situation might be helped if he disclosed the company's current progress, B calls C, an outside lawyer for XYZ. B calls a conference at which A, B, and C discuss the matter of company disclosure. They decide that it would be helpful to have the opinion of an outside consultant concerning progress of the project. They bring in D, a world-renowned researcher in cancer. He confirms A's estimate of the complexity of the remaining research and the possibility that it could take at least five years to know if something substantial would come from the project. When asked her opinion, C indicates that she thinks disclosure is not required and might even be misleading. Based on her opinion, all concur in the decision to delay an announcement.

S is a shareholder. On February 1, five days after the last meeting between A, B, and C, S sells 1,000 shares of XYZ at $5 per share. This is a transaction over the New York Stock Exchange.

In the meantime, B feels "in his bones" that A is on the verge of a dramatic breakthrough in cancer therapy. On February 10, he buys 1,000 shares on the exchange at $5 per share.

On the morning of March 1, A bursts into B's office with news that working nonstop, he has miraculously succeeded in separating an element from the cancerous cells that, when injected into dogs with eye cancer, seems immediately to go to work curing the diseased cells. Word has already leaked out to the research staff; by midafternoon, the XYZ stock is trading at $10 per share. C is called in and issues a careful news release indicating that as of March 1, the company has made progress in separating an element from cancerous cells of cattle that seems to have an effect in curing eye cancer in animals, but that nothing is known in the way of definitive research or what the possible effect may be on human beings.

The news release is sent to all shareholders and given to the major news services. By March 15, the stock has gone to $20 per share. By March 30, it is $25 per share. S checked with her broker on March 1 about her holdings and was told that XYZ stock had taken off, based on some cancer research breakthrough.

After checking into the facts, S hires you as an attorney and asks you to sue B, C, and XYZ under rule 10b-5. By the time the suit is brought, the stock of XYZ is selling at $30 per share.

While you are waiting to come to trial (18 months after the filing of the complaint), XYZ announces that further research indicates that there are harmful side effects from the extract and that all further research based on the extract has been discontinued. Within 24 hours, the stock of XYZ is trading at $3 per share.

C and her law firm have been counsel to XYZ for 10 years. C's name has appeared in XYZ's annual reports, registration statements, etc. Three months before she was asked for her opinion about whether to disclose the initial research findings, C resigned as a member of XYZ's board of directors.

Discuss the merits of S's lawsuit against B, C, and XYZ under rule 10b-5. Do not consider the measure of damages or contribution among parties, if you find one or more persons liable.

## SAMPLE EXAM QUESTION VII

On December 15, the federal government issued new regulations, making the curing of tobacco more expensive.

On January 1 of the next year, X Corp., a conglomerate that had been very active in buying other companies, was approached by D, a shareholder in Y Corp., about buying D's 10% interest in Y Corp.'s common stock. Y Corp. is a small tobacco company. C, Y Corp.'s president, is 68 years old. He is also chairman of the board of directors. He owns 250 shares of Y Corp.'s 1,574,354 outstanding shares and has had an option to purchase 50,000 additional shares for many years. (The market price of the company's stock has never risen substantially above the option exercise price, which is now $14 per share. The market price of the company's stock is now at $8 per share.) The rest of the board is composed of C's cronies, who have been on the board for an average of 10 years; their average age is 66. The rest of the management (i.e., the key officers) are all around age 60. D is the largest shareholder of Y Corp. and has been trying to get C to either get new management or to sell the company. The earnings per share of the company have been dropping for the last five years and are now at 80 cents per share. The multiple of 10 times earnings for the stock price is just a little below the industry average.

D, finally tiring of feuding with C about the future of the company, has sought out X Corp. and offered the stock for sale. D tells the management of X Corp. that the new government regulations may have raised the value of Y Corp.'s inventory. He therefore offers his stock for $12 per share. The book value of the stock is $8 per share. X Corp. already owns a cigarette manufacturer (of the Superman brand), and, aware of the recent government regulation, its management has been looking for a tobacco company to buy.

After an investigation of Y Corp. (which involves no contact with its management), X Corp. buys D's stock for $12 per share. At the closing of the sale, on January 15, D has a conversation with the vice president of acquisitions for X Corp., suggesting that it would make a lot of sense for X Corp. to buy Y Corp. for a premium over the market price of the Y stock and then to liquidate Y Corp. The vice president of X Corp. makes no response.

The minutes of a directors' meeting of X Corp., held on January 30, indicate that the directors (including the vice president of acquisitions) authorized a tender offer for Y Corp.'s shares at $10 per share. The reason for the acquisition is stated to be that X Corp., concerned about the possible increased tobacco costs to its cigarette manufacturer, is seeking a stable source of tobacco.

The vice president of acquisitions of X Corp. then approaches C and indicates that X Corp. intends to bid for the shares of Y. During a lengthy discussion, the vice president makes it known that if C is willing to cancel his 50,000 stock options, once the acquisition is complete, X Corp. will see to it that C is given a five-year management contract at a substantial increase in salary. C gives his tentative agreement to this plan.

On February 15, X Corp. makes a cash tender offer for all of the Y stock at $10 per share (the market price being $8 per share). The offer states that it is contingent on the tender of at least 67% of the stock. In fact, 68% of the stock is offered, which X Corp. accepts. The tender offer discloses to Y shareholders all relevant financial information about X Corp., its management, the fact that an X Corp. subsidiary is in the cigarette manufacturing business, that over the past five years it had sought to expand sales and earnings by buying other companies in related businesses, that it has offered a five-year management contract to C, and that it is offering a price in excess of recent market values of Y's stock.

On February 28, a board meeting of Y Corp. is held. All directors except C resign. New directors are elected by X Corp. C gives up his stock options and is given a five-year management contract at a substantial increase over his present salary. A discussion is then held concerning the future of Y Corp. and ways to improve the running of the business are discussed in detail.

A month later, there is another board meeting of Y Corp., at which X Corp. has its nominees pass a resolution to liquidate Y Corp. State law requires a two-thirds vote of the shareholders, which X Corp. gets by voting its own shares. Y Corp. is liquidated within 30 days. It turns out that the value of its tobacco inventory is worth 100% more than its stated book value, which brings the book value of each Y share to $16 per share.

The shareholders that sold to X Corp. in its tender offer bring a class action against X Corp. under rule 10b-5 of the 1934 Act. After discovery, plaintiffs stipulate that X Corp. did not receive any inside information from Y Corp. (or key persons associated with Y) in making its tender offer.

In discussing the issues in the above fact situation, consider only rule 10b-5 as applicable to the case. (If you find a cause of action, do not discuss the measure of damages.)

## SAMPLE EXAM QUESTION VIII

A, who has a net worth of $150 million, buys on the stock exchange 5.1% of XYZ Corp. common stock. A has a history of taking companies over through tender offers. As soon as he completes the purchase, he files a section 13(d) information report with the S.E.C., as required under the 1934 Act, completing responses to all of the questions asked. In the report, A says he has no present intention to take over XYZ. But speculators, suspecting that A will make a move to take over XYZ, begin buying the XYZ stock in the market. The stock moves very rapidly from $5 per share to $10 per share. In the meantime, A goes back to running his other enterprises. A year goes by, and the stock of XYZ falls back to $5 per share. A now makes a tender offer for 51% of the XYZ stock at a price of $7.50 per share. In the section 14(d) information report required under the 1934 Act, A indicates that it is his present intention to gain control and remove the management of XYZ for incompetency. B, a former shareholder of XYZ that sold out at $5 per share shortly before A's tender offer, now sues A for damages for a misleading section 13(d) report. Who wins?

# ANSWER TO SAMPLE EXAM QUESTION I

The bank appears to be an underwriter who sold securities unlawfully without registration. A initially appears to be a "control person," since she is in a position to influence the direction of XYZ. Thus, the bank is potentially an underwriter of A's securities since it may be held to have "purchased" the securities from an issuer with a view toward distribution to the public. (Under section 2(11) of the 1933 Act, control persons, like A, are held to be "issuers" for purposes of determining those who are underwriters.) The 1933 Act requires underwriters to comply with the registration provisions of the Act unless they can distribute the securities in the offering under some exemption.

Before the bank can be found to be an underwriter, it must first be determined whether A's having left XYZ changes her status as a control person, so that the bank can claim that it is no longer selling for an issuer. The answer is ***probably not***. A still owns 25% of the company's stock, which is probably enough to be influential in the direction of the company.

The next issue concerns the status of the loan. If it is spurious (*i.e.*, a device merely to give A cash for her securities), then it is clear under *Guild Films* that the bank may be held as an underwriter. Here, the loan probably was not spurious. A's motivation was to get rid of her stock since she knew the company was in financial trouble, and she probably did not have time to register the stock before it fell in price. The bank would never have gone along with a pledge with this knowledge. Additionally, the loan was probably not a weak loan: The stock was pledged and A had the real estate she bought with the loan (and probably other property as well), so the bank had adequate security for the loan. But even if the loan was bona fide, that does not clear the bank. The S.E.C.'s position would be that the stock should have been registered before being sold. Here, the results of the sale would seem to support the S.E.C.'s position. Shortly after the sale, XYZ's difficulties were revealed and the stock dropped in price. Had the bank registered the securities, an investigation of XYZ would have revealed its problems, and the public would not have purchased overpriced securities. Hence, the bank should have gone after A for other security or to force her to register the stock before the sale, sold the securities in accordance with SA Rule 144, or have taken a loss on the loan.

# ANSWER TO SAMPLE EXAM QUESTION II

The issue is whether or not a security is involved. There are several tests for a security, each one of which must be considered:

| | Test | Answer | Analysis |
|---|---|---|---|
| a. | Is it listed as a security in section 2(1) of the Act? | No | |
| b. | Is it an investment contract? | Probably Yes | The critical issue here concerns the degree of participation and effort by the company. *S.E.C. v. Koscot* held |
| | 1) Is it an investment with the expectation of profit? | Yes | that the program for solicitation of distributors was an investment contract and could be separated from |
| | 2) Are the essential management functions performed by the promoter with the investor passive? | Yes | the sale of the product involved. A similar situation is present here. There is an investment of money, a return depends primarily on |

3) Is there a "common enterprise"?  Yes

recruiting other distributors, the efforts of the company are an important part of this recruiting process, and finally, the success of the scheme as a whole is dependent on the essential managerial efforts of the company. Also, there is a "common enterprise" in that the efforts of management *and* the investor are necessary to the success of the scheme.

Counterarguments would be that the investors have to work very hard to make a profit and therefore the analogy should be to the purchase of a franchise. Investors are even called "independent contractors" and warned of the difficult work involved. They are given recruiting materials but are not assisted in the actual recruiting. Also, the conservative definition of a "common enterprise" is an investment by a group of investors whose pool of capital is necessary to fund the development of the scheme.

Nevertheless, the tendency is to find a security in this type of case, if the company is involved in performing at least some of the management functions critical to the success of the scheme. Thus, given the company's advertising program, the week's training course, the fact that its product is inferior, and the above trend, it appears that the weight of the arguments is in favor of finding a security.

c. Do the investors need the protection of the Act?  Yes

The persons enlisted here appear to be relatively unsophisticated and the program involves a large number of people.

d. Are the investors contributing risk capital?  Hard to tell

Without more facts this test could not be applied. Possibly the contributions to buy distributorships are being used to provide the risk capital to start the company (*i.e.*, to manufacture inventory, etc.). If so, then this would also meet the "common enterprise" test.

# ANSWER TO SAMPLE EXAM QUESTION III

The issue here concerns what must be included in the registration statement, and what (under section 11) is a "fact" and a "material" fact.

The registration statement must include all of those facts that a reasonable investor would consider material in making an investment decision whether to buy the company's securities being offered. Traditionally, the S.E.C. indicated that only historical "hard" facts should be included, and (although relevant to investors) opinions like projected earnings should not be included. Hence, QRS would argue that all investors should take with a grain of salt the projected earnings in the registration statement (since it was only an opinion and not to be relied on), and there should be no recovery. However, including a projection in the registration statement, and an optimistic one at that, is almost certain to have an effect on the sale of the securities. The S.E.C. has more recently indicated that, although a company need not include such projections, if it does so, it must follow certain standards to avoid liability.

There are no facts to indicate that the company did not follow a reasonable format in presenting its projection. But there is a question as to whether it has presented enough information for an investor to judge whether the estimate was reasonable and probably accurate. The company probably should have indicated that its estimate was "optimistic" and that it was experiencing cost overruns and delays on its government contracts. Perhaps the company should have included another "pessimistic" projection. There is no basis from the facts given to question the good faith of the company, since it may have had a reasonable basis for believing it could get the contracts back on schedule.

It appears that there is liability under section 11 here for failure to disclose sufficient information on which an investor could base an investment decision.

# ANSWER TO SAMPLE EXAM QUESTION IV

The issue here is whether this is a private offering of securities pursuant to section 4(2) and thereby exempt from registration under section 5 of the 1933 Act. The availability of the section 4(2) exemption turns on whether, considering all the circumstances of the offering, the potential purchasers need the protection of the 1933 Act. That question, in turn, depends on a number of factors:

1) *Manner of offering and number of offerees:* First, was the offering conducted in a "public" manner, reaching a large number of offerees (which would make it likely that at least some of the offerees need 1933 Act protection)? Here, it seems that the offering was not conducted in a public manner: no advertising was used, and there was no general solicitation. Likewise, the number of offerees was relatively small.

2) *Sophistication of the offerees:* Also relevant to the need for 1933 Act protection is the relative sophistication of the offerees, *i.e.*, their knowledge, experience, ability to bear the risk of the investment, and their ability to properly evaluate the merits of the securities offered. Here, there seem to be some questions that might be raised, especially with respect to F: B, C, D, and E have all participated in similar transactions before, and are

"experienced executives" who presumably know a great deal about the risks (and benefits) of transactions like this one. F, however, has never incorporated a business, and evidently is far less experienced than the others. On the other hand, F is investing only $300 (3,000 × 10 cents), and therefore very likely can easily bear the risk of the investment. Moreover, F is a lawyer, and perhaps even a relatively unsophisticated lawyer is more savvy in business matters than a lay person.

From a policy perspective, this is a "seed capital" sort of transaction, with a small group of people putting up the initial cash to get a business started. If the S.E.C. were to require all such transactions to be registered, economic growth would suffer tremendously.

On balance, then, while F does not seem to meet precisely the criteria for a private placement investor, F is also not clearly unsuitable. This factor alone should not make the exemption unavailable.

3) *Type of information provided:* Another important factor examined in section 4(2) cases is the nature and amount of information provided. If the information is both qualitatively and quantitatively equivalent to the information that would be contained in a 1933 Act registration statement, or if the offerees at least had access to such information on request, the offering will be more likely to qualify under section 4(2). Here, however, that does not seem to be the case. Certainly F does not have access to this kind or amount of information, and it is at least questionable whether B, C, D, and E had such access. On balance, the information requirement has not been met in this case.

4) *Resale restrictions:* Appropriate restrictions on resale have been imposed on the securities to prevent their secondary distribution to the public by the initial participants.

5) *Other factors:* The remaining factors favor the exemption's availability in this case. The total dollar value of the offering is relatively small ($10,000); the securities were offered only to a reasonably homogenous group; and the securities, while marketable in theory, because they are relatively cheap, have been restricted and therefore are essentially unmarketable without the called-for legal opinion.

In conclusion, while not all the requirements of section 4(2) were met here, many businesses are formed this way. Given the small dollar amount involved, and the nature of the participants, all of whom have some professional tie to the issuer, it is likely that a court would apply 1933 Act section 4(2) and find the transaction exempt from registration.

## ANSWER TO SAMPLE EXAM QUESTION V

1.  No. Rule 144, which sets forth objective criteria for those wishing to prove investment intent after purchasing and holding privately offered securities, is not available to X. One technique by which rule 144 achieves its goal of assuring the necessary investment intent is by requiring a purchaser to bear the full economic risk of the investment for two years before reselling. This two-year holding period is tolled until the purchaser has paid for the securities in full (because until the securities have been paid for, the risk of ownership is not really on the buyer). Although X acquired the securities two years ago, X has not yet paid the note delivered in exchange for the securities, and therefore the holding period requirement has not been satisfied.

    Rule 144(d)(2) provides that the holding period will commence if the securities are paid with a promissory note that (i) provides for full recourse against the purchaser of the securities, and (ii) is secured by collateral other than the securities purchased, having a fair market value at least equal to the purchase price. Neither of these requirements is met here, however. Finally, even if both requirements were met, rule 144(d)(2)(iii) requires that any note given in payment be paid in full before the securities are sold. Therefore, even if X had paid with a note otherwise meeting the requirements of rule 144, X would not be permitted to sell under the rule until the note is paid.

2. No. Rule 144 requires that collateral be equal in value to the outstanding amount of the loan *at all times* during the holding period. The holding period of rule 144 is tolled any time the value of the collateral drops below the amount of the debt—which it did here for a period of six months. Only in this way is X, the purchaser, subject to the full risk of having *purchased* the securities, rather than leaving that risk with the issuer.

3. Yes. Here, X (the purchaser) and the bank, but not the issuer (Y), bear the risk of the purchase of the securities; Y already has received the purchase price. Therefore, after two years X may use rule 144 to sell the securities.

## ANSWER TO SAMPLE EXAM QUESTION VI

The first issue is whether any of the defendants is an "insider." The corporation (XYZ) is. So is B, the president. But is C such an insider? She has resigned from the board and only represents the corporation as its outside attorney. Still, as such, she was given access to the company's inside information, and was bound by a fiduciary duty to the company, and therefore she is an insider.

Moving on, then, the next question is whether XYZ and C, neither of whom traded in securities, can be liable in this case. Certainly the issuer, XYZ, can be liable, as was the issuer in the *Texas Gulf Sulphur* case. But can C be liable? Although at one time, an aiding and abetting theory might have resulted in C's liability, aiding and abetting is no longer available to private plaintiffs in rule 10b-5 cases (after the *Central Bank* decision). The facts do not support an inference of fraudulent intent on C's part. In the absence of any trading by C, then, it is unlikely that C can be liable under rule 10b-5.

B, on the other hand, traded in XYZ stock, albeit before the most promising information about the cancer therapy was known to anyone. The next issue, then, is whether B was under a duty to disclose the information in his possession on February 10 about A's research into cancer treatments. Was that information a "material fact"? But there remains the issue of whether or not she must disclose material facts in her possession, even if she does not trade in the stock. *Texas Gulf Sulphur* might seem to indicate that the answer is "No."

Facts are material when a reasonable investor would want to know the information and would give it significance in making an investment decision. *Texas Gulf Sulphur* and *Basic* indicated that in making this determination, the probability of the fact actually coming to fruition should be considered along with the magnitude of the impact of such a fact on the market for the company's securities. Here, the impact of a cancer cure would be phenomenal, much like the discovery of ore in the *Texas Gulf Sulphur* case, or the takeover in *Basic*, or perhaps greater than both. But the probability of the cure becoming a reality is very small indeed. So it is a close question, whether the company should have been required to issue a very cautionary press release, or whether, having checked out the probabilities, the chances for a cure were too remote to require disclosure. Certainly the chances of the cancer cure becoming reality were much smaller than the ore discovery becoming reality in *Texas Gulf Sulphur*.

Assuming that the press release should have been issued, there is still the issue of whether or not S can prove the necessary scienter to recover from B or XYZ. *Hochfelder* would seem to require that B have acted with the intent to defraud (with the possibility that reckless conduct would qualify). Here, it appears that the most that can be charged is bad judgment (possibly negligence).

Assuming that the required state of mind can be proved, the plaintiff will have no difficulty establishing that the non-disclosure was "in connection with" a sale of securities. The privity requirement, on the other hand, may present a problem, at least with respect to the case against B: there really is no connection between B's trades and the plaintiff's trades, and some courts would not permit S to recover against B for that reason. XYZ, of course, has not traded at all, and so if a recovery against it is possible, it will be because no privity is required in an action against the issuer (as was the case in *Texas Gulf Sulphur*).

Reliance and causation are the remaining elements, and because this case involves nondisclosure rather than an affirmative misstatement, the courts are likely not to be too strict in interpreting these requirements.

In conclusion, the weakest links in the plaintiff's case are materiality and, with respect to the case against B and C (the latter having never traded in XYZ stock so far as we know), privity. The case does not look strong, and the outcome is in doubt.

# ANSWER TO SAMPLE EXAM QUESTION VII

The overall rationale of rule 10b-5 is to protect the public interest in the integrity and fairness of the securities markets and securities transactions by ensuring that interstate purchase and sale transactions involving securities are free from fraud.

There are several elements that a private plaintiff must prove to sustain a rule 10b-5 cause of action: a security; a purchase or sale; fraud in connection with the purchase or sale; a material fact, if the fraud is misrepresentation or omission of a fact; reliance; scienter; causation; and possibly privity.

The main issues here concern whether there is an omission of a material fact and, if so, whether there was the required scienter.

a.  **Material Fact?**

   1)  Was it an omission of a material fact to fail to disclose that a new government regulation made the curing of tobacco more expensive and that, therefore, Y Corp.'s inventory of tobacco was worth much more in market value than its book value?

      a)  *Arguments that it is not a material fact:* The information is public knowledge (D, a Y Corp. shareholder knew about it; why should X Corp. have to specifically inform other Y Corp. shareholders about it?). X Corp. should not have to disclose information about another company to that company's shareholders (it should only have to disclose information about its own company). X Corp. is not an insider here, so it has no duty to disclose information about Y Corp. to Y shareholders. Information about a company's market value of inventory is just an "opinion," not a fact, so no disclosure is required.

      b)  *Arguments that it is a material fact:* X Corp. owned 10% of the Y stock at the time of the offer and had had meetings with Y Corp. management, so it is an insider and as such has a special duty to Y shareholders to disclose what it knows that affects their interests. The *Leasco* case might be authority that X Corp. must disclose information it knows about the company to be acquired, although that was a 1933 Act (section 11) case, not a rule 10b-5 case. X Corp. may have bought off Y's management, so it has a duty to protect Y shareholders. Inventory of tobacco has an easily ascertainable value in the market and is not as speculative as real estate is; therefore, it is a fact and must be disclosed.

2) Even assuming there was no omission of a material fact in failing to disclose the inventory value, was it an omission of a material fact to fail to disclose the intent to liquidate Y Corp.?

   a) ***Arguments that it was:*** The intent to liquidate would have warned Y shareholders that there was greater value in Y Corp.'s assets than appeared on the books. There was clear intent to liquidate, as shown by X Corp.'s purchase of 68% of the stock and the fact that Y Corp. was liquidated shortly after its acquisition.

   b) ***Arguments that it was not a material fact:*** There was no intent to liquidate at the time of the tender offer, as shown by the board minutes of X Corp., the giving of a five-year management contract to C, and the meeting on ways to make Y Corp. run effectively. Even if there was intent, it was not material since many companies buy other companies and liquidate them afterward— disclosure of such an intent would have told the Y shareholders nothing about a higher intrinsic value than was shown on the books.

b. **Scienter?** Was there intentional conduct (or possibly reckless conduct)? Certainly X Corp. and its key executive knew about the higher inventory value, and if it is shown that they had the intent to liquidate Y Corp., then it could reasonably be inferred that they purposefully failed to disclose this information to Y shareholders.

c. **Privity?** If it is required in rule 10b-5 causes of action, it exists here since X Corp. purchased the shares directly from Y shareholders.

d. **Purchase or Sale of a Security?** Yes. Y shareholders sold to X Corp., and the alleged fraud was directly connected with the sale.

e. **Reliance?** Would the Y shareholders have relied on the material undisclosed information had it been disclosed? Probably yes.

f. **Causation?** Did the failure to disclose cause the loss to Y shareholders? In cases of deceptive omission, showing materiality proves causation in fact, unless X Corp. can show that some other cause was responsible for the loss.

## ANSWER TO SAMPLE EXAM QUESTION VIII

The problem here is that the facts are subject to several interpretations as to what A's real intent was at the time he completed the purchase of 5.1% of XYZ's common stock. Section 13(d) of the 1934 Act requires that the party acquiring equity securities of the issuer disclose his ***present*** intent with respect to the company ("present intent" including changes to be made in management, whether a tender offer for control is contemplated, etc.). A knew that the speculators would begin buying the stock as soon as they found out he had acquired an interest in XYZ. His past history included a pattern of buying an interest in a company and then finally tendering for control of the whole company, paying a premium for the stock over its then market price. So perhaps A had this intention when he filed the 13(d) report to take over XYZ. But even if he had such intent, **when** did he intend to take control? In a month? Six months? A year? Or only when the stock price sagged after the speculators gave up and sold out? If he knew when the report was filed that he wanted to buy XYZ and would do so when the stock price began to drop, was this present intention? And must it have been disclosed? On the other hand, A may not have had a present intention to buy XYZ. Perhaps he bought the 5.1% purely as an investment. A might argue that only after he saw the bad management of XYZ did he form the intention to take over personal control. It is up to the court to make the factual determination about A's intention (a material fact) and whether or not A misrepresented it. This is a very difficult determination in the setting of tender offers, where the nature of business conditions can change a person's mind overnight. It is also difficult in that it raises the question of whether a person's intention to do something only after the passage of a significant period of time requires disclosure of this intention as a **current** material fact.

# TABLE OF CITATIONS TO SECURITIES ACT OF 1933

| Section | Text Reference |
|---|---|
| 2(1) | §§124, 127, 133, 140 |
| 2(3) | §§159, 160, 473 |
| 2(4) | §132 |
| 2(7) | §§63, 1854 |
| 2(10) | §§177, 178, 515 |
| 2(10)(b) | §179 |
| 2(11) | §§93, 94, 96, 101, 102, 105, 106, 331, 335, 378, 578, 581, 591 |
| 2(12) | §§117, 317 |
| 2(15) | §361 |
| 3 | §§303, 362, 459 |
| 3(a)(2) | §§304, 700 |
| 3(a)(3) | §305 |
| 3(a)(4) | §306 |
| 3(a)(5) | §307 |
| 3(a)(6) | §308 |
| 3(a)(7) | §534 |
| 3(a)(8) | §§154, 309, 310 |
| 3(a)(9) | §§486, 488, 489, 491, 498, 536, 588 |
| 3(a)(10) | §§495, 496, 498, 510, 536, 588 |
| 3(a)(11) | §§313, 440, 444, 445, 446, 448, 451, 457, 459, 588 |
| 3(b) | §§360, 362, 363, 365 |
| 4(1) | §§91, 116, 122, 315, 540, 579, 580, 584, 588 |
| 4(2) | §§314, 341, 342, 343, 350, 357, 359, 360, 363, 365, 385, 444, 459, 579, 580, 582, 588, 602 |
| 4(3) | §§118, 201, 315, 316, 318, 319, 320, 323 |
| 4(3)(B) | §320 |
| 4(3)(C) | §325 |
| 4(4) | §§204, 326, 336, 572 |
| 4(5) | §314 |
| 4(6) | §§360, 361, 378, 551 |
| 5 | §§87, 91, 92, 119, 123, 157, 303, 316, 342, 370, 381, 405, 440, 473, 486, 504, 510, 515, 540, 546, 618, 619, 621, 687, 688, 690, 694, 695, 698, 699, 700, 1410, 1411, 1733 |
| 5(a) | §§158, 176 |
| 5(a)(1) | §193 |
| 5(a)(2) | §199 |
| 5(b)(1) | §§177, 195 |
| 5(b)(2) | §§88, 183, 186, 194, 198, 199 |
| 5(c) | §§158, 161, 169, 170, 171, 173 |
| 6 | §216 |
| 6(a) | §§285, 646 |
| 7 | §§216, 226 |

| Section | Text Reference |
|---|---|
| 7(b) | §297 |
| 8 | §§190, 1551 |
| 8(b) | §276 |
| 8(d) | §277 |
| 8(e) | §§268, 269 |
| 8A(c)(2) | §631 |
| 8A(e) | §633 |
| 10 | §195 |
| 10(a) | §§178, 194, 197, 198, 515 |
| 10(a)(3) | §§207, 295 |
| 10(b) | §§178, 184, 515, 1418, 1420 |
| 11 | §§208, 261, 293, 294, 621, 625, 643, 644, 645, 649, 650, 651, 658, 662, 663, 664, 666, 686, 695, 696, 710, 711, 718, 732, 734, 748, 922, 923, 980, 1409, 1422, 1430, 1438, 1446, 1463, 1464, 1766 |
| 11(a) | §§644, 652, 657, 659, 662, 663 |
| 11(c) | §666 |
| 11(e) | §§679, 681, 685 |
| 11(e)(3) | §683 |
| 11(f) | §§686, 734 |
| 11(g) | §684 |
| 12 | §§41, 208, 980, 1422, 1465 |
| 12(1) | §§621, 626, 687, 688, 689, 690, 691, 692, 693, 695, 696, 698, 714, 715, 718, 739, 922, 1410, 1411, 1412, 1438, 1912 |
| 12(2) | §§294, 622, 626, 699, 700, 701, 703, 704, 707, 708, 710, 714, 715, 716, 717, 718, 721, 922, 924, 1412, 1438, 1766 |
| 13 | §662 |
| 14 | §739 |
| 14(e) | §§1065, 1066, 1067 |
| 15 | §§689, 1422, 1424, 1426, 1430 |
| 17 | §§139, 622, 718, 730, 980, 1064, 1414 |
| 17(a) | §§208, 635, 719, 721, 723, 925, 1065, 1467, 1563, 1777, 1778, 1829 |
| 17(a)(1) | §§718, 720, 723, 925, 1066, 1471, 1779 |
| 17(a)(2) | §§718, 720, 925, 1066, 1471, 1779 |
| 17(a)(3) | §§718, 720, 925, 1066, 1471, 1779 |
| 18 | §1888 |
| 20 | §1549 |
| 20(a) | §§634, 1502 |
| 20(b) | §634 |
| 20(d) | §628 |
| 24 | §§635, 1562 |

# TABLE OF CITATIONS TO SECURITIES ACT RULES

# TABLE OF CITATIONS TO
# SECURITIES EXCHANGE ACT OF 1934

# TABLE OF CITATIONS TO
# SECURITIES EXCHANGE ACT RULES

| Rule | Text Reference |
|---|---|
| 3a51-1 | §298 |
| 3b-3 | §1711 |
| 10a-1(c) | §1717 |
| 10b-5 | §§139, 643, 721, 782, 795, 796, 797, 798, 799, 800, 801, 802, 805, 806, 807, 808, 810, 811, 812, 813, 814, 815, 816, 818, 827, 834, 835, 836, 837, 838, 854, 856, 858, 861, 863, 865, 868, 869, 870, 873, 874, 876, 878, 880, 881, 883, 884, 885, 886, 888, 889, 890, 891, 894, 900, 907, 908, 909, 910, 911, 912, 915, 917, 918, 919, 920, 921, 922, 923, 924, 925, 926, 927, 931, 932, 933, 935, 936, 938, 940, 942, 943, 944, 946, 948, 955, 957, 960, 968, 969, 977, 981, 983, 988, 1051, 1057, 1058, 1059, 1063, 1064, 1065, 1066, 1067, 1068, 1251, 1252, 1257, 1271, 1285, 1286, 1310, 1415, 1417, 1418, 1420, 1425, 1435, 1436, 1439, 1448, 1449, 1450, 1451, 1468, 1471, 1571, 1725, 1727, 1728, 1763, 1766, 1777, 1778, 1798, 1820, 1828, 1829, 1881 |
| 10b-5(1) | §881 |
| 10b-5(2) | §881 |
| 10b-5(3) | §881 |
| 10b-6 | §§1095, 1723, 1739, 1740, 1760, 1762, 1763, 1766 |
| 10b-6(a) | §1746 |
| 10b-6(c)(3) | §1748 |
| 10b-6(f) | §§1095, 1757 |
| 10b-6A | §1744 |
| 10b-7 | §§1723, 1739, 1740, 1745, 1750, 1751, 1762, 1763 |
| 10b-7(g) | §§1753, 1758 |
| 10b-7(j) | §1752 |
| 10b-7(k) | §1754 |
| 10b-8 | §§1723, 1739, 1740, 1745, 1762, 1763 |
| 10b-10 | §§1799, 1807 |
| 10b-13 | §1032 |
| 10b-18 | §§1089, 1090, 1091, 1092, 1093, 1094 |
| 10b-18(c) | §1089 |
| 10b-21 | §1719 |
| 11a-1 | §1669 |

| Rule | Text Reference |
|---|---|
| 11b-1 | §1662 |
| 11Aa3-1 | §569 |
| 12g-1 | §744 |
| 12g3-2(b) | §§1871, 1872, 1873 |
| 12h-3 | §749 |
| 13a-1 | §751 |
| 13a-11 | §751 |
| 13a-13 | §751 |
| 13d-1 | §767 |
| 13d-3(d)(1) | §994 |
| 13e-1 | §1096 |
| 13e-3 | §1098 |
| 13e-4 | §1088 |
| 13f-1 | §770 |
| 14a-1 | §§1131, 1152 |
| 14a-1(l) | §§1147, 1236 |
| 14a-2 | §1230 |
| 14a-2(a)(1) | §1229 |
| 14a-2(a)(2) | §1232 |
| 14a-2(a)(6) | §1233 |
| 14a-2(b) | §§1244, 1245 |
| 14a-2(b)(1) | §§1244, 1245 |
| 14a-2(b)(2) | §1231 |
| 14a-2(b)(3) | §1229 |
| 14a-3 | §§1137, 1146, 1151, 1154, 1229 |
| 14a-3(a) | §1155 |
| 14a-3(f) | §1248 |
| 14a-3(g) | §1247 |
| 14a-4 | §§1137, 1229 |
| 14a-4(f) | §§1155, 1156 |
| 14a-5 | §§1137, 1229 |
| 14a-6 | §§513, 1137, 1161, 1229 |
| 14a-6(a) | §1165 |
| 14a-6(g) | §1247 |
| 14a-7 | §§1182, 1226 |
| 14a-7(b) | §1183 |
| 14a-8 | §§1139, 1186, 1229 |
| 14a-8(a) | §1187 |
| 14a-8(b) | §1187 |
| 14a-8(c) | §§1186, 1201 |
| 14a-8(c)(7) | §§1210, 1212, 1213 |
| 14a-8(d) | §1201 |
| 14a-9 | §§827, 1138, 1152, 1168, 1204, 1242, 1249, 1257, 1265, 1271 |
| 14a-10 | §1129 |
| 14a-11 | §§1176, 1178, 1229 |

# TABLE OF CASES

# INDEX

# Notes

# gilbert LAW SUMMARIES

AMERICA'S BEST SELLING OUTLINES

## Bankruptcy

**By Professor Ned W. Waxman, College of William and Mary**

Participants in the Bankruptcy Case; Jurisdiction and Procedure; Commencement and Administration of the Case (including Eligibility, Voluntary Case, Involuntary Case, Meeting of Creditors, Debtor's Duties); Officers of the Estate (including Trustee, Examiner, United States Trustee); Bankruptcy Estate; Creditor's Right of Setoff; Trustee's Avoiding Powers; Claims of Creditors (including Priority Claims and Tax Claims); Debtor's Exemptions; Nondischargeable Debts; Effects of Discharge; Reaffirmation Agreements; Administrative Powers (including Automatic Stay, Use, Sale, or Lease of Property); Chapter 7- Liquidation; Chapter 11- Reorganization; Chapter 13-Individual With Regular Income; Chapter 12- Family Farmer With Regular Annual Income.
ISBN: 0-15-900164-1    Pages: 356    $19.95

## Basic Accounting for Lawyers

**By Professor David H. Barber**

Basic Accounting Principles; Definitions of Accounting Terms; Balance Sheet; Income Statement; Statement of Changes in Financial Position; Consolidated Financial Statements; Accumulation of Financial Data; Financial Statement Analysis.
ISBN: 0-15-900004-1    Pages: 136    $16.95

## Business Law

**By Professor Robert D. Upp, Los Angeles City College**

Torts and Crimes in Business; Law of Contracts (including Contract Formation, Consideration, Statute of Frauds, Contract Remedies, Third Parties); Sales (including Transfer of Title and Risk of Loss, Performance and Remedies, Products Liability, Personal Property Security Interest); Property (including Personal Property, Bailments, Real Property, Landlord and Tenant); Agency; Business Organizations (including Partnerships, Corporations); Commercial Paper; Government Regulation of Business (including Taxation, Antitrust, Environmental Protection, and Bankruptcy).
ISBN: 0-15-900005-X    Pages: 295    $16.95

## California Bar Performance Test Skills

**By Professor Peter J. Honigsberg, University of San Francisco**

Hints to Improve Writing; How to Approach the Performance Test; Legal Analysis Documents (including Writing a Memorandum of Law, Writing a Client Letter, Writing Briefs); Fact Gathering and Fact Analysis Documents; Tactical and Ethical Considerations; Sample Interrogatories, Performance Tests, and Memoranda.
ISBN: 0-15-900152-8    Pages: 216    $17.95

## Civil Procedure

**By Professor Thomas D. Rowe, Jr., Duke University, and Professor Richard L. Marcus, U.C. Hastings**

Territorial (personal) Jurisdiction, including Venue and Forum Non Conveniens; Subject Matter Jurisdiction, covering Diversity Jurisdiction, Federal Question Jurisdiction; Erie Doctrine and Federal Common Law; Pleadings including Counterclaims, Cross-Claims, Supplemental Pleadings; Parties, including Joinder and Class Actions; Discovery, including Devices, Scope, Sanctions and Discovery Conference; Summary Judgment; Pretrial Conference and Settlements; Trial, including Right to Jury Trial, Motions, Jury Instruction and Arguments, and Post-Verdict Motions; Appeals; Claim Preclusion (Res Judicata) and Issue Preclusion (Collateral Estoppel).
ISBN: 0-15-900272-9    Pages: 447    $19.95

## Commercial Paper and Payment Law

**By Professor Douglas J. Whaley, Ohio State University**

Types of Commercial Paper; Negotiability; Negotiation; Holders in Due Course; Claims and Defenses on Negotiable Instruments (including Real Defenses and Personal Defenses); Liability of the Parties (including Merger Rule, Suits on the Instrument, Warranty Suits, Conversion); Bank Deposits and Collections; Forgery or Alteration of Negotiable Instruments; Electronic Banking.
ISBN: 0-15-900009-2    Pages: 222    $17.95

## Community Property

**By Professor William A. Reppy, Jr., Duke University**

Classifying Property as Community or Separate; Management and Control of Property; Liability for Debts; Division of Property at Divorce; Devolution of Property at Death; Relationships Short of Valid Marriage; Conflict of Laws Problems; Constitutional Law Issues (including Equal Protection Standards, Due Process Issues).
ISBN: 0-15-900235-4    Pages: 188    $17.95

## Conflict of Laws

**By Dean Herma Hill Kay, U.C. Berkeley**

Domicile; Jurisdiction (including Notice and Opportunity to be Heard, Minimum Contacts, Types of Jurisdiction); Choice of Law (including Vested Rights Approach, Most Significant Relationship Approach, Governmental Interest Analysis); Choice of Law in Specific Substantive Areas; Traditional Defenses Against Application of Foreign Law; Constitutional Limitations and Overriding Federal Law (including Due Process Clause, Full Faith and Credit Clause, Conflict Between State and Federal Law); Recognition and Enforcement of Foreign Judgments.
ISBN: 0-15-900011-4    Pages: 260    $18.95

## Constitutional Law

**By Professor Jesse H. Choper, U.C. Berkeley**

Powers of Federal Government (including Judicial Power, Powers of Congress, Presidential Power, Foreign Affairs Power); Intergovernmental Immunities, Separation of Powers; Regulation of Foreign Commerce; Regulation of Interstate Commerce; Taxation of Interstate and Foreign Commerce; Due Process, Equal Protection; "State Action" Requirements; Freedoms of Speech, Press, and Association; Freedom of Religion.
ISBN: 0-15-900265-6    Pages: 335    $19.95

## Contracts

**By Professor Melvin A. Eisenberg, U.C. Berkeley**

Consideration (including Promissory Estoppel, Moral or Past Consideration); Mutual Assent; Defenses (including Mistake, Fraud, Duress, Unconscionability, Statute of Frauds, Illegality); Third-Party Beneficiaries; Assignment of Rights and Delegation of Duties; Conditions; Substantial Performance; Material vs. Minor Breach; Anticipatory Breach; Impossibility; Discharge; Remedies (including Damages, Specific Performance, Liquidated Damages).
ISBN: 0-15-900014-9    Pages: 326    $19.95

## Corporations

**By Professor Jesse H. Choper, U.C. Berkeley, and Professor Melvin A. Eisenberg, U.C. Berkeley**

Formalities; "De Jure" vs. "De Facto"; Promoters; Corporate Powers; Ultra Vires Transactions; Powers, Duties, and Liabilities of Officers and Directors; Allocation of Power Between Directors and Shareholders; Conflicts of Interest in Corporate Transactions; Close Corporations; Insider Trading; Rule 10b-5 and Section 16(b); Shareholders' Voting Rights; Shareholders' Right to Inspect Records; Shareholders' Suits; Capitalization (including Classes of Shares, Preemptive Rights, Consideration for Shares); Dividends; Redemption of Shares; Fundamental Changes in Corporate Structure; Applicable Conflict of Laws Principles.
ISBN: 0-15-900342-3    Pages: 308    $19.95

## Criminal Law

**By Professor George E. Dix, University of Texas**

Elements of Crimes (including Actus Reus, Mens Rea, Causation); Vicarious Liability; Complicity in Crime; Criminal Liability of Corporations; Defenses (including Insanity, Diminished Capacity, Intoxication, Ignorance, Self-Defense); Inchoate Crimes; Homicide; Other Crimes Against the Person; Crimes Against Habitation (including Burglary, Arson); Crimes Against Property; Offenses Against Government; Offenses Against Administration of Justice.
ISBN: 0-15-900217-6    Pages: 271    $18.95

## Criminal Procedure

**By Professor Paul Marcus, College of William and Mary, and Professor Charles H. Whitebread, U.S.C.**

Exclusionary Rule; Arrests and Other Detentions; Search and Seizure; Privilege Against Self-Incrimination; Confessions; Preliminary Hearing; Bail; Indictment; Speedy Trial; Competency to Stand Trial; Government's Obligation to Disclose Information; Right to Jury Trial; Right to Counsel; Right to Confront Witnesses; Burden of Proof; Insanity; Entrapment; Guilty Pleas; Sentencing; Death Penalty; Ex Post Facto Issues; Appeal; Habeas Corpus; Juvenile Offenders; Prisoners' Rights; Double Jeopardy.
ISBN: 0-15-900347-4    Pages: 271    $18.95

## Dictionary of Legal Terms

**Gilbert Staff**

Contains Over 3,500 Legal Terms and Phrases; Law School Shorthand; Common Abbreviations; Latin and French Legal Terms; Periodical Abbreviations; Governmental Abbreviations.
ISBN: 0-15-900018-1    Pages: 163    $14.95

## Estate and Gift Tax

**By Professor John H. McCord, University of Illinois**

Gross Estate Allowable Deductions Under Estate Tax (including Expenses, Indebtedness, and Taxes, Deductions for Losses, Charitable Deduction, Marital Deduction); Taxable Gifts; Deductions; Valuation; Computation of Tax; Returns and Payment of Tax; Tax on Generation-Skipping Transfers.
ISBN: 0-15-900019-X    Pages: 283    $18.95

## Evidence

**By Professor Jon R. Waltz, Northwestern University, and Roger C. Park, University of Minnesota**

Direct Evidence; Circumstantial Evidence; Rulings on Admissibility; Relevancy; Materiality; Character Evidence; Hearsay and the Hearsay Exceptions; Privileges; Competency to Testify; Opinion Evidence and Expert Witnesses; Direct Examination; Cross-Examination; Impeachment; Real, Demonstrative, and Scientific Evidence; Judicial Notice; Burdens of Proof; Parol Evidence Rule.
ISBN: 0-15-900020-3    Pages: 359    $19.95

## Federal Courts

**By Professor William A. Fletcher, U.C. Berkeley**

Article III Courts; "Case or Controversy" Requirement; Justiciability; Advisory Opinions; Political Questions; Ripeness; Mootness; Standing; Congressional Power Over Federal Court Jurisdiction; Supreme Court Jurisdiction; District Court Subject Matter Jurisdiction (including Federal Question Jurisdiction, Diversity Jurisdiction); Pendent and Ancillary Jurisdiction; Removal Jurisdiction; Venue; Forum Non Conveniens; Law Applied in the Federal Courts (including Erie Doctrine); Federal Law in the State Courts; Abstention; Habeas Corpus for State Prisoners; Federal Injunctions Against State Court Proceedings; Eleventh Amendment.
ISBN: 0-15-900232-X    Pages: 310    $19.95

## Future Interests & Perpetuities

**By Professor Jesse Dukeminier, U.C.L.A.**

Reversions; Possibilities of Reverter; Rights of Entry; Remainders; Executory Interest; Rules Restricting Remainders and Executory Interest; Rights of Owners of Future Interests; Construction of Instruments; Powers of Appointment; Rule Against Perpetuities (including Reforms of the Rule).
ISBN: 0-15-900218-4    Pages: 219    $17.95

## Income Tax I - Individual

**By Professor Michael R. Asimow, U.C.L.A.**

Gross Income; Exclusions; Income Splitting by Gifts, Personal Service Income, Income Earned by Children, Income of Husbands and Wives, Below-Market Interest on Loans, Taxation of Trusts; Business and Investment Deductions; Personal Deductions; Tax Rates; Credits; Computation of Basis, Gain, or Loss; Realization; Nonrecognition of Gain or Loss; Capital Gains and Losses; Alternative Minimum Tax; Tax Accounting Problems.
ISBN: 0-15-900266-4    Pages: 312    $19.95

For more information visit our World Wide Web site at http://www.gilbertlaw.com or write for a free 32 page catalog:
Harcourt Brace Legal and Professional Publications, 176 West Adams, Ste. 2100, Chicago, Illinois 60603

# LAW SCHOOL LEGENDS SERIES

## America's Greatest Law Professors on Audio Cassette

Wouldn't it be great if all of your law professors were law school legends? You know — the kind of professors whose classes everyone fights to get into. The professors whose classes you'd take, no matter what subject they're teaching. The kind of professors who make a subject sing. You may never get an opportunity to take a class with a truly brilliant professor, but with the Law School Legends Series, you can now get all the benefits of the country's greatest law professors…on audio cassette!

### Administrative Law
**Professor To Be Announced**
**Call For Release Date**

TOPICS COVERED (Subject to Change): Classification Of Agencies; Adjudicative And Investigative Action; Rule Making Power; Delegation Doctrine; Control By Executive; Appointment And Removal; Freedom Of Information Act; Rule Making Procedure; Adjudicative Procedure; Trial Type Hearings; Administrative Law Judge; Power To Stay Proceedings; Subpoena Power; Physical Inspection; Self Incrimination; Judicial Review Issues; Declaratory Judgment; Sovereign Immunity; Eleventh Amendment; Statutory Limitations; Standing; Exhaustion Of Administrative Remedies; Scope Of Judicial Review.
**3 Audio Cassettes**
ISBN 0-15-900189-7          $39.95

### Agency & Partnership
**Professor Richard J. Conviser**
**Chicago Kent College of Law**

TOPICS COVERED: Agency: Creation; Rights And Duties Of Principal And Agent; Sub-Agents; Contract Liability–Actual Authority: Express And Implied; Apparent Authority; Ratification; Liabilities Of Parties; Tort Liability–Respondeat Superior; Frolic And Detour; Intentional Torts. *Partnership:* Nature Of Partnership; Formation; Partnership By Estoppel; In Partnership Property; Relations Between Partners To Third Parties; Authority of Partners; Dissolution And Termination; Limited Partnerships.
**3 Audio Cassettes**
ISBN: 0-15-900351-2          $39.95

### Antitrust Law
**Professor To Be Announced**
**Call For Release Date**

TOPICS COVERED (Subject to Change): How U.S. Antitrust Lawyers And Economists Think And Solve Problems: Antitrust Law's First Principle — Consumer Welfare Opposes Market Power; Methods Of Analysis — Rule Of Reason, Per Se, Quick Look; Sherman Act Section 1 — Civil And Criminal Conspiracies In Unreasonable Restraint Of Trade; Sherman Act Section 2 — Illegal Monopolization And Attempts To Monopolize; Robinson Patman Act Price Discrimination And Related Distribution Problems; Clayton Act Section Section 7 — Mergers And Joint Ventures; Antitrust And Intellectual Property; U.S. Antitrust And International Competitive Relationships — Extraterritoriality, Comity, And Convergence; Exemptions And Regulated Industries; Enforcement By The Department Of Justice, Federal Trade Commission, National Association Of State Attorneys General, And By Private Litigation; Price And Non-Price Restraints.
**2 Audio Cassettes**
ISBN: 0-15-900341-5          $39.95

### Bankruptcy
**Professor Elizabeth Warren**
**Harvard Law School**

TOPICS COVERED: The Debtor/Creditor Relationship; The Commencement, Conversion, Dismissal and Reopening Of Bankruptcy Proceedings; Property Included In The Bankruptcy Estate; Secured, Priority And Unsecured Claims; The Automatic Stay; Powers Of Avoidance; The Assumption And Rejection Of Executory Contracts; The Protection Of Exempt Property; The Bankruptcy Discharge; Chapter 13 Proceedings; Chapter 11 Proceedings; Bankruptcy Jurisdiction And Procedure.
**4 Audio Cassettes**
ISBN: 0-15-900273-7          $45.95

### Civil Procedure
**By Professor Richard D. Freer**
**Emory University Law School**

TOPICS COVERED: Subject Matter Jurisdiction; Personal Jurisdiction; Long-Arm Statutes; Constitutional Limitations; In Rem And Quasi In Rem Jurisdiction; Service Of Process; Venue; Transfer; Forum Non Conveniens; Removal; Waiver; Governing Law; Pleadings; Joinder Of Claims; Permissive And Compulsory Joinder Of Parties; Counter-Claims And Cross-Claims; Ancillary Jurisdiction; Impleader; Class Actions; Discovery; Pretrial Adjudication; Summary Judgment; Trial; Post Trial Motions; Appeals; Res Judicata; Collateral Estoppel.
**5 Audio Cassettes**
ISBN: 0-15-900322-9          $59.95

### Commercial Paper
**By Professor Michael I. Spak**
**Chicago Kent College Of Law**

TOPICS COVERED: Introduction; Types Of Negotiable Instruments; Elements Of Negotiability; Statute Of Limitations; Payment-In-Full Checks; Negotiations Of The Instrument; Becoming A Holder-In-Due Course; Rights Of A Holder In Due Course; Real And Personal Defenses; Jus Teril; Effect Of Instrument On Underlying Obligations; Contracts Of Maker And Indorser; Suretyship; Liability Of Drawer And Drawee; Check Certification; Warranty Liability; Conversion Of Liability; Banks And Their Customers; Properly Payable Rule; Wrongful Dishonor; Stopping Payment; Death Of Customer; Bank Statement; Check Collection; Expedited Funds Availability; Forgery Of Drawer's Name; Alterations; Imposter Rule; Wire Transfers; Electronic Fund Transfers Act .
**3 Audio Cassettes**
ISBN: 0-15-900275-3          $39.95

### Conflict Of Laws
**Professor Richard J. Conviser**
**Chicago Kent College of Law**

TOPICS COVERED: Domicile; Jurisdiction; In Personam, In Rem, Quasi In Rem; Court Competence; Forum Non Conveniens; Choice Of Law; Foreign Causes Of Action; Territorial Approach To Choice/Tort And Contract; "Escape Devices"; Most Significant Relationship; Governmental Interest Analysis; Recognition Of Judgments; Foreign Country Judgments; Domestic Judgments/Full Faith And Credit; Review Of Judgments; Modifiable Judgments; Defenses To Recognition And Enforcement; Federal/State (Erie) Problems; Constitutional Limits On Choice Of Law.
**3 Audio Cassettes**
ISBN: 0-15-900352-0          $39.95

### Constitutional Law
**By Professor John C. Jeffries, Jr.**
**University of Virginia School of Law**

TOPICS COVERED: Introduction; Exam Tactics; Legislative Power; Supremacy; Commerce; State Regulation; Privileges And Immunities; Federal Court Jurisdiction; Separation Of Powers; Civil Liberties; Due Process; Equal Protection; Privacy; Race; Alienage; Gender; Speech And Association; Prior Restraints; Religion—Free Exercise; Establishment Clause.
**5 Audio Cassettes**
ISBN: 0-15-900319-9          $45.95

### Contracts
**By Professor Michael I. Spak**
**Chicago Kent College Of Law**

TOPICS COVERED: Offer; Revocation; Acceptance; Consideration; Defenses To Formation; Third Party Beneficiaries; Assignment; Delegation; Conditions; Excuses; Anticipatory Repudiation; Discharge Of Duty; Modifications; Rescission; Accord & Satisfaction; Novation; Breach; Damages; Remedies; UCC Remedies; Parol Evidence Rule.
**4 Audio Cassettes**
ISBN: 0-15-900318-0          $45.95

### Copyright Law
**Professor Roger E. Schechter**
**George Washington University Law School**

TOPICS COVERED: Constitution; Patents And Property Ownership Distinguished; Subject Matter Copyright; Duration And Renewal; Ownership And Transfer; Formalities; Introduction; Notice, Registration And Deposit; Infringement; Overview; Reproduction And Derivative Works; Public Distribution; Public Performance And Display; Exemptions; Fair Use; Photocopying; Remedies; Preemption Of State Law.
**3 Audio Cassettes**
ISBN: 0-15-900295-8          $39.95

### Corporations
**By Professor Therese H. Maynard**
**Loyola Marymount School of Law**

TOPICS COVERED: Ultra Vires Act; Corporate Formation; Piercing The Corporate Veil; Corporate Financial Structure; Stocks; Bonds; Subscription Agreements; Watered Stock; Stock Transactions; Insider Trading; 16(b) & 10b-5 Violations; Promoters; Fiduciary Duties; Shareholder Rights; Meetings; Cumulative Voting; Voting Trusts; Close Corporations; Dividends; Preemptive Rights; Shareholder Derivative Suits; Directors; Duty Of Loyalty; Corporate Opportunity Doctrine; Officers; Amendments; Mergers; Dissolution.
**4 Audio Cassettes**
ISBN: 0-15-900320-2          $45.95

### Criminal Law
**By Professor Charles H. Whitebread**
**USC School of Law**

TOPICS COVERED: Exam Tactics; Volitional Acts; Mental States; Specific Intent; Malice; General Intent; Strict Liability; Accomplice Liability; Inchoate Crimes; Impossibility; Defenses;

Insanity; Voluntary And Involuntary Intoxication; Infancy; Self-Defense; Defense Of A Dwelling; Duress; Necessity; Mistake Of Fact Or Law; Entrapment; Battery; Assault; Homicide; Common Law Murder; Voluntary And Involuntary Manslaughter; First Degree Murder; Felony Murder; Rape; Larceny; Embezzlement; False Pretenses; Robbery; Extortion; Burglary; Arson.

**4 Audio Cassettes**
ISBN: 0-15-900279-6      $39.95

## Criminal Procedure

**By Professor Charles H. Whitebread**
**USC School of Law**

TOPICS COVERED: Incorporation Of The Bill Of Rights; Exclusionary Rule; Fruit Of The Poisonous Tree; Arrest; Search & Seizure; Exceptions To Warrant Requirement; Wire Tapping & Eavesdropping; Confessions (Miranda); Pretrial Identification; Bail; Preliminary Hearings; Grand Juries; Speedy Trial; Fair Trial; Jury Trials; Right To Counsel; Guilty Pleas; Sentencing; Death Penalty; Habeas Corpus; Double Jeopardy; Privilege Against Compelled Testimony.

**3 Audio Cassettes**
ISBN: 0-15-900281-8      $39.95

## Evidence

**By Professor Faust F. Rossi**
**Cornell Law School**

TOPICS COVERED: Relevance; Insurance; Remedial Measures; Settlement Offers; Causation; State Of Mind; Rebuttal; Habit; Character Evidence; "MIMIC" Rule; Documentary Evidence; Authentication; Best Evidence Rule; Parol Evidence; Competency; Dead Man Statutes; Examination Of Witnesses; Present Recollection Revived; Past Recollection Recorded; Opinion Testimony; Lay And Expert Witness; Learned Treatises; Impeachment; Collateral Matters; Bias, Interest Or Motive; Rehabilitation; Privileges; Hearsay And Exceptions.

**5 Audio Cassettes**
ISBN: 0-15-900282-6      $45.95

## Family Law

**Professor To Be Announced**

TOPICS COVERED (Subject to change): National Scope Of Family Law; Marital Relationship; Consequences Of Marriage; Formalities And Solemnization; Common Law Marriage; Impediments; Marriage And Conflict Of Laws; Non-Marital Relationship; Law Of Names; Void And Voidable Marriages; Marital Breakdown; Annulment And Defenses; Divorce — Fault And No-Fault; Separation; Jurisdiction For Divorce; Migratory Divorce; Full Faith And Credit; Temporary Orders; Economic Aspects Of Marital Breakdown; Property Division; Community Property Principles; Equitable Distribution; Marital And Separate Property; Types Of Property Interests; Equitable Reimbursement; Alimony; Modification And Termination Of Alimony; Child Support; Health Insurance; Enforcement Of Orders; Antenuptial And Postnuptial Agreements; Separation And Settlement Agreements; Custody Jurisdiction And Awards; Modification Of Custody; Visitation Rights; Termination Of Parental Rights; Adoption; Illegitimacy; Paternity Actions.

**3 Audio Cassettes**
ISBN: 0-15-900283-4      $39.95

## Federal Courts

**Professor To Be Announced**

TOPICS COVERED (Subject to change): History Of The Federal Court System; "Court Or Controversy" And Justiciability; Congressional Power Over Federal Court Jurisdiction; Supreme Court Jurisdiction; District Court Subject Matter Jurisdiction—Federal Question Jurisdiction, Diversity Jurisdiction And Admiralty Jurisdiction; Pendent And Ancillary Jurisdiction; Removal Jurisdiction; Venue; Forum Non Conveniens; Law Applied In The Federal Courts; Federal Law In The State Courts; Collateral Relations Between Federal And State Courts; The Eleventh Amendment And State Sovereign Immunity.

**3 Audio Cassettes**
ISBN: 0-15-900296-6      $39.95

## Federal Income Tax

**By Professor Cheryl D. Block**
**George Washington University Law School**

TOPICS COVERED: Administrative Reviews; Tax Formula; Gross Income; Exclusions For Gifts; Inheritances; Personal Injuries; Tax Basis Rules; Divorce Tax Rules; Assignment Of Income; Business Deductions; Investment Deductions; Passive Loss And Interest Limitation Rules; Capital Gains & Losses; Section 1031, 1034, and 121 Deferred/Non Taxable Transactions.

**4 Audio Cassettes**
ISBN: 0-15-900284-2      $45.95

## Future Interests

**By Dean Catherine L. Carpenter**
**Southwestern University Law School**

TOPICS COVERED: Rule Against Perpetuities; Class Gifts; Estates In Land; Rule In Shelley's Case; Future Interests In Transferor and Transferee; Life Estates; Defeasible Fees; Doctrine Of Worthier Title; Doctrine Of Merger; Fee Simple Estates; Restraints On Alienation; Power Of Appointment; Rules Of Construction.

**2 Audio Cassettes**
ISBN: 0-15-900285-0      $24.95

## Law School ABC's

**By Professor Jennifer S. Kamita**
**Loyola Marymount Law School, and**
**Professor Rodney O. Fong**
**Golden Gate University School of Law**

TOPICS COVERED: Introduction; Casebooks; Hornbooks; Selecting Commercial Materials; Briefing; Review; ABC's Of A Lecture; Taking Notes; Lectures & Notes Examples; Study Groups; ABC's Of Outlining; Rules; Outlining Hypothetical; Outlining Assignment And Review; Introduction To Essay Writing; "IRAC"; Call Of The Question Exercise; Issue Spotting Exercise; IRAC Defining & Writing Exercise; Form Tips; ABC's Of Exam Writing; Exam Writing Hypothetical; Practice Exam And Review; Preparation Hints; Exam Diagnostics & Writing Problems.

**4 Audio Cassettes**
ISBN: 0-15-900286-9      $45.95

## Law School Exam Writing

**By Professor Charles H. Whitebread**
**USC School of Law**

TOPICS COVERED: With "Law School Exam Writing," you'll learn the secrets of law school test taking. In this fascinating lecture, Professor Whitebread leads you step-by-step through his innovative system, so that you know exactly how to tackle your essay exams without making point draining mistakes. You'll learn how to read questions so you don't miss important issues; how to organize your answer; how to use limited exam time to your maximum advantage; and even how to study for exams.

**1 Audio Cassette**
ISBN: 0-15-900287-7      $19.95

## Professional Responsibility

**By Professor Erwin Chemerinsky**
**USC School of Law**

TOPICS COVERED: Regulation of Attorneys; Bar Admission; Unauthorized Practice; Competency; Discipline; Judgment; Lawyer-Client Relationship; Representation; Withdrawal; Conflicts; Disqualification; Clients; Client Interests; Successive And Effective Representation; Integrity; Candor; Confidences; Secrets; Past And Future Crimes; Perjury; Communications; Witnesses; Jurors; The Court; The Press; Trial Tactics; Prosecutors; Market; Solicitation; Advertising; Law Firms; Fees; Client Property; Conduct; Political Activity.

**3 Audio Cassettes**
ISBN: 0-15-900288-5      $39.95

## Real Property

**By Professor Paula A. Franzese**
**Seton Hall Law School**

TOPICS COVERED: Estates—Fee Simple; Fee Tail; Life Estate; Co-Tenancy—Joint Tenancy; Tenancy In Common; Tenancy By The Entirety; Landlord-Tenant Relationship; Liability For Condition Of Premises; Assignment & Sublease; Easements; Restrictive Covenants; Adverse Possession; Recording Acts; Conveyancing; Personal Property—Finders; Bailments; Gifts; Future Interests.

**4 Audio Cassettes**
ISBN: 0-15-900289-3      $45.95

## Remedies

**By Professor William A. Fletcher**
**University of California at Berkeley, Boalt Hall School of Law**

TOPICS COVERED: Damages; Restitution; Equitable Remedies (including Constructive Trust, Equitable Lien, Injunction, and Specific Performance); Tracing; Rescission and Reformation; Specific topics include Injury and Destruction of Personal Property; Conversion; Injury to Real Property; Trespass; Ouster; Nuisance; Defamation; Trade Libel; Inducing Breach of Contract; Contracts to Purchase Personal Property; Contracts to Purchase Real Property (including Equitable Conversion); Construction Contracts; and Personal Service Contracts.

**3 Audio Cassettes**
ISBN: 0-15-900353-9      $45.95

## Sales & Lease of Goods

**By Professor Michael I. Spak**
**Chicago Kent College of Law**

TOPICS COVERED: Goods; Contract Formation; Firm Offers; Statute Of Frauds; Modification; Parol Evidence; Code Methodology; Tender; Payment; Identification; Risk Of Loss; Warranties; Merchantability; Fitness; Disclaimers; Consumer Protection; Remedies; Anticipatory Repudiation; Third Party Rights.

**3 Audio Cassettes**
ISBN: 0-15-900291-5      $39.95

## Secured Transactions

**By Professor Michael I. Spak**
**Chicago Kent College of Law**

TOPICS COVERED: Collateral; Inventory; Intangibles; Proceeds; Security Agreements; Attachment; After-Acquired Property; Perfection; Filing; Priorities; Purchase Money Security Interests; Fixtures; Rights Upon Default; Self-Help; Sale; Constitutional Issues.

**3 Audio Cassettes**
ISBN: 0-15-900292-3      $39.95

## Torts

**By Professor Richard J. Conviser**
**Chicago Kent College of Law**

TOPICS COVERED: Essay Exam Techniques; Intentional Torts—Assault; Battery; False Imprisonment; Intentional Infliction Of Emotional Distress; Trespass To Land; Trespass To Chattels; Conversion; Defenses; Defamation—Libel; Slander; Defenses; First Amendment Concerns; Invasion Of Right Of Privacy; Misrepresentation; Negligence—Duty; Breach; Actual And Proximate Causation; Damages; Defenses; Strict Liability; Products Liability; Nuisance; General Tort Considerations.

**4 Audio Cassettes**
ISBN: 0-15-900185-4      $45.95

## Wills & Trusts

**By Professor Stanley M. Johanson**
**University of Texas School of Law**

TOPICS COVERED: Attested Wills; Holographic Wills; Negligence; Revocation; Changes On Face Of Will; Lapsed Gifts; Negative Bequest Rule; Nonprobate Assets; Intestate Succession; Advancements; Elective Share; Will Contests; Capacity; Undue Influence; Creditors' Rights; Creation Of Trust; Revocable Trusts; Pourover Gifts; Charitable Trusts; Resulting Trusts; Constructive Trusts; Spendthrift Trusts; Self-Dealing; Prudent Investments; Trust Accounting; Termination; Powers Of Appointment.

**4 Audio Cassettes**
ISBN: 0-15-900294-X      $45.95

**All titles available at your law school bookstore
or call to order: 1-800-787-8717**

# Current & Upcoming Titles

 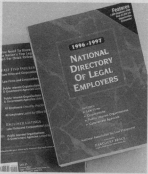 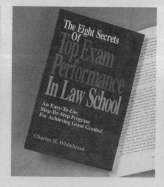 

## Gilbert's Pocket Size Law Dictionary
### Gilbert

A dictionary is useless if you don't have it when you need it. If the only law dictionary you own is a thick, bulky one, you'll probably leave it at home most of the time — and if you need to know a definition while you're at school, you're out of luck!

With Gilbert's Pocket Size Law Dictionary, you'll have any definition you need, when you need it. Just pop Gilbert's dictionary into your pocket or purse, and you'll have over 3,500 legal terms and phrases at your fingertips. Gilbert's dictionary also includes a section on law school shorthand, common abbreviations, Latin and French legal terms, periodical abbreviations, and governmental abbreviations.

With Gilbert's Pocket Size Law Dictionary, you'll never be caught at a loss for words!

**Available in your choice of 4 colors, $7.95 each:**
- Black    ISBN: 0-15-900255-9
- Blue    ISBN: 0-15-900257-5
- Burgundy    ISBN: 0-15-900256-7
- Green    ISBN: 0-15-900258-3

**Limited Edition: Simulated Alligator Skin Cover**
- Black    ISBN: 0-15-900316-4   $7.95

## What Lawyers Earn: Getting Paid What You're Worth
### NALP

"What Lawyers Earn" provides up-to-date salary information from lawyers in many different positions, all over the country. Whether you're negotiating your own salary — or you're just curious! — "What Lawyers Earn" tells you how much lawyers really make.
ISBN: 0-15-900183-8     **$17.95**

## The 100 Best Law Firms To Work For In America
### Kimm Alayne Walton, J.D.

An insider's guide to the 100 best places to practice law, with anecdotes and a wealth of useful hiring information. Also included are special sections on the top law firms for women and the best public interest legal employers.
ISBN: 0-15-900180-3     **$19.95**

## The 1996-1997 National Directory Of Legal Employers
### NALP

The National Association for Law Placement has joined forces with Harcourt Brace to bring you everything you need to know about 1,000 of the nation's top legal employers, fully indexed for quick reference.
It includes:
- Over 22,000 job openings.
- The names, addresses and phone numbers of hiring partners.
- Listings of firms by state, size, kind and practice area.
- What starting salaries are for full time, part time, and summer associates, plus a detailed description of firm benefits.
- The number of employees by gender and race, as well as the number of employees with disabilities.
- A detailed narrative of each firm, plus much more!

The National Directory Of Legal Employers has been published for the past twenty years, but until now has only been available to law school career services directors, and hiring partners at large law firms. Through a joint venture between NALP (The National Association For Law Placement) and Harcourt Brace, this highly regarded, exciting title is now available for students.
ISBN: 0-15-900179-X     **$49.95**

## Proceed With Caution: A Diary Of The First Year At One Of America's Largest, Most Prestigious Law Firms
### William R. Keates

In "Proceed With Caution" the author chronicles the trials and tribulations of being a new associate in a widely coveted dream job. He offers insights that only someone who has lived through the experience can offer. The unique diary format makes Proceed With Caution a highly readable and enjoyable journey.
ISBN: 0-15-900181-1     **$17.95**

## The Eight Secrets Of Top Exam Performance In Law School
### Charles Whitebread

Wouldn't it be great to know exactly what your professor's looking for on your exam? To find out everything that's expected of you, so that you don't waste your time doing anything other than maximizing your grades?

In his easy-to-read, refreshing style, nationally-recognized exam expert Professor Charles Whitebread will teach you the eight secrets that will add precious points to every exam answer you write. You'll learn the three keys to handling any essay exam question, and how to add points to your score by making time work for you, not against you. You'll learn flawless issue spotting, and discover how to organize your answer for maximum possible points. You'll find out how the hidden traps in "IRAC" trip up most students… but not you! You'll learn the techniques for digging up the exam questions your professor will ask, before your exam. You'll put your newly-learned skills to the test with sample exam questions, and you can measure your performance against model answers. And there's even a special section that helps you master the skills necessary to crush any exam, not just a typical essay exam — unusual exams like open book, take home, multiple choice, short answer, and policy questions.

"The Eight Secrets of Top Exam Performance in Law School" gives you all the tools you need to maximize your grades — quickly and easily!
ISBN: 0-15-900323-7     **$9.95**

## Guerrilla Tactics for Getting the Legal Job of Your Dreams
### Kimm Alayne Walton, J.D.

Whether you're looking for a summer clerkship or your first permanent job after school, this revolutionary new book is the key to getting the job of your dreams!

"Guerrilla Tactics for Getting the Legal Job of Your Dreams" leads you step-by-step through everything you need to do to nail down that perfect job! You'll learn hundreds of simple-to-use strategies that will get you exactly where you want to go.

"Guerrilla Tactics" features the best strategies from the country's most innovative law school career advisors. The strategies in "Guerrilla Tactics" are so powerful that it even comes with a guarantee: Follow the advice in the book, and within one year of graduation you'll have the job of your dreams… or your money back!

Pick up a copy of "Guerrilla Tactics" today…and you'll be on your way to the job of your dreams!
ISBN: 0-15-900317-2     **$24.95**

## Checkerboard Careers: How Surprisingly Successful Attorneys Got To The Top, And How You Can Too!
### NALP

Fast paced and easy to read, "Checkerboard Careers" is an inspirational guide, packed with profiles and monologues of how successful attorneys got to the top and how you can, too.
ISBN: 0-15-900182-X     **$17.95**

---

## FREE! Gilbert Law Summaries 1st Year Survival Manual

**Available from your BAR/BRI Bar Review Representative or write:**

Gilbert Law Summaries
176 West Adams, Ste. 2100
Chicago, Illinois 60603

**Also available on our World Wide Web site at
http://www.gilbertlaw.com**

---

**To Order Any Of The Items In This Publications Catalog, Call Or Write:**
Harcourt Brace Legal and Professional Publications, 176 West Adams, Ste. 2100, Chicago, Illinois 60603

# 1-800-787-8717

## Legalines

*Summary of Subjects Available*

■ Administrative Law

■ Antitrust

■ Civil Procedure

■ Commercial Law

■ Conflict of Laws

■ Constitutional Law

■ Contracts

■ Corporations

■ Criminal Law

■ Criminal Procedure

■ Decedents' Estates & Trusts

■ Domestic Relations

■ Enterprise Organization

■ Estate & Gift Taxation

■ Evidence

■ Family Law

■ Federal Courts

■ Income Tax

■ Labor Law

■ Partnership & Corporate Taxation

■ Property

■ Real Property

■ Remedies

■ Sales & Secured Transactions

■ Securities Regulation

■ Torts

■ Wills, Trusts & Estates

# Current & Upcoming Software Titles

### Gilbert Law Summaries
*Interactive Software For Windows*
Gilbert's Interactive Software features the full text of a Gilbert Law Summaries outline. Each title is easy to customize, print, and take to class. You can access the Lexis and Westlaw systems through an icon on the tool bar (with a valid student I.D.), as well as CaseBriefs Interactive Software, and Gilbert's On-Screen Dictionary Of Legal Terms (sold separately).

| | | |
|---|---|---|
| **Administrative Law** 0-15-900205-2 | Asimow $27.95 | |
| **Civil Procedure** 0-15-900206-0 | Marcus, Rowe $27.95 | |
| **Constitutional Law** 0-15-900207-9 | Choper $27.95 | |

| | | |
|---|---|---|
| **Contracts** 0-15-900208-7 | Eisenberg $27.95 | |
| **Corporations** 0-15-900209-5 | Choper, Eisenberg $27.95 | |
| **Criminal Law** 0-15-900210-9 | Dix $27.95 | |
| **Criminal Procedure** 0-15-900211-7 | Marcus, Whitebread $27.95 | |
| **Evidence** 0-15-900212-5 | Kaplan, Waltz $27.95 | |
| **Income Tax 1** 0-15-900213-3 | Asimow $27.95 | |
| **Property** 0-15-900214-1 | Dukeminier $27.95 | |
| **Secured Transactions** 0-15-900215-X | Whaley $27.95 | |
| **Torts** 0-15-900216-8 | Franklin $27.95 | |

### CaseBriefs
*Interactive Software For Windows*
Each title is adaptable to *all* casebooks in a subject area. For example, the Civil Procedure CaseBriefs title is adaptable to Civil Procedure by Cound, Hazard, Yeazell, etc... Simply select the casebook you're using when installing the software, and the program will do the rest! CaseBriefs is easy to customize, print, and take to class. You can access the Lexis and Westlaw systems through an icon on the tool bar (with a valid student I.D.), as well as Gilbert Law Summaries Interactive Software, and Gilbert's On-Screen Dictionary Of Legal Terms (sold separately).

| | |
|---|---|
| **Administrative Law** 0-15-900190-0 | Adaptable To All Casebooks $27.95 |
| **Civil Procedure** 0-15-900191-9 | Adaptable To All Casebooks $27.95 |
| **Conflict Of Laws** 0-15-900192-7 | Adaptable To All Casebooks $27.95 |
| **Constitutional Law** 0-15-900193-5 | Adaptable To All Casebooks $27.95 |

| | |
|---|---|
| **Contracts** 0-15-900194-3 | Adaptable To All Casebooks $27.95 |
| **Corporations** 0-15-900195-1 | Adaptable To All Casebooks $27.95 |
| **Criminal Law** 0-15-900196-X | Adaptable To All Casebooks $27.95 |
| **Criminal Procedure** 0-15-900197-8 | Adaptable To All Casebooks $27.95 |
| **Evidence** 0-15-900198-6 | Adaptable To All Casebooks $27.95 |
| **Family Law** 0-15-900199-4 | Adaptable To All Casebooks $27.95 |
| **Income Tax** 0-15-900200-1 | Adaptable To All Casebooks $27.95 |
| **Property** 0-15-900201-X | Adaptable To All Casebooks $27.95 |
| **Remedies** 0-15-900202-8 | Adaptable To All Casebooks $27.95 |
| **Torts** 0-15-900203-6 | Adaptable To All Casebooks $27.95 |
| **Wills, Trusts & Estates** 0-15-900204-4 | Adaptable To All Casebooks $27.95 |

**Gilbert's On Screen Dictionary Of Legal Terms:**
Features over 3,500 legal terms and phrases, law school short-hand, common abbreviations, Latin and French legal terms, periodical abbreviations, and governmental abbreviations.

ISBN: 0-15-900-311-3    Macintosh    $24.95
ISBN: 0-15-900-308-3    Windows    $24.95

**All titles available at your law school bookstore**
**or call to order: 1-800-787-8717**